Finiteness

Finiteness

Theoretical and Empirical Foundations

Edited by
IRINA NIKOLAEVA

UNIVERSITY PRESS

OXFORD
UNIVERSITY PRESS

Great Clarendon Street, Oxford OX2 6DP

Oxford University Press is a department of the University of Oxford.
It furthers the University's objective of excellence in research, scholarship,
and education by publishing worldwide in

Oxford New York

Auckland Cape Town Dar es Salaam Hong Kong Karachi
Kuala Lumpur Madrid Melbourne Mexico City Nairobi
New Delhi Shanghai Taipei Toronto

With offices in

Argentina Austria Brazil Chile Czech Republic France Greece
Guatemala Hungary Italy Japan Poland Portugal Singapore
South Korea Switzerland Thailand Turkey Ukraine Vietnam

Oxford is a registered trade mark of Oxford University Press
in the UK and in certain other countries

Published in the United States of America
by Oxford University Press Inc., New York

British Library Cataloguing in Publication Data
Data available

Library of Congress Cataloging in Publication Data
Data available

Typeset by SPI Publisher Services, Pondicherry, India
Printed in Great Britain
on acid-free paper by
Biddles Ltd., King's Lynn, Norfolk

ISBN 978-019-921373-3 (hbk)
ISBN 978-019-921374-0 (pbk)

1 3 5 7 9 10 8 6 4 2

Contents

Part IV Finiteness in Diachrony and Language Acquisition

Contents

Part IV Finiteness in Diachrony and Language Acquisition

Acknowledgements

The editor is greatly indebted to Frans Plank, who solicited several contributions and participated in the early editorial work on the volume. For illuminating discussions on finiteness and related questions I thank Ellen Brandner, Frans Plank, and Susanne Trissler, as well as the participants and the audience at the Finiteness Conference (University of Konstanz, May 2001), most importantly, Maria Koptjevskaja-Tamm and Nigel Vincent. Many thanks go to the people who have provided practical help during the preparation of the book: David Atfield, Thomas Mayer, and especially, Simon Carne. I am also very grateful to the Oxford University Press reviewers whose comments helped enormously to improve the volume, and to John Davey for his assistance in solving editorial questions. This work has been partly supported by the Deutsche Forschungsgemeinschaft through Sonderforschungsbereich 471 at the University of Konstanz (Project A11).

Authors

DAVID ADGER is Reader in Linguistics at Queen Mary, University of London. He is author of *Core Syntax* (2003), co-editor of Oxford Studies in Theoretical Linguistics, and has published on syntactic theory and the interfaces between syntax and other components of grammar in such journals as *Language, Linguistic Inquiry* and *Natural Language and Linguistic Theory.*

WALTER BISANG was educated in Zürich and London, where he studied General Linguistics, Chinese language and culture, Georgian, Thai, and Khmer. Since 1992 he has been Professor of General and Comparative Linguistics in Mainz (Germany). His research interests include typology and language universals, formal vs. functional linguistics, grammaticalization, language contacts, and areal typology. He has worked on East and mainland Southeast Asian languages, Caucasian languages, Austronesian languages, and Yoruba.

SONIA CRISTOFARO received her Ph.D. in Linguistics at the University of Pavia in 1998, and is now Associate Professor of Linguistics at the same university. Her main research areas are typology, cognitive linguistics, and historical linguistics. Her publications include a book on complementation in Ancient Greek (*Aspetti della complementazione frasale in greco antico,* 1996) and a book on the typology of subordination (*Subordination,* 2003).

NICHOLAS EVANS is Professor of Linguistics at the University of Melbourne. His interests range from semantics, historical linguistics, and the mutual influence of language and culture to morphosyntax and language typology. He has carried out fieldwork on a range of Australian Aboriginal languages. He has written grammars of Kayardild and Bininj Gun-wok, dictionaries of Kayardild and Dalabon, and co-edited books on the archaeology and linguistics of the Australian continent, polysynthesis, and challenges in grammar writing.

PETRA GRETSCH studied general linguistics, psychology, and computer science at the Universities of Tübingen and Edinburgh. She worked at the Linguistics Departments of Tübingen and Konstanz. After receiving a grant for the *Graduiertenkolleg Integriertes Linguistikstudium* she finished her dissertation in Tübingen. In 1998 she became a staff member at the Max Planck Institute for Psycholinguistics at Nijmegen, working in the field of language acquisition.

ELENA KALININA received her MA (1995) and Ph.D. (1998) at the Department of Theoretical and Applied Linguistics of Moscow State University. She has been working at the same department since 1999, first as Research Fellow and then—from 2003—as

Assistant Professor. Her research interests lie in the domain of syntactic typology and the minority languages of Russia, in particular Caucasian and Tungus languages.

JAKLIN KORNFILT is Professor of Linguistics at Syracuse University. She has published on syntactic and morphological theory, and on Turkish and Turkic; she is also interested in German and the Germanic languages. Her Turkish grammar (*Turkish*) was published in 1997. Her current work focuses on questions of mixed categories, on relative clauses, and on the syntax and morphology of case—particularly of subject case.

ADAM LEDGEWAY is Senior Lecturer in Romance Philology at the University of Cambridge and a Fellow of Downing College, where he teaches comparative Romance linguistics, Italian linguistics, and Italian dialectology. He works and publishes on the history and structure of the Romance languages, in particular Italian and the dialects of Italy. His research is channelled towards bringing together traditional Romance philological scholarship and the insights of recent generative syntactic theory. He has published on such topics as perfective auxiliary selection, object marking, complementation, deictic systems, and the fine structure of the left periphery.

IRINA NIKOLAEVA has a Ph.D. in Linguistics from the University of Leiden and is currently Research Associate at the University of Oxford. Her interests lie in the field of syntax, morphology, typology, lexicalist theories of grammar, and documentation of endangered languages. She has published several books on Uralic, Altaic, and Palaeosiberian languages and linguistics based on extensive fieldwork, as well as papers on the syntax–semantics and syntax–information structure interface, phonology, and historical-comparative linguistics.

CLIVE PERDUE is Head of the Research Group *Structures formelles du language* (CNRS and Université Paris 8), and is a founding member of the European network The Structure of Learner Varieties, coordinated by the Max Planck Institute for Psycholinguistics, which investigates child, bilingual, and adult language acquisition from a crosslinguistic perspective.

DAVID M. PERLMUTTER received his Ph.D. in Linguistics from MIT. He has taught linguistics at Brandeis University, MIT, the University of California at San Diego, and three Linguistic Society of America Summer Linguistics Institutes. The central theme of his work has been to confront linguistic theory with data from a wide range of languages. Highlights include the development of Relational Grammar with Paul Postal and others, the Unaccusative Hypothesis, and evidence for syllable structure in American Sign Language. He served as President of the LSA in 2000.

PETER SELLS received his Ph.D. from the University of Massachusetts at Amherst and is now Professor of Linguistics and Asian Languages at Stanford University, where he has taught for many years. His research focuses on the theoretical and typological properties of syntax and morphology in a variety of languages.

NINA SUMBATOVA was educated at Moscow State University and the Institute of Linguistics of the Russian Academy of Sciences. Since 1998 she has been Associate Professor of the Russian State University for the Humanities. She has mainly worked and written on Kartvelian and Nakh-Daghestanian languages. Her linguistic interests include the typology of verbal categories, information structure, and the documentation of endangered languages.

Abbreviations

I, II	noun classes I and II	AUG	augmented (number)
A	transitive subject, actor	AUX	auxiliary
ABL	ablative		
ABS	absolutive	BEN	benefactive
ACC	accusative	BL	blunt
ACT	actual	C, COMP	complementizer
AD	localization 'near'	CARD	cardinal
ADJ	adjective	CAUS	causative
AdjP	Adjectival Phrase	CIT	citative
ADP	prefix deriving from original adverbial function	CL	class marker
		CM	conjugation marker
ADV	adverb	CNT	contentive
AFF	affective	COBL	complementizing oblique
Agr	agreement		
AgrP	Agreement Phrase	COH	coherence particle
AgrSP	Subject Agreement Phrase	COMPL	completive
		COND	conditional
AH	addressee honorific	CONJ	conjunctive
ALL	allative	CONT	contemporative
AN	action nominal	COP	copula
ANIM	animate	CP	Complementizer Phrase
ANTIPASS	antipassive	CSL	causal converb
AOBL	oblique case of the attributive	CVB	converb
AOR	aorist	D	determiner
APPR	apprehensive; 'lest' inflection	DAT	dative
		DEC	declarative
ART	article	DEF	definite
ASC	associative	DEM	demonstrative
ATR	attributive, attribute	DIR	directional marker

DP	Determiner Phrase	IMM	immediate
DS	different subject	IMP	imperative
DTR	detransitive	IMPL	implicated clause
DUB	dubitative	I, INFL	inflection(al head)
DYN	dynamic	IN	localization 'inside'
		INCH	inchoative
ECM	Exceptional Case Marking	INCL	inclusive
		INCOMPL	incomplete
EL	elative	IND	indicative
EM1	epistemic marker 1	INDF	indefinite
EM2	epistemic marker 2	INDIR	indirect
EMPH	emphatic	INF	infinitive
ERG	ergative	INFER	inferential
ESS	essive	INS	instrumental
		INT	intensifier
F	feminine	INTER	localization 'between'
Fin	finiteness	INTERJ	interjection
FIN	finite	INTR	intransitive
FinP	Finiteness Phrase	IntSBJV	interrogative subjunctive
FN	factive nominalization	IP	Inflectional Phrase
FOC	focus	IPFV	imperfective
FocusP	Focus Phrase	IQ	indirect question
ForceP	Force Phrase	IRR	irrealis
FUT	future		
FUTFN	future factive nominalization	JUSS	jussive
		K	Case
GEN	genitive	KP	Case Phrase
GER	gerund		
GNR.PRS	general present	L1	first language
		L2	second language
H	human	LAT	lative
HAB	habitual	LDR	long-distance reflexive
HORT	hortative	LF	logical form
HPL	human plural	LOC	locative
HYP	hypothetical mood	LOG	logophoric

M	masculine	OPT.N	optative noun
M-finiteness	morphological finiteness	ORIG	origin
MA	male addressee		
MABL	modal ablative	P	possessor
MC	main clause	PARTV	partitive
MOD	modification marker	PASS	passive
MOD.OBL	modus obliquus	PAT	patient
MoodP	Mood Phrase	PF	Phonological Form
MPROP	modal proprietive	PFV	perfective
MSD	masdar	PL	plural
		POL	polite
N	neuter	POSS	possessive
N1	non-human class 1	POSTLAT	postlative
N2	non-human class 2	POT	potential
NCUR	noncurative	POT.IMP	potential imperative
NEG	negation	POT.INF	potential infinitive
NegP	Negation Phrase	PQ	polar question
NFIN	nonfinite	PRET	preterite
NFN	non-factive nominaliza-tion	PRH	prohibitive
		PRIV	privative
NFUO	nonfinite utterance organization	pro	null pronominal
NH	non-human	PRO	null anaphoric pronominal
NMLZ	nominalizer	PROG	progressive
NOC	non-obligatory control	PROP	proprietive
NOM	nominative	PROPS	propositive
NPI	negative polarity item	PRS	present
NPL	non-human plural	PRSPR	present progressive
NPST.PROG	non-past progressive	PRS.PTCP	present participle
		PRT	particle
O	object (agreement)	PST	past
OBL	oblique (stem)	PST.CONT	past continuous
OBLG	obligative	PST.PTCP	past participle
OC	obligatory control	PTCP	participle
OPT	optative		

PUN	punctual	SUB	subordinator
PURP	purposive	SUBOR	subordinate
		SUG	suggestive
Q	question	SUP	localization 'on, above'
RE	epistemic particle	T	tense
REFL	reflexive	TAM	tense/aspect/modality
REL	relative	TC	topic-contrast particle
REM	remote	TEMP	temporal converb
REPET	repetitive	THM	thematic
RES	resultative	TL	target language
RESTR	restrictive	TOP	topic
RQ	requestive mood	TR	transitive
		TRANST	transition
S	subject		
S-finiteness	semantic finiteness	UG	Universal Grammar
SAE	Standard Average European	UQ	universal quantifier
SBJV	subjunctive	V	verb
SEQ	sequential	V2	verb second
SFI	second form of the infinitive	V.DAT	verbal dative case
		VEG	vegetable class
SG	singular	V.I.ALL	verbal intransitive allative case
SH	subject honorific		
SOR	subject-to-object raising	VN	verbal noun
Spec	specifier	VNP	Verbal Noun Phrase
SPN	supine	VOC	vocative
SR	switch-reference	VOL	volitional
SS	same subject	VP	Verb Phrase
SSC	Specified Subject Condition	VRB	verbalizing suffix
STAT	stative	XP	syntactic phrase

1

Introduction

IRINA NIKOLAEVA

The notion of finiteness originates in the grammatical tradition of late antiquity. The term 'finite' adopted in European linguistics goes back to the Latin *finitus*, the perfective participle of the verb *finio* 'finish, limit, set bounds to, determine'. One of the meanings of *finitus* is 'definite' or 'determined' in the sense 'referring to a particular person' (Sauter et al. 1968: 705). The term was first applied to personal pronouns (*pronomina finita*) and then to verbs expressing person and number. The system of verbal forms was accordingly divided into two classes: *verba finita*, i.e. forms defined or determined by person and number, and *verba infinita*, i.e. personally undetermined forms. The latter category in Latin includes infinitives, participles, gerunds and supines. Such usage became standard, especially after the influential *Institutiones grammaticae* by Priscianus Caesariensis (*c.*500 AD).

Following this tradition, most descriptive grammarians think of finiteness as a property of a verb. Although in Latin the finite/nonfinite distinction was initially motivated by the presence/absence of agreement (person and number), later other verbal categories were taken into account, most importantly tense. Huddleston (1988: 44) defines the finite verb as a verb 'limited by properties of person, number and tense', and in Hogg (1992: 541) the term 'finite' describes 'a verb which is marked for tense and number'. Yet it has long been noticed that the inflectional approach to finiteness is too narrow to have a universal application. Although in most European languages the relevant categories correlate, they often conflict with each other in a broader cross-linguistic perspective. In a number of languages the forms usually classified as nonfinite lack some categories but not others. For example, in Kannada infinitives are uninflected, but participles, gerunds, and dependent conditionals take tense (though not agreement). The tense opposition on participles is shown in the following examples from Sridhar (1990).

(1) a. na:yi   maguvannu   kaccitu
        dog   child.ACC   bite.PST.3SG.N
        'The dog bit the child.'

   b. [maguvannu   kaccida]   na:yi
        child.ACC   bite.PST.PTCP   dog
        'the dog which bit the child'

(2) a. aŋgaDiya   hinde   go:Daunide
        shop.GEN   behind   warehouse.be.PRS.3SG.N
        'There is a warehouse behind the shop.'

   b. [hinde   go:Daun   iruva]   aŋgaDi
        behind   warehouse   be.PRS.PTCP   shop
        'the shop behind which there is a warehouse'

The same form may have different inflections in different syntactic contexts: in Northern Khanty and Mansi (Uralic) clausal nominalizations inflect for agreement in complement and adverbial clauses, but not in relative clauses, cf. the Northern Khanty examples:

(3) a. [ma   xo:t   we:r-m-e:m   jupina]
        I   house   make-NMLZ-1SG   after
        'after I built the house'

   b. [ma   we:r-əm]   xo:t-e:m
        I   make-NMLZ   house-1SG
        'the house I built'

The traditional approach has no principled grounds for establishing which feature is responsible for finiteness. Moreover, neither tense nor agreement is a universal category, so whichever is chosen will be absent in a number of languages. If agreement is taken to be the relevant category, languages like Japanese, where verbs inflect for tense but not agreement, lack finiteness altogether. If tense is the decisive feature, the finite/nonfinite opposition appears to be absent in languages like Lango, where verbs do not inflect for tense (Noonan 1992).

Some grammarians additionally consider the form's syntactic function, based on the assumption that nonfinite verbs occur exclusively or predominantly in dependent contexts. *A Dictionary of Grammatical Terms* defines the notion 'finite' as follows (Trask 1993: 103–4):

Denoting a form of a verb or auxiliary which can in principle serve as the only verb form in a sentence and which typically carries the maximum in morphological marking for such categories as tense and agreement permitted in a language.

A similar definition is suggested in Matthews (1997):

> Traditionally a verb, e.g. in Latin and Greek, inflected for person and number. Now more generally of any verb whose form is such that it can stand in a simple declarative sentence.

This definition reflects the widespread view that only finite verbs are able to form an independent utterance and that each independent utterance must have one and only one finite verb. This idea also has ancient roots, harking back to Stoic logic (Luhtala 2000).

However, distributional and inflectional criteria may conflict with each other. Languages like West Greenlandic exhibit dependent-only forms that do not show any reduction of finiteness features. For example, the so-called 'contemporative mood' used in complement clauses takes tense and agreement (Fortescue 1984):

(4) niriursui-vunga   [aqagu   urni-ssa-llutit]
     promise-IND.1SG   tomorrow   come.to-FUT-CONT.1SG.2SG
     'I promise to come to you tomorrow.'

On the other hand, imperatives, which tend to have little inflection even in languages with rich inflectional morphology, are limited to main/independent clauses. Moreover, typological studies have demonstrated that in a sizable number of languages arguably nonfinite forms with reduced tense and agreement can function as the only predicate in a clause (Kalinina 2001d). Summing it up, Johns and Smallwood (1999) show that among eight possible combinations of three finiteness features, main clausehood (MC), tense (T), and agreement (Agr) marking, at least four are associated with the term 'nonfinite' in descriptive practice: −MC −T −Agr (English infinitives), −MC −T +Agr (European Portuguese infinitives), −MC +T −Agr (Tamil and Lezgian participles), and +MC −T −Agr (Russian and Middle Welsh infinitives). So tense/mood/agreement morphology and dependent/independent status appear to be empirically independent parameters, although there may be implicational correlations between them: for all languages, if person and/or number and/or tense are marked on dependent forms, then they are also marked on independent forms (Vincent 1998).

Neither distributional nor inflectional criteria are applicable to languages without inflectional morphology such as Chinese or Vietnamese, or languages like Slave, where the same verbal form is used in all syntactic contexts and subordination is indicated by position alone (Rice 1989). Taken together, these facts indicate that the traditional notion of finiteness is ill-defined (cf. Joseph 1983). The question is then whether it is altogether a universally valid concept.

The development of syntactic theory starting from the 1960s led to an obvious departure from traditional assumptions. Finiteness was reanalysed as something more abstract, essentially a clausal category that is only secondarily reflected in the form of the verb. This significant conceptual move overcame objections of the sort raised above and made it possible to maintain the universality of the finite/nonfinite distinction. It also raised further questions, some of which are internal to the architecture of a particular theory whereas others are more general in nature.

In generative syntax the idea that finiteness somehow represents the whole clause was implemented by assigning it the status of a clausal head. Since in this syntactic tradition grammatical categories can only be defined if they occupy a place in the hierarchical phrase structure, finiteness has a structural corollary: it corresponds to a position on a tree from where it dominates the rest of the clause. In early transformational grammar it was represented as the AUX(iliary) node, whereas in the later versions of the theory AUX was replaced by INFL(ection) or I. In the Principles and Parameters framework this category is a carrier of information about tense and agreement represented either as its features (Chomsky 1981; 1986a) or subconstituents (Pollock 1989). The finiteness opposition is realized as the distinction between the finite and nonfinite I: the former is positively specified for tense or agreement and the latter is not. The subject–verb agreement is essentially thought of as agreement between the subject and finiteness (INFL), although tense and agreement are morphologically expressed on the verb due to head movement operations and merging of inflectional elements with the verb. This account provides a unitary characterization of the clausal syntax based on the notion of finiteness, reflecting the traditional view that finiteness is associated with the richness of specification for other grammatical features.

The structural finite/nonfinite distinction has a number of far-reaching consequences for a wide variety of syntactic phenomena. Finiteness correlates with the presence of an overt subject in the nominative case. This correlation was first explained in detail in the government-based Case Theory of the early 1980s. In fact, the initial motivation for Case Theory came from the recognition of nonfinite contexts, where nominative subjects are ruled out. In the traditional Government and Binding view, the Case Filter (Chomsky 1981) requires that every overt NP bear an abstract Case, which may or may not be phonologically realized. The Case is assigned in a particular structural configuration. The relation between the nominative subject and finiteness is represented as the Spec–head relation. The finite and nonfinite INFL have different Case assigning properties. The finite INFL assigns the nominative Case to its specifier under government. The phonologically null subjects in pro-drop languages (*pro*), as well as expletive subjects in the SpecIP position, all bear the nominative Case. The earlier versions of the theory required positive specification for both tense and agreement for I to function as a Case-licenser, but it has also been suggested that in some languages only agreement defines the realization of finiteness (George and Kornfilt 1981; Fisher 1988) or that the choice of Case-assigner may vary (Koopman and Sportiche 1991). After IP was split into several functional heads, the agreement head (AgrS) has usually been held responsible for finiteness.

The nonfinite INFL is not a governor and does not assign Case. As the specifier of a nonfinite clause is not a Case-marked position, it cannot host phonologically realized NPs; only empty categories such as PRO can appear there. Thus, in standard Government and Binding Theory the difference between finite and nonfinite clauses is reflected in the following two configurations.

(5)   a.

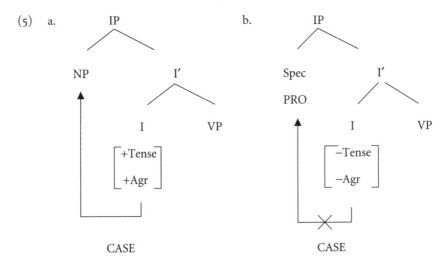

A great deal of research has been devoted to the analysis of nonfinite structures which were shown to fall into the following main types: (i) null subject clauses, including control and raising structures; (ii) ECM contexts where the subject receives its Case from the main verb; and (iii) overt non-nominative subjects where Case comes from the complementizer, e.g. *for* in English. Thus, finiteness has played a prominent role in explaining the occurrences of overt subjects, expletives, *pro*, and PRO.

Another area of syntax where the notion of finiteness proved to be important is the distribution of referential expressions and anaphoric elements, i.e. sentence-internal anaphors and personal pronouns. As known since Tense-S

Condition and Specified Subject Condition originally formulated in Chomsky (1973), the syntax imposes some kind of ban on antecedent–anaphor relation across the boundary of a finite clause and an intervening subject. To put it differently, a dependent finite clause represents an opaque domain in that it is not accessible to certain rules operating in the main clause, whereas a nonfinite clause is syntactically transparent in this sense. In the classical Binding Theory (Chomsky 1981) this is expressed with the idea that an anaphor must find an antecedent (i.e. must be bound) in the local domain determined, at least in some languages, either by the subject or the finite INFL. The nonfinite INFL does not define a binding domain; therefore in nonfinite clauses the anaphors are bound by the next available binder, the main subject. The distribution of bound anaphors is further tied to other grammatical phenomena such as pronominal binding, wh-movement, NP-movement, and control of PRO, and can be thought of as part of the general theory of empty and lexical categories.

The research along these lines maintains that the manifestations of finiteness are interdependent, as required by the general principles of grammar. Finiteness is a binary morphosyntactic category of the clause that (i) regulates tense and agreement on the verb, (ii) controls the realization of the subject argument, and (iii) creates domains opaque for some syntactic rules. This captures many important generalizations; however, there are well-known cases where the relevant properties do not come together as predicted by the theory.

An early problem was provided by European Portuguese, where infinitives inflect for agreement. In Welsh all infinitives agree with pronominal subjects, but the infinitives embedded under epistemic/declarative verbs and the infinitives embedded under the verbs of volition differ in terms of binding (Tallerman 1998). This leads to the parametrization of the idea that overt agreement is needed for the identification of finiteness. Independent nominative subjects are licensed in arguably nonfinite clauses defined by uninflected verbs in Québec French infinitival conditionals (Martineau and Motapanyane 1996) and West Flemish adverbial infinitives (Haegeman 1986). On the contrary, in Modern Greek and other Balkan languages some fully inflected subjunctives are syntactically transparent and form control and raising structures (Felix 1989; Anderson 1997; Roussou 2001). Relating finiteness to inflection predicts that languages without inflectional morphology do not have a structural distinction equivalent to that of finite/nonfinite; but a number of such languages seem to exhibit the relevant syntactic effects. One example is Khmer, where clauses embedded under verbs of saying can have an overt subject, while clauses embedded under volitional verbs cannot (Fisher 1988). Similar facts have been observed in Modern Standard Chinese (Huang 1984; Li 1990; Tang 2000).

Such cases require additional assumptions that are sometimes difficult to check on independent grounds. For instance, Haegeman (1986) argues that in West Flemish the nominative Case is assigned by the preposition selecting a relevant complementizer, and a compatible analysis of Portuguese was proposed in Raposo (1987). Although each individual case can be handled in one way or another, taken together they considerably weaken the universality of the finite/nonfinite distinction as far as the relation between syntax and morphology is concerned. Some authors have therefore concluded that the morphological form of the verb is not a suitable criterion for establishing the finite/nonfinite nature of the dependent clause (e.g. Vincent 1998; Ledgeway 1998).

This conclusion is in line with the functional literature, which has long recognized that properties involved in the definition of finiteness are not universal because finiteness has different morphosyntactic realizations across languages (e.g. Noonan 1985; Palmer 1986). Unlike early formal theories, which said little or nothing about the content of this category, functionalism has always attempted to provide it with a conceptual motivation. Givón (1990; 2001) suggests that dependent events, by virtue of lacking an independent perspective, are not conceptualized as independent processes and may possibly be conceptualized as components of main events. The thematic dependence of an event on its context correlates with the syntactic dependence of the clause. In other words, the degree of integration of a dependent event into a higher clause is iconically reflected at the morphosyntactic level by the degree of downgrading of the dependent clause with respect to the prototypical main clause. The stronger the semantic bond between the two events, the more extensive will be the syntactic integration of the two clauses into a single clause. Finiteness, then, is the 'systematic grammatical means used to express the degree of integration of a clause into its immediate clausal environment' (Givón 1990: 853). The structural reduction of a clause involves the loss of verbal properties (such as tense, aspect, mood, or person/number marking) and the acquisition of nominal properties (such as case, co-occurrence with determiners, omission of verbal arguments or their encoding as possessors or obliques) on the part of the verb describing the dependent event. The downgrading occurs on a language-specific basis, so the degree to which the nonfinite (nominalized) clause differs from the finite clause is a matter of considerable cross-linguistic variation. Since finite/nonfinite are just two extremes on the functionally motivated scale of desententialization and there are many intermediate situations, mismatches of the sort mentioned above are not problematic from a functionalist perspective.

One fundamental difference between the functional and formal approaches to finiteness is that the former is primarily concerned with its overt clause-internal manifestations in terms of the opposition between the prototypical (morphological) properties of nouns and prototypical (morphological) properties of verbs. The nature of the data shapes the conclusion: if finiteness is defined by a cluster of parameters, it is bound to be graduated given the range of cross-linguistic variations, so many functionalists view it as a scalar phenomenon. In this view, no decision is needed as to what features are crucial for finiteness. In contrast, under the formal approach the main question has always been which feature is responsible for the formation of opaque domains, subject licensing, and the related phenomena of control and raising, which tends to lead to a binary understanding of finiteness. This implies that if the notion of finiteness has a cross-linguistic applicability, its nature must be viewed as somewhat more complex. Both the gradual and binary nature of finiteness can be captured by making a principled distinction between an abstract binary category that regulates certain syntactic processes, on the one hand, and its individual morphological manifestations, on the other.

The recent versions of generative syntax have given up the strong isomorphism between syntactic structure and morphology, and maintain that clausal finiteness correlates with tense and agreement inflection on a language-particular basis. Although the highest clausal level headed by a complementizer was not at first considered responsible for the realization of finiteness, finiteness was recently associated with the complementizer domain (CP) rather than the inflectional domain (IP). Theory-neutral evidence for this contention comes from the fact that inflectional categories can be spelled out at C and that in a number of languages the choice of a complementizer correlates with the finiteness of the clause it introduces. Vincent (1997; 1998) argues, on the basis of analysis of complementation in Italian dialects, that finiteness may be signalled on the main verb (in IP), on C, or by a combination of the two. There are also suggestions that finiteness is an operator in C which has to be realized in order to license the nominative Case (Platzack and Holmberg 1989) or that it requires incorporation of I into C (Kayne 1994: 95). Rizzi (1997) proposed an influential system where finiteness is a theoretical primitive structurally independent of tense and located at the highest sentential level. It is still contributed by only one functional head (FinP), a subconstituent of the split CP, but is not reduced to the presence of agreement or tense. Instead, it constitutes a more basic property of the C system that interacts with functional heads in the IP domain.

With the development in the 1990s of Checking Theory as a general theory of how functional heads license lexical categories, the finiteness features were interpreted as abstract morphosyntactic properties, whose function is to regulate the syntactic distribution of DPs rather than the morphological features overtly realized on the verb. In this view, finiteness has to do with the appearance of the overt subject licensed by the mechanism of feature checking. Since the notion of government was no longer conceptually desirable, feature checking was characterized in terms of a single X-bar-theoretic configuration, the Spec–head relation with one of the functional categories. In early versions of Minimalism, the subject's nominative Case in finite clauses was checked against AgrS, and PRO was assumed to bear the null Case checked via Spec–head agreement with the nonfinite INFL (Chomsky and Lasnik 1993; Radford 1997). In other versions finiteness basically reduces to the presence of a categorial D-feature on Tense (Chomsky 1995b: ch. 4). Roberts and Roussou (2002) argue that both Tense and AgrS relate to operators or properties of C forming a (C, AgrS, T) dependency where T is bound both by C and AgrS. In finite clauses T is identified by a strong D-feature at the AgrS level, whereas in nonfinite clauses AgrS does not project or is somehow inactive. The way in which AgrS is parametrically realized (either as a head or a specifier) depends on the morphological properties of a particular language, giving rise to different typological patterns.

If clausal finiteness is a syntactic primitive represented as a feature or position on the tree, depending on one's syntactic assumptions, the question is whether it conveys interpretation-relevant information. In other words, is this category purely syntactic or both syntactic and semantic? The functional content of finiteness has been a matter of some debate. Hoekstra and Hyams (1998a) and Hoekstra et al. (1999) argue that it has to do with the event being situated in a particular temporal interval. The temporal reference is fixed through an operator assumed to be located in C. The notion of finiteness refers to this fixation, and makes visible a chain between the operator and the verb, or more specifically, the Tense position. Languages vary in how finiteness is expressed. For example, in Dutch a present tense verb is overtly marked for number but not for person or tense, so it is number morphology that makes a Tense chain visible. Bianchi (2000; 2003) also relates finiteness to temporal anchoring. A finite verb encodes the relation of event time or reference time to speech time, whereas infinitives show no sensitivity to this relation. She implements this idea in Rizzi's system, assuming that speech time is syntactically represented in FinP where it licenses the nominative Case. According to Roussou (2001), the role of FinP has to do with quantification over time intervals and possible worlds, and consists in providing an anchoring point to the speech time. In this sense finiteness is context-dependent, and belongs together with deixis. If this is true, the finite/nonfinite nature of a complement is basically determined by its semantics, i.e. by the selecting predicate or other operator in the matrix clause. One would not expect to find a fundamental difference in finiteness between the same semantic types of complement in different languages, as appears to be the case.

It has also been suggested that the category crucially associated with finiteness is modality (Holmberg et al. 1993; Vincent 1998) or an even more rudimentary semantic property referred to as assertion. The latter idea is present in many studies on V2 in Germanic, since the movement of the finite verb into the V2 position appears to be a strategy to encode the assertive force (e.g. Platzack and Holmberg 1989; Wechsler 1991; Brandner 2004). It is also explored in detail by Klein (1994; 1998), who argues that the main function of finiteness as a category is to relate the descriptive content of an utterance to its topic component, in particular to the time span about which the assertion is made. The range of syntactic, semantic, and pragmatic phenomena depending on the presence of finiteness in Klein's sense is considerably broader than has usually been thought, some of them pertaining to reference and information structure.

What emerges from the picture sketched above is that there seem to be some cross-linguistically valid correlations between subject requirement, subject agreement, tense, syntactic opacity, and independent clausehood. These properties are associated with the category of finiteness, but the syntactic nature of this connection and the content of the category itself are a matter of discussion. The aim of the present volume is to shed light on this category by focusing on the following interrelated questions:

(1) Is finiteness an elementary notion, and if not, can it be reduced to other more basic properties?

(2) Is the finite/nonfinite distinction universal?

(3) Is there a consistent cross-linguistic realization of finiteness?

(4) How do different grammatical theories represent finiteness?

(5) Assuming finiteness is elementary, does it have any structure-independent motivation?

(6) Assuming finiteness is not elementary, are there any universally predictable patterns that render such a derived category meaningful?

(7) What about finiteness is subject to change?

(8) How is finiteness acquired by language learners?

Some of these questions were originally formulated by Frans Plank at the Conference on Finiteness that took place on 11–13 May 2001 at the University of Konstanz. Earlier versions of several chapters included in this volume were presented as papers at this conference.

The first part of the book, 'Finiteness in Formal Theories', deals with the role finiteness plays in syntax and how it is handled by different theoretical approaches. The chapters in this part have a fairly similar structure: they start with a brief overview of previous works on finiteness conducted within the relevant framework, and then provide the author's original contribution in the form of a case study.

David Adger's chapter surveys the recent literature on finiteness completed within the Minimalist Programme, and examines in the minimalist perspective the role finiteness plays in three syntactic domains roughly defined by three functional heads, C, T, and V. The author maintains, following Rizzi (1997), that there is positional evidence for a low complementizer position Fin. This position is associated with the interpretable feature [± finite] responsible for the interpretation of the lower clause as anaphoric with respect to the speech event denoted by the higher clause. The questions central to the chapter are whether Fin bears features other than [± finite] and whether [± finite] is associated with the syntactic effect of subject licensing. The chapter shows that in Irish the C-domain expresses more rudimentary temporal information than that found on finite verbs: the complementizer is marked as past/non-past, while the finite verb opposes past, present, and future. The complementizer is located in Fin, which suggests that Fin is associated with tense-related features. Similarly, West Flemish data demonstrate that Fin is able to host agreement. In Gaelic the clause can be truncated at the VP level, removing Fin, while subjects can be licensed by the features T and Agr, which may appear lower in the clause. This means that subject licensing must be divorced from the feature [± finite], and that the clausal expression of finiteness must be disassociated from its morphological expression as tense and agreement. Adger concludes that the inflectional features of the verb are duplicated on Fin; however, the relationship between the featural specification of Fin and that of the T-domain is largely language-specific.

The contribution from Peter Sells addresses the treatment of finiteness in the non-transformational theories of Head-Driven Phrase Structure Grammar (HPSG) and Lexical-Functional Grammar (LFG). The main insight of this contribution is partly similar to Adger's in the sense that Sells provides a conceptual distinction between finiteness as a property of a clause, on the one hand, and its overt morphosyntactic expression by a 'finite' verbal form, on the other. Non-transformational theories have necessary tools to express the distinction between the surface form or position of a given morphosyntactic element and the grammatical information it expresses. Clausal finiteness is represented as the abstract feature FINITE with an interpretational foundation related to assertiveness and the expression of the declarative speech act, while the 'morphological' finiteness corresponds to Finite, a value of a Form feature that verbs and perhaps other lexical items can have. The relationship between the two is illustrated by several case studies.

Sells analyses two types of Japanese complement clause, showing that while both are Finite in terms of morphology, only one type is actually a full clausal unit that can have a subject. In Japanese, morphological finiteness is not exclusively associated with a syntactic category such as IP, CP, or FinP, and carries none of the semantic or pragmatic functions of FINITEness. On the contrary, Swedish has clauses that are truly FINITE but lack a Finite form expressing this information. The finite auxiliary *ha*, encoding the information about FORCE and TENSE, can be deleted in the presence of the modal words *kanske* and *manne* 'maybe' located in the V2 position. Sells suggests that in such cases, even though there is no tensed verb, a hearer could recover the finiteness of the clause, as it is clearly recognizable as expressing assertion and has a nominative subject. This argues for the presence of the grammatical category FINITE, which in Swedish does not necessarily have to be expressed by [Form: Finite]. The chapter further shows that grammatical phenomena can be sensitive to either morphological or clausal finiteness.

The conclusions of the two chapters summarized above are by and large compatible, in spite of the different initial assumptions. In both chapters the notion of finiteness is essentially decomposed into the syntactic aspect provided with an interpretational foundation, on the one hand, and the morphological aspect, on the other. The nature of the relationship between the two is largely arbitrary and depends on the individual language. The chapters collected in the second part of the volume, 'Finiteness in Functional Theories and Typology', pose a different but related question: what typological generalizations can be made from the patterns of the overt (morphological) manifestations of (clausal) finiteness?

Following other functional literature, Sonia Cristofaro focuses her attention on the cross-linguistic distribution of a number of phenomena, such as the presence of tense, aspect, mood, and agreement distinctions on the verb, the expression of these distinctions by means of special verbal forms not used in independent clauses, the presence of nominal morphology on the verb, the ability of the verb to take overtly expressed arguments, and the coding of arguments as possessors. Based on the data collected within a larger typological project on subordination (Cristofaro 2003), the chapter shows that these phenomena follow predictable patterns and are linked by a number of implicational correlations across languages. The correlation patterns appear to obey a number of principles of form–function correspondence which have been suggested in functionally oriented literature, and which pertain to the cognitive status of the state of affairs expressed by the relevant clause and the type of semantic relationship between the main and dependent clauses. However, the individual combinations of morphosyntactic properties involved in the definition of finiteness are entirely language- and construction-specific, as ensured by the very nature of implicational correlations. Based on this argument, Cristofaro speculates that one should abandon the idea of finiteness as a single category which can be defined through a number of formal properties. Instead, manifestations of finiteness could be viewed as a realization of a cross-linguistic tendency. This conclusion departs from other functionalist approaches discussed in the chapter (in particular, Givón 1990), which treat finiteness as a cross-linguistically and cross-constructionally valid category encompassing any property that involves deviation from the independent clause pattern.

Walter Bisang's chapter aims to demonstrate how finiteness can be described as a discrete binary phenomenon from a functional perspective. Bisang discusses the categories that can be morphologically expressed on the verb in the world's languages from the perspective of obligatoriness. A category represented by a paradigm is obligatory if the speaker is forced overtly to express a certain value or subcategory of that paradigm. The concept of finiteness argued for in the chapter is crucially based on the idea that the finite/nonfinite distinction depends on the obligatory linguistic expression of certain cognitive domains such as tense, illocutionary force, person, and politeness. If a category is general enough to occur obligatorily in every independent sentence, it gets reanalysed as a reliable indicator of sentencehood.

Languages create asymmetries between main/independent and dependent clauses. An asymmetry arises if a cognitive domain that is obligatorily expressed in an independent clause cannot occur at all, or can only occur with a reduced set of subcategories in a dependent clause. Asymmetries of this kind are far from being universal. There are languages like Chinese or Vietnamese with no obligatory categories, and languages with rich verbal morphology which do not show any asymmetry of obligatory categories. The notion of finiteness is only relevant for those languages that demonstrate a morphological asymmetry between independent and dependent clauses. Such languages can be effectively characterized as finite, although both the categories involved in the asymmetry and the means of their overt expression can differ. According to Bisang, finiteness, then, is an open concept in the sense that it can involve any category that overtly marks structural independence at the highest level of sentencehood. It is discrete but not universal, neither in the sense of individual grammatical categories that are used for its expression nor in the sense that it must be marked in some way in every language. From a cognitive perspective, it can be viewed as a device which helps the human parser to recognize sentences as maximal syntactic units.

Unlike the previous two chapters, Irina Nikolaeva's contribution does not attempt to present a definition of finiteness, and is concerned with independent rather than dependent clauses. The purpose of the chapter is to present evidence that some types of independent clauses prefer nonfinite patterns while others do not, and to provide an explanation for this fact. The reduction of finiteness in independent clauses appears to correlate with the content of the clause. Imperatives and hortatives/jussives systematically demonstrate properties that are commonly thought of as diagnostics of nonfiniteness: they tend to have reduced tense/agreement morphology compared to declarative clauses and rarely allow overt subjects. However, the combinations of these properties differ considerably across languages, which shows that they cannot be reduced to a common syntactic source. The analyses that relate finiteness in independent clauses to the presence/absence of a single syntactic element (a feature or a functional head) cannot account for the range of cross-linguistic data.

The author suggests, partly in line with Cristofaro's chapter, that the reduction of finiteness in independent clauses should be understood as a cross-linguistic tendency motivated by the functional pressure for economic expression. Crucial for the chapter are the notion of constructional meaning, as employed in Construction Grammar, and the separation of the information associated with the verbal form from the information associated with the syntactic construction. The chapter introduces the principle of Constructional Economy, which prevents the doubling of constructional meaning by inflectional or phrasal means within the same construction. For example, the semantics of imperatives imposes heavy restrictions on the available subjects because there is a strong connection between the subject and the addressee. This requirement directly follows from the meaning of the imperative construction and is inherently incorporated into its syntactic representation, whereas Constructional Economy prevents predictable information from being overtly expressed. This accounts for the fact that imperatives tend to lack subjects and agreement morphology. As a functional tendency, Constructional Economy applies to some languages and constructions but not others, and can only determine the likelihood of certain patterns. The ultimate shape of a construction follows from its individual grammaticalization path, so we can expect to find a lot of cross-linguistic variations.

The authors of Part II basically agree that the relationship between the morphosyntactic aspects of finiteness and semantics is not unmotivated.

Nonfinite or 'less finite' patterns tend to correlate with some kind of semantic reduction and predictability. This is ensured by such functional factors as economy of expression, reliability of occurrence, and facilitation of parsing.

While the second part of the volume is concerned with cross-linguistic variations in the realization of finiteness, the third part contains chapters that discuss the finite/nonfinite opposition in individual languages.

The contribution of Elena Kalinina and Nina Sumbatova examines the languages of the Nakh-Daghestanian (East Caucasian) group. The chapter argues that none of the traditional approaches to finiteness yields satisfactory results when applied to the Daghestanian data. First, the Daghestanian situation differs from the situation in typical European languages in that the finite categories obligatorily expressed in the clause are not necessarily hosted by the verb, but are rather associated with the focus constituent. The focus constituent bears a special marker which expresses illocutionary force, tense, mood, and subject agreement. Thus, the verb is deprived of its central role in the definition of finiteness. Second, there is no strict contrast between the verbal forms used in main/independent clauses and the verbal forms used in dependent contexts. As mentioned above, this opposition is often taken to be the basis of the finite/nonfinite distinction in traditional grammars. However, in Daghestanian the verbal forms are contrasted on the basis of the illocutionary force and information structure of the clause where they appear. The forms traditionally labelled as 'finite' are confined to declarative and interrogative sentences. These forms enter the domain of the wide focus, but are impossible in sentences with narrow focus, which extends over one non-predicate constituent, and in some languages also in thetic utterances. In other words, the 'finite' forms are used to express the assertive part of the proposition. The so-called 'nonfinite' forms fulfil several functions: (i) they are used in declarative and interrogative sentences with narrow focus where they belong to the presuppositional part of the proposition, whereas the finite categories are hosted by the focus constituent, (ii) they can head independent non-declarative non-interrogative clauses which lack focus markers altogether, and (iii) they are used as dependent predicates in relative clauses and factive complement clauses. So the distribution of verbal forms in the languages of Daghestan cuts across the traditional dependent/independent contrast. Rather, verbal forms are opposed as expressing assertions or presuppositions. Forms expressing presuppositions typically lack finite categories, but can equally occur in dependent and main/independent clauses. The chapter ends up with some speculations about the nature of finiteness in Daghestanian.

The main question addressed in David Perlmutter's chapter is what syntactic effects are associated with finite and nonfinite clauses and how they differ in an individual language. Perlmutter analyses Russian, a language where the distinction between finite and nonfinite clauses is uncontroversial, as these clauses are consistently headed by inflected verbs and uninflected infinitives, respectively. Russian has three constructions whose distribution is sensitive to the finite/nonfinite contrasts: the Impersonal Construction and the so-called Unspecified *they* Construction occur in finite but not in nonfinite clauses, whereas the Unspecified Human Subject Construction occurs only in nonfinite clauses. The purpose of the chapter is to explain these patterns.

The chapter argues that the relevant distribution follows from two factors. On the one hand, the constructions in question have phonologically null subjects whose lexical properties play the key role in explaining the constructions' distribution. The semantic and morphosyntactic representations of null subjects are distinct: the Impersonal Construction and the Unspecified *they* Construction require their null subjects to be in the nominative case, while in the Unspecified Human Subject Construction the null subject must be in the dative. On the other hand, Russian imposes an independent syntactic requirement that the subjects of finite and nonfinite clauses be nominative and dative, respectively. This makes finite clauses compatible with those constructions that require the nominative subject, and nonfinite clauses compatible with those constructions that require the dative subject. A corollary of this analysis is that the gaps in the distribution of various constructions are not to be included among the properties of finite and nonfinite clauses in Russian. Finite and nonfinite clauses do not differ in the classes of construction they allow. Instead, they differ in the case they require of their subjects, as is well attested cross-linguistically. A careful distinction is needed between the empirical properties of the finite/nonfinite contrast and the phenomena that may be correlated with it but follow from other independent syntactic properties in a particular language.

Jaklin Kornfilt takes a rather different view. She presents evidence from Turkish that not only the nominative but also the genitive subject Case can be an expression of finiteness. This contrasts with the standard assumptions on the connection between finiteness and the licensing of the nominative Case. The genitive in Turkish is licensed clause-internally and is dependent on the categorial features of the predicate inflection within that clause. This further suggests that finiteness is not dependent on a particular morphological case of the subject but, more generally, on the presence of the subject Case as a syntactic notion, while the morphological realization of the latter may depend on a number of independent factors.

The second major point the chapter makes is that, although some approaches have taken tense to be the property determining finiteness of a clause, in Turkish and some other languages agreement shows up independently from tense and licenses the subject Case. Tense cannot determine finiteness by itself, i.e. without the presence of agreement, and where it plays a role in Turkish, that role is secondary. As in Adger's chapter, syntactic finiteness corresponds to a distinct position in the clausal architecture which can be sensitive to different morphological features across languages, either tense or agreement. Unlike tense, however, agreement does not have a semantic interpretation and cannot represent a clause's temporal independence. If semantic finiteness relates to temporal independence, as has been argued in various places, this suggests that semantic and syntactic finiteness, while coinciding in many instances, do not always go hand in hand.

The last part of the volume deals with diachronic issues and the role finiteness plays in linguistic change and linguistic development. Adam Ledgeway analyses three distinct subordination types in the dialects of southern Italy which have been subject to change. Crucially, changes in finiteness may operate at different levels: at the level of morphology, at the level of syntax, or at both levels, whereas morphology does not mirror all structural distinctions. The Neapolitan asyndetic structures consisting of the paratactic sequence of two juxtaposed imperatives demonstrate a shift from the less finite to the more finite both in morphology and syntax. However, the loss of person marking on Neapolitan infinitives observed by the second half of the seventeenth century has had no effect on their syntax. Similarly, southern Calabrian clauses headed by a complementizer derived from MODO 'now' have been decategorialized from finite to inflected infinitival clauses, despite not exhibiting any loss in the morphological realization of finiteness.

On the basis of this data Ledgeway concludes, rather similarly to other chapters in the volume, that finiteness has distinct and sometimes unrelated manifestations in different areas of the grammar. Moreover, syntactic correlates of finiteness such as destructuring, categorial changes, and nominative-licensing ultimately follow from deeper semantic distinctions. For instance, the categorial shift from the complementizer to the infinitival marker undergone by the reflexes of MODO highlights an increased degree of semantico-pragmatic integration between matrix and embedded clauses, and the reduced autonomy of the latter. So syntactic manifestations of finiteness have a semantic corollary related to the degree of semantic autonomy borne by individual clauses. This latter conclusion mirrors the functionalist understanding of finiteness as represented by the works of Givón and by Cristofaro's chapter in this volume, although, unlike the latter, it is based on the diachronic analysis of two related dialects rather than on an analysis of a typologically informed language sampling.

Nick Evans examines insubordination, which he defines as 'the conventionalized main-clause use of formally subordinate clauses'. The chapter provides a typological survey of formal manifestations of insubordination, showing that insubordinated constructions can involve main-clause subjunctives, subordinate word order, complementizers, subordinating conjunctions, logophoric pronouns, switch-reference markers, and nonfinite verbal forms such as infinitives. Evans describes the range of functions fulfilled by insubordinated constructions which include expressions of interpersonal coercion and modal and evidential meanings, as well as the marking of various discourse contexts such as negation, contrastive statements, and reiteration. The chapter further examines the development of insubordinated constructions through a three-step diachronic process: (i) the ellipsis of the main clause, (ii) the conventionalized restriction of interpretation of ellipsed material, and (iii) the development of conventionalized main-clause use. At the first stage the insubordinated clauses can perhaps be analysed as underlying subordinate clauses whose main clause has been ellipsed but can plausibly be restored for analytic purposes. At the second stage insubordinated clauses acquire greater semantic specificity, so that certain logically possible 'restored' meanings or functions are never found; and by the final stage they become fully independent main clauses.

Insubordination is an important diachronic phenomenon because of the unusual way the direction of change runs: from a subordinate clause to main clause. It raises several issues concerning finiteness. The most important question is whether the main-clause status entails finiteness, so that the change from subordinate to main entails changes in finiteness as part of the reanalysis process. If the presence of a nonfinite form is an indicator of nonfiniteness, insubordinated clauses involving nonfinite forms remain nonfinite. In this case Evans's material suggests that finiteness and the main-clause status do not necessarily correlate, as is also shown in Nikolaeva's and Kalinina and Sumbatova's contributions. Alternatively, if the verbal form is not an indicator of finiteness, other criteria for the finite/nonfinite distinction in independent clauses must be found, perhaps along the lines suggested in Sells's chapter.

The book concludes with a joint chapter by Petra Gretsch and Clive Perdue devoted to the acquisition of finiteness, the question that gave rise to intense debate in the 1990s. Children are known to produce root infinitives for some period of time. This fact requires an explanation, given that in the adult speech root infinitives are rather exceptional. In the research conducted within various versions of generative grammar, children's root infinitives follow from the absence or underspecification of a syntactic element responsible for finiteness. The alternative view Gretsch and Perdue intend to defend treats finiteness as a multi-level phenomenon. Following Lasser (1997), they distinguish the overt form that finiteness takes and the function it serves, Morphological and Semantic finiteness, respectively. After Klein (1994; 1998), Semantic finiteness is understood as the carrier of assertion, which involves two pragmatic operations: the anchoring of the utterance in the discourse world and the linking of the state of affairs described by the predicate to the topical part of the utterance.

The case studies concentrate on the acquisition of finiteness in L1 German and L2 Dutch, English, and German. Under the standard assumptions, child learners quickly develop inflectional verbal morphology, while adult learners do not; but the authors show that there are more similarities in L1 and L2 acquisition than is usually thought. They propose a common stage model for early L1 and L2 development. At the first stage, utterances consist of a topic, a predicate and a linking element which expresses the relationship between them. The class of linkers includes the expressions of positive or negative assertion, scope particles, and modal phrases. At the second stage, the relation between the predicate and the topic is grammaticalized: finite verbs and auxiliaries start expressing both tense and assertion. As they serve as grammatical linking devices, non-verbal linkers can no longer be used as validators of the topic–predicate relation. So the acquisition of the formal and functional side of finiteness does not go hand in hand. This fact is not surprising as far as adult learners is concerned: since they are familiar with Semantic finiteness from the knowledge of their L1, their learning task consists in acquiring new means to mark it formally. But for children, too, acquiring the formal and functional aspects of finiteness represents two independent learning tasks. The similarity in L1 and L2 acquisition, then, confirms the theoretical considerations that keep two aspects of finiteness apart.

Part I
Finiteness in Formal Theories

2

Three domains of finiteness: a Minimalist perspective

DAVID ADGER

2.1 Introduction

This chapter[1] examines the role that the traditional notion of finiteness has played in analyses of clause structure and argument licensing in the development of the Minimalist Programme. I focus on three broad domains: the upper, middle, and lower areas of clause structure which roughly correspond to the A-bar, A, and theta-positions of Government and Binding theory, and their corresponding heads, C, T, and V. Following the general format of this volume, the initial sections are intended as a (selective) reading of recent work on this topic, and I use and extend the conclusions from this in the final section.

It is important, at the outset, to emphasize that there is no guarantee that the traditional notion of finiteness will find any place in a theory of language: it names a possibly open-ended set of phenomena and may very well have no satisfactory definition (see Cristofaro, Chapter 4 below, for a similar point in a very different framework). Within generative grammar, the question is not what finiteness is, but whether providing an insightful account of the phenomena requires such a notion in the first place. If it does, then there is no expectation that the notion will be unitary or that it will correspond in any deterministic way to the traditional idea. I shall argue here that there is a particular structural position which often hosts elements which have been traditionally categorized as marking finiteness; I'll further suggest that this position hosts a feature whose interpretation has to do with dependence on the speech event. Finally, I'll argue that this same position may host information about tense and agreement which is essentially parasitic on

[1] I would like to thank the participants of the Celtic Linguistics Conference in Dublin 1995 for comments on a very early version of the last sections of this chapter. Many thanks also to Gillian Ramchand for comments on a previous version of those sections, and to two anonymous referees for comments on the chapter as a whole.

information elsewhere in the clause, and that this tense and agreement information impacts upon the kinds of subject that are licit in an embedded clause. In this way the notion of finiteness is deconstructed into antecedent notions that do have a definition within the theoretical system. The question is then to what extent these notions themselves are required, and if so, whether their definitions are correct. These deeper questions I will not tackle here.

2.2 Background concepts

Traditional grammatical categories such as tense, case, number, etc. are usually conceptualized, within current approaches to generative grammar, as properties of lexical items (almost all of these approaches take the lexical item as the basic unit of syntax). Within the Principles and Parameters framework, and more specifically within the research programme which goes under the rubric of the Minimalist Programme (Chomsky 2000; 2001b; 2004), lexical items are taken to be no more than sets of such properties. We will assume that these properties can be notated as feature–value pairs of the form [feature:value]. For example, we will assume that a first person singular pronoun in a language like English has something like the structure in (1):

(1)   [person:1, number:sing, case: , . . .]

Here we have **valued** person and number features, which contribute to the semantic interpretation of the item. Features which contribute to semantic interpretation are called **interpretable features**. We also have an **unvalued** case feature, notated [case:]. This case feature does not contribute to the interpretation, and is said to be **uninterpretable**. Such uninterpretable features receive a value during the course of the syntactic derivation by **matching** with another instance of the feature, and thereby receiving a value. Once valued, such features are removed from the syntactic representation (they **delete**)—see Chomsky (2001b).

Lexical items can be fairly abstract, and need not correspond to the classical major categories of N, V, A, and P. In fact, much of the syntactic 'work' in this framework is done by abstract lexical items called **functional categories**, which combine with projections of the lexical categories to create a fairly rich architecture above them. These functional categories host semantic information which is traditionally associated with the 'minor' categories of traditional grammar: tense, definiteness, aspect, number, etc. The extent to which these minor categories are represented as features bundled in lexical items with other features, or, on the other hand, the extent to which they project independent syntactic structure, is an open question, and possibly an area of parametric variation.

A lexical item, then, will be affected by a syntactic derivation in a way that is determined by how its features interact with the features of other lexical items. If, for example, (1) combines with a preposition bearing the valued case feature [case:acc], its own case feature will be valued as [case:acc]:[2]

(2) P[case:acc] ... [person:1, number:sing, case:] → P[case:acc] ... [person:1, number:sing, case:acc]

Neither case feature is interpretable, and so both delete from the syntactic representation, deletion marked here with a strikethrough, following Pesetsky and Torrego (2001):

(3) P[~~case~~:acc] [person:1, number:sing, ~~case~~:acc]

However, the case features can be accessed by the morphophonological component which will ensure that the output has the appropriate morphological case form (i.e. in English *me* rather than *I*). This same technology is intended to encompass all other syntactic dependencies.

Within such a framework a number of questions arise about finiteness. First, is finiteness a feature? If so, is it an interpretable feature, and what is its interpretation? How does the finiteness property relate to other features such as tense and agreement (is it derivable from them, or does it enter into valuing-style dependencies with them?). Does finiteness project independently in clausal structure? If so, what is its distribution? What kind of a role does it play in the argument licensing dependencies of case and selection?

The rest of this chapter addresses these questions, via an examination, synthesis, and extension of recent work on these topics. Following Bianchi (2003), I'll suggest that there is a functional category which expresses whether certain aspects of the semantics of a clause are temporally anaphoric or not, and which does so by means of a feature, which we might call [finite: ±], giving a semantic interpretation to this traditional idea. This functional category is responsible for manifestations of what we commonly think of as finiteness, as it may bear uninterpretable features of tense and agreement which are parasitic on specifications which arise elsewhere in the sentence. I'll argue that this functional category does project independently in a particular position in the clause, following Rizzi (1997), and will follow him in terming

---

[2] I follow, here, the implementation of Adger (2003). Chomsky (2001b) has proposed that case valuation is a sort of side effect of the checking of person and number features. We return to this in section 2.4.1.

this category Fin. I combine these ideas with a suggestion of Landau (2004) that the relation of subject licensing and finiteness is one which ties together the possibility of independent temporal reference with the possibility of independent nominal reference.

It follows from this set of ideas that, although there is just one way to be finite (which is to be specified as [finite:+]), there is more than one way to be non-finite. The clause could have a Fin projection with the specification [finite:−]; alternatively, it could lack the Fin projection altogether: that is, the clause could be **truncated** below this position because of the properties of the selecting predicate (Rizzi 1994a; Wurmbrand 2003). The clausal level at which truncation takes place leads to different kinds of nonfiniteness—nonfinite TP vs. nonfinite VP, for example. For both types of construction, the question of subject licensing arises. If the possibility of a referentially independent subject depends on independent temporal reference, how do languages license subjects in these domains? One familiar example comes from ECM constructions, which are truncated at T and where the licensing of the subject is clause-external. I provide new data from Scottish Gaelic where clauses are truncated at the VP layer, and the licensing of the subject has to be VP-internal, with concomitant effects on the temporal interpretation of the construction.

As discussed in the introduction to this volume, and in Kornfilt (chapter 9 below), generative grammar took traditional ideas of morphosyntactic finiteness and reified them as structures where finiteness is a property of an independently projecting functional category and is only secondarily realized on the verb itself. Although the idea has much earlier roots, since the late 1970s transformational grammar has assumed that the head of the clause is a syntactic element capable of bearing tense and agreement features. This syntactic element was originally termed INFL, later shortened to just I. Under the assumption that this element is the head of the clause, and the notion that syntactic phrases are endocentric, we are led to the following type of structure:

(4)

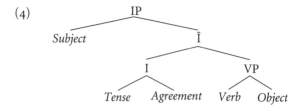

This approach allowed analysts at the time to treat finiteness as a general clausal property which is related to the richness of specification of tense and/or agreement properties on the clausal head I. The fact that these properties are morphologically manifested on verbal elements can be dealt with by the idea that certain verbs move to I (in English, just the topmost auxiliary, but in other languages also main verbs), or alternatively, that I lowers to the verb. A nonfinite clause would then be one where, rather than Infl being specified for tense and agreement features, it is either unspecified or negatively specified for these features.

This treatment of finiteness as richness of specification of tense and agreement on a clausal head essentially deconstructs the notion of finiteness and renders the idea of a finiteness feature irrelevant. Unlike some other traditional grammatical properties which were reified as features, finiteness is, from this theoretical perspective, simply an epiphenomenon arising from the presence or absence of other features.

This approach allowed a fairly successful implementation of an important generalization about finite and nonfinite clauses in many languages: overt subjects with nominative case are restricted to finite clauses. In terms of the theoretical viewpoint just outlined, the relation between nominative case and finiteness is natural, since the element bearing nominative case (the subject) is in a special structural relation (specifier) with the element bearing the features related to finiteness (I). However, a new question then arises as to whether nominative case is associated with a positive specification for tense features or for agreement features.

We can see the evidence for the nominative–finiteness correlation quite directly. The structure of finite clauses clearly shows that, when a clause bears tense and agreement information, a nominative subject is licensed:

(5)   He leaves early every day.

However, in an infinitive, a nominative subject is impossible:[3]

(6)   *I planned he to leave early every day

Theorists working within the Government and Binding framework captured this idea by something like the following (see Kornfilt, Chapter 9 below, for discussion):

(7)   I[tense:+, Agr:+] assigns nominative case to its specifier

This proposal now extends naturally to a potential challenge for the original generalization which is raised by languages like European Portuguese, where a nominative subject is, in fact, possible in an infinitive just when the infinitive

---

[3] We leave aside accusative subjects in infinitives. See section 2.4.2 for discussion.

is inflected for agreement (see Raposo 1987 for Portuguese and George and Kornfilt 1981 for similar data from Turkish inflected gerunds):

(8) É correto nós   ignor-ar-mos   isto.
     is right   us.NOM   ignore-INF-1.PL   this
     'It is right for us to ignore this.'

We can capture the data by assuming that universally the following holds:

(9) [Agr:+] assigns nominative case to its specifier

In addition we have the following parametric difference:

(10) [tense:−] implies [Agr:−]

(10) would be inactive in European Portuguese, Turkish, etc. but would constrain the featural composition of I in English, French, etc.

From the late 1980s, a number of arguments appeared, most famously those in Pollock (1989), which pointed towards splitting up previously atomic syntactic categories into their constituent features and allowing these features themselves to project as heads (essentially an extension of the proposal that inflectional features on the verb were actually hosted by an independently projecting I node). Pollock's contribution was to argue that the constituent parts of I (tense and agreement) should themselves both be allowed to project as headed phrases, part of clause structure. His specific proposal was that the tense features project a head (let us term it T) which selects an AgrP. The basis of this suggestion was essentially that it provided extra positions which acted as landing sites for verb movement:

(11)

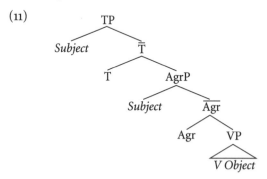

Belletti (1990), on the basis of pursuing a transparent relationship between the internal morphological structure of words and the syntactic structure of clauses (the Mirror Principle of Baker 1988), suggested that AgrP selects TP rather than the structure in (11), while Chomsky (1991) suggested that there were two AgrPs, one below T, which is associated with object agreement, and one above, associated with subject agreement:

(12)

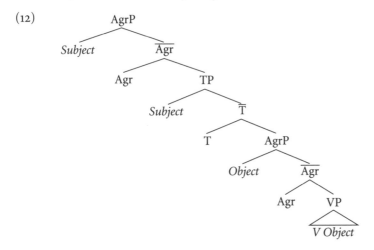

If we assume that a negative specification for tense is what is at the core of an infinitive, then the parametric difference between European Portuguese and other languages can now be thought of in two different ways: either as negative specification for Agr features when Agr is selected by T (in Pollock's system), or simply as truncation of the clause at the T level in infinitives (in Belletti's or Chomsky's systems). We return later to the possibility that these two ways of creating a nonfinite clause (negative specification vs. truncation) are both realized in language.

So far we have looked at finiteness only within the IP layer of the clause. Over the past decade or so, however, researchers working within the Minimalist Programme have tended to think of the clause as consisting of three different domains: the IP domain, which is the primary locus of tense, agreement and case; the VP domain, which is mainly concerned with relating arguments to the lexical properties of the verb (such as theta-role assignment, aspectual structure, etc.); and the CP layer, which is concerned with the 'edge' of the clause, where topic, focus, wh-movement and other (quasi)-quantificational notions are canonically expressed (see especially Rizzi 1997 and, for a good overview, Haegeman 1997).

2.3 Finiteness and the CP domain

Rizzi (1997) proposes that the CP domain of clause structure is configured in the following fashion:

(13)

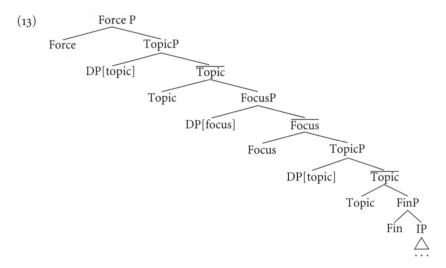

The topmost projection, ForceP, is where features related to the semantic force of the clause (as an assertion, an order, a question, etc.) reside. The lowest projection within this domain, FinP, is the one most closely related to the IP layer of clause structure, and it is the most relevant for us here. The head Fin encodes whether the clause is finite or not. For Rizzi, finiteness is to be understood as a more rudimentary specification for mood, tense, and agreement than is found in the IP domain. Rizzi does not provide an independent semantics for the Fin head, endowing it with essentially formal (uninterpretable) features.

Of the remaining projections, Focus does not mark a property of the clause as a whole, but rather serves as a landing site for focalized phrases. The Topic projections, between which FocusP is sandwiched, host backgrounded or topicalized XPs.

If we accept Rizzi's proposals for the position of topics and focalized XPs, we then have an argument that the complementizers usually analysed as finite and nonfinite in Italian are actually realizations of Force and Fin. Consider the following examples:

(14) Credo che,   il tuo libro, loro lo apprezzerebbero molto.
      I.think that[+fin] the your book them it will.appreciate   much
      'I think that they will appreciate your book very much.'

(15) *Credo, il tuo libro, che   loro lo apprezzerebbero molto
      I.think   the your book that[+fin] them it will.appreciate   much

Here we see that it is impossible to topicalize to a position to the left of the complementizer *che*, leaving a clitic within the lower domain, but it is possible to topicalize to its right. This contrasts with the behaviour of the nonfinite complementizer *di*:

(16) *Credo di,   il   tuo   libro, apprezzar-lo molto
       I.think that[-fin] the   your   book   appreciate-it much
       'I think that they will appreciate your book very much.'

(17) Credo, il   tuo   libro, di   apprezzar-lo molto.
       I.think the   your   book   that[-fin] appreciate-it much
       'I think that they will appreciate your book very much.'

In these examples, topicalization is impossible in the latter case. If *di* is in the same structural position as *che*, this is mysterious. However, if *di* is a realization of Fin, then we immediately rule out (16), since there is no topic position to the right of Fin, only one to the left:

(18) Credo $[_{ForceP}[_{TopP}[_{FinP}$ di $[_{TP}$ ...

There is an interesting contrast between these cases in Italian and topicalization in nonfinite clauses in English, which seems to be generally barred (Hooper and Thompson 1973; Haegeman 2004):

(19) a. I decided that, your book, we should all read first.
       b. *I decided, your book, to read first

Emonds (2004) points out that the same effect holds for Negative Preposing:

(20) a. I promised that only until five would we work.
       b. *We will propose only until five to work

One plausible analysis is that, since the higher verb selects a nonfinite verb form in this case, it selects Fin directly. This would capture the idea that infinitival clauses, which require special selection, are structurally reduced (as first proposed in this context by Hooper and Thompson 1973):[4]

(21) ... propose $[_{FinP}[_T$ to work...

What of *for* in English? This complementizer rejects topics completely:

(22) a. *I propose, these books, for John to read
       b. *I propose for, these books, John to read

---

[4] Note that the higher predicate can select a full CP which allows both finite and infinitive CP, as happens in wh-questions:

(i) a. I decided who I should invite.
     b. I decided who to invite.

Clearly, then, some infinitives have higher structure than just Fin, since wh-movement presumably targets FocusP.

Our explanation can be directly extended to this case. (22b) is ruled out on the assumption that *for* is Fin. If Fin is selected directly by the higher clause, then, once again, no topic projection can intervene.[5]

This explanation also extends to the fact that topicalization in Italian is degraded in raising infinitivals, in contrast to the control cases we saw above. Rizzi gives:

(23) *?Gianni   sembra,   il   tuo   libro,   conoscer-lo bene
        Gianni   seems,   the   your   book,   know-it   well
        'Gianni seems to know your book well.'

In this case the higher predicate directly selects IP, so there is no CP domain, no nonfinite C, and no position for a fronted topic. The data seem to be replicated with raising predicates in English:

(24) *John seems, your book, to like best

This argument, then, suggests that the CP layer above Fin can be truncated. The question that still needs to be answered is why (17) is grammatical in Italian. We return to this directly below.

There is further evidence from Welsh for a split between the Force and Fin heads in CP. Tallerman (1996) provides examples where a topicalized XP is sandwiched between two complementizer-like elements (marked in bold here), and she treats these as examples of CP recursion (see also Rouveret 1994; following Tallerman I have glossed the particle that occurs after the topic simply as PRT):

(25) a. Dywedais i **mai** ['r dynion a   fuasai'n   gwerthu'r ci]
          said   I MAI the men   PRT would-Asp sell-the   dog
          'I said that it's the men who would sell the dog.'

      b. **Ai** [ceffyl a   fuasai hi'n   gwerthu]
          AI   horse PRT   would   she-Asp   sell
          'Is it the horse that she'd sell?'

      c. **Nid** [y   dyn   a   ddaeth]
          NEG   the man   PRT   came
          'It wasn't the man who came.'

Roberts (2005) reanalyses these examples as having the higher particle being Force, followed by a Topic, with the lower element (*a*) being Fin.

---

[5] This is not what Rizzi suggests: he proposes that *for* is syncretic for both Force and Fin, and that the (b) example is ruled out because of a case adjacency effect between *for* and the accusative subject.

We have now seen some evidence for a specialized position in clause structure in the C domain which hosts a head which marks nonfiniteness (e.g. *di* in Italian, *for* in English). There also appears to be a case where we see both Force and Fin projections realized at the same time in Welsh. The obvious follow-on question is what features characterize the Fin head.

Looking first at English, the embedding complementizers *that* and *for* mark whether the IP domain is tensed or non-tensed:

(26)   a. I said that he was ungrateful.
       b. *I said that he to be ungrateful

(27)   a. I asked for him to be there.
       b. *I asked for he was there

This seems to be the most rudimentary finiteness distinction made in the C-system: [tense:+] or [tense:−]. Interestingly, the semantic interpretation of the non-tensed cases is, in some sense, modal. For example, Stowell (1982) argues that certain infinitives express an 'unrealized future', accounting for the contrast below:

(28)   a. I remembered today that I locked the door yesterday.
       b. *I remembered today to lock the door yesterday
       c. I remembered today locking the door yesterday.

(28b) is ruled out, as the infinitive expresses an unrealized future which is incompatible with the adverbial. One might adopt the idea that the interpretation of some feature on Fin is some kind of modal anchoring to the higher tense so that the event of locking is understood to be future with respect to the event of remembering. This would allow us to associate an interpretation with the Fin head for which we have so far just given positional argumentation.

In fact such an interpretation has been proposed for Fin by Bianchi (2003). Bianchi argues that the meaning of finiteness relates to the way that both the tense and the logophoric centre of the clause are identified. The logophoric centre of the clause is to be understood as involving the relation between the speaker and the subject of the clause (so that, for example, whether the subject is first, second, or third person specifically depends on whether the referent is identical to the speaker, addressed by the speaker, or neither). Bianchi suggests that in nonfinite clauses the identification of the temporal and logophoric centres of the clause must be determined anaphorically (i.e. via the temporal and logophoric centres of another clause). In the finite case, they can be independently specified. The specific idea is that Fin, which syntactically identifies this area of clause structure, is semantically interpreted as introducing a variable for the speech event which is identified deictically (finite) or anaphorically (nonfinite). Bianchi ties in this idea to the licensing of nominative case, which for her depends on the person features which provide the logophoric centre in Fin.

If Bianchi is right, we can conclude that Fin contains an interpretable feature which we can call [finite: $\pm$] and which provides these meanings, in much the same way that T bears an interpretable feature that marks semantic tense. We can then ask the question of whether Fin bears other (perhaps uninterpretable) features.

Evidence that it does comes from languages which seem to express more than a simple tensed/non-tensed distinction in C. Cottell (1995) argues that, in Irish, richer temporal information than just finiteness can be expressed in the C-domain. She gives the following examples:

(29) Deir   sé   go   dtógfaidh   sé   an   peann.
      say.PRS he   that take.FUT   he   the   pen
      'He says that he will take the pen.'

(30) Deir   sé   gur   thóg   sé   an   peann.
      say.PRS he   that.PST take.PST he   the   pen
      'He says that he took the pen.'

Here we see that the verb inflects for future versus past, and we can also see that the complementizer marks for past or non-past. This distinction can be seen across a whole range of complementizer-like elements in the language, including relative particles, negative complementizers, and complementizers signalling temporal relations like *sula/sular* 'before':

(31) Rith   leat   sula   bhfeicfear   tú.
      run   with.you   before   see.PASS   you
      'Run along before you are seen.'

(32) D'éag   sé   sular   thánig   an   sagart.
      die.PST   he   before.PST   come.PST   the   priest
      'He died before the priest came.'

What we seem to have here is a tense feature on the complementizer, which, interestingly, still marks a more rudimentary distinction than that seen on the finite verb: rather than past, present, and future, we simply have a past/non-past distinction. The feature on C is dependent on the interpretable tense feature hosted by T.

There is good evidence that the tensed complementizers in Irish are actually lower than one might expect. McCloskey (1996) provides the following kind of example:

(33) Deiridís   [an chéad Nollaig   eile   [go   dtiocfadh
      they.would.say   the first   Christmas other   that would.come
      sé   aníos]]
      he   up
      'They used to say that next Christmas he would come up.'

Note the difference between the English translation and the structure of the Irish sentence. In English the adverbial *next Christmas* appears after the complementizer *that*, while in Irish the corresponding adverbial appears before the complementizer. McCloskey argues, on the basis of the assumption that adjunction to a CP argument is impossible (Chomsky 1986a), that the adverb in Irish is actually adjoined lower than the outermost layer of CP, and that the complementizer subsequently lowers. As pointed out by Ian Roberts (2005) this can be elegantly updated in Rizzi's system by assuming that the complementizer here is in Fin, rather than Force. Putting this together with Cottell's suggestion of tense features on the complementizer, we see, once again, the expression of some tense-related feature on Fin.

Tense is not the only I-system feature that has been argued to appear on Fin. It has long been observed that agreement features also appear on C (Bayer 1983/4). The following examples are from West Flemish (Haegeman 1992):

(34) a. dan-k   (ik)   goan
         that-1SG   (I)   go
         'that I go'

      b. da-se   (zie)   goat
         that-3SG.F   (she)   goes
         'that she goes'

      c. dan-ze   (zunder)   goan
         that-3PL   (they)   go
         'that they go'

Haegeman (2004) suggests that the existence of these φ-features on Fin provides the answer to the question we left open above: why is topicalization possible in Italian control structures while it is not in English control structures? Note that the kind of topicalization involved in Italian requires a clitic element which doubles the features of the argument. Moreover, this clitic appears as part of the I-system (printed here in bold):

(35)   Credo   **il**   **tuo**   **libro**   di   apprezzar-**lo**   molto.
       I.think   the   your   book   that[-fin]   appreciate-it   much
       'I think that they will appreciate your book very much.'

Since features of the I system can be replicated on Fin, the features of this clitic can appear on Fin. Haegeman tentatively proposes that the topicalized element is licensed by being in a relation with these features. In contrast, topicalization in English does not involve a clitic, and so no copying of features to Fin is possible, hence topicalization in control clauses is ungrammatical.

Finally, let us turn to how to capture the relationship between the featural specification of Fin and that of the I domain. Assuming that the interpretation of the Fin head is as discussed above, we can capture the (cross-linguistically variable) duplication of I-system features on Fin by endowing it with unvalued tense and agreement features:

(36)   Fin[Tense: , Agr: , finite: $\pm$]

When Fin Merges with the highest element in the I domain, its unvalued features Agree with the features of the lower heads, and are valued. They do not contribute to the interpretation, but they allow particularized morphological expression of the features of the I-domain on C.

What we have seen in this section is evidence for a functional category in a position in the highest layer of clause structure which is associated with a particular kind of semantic force (essentially, whether it links anaphorically or deictically to the speech event). In some languages this functional category may also bear features which derive from elsewhere in the clause (specifically, tense and agreement features). I also argued, on the basis of possibilities for topicalization, that clauses could be truncated when the higher predicate selects Fin directly. In the next section we will explore what happens when Fin itself is absent.

2.4 Finiteness and subject licensing in TP

We have just seen that there is a relationship between the Fin head and the agreement features which appear in the T domain. This brings us back to the generalization, briefly discussed in section 2.2, that nominative case licensing for the subject seems to depend on finiteness, however construed. In nonfinite clauses, the subject apparently cannot receive nominative case, and may in fact be null. We saw how this had been attributed to the nominative case assigning properties of Agr. In this section we will explore how this idea has been updated to deal with the concerns of the Minimalist Programme, and how its relevance to null subjects in infinitives has been challenged.

Before we address examples with null subjects, let us briefly consider how case checking of the subject works in finite clauses.

2.4.1 *Case licensing and finite T*

In section 2.2, we proposed that nominative case was checked by agreement features. Early versions of minimalism adopted this idea, endowing Agr heads with both uninterpretable agreement features (to be checked with the interpretable agreement features on argument DPs) and with valued uninterpretable case features. The latter check with uninterpretable case features on the DP. Updating this slightly, we have a derivation like the following:

(37) a. Agr[agr: , case:nom] ... DP[agr:3pl, case:] →
      b. Agr[~~agr~~:3pl, ~~case~~:nom] ... DP[agr:3pl, ~~case~~:nom]

The Agr features on the Agr head are checked and deleted (since they are semantically uninterpretable), as are all the case features. These features, however, are interpreted by the morphology, and may then determine the particular morphological form of the morphemes once they are spelled out.

2.4.2 *Licensing subjects in infinitives*

Within Government and Binding theory (see e.g. Chomsky 1981; 1986b), the null subject of certain nonfinite clauses is termed PRO. The distribution of PRO is restricted to nonfinite clauses by a constraint known as the PRO theorem, which requires PRO to be ungoverned. The only syntactic position where arguments can appear and which is ungoverned is the subject position of nonfinite clauses, hence we rule out examples where PRO is the subject of a finite clause:

(38) *Zelda believed PRO was unhappy

Moreover, since Case is assigned under government in this theory, and since the subject position of infinitives is ungoverned, overt case-marked DPs cannot appear as the subject of an infinitive (unless there is some other governor):

(39) *Zelda tried her to be happy

However, the theory of Case in later GB tied case-marking to theta-role assignment using the notion of **visibility**: a DP is only visible for theta-role assignment if it is case-marked. This notion of visibility played an important explanatory role in the theory (see Chomsky 1986b), but is clearly incompatible with the theory of PRO just outlined: PRO is an argument, and so must receive Case to be visible for theta-role assignment. However, PRO's distribution precisely depends on its being ungoverned, and hence, unmarked for Case (see Martin 2001 for discussion).

Moreover, the notion of government in the Minimalist Programme is, as Chomsky (1993) pointed out, problematic. It is an extra concept defined over and above the basic phrase structural relations of specifier and complement.

Chomsky and Lasnik (1993) solve these problems by the suggestion that the element in the subject position of nonfinite T could indeed be assigned case, but the particular case assigned had the property of realizing the case-marked DP as null (i.e. as PRO). Chomsky and Lasnik term this case **null case**.

Of course, as pointed out by Watanabe (1993) and Martin (2001), this theory now predicts that all infinitives will allow PRO and that overt DPs will never be allowed in an infinitive. This is clearly incorrect. (40) is an example of a so-called raising infinitive, while (41) is the construction usually termed an ECM infinitive:

(40)   *It seems to Naomi PRO to be happy

(41)   Naomi believes Zelda to have eloped.

In (40) we have a nonfinite clause with a PRO subject, but the sentence is ungrammatical; in (41) we have a nonfinite clause with an overt subject. Martin (2001) proposes to solve this problem by the idea that T in raising clauses (40) cannot check any case, while null case is checked in control clauses. On the assumption that PRO is endowed with null case lexically, this case will never be checked in an example like (40), but it will be in cases like (42) (so-called control infinitives):

(42)   Naomi tried PRO to be happy.

Martin bases this distinction on the fact, noted by Stowell (1982), that raising and control infinitivals appear to have a different kind of specification for tense. Martin proposes that T in control infinitivals is [tense:+] and that this can check null case on PRO in (42). Exceptional Case Marking examples like (41) can then be dealt with by assuming that verbs like *believe* can directly select TP rather than CP, and that the accusative case of the subject is then derived by movement to a higher position (Martin's suggestion, following Lasnik and Saito 1992), or via Agree (see e.g. Adger 2003).

Note that this discussion is predicated on the idea that T (or perhaps C) bears a valued case feature ([case:null]). However, this proposal turns out to be empirically problematic as well as conceptually weak—null case clearly has no interface motivation. As has been known for some time, languages with case concord show that PRO bears case (see Sigurðsson 1996):

(43) Strákarnir   vonast til að PRO vanta ekki alla í skólann
      boys.NOM.DEF hope   for PRO to.lack not all in school
      'The boys hope not to all be absent from school.'

In this example, the floating quantifier *alla*, 'all', agrees in case with the subject of the clause, as is usual for such quantifiers. However, the subject is non-overt PRO. Note that PRO does not bear the same case as its controller (*The boys*, which is nominative), so this cannot be a situation involving case transmission of some kind. The only non-stipulative explanation for accusative case on the quantifier is that PRO bears accusative case and the quantifier agrees with it. Similar examples have been found in Russian, Hungarian, and Greek (see Landau 2004 for examples and references). This kind of data strongly suggest that a null case approach to the distribution of PRO is incorrect.

Landau (2004) proposes an alternative that is worth exploring. He derives the licensing of PRO vs. overt NPs in embedded finite and nonfinite clauses from the interaction of semantically interpretable features on the NP and on the clausal heads. His main suggestion is that, if the clausal heads C or T bear positive specifications for tense and agreement features (which he notates as [T] and [Agr]), then they become instantiated with an uninterpretable feature [R], which needs to be checked by an interpretable [R] feature on an NP. The function of this feature is to mark an NP as independently referential [R:+] or obligatorily anaphoric [R:−]. Following an old insight of Borer (1989), PRO is taken to be a sort of anaphor, and is hence [R:−].

With this in place, and simplifying considerably, the following analysis is possible: finite clauses contain an inflectional head (I) with a positive specification for the T and Agr features. It follows that this head is endowed with the uninterpretable feature [R:+] which has to be checked by an interpretable feature [R:+]. This forces an independently referential subject to appear, and rules out PRO (which would have an [R:−] feature).

(44) a. *Anson said that PRO left
      b. Anson said that *I[T:+, Agr:+, R:+] PRO[R:−]

A control clause, on the other hand, has a specification for a C bearing uninterpretable [T:−] (this derives from the requirements of the selecting predicate). This must check with an interpretable [T:−] on I, and it follows that I will bear an uninterpretable [R:−]. From this, it follows that only PRO is possible as a subject.

(45) a. Anson would prefer PRO to leave.
      b. Anson would prefer C[T:−] I[T:−, Agr:−, R:−] PRO[R:−]

In a raising or ECM infinitive, there is no C layer. Landau argues on the basis of the semantics of these clauses that they do contain a positive specification for T, but that they lack Agr. It follows that there is no uninterpretable [R] feature to be checked at all, so an overt subject is possible in an ECM clause.

(46) a. Anson believed [Jill to be a producer]
      b. Anson believed I[T:+] Jill[R:+] . . .

Whether this overt subject remains in situ or raises depends upon the case-marking potential of the higher verb: if the verb assigns accusative, then an ECM structure will result, as above; if it lacks accusative, then a raising structure will be generated:

(47) a. Jill seems [*t* to be a producer]
      b. Jill[R:+] seems I[T:+] *t* . . .

Landau's system also extends to control into subjunctives in a range of different languages in a way that is not directly relevant here. What is important for us is the fact that the system is consistent with the conclusions we have come to so far: we can take Landau's C to be Fin, and we have already motivated the idea that Fin can contain uninterpretable tense and agreement features. The notion that the tense feature on Fin is a simple binary [T] feature captures the reduced temporal distinctions that can be made at this position in the clause. The crucial intuition about subject licensing is that the anaphoric nature of the subject (whether it is PRO or not) does not depend on the interpretable feature [finite: ±] on Fin, but rather on the interplay of interpretable and uninterpretable features of tense, agreement, and referentiality. Unlike in earlier approaches, finiteness is not necessarily reduced to just tense and agreement, but just tense and agreement are relevant for the licensing of different kinds of subjects. Which features are available for licensing subjects depends on the presence of the Fin head, and the specifications of the I head. If the Fin head is absent, then what matters is just the specification of I. In the next section we will explore what happens when we truncate the clause lower than I, and we will see that the mechanisms for argument licensing in this kind of nonfinite domain are just the same: the presence of both T and Agr is required.

2.5 Finiteness and subject licensing in the absence of T

We have seen that tense and agreement features appear on Fin and on T. These features seem to be implicated in the selection of the clause and in the licensing of the subject. Landau's system ties down the possibility of having a referential subject to the presence of both tense and agreement features. In this section I'll present some new data from Scottish Gaelic, a language which lacks infinitives. I'll argue that the distribution of overt and PRO subjects in this language provides some further motivation for Landau's approach to subject licensing.[6]

2.5.1 *Finite and nonfinite clauses in Scottish Gaelic*

Finite clauses in Scottish Gaelic are VSO in structure. This order is usually assumed to derive from an underlying SVO order, with raising of the verb to some functional position above the position of the subject—we'll assume to T (see McCloskey 1996 and references therein for Irish, and Adger 1994 for Scottish Gaelic):

(48) Bhuail$_j$ mi t$_j$ an   cat
      strike.PST I   the cat
      'I struck the cat.' (SG)

Finite tense can also be marked by the auxiliary *bith*, 'be', which appears in its suppletive present form in the next example (see below for the VN gloss of verbal nouns in Gaelic):

(49) Tha   Calum   ag   òl   an   ti.
      be.PRS   Calum   PROG   drink.VN   the tea
      'Calum is drinking the tea.' (SG)

Following Adger and Ramchand (2003), I'll assume that in such examples the auxiliary is in T; that is, it bears a categorial T feature and is Merged in this position to satisfy the requirement that the T projection in clausal structure be instantiated. I'll also adopt their position that the subject is introduced by a predicative head, Pred, which can be null, but here marks for aspect (roughly, but not quite, progressive). See also Bowers (1993) and Svenonius (1994). This

---

6 The idea of truncation at this lower level is also implicated in the analysis of restructuring verbs in Germanic and Romance. See especially Wurmbrand (2003) and references there.

gives us the following structure, with T selecting a PredP with an internal subject (this is parallel to the standard VP-internal subject structures motivated by Koopman and Sportiche (1991) among many others):

(50)

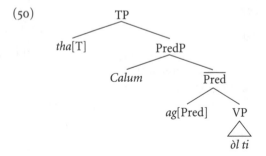

The nonfinite form of the verb here consists just of the **verbal noun** (VN), a nominalized verb form.

Subordinate clause types come in a variety of forms. Focusing our attention on argument clauses, finite subordinate clauses are obligatorily headed by a complementizer, which triggers a particular morphological form (the dependent form) of the finite verb, marked in the example below with the past dependent particle *do*:

(51)   Thuirt   mi   gun   do bhuail   mi   an   cat.
        Say.PST   I   that   strike.PST I   the   cat
        'I said that I struck the cat.'

(52)   Dh'fhaighnich   mi   an   do bhuail   thu   an   cat.
        Ask.PST   I   if   strike.PST   you   the   cat
        'I asked if you struck the cat.'

There is just one major type of nonfinite subordinate argument clause, which is headed by the verbal noun. At its simplest, this clause consists just of the verbal noun:

(53)   a. Tha   mi   airson   ithe.
           be.PRS   I   for   eat.VN
           'I want to eat.'

        b. Dh'fheuch   sinn   ri   coiseachd.
           try.PST   we   to   walk.VN
           'We tried to walk.'

        c. 'S   fheàrr   do   dh' Anna   seinn.
           is   better   to   Anna   sing.VN
           'Anna prefers to sing.'

    d. Bu   toigh   leam   falbh.
       be.COND liking with.me leave.VN
       'I'd like to leave.'

    e. Dh'iarr   e   orm   leumnaich.
       ask.PST he   on.me   jump.VN
       'He asked me to jump.'

A wide range of structures take these verbal nouns as complements. The examples in (b) and (e) show cases where finite verbs have a VN complement (the verb having raised to T). The (c) and (d) examples show adjectival and nominal heads, respectively, taking VN complements; we assume that these too are dissociated from their VN argument by some movement process. The (a) example shows a preposition taking a VN complement.

The examples above are all interpreted in the following way: one of the DPs in the higher clause is interpreted as the 'subject' of the VN, giving a classic case of a control structure.

If the verbal noun is transitive, then the object appears in a position preceding the verbal noun and the verbal noun itself is prefixed with a particle, glossed here as just PRT; we will see immediately below that this particle can inflect for agreement features.

(54) a. Tha   mi   airson cèic agus aran   ithe.
         be.PRS I   for   cake and   bread eat.VN
         'I want to eat cake and bread.'

      b. 'S fheàrr do dh' Anna òran Gàidhlig a   sheinn.
         is better to   Anna   song Gaelic   PRT sing.VN
         'Anna prefers to sing a Gaelic song.'

Adger (1996) argues that these structures involve movement from a post-VN position into the specifier of an Agr head, which is realized by the particle *a* in (54b). The arguments for this analysis come from the behaviour of pronominal objects with emphatic particles in these constructions. Emphatic particles usually attach directly to a pronoun, as in (55):

(55) Bhuail   mi iad-fhèin.
     strike.PST I   them-EMPH
     'I struck *them*.'

If we examine the behaviour of pronominal objects in VN constructions, we see that the particle which precedes the VN inflects for person, number, and gender features. The full pronoun itself does not appear; rather, we have a null pronoun occurring with rich agreement:

(56) 'S fheàrr do dh' Anna an   seinn.
      is   better to   Anna   PRT.3PL sing.VN
      'Anna prefers to sing them.'

If we combine these two constructions, we find the following:

(57) 'S fheàrr do dh' Anna an   seinn-fhèin.
      is   better to   Anna   PRT.3PL sing-EMPH
      'Anna prefers to sing *them*.'

Here, the emphatic particle is stranded in a position to the right of the VN. This gives us evidence that the base position for the object is to the right of the VN, and that argument DPs (and perhaps pronominals) move from there to a leftwards position. More concretely, we have the following structure:

(58)

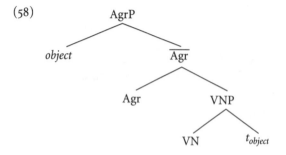

Full nominal arguments, as opposed to pronouns, trigger a default particle, with no agreement:

(59) 'S fheàrr do dh' Anna òrain   Gàidhlig
      is   better to   Anna   song.PL Gaelic
      a/*an   sheinn
      PRT.3SG.M/*PRT.3PL   sing
      'Anna prefers to sing Gaelic songs.'

The different behaviour of pronouns and full DPs is a well-known characteristic of the Celtic languages (see Adger 2000 for Gaelic and Hale and McCloskey 1984 for Irish)—descriptively, rich agreement occurs with null pronominals, while overt NPs occur with a default form of agreement.

In SG, subjects are not allowed in VN clauses, except in one specific case:[7]

(60) *Bu toigh leam   sibh/Màiri   an   doras a   dhùnadh
       be   liking with.me you/Mary   the door   PRT shut.VN
       'I'd like you/Mary to shut the door.'

---

[7] The preferred alternative is to use a finite clause with a conditional verb form.

(61) Bu toigh leam   sibh/Màiri a   bhith a'   dùnadh an dorais.
      be liking with.me you/Mary PRT be.vn prog shut.vn the door.GEN
      'I'd like you/Mary to be shutting the door.'

(62) *Bu toigh   leam   sibh/Màiri a   dhùnadh an   dorais
      be   liking with.me you/Mary PRT shut.vn   the door.GEN
      'I'd like you/Mary to shut the door.'

One way of just describing what is going on is the following: in a structure
like (61), a subject may be inserted only if the sequence *a bhith* follows it, in
which case the form of the verb also changes in that it is inflected with an
aspectual particle *a'* (which sometime surfaces as *ag*) giving rise to a progressive construction.[8] Other aspectual particles are possible here too, with a
different interpretation:

(63) Bu toigh   leam   sibh/Màiri a   bhith air   an   doras
      be liking   with.me you/Mary PRT be.vn PRF the door
      a   dhùnadh.
      PRT close.vn
      'I'd like you/Mary to have shut the door.'

Note that with the perfect particle seen in (63), the object moves into [Spec,
AgrP], rather than remaining post-VN. This also holds for other aspectual
particles, such as prospective *gu(s)*, and true progressive *ri(s)*.

The same descriptive characterization about the ability of *a bhith* to license
subjects also captures the behaviour of intransitives:

(64) *Bu toigh leam   sibh/Màiri (a)   choiseachd don   sgoil
      be   liking with.me you/Mary (PRT) walk.vn   to.the school
      'I'd like you/Mary to walk to the school.'

(65) Bu toigh leam   sibh/Màiri a   bhith a'   coiseachd
      be liking with.me you/Mary PRT be.vn prog walk.vn
      don   sgoil.
      to.the school
      'I'd like you/Mary to walk to the school.'

The collocation of elements *a bhith* appears to select an aspectually
headed phrase (the PredP discussed above). It cannot be followed by a simple
AgrP:

---

[8] I have translated this construction with an English progressive, which here has a slightly awkward
feel. There is no such awkwardness in the Gaelic case, as the interpretation of *ag* is not quite
progressive. See Ramchand (1997) and Adger (1996) for discussion.

(66) *Bu toigh leam   sibh/Màiri a   bhith an doras a   dùnadh
      be liking with.me you/Mary PRT be.VN the door PRT close.VN

The question we would like to answer is what the syntax of this construction is and why it licenses subjects.

Morphologically, *a bhith* consists of the verbal noun form of the tense bearing auxiliary *bith* 'be', preceded by a particle which appears to be the same as the agreement particle discussed above. We will see that, following Landau's intuition, a referential subject is licensed here because we have both a T feature contributed by the auxiliary and an Agr feature contributed by the particle. First, however, we will see that VN clauses in general lack a T projection.

2.5.2 *Are verbal noun clauses infinitives?*

What distinguishes an infinitival from a finite clause? In familiar languages like English the answer seems to be fairly clear. There are at least the following diagnostics:

1. Infinitival clauses are often marked by special morphology (non-affixal *to* in English, or nonfinite inflection on the verb in, for example, Romance languages).
2. The verb form (and indeed the clause) is invariant for agreement and tense distinctions (putting aside inflected infinitives—see section 2.2).
3. Infinitival clauses may have a special complementizer (Fin—see section 2.3).
4. The subject position is restricted in form—it cannot be a nominative NP.
5. At least some infinitival clauses (control clauses) may be questioned, relativized, passivized, etc. in much the same way as finite clauses, because they have much the same functional structure, differing mainly in the featural specification of heads. However, some nonfinite clauses (ECM/raising constructions) have a reduced structure, lacking the projections associated with the C layer.
6. Infinitival clauses are either selected or permitted in particular syntactic contexts: control predicates; raising predicates; ECM; certain clausal subjects.

In what follows, I will argue that there is no T position in verbal noun clauses so they are truncated, in much the same way as raising and ECM complements. The question then arises as to how they license overt subjects in the restricted environment discussed above. However, while ECM and raising clauses are truncated just below Fin, I will argue that VN clauses are truncated below T.

2.5.3 *Verbal noun clauses lack T*

There seems little prima facie evidence that VN clauses are infinitives. Firstly, there is no special infinitival form for a verb in Scottish Gaelic, unless one counts the VN form itself as such. But the VN form is used in a number of other contexts, most importantly as the nominalization of the verb, and in such contexts it behaves entirely like a noun, with gender and number features and case requirements (see e.g. Calder 1990).

Secondly, there appears to be no infinitival complementizer in Scottish Gaelic, at least none that plays the role of a simple subordinator. The translation of a nonfinite clausal subject in English must be a finite clause in SG (usually in a morphological paradigm called the conditional in traditional grammars):

(67) Biodh   snog nam phòsadh   Iain Màiri.
      be.COND nice if   marry.COND   Iain Mary
      'For Ian to marry Mary would be nice.'

Related to this, VN complement clauses never have a complementizer, while finite ones always do.[9]

It appears, then, that simply identifying VN clauses in Gaelic with infinitival clauses in English is not helpful. They have no dedicated morphological marking, there does not seem to be a nonfinite subordinating complementizer in the language, and, as we saw in the previous section, the restrictions on overt subjects seem to be rather different from those on overt subjects in English.

What, then, are VN clauses? I would like to propose that they are simply untensed verb phrases, and so they do not contain T, or C, or any other functional head associated with these domains of clause structure. This view is

---

[9] Temporal adjuncts do have a subordinating element that appears with VN clauses, suggesting that perhaps they could be taken as nonfinite subordinating complementizers:

(ii) An dhèidh do Dhaibhidh na   leabharaichean a   leughadh, chuir   e
      after   to David   the books   PRT read.VN   put.PST he
      sìos   iad
      down   them
      'After David read the books, he put them down.'

Importantly, the case licensing of the subject here has a special syntax involving the insertion of a prepositional element *do*.

compatible with the observations made above, since if a clause lacks T (and hence C) there can be no [Spec, TP] to receive case, no head to host an infinitival marker, no tense-related agreement marking, and no subordinating complementizer. I do however assume that the arguments offered above are correct and that these VNs may project a case licensing Agr head. The distinction between this head and the other functional heads which cannot appear in a VN clause is that the Agr head has no semantic effect on the projection it combines with. So whereas T might be seen as binding an event variable, and C as introducing a propositional variable, Agr behaves simply as a case licenser:[10]

(68)

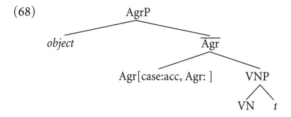

Agr has its unvalued agreement features valued by the features of the object, and the object moves to the specifier of Agr. Agr also Matches in case features with the object, valuing the object's case feature as accusative.

I proposed above that verb phrases were actually PredPs, so we can extend (68) to (69):

(69)

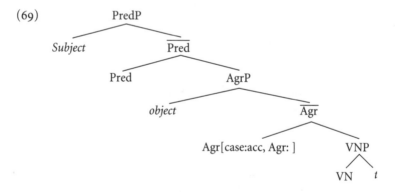

Note that this analysis extends the 'truncation' perspective on the selection of nonfinite clauses discussed in previous sections of this chapter. Rather than

---

[10] In fact, it would be possible to combine the Agr features with the VN itself, either lexically, or via head movement of the VN to Agr. I know of no evidence that suggests that this occurs, but it is a theoretical option. If Agr is just adjoined to the VN lexically (i.e. it is not a separate syntactic head), then the selected projection is, of course, just VN. See Sells and McCloskey (1988) for discussion.

truncating at Fin (Control clauses) or just below (raising and ECM clauses), we truncate at the VP (PredP) level. In terms of their broad semantics, VP/PredP and CP are both propositional, so it should come as no surprise that languages differ in whether s-selection for a proposition is met by either of these two categories (in Minimalist terms, they are both **phases**, and Pred is a generalized version of the 'little v' of Chomsky 1995b, Kratzer 1996, and many others).

2.5.4 *Consequences of lack of T*

This view of the status of VN clauses has a number of immediate predictions. First, it predicts that VN clauses in Scottish Gaelic will be unable to undergo syntactic processes that require TP or CP. If our hypothesis is correct, there should be no 'infinitival' constituent questions (movement to/A-bar binding from [Spec, CP]) and no 'infinitival relatives' (ditto). The question of passivization is slightly more complicated, since there are a number of passive forms in SG, some of which involve T while others do not. I will show that precisely the former group are disallowed in VN clauses, while the latter group are well-formed. This is further evidence for the hypothesis described above.

Taking constituent questions first, (70) and (71) show that it is impossible to extract to a position at the start of a VN clause; the only possibility is a paraphrase with a finite clause:

(70)   *Cha   robh   fhios   agam   dè   a   dhèanamh
        NEG   was   knowledge   at.me   what   PRT   do.VN
        'I didn't know what to do.'

(71)   Cha   robh   fhios   agam   dè   dhèanainn.
        NEG   was   knowledge   at.me   what   do.COND.1.SG
        'I didn't know what to do.'

The same pattern is observed with adjunct questions.[11] These data are replicated with relatives (I give non extraposed relatives for ease of exposition; Gaelic speakers prefer to extrapose relative clauses in general, but this does not affect the judgements reported here):

(72)   *Tha am bòrd air   an t-seacaid agad   a   chur   a-muigh
        is   the table on.it   the jacket   at.you PRT   put.VN   outside
        'The table to put your jacket on is outside.' (pied-piped version)

---

[11] Jim McCloskey has pointed out to me that in some dialects of Irish, some adjunct questions are well formed with VNs. I have no explanation for this as yet.

(73) *Tha am bòrd an t-seacaid agad   a   chur   air   a-muigh
      is   the table the jacket   at.you PRT put.VN on.it outside
      'The table to put your jacket on is outside.' (non-pied-piped version)

These data strongly argue for the lack of at least a CP projection in VN clauses, which follows from the idea that these clauses are truncated below TP.

A number of different types of passivization in SG provide further evidence that the view we are taking here of VN clauses is the correct one. We will concentrate on three types of passivization: morphological, the *rach*-passive, and A-movement passives.

(i) Each verb in SG has a tensed passive form. For example, corresponding to the active:

(74) Dhùin   Daibhidh an   doras.
      shut.PST David   the   door
      'David shut the door.'

we have

(75) Dhùineadh   an   doras.
      shut.PST.PASS the   door
      'The door was shut.'

On the well-motivated assumption that the finite verb here is in T, this suggests that there is a passive form of T to which the finite verb raises.

All verbs in SG have a VN form, but there is no 'passive' VN form. That is, although there is a VN clause corresponding to (74) (e.g. 76), there is no morphologically distinct form corresponding to (75) (e.g. 77).

(76) Feumaidh Dàibhidh an   doras a   dhùnadh.
      must   David   the   door   PRT   close.VN
      'David must close the door.'

(77) *Feumaidh an   doras a   dhùnadh
      must   the   door   PRT   close.VN
      'The door must be closed.'

A number of verbs do have a passive participle type form, which is used with the auxiliary:

(78) Tha   an   doras dùinte.
      is   the   door   closed.PST.PTCP
      'The door is closed.'

However, the -*te* morphology is fairly unproductive, so while *dùinte* 'closed' is fine, similar formations on other verbs are extremely awkward, and speakers much prefer to use the passive formation discussed below in (iii). Moreover such examples look like adjectives in undergoing comparative formation and modification by intensive particles:

(79) Tha   an   doras   nas   dùinte.
     is   the   door   more   closed
     'The door is more closed.'

(80) Tha   an   doras   glè   dhùinte.
     is   the   door   very   closed
     'The door is very closed.'

This gap in the paradigm falls out of our claim that VN clauses lack functional structure from T up.

(ii) An alternative passive form is the *rach*-passive. This is formed from the verb *rach* 'go' plus a VN clause. The *rach*-passive counterpart of our example is:

(81) Chaidh   an   doras   a   dhùnadh.
     go.PST   the   door   PRT   shut.VN
     'The door was/got shut.'

where *chaidh* is the suppletive past of *rach*. Note that once again the passivization takes place in T (there is immediate morphological evidence for this in the past tense form of the verb). Our hypothesis that there is no T in VN clauses predicts that *rach*-passives are not possible in VN-clauses. This turns out to be the case.

First, a brief comment about the structure of examples like (81). There are three possibilities. The apparent subject *an doras* may be in the [Spec, AgrP] position in the lower VN clause with a null expletive as the subject of the matrix verb *chaidh*:

(82)   Chaidh *expl* [$_{AgrP}$ an doras a dhùnadh]

Another possibility is that the subject has raised into a specifier position in the upper clause (perhaps [Spec, TP]) and the verb has raised further into AgrS (as in the system of Bobaljik and Carnie 1996) or perhaps into Fin in a system like that argued for in previous sections of this chapter:

(83)   [$_{AgrSP/FinP}$ chaidh [$_{TP}$ an doras [$_{AgrP}$ t a dhùnadh]]]

Finally, it could be the case that the VN clause itself is the subject of *chaidh*:

(84) [$_{TP}$ chaidh$_i$ [$_{VP}$ [an doras a dhùnadh] t$_i$]]

So, depending on the right analysis, the subject is either (i) a null expletive, (ii) *an doras*, or (iii) the VN clause itself.

Let us briefly recapitulate what we have discovered about the descriptive relationship between finite clauses and VN clauses. Essentially, in a VN clause the subject appears before *a bhith*, then there is an aspectual particle and the verb appears in its VN form. The position of the object with respect to the verb is determined by the aspectual particle. The simple aspectual particle *a'* (sometimes realized as *ag*) has no effect on VO order, while other aspectual particles like the perfect particle *air* cause the object to front, giving an OV order.

Given this discussion, our hypothesis that VN clauses lack T predicts that none of the following should be grammatical, no matter what the right analysis of (81) is:

(85) *Bu   toigh leam   a   bhith   a'   dol   an   doras
      be.COND liking with.me   PRT   be.VN   PROG go.VN the   door
      a   dhùnadh
      PRT   shut.VN
      (expletive subject)

(86) *Bu   toigh leam   an   doras a   bhith   a'   dol
      be.COND liking with.me   the   door   PRT   be.VN   PROG go.VN
      a   dhùnadh
      PRT   shut.VN
      (*an doras* subject)

(87) *Bu   toigh leam   an doras a   dhùnadh a   bhith a'
      be.COND liking with.me   the door PRT   shut.VN PRT   be.VN PROG
      dol   (VN clause subject)
      go.VN

In each of these examples, we have taken a construction which selects a VN clause and attempted to create a passive using the *rach* passive strategy. As is obvious from the grammaticality judgements shown, our hypothesis makes the correct prediction. There is simply no VN version of the *rach*-passive, since the *rach*-passive makes crucial use of T and there is no T in a VN clause.

(iii) The aspectual passive: another commonly used passive form in SG is one where an aspectual particle signalling perfect aspect is followed by an agreement particle, inflected for φ-features agreeing with the (surface) subject. This type of example typically is ambiguous between a passive and an active reading:

(88)   Tha   Dàibhidh   is   Màiri   air   am   marbhadh
       is   David   and   Mary   PRF   PRT.3PL   kill.VN
       'David and Mary have murdered them.' *or*
       'David and Mary have been murdered.'

I shall assume that the active reading arises when the structure involves a *pro* in the specifier of AgrP, while the passive reading arises when there is a DP trace of the surface subject in this specifier:[12]

(89)   Tha [Dàibhidh is Màiri]$_i$ air pro$_j$ am marbhadh (active)

(90)   Tha [Dàibhidh is Màiri]$_i$ air t$_i$ am marbhadh (passive)

Note that this type of passive does not involve TP at all. The auxiliary verb *tha* is not affected by the operation. Our current hypothesis therefore predicts that this type of passive should be available in VN clauses, and indeed it is:

(91)   Bu   toigh   leam   Dàibhidh   is   Màiri   a   bhith   air
       be.COND   liking   with.me   David   and   Mary   PRT   be.VN   PRF
       am   marbhadh
       PRT.3PL   kill.VN
       'I would like David and Mary to be murdered.'

In summary then, we have seen that when passive is an operation that crucially relies on T, it is not available in a VN clause, whereas when it does not involve T it *is* available. This is strong evidence for the view that VN clauses are truncated at T, evidence which is backed up by the lack of CP processes like constituent question formation and relativization.

Let us finally turn to the main problem at hand: the licensing of subjects in VN-clauses. Recall that an overt subject is barred in a simple VN clause:

(92)   *Bu   toigh   leam   Màiri   an   doras   a   dhùnadh
       be.COND   liking   with.me   Mary   the   door   PRT   shut.VN
       'I'd like Mary to shut the door.'

(93)   *Bu   toigh   leam   Màiri   (a)   falbh
       be.COND   liking   with.me   Mary   (PRT)   leave.VN
       'I'd like Mary to leave.'

---

[12] Of course, this analysis of passive leaves open the question of why this A-movement takes place, given that a *pro* can occur here, and so this is presumably a case position. We leave this problem aside, since, for the current argument, what is important is that this version of passive does not involve the T node, but rather structure below T.

(94) Bu   toigh   leam   falbh
      be.COND   liking   with.me   leave.VN
      'I'd like to leave.'

One simple possibility is that this effect is due to case. On a classical GB account, there is no case governor, hence only PRO is available. A null case story is rather less plausible; we could say that Pred bears a null case feature forcing a PRO to appear in a PredP, but since Pred also appears in finite clauses, we would have to tie the absence of null case on Pred to the absence of T (or else we would have a case conflict between the nominative case of T and the hypothesized null case on Pred). This is certainly possible, but is rather an odd stipulation.

Futhermore, neither approach gives us any immediate insight into why a subject is licensed in a clause with *a bhith*:[13]

(95) Bu   toigh   leam   Màiri   a   bhith   a'   dùnadh
      be.COND   liking   with.me   Mary   PRT   be.VN   PROG   shut.VN
      an   dorais.
      the   door.GEN
      'I'd like Mary to shut the door.'

However, Landau's proposal—that presence of both T and Agr features is required to license a referential subject—allows us to predict exactly this result. Recall that the auxiliary *bith* is a realization of T (i.e. it bears a categorial T feature). Moreover, it is a verbal noun form of the T auxiliary. As we have seen, verbal nouns allow the projection of an Agr node for case-licensing purposes; it follows that we can project an AgrP structure above *bith*. Since *bith* is T, it selects PredP directly. This gives us the following structure:

(96)

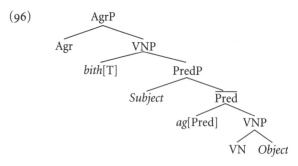

---

[13] There is a complex set of data concerning when overt subjects are licensed in various dialects of Irish. In Ulster Irish, examples like (92) and (93) are well formed, while in Munster Irish only (93) is well formed. I take the latter fact to indicate that the Agr node is Merged higher than the base subject position, and that the subject may therefore be licensed by it (correctly predicting accusative case). Any object will then be forced to be licensed in another fashion, which appears to be correct (such objects receive genitive case). In Ulster Irish, it may be the case that a full TP structure is generated.

We now have both a T feature and Agr features immediately above the subject. On the assumption that both have a positive specification, the presence of both T and Agr features instantiates an uninterpretable [R] feature on the VN. This feature requires a referential NP argument if it is to be eliminated, predicting the presence of an overt subject. The usual mechanism for case licensing the subject causes raising to the specifier of Agr, in a parallel fashion to raising of the object to the specifier of Agr:

(97)

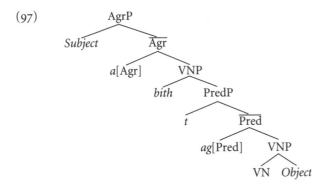

We then correctly derive VNPs with subjects as in (98)

(98) Bu   toigh   leam   Màiri   a   bhith   a'   dùnadh
      be.COND   liking with.me   Mary   PRT   be.VN   PROG   shut.VN
      an   dorais.
      the   door.GEN
      'I'd like Mary to be shutting the door.'

This analysis also predicts the impossibility of an overt subject in the absence of *a bhith* in a verbal noun clause. Since VN clauses lack T, there is no higher case assigner for such a subject:

(99) *Bu   toigh   leam   Màiri   a'   dùnadh   an   dorais
      be.COND   liking with.me   Mary   PROG shut.VN the   door.GEN
      'I'd like Mary to shut the door.'

Notice that we also predict that these cases will have a different temporal interpretation from the simple VN clauses which lack *a bhith*, since *a bhith* clauses have an extra (interpretable) T feature. This is correct: these are the only clauses which license subjects and they are the only nonfinite clauses which have a special temporal interpretation (this is the 'progressive' interpretation we remarked on earlier).

We now need to inquire about the status of cases where there is no overt subject:

(100) Bu   toigh   leam   an   doras   a   dhùnadh.
       be.COND   liking with.me   the door   PRT   close.VN
       'I'd like to shut the door.'

These constructions could plausibly involve either control or raising, with a PRO or a trace in the PredP subject position. The proposal defended here allows either a control or a raising analysis (or indeed more radical alternatives), and I will not choose between them here.[14]

Interestingly, the Agr head that appears above *b(h)ith* cannot have rich agreement. When a pronominal subject appears in this construction, it cannot appear as *pro* and trigger rich agreement, in contrast to the object of a VN clause:

(101) Tha   e   doirbh   bhur   glacadh.
       is   it   difficult PRT.2PL   catch.VN
       'It is difficult to catch you.'

(102) *Bu   toigh   leam   bhur   b(h)ith   a'   dùnadh
       be.COND   liking with.me   PRT.2PL   be.VN   PROG   shut.VN
       an   dorais
       the door.GEN
       'I'd like you to be shutting the door.'

Instead, pronouns appear in their overt form with a default agreement:

(103) Bu   toigh   leam   sibh   a   bhith   a'   dùnadh
       be.COND   liking with.me   you   PRT   be.VN   PROG   shut.VN
       an   dorais
       the door.GEN
       'I'd like you to be shutting the door.'

What this suggests is that the Agr which projects above *bith* here is not fully specified for its agreement features: it does not have the full set of phi-features needed to license *pro*. Let us assume that the Agr head here bears only a default specification for agreement features [Agr:3s]. This is not enough to license a *pro*, ruling out (102). However, an overt full pronoun is case-licensed

---

[14] McCloskey (1984) argues that in corresponding Irish cases the subject has raised to the complement of the higher preposition. The arguments he uses for the most part do not extend to the Gaelic constructions, and in fact the syntax of the two languages is rather different in this area (Irish allowing a variety of overt subjects in the analogous constructions).

in such a structure, since it bears interpretable agreement features, just like an overt DP.

What will such a default value mean for Landau's proposal as applied here? We have already proposed that [Agr:−] triggers the appearance of [R:−], and that [AGR:+] (in combination with [T:+]) triggers the appearance of [R:+]. A plausible extension of this idea is that Agr bearing a default specification triggers the appearance of an uninterpretable *unvalued* R feature [R:]. This is then compatible with either a fully referential NP or an anaphoric one, i.e. PRO.

If this is correct, we expect to see an unusual situation: there should be no complementarity between full DP and PRO in these structures. This turns out to be correct:

(104) Bu   toigh liam   a   bhith a'   dùnadh an dorais
       be.COND liking with.me PRT be.VN PROG shut.VN the door.GEN
       'I'd like to be shutting the door.'

This final section has extended the ideas discussed in the previous sections to cases where nonfinite structures arise via truncation of T. We saw, however, that in Gaelic the T feature could be reintroduced in a verbal noun structure, and the featural configurations for subject licensing reconstituted within the truncated structure.

2.6 Conclusion

This chapter has surveyed some recent literature within the Minimalist Programme which has been concerned with the notion of finiteness, and has extended these ideas to a new domain. I have suggested that there is good positional evidence for a low complementizer position Fin. I have also argued that there are reasons to associate this position with a feature, and that this feature determines the interpretation of the lower clause as anaphoric to the speech event of the higher clause (following Bianchi). I proposed that we call this feature [finite: ±]. It is akin, but not identical, to the notion of S-finiteness discussed by Gretsch and Perdue (Chapter 12 below).

There is also evidence that Fin may bear uninterpretable tense and agreement features. Landau suggests that it is the behaviour of these features that is responsible for subject licensing, and the effects of this can be seen when the C layer is removed, truncating the clause at TP. I showed a particularly radical case of this kind of truncation in Gaelic, where the clause can be truncated at the VP level, thus removing not only Fin but T as well. In this case too, though, subjects can be licensed in a way that depends on the formal features

T and Agr. This strongly argues for divorcing subject licensing from the interpretable feature [finite]. These uninterpretable features might be thought of as an execution within current syntactic theory of the structural correlates of M-finiteness, as also discussed by Gretsch and Perdue.

The distinction between the uninterpretable features [T] and [Agr] on Fin and the interpretable [finite] feature also argues for a divorce between the clausal expression of finiteness and its morphological expression as tense and agreement features (see Sells, Chapter 3 below). The [T] and [Agr] features, we have seen, are not confined to the Fin projection, and in fact may appear very low down in the clause.

I have argued, in line with expectations, that there is no clear mapping from the traditional notion of finiteness to the categories of formal grammar. There are phenomena, and there are attempted explanations of those phenomena which are embedded within a theoretical system. Typically, the terms in which the explanation is couched will be far removed from the terms in which the original phenomenon was described, and I believe this is the case for finiteness.

3

Finiteness in non-transformational syntactic frameworks

PETER SELLS

3.1 Introduction

3.1.1 *Overview: finiteness, and its expression*

In this chapter, I consider different possible uses of the term 'finite':

(1)   a. finite as a value of a form feature of verbs;
       b. finite as a formal grammatical property of clauses (typically expressed by a finite form);
       c. finite as a formal property that certain elements may be sensitive to, such as agreement, complementizer selection, or the presence or form of negation;
       d. finite as a property of clauses used to make an assertion.

I will discuss some aspects of the treatment of finiteness in its various facets given in (1) in the non-transformational theories of Head-Driven Phrase Structure Grammar (HPSG) and Lexical-Functional Grammar (LFG).[1]

Due to the way that syntactic information is represented in these approaches, it can be stated at the outset that finiteness is considered to really be a property of a clause. From this starting point, my purpose here is to show what other aspects of clausal structure or interpretation may express or interact with finiteness. This means that we must be careful to recognize the

The material in this chapter on Swedish was presented at the Conference on Finiteness held at the University of Konstanz in 2001. I am grateful to Irina Nikolaeva and three anonymous reviewers for very useful comments and suggestions on the chapter, helping it attain its present form. All responsibility for errors and misinterpretations remains with me.

[1] See Pollard and Sag (1994) and Sag et al. (2003) for introductory presentations on HPSG; Bresnan (1982) and Bresnan (2001) for LFG; Ackerman and Webelhuth (1998) and Andrews and Manning (1999) offer hybrid formalisms that are inspired by aspects of both of these major approaches.

conceptual distinction between finiteness as a property of a clause and its overt morphosyntactic expression (typically as tense marking on a verb) in a 'finite' morphological form—the clear distinction in (1a/b). In this regard my approach is similar to that of Nikolaeva (2003), though with a focus on the theoretical mechanisms that can allow one to present analyses which are not forced to reduce finiteness to only one of the characterizations in (1). I will argue that non-transformational theories have as a necessary design feature the distinction between the surface form or position of a given morphosyntactic element and the grammatical information that that element expresses.[2]

The chapter is organized as follows: in the rest of this section I discuss transformational and non-transformational approaches to clausal features such as finiteness, illustrating the more flexible relation between function and form that has been recognized explicitly in the latter group. In sections 3.2 and 3.3 I offer arguments from Japanese and Swedish respectively that the notion of a finite verb form is (empirically and) conceptually distinct from the notion of a finite clause. In section 3.4 I show briefly how other grammatical phenomena, such as the distribution of complementizers and of negation, are sensitive to one or other notion of finiteness. Finally, section 3.5 contains a brief summarizing conclusion and a consideration of the nature of clausal finiteness.

3.1.2 *Clausal finiteness*

Transformational approaches to morphosyntax typically deal with the distribution of information in the clause through fixed structures and the mechanism of movement: for example, in the approach to tense marking in the GB system of Chomsky (1981; 1986a), the tense information in a clause is associated with the INFL position (and also with its X′-projected nodes I′ and IP). A verb root would end up hosting this tense information as an inflected word via the mechanism of head movement of the V up to INFL as in (2) (see e.g. Travis 1984; Baker 1988), or by lowering of the inflectional affix in INFL onto V (Chomsky 1981). Through these mechanisms, tense is considered to be a property of the clause (by assumption here, the IP), even though morphologically the tense inflection is located on V in a language like English, where the INFL affix lowers into VP (due to arguments by Emonds 1978 on English vs. French; see also Swedish in (24) below, where the finite verb is clearly VP-internal). Hence the surface position of tense can be quite low in the overall structure.

---

[2] This distinction also figures prominently in recent papers devoted to the acquisition of finiteness (see Dimroth and Lasser 2002: 647 ff. and Gretsch and Perdue, ch. 12 below). (See section 3.5.2.)

(2)

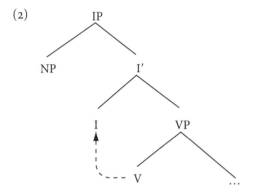

The specific role of finiteness in the clause has been treated by factoring out the CP domain, following an influential paper by Rizzi (1997, esp. 283–5). Rizzi argues that finiteness is located in the head of the phrase FinP, which is structurally higher than IP. What has been called IP may itself be internally complex, perhaps consisting of AgrP, TenseP, NegP, and so on, as proposed by Pollock (1989). A standard argument for the distinction between finiteness and tense (and so, on this type of approach, FinP vs. TenseP) is the fact that complementizers like English *that* and *for* classify clauses as finite or nonfinite, but are not sensitive to tense: there is no 'past tense' complementizer, for example. Hence, in Rizzi's approach, verbs with tense would be associated with Tense(P), while complementizers would be higher in the structure associated with Fin(P)—or even higher (see Adger, chapter 2 above). Exactly how these morphemes spell out in a given language would be subject to different possibilities of head movement. In Japanese, for instance, verb stems combine morphologically both with tense markers and with complementizers, among other suffixes:

(3)   a. tabe   -ru   -to
          eat   -Prs   -that
          'that (someone) eats'
      b. tabe   -ta   -to
          eat   -Pst   -that
          'that (someone) ate'

The complementizer -*to* is restricted to combination with finite verbs, but is not sensitive to tense, a property it shares with the English *that*. Consequently, the assumption from Rizzi's work is that a complementizer will be generated in a Fin node, and may or may not surface as an independent form (e.g. -*to* vs. *that*) depending on details of morphological processes which are fed by movement.

Rizzi's proposal for factorization of the features of the clause also covers Force—declarative, interrogative, or imperative, in the main cases. Not only does his proposal distinguishes Fin(ite) and Force as syntactic entities, it places Force as the highest syntactic projection and Fin as the lowest projection (within the 'CP-domain'), as shown in (4) (see Adger, chapter 2, Example (13) above):

(4)   Rizzi's Expanded CP

$[_{\text{ForceP}} \cdots \cdots [_{\text{FinP}} \cdots [_{\text{TP}} \cdots]]]$

The categories intermediate between ForceP and FinP, which are not relevant here, include Focus(P) and Topic(P). The ForceP part of Rizzi's proposal will correspond to what I describe below as grammatical information—abstract information that typically has no dedicated form (for example, there is no dedicated Imperative form of the verb in English; a finite clause may be used to make an Assertion, but need not be, and so on; see e.g. Sadock and Zwicky 1985).

In contrast, FinP corresponds much more closely to morphological information: as an illustration, Roberts and Roussou (2002: 142) present an account of V2 declarative clauses which requires that T(ense) is moved to the Fin head of FinP and that these features are spelled out in that position. For them, a V2 clause involves overt realization of SpecFinP and Fin, with a finite/tensed verb in the second position.[3] And it is this overt structure that indicates that a clause has the Force of a declarative (say, assertive force).

In fact, Roberts (2004) concludes that there is no ForceP in root declarative clauses (as there is no syntactic evidence for it, declaratives being rooted in FinP), and therefore that a declarative clause type is the unmarked clause type. In other words, a clause will be interpreted as declarative unless there is a positive indication that it is either interrogative or imperative (see pp. 305, 314). In Roberts's account of V2, the V2 structure is pure form, driven by the need of the Fin head to be overt, and the connection to the semantic or pragmatic Force is left as an implication. This appears to be a necessary conclusion in the Minimalist approach, or at least in the factorization of CP into Force and Fin, because it is assumed that features on heads only exist if they have syntactic consequences—in other words, if they trigger movement. As there is no evidence of the syntactic effect of Force in root V2 clauses (by Roberts's argument, they are rooted in FinP), it has to be assumed that Force is absent. Hence there may be only an implicit relation between a clausal property (expressing an Assertion) and the morphosyntax of the clause.

Non-transformational approaches offer a different point of view on the relation between form (e.g. Finiteness) and function (e.g. semantic or

---

[3] As I show below in section 3.3, in Swedish it is sometimes the case that the overt realization of Finite is in a different position from the overt realization of Tense.

pragmatic FORCE). First, such approaches do not countenance word formation in the syntax, or movement to collect or check features, as they are committed to the Lexicalist Hypothesis proposed in Lapointe (1985). Second, they make a distinction between abstract properties which characterize linguistic objects and whatever is the overt linguistic expression of those properties. The resulting constructional approach is perhaps more readily evident in the actual practice of HPSG, so I begin by presenting some ideas from that framework, concerning clausal properties and clausal features. This means that it is not necessary to assume a 1–1 correspondence between clausal properties and the morphosyntactic heads which express them (compare the pure interpretation of Rizzi's proposals described above: every finite clause used with some communicative effect should have a Force head and a Fin head). I shall return to this point shortly.

Elaborating on the first point above, about the Lexicalist Hypothesis, words are inserted into syntactic structures in their fully inflected (surface) forms and share their information with the structure containing them. Research in non-transformational approaches has therefore considered various ways of dealing with information shared between a single word and the clause containing it, but in most cases there is a simple and direct approach:

(5)   For inflectional features, the verb is the head of the clause.

This statement actually recalls the original development of X'-theory in Jackendoff (1977), in which V was the X' head of S for precisely the reasons of information sharing. This is accomplished by 'feature percolation', whereby any relevant feature specification on V is similarly specified on the maximal projection of V (VP or S). In HPSG analyses, for example, a verb shares its finiteness information with the clause in virtue of being the head. In a slightly different architecture, LFG accomplishes the same thing, by associating information on V directly with the clause at the f-structure level.

So, on these approaches, *that* in English is a complementizer which combines with a finite clause, while -*to* in Japanese (see 3) is a 'complementizer' which combines with a finite verb (compare with the HPSG analysis of *that* in 35 below); but as a finite verb necessarily heads a finite clause, both *that* and -*to* will have the syntactic effects of signalling an embedded clause that must be finite. And this is true regardless of whether the complementizing form is structurally located in C, V, or some other clausal node. The same property holds for other clausal features (see Sells 1995).[4]

---

[4] This is not to say that every kind of grammatical information flows from head to clause (see e.g. Pollard and Sag 1994; Andrews and Manning 1999); but this is true for feature specifications of finiteness or tense.

Now I turn to the second point mentioned at the beginning of this subsection. Exactly how information flows between different parts of a single representation (HPSG) or between different representations (LFG) is an important aspect of these non-transformational approaches. I first present some simple characterizations of declarative and imperative clauses in HPSG, to illustrate how abstract grammatical information and overt linguistic form can be related, and then I discuss the two parts of the syntactic representation in LFG, leading me to look in more detail at exactly what the information is that is flowing around (in some cases, only apparently).

HPSG approaches typically associate morphosyntactic form with semantic and pragmatic information either through lexical entries or through 'types', which declare necessary types of information for a given linguistic object (usually, a somewhat abstract object). The definition of a 'declarative' clause could be stated as in (6), using aspects of the proposals in Ginzburg and Sag (2000: 42–3) and the related analyses in Sag et al. (2003):[5]

(6)   *declarative-cl:*

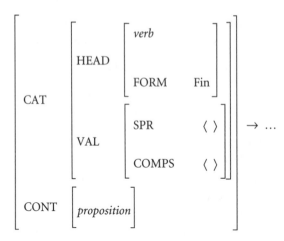

The key in (6) is the way the rule mentions both syntax and semantics. The type *declarative-cl* requires that the semantics of a *proposition* type be expressed by a syntax which is headed by a Finite form with empty VALENCE lists of COMPS and SPR. The requirement for empty lists means that the verb must have combined with all its arguments, and therefore the structure is syntactically (and semantically) complete. Thus (6) says that a declarative clause is headed by a finite verb which has all of its arguments in place, and has a proposition type of meaning. (See also Sag et al. 2003: 479.)

---

[5] I assume that verbs have a morphological Form feature, one value of which is Finite (see e.g. Gazdar et al. 1985: 23 ff. or Sag et al. 2003: 246 ff.).

Ultimately, it is necessary to recognize that Force is associated not with particular forms but rather with constructions—a point made strongly in Nikolaeva (2003) (see also the discussion of Roberts and Roussou 2002 above). In representations like those above, there are places to express these associations—in the constraints that relate CAT and CONT, and then the constraints that relate CONT and actual illocutionary Force, which I now come to. However, they are associations, not equivalences.

Following a general strategy laid out by Portner (1997), Ginzburg and Sag (2000) classify the contents of different clause types and then specify which illocutionary forces can embed them at the root level, as in (7). Portner draws analogies between verbs taking different kinds of embedded clause complement (e.g. *think* takes a proposition and *wonder* takes a question) and what happens at the root level (one asserts a proposition and asks a question, and not vice versa).

(7) a. *assert-rel* ⇒ [MSG-ARG *proposition*]
     b. *ask-rel* ⇒ [MSG-ARG *question*]
     c. *order-rel* ⇒ [MSG-ARG *outcome*]

In (8) I show a simplified definition of *root-cl* from Ginzburg and Sag (2000: 267), where the values of *illoc-rel* are those indicated in (7):

(8) *root- cl:*

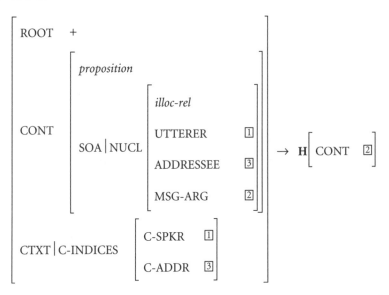

Thus a root clause is characterized as an illocutionary act, roughly of the form 'I *illoc-rel* to you that P' (the left-hand side of the rule) where P is the actual content of the clause (the right-hand side of the rule, tagged ②). For an assertion, (7a) says that the type of P has to be *proposition,* and so on.[6]

In English, a declarative is a clause headed by a verb which has combined with all its arguments and is a proposition semantically. A declarative clause in a V2 language might be characterized slightly differently in its syntax: it not only needs a finite verb, but the finite verb must be in second position. For example, Kathol (2000: 140ff.) offers some very simple type declarations for German which characterize a root declarative clause as a structure that has the semantics of a declarative, a finite verb in second position, and some non-verbal constituent in the initial position (compare with the LFG structures in 29 below).

Now I consider an imperative; (9) is a rule which declares what it is to be an imperative clause, while also showing the specific English construction for expressing an imperative:

(9)   *imperative-cl:*

$$
\begin{bmatrix}
\text{CAT} & \begin{bmatrix} \text{VAL} & \begin{bmatrix} \text{SPR} & \langle\ \rangle \end{bmatrix} \end{bmatrix} \\[2ex]
\text{CONT} & \begin{bmatrix} outcome \\[1ex] \text{SOA} & \boxed{1} \end{bmatrix}
\end{bmatrix} \rightarrow
$$

$$
\begin{bmatrix}
\mathbf{H} & \begin{bmatrix}
\text{CAT} & \begin{bmatrix}
\text{HEAD} & \begin{bmatrix} verb \\[1ex] \text{FORM} & \text{Base} \end{bmatrix} \\[2ex]
\text{VAL} & \begin{bmatrix} \text{SPR} & \langle\ \text{NP [PER 2]}\ \rangle \\[1ex] \text{COMPS} & \langle\ \rangle \end{bmatrix}
\end{bmatrix} \\[4ex]
\text{CONT} & \boxed{1}
\end{bmatrix}
\end{bmatrix}
$$

First, we can see in (9) that the semantic type is *outcome,* the type of an imperative and the appropriate type for an illocutionary act of ordering. This meaning is associated by the rule with the 'Base' form (a term I borrow

---

[6] The mention of SOA (state-of-affairs) and NUCL (nucleus) in (8) are technical details of the Ginzburg and Sag (2000) analysis which I gloss over here.

from Gazdar et al. 1985), the uninflected citation form of the verb. So while a finite form like *eats* or *brought* will head a declarative, an imperative will be headed by *eat* or *bring*. There is no specific imperative form of the verb in English. Second, (9) shows that the construction for an imperative clause is one that requires no SPR or COMPS arguments—it is complete—but which consists of a single daughter which would combine with a SPR that is second person. So, what (9) says is that the grammar allows a nonfinite Base form VP that would have taken a second person subject to function by itself as a full sentence (with all VALENCE values satisfied), and this is exactly correct for the form of an imperative sentence in English. In turn, the meaning of such a structure can be the message conveyed in an ordering speech act, according to (7c) and (8).

Details aside, the main point I wish to illustrate here is that there is no necessary morphological relationship between the form of the verb, clausal properties such as 'finite' or 'declarative', and illocutionary force such as assertion; these clausal properties are defined constructionally.

3.1.3 *Clausal finiteness and the architecture of grammar*

I move now to the LFG account of grammatical information and its expression, which will provide more of the technical background to the points I wish to make concerning the different natures of 'finiteness'. LFG provides two separate representations for each example: for the English example (10a), the constituent structure is in (10b) and the functional structure is in (10c). (These terms are usually shortened to 'c-structure' and 'f-structure'.)

(10) a. Anna often reads novels.

b. C-structure: c. F-structure:

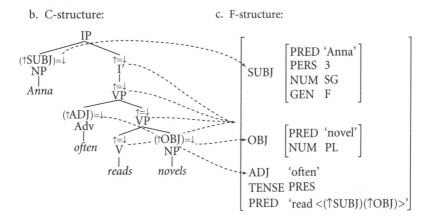

The arrows connecting the c- and f-structures are not part of the formal representation, but simply depict graphically the information flow that the annotations (such as '↑ = ↓') on each node define. For example, the annotation '(↑ SUBJ) = ↓' means that the information associated with a node so marked is the value of the SUBJ attribute in the f-structure. The annotations in (10b) show that SpecIP is the subject position, complement-of-V is the object position, and a position adjoined to VP is an adjunct. These define how the information associated with these positions contributes to the whole f-structure. Finally, any node annotated ↑ = ↓ contributes its information directly to the whole f-structure nucleus. So, while the information that the clause is present tense is associated with a TENSE PRES specification on the verb *reads*, this information becomes a property of the whole clause (nucleus) in virtue of the ↑ = ↓ annotations. In particular the arrow from V to the f-structure shows that any information that V has becomes directly part of the whole f-structure. In the c-structure, V is the head of VP but it is not the head of IP; but as far as the f-structure information goes, V is the 'head' (strictly, it is *a* head) of the clause nucleus. F-structure attributes represent the abstract grammatical information conveyed by a variety of surface forms, and f-structures are considered to be largely universal in their main properties, providing the core of semantic interpretation. In the present context, the examples in (10a), (11), and (12) all correspond to essentially the same f-structure, the one in (10c), and hence are (rough) translation equivalents of each other.

While complements, specifiers, and adjoined phrases are associated with some grammatical function (such as SUBJ or ADJ), all other nodes are annotated ↑ = ↓ (see Bresnan 2001: ch. 6). Hence, even though the French c-structure in (11) differs from the English structure in (10b), due to the higher position of the finite verb in French (the finite verb is in I rather than V), the information flow to f-structure will give the same f-structure (10c):

(11)

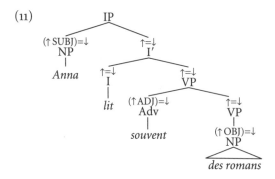

In LFG, maximal projections need not have an overt head in the c-structure; hence there is no I head of IP in the English c-structure, and no V head of VP in the French c-structure, in these particular examples.

Finally, even the radically different c-structure in (12) for a Swedish V2 clause will give the same f-structure (10c). Here, the finite verb is in C, its canonical position in a V2 clause, and hence IP and VP have no c-structure heads. Nevertheless, IP is present so that the subject can be expressed (it is SpecIP) and VP must be present to host the VP-internal adverb *ofta*.

(12)

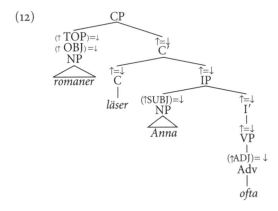

This example has a topicalized object, but apart from the addition of that topic information (predictable as one of the functional options for SpecCP), the c-structure in (12) will determine the f-structure in (10c) by the regular principles of LFG (see Bresnan 2001 and Sells 2001).

Focusing on finiteness, what has been described so far in this section is the simplest and most direct approach: the information about finiteness is shared between the morphosyntactic element that expresses it and the clause. I have illustrated this above with respect to [FORM Fin] in HPSG and with respect to TENSE in LFG.[7] However, as I mentioned above, clausal finiteness and its expression do not always match up perfectly. In fact, a similar kind of mismatch arose in the HPSG treatment of the imperative in (9): the verbal form in English is Base (there is no 'Imperative' form of English verbs) marking a subjectless sentence as an imperative clause, with the semantic property of being an outcome. Under such an account, notably, there is no 'imperative' feature at all, either to be a kind of morphology that a verb has or to be a property of clauses that have outcome-type meanings.

---

[7] Apart from my own work in Sells (2004; 2005), the specific attribute FINITE has not figured in LFG analyses, to my knowledge.

I address this mismatch issue in more detail in the following two major sections of the chapter. Following the representational system of Sadler and Spencer (2001), I will indicate clausal finiteness as involving the feature specification FINITE+. A finite form in the morphology, on the other hand, will have a Form feature specified for the value Finite. In other words, grammatical information is represented by names in capital letters, while morphological features due to morphological form are represented by names with an initial capital. FINITEness may be associated with clausal pragmatic functions such as making an assertion (see section 3.3 below); contrastingly, Finite-ness is pure form, and has no (inherent) interpretation. I will tentatively assume that there is usually a transparent realizational relationship as follows (see Sadler and Spencer 2001):

(13)   The grammatical information [FINITE +] is expressed by [Form:Finite].

For simplicity, I will refer to the two types of linguistic feature-value pairs as 'FINITE' and 'Finite'.[8] A parallel distinction is necessary between TENSE and Tense: it is not uncommon for a periphrastic form involving a Present form to be used to express TENSE PAST, as in the Latin example in (14) from Sadler and Spencer (2001):

(14)   Clodia laudata   est
        Clodia praise.Ptcp.F.Nom.Sg be.Prs
        'Clodia was praised.'

This example has a simple past interpretation, but the grammatical specification TENSE PAST finds its expression as a present perfective.[9] This is a problem for standard morpheme-based accounts, as somehow we have to make 'present' and 'participle' into 'past'. What is crucial here is that the exponent is constructional—it is syntactically complex, and it cannot be said that either part of the construction is directly carrying the relevant grammatical information. So, for this case, Sadler and Spencer argue for a constructional realization of the TENSE PAST information: the construction means TENSE PAST, but no parts of the construction contain (parts of) that information.

[8] The standard HPSG notational system does not distinguish grammatical and morphological representations in this way, using e.g. 'FORM' for what I am representing as 'Form'. However, the conceptual distinction that I am making is as easily formulated in HPSG as in LFG (see Ackerman and Webelhuth 1998, and the realizational approaches in Erjavec 1994 and Monachesi 2001). I also adopt the LFG terminology 'attribute' for grammatical information, and reserve 'feature' for morphological form information. Similarly, as I am distinguishing the information in an attribute like PAST from the feature Pst that might express it, the glossing in my examples departs from the usual convention of using small capitals for features of form.

[9] A Swedish example with similar properties appears below in (33a).

Facts like these have been a major motivation for the conceptual split between grammatical and morphological features. Ackerman and Webelhuth (1998) formulate such an approach, motivating it this way: 'by not arbitrarily tying functions to certain forms, form does not take primacy over function...we can capture generalizations across grammatical units performing the same functions even if the units are expressed very differently either in their phrasal or their morphophonological makeup' (pp. 141–2). One such generalization they describe this way: '[the approach]...finally, ensures that each finite predicate in German, be it expressed synthetically or analytically [= periphrastically—*PS*], will be marked for exactly one of the available tenses, and that its categorial head bears one of the six possible tense-aspect combinations' (p. 197). The general situation they describe can be seen in the Latin periphrastic expression of PAST tense above, which involves a Present form and a Participle form (and no Past form). In such periphrastic expressions, we never seem to find a sequence of nonfinite forms doing duty for an expected finite form, or for two finite forms to stand for one (e.g. a sequence of Aux[Pres] + V[Pres] meaning 'PAST of V'). So the finiteness of the clause is faithfully preserved and expressed just once, regardless of whether the expression is synthetic or periphrastic.

This all leads to the following conclusion: the correspondence between grammatical information and expression as linguistic form (f-structure and c-structure in LFG) is not just the simplest kind of information flow of pre-specified (that is, morphemic) information. Rather, there is a characterization of clausal grammatical information and there are correspondences to its expression in morphosyntactic form, as illustrated schematically in (15):

(15)   a. Grammatical information   b. Overt structure

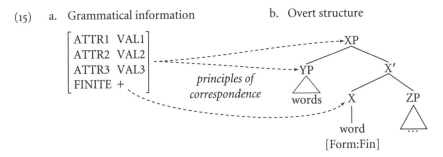

The 'principles of correspondence' are the realizational rules of realizational morphology. In the first instance, as indicated in (15), FINITE + might be expressed by one word whose Form feature has the Finite value; but there may be more complex constructional expressions, such as with the Latin

example above (see e.g. Stump 2001; Ackerman and Webelhuth 1998; Sadler and Spencer 2001; and Sadler and Nordlinger 2004 for many different examples).

3.2 Morphological finiteness: Japanese

In this section and the next I illustrate the distinction between the abstract grammatical attribute FINITE and the morphological feature Finite through consideration of the following situations: first, where a language uses Finite forms in clauses that do not appear to carry any of the pragmatic functions associated with FINITEness; and second, where a language has clauses that are truly FINITE but which lack a Finite form expressing this information.

In Sells (1996) I argued that morphological finiteness was not exclusively associated with a given syntactic category such as IP or CP (or FinP), in Japanese at least. The constructions at issue involve clause-like complements to nouns, which exhibit the properties of raising and control structures (for extensive discussion, see Nakau 1973). One control construction is formed with *koto-ni suru*, illustrated in (16a); this involves one use of the noun *koto* (lit. 'fact') and the verb *suru* (lit. 'do'). Overt expression of the controlled position by the reflexive *zibun* is also allowed, as in (16b), and the control is obligatory, as (16c) shows.

(16) a. taroo-wa   [tookyoo-ni ik-u]   koto-ni   sita
        Taroo-Top   [Tokyo-to   go-Prs]   fact-Dat do.Pst
        'Taroo decided to go to Tokyo.'

      b. taroo$_i$-wa   [zibun$_i$-ga   tookyoo-ni   ik-u]   koto-ni   sita
        Taroo$_i$-Top   [self$_i$-Nom   Tokyo-to   go-Prs]   fact-Dat do.Pst
        'Taroo decided ('for himself') to go to Tokyo.'

      c. *taroo-wa   [hanako-ga   tookyoo-ni ik-u]   koto-ni   sita
        Taroo-Top   [Hanako-Nom   Tokyo-to   go-Prs] fact-Dat do.Pst
        'Taroo decided for Hanako to go to Tokyo.'

For (16a), the standard assumption is that there is a null pronominal subject (corresponding to the overt subject *zibun* in 16b). This means that the bracketed parts of the examples are embedded clauses. What is of importance here is that these are finite clauses, a characteristic property of all noun-modifying clauses in Japanese, even control and raising complements (which are by contrast nonfinite in English). They are 'full' clauses in terms of having subjects, and of being finite. It is a morphological property of Japanese that noun–complement clauses must be finite (see Sells 1995).

The idea that there are two clauses present in the control examples in (16) is reinforced by an additional diagnostic: the *sika . . . na(i)* construction, which is one way of expressing the meaning of 'only' (rather like *ne . . . que* in French). The particle *sika* is a negative polarity item, and attaches to the constituent that is the focus of the 'only' meaning; at the same time the negative marker-*(a)na(i)* appears on the verb, as seen in (17), where both forms are underlined. To a first approximation, *sika* and the negative element must be in the same clause (Muraki 1978; McCawley and Momoi 1986; Miyagawa 1987).

(17) taroo-wa   tookyoo-ni-<u>sika</u>   ik-<u>ana</u>-katta
      Taroo-Top   Tokyo-to-*sika*   go-Neg-Pst
      'Taroo went only to Tokyo.'

A more accurate statement of the constraint is given in Sagawa (1978), who argues that the Specified Subject Constraint (SSC) of Chomsky (1973) applies to *sika . . . na(i)*: an intervening subject blocks licensing of the *sika . . . na(i)* construction. The following examples, adapted from Muraki (1978), show that this is correct.

(18) a. *John-wa [Mary-ga   ryoori-no   hon-<u>sika</u> yom-u]   koto-o
         John-Top [Mary-Nom cooking-Gen book-*sika* read-Prs] fact-Acc
         nozondei-<u>na</u>-i
         hope-Prog-Neg-Prs
         'John hopes that Mary will read only cookbooks.'

      b. John-wa   [Mary-<u>sika</u> ryoori-no   hon-o   yomu]   koto-o
         John-Top [Mary-*sika* cooking-Gen book-Acc read-Prs] fact-Acc
         nozondei-<u>na</u>-i
         hope-Prog-Neg-Prs
         'John hopes that only Mary will read cookbooks.'

In (18a), the intervening subject *Mary-ga* blocks the *sika . . . na(i)* relation; the example is acceptable if *sika* is replaced by the accusative case marker -*o*, but it has a different meaning. However, (18b) is good, with *sika* on the subject itself, even though *sika* and negation are not clause-mates. This is evidence for replacing the clause-mate condition with one referring to an intervening subject, namely the SSC. Following on from these observations, the fact that (19b) is unacceptable indicates that the bracketed embedded clause has a subject, even if that subject is not overt.

(19) a. taroo-wa   [tookyoo-ni-<u>sika</u>   ik-<u>ana</u>-i]   koto-ni   sita
         Taroo-Top   [Tokyo-to-*sika*   go-Neg-Prs]   fact-Dat   do.Pst
         'Taroo decided to go only to Tokyo.'

b. *taroo-wa   [tookyoo-ni-<u>sika</u>   ik-u]   koto-ni   si-<u>na</u>-katta
Taroo-Top   [Tokyo-to-*sika*   go-Prs]   fact-Dat   do-Neg-Pst
'Taroo decided to go only to Tokyo.'

Crucially, the fact that (19b) patterns with (18a) shows that there is a subject in the bracketed part of (19b), even though the subject is not overt. (19a) shows that *sika...na(i)* is acceptable in the control complement, as long as the SSC is respected.

The facts just discussed are thrown into relief by a contrasting construction involving *koto-ga aru* (*aru* 'exist'), shown in (20). In conjunction with an embedded predicate in the past tense form, this expresses a meaning of there having been an experience of something (literally, that 'the fact of having done something exists').

(20)   taroo-wa   [tyuugoku-ni   itta]   koto-ga   ar-u
Taroo- Top   [China-to   go.Pst]   fact-Nom   exist-Prs
'Taroo has been to China.'

This is a raising construction, as seen in the fact that there are no thematic restrictions on the subject. Although the examples in (21) are a little strange in isolation, given the right context they are perfect. (21a,b) involve raising of idiom chunks.

(21)   a.   (Sahara-sabaku-ni-mo)   ame-ga   [hutta]   koto-ga   ar-u
(Sahara desert-in-even)   rain-Nom   [fall.Pst]   fact-Nom   exist-Prs
'Even in the Sahara desert, rain has fallen.'

b.   ?musi-ga   [sirase-ta]   koto-ga   ar-u
bug-Nom   [report-Pst]   fact-Nom   exist-Prs
'I have had a hunch.'

c.   ?hanasi-ni   hana-ga   [sai-ta]   koto-ga   ar-u
speech-Dat   flower-Nom   [bloom-Pst]   fact-Nom   exist-Prs
'Conversation has blossomed.'

Unlike the control construction, the subject of the complement cannot be expressed by *zibun*, as in (22a). The unacceptability of this example shows that the lowest subject cannot be overtly expressed (removing *zibun-ga* makes the example acceptable). An additional fact about *koto-ga aru* is that the split expression of *sika...na(i)* is acceptable, as in (22b) (compare with 19b). The negative form of *aru* is *nai*.

(22)   a.   taroo$_i$-wa   [(*zibun$_i$-ga) tyuugoku-ni itta]   koto-ga   ar-u
Taroo$_i$-Top   [(self$_i$-Nom) China-to   go.Pst]   fact-Nom exist-Prs
'Taroo has been to China.'

b. taroo-wa   [tyuugoku-ni-<u>sika</u>   itta]   koto-ga   <u>na</u>-i
   Taroo-Top   [China-to-*sika*   go.Pst]   fact-Nom   exist.Neg-Prs
   'Taroo has been only to China.'

The bracketed part of (22b) is clearly a finite constituent, as it is uncontroversially a past tense form. However, it does not have a subject, not even a covert one; more precisely, it does not have a subject position. From this, two related properties follow: there is no position to host *zibun*, and there can be no subject to block the split expression of *sika . . . na(i)*.

In Sells (1996) I argued that these constituents in raising constructions are VPs, verbal categories lacking a subject (position). In this they contrast with the control complements in examples like (16), which are true clauses. It is important to understand what this difference is, as it does not map onto the standard distinction between VP and IP in languages like English or Swedish. For example, I am not aware of any adverbials which are licensed in the putative IP complements in Japanese but not in the VP complements. However, if such adverbials were sensitive to the morphological property of Finiteness (see section 3.4 below), we would expect no difference between the two complement types. In fact, postulating functional categories such as IP leads to a series of failed predictions for a language like Japanese (see Sells 1995), so we would be surprised to find any hierarchical effects of structure in the first place.[10]

So, while both types of complement discussed in this section are Finite in terms of morphology, only the control type is actually a full clausal unit, as shown by the tests above. The morphologically Finite form is uncontroversially a necessity of Japanese combinatoric syntax—a Finite form of some kind must be there to connect a verb-headed structure, of whatever size, to a following noun. However, the Finite marking carries none of the semantic clausal functions of FINITEness, for control and raising complements are neither (necessarily) declarative nor assertive.[11] Additionally, morphological Finiteness need not be associated with a full clause syntactically. In the *koto-ga aru* construction the morphological past tense has a semantic function—and may in fact be better considered to be perfective aspect rather than past tense—but it does not have the communicative or pragmatic function associated with clausal FINITEness.

---

[10] While there is strong positional evidence for specifier and head positions within CP and IP in languages like English or Swedish, distinct from positions within VP, such evidence is lacking in Japanese.

[11] This is evidenced by the fact that such complements are expressed as nonfinite constituents in most languages.

While it may be the case that there is an implication that FINITE constituents necessarily have a subject (i.e. are clauses), the evidence in this section shows that Finite constituents need not be clausal, and need not have subjects. Hence the mapping from morphological features to clausal properties is imperfect.

3.3 Clausal finiteness and its expression: Swedish

In the previous section I illustrated a case where morphological Finiteness on embedded constituents is required by external constraints on those constituents, but apparently has none of the canonical assertive or declarative functions associated with FINITEness internal to those constituents. In this section I consider full clauses in Swedish which show all the properties of FINITE clauses but which display non-canonical expression of this property in terms of overt finite or tensed verbs. This section continues the discussion of the architecture of the grammar from section 3.1.3 above.

3.3.1 *V2 clauses*

Swedish main clauses are V2 clauses, a familiar property in all of the modern Germanic languages. For example, in (23), the finite verb *har* precedes the negative adverb *inte* which itself is located at the left edge of VP. That VP is headed by what is known as the Supine form of the verb, *rest*.

(23)   Erik har   inte   rest   än.
       Eric have.Prs not   go.Spn   yet
       'Eric has not gone yet.'

Compare the word order in (24) with the relative position of negation and the finite verb in an embedded non-V2 clause:

(24)   ...att   Erik   inte   har   rest   än.
       ...that   Eric   not   have.Prs go.Spn yet
       '...that Eric has not gone yet.'

The finite verb *har* is VP-internal in (24), and hence following the negative *inte*; as the order is the opposite in (23), it is standardly assumed that the finite verb in V2 clauses is external to VP, located in the head of one of the functional projections IP or CP (see (29) below).

The second position in a V2 clause is usually considered to be exclusively a finite verb position, but this is not quite accurate, for Swedish at least. For example, the adverb *kanske* ('maybe') can occupy this position, as in (25) from Holmberg and Platzack (1995: 50) (see also Vikner 1995: 45ff.; Egerland 1998; Kathol 2000: 278ff.). This form is derived historically from a collocation meaning 'can happen', but like *maybe* in English, it is not transparent synchronically. Nevertheless, it can carry the clause-typing function in a V2 clause otherwise associated with a finite verb.

(25) Erik kanske inte har   (*inte) rest   än.
      Eric maybe not have.Prs (*not) go.Spn yet
      'Eric maybe has not gone yet.'

Here the placement of negation relative to the finite verb *har* shows once again that that verb is within VP, rather than occupying a higher inflectional position in I or C. Now, what is the sense of finiteness in the second position? Clearly *kanske* is not marking TENSE, but it can be considered to have a Finite value for a Form feature due to its historical origin from a verb, and it is this property that allows it to appear in second position. (26) presents a similar example, from Egerland (1998).

(26) Det kanske han inte gjorde.
      it maybe he   not do.Pst
      'Perhaps he did not do it.'

The initial constituent in this example, being a non-subject, will be located in SpecCP (see 29 below). The indication that the clause is finite for the purpose of V2 comes from *kanske*, in the head C of CP, while the information of past tense in the clause is expressed by the V within VP.

Yes–No interrogatives, which effectively are 'V1' clauses, can also have their clause-typing function expressed by the non-verbal form *månne* (see Vikner 1995: 45). The examples in (27) are essentially equivalent, with a Finite form in initial position in either case.

(27) a. Har   Sara varit   här?
         have.Prs Sara be.Spn here
         'Has Sara been here?'

      b. Månne Sara har   varit   här?
         Q   Sara have.Prs be.Spn here
         'Has Sara been here?'

These facts show that the expression of the clause type by the element in the second position (or initial position in a Yes–No interrogative) is not determined by the values PRES or PAST of the attribute TENSE, which are the only 'finite' possibilities for verbs in Swedish (see Sells 2001). Rather, there is some formal marking feature [Form:Finite], which is present not only on all finite verbs but also on *kanske* and *månne*, and it is this feature which must be present in a V2 clause or a V1 interrogative. These examples show that 'finite' is not just a convenient label for 'present or past', but is a separate morphological property.

So far, I have concentrated only on the overt form of V2 and V1 clauses. Now I will investigate whether Swedish provides any evidence for the clausal FINITE attribute, in addition to the evidence just presented for [Form:Finite]. However, to get to that point, we need to consider what finite clauses are used for.

At the level of the main clause, finiteness has been connected with the notion of assertion (e.g. Klein 1998). Klein makes a stronger claim, that 'being the carrier of [assertion] is the main function of finiteness...the distinction between finite and nonfinite forms is not a mere surface phenomenon. It reflects the presence or absence of an abstract operator in the representation of an utterance' (1998: 225). Relevant in this context is the discussion in Dimroth (2002) of examples of repeated assertions from non-native adult learners of German, which involve stressed *auch* ('also') (see 28):

stressed finite auxiliaries that have almost no lexical meaning... just encode that the state of affairs rendered by the expressions in their scope does indeed hold for some given topic element... In case a given state of affairs is said to apply to more than one topic, the function of additive words and the function of finiteness marking seem therefore to be closely related. In such a context of repeated assertion as expressed by stressed *auch*, the simple assertive relation can even be seen as redundant. (Dimroth 2002: 900)

(28) a. die   *sind*   runnergefallen von   dem   wagen
          they   be.Pres   fall.Ptcp   from the.Dat   car
          'they have fallen from the car'

      b. und der   mann   *AUCH*   runnergefallen
          and the.Nom   man   ALSO   fall.Ptcp
          (lit.) 'and the man also fallen'

Interestingly, Andersson (1985) and Wechsler (1991) have argued that Swedish V2 structures have the function of marking what they call 'Speaker's Assertion'. Although I cannot address the precise pragmatic nature of assertion, I will assume that there is some clausal information [FORCE ASSERT] which is expressed through V2 and the notion of morphological finiteness.[12] In the Germanic languages this expression involves one or both of the two particular syntactic structures in (29):

---

[12] For now, I will assume that this illocutionary information will be expressed in f-structure in LFG—assuming that there are force types such as asserting, asking, and ordering (see section 3.1.2 above). See also section 3.5.2.

(29) [FORCE ASSERT] is expressed by a or b:

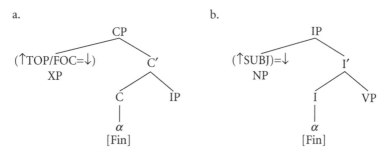

In Sells (2001) I argue that Swedish shows different syntactic structures for non-subject-initial and subject-initial V2 clauses, the former involving CP and the latter IP (see also Travis 1991; Branigan 1996; and Zwart 1997), as in (29). The fact that there are two structures, with common functions, highlights the relevance of form—an overt specifier and a following Finite form—over any particular 'cartographic' structure such as CP or IP for expressing FORCE (cf. the discussion in section 3.1.2).

The central role of the word bearing [Form:Finite] is seen in an unusual kind of V2 clause in Swedish, in which there are two apparently tense-inflected verbs, one to mark the V2 structure and one expressing TENSE. The rather surprising examples like (30) have a focused tensed verb in first position and the supporting verb *gör* ('do') in the second position, also in its tensed form.

(30) Skriver   gör   han   sällan.
      write.Prs do.Prs   he   seldom
      'He seldom WRITES.'

Most of the Germanic languages do not allow a tensed verb in the initial position of a V2 clause, but Swedish does. If we understand that the function of the first tensed verb is to express the grammatical TENSE of the clause, while the function of the second is to provide the Finite value (for the V2 structure), the grammatical properties of the example are no longer surprising.[13]

---

[13] It is not that the second verb has some TENSE information that remains 'unused'; on a realizational view the word only has pure form specifications, being Finite and Present. How these correspond to the grammatical clausal information of FINITE and TENSE is determined by the (non-trivial) principles of correspondence (alluded to in (15)).

(29) represents some of the principles of correspondence schematized in (15), in this case for [FORCE ASSERT]; they are constructional expressions, involving the specification [Form:Finite]. However, it is far from obvious that they are also expressing the information [FINITE +], as we have had no need to mention the FINITE attribute in the account so far.

3.3.2 *Ha-deletion*

What I have actually shown above is that the syntax of Swedish involves the grammatical attributes FORCE and TENSE, expressed by overt forms which are specified for Form and Tense features. In fact, despite the topic of this chapter, there has been no evidence yet for the grammatical attribute FINITE in this section. None of the analyses sketched above has crucially referred to this attribute, rather they make reference to the Form value Finite, rather than to an abstract finiteness attribute of the clause. In this subsection, I will show that there is in fact positive evidence for the grammatical attribute FINITE, at least in Swedish.

The auxiliary *ha* ('have') expresses past tense or perfective aspect in construction with a main verb in its Supine form. *Ha* is optional in certain contexts, characterized in the generative literature by a hypothesized rule of '*Ha*-deletion'. For example, following a modal, nonfinite *ha* can be optionally present, but *har* cannot be absent when it is in second position in a main clause (see den Besten 1983; Platzack 1986; Holmberg 1986), as shown by the contrast in the examples in (31).

(31) a. Han   måste   (ha)   varit   sjuk.
          he   must.Pst (have.Bse) be.Spn   sick
          'He must have been sick.'

      b. Han   *(har)   varit   sjuk.
          he   *(have.Prs) be.Spn   sick

In certain main clauses in Swedish the forms *kanske* and *månne* can fulfil the clause-marking functions, as we saw above. With such non-verbs in the crucial second position, the finite verb *har* becomes optional, as shown in (32) and (33):

(32) a. Sara kanske   (har)   varit   här.
          Sara maybe   (has)   be.Spn   here

      b. Månne Sara   (har)   varit   här?
          Q   Sara   (has)   be.Spn   here

(33) a. Allan kanske (har)   redan   ätit   frukost.
          Allan maybe (have.Prs)   already   eat.Spn   breakfast
          'Maybe Allan ate/has eaten breakfast already.'

b. Kanske han snart (har) skrivit sin bok?
   maybe he soon (have.Prs) write.Spn his book
   'Will he maybe soon have written his book?'

The examples in (33), without *har*, are cited in Platzack (1986: 202). With the background of the discussion of *kanske* above, it is clear that *ha* must be present if it is the only candidate for marking finiteness in the second position in a V2 clause (as in 31b), but if something else is available for this purpose, then *ha* can be absent. This is true, even though *ha* might be the only tense-expressing verb in the clause. With *ha* absent, these are main clauses without a formally tensed verb in them.

Finite *ha* is also optional in embedded clauses, which are not subject to the V2 requirement. Once again there is no formally finite verb in the embedded clause in the version of (34) without *har*.

(34) Jag tror att han (har) varit sjuk.
     I think.Prs that he (have.Prs) be.Spn sick
     'I think that he was/has been sick.'

In each of the *ha*-less examples, the clause in which *ha* would have appeared has an interesting property: the fact that it is 'supposed' to be finite is still evident. In other words, even though there is no tensed verb, a hearer could recover the finiteness of the clause. Perhaps surprisingly, though, as the omitted verb could have been *har* (Present) or *hade* (Past), the tense of the *ha*-less clause cannot be recovered.

The finiteness information can be recovered in the following ways. The clauses that are V2 clauses with *kanske* in the second position are clearly recognizable as expressing assertions, and assertions are associated with finiteness.[14]

In examples like (34), Julien (2000) observes that the finiteness of the embedded clause is recoverable from the fact that the subject is nominative (the pronoun *han*), for nominative subjects are only possible in finite clauses in Swedish. So in all these examples without a finite verb in them, the fact that the clause is one that is finite is evident from other clues in the structure or context (for details, see Sells 2005).

At this point, we finally see evidence for a grammatical FINITE attribute: a 'finite' clause in Swedish cannot be unequivocally characterized as having a [Form:Finite] word in it. Nevertheless, there is a clear intuition as to which

---

[14] The German data discussed by Dimroth (see p. 78) are interesting in this context—are examples like (28b) truly nonfinite (now that we know that there is no simple relation between FINITE and its expression)?

clauses are finite and which ones are not. Formally, then, this means that all finite clauses are FINITE +, a specification which is matched by a Finite form in the overt structure, except in cases of *Ha*-deletion. The use of FINITE + seems to be the only way to make sense of these linguistic intuitions (though see section 3.5.2). Consider the subject in the *ha*-less version of (34): it is in the nominative case, and we would want to say that the nominative case is only possible in finite clauses; but we must mean here 'clauses that are FINITE +', and not 'clauses that have a [Form:Finite] word in them', as the latter is not true for this example.

3.4 Other finite-sensitive phenomena

In this section I briefly discuss some different parts of syntax that are sensitive to one or other aspect of finiteness, with the goal of reinforcing the idea that grammatical and morphological finiteness must be distinguished. Here I focus on complementizers, and negation, though of course there are many phenomena whose analysis typically refers to finiteness, subject–verb agreement being almost a prototypical instance; and in many languages anaphor binding is constrained by finite domains (see e.g. Wexler and Manzini 1987; Dalrymple 1993).

3.4.1 *Complementizers*

Complementizers are sometimes classified by a language for finite or non-finite clauses (e.g. *that* vs. *for* in English), but do not seem to be sensitive to particular tenses within the finite realm (e.g. no complementizer exclusively for future tense). For example, (35) is an HPSG entry for *that* (cf. Ginzburg and Sag 2000: 46; Sag et al. 2003: 343ff.):

(35)   Lexical entry for *that*

$$
\begin{bmatrix}
\text{CAT} & \begin{bmatrix} \text{HEAD} & [comp] \end{bmatrix} \\
\text{CONT} & \boxed{1}\,proposition \\
\text{ARG-ST} & \left\langle \begin{bmatrix} \text{FORM} & \text{Fin} \\ \text{SPR} & \langle\,\rangle \\ \text{CONT} & \boxed{1} \end{bmatrix} \right\rangle
\end{bmatrix}
$$

This says that *that* is a complementizing head which selects for a Finite form that is saturated with respect to its specifier—in other words, a full clause. The complementizer shares its content (meaning) with the content of the clause it selects, and constrains that content to be of the type *proposition*. The Japanese 'complementizer' *-to* discussed in section 3.1.2 would have a similar entry, except that it would not specify anything about the saturation of the arguments of its verbal host: in fact, it would combine with a finite verb before that verb combined with any of its arguments.

The Swedish relative complementizer *som* is like *that* in English in that it only introduces finite clauses:

(36) Vi   talade   med dom$_i$ som t_i (hade)   kommit.
      we   talk.Pst with them$_i$ who t_i (have.Pst) come.Spn
      'We talked with those who had come.'

(36), from Julien (2000), shows that *Ha*-deletion is possible in *som*-clauses. So, once again, this means that *som* must be sensitive to the FINITEness of the clause it introduces, regardless of whether there are any Finite forms in that clause. In other words, an entry rather like (35) would not be correct for *som*; the entry would require reference not to a Finite form, but to the more abstract notion of FINITEness discussed in section 3.3. (See also section 3.5.2.) On the other hand, the Swedish complementizer *att* can introduce both finite and infinitive complements, and so is a marker only of subordination.

I also argued above that the presence of a nominative subject indicates a finite clause in Swedish (see 34), but it must be recognized that other languages may not have this property—certain nonfinite clauses in Portuguese may have nominative subjects, for example (see Adger, Chapter 2 above), so nominative case would predict nothing about finiteness in that language.

3.4.2 Negation

Negation is strongly implicated with finiteness in many languages, for example the difference between the expression of English and French clausal negation discussed by Emonds (1978). English clausal negation requires a finite auxiliary to precede *not*, while in French all finite verbs may take a negative adverb *pas*, with the preverbal marker *ne* playing only a subsidiary role:

(37)   a. She has not read the book.
     b. Elle n'a pas lu le livre.
     c. She does not read the book.
     d. Elle ne lit pas le livre.

The first two examples are parallel, but the languages diverge in the last two: assuming that there is an abstract position for tense (now considered to be I, the head of INFL) right in front of the position of *not/pas*, English requires the dummy auxiliary *do* in that position, with the main verb in VP, while French allows the main verb to appear directly in the pre-*pas* position.

Here I present a sketch of the HPSG analysis of these and related facts, due to Kim (2000) and Kim and Sag (2002)—though I begin with a minor digression from the generalizations just described. First of all, for English, the prototypical expression of a negative adverb is as a VP modifier, like many other adverbs. This provides a plausible analysis of examples like those in (38), with the structure shown:

(38)   a. Max has [$_{VP}$ not [$_{VP}$ eaten kimchee]].
     b. Max has [$_{VP}$ never [$_{VP}$ eaten kimchee]].

Taking a view of syntax which does not use empty categories, this straightforwardly explains why an example like (39) is bad: *never* has no VP to modify.

(39)   *Sam has eaten kimchee, but Max has never.

However, there is one adverb that can be stranded preceding a 'VP-Deletion' site, in contrast to *never*, namely *not*:

(40)   Sam has eaten kimchee, but Max has not.

To account for this, Kim (2000) and Kim and Sag (2002) proposed that *not* can function either as a VP-adverbial, as in (38b), or as a complement selected by an auxiliary, in (40). Hence *not* would be sanctioned in the structure in (40) by the preceding auxiliary verb. To allow for this possibility, there is a lexical rule which adds negation as a complement to the auxiliary verb, even though the negation functions semantically as a modifier on the verb's meaning. As an auxiliary in English already takes a nonfinite VP complement, the output of the lexical rule will be an auxiliary verb which takes two complements, though only the VP will be a semantic argument of the auxiliary. The rule in (41) is slightly adapted from Kim (2000: 119, 143):

(41)   English Finite Negation Lexical Rule

$$
\begin{bmatrix}
\text{CAT} & \begin{bmatrix}
\text{HEAD} & \begin{bmatrix} verb \\ \text{FORM} \quad \text{Fin} \\ \text{AUX} \quad + \end{bmatrix} \\
\text{COMPS} \quad \boxed{1}
\end{bmatrix} \\
\text{CONT} \quad \boxed{2}
\end{bmatrix}
\Rightarrow
\begin{bmatrix}
\text{COMPS} \quad \langle\, \text{Neg:}\,\boxed{3}\,\rangle \oplus \boxed{1} \\
\text{CONT} \quad \boxed{3}\begin{bmatrix} \text{ARG} \quad \boxed{2} \end{bmatrix}
\end{bmatrix}
$$

The rule says that a finite auxiliary verb adds an extra negative complement, and that the meaning of the negative complement is a modifier on the
original meaning of the auxiliary verb. For 'VP-Deletion', another lexical rule
would map an auxiliary with a VP complement to a new form of the verb
lacking that complement; if that rule followed (41), the auxiliary verb would
have a negative complement, but no VP complement, which is exactly what is
required for (40).[15]

In contrast to English, in French all finite verbs may take a negative
complement *pas*, so there is no AUX + restriction on the rule; otherwise it
is identical:

(42)   French Finite Negation Lexical Rule

$$
\begin{bmatrix}
\text{CAT} & \begin{bmatrix}
\text{HEAD} & \begin{bmatrix} verb \\ \text{FORM} \quad \text{Fin} \end{bmatrix} \\
\text{COMPS} \quad \boxed{1}
\end{bmatrix} \\
\text{CONT} \quad \boxed{2}
\end{bmatrix}
\Rightarrow
\begin{bmatrix}
\text{COMPS} \quad \langle\, \text{Neg:}\,\boxed{3}\,\rangle \oplus \boxed{1} \\
\text{CONT} \quad \boxed{3}\begin{bmatrix} \text{ARG} \quad \boxed{2} \end{bmatrix}
\end{bmatrix}
$$

The details of the analysis are not important; what matters is that the rule in
either language refers to Finite—the morphological form—a Finite form can
host a stranded negation. This in turn means that we can show that the
English auxiliary *better* is a Finite form (cf. Sag et al. 2003: 414)—it can

---

[15] For a fuller account of the English auxiliary system see Sag et al. (2003: 406ff.).

precisely host a stranded negation, as in (43),[16] although it cannot appear in nonfinite contexts, as shown by the unacceptability it causes in the examples in (44):

(43)   . . . said he might touch on it on his next album. 'He better not, or he'll get his career ended. Cause ain't no head up with me, Cube . . .'.

(44)   a. I thought about (*better) leaving.
        b. We decided to (*better) stay.

One possible account of these facts would propose that *better* has no Form feature, but is somehow able to appear in FINITE clauses. However, a simpler and more accurate account is that *better* is [Form:Finite] (just like Swedish *kanske* discussed above). This categorization confirms that the lexical rules for negation refer to Finite rather than FINITE.

3.5 Conclusion

3.5.1 *Different notions of 'finiteness'*

In this chapter I have considered different uses of the term 'finite':

(45)   a. Finite as a value of a Form feature that verbs and perhaps a few other lexical items have;
        b. FINITE as a formal grammatical property of clauses (typically expressed by a Finite form, but there are exceptions);
        c. 'finite' as a formal property that certain elements may be sensitive to, such as agreement, complementizers, and negation;
        d. 'finite' as a property of clauses used to make an assertion.

Clearly (45a) has fairly strong validity: languages have Finite forms (usually verbs), though not all languages have distinguished Finite forms. The grammatical attribute FINITE in (45b) seems to underlie much of what linguists have in mind when they talk about finiteness, in which case it is surprising how hard it is to find truly positive evidence of it. I argued above that *Ha*-deletion provides the evidence for FINITE vs. Finite.[17] The sense of 'finite' in (45c) can be either FINITE (for complementizers) or Finite (for negation); and for (45d), the only sense is FINITE, for the German and Swedish data

---

[16] Example verified using Google, at www.the411online.com/mack10.html, 19 Mar. 2005.

[17] Possibly, the discussion following on from the Latin example (14) provides other evidence, regarding the independence of finiteness from tense; that discussion could be taken to imply that there is a FINITE attribute which is always expressed by a Finite form, regardless of how TENSE is expressed. Cf. the quote from Ackerman and Webelhuth (1998) on p. 71 above.

above showed some examples of assertive clauses which lack any Finite verb form. Clearly, the grammar needs to recognize both uses of the term 'finite'; it is clear also that the correspondence between the two may be imperfect.

3.5.2 *The grammatical representation of clausal properties*

The concept of morphological finiteness is relatively straightforward: certain (inflectional) forms are classified as finite forms. Gretsch and Perdue (Chapter 12 below) use the term 'M-finiteness' for this notion, corresponding to my use of 'Finite form'.

However, it is less clear exactly where in the grammar we should locate the other notion, FINITEness, as I have used it here. In the HPSG partial analyses of clausal force sketched in section 3.1.2, there was no mention of 'finite' or 'force' in the semantic parts of the rules. In the LFG analyses, I used the attributes FINITE and FORCE in the f-structures, to display them explicitly as clausal properties. If these attributes were argued to be more properly semantic, an issue I address immediately below, the projection architecture of LFG (see e.g. Dalrymple 2001 on mapping to semantics) would allow them to be part of the correspondence between the semantics and the c-structure, without the f-structure mediation I assumed here.

The notion of FINITEness is closely related to 'C(onstructional)-finiteness' in Nikolaeva (2003), and 'S(emantic)-finiteness' in Gretsch and Perdue (Chapter 12 below). Nikolaeva associates C-finiteness with 'deep tense', a property of a clause used to assert a proposition located at some time with respect to the speech time. Gretsch and Perdue associate the notion of S-finiteness with the notion of anchoring the referents of an utterance, in order that an assertion can be made (following Lasser 1997 and Klein 1998).[18] They suggest that M-finiteness always implies S-finiteness, but I have argued above that Japanese counterexemplifies such a strong universal claim. They note that the absence of M-finiteness does not imply the absence of S-finiteness, and the discussion of Swedish above supports this.

It seems to me that FINITE as an intermediary syntactic feature is necessary, for there is no purely semantic notion of finiteness that delineates exactly the right set of cases. Although the most prominent idea has been that FINITEness goes together with assertion, Nikolaeva (2003) observes that while assertion implies C-finiteness—perhaps by definition—non-assertion does not imply the absence of C-finiteness. The reason for this is that interrogatives have the

---

[18] A somewhat similar conception of the nature of finiteness due to Bianchi (2003) is mentioned in Adger (Ch. 2 above).

hallmarks of being C-finite, syntactically and morphologically, but are definitely not assertions.

In Ginzburg and Sag (2000) there is a close relation between the meanings of declaratives and interrogatives. Declaratives are propositions, while questions are propositions with an abstracted parameter, the focus of the question; both are built from realis states-of-affairs. These two types differ from imperatives, which are built from irrealis states-of-affairs. Realis states-of-affairs either describe or are resolved by the situation in a real world at a given time. Contrastingly, irrealis states-of-affairs precisely lack the index which would anchor them in a real world at a given time. Thus, it would seem plausible to analyse propositions and questions as involving an abstract syntactic feature FINITE; both would canonically be expressed by clauses with finite verbal heads, but there could be other possibilities (cf. the expression of a question by *månne* with no Finite verb in 32b). However, only propositions, the meaning of one type of FINITE form, would be the basis of assertions.

Part II

Finiteness in Functional Theories and Typology

4

Deconstructing categories: finiteness in a functional-typological perspective

SONIA CRISTOFARO

4.1 Introduction

This chapter examines the notion of finiteness in a functional-typological perspective, with particular regard to the status of finiteness and nonfiniteness as cross-constructionally and cross-linguistically relevant categories.

Finiteness and nonfiniteness, as defined in functionally oriented theories of grammar, do not correspond to internally consistent classes. As the various properties that are taken as distinctive for finiteness and nonfiniteness do not always combine with the same properties from one construction to another, finiteness and nonfiniteness encompass a variety of entities that are similar with respect to some properties but differ with respect to other properties.

At the same time, however, the various properties that are regarded as distinctive for finiteness and nonfiniteness occur in predictable correlation patterns from one construction to another. This chapter examines the cross-linguistic distribution of a number of such properties, such as presence vs. absence of tense, aspect, mood, and person agreement distinctions on the verb, expression of these distinctions by means of special forms not used in independent clauses, presence of nominal morphology (such as case marking or adpositions) on the verb, impossibility for the verb to take overtly expressed arguments, and coding of arguments as possessors. On the basis of data collected within a larger typological project on subordination (Cristofaro 1998; 2003), it will be shown that these properties are linked by a number of implicational correlations, that can be accounted for in terms of various principles of form–function correspondence. These principles have been elaborated to various extents in functionally oriented literature, and pertain to the cognitive status of the state of affairs expressed by the relevant clause and the semantic relationship between this clause and the clauses with which it combines.

The chapter will argue that the logical consequence of these facts is that finiteness and nonfiniteness cannot be regarded as cross-constructionally and cross-linguistically valid grammatical categories, that is, categories that are arguably part of a speaker's linguistic knowledge and are manifested in different constructions in different languages. Instead, the various properties that are taken as distinctive for finiteness and nonfiniteness correspond to a number of language-specific and construction-specific grammatical categories. As individual properties and combinations thereof appear to be motivated in terms of different principles, it is even doubtful that finiteness and nonfiniteness may be cross-linguistically and cross-constructionally appropriate descriptive categories. This conclusion is in accordance with recent proposals in typological research, according to which grammatical categories and relations are construction-specific and language-specific, and universals of grammar are rather found in a number of principles of form–function correspondence manifested in individual categories and relations (Dryer 1996; 1997; Croft 2001).

4.2 Finiteness in functionally oriented theories of grammar

The issue of finiteness has been addressed in detail in a number of functionally oriented theories of grammar, such as the functional-typological approach (as exemplified in Givón 1984; 1990; 2001), Cognitive Grammar (Langacker 1987a; 1991b), Functional Grammar (Dik 1997a; 1997b), and Systemic Functional Theory (Halliday 1994). Linguists working within these theories have developed two basic approaches to finiteness. On one view, finiteness is defined in terms of presence or absence of particular properties or their combinations. On another view, finiteness and nonfiniteness are scalar categories defined in terms of a variety of properties that may combine in different ways from one construction to another.

The first approach is exemplified by the work of Langacker (1991b) and Halliday (1994). On the basis of English verb forms, they define finiteness in terms of grammatical specification for tense and modality on the verb, as found with indicative, conditionals, and forms introduced by modal verbs such as *can, may, must,* and the like. Grammatical specification for tense and modality is regarded as a device to locate the state of affairs being described with respect to the speech act situation.[1]

---

[1] By 'state of affairs' is meant here, following the Functional Grammar usage, the conception of something that can be the case in some world, as defined by a nuclear predication consisting of a predicate and its terms (Dik 1997a).

Langacker's notion of finiteness is based on the two notions of process and grounding (Langacker 1987a; 1987b; 1991b). Processes are cognitive entities prototypically encoded by verbs, and involving a continuous series of states representing different phases of the process itself and construed as occupying a continuous series of points in conceived time. Each of these states remains active only momentarily during cognitive processing, and begins to decay as the following scene enters into consciousness. For example, an action like 'enter' corresponds to a process involving an entity (in Langacker's terms, a trajector) progressing from an out-relation to an in-relation with respect to some landmark (Langacker 1987a: 244–5). The progression involves an indefinite number of component phases, that the conceptualizer processes individually in a non-cumulative fashion. This mode of cognitive processing is described by Langacker (1987b: 72) as sequential scanning. Sequential scanning crucially pertains to the occurrence of changes and events through time (Langacker 1991a: 79).

According to Langacker, finite clauses designate a grounded entity of a process type. Grounding is a semantic function whereby a cognitive entity is located with respect to the ground, i.e. the speech event, its participants, and its immediate circumstances. The ground is the vantage point from which a linguistically coded scene is viewed (Langacker 1987a: 126–9; 1991b: 441). For processes, grounding is obtained through the specification of tense and modality on the verb designating the process. Tense locates the designated process with respect to the time of the speech event, while modality locates the designated process with respect to known reality. In English, for instance, absence of modal verbs indicates that the speaker accepts the designated process as a part of known reality, while presence of a modal verb (such as *will, may, must, should*) places it in the realm of irreality.

Similarly, Halliday (1994: 72–5) identifies finiteness with a so-called finite operator, which is one of a small group of verbal operators expressing tense (e.g. *is, has*) or modality (e.g. *can, must*). The finite operator combines with the subject element (as represented for instance by pronouns such as *he*) to form the constituent Mood, as manifested in categories such as the Indicative. The function of the finite operator is to circumscribe the proposition, that is, bring the proposition down to earth, so that it is something that can be argued about. The finite operator does so by relating the proposition to its context in the speech event, with reference to either the time of speaking or the speaker's judgement. The time of speaking is indicated by temporal elements such as *was* in *An old man was crossing the road*, while the speaker's judgement is indicated by modal elements such as *can't* in *It can't be true*. In addition to expressing tense or modality, the finite operator also indicates positive or negative polarity; in fact, each of the temporal or modal elements appears in both positive and negative form, e.g. *did/didn't, can/can't.*

In the other major functionally oriented approach to finiteness, exemplified by the work of Givón (1990: ch. 19; 2001: ch. 18) and Dik (1997b: 144–68), finiteness is identified with conformity to the independent clause pattern. A verb or clause may be more or less finite depending on how many properties it displays that deviate from this pattern.

In Givón's model, finiteness is a clausal category defined in terms of a clause's degree of similarity to the prototype transitive main clause. Similarity is measured in terms of features pertaining to the verb, such as tense, aspect, mood, pronominal agreement, and nominalizing affixes, and features pertaining to verb arguments, such as the case of subject and object. Nonfinite clauses may lack tense, aspect, mood, or person agreement marking, or display a reduction in the number of distinctions pertaining to these categories. In addition, they may display nominalizing affixes, as is the case with forms such as participles, infinitives, and nominalizations. Also, the subject of a nonfinite clause may bear dative/benefactive or genitive marking, and the object may bear genitive marking.

Similarly, Dik regards a finite verb form as one that can be specified for the same distinctions which are also characteristic of main-clause predicates. Nonfinite verb forms, on the other hand, cannot normally be used as the main verb of a clause. Nonfinite verb forms typically lack agreement for person, number, and gender for the subject, are not inflected, or display reduced inflection for tense, aspect, and mood, and have certain properties in common with adjectival or nominal predicates.[2]

In spite of their differences, the two approaches just described appear to have similar implications for the definition of finiteness and nonfiniteness.

The various properties that are taken as distinctive for finiteness and nonfiniteness in these approaches do not make it possible to define internally consistent classes, either cross-linguistically or within individual languages. For example, as far as Langacker's and Halliday's definitions of finiteness are concerned, verb forms that are not specified for tense may or may not be specified for modality, and vice versa, in a number of languages (see Cristofaro 2003: appendix 4 and references therein for extensive exemplification on such languages). Also, not all languages have verb forms inflected for tense and modality, but all languages presumably

---

[2] Similar classifications of verb forms are used in Stassen (1985), Haspelmath (1995), and Hengeveld (1998), although these works are not specifically concerned with defining finiteness and nonfiniteness.

have a means for grounding states of affairs. Therefore grounding may or may not be associated with specification for tense and modality from one language to another. In this respect, Langacker's and Halliday's approach is reminiscent of generative treatments of finiteness, where finiteness corresponds to a node in clause structure that specifies tense and agreement, and additional machinery is needed to account for languages that have no tense or agreement (see Nikolaeva, Chapter 1 above, and Kornfilt, Chapter 9 below, for an overview).

These facts mean that, if finiteness and nonfiniteness are defined in terms of any of the three properties of inflection for tense, inflection for modality, and grounding, they will encompass a number of constructions that share the selected property, but may differ with respect to the other two properties. In addition, the selected properties may not be relevant to all languages.

More generally, as repeatedly pointed out in the literature on finiteness (Joseph 1983: ch. 1; Koptjevskaja-Tamm 1993a; Nikolaeva, Chapter 1 above), the various properties that are taken as evidence of conformity to or deviation from the independent clause pattern do not combine in the same way from one construction to another, either cross-linguistically or within individual languages. Verb forms not inflected for some particular parameter may or may not be inflected for some other parameter and may or may not display verbal or adjectival morphology from one construction to another, both cross-linguistically and within individual languages. Also, verb forms with reduced inflectional potential may or may not be able to occur in independent clauses (Kalinina and Sumbatova, Chapter 7 below; Evans, Chapter 11 below).

Thus, if finiteness and nonfiniteness are defined in terms of conformity to vs. deviation from the independent clause pattern, as is the case in Givón's and Dik's approach, they will encompass a variety of entities that are similar with respect to some properties (e.g. absence of inflection for some particular verbal parameter), but differ with respect to other properties (e.g. inflection for other verbal parameters, presence vs. absence of nominal or adjectival morphology on the verb, or ability to occur in an independent clause).

In what follows, it will however be shown that the cross-constructional distribution of these properties obeys a number of universal, functionally motivated implicational patterns, and the theoretical implications of these facts for the status of finiteness and nonfiniteness as cross-constructionally and cross-linguistically relevant categories will be discussed.

4.3 Finiteness and nonfiniteness: correlations between individual properties

In this section, a number of cross-linguistic correlation patterns between various properties usually associated with finiteness and nonfiniteness will be presented. These correlation patterns were observed in a cross-linguistic study of subordination systems, based on an eighty-language sample (Cristofaro 1998; 2003; for the sample, see Appendix 1 below). The primary goal of this study was to define implicational patterns in the cross-linguistic coding of various types of subordination relation, as manifested in complement, adverbial, and relative sentences. By 'subordination relation' is meant, following Langacker (1991b: 346–7), a particular way to construe the cognitive relationship between two states of affairs, such that one of the two (the dependent state of affairs) is construed in the perspective of the other (the main state of affairs). The details of this definition need not concern us here, but will be taken up in section 4.4.1. It should however be pointed out that the cognitive situation defined here as subordination underlies all the sentence types usually identified as complement, adverbial, and relative sentences, plus some other sentence types having a different formal structure but the same semantic and pragmatic implications (Cristofaro 2003: ch. 2).

For each of the subordination relation types taken into account, the structure of the clause coding the dependent state of affairs (the dependent clause) was examined. Attention was focused on the following properties:

(i) Presence vs. absence of the categorial distinctions normally allowed to verbs in the language, such as tense, aspect, mood, or person agreement distinctions referring to A, S, and O (after Dixon's 1994 terminology) arguments. This is illustrated in (1) and (2) below. In the Punjabi sentence in (1), the verb coding the dependent state of affairs is not marked for tense, aspect, mood, or person agreement:

Punjabi (Indo-European)

(1) *Māi*   **Tur**   *sakdaa*   *āā*
     I   walk   able.PRS.M   am
     'I can walk.' (Bhatia 1993: 263)

In the Huallaga Huánuco Quechua sentence in (2), the verb coding the dependent state of affairs is not inflected for tense, mood and person agreement, but inflects for aspect:

Huallaga (Huánuco) Quechua (Amerindian, Andean)

(2) *[Aywa-**yka**-q-ta]*   *rika-shka-:*
     go-IPFV-SUB-O   see-PERF-1
     'I saw him going.' (Weber 1989: 116)

(ii) Coding of categorial distinctions on verbs by means of special forms not used in independent clauses, as found for instance in so-called dependent moods and subjunctives. Another case in point is represented by those languages where the verb forms used in dependent clauses display possessive person agreement affixes instead of the normal person agreement affixes found in independent clauses. This is for instance the case in Huallaga (Huánuco) Quechua:

Huallaga (Huánuco) Quechua (Amerindian, Andean)

(3) *[allaapa-ta*   *miku-shpa-**yiki**]*   wira   ka-nki-paq
     much-O   eat-TRANST-2P   fat   be-2FUT-FUT
     'If you eat much/many, you will be fat.' (Weber 1989: 119)

(iii) Presence vs. absence of case marking or adpositions on verbs, as in example (4):

Tamil (Elamo-Dravidian)

(4) *ava*   **vizzuntatunaale**   *azutaa*
     she   fall.PST.NMLZ.INS   weep.PST.3F.SG
     'Because she fell, she cried.' (Asher 1985: 21)

(iv) Impossibility for the verb to take overtly expressed arguments, as is for example the case with infinitives in Lango:

Lango (Nilo-Saharan)

(5) *àmìttò*   *[cwɛ̀*   *kàttò*   *rwòt]*
     1SG.want.PROG   fat.INF   exceed.INF   king
     'I want to be fatter than the king.' (Noonan 1992: 212)

(v) Coding of arguments as possessors, as in the following sentence from Hixkaryana:

Hixkaryana (Amerindian, Ge-Pano-Carib)

(6) *[Waraka*   *wya*   *honyko*   *wonɨr]*   *xe*   *wehxaha*
     Waraka   by   peccary   shooting.of   desire   I.am
     'I want Waraka to shoot peccary.' (Derbyshire 1979: 92)

Cross-linguistic investigation shows that these properties are linked by a number of implicational correlations (Cristofaro 2003: ch. 10; the relevant data are reported in Appendix 2 below). Although these correlations basically correspond to patterns observed in previous literature (such as the Deverbalization Hierarchy presented in Croft 1991: 83; see also Comrie 1976; Koptjevskaja-Tamm 1993b; Givón 1990: ch. 19), they have never before been systematically investigated in a large-scale cross-linguistic sample.

A first set of implicational correlations concerns absence of tense, aspect, or mood distinctions, or expression of these distinctions differently from independent clauses. Properties such as presence of case marking or adpositions on the verb, coding of arguments as possessors, absence of person agreement distinctions, expression of person agreement distinctions by means of special forms not used in independent clauses, and impossibility for the verb to take overtly expressed arguments all entail absence of tense, aspect, or mood distinctions, or expression of these distinctions by means of special forms not used in independent clauses. The relevant correlations are as follows (henceforth, T/A/M = tense, aspect, or mood):[3]

(7)   Case marking/ adpositions on the verb → T/A/M not expressed ∨ special T/A/M forms

(8)   Arguments expressed as possessors → T/A/M not expressed ∨ special T/A/M forms

(9)   Person agreement not expressed → T/A/M not expressed ∨ special T/A/M forms

(10) Special person agreement forms → T/A/M not expressed ∨ special T/A/M forms

(11) Arguments not expressed → T/A/M not expressed

A second set of implicational correlations concerns the relationship between absence of person agreement distinctions on the verb, or expression of these distinctions differently from independent clauses, and properties such as presence of case marking or adpositions on the verb, coding of arguments as possessors, and impossibility for the verb to take overtly expressed arguments:

(12) Case marking/ adpositions → Person agreement not expressed

The data for this implicational correlation are reported in Table 4.6 in Appendix 2 below. As can be seen from that table, the implicational

---

[3] The basic logic concepts and symbols used in this paper are illustrated in a number of textbooks, such as Allwood et al. (1977).

correlation has fourteen exceptions. Many of these are cases where person agreement distinctions are expressed by means of special agreement forms. In fact, a frequency correlation exists between presence of case marking or adpositions on the verb and use of special agreement forms to express person agreement distinctions. Presence of case marking or adpositions on the verb is usually associated with absence of person agreement distinctions. However, if person agreement distinctions are expressed, the percentage of special person agreement forms is higher than when no case marking or adpositions are present. Conversely, the percentage of case-marking adpositions is higher when person agreement distinctions are expressed by special forms than when they are expressed as in independent clauses. The relevant percentages are reported in Table 4.7 in Appendix 2 below.

(13)   Arguments expressed as possessors → Person agreement not expressed ∨
         Special person agreement forms
(14)   Arguments not expressed → Person agreement not expressed

Finally, there is an implicational relationship between coding of arguments as possessors and presence of case marking or adpositions on the verb:

(15)   Arguments expressed as possessors → Case marking/ adpositions

A frequency hierarchy can also be established concerning the relative frequency of each individual phenomenon with respect to the others (>> = more frequent than; for details about the procedure followed in establishing this hierarchy, the reader is referred to Cristofaro 2003: ch. 10):

(16)   Lack of T/A/M distinctions (131 cases) >> Lack of person agreement
         distinctions (114 cases), lack of overtly expressed arguments (104 cases)
         >> Case marking/ adpositions (53 cases), special T/A/M forms (56
         cases) >> Special person agreement forms (24 cases), coding of
         arguments as possessors (16 cases)

4.4 Explaining the observed correlations

4.4.1 *The cognitive status of dependent states of affairs*

Most of the properties involved in the observed implicational and frequency correlations have been accounted for in functional-typological literature in terms of the discourse function and the cognitive status of the states of affairs being described. The basic idea underlying this approach, which has been formulated in three major versions (Hopper and Thompson 1984; 1985;

Langacker 1987a: chs. 5–7; 1987b; 1991: ch. 10; Croft 1991; 2001: ch. 2), is that nouns and verbs have different prototypical discourse or cognitive functions. Whenever a verb is not being used in its prototypical discourse or cognitive function, it fails to display the full range of categorial distinctions (such as tense, aspect, mood, or person agreement distinctions) that are found in the prototypical function, and it may display some of the properties that are characteristic of nouns in their prototypical function, such as case marking, coding of arguments as possessors, or possessive person agreement.

This approach can also be used to account for at least some of the observed correlations. In particular, Langacker (1987a: chs. 5–7; 1987b; 1991: ch. 10) establishes a distinction between nouns and verbs in terms of the cognitive difference between things and processes. While verbs, as was pointed out in section 4.2, prototypically encode processes (sequentially scanned entities), nouns prototypically encode things. Things, as opposed to processes, are sets of interconnected entities construed summarily as a unitary whole. For instance, the cognitive processing of a red spot on a white wall includes a set of cognitive events, each corresponding to a colour sensation associated with a distinct location on the visual field. However, these cognitive events are interconnected, so that what the viewer perceives is a unitary whole, not an array of individual red dots. This mode of cognitive processing is described by Langacker (1987b: 63, 72) as summary scanning.

As was mentioned in section 4.3, in Langacker's model subordination is a cognitive situation whereby one of two linked states of affairs is construed in the perspective of another state of affairs. More specifically, Langacker argues that dependent states of affairs (or, in Langacker's terms, processes)[4] lack an autonomous profile. By profile Langacker (1987a: 183–9) means that part of a scene that is obligatorily accessed, and accorded special cognitive prominence. In subordination, the profile of the scene coincides with the profile of one of the linked states of affairs, which overrides the profile of the other state of affairs. For instance, as Langacker (1991b: 436–7) observes, a typical complement construction like *I know she left* designates the process of knowing, not of leaving. Likewise, *Alarms ringing, the burglar fled* designates the act of fleeing, not of ringing, and *The skirt she bought was too tight* designates the skirt, not the act of buying.

---

[4] Langacker's notion of process overlaps with the notion of state of affairs in that both refer to a predication consisting of a predicate and its terms and denoting something that can be the case in some world. The notion of state of affairs as such, however, has no implications for the way in which this entity is conceptualized. In fact, a process can be regarded as a sequentially scanned state of affairs.

Langacker (1991b: 439–41) argues that lack of an autonomous processual profile on the part of the dependent state of affairs leads to different conceptualization of that state of affairs. Only the state of affairs that is profiled gets the sequential, state-by-state scanning characteristic of processes, while the non-profiled state of affairs is construed holistically as a component of the profiled state of affairs, and scanned summarily as a unitary entity.

It appears reasonable to assume that the fact that the dependent state of affairs is construed as a unitary whole and integrated as a component of the main state of affairs may lead to conceptualization of this state of affairs as a thing, because things too are scanned summarily and construed as a unitary whole. As a result, since things are prototypically encoded by nouns, the verb may display typical nominal properties such as presence of case marking or adpositions. The presence of special person agreement forms can also be regarded as evidence that the dependent state of affairs is conceptualized as a thing, because these forms are in virtually all cases possessive forms (see example 3 above), and possessive agreement forms are a nominal property (see e.g. Seiler 1983). In fact, the existence of implicational and frequency correlations between presence of case marking or adpositions, presence of special person agreement forms, and coding of arguments as possessors (13 and 15 above; Table 4.6 below) can be regarded as evidence that all of these properties reflect conceptualization of the dependent state of affairs as a thing.

These properties all entail absence of tense, aspect, or mood distinctions, or expression of these distinctions by means of special forms not used in independent clauses (7, 8, and 10 above). This may be related to the absence of sequential scanning. As was pointed out in section 4.2, sequential scanning pertains to the fact that processes are conceptualized as occurring through time. Properties such as tense, aspect, and mood distinctions also pertain to occurrence of processes through time: tense pertains to location of a process along a time axis, aspect pertains to the internal temporal constituency of a process, and mood pertains to actuality, i.e. the possible realization of a process at some point in time (Chung and Timberlake 1985). Hence one may assume that tense, aspect, and mood distinctions are directly connected with sequential scanning, and they may be missing when there is no sequential scanning, as is the case when the dependent state of affairs is conceptualized as a thing.

On the other hand, since in this case the cognitive status of the dependent state of affairs is very different from that of independent states of affairs, which are usually conceptualized as processes, one may assume that, if tense, aspect, and mood distinctions are expressed at all, they are not expressed in the same way as in independent clauses. This may explain why the properties that are related to conceptualization of the dependent state of affairs as a thing entail either absence of tense, aspect, or mood distinctions, or expression of these distinctions by means of special forms.

A similar line of reasoning may be used to account for the fact that presence of case marking or adpositions on the verb and coding of arguments as possessors entail absence of person agreement distinctions, or coding of these distinctions by means of special forms (12, 13). Unlike tense, aspect, and mood distinctions, person agreement distinctions do not refer to the occurrence of states of affairs through time, but rather to the entities taking part in the state of affairs. Even if they are scanned summarily rather than sequentially, dependent states of affairs are still relational, that is, they still involve a number of participants. So in principle there is no reason why verbs coding dependent states of affairs should not refer to these participants by means of person agreement distinctions. Person agreement distinctions, however, are a distinguishing property of verbs with respect to nouns.[5] If the dependent state of affairs is conceptualized as a thing, as indicated by presence of case marking or adpositions on the verb and coding of arguments as possessors, one may assume that this is reflected at the level of verb form by absence of typical verbal properties such as person agreement (or presence of nominal properties such as possessive agreement).

The fact that person agreement distinctions are a typical verbal property may also explain why absence of person agreement distinctions entails absence of tense, aspect, or mood distinctions, or expression of these distinctions by means of special forms. Typical verbal properties are missing when the relevant state of affairs is not conceptualized as a process, and absence of processual properties is directly reflected by absence of tense, aspect, or mood distinctions, or coding of these distinctions by means of special forms (though see section 4.4.2 below for an alternative explanation for this correlation).[6]

---

[5] This refers to person agreement for arguments. In a number of languages, nouns also display person agreement distinctions, but these refer to the person of the possessor, not arguments such as A, S, or O. Seiler (1983) shows that in these languages the same markers can be used to express the person of the possessor on nouns and the person of arguments on verbs. However, as is argued by Seiler, this is because of a number of conceptual similarities between agent and possessor in a relation of alienable possession, and experiencer and possessor in a relation of inalienable possession. This does not mean that possessor agreement on nouns should be regarded as the same thing as argument agreement on verbs, although the two can be expressed by the same markers.

[6] Hopper and Thompson (1984; 1985) and Croft (1991: chs. 2, 3) also propose models where a connection is established between the dependent status of particular clauses and the fact that the verb in those clauses lacks typical verbal properties and displays nominal properties (neither of these models adopts any specific definition of subordination, however). Hopper and Thompson argue that verbs are prototypically used in discourse to report discrete events, while nouns are prototypically used to refer to discourse-manipulable participants. Properties such as absence of inflectional distinctions and presence of nominal morphology on the verb are found when verbs do not report

Finally, the cognitive status of dependent states of affairs also makes it possible to account for at least some aspects of the frequency hierarchy in (16). The cognitive status of dependent states of affairs leads to summary rather than sequential scanning of these states of affairs. This may explain why absence of the grammatical properties directly related to sequential scanning, namely tense, aspect, and mood distinctions, is the most frequent phenomenon in the coding of subordination.

On the other hand, the cognitive status of dependent states of affairs may, but need not, lead to conceptualization of those states of affairs as things. Conceptualization of dependent states of affairs as things originates from a number of cognitive similarities between dependent states of affairs and things. Like things, dependent states of affairs are scanned summarily rather than sequentially. Also, dependent states of affairs are integrated in the perspective of the main state of affairs, which means that, just like things, they can be conceptualized as components of that state of affairs. However, there are a number of differences between dependent states of affairs and things. For instance, dependent states of affairs are relational, i.e. involve a number of entities taking part in the state of affairs, while things are non-relational. This means that, while summary scanning of dependent states of affairs is a direct result of the cognitive status of these states of affairs, conceptualization of dependent states of affairs as things is not. This may explain why the grammatical properties that are directly related to conceptualization of the dependent state of affairs as a thing, namely presence of case marking and adpositions on the verb, use of special (possessive) person agreement forms, and coding of arguments as possessors, are the least frequent properties in the cross-linguistic coding of subordination.

4.4.2 *Information recoverability*

Some of the observed correlations cannot be accounted for in terms of the cognitive status of dependent states of affairs. For example, there does not seem to be any connection between the cognitive status of dependent states of affairs and the fact that verb arguments cannot be expressed overtly. Just like person agreement distinctions, verb arguments pertain to relationality, i.e. the fact that an event involves a number of entities that take part in it. As was

---

discrete discourse events, as is the case with certain types of subordinate clause. Similarly, Croft argues that typical verbal and nominal properties are based on prototypical combinations of semantic class and pragmatic function of lexical roots, and fail to appear in non-prototypical combinations, as manifested in certain types of subordinate clause. Neither of these approaches, however, directly addresses the issue of why specific individual properties should be missing in particular non-prototypical situations, nor why there should be correlations between different properties.

mentioned in the previous section, even if they are scanned summarily rather than sequentially, dependent states of affairs are still relational, that is, they still involve a number of entities taking part in the event. This means that the cognitive status of the dependent event cannot account for the implicational correlation between impossibility for the verb to take overtly expressed arguments and other properties such as absence of tense, aspect, mood, and person agreement distinctions (11, 14).

However, arguments are usually not expressed when main and dependent states of affairs share a participant, and thus there is no need for overt reference to this participant in both of the linked clauses (see Cristofaro 2003 for extensive cross-linguistic data). This reflects an economic principle of information recoverability whereby information that is recoverable from the context is not expressed overtly. This principle has proved effective for a large number of phenomena in a wide variety of languages (see e.g. Croft 2003 for extensive discussion of this principle in relation to markedness).

Absence of tense, aspect, and mood distinctions has been related to information recoverability too (Haiman 1985; Noonan 1985; Cristofaro 2003). In a number of semantic relations between states of affairs, particular semantic features of these states of affairs, such as time reference, aspect, and mood value, are predetermined. As a result, these features need not be overtly specified, and verb forms not specified for the corresponding categorial distinctions may be used in the relevant clauses.

For example, in purpose relations involving motion verbs, as exemplified in:

(17)   We went to the market to buy fish.

the state of affairs expressed by the motion verb and the state of affairs corresponding to the purpose of motion are in a fixed temporal sequence, so the time reference of either of the two states of affairs can be determined on the basis of that of the other state of affairs. As a result, time reference can be specified for one event only, while verb forms not specified for tense can be used in the clause expressing the other event.

All the subordination relations involving sharing of participants between main and dependent state of affairs also involve predetermination of the time reference, aspect, and mood value of the dependent state of affairs. For instance, phasal predicates such as 'begin', 'stop', or 'continue' entail that the main and dependent states of affairs are brought about by the same entity and take place at the same time, and that the dependent state of affairs is ongoing at the moment the main state of affairs takes place. In this case, there is no need to specify either the participants or the time reference, aspect, or mood value of the dependent state of affairs.

On the other hand, there are a number of subordination relation types, such as temporal relations, that entail predetermination of the time reference, aspect, and mood value of the dependent state of affairs, but not sharing of participants between main and dependent state of affairs (for detailed discussion of these issues with respect to various types of subordination relation, the reader is referred to Cristofaro 2003: chs. 5, 6). This is, for instance, the case with temporal anteriority relations of the type exemplified in (18), where the time reference, aspect, and mood value of the dependent state of affairs are predetermined, but main and dependent state of affairs may not share any participants (in fact, in 18, they don't).

(18)   I wrote him after they called.

In this case, there is no need overtly to specify the time reference, aspect, and mood value of the dependent state of affairs. However, the participants of the dependent state of affairs should be specified overtly, as their identity is not predetermined.

Since the relation types involving sharing of participants between the main and the dependent state of affairs are a subset of those involving predetermination of the time reference, aspect, and mood value of the dependent state of affairs, one would expect that, in all the cases where arguments are not expressed overtly, tense, aspect, or mood distinctions are not expressed either, but that tense, aspect, or mood distinctions may not be expressed even when arguments and person agreement distinctions are expressed. This is exactly what happens in the implicational correlation patterns illustrated in (11) above.

This also provides an additional motivation for the implicational correlation between absence of tense, aspect, or mood distinctions and absence of person agreement distinctions (9). This correlation was accounted for in section 4.4.1 in terms of the cognitive status of dependent states of affairs. However, person agreement distinctions cross-reference the participants of a state of affairs on the verb, and their cross-linguistic distribution also appears to be related to sharing of participants between main and dependent state of affairs (see Cristofaro 2003: chs. 5, 6 for extensive cross-linguistic data and discussion). Hence this correlation may be accounted for in the same way as the correlation between absence of tense, aspect, or mood distinctions and the inability of the verb to take overtly expressed arguments. In all the cases where the time reference, aspect, and mood value of the dependent state of affairs need not be expressed because they are predetermined, there is no need to cross-reference the participants of the dependent state of affairs by means of person agreement, because these participants are the same as those of the main state of affairs. The reverse, however, does not hold: there are cases where the time reference, aspect, and mood value of the dependent state of affairs are not expressed because they are predetermined, but the participants of the dependent state of affairs are cross-referenced by person agreement, because their identity is not predetermined.

4.4.3 *Semantic integration*

Absence of tense, aspect, mood, and person agreement distinctions, as well as inability of the verb to take overtly expressed arguments, have also been related to an iconic principle which Newmeyer (1992: 762–3) labels iconicity of independence. In a number of semantic relations between states of affairs, these states of affairs are semantically integrated, that is, the boundaries between them are eroded to some extent. For example, the two states of affairs may be part of the same event frame, as is the case in a sentence like:

(19)   I started teaching in October.

where starting to teach and teaching are actually part of the same action. Semantic integration is also obtained in relations of direct causation, as exemplified in:

(20)   She made him buy a desktop computer.

where somebody's manipulating somebody else into buying a computer and buying a computer are obviously tightly interconnected.

Absence of tense, aspect, mood, or person agreement distinctions, and absence of overtly expressed arguments, result in non-specification of information about the corresponding semantic features of the state of affairs being expressed. As a result, the relevant clause depends on other clauses for the specification of this information. Syntactic dependency between clauses is argued to iconically reflect semantic integration between the states of affairs they express. In fact, this principle is invoked by Givón (1980) to account for the occurrence of verb forms with reduced inflectional potential in various types of complement clauses cross-linguistically. In Cristofaro (2003) it is argued that semantic integration also plays a role in a number of implicational correlations concerning verb forms with reduced inflectional potential and inability of the verb to take overtly expressed arguments in various types of complement, adverbial, and relative clause.

Thus, there appear to be at least three motivations for absence of tense, aspect, mood, or person agreement distinctions, and inability of the verb to take overtly expressed arguments: the cognitive status of dependent states of affairs, information recoverability, and semantic integration.[7] On the other hand, there does not seem to be any direct connection between the latter two principles and properties such as case marking or adpositions on the verb, presence of special (possessive) person agreement forms, and coding of arguments as possessors.[8] These properties appear to reflect the cognitive status of the dependent state of affairs only, and this may be another reason why they are less frequent than absence of tense, aspect, mood, or person agreement distinctions, and inability of the verb to take overtly expressed arguments, as manifested in the frequency hierarchy in (16).

4.5 Concluding remarks: finiteness, grammatical categories, and universal principles

Functionally oriented theories of grammar generally assume finiteness and nonfiniteness to be categories relevant to a number of different constructions in different languages.

---

[7] The analysis of absence of tense, aspect, and mood distinctions in terms of information recoverability and semantic integration may appear to be in contrast with the analysis of this phenomenon in terms of the cognitive status of dependent states of affairs. In the former case, it is assumed that tense, aspect, and mood distinctions are relevant to dependent states of affairs, and they are not expressed because of information recoverability or semantic integration. In the latter case, it is assumed that tense, aspect, and mood distinctions are not relevant to dependent states of affairs because these states of affairs lack an autonomous processual profile. These two analyses, however, pertain to different functional domains. Tense, aspect, and mood distinctions reflect intrinsic semantic features of states of affairs in general, namely the fact that states of affairs occur through time, and they may not be expressed on dependent states of affairs because of information recoverability and semantic integration. The intrinsic semantic features of a particular scene are in principle independent of the way that scene is conceptualized, that is, the perspective imposed on that scene by the speaker (although of course there is a connection between the two: see on this point Croft 1991: 99–100). The fact that states of affairs occur through time is not relevant to the conceptualization of dependent states of affairs, because these states of affairs are not conceptualized as processes in their own right. This may be reflected by absence of tense, aspect, and mood distinctions, independently of the fact that these distinctions also reflect intrinsic semantic features of dependent states of affairs. On the other hand, even if tense, aspect, and mood distinctions are not relevant to the way dependent states of affairs are conceptualized, verbs coding dependent states of affairs may still display tense, aspect, and mood distinctions, because these distinctions are relevant to the semantics of dependent states of affairs.

[8] The principle of information recoverability appears to be the basis of Givón's notion of finiteness, in that he states that the more predictable a clausal feature is vis-à-vis its immediate clausal context, the more likely it is to be left unmarked, i.e. less finite (Givón 1990: 876). Givón, however, includes within nonfiniteness any property involving deviation from the prototype transitive main clause pattern, including coding of arguments as possessors and presence of case marking or adpositions on the verb. As these properties are not clearly amenable to an explanation in terms of information recoverability, they should not be regarded as relevant to the distinction between finiteness and nonfiniteness on this view. On the other hand, if one assumes (as Givón actually does) that nonfiniteness encompasses any phenomenon leading to deviation from the independent clause pattern, information recoverability cannot be an overall explanation for nonfiniteness.

In section 4.2 it was, however, shown that finiteness and nonfiniteness, as defined in these theories, do not correspond to internally consistent classes. The question then arises as to why categories such as finiteness and nonfiniteness should be posited in the first place. In principle, a particular linguistic category can be posited either because there is evidence that that category is a grammatical category (i.e. a category that has a role in the grammar of a particular language, and is part of the linguistic knowledge of the speakers of that language), or because it represents an adequate description of particular facts of the language (independently of how those facts are represented in a speaker's mental grammar).

Neither of these motivations, however, appears to apply in the case of finiteness and nonfiniteness. In discussing a number of putative grammatical categories and relations (such as parts of speech and subject), Dryer (1996; 1997) and Croft (2001) have extensively argued that, if the entities falling within a putative grammatical category or relation do not display the same range of properties from one construction to another, there is no reason to assume that these constructions instantiate the same grammatical category in a speaker's linguistic knowledge. Instead, one should assume that the various constructions in which these entities are manifested instantiate distinct grammatical categories. These categories are construction-specific, because they are not the same from one construction to another, and language-specific, because they are not the same from one language to another.

The same arguments apply to finiteness and nonfiniteness. As the various entities that fall within finiteness and nonfiniteness display different properties from one construction to another, there is no reason to assume that these entities instantiate the same grammatical category in each case. This holds both cross-linguistically and within individual languages. It follows that finiteness and nonfiniteness do not correspond to grammatical categories that are manifested in different constructions in different languages, but rather to a number of language-specific and construction-specific grammatical categories. On this view, for example, verb forms that are not inflected for some particular parameter, but differ in their other properties (such as inflection for other parameters, presence of nominal morphology, or ability to occur in independent clauses), should be regarded as instances of different grammatical categories, both cross-linguistically and within individual languages.

In addition to that, the various properties involved in the notions of nonfiniteness, as well as the correlations between these properties, may be motivated in terms of different principles of form–function correspondence. For example, while properties such as presence of case marking or adpositions on the verb arguably originate from the cognitive status of the states of affairs being encoded, other properties may also be motivated in terms of principles such as semantic integration and information recoverability. Similarly, some property combinations (e.g. case marking or adpositions on the verb and absence of tense, aspect, or mood distinctions) are motivated in terms of the cognitive status of the dependent state of affairs, while others (e.g. impossibility for the verb to take overtly expressed arguments and absence of tense, aspect, mood, or person agreement distinctions) are motivated in terms of information recoverability.

This suggests that there is actually no particular reason to use finiteness and nonfiniteness as descriptive cover terms for the various properties and their combinations. These properties and combinations cannot be regarded as manifestations of the same general phenomenon, and thus there appears to be no reason why they should be grouped together for descriptive purposes.

Thus, the notions of finiteness and nonfiniteness do not provide either an adequate account of a speaker's linguistic knowledge or an adequate description of particular phenomena in individual languages. In this respect, finiteness and nonfiniteness are not cross-linguistically relevant categories, and not even categories relevant to different constructions within particular languages.

However, a number of cross-linguistically and cross-constructionally valid principles exist that motivate both the presence of the various properties involved in finiteness and nonfiniteness in particular clause types (dependent clauses) and the attested combinations and relative frequency of these properties. This confirms that, as argued in recent typological proposals on grammatical categories and relations (Dryer 1996; 1997; Croft 2001), universals of grammar do not correspond to categories and relations defined in terms of individual properties, but are rather found in the principles of form–function correspondence governing the cross-linguistic and cross-constructional distribution of individual properties.

Appendix 1. Languages in the sample

Acehnese, Ainu, Akan, Arabic (Gulf), Arapesh, Banda Linda, Barasano, Basque, Berbice Dutch Creole, Borana, Burushaski, Canela-Krahô, Chinese (Mandarin), Diegueño, Djapu, Egyptian (Ancient), Finnish, Fula, Gimira, Greek (Classical), Greenlandic (West), Gumbayinggir, Guugu Yimidhirr, Hixkaryana, Hittite, Hmong Njua, Ho, Hurrian, Italian, Jacaltec, Japanese, Kanuri, Karimojong, Kayardild, Khasi, Kobon, Kolokumi, Krongo, Lango, Lezgian, Limbu, Makian (West), Maŋarayi, Maori, Maricopa, Muna, Nama,

Nandi, Ngbaka, Nung, Paiwan, Paumarí, Pero, Pirahã, Punjabi, Quechua
(Huallaga Huánuco), Resigaro, Retuarã, Sawu, Shipibo-Conibo, Shoshone
(Tümpisa Panamint), Slave, Songhay, Sumerian, Supyire, Tagalog, Tamazight,
Tamil, Tanghkul Naga, Tarascan, Tok Pisin, Turkish, Tzutujil, Ute, Vai, Viet-
namese, Wargamay, Wayãpi, Yidiɲ, Yoruba.

Appendix 2. Data supporting the observed correlations

In this appendix, a number of tables are presented that illustrate the data
supporting the correlation patterns discussed in section 4.3 (these tables
reproduce those of Cristofaro 2003: ch. 10). As can be seen from these tables,
the proposed implicational correlations are not free from exceptions—i.e. all
of the logically possible combinations of the relevant properties are attested.
This situation is actually quite frequent in cross-linguistic research. In this
case, one can still establish an implicational correlation between the relevant
properties, provided that one of the four cases is significantly rarer than the
others. One has then to develop some criteria to decide how rare the relevant
case should be in order to regard the candidate implicational correlation as
valid (see on this point Stassen 1985: 20–1). It should be pointed out in this
connection that not all of the four logically possible combinations of two
given properties are equally significant in establishing an implicational correlation between these two properties. For instance, given two properties A
and B, the cases where both properties are present (A & B) or neither
phenomenon is present ($\sim$A & $\sim$B) support either an implication of the
form A $\rightarrow$ B or one of the form B $\rightarrow$ A. Thus, they are not relevant in
establishing the implicational correlation between A and B. Implicational
correlations are revealed by the other two logically possible combinations of
A and B. If $\sim$A & B occurs, while A & $\sim$B does not occur or is rather rare, then
A and B are linked by an implicational relationship of the form A $\rightarrow$ B. If A &
$\sim$B occurs, while $\sim$A & B does not occur or is rather rare, then A and B are
linked by an implicational relationship of the form B $\rightarrow$ A. Thus, only the cases
where one of the two relevant properties is present, while the other is absent,
are truly significant for implication. The general criterion adopted in this
study for regarding a candidate implicational correlation as valid is therefore
based on these two cases. An implicational correlation is regarded as valid if
the number of occurrences of one of the two significant cases is no more
than one third of the number of occurrences of the other significant case.

For each table, the corresponding implication is reported, along with
the number of significant cases supporting the implication and the number
of significant cases contradicting it. The table concerning the frequency

correlation between presence of case marking or adpositions on the verb and absence of person agreement distinctions (Table 4.7) reports the percentages of each of the logically possible combinations of the properties involved in the correlation.

In the tables, the notation T/A/M is used to mean 'tense, aspect, or mood distinctions', and the notation TAM is used to mean 'tense, aspect, and mood distinctions'. Thus, for instance, the notation 'T/A/M not expressed' means that tense, aspect, or mood distinctions are not expressed, while the notation 'TAM expressed' means that tense, aspect, and mood distinctions are all expressed.

TABLE 4.1. Case marking/adpositions on verbs vs. expression of tense, aspect, and mood distinctions

	T/A/M not expressed	TAM expressed: no special forms	T/A/M expressed: special forms
Case marking/ adpositions	74	7	22
No case marking/ adpositions	147	135	58

Implication: Case marking/adpositions → T/A/M not expressed ∨ special T/A/M forms (7).

Significant cases
Cases supporting the implication:
No case marking/adpositions and T/A/M not expressed   147
No case marking/adpositions and special T/A/M forms   58
Cases contradicting the implication:
Case marking/adpositions and TAM expressed: no special forms   7

TABLE 4.2. Coding of arguments as possessors vs. expression of tense, aspect, and mood distinctions

	T/A/M not expressed	TAM expressed: no special forms	T/A/M expressed: special forms
Arguments expressed as possessors	24	1	6
Arguments expressed as in independent clauses	77	132	44

Implication: Arguments expressed as possessors → T/A/M not expressed ∨ special T/A/M forms (8).

Significant cases
Cases supporting the implication:
Arguments expressed as in independent clauses and T/A/M not expressed   77
Arguments expressed as in independent clauses and special T/A/M forms   44
Cases contradicting the implication:
Arguments expressed as possessors and TAM expressed: no special forms   1

TABLE 4.3. Absence of person agreement distinctions vs. expression of tense, aspect and mood distinctions

	T/A/M not expressed	TAM expressed: no special forms	T/A/M expressed: special forms
Person agreement not expressed	100	9	33
Person agreement expressed	28	80	19

Implication: Person agreement not expressed → T/A/M not expressed ∨ special T/A/M forms (9).

Significant cases
Cases supporting the implication:
  Person agreement expressed and T/A/M not expressed   28
  Person agreement expressed and special T/A/M forms   19
Cases contradicting the implication:
  Person agreement not expressed and TAM expressed: no special forms   9

TABLE 4.4. Use of special forms to express person agreement distinctions vs. expression of tense, aspect, and mood distinctions

	T/A/M not expressed	TAM expressed: no special forms	T/A/M expressed: special forms
Person agreement expressed: special forms	17	1	8
Person agreement expressed: no special forms	39	78	13

Implication: Special person agreement forms → T/A/M not expressed ∨ special T/A/M forms (10).

Significant cases
Cases supporting the implication:
  Person agreement expressed: no special forms and T/A/M not expressed   39
  Person agreement expressed: no special forms and special T/A/M forms   13
Cases contradicting the implication:
  Person agreement expressed: special forms and TAM expressed: no special forms   1

TABLE 4.5. Absence of overtly expressed arguments vs. absence of tense, aspect, and mood distinctions

	T/A/M not expressed	TAM expressed
Arguments not expressed	127	49
Arguments expressed	117	150

Implication: Arguments not expressed → T/A/M not expressed (11).

Significant cases
Cases supporting the implication:
  Arguments expressed and T/A/M not expressed   117
Cases contradicting the implication:
  Arguments not expressed and TAM expressed   49

TABLE 4.6. Case marking/adpositions on verbs vs. absence of person agreement distinctions

	Person agreement not expressed	Person agreement expressed
Case marking/ adpositions	43	14
No case marking/ adpositions	69	125

Implication: Case marking/adpositions → Person agreement not expressed (12).

Significant cases
Cases supporting the implication:
   No case marking/adpositions and person agreement not expressed   69
Cases contradicting the implication:
   Case marking/adpositions and person agreement expressed   14

TABLE 4.7. Case marking/adpositions on verbs vs. use of special forms to express person agreement distinctions

	Person agreement expressed: special forms	Person agreement expressed: no special forms
Case marking/ adpositions	6	8
No case marking/ adpositions	17	108

Frequency correlations: The percentage of special person agreement forms is higher when the verb displays case marking/adpositions than when this is not the case. The percentage of case marking/adpositions is higher when person agreement distinctions are expressed by special forms than when they are expressed as in independent clauses.

Percentages of individual combinations		%
Case marking/adpositions	Special person agreement forms	43
	Person agreement expressed as in independent clauses	57
No case marking/adpositions	Special person agreement forms	14
	Person agreement expressed as in independent clauses	86
Special person agreement forms	Case marking/adpositions	26
	No case marking/adpositions	74
Person agreement expressed as in independent clauses	Case marking/adpositions	7
	No case marking/adpositions	93

TABLE 4.8. Coding of verb arguments as possessors vs. expression of person agreement distinctions

	Person agreement not expressed	Person agreement expressed: no special forms	Person agreement expressed: special forms
Arguments expressed as possessors	13	2	4
Arguments expressed as in independent clauses	23	95	7

Implication: Arguments expressed as possessors → Person agreement not expressed ∨ special person agreement forms (13).

Significant cases
Cases supporting the implication:

Arguments expressed as in independent clauses and person agreement not expressed   23
Arguments expressed as in independent clauses and special person agreement forms   7

Cases contradicting the implication:

Arguments expressed as possessors and person agreement expressed: no special forms   2

5

Categories that make finiteness: discreteness from a functional perspective and some of its repercussions

WALTER BISANG

5.1 Introduction

Functional approaches describe finiteness as a scalar phenomenon, while formal theories take finiteness as a discrete phenomenon. From the perspective of functional-typological findings, finiteness must be defined not in terms of an individual universal morphological property or parameter but rather in terms of a cluster of parameters (see Cristofaro, Chapter 4 above). These parameters then form the basis for establishing a scale for situating individual patterns of how finiteness is realized in individual languages (Givón 1990; Dik 1997a; Hengeveld 1998; Cristofaro, Chapter 4 above). Since formal approaches focus on syntactic effects of properties or features, a scalar analysis is impossible—features are discrete and they are integrated into a binary system which determines whether a certain effect takes place or not. In Rizzi's (1997) analysis of the CP-domain, finiteness clearly plays a role in the projection closest to IP, i.e. in FinP. The features that can appear on Fin are T and Agr. On a general level, the question then is how finiteness can be reflected in the geometry of interpretable and uninterpretable features of T- and Agr-features somewhere in the C- and in the T-domains (for more details, see Adger, Chapter 2 above).

In the present chapter, I try to show how finiteness can be described as a discrete, binary phenomenon from a functional perspective (also see Bisang 1998; 2001a). For that purpose, I look at the categories that can be morphosyntactically expressed in independent vs. dependent clauses in the framework of obligatoriness and asymmetry. In this context, finiteness will be defined in terms of morphosyntactic indicators of sentencehood. If a language has an overt morphosyntactic marker from which the human parser can derive the independent status of a grammatical structure that language makes a finite/nonfinite distinction (also see Maas 2004: 361, who defines 'semantic finiteness' as 'a condition for an independent interpretation of a sentence'). If there is no such indicator in a language there is no finite/nonfinite distinction in that language. In that sense, finiteness is not a universal category.

The structure of the chapter will be as follows. In the second section, I will first introduce scalar approaches as they are discussed in functional typology (section 5.2.1). Since the chapter by Cristofaro presents an excellent survey of functional approaches to finiteness, I can limit myself to the presentation of scalarity. In section 5.2.2, I will explain in what way discreteness can be used in a functional framework. Given the extensive introduction of finiteness from the perspective of the minimalist programme and its predecessors in Adger (Chapter 2 above), I will not provide any extra section on finiteness from a generative perspective in this chapter.

The concept of finiteness adopted here is crucially based on the idea that the finite/nonfinite distinction depends on the obligatory expression of certain cognitive domains such as tense, illocutionary force, person, and politeness. Such an asymmetry arises if a cognitive domain that is addressed obligatorily in an independent clause or sentence cannot occur in the dependent clause, irrespective of whether that domain is expressed morphologically or syntactically. The concepts of obligatoriness, asymmetry, and some cognitive domains involved in finiteness will be the topic of section 5.3.

Section 5.4 will show that the use of markers from the cognitive domains of tense, agreement, illocutionary force, and politeness as indicators of finiteness is not arbitrary as is often stated in functional approaches. Their use in the context of finiteness is motivated by their semantic generality in terms of Bybee (1985). For a marker to be obligatory, it must be semantically general enough to be compatible with each of its potential hosts.

The conclusion in section 5.5 will sketch some repercussions of my approach to finiteness. The lack of any category that is universally used for expressing finiteness can be seen as a consequence of regrammaticalization (exaptation, hypoanalysis). From this perspective, semantic/pragmatic definitions such as the one by Klein (1994; 1998; forthcoming) in terms of tense and assertion may reflect only *one* possible solution adopted in many Indo-European languages. Other languages select other semantic domains to express finiteness. Finally, the fact that finiteness does not need to be pervasively marked through the whole system of a language (see the case of insubordination, Evans, Chapter 11 below, or the case of root sentences, Lasser 2002) can be explained by properties of the human parser. Human parsers do not need 100 per cent obligatoriness to reanalyse a marker of a certain category.

5.2 Scalarity vs. discreteness

This section deals with scalar approaches in functional typology (5.2.1) and with the definition of discreteness and its usefulness for a typological account of finiteness (5.2.2).

5.2.1 *Finiteness as a scalar phenomenon in functional typology*

Givón (1990: 852–91) presents the most detailed study on finiteness as a scalar phenomenon. In his view (p. 853), finiteness as a property of the clause is a syntactic reflection of the degree with which a clause is integrated into 'its immediate clausal environment'. In this function, it is part of clausal dependency which is 'ultimately a matter of discourse coherence':

(1)   Properties of finiteness (Givón 1990: 853)
      Clausal domain: finiteness is a property of the clause (rather than of the verb).
      Complexity and scalarity: finiteness is a complex, multi-featured, scalar grammatical meta-phenomenon (rather than a single, discrete, binary feature).
      Coding function: Finiteness is the systematic grammatical means used to express the degree of integration of a clause into its immediate clausal environment. The syntactic dependence of the clause—i.e. its finiteness—is thus used to code thematic dependence of an event/state on its discourse context.
      Scope of dependency: While some clause-dependencies (such as V-complements, sentential subjects, or relative clauses) may be expressed in terms of purely syntactic relations, clausal dependency—like event integration—is ultimately a matter of discourse coherence. Syntactic dependencies are but a restricted subset of discourse-pragmatic dependency.

The list of features under (2) are the 'main syntactic features' determining the degree of finiteness of a given clause in comparison to a 'prototype transitive main clause' in terms of Givón (1990: 853). Since the use of a topic marker is another feature relevant to finiteness as a scalar phenomenon not mentioned by Givón, I add it as a sixth feature to the list of Givón's five features (see Bisang 2001a: 1401–2):

(2)   Tense/aspect/modality
Pronominal ('grammatical') agreement
Nominalizing affixes
Case marking of the subject and object
Articles, determiners
Use of a topic marker

In the context of the first feature, i.e. tense/aspect/modality, Givón (1990: 854) presents the following two scales:

(3)   Scale of finiteness of tense/aspect/modality:
more finite   >   less finite

terminated   >   non-terminated
realis   >   irrealis
punctual   >   durative
in-sequence   >   anterior

(4)   Finiteness ranking of tense/aspect/modality:
most finite: Tense
            Modality
            Aspect
least finite: Negation

Subjunctives as we find them in French, Greek, or Latin are an example of the 'realis > irrealis' scale in (3). In most languages, the subjunctive denotes some modality of irrealis or intention. As the scale predicts, the subjunctive rarely occurs in matrix clauses in the three languages mentioned above. If we find it in this function, it is used to express a wish in French (5) or an exhortation to the first person plural in Classical Greek (6):

(5)   Dieu   vous   bénisse!
God   2PL   bless.CONJ.PRS.3SG
'May God bless you!'

(6)   Iōmen.
go.CONJ.PRS.1PL
'Let's go!'

The subjunctive (or conjunctive) of Classical Greek can also be used as an example of the hierarchy under (4). This form, which is mostly used in dependent clauses, does not mark tense distinction as the forms of the indicative do, but it still follows two separate paradigms for the distinction of aspect as expressed by the forms of present and aorist in traditional terminology.

Other scale-based approaches are described by Noonan (1985) and Henge-veld (1998). To conclude this section, I shall briefly sketch Hengeveld's (1998) findings on adverbial subordination based on a sample of forty-five European languages. In order to avoid the problem of having to define finiteness cross-linguistically, Hengeveld (1998) departs from the notion of dependency. Independent verb forms may be used in matrix clauses while dependent forms are only used in subordinate constructions (Hengeveld 1998: 339). The conditions under which independent vs. dependent verbal forms are employed is described in four hierarchies. The first hierarchy is defined by the parameter of entity types in terms of Lyons (1977: 442–7) and Dik (1997a). Linguistic units may refer to entities of five different types, beginning with the zero order to which belong properties or relations. First-order entities are individuals. They are evaluated in terms of existence. Since first-order entities are limited to noun phrases, they are of no relevance to adverbial subordin-ation. Second-order entities denote states of affairs, i.e. predicates with their arguments and satellites. They can be evaluated in terms of their reality. Third-order entities refer to propositional contents and can be evaluated in terms of truth. While a second order is an extensional object, a propositional content is an intentional object. Propositional contents 'are entities of the kind that may function as the objects of such so-called propositional attitudes as belief, expectation and judgement' (Lyons 1977: 445). Finally, the fourth order reflects the level of speech acts. They can be evaluated in terms of informativeness. These four entity types are linked in the following way to the semantics of adverbial subordination:

(7) *Zero order*
     Means
     Second order
     Cause, simultaneity, addition, anteriority, potential circumstance, purpose, unreal circumstance, negative circumstance
     Third order
     Reason, concession, potential condition, unreal condition
     Fourth order
     Explanation

The use of independent vs. dependent forms within the above four entity types is determined by the following hierarchy:

(8) Entity Type Hierarchy (Hengeveld 1998: 359)
     zero order > second order > third order > fourth order
     dependent verb form   >   independent verb form

This hierarchy reads as follows:

If a language uses a dependent verb form for the expression of an adverbial clause designating an entity of a certain order, then it will also use a dependent form for the expression of adverbial clauses designating entities of lower orders, and vice-versa for independent verb forms. (Hengeveld 1998: 359)

The other three hierarchies refer to the correlation between independent vs. dependent marking and time-dependency (9), factuality (10), and presupposedness (11). The parameter of time-dependency only applies to second-order entity types. It is based on the question of whether the adverbial clause depends on the time reference expressed in the matrix clause. The factuality hierarchy describes the use of independent vs. dependent verb forms for the expression of a factual clause designating an entity of a certain order. In an analogous way, the presupposedness hierarchy deals with the use of independent vs. dependent verb forms for the expression of presupposed vs. non-presupposed adverbial clauses.

(9)   Time-dependency hierarchy (Hengeveld 1998: 377)
      dependent time reference > independent time reference
      dependent verb form   >   independent verb form

(10) Factuality hierarchy (Hengeveld 1998: 365)
      factual   >   nonfactual
      dependent verb form >   independent verb form

(11) Presupposedness hierarchy (Hengeveld 1998: 353, 371)
      presupposed   >   nonpresupposed
      dependent verb form >   independent verb form

The validity of Hengeveld's (1998) four hierarchies depends on the existence of a morphological distinction between dependent and independent verb forms. It does not apply to languages in which this distinction does not show up morphologically.

5.2.2 Discreteness

In both formal and functional approaches, finiteness is understood as a phenomenon that is related to the clause. From a formal perspective, the categories that define finiteness are discrete or binary morphosyntactic categories. Their presence or their absence is crucial for certain morphosyntactic effects to take place. In the classical Government and Binding approach (Chomsky 1981; George and Kornfilt 1981), these effects are concerned with tense and verb agreement, the realization of the subject, and the creation of domains that are inaccessible for certain syntactic rules. In the minimalist approach, the features involved with finiteness (T and Agr) trigger certain syntactic effects within assumptions concerning the feature geometry in Universal Grammar. If there is a cross-linguistic mismatch of these features, the universal status of finiteness as an independent category is at stake.

Functional typology looks at finiteness from another perspective. In general, typology is interested in the morphosyntactic patterns that are used for the expression of certain semantic or pragmatic structures. Croft (2003) presents the following standard research strategy in typology:

(12)   Standard strategy for typological research (Croft 2003: 14)
    (i)   Determine the particular semantic(-pragmatic) structure or situation type that one is interested in studying.
    (ii) Examine the morphosyntactic construction(s) or strategies used to encode that situation type.
    (iii) Search for dependencies between the construction(s) used for that situation and other linguistic factors: other structural features, other external functions expressed by the construction in question, or both.

In terms of Givón (1990: 853), the semantic basis is '[T]he *thematic dependence* of an event/state on its discourse context', while finiteness itself reflects '[T]he *syntactic dependence* of the clause [italics his]', and is thus related to the morphosyntactic expression format of thematic dependence. If the prototypical independent event is the 'transitive main clause', finiteness can be measured against the degree of (morphosyntactic) similarity to this prototype (see Givon 1990: 853). Like Givón's (1990) analysis, Hengeveld's (1998) analysis is also based on dependency. The only difference is that Hengeveld's (1998) notion of finiteness has no semantic basis. He only looks at the distribution of verb forms across matrix clauses (independent clauses) and subordinate clauses (dependent clauses).

On the basis of the cross-linguistic range of expression formats for a certain linguistic phenomenon, it is possible to look for dependencies between these formats (or constructions in terms of Croft 2003; see 12 (iii) above). In the case of finiteness, this yields hierarchies as discussed in section 5.2.1 (Givón 1990; Hengeveld 1998). These hierarchies are scalar, i.e. they consist of a number of different parameters arranged within a continuum.

The scalarity of finiteness as it is discussed in functional typology is the result of cross-linguistic comparison. This leads to the question of whether scalarity matters if one looks at individual languages. If finiteness is defined in terms of the categories that are to be morphologically or syntactically expressed in independent vs. dependent clauses of individual languages, it turns out that finiteness is a discrete or binary phenomenon. Thus, if finite clauses differ from certain types of nonfinite clause in an individual language by the presence of a tense marker, there is a discrete criterion for finiteness. If the tense marker is present [+tense] the clause is [+finite], if not the clause is [−finite]. In the case of finite verbs vs. nonfinite participial-adjectival verbs in Hebrew as discussed by Givón (1990: 857), the crucial category is person. While both verbal forms are marked for gender and number, only finite verbs are marked for person. In this case, the asymmetry between finite and nonfinite is based on person.

From such a discrete perspective, a typologist can look at the categories involved in establishing finite vs. nonfinite asymmetries. The examples that will be discussed in section 5.3.3 only cover those cases in which the asymmetry is based on a single grammatical category and its morphosyntactic expression. The categories discussed will be tense, illocutionary force, person, and politeness. Of course, there are many more cases in which a single marker reflects a combination of more than one category (see Cristofaro, Chapter 4 above) but I shall not discuss them because only those instances which clearly express a single category can be used to prove the relevance of that category for finiteness.

A look at the categories involved in the creation of the asymmetry between finite and nonfinite clauses reveals that there is no universal category of finiteness (see also the conclusion of Cristofaro, Chapter 4). This is in line with typological findings in general. In spite of this, the selection of the categories that can mark finiteness is not arbitrary, it is motivated. A category needs to fulfil two conditions to get involved in the expression of finiteness: it needs to be semantically general enough to be compatible with any event/state (Bybee 1985) and it needs to be obligatory. As soon as it is obligatory, it is reliable enough to be associated by the human parser with the syntactic structure of a clause and can thus be reanalysed as an indicator of finiteness. This will be explained in more detail in the two sections that follow.

5.3 Obligatoriness and its role in the finite/nonfinite asymmetry

This section deals with obligatoriness in general (5.3.1) and the relation between finiteness and obligatoriness (5.3.2). The last section will deal with some of the categories involved in the formation of finite/nonfinite asymmetries, i.e. tense (5.3.3.1), illocutionary force (5.3.3.2), person (5.3.3.3), and politeness (5.3.3.4).

5.3.1 *Obligatoriness*

Obligatoriness is here defined in terms of paradigms (e.g. aspect), not in terms of individual grammatical functions (e.g. perfective) (see also Bisang 2004). This definition is based on Lehmann (1995), who presents obligatoriness under the heading of 'transparadigmatic variability'—one of his parameters for measuring the autonomy of a linguistic sign and thus its degree of grammaticalization:

> By this [i.e. transparadigmatic variability] we mean the freedom of the language user with regard to the paradigm as a whole. The paradigm represents a certain category, and its members, the subcategories (or values) of that category. There may then be a certain freedom in either specifying the category by using one of its subcategories, or leaving the whole category unspecified. To the extent that the latter option becomes constrained and finally impossible, the category becomes obligatory. We shall therefore use the term **'obligatoriness'** as a—more handy—converse equivalent of 'transparadigmatic variability'. (Lehmann 1995: 139)

The paradigm approach to obligatoriness is preferable to Bybee's (1997) notion of obligatoriness. In her definition, obligatoriness allows 'the inference that if X is not present, not-X is meant, which creates a zero and thus an obligatory category' (p. 34). This definition is only possible in the special situation where there is zero-marking. It is systematically unable to account for the emergence of a language with an obligatory grammatical category consisting of two or more equally marked subcategories. If a language reaches a stage in which it has two non-obligatory markers for two different subcategories (e.g. perfective vs. imperfective as two subcategories of aspect) it would be impossible for that language to develop a system in which both subcategories must be marked obligatorily, because this would imply that it overcomes a stage of contradictory inferences in which the absence of each marker entails the meaning of the other marker, i.e. the absence of the perfective marker triggers imperfective meaning while the absence of the imperfective marker produces a perfective interpretation. In the development of a grammatical system, this deadlock can be overcome only if at some stage the individual products of grammaticalization are subsumed under one cognitively/semantically coherent paradigm such as aspect or tense with obligatory status. In such a paradigm, a zero-position, if present at all, becomes unambiguously interpretable.

5.3.2 *Obligatoriness and finiteness*

If obligatoriness in the sense of Lehmann (1995) is applied to independent clauses, languages can create asymmetries in the sense that a finite clause has to be marked for a given grammatical category which cannot occur at all or which can occur only with a reduced set of subcategories in the nonfinite clause. In section 5.3.3, I will discuss the following categories that can be used for this purpose:

(13)   Categories that can be relevant to finiteness from a cross-linguistic perspective:

tense
illocutionary force
person
politeness

In Bisang (1998: 739–47; 2001a: 1405–7), I call the asymmetry that is based on the categories in (13) 'minus-asymmetry' because it is based on a reduction of the number of possible categories from the matrix clause to the subordinate clause. The other type of asymmetry, i.e. plus-asymmetry, is formed by the obligatory addition of information to the nonfinite clause in comparison to the matrix clause. Since I deal with plus-asymmetry in more detail in Bisang (1998: 746–51), I will not discuss it here. I would only like to mention the categories involved, i.e. special markers of subordination, markers of case, and markers of person.

Forms which exclusively mark clause-combining such as markers of sequentiality or of adverbial subordination need special treatment. If they are combined with the omission of a category which is obligatory in the verb form of the main clause I shall subsume them under the heading of minus-asymmetry (see examples 14 and 15 from Japanese). If they are added to a form which could otherwise also occur in the function of a main clause, I treat them as a case of plus-asymmetry.

5.3.3 *Examples of minus-asymmetry*

5.3.3.1 *Finiteness and tense*   In Japanese, the only forms which are clearly nonfinite as well as dependent in the sense that they cannot occur alone in a main clause are converb forms. Converb forms cannot occur with tense marking (for the relevance of politeness, see section 5.3.3.4), while finite forms must take a tense marker. The two most common tense markers are -*(r)u* for present and -*ta*/-*da* for past. Within the same morphological pattern we also find two forms which are much less frequent, the future/dubitative form and the imperative. Thus, asymmetry is established by giving up the [± past] distinction (or by leaving out the tense-mood categories of the future/dubitative or the imperative). In example (14), the converb forms *it-te* 'going' and *at-te* 'meeting' do not contain any information concerning tense. The hearer has to wait for the matrix verb *tabe-ru* 'eat-PRS' to know where the converb forms are situated in time. As we can see from (15), the lack of tense is crucial for converbs. Any other grammatical category such as passive, causative, volition, or negation is compatible with this formal category of the verb, even though the form presented in (15) is very rare.

(14) Koobe e   it-te,   tomodati ni   at-te,   issyo-ni
      Koobe DIR   go-CVB   friends   DAT   meet-CVB   together-DAT
      gohan o   tabe-ru.
      meal   ACC   eat-PRS
      '[I] go to Kobe, meet my friend, and [we] eat together.'

(15) Yame-sase-rare-taku-nakere-ba,   yoku hatarai-te   kudasai.
      quit-CAUS-PASS-VOL-NEG-COND   well work-CVB   please
      'If [you] don't want to be dismissed, do your work.'

5.3.3.2 *Illocutionary force and minus-asymmetry*   In Abkhaz (Hewitt 1979; 1987), finite forms are characterized by the suffixes *-(y)t'* or *-n* (the only exception being future I in *-p'*—see Hewitt 1987) and the suffixes *-ma, -w* in neutral yes-no questions and *-y* in yes-no questions uttered against presupposed answers. These illocutionary-force suffixes are omitted (conjugation group I) or replaced by *-z* (conjugation group II) in nonfinite forms (see Table 5.1). The nonfinite forms are used with relative clauses as in examples (16) and (17), with dependent clauses as in examples (18) and (19) and with wh-questions which are formed by clefting. The finite form that corresponds to the relative form in (16) is *yə-y-ba-ø-yt'* 'he saw them [3.PL.P-3.SG.A-see-AOR-FIN]'. As we can see, this form is clearly marked for finiteness by *-yt'*. This also applies to the other independent forms in examples (17) to (19).

TABLE 5.1. Paradigm with the verbal root *-ca-* 'go' in Abkhaz (Hewitt 1979; 1987)

Group I	Finite	Nonfinite	Group II	Finite	Nonfinite
PRS	s-ca-wa-(y)t'	yə-ca-wà	IPFV	s-ca-wa-n	yə-ca-wà-z
AOR	s-ca-(y)t'	yə-cà	PST.INDF	s-ca-n	yə-cà-z
FUT.I	s-ca-p'	yə-ca-rà	COND.I	s-ca-rə̀-n	yə-ca-rə̀-z
FUT.II	s-ca-ṣ-t'	yə-cà-ṣa	COND.II	s-cà-ṣa-n	yə-cà-ṣa-z
PFV	s-ca-x̀à-yt'	yə-ca-x̀à-w	PL.PFV	s-ca-x̀à-n	yə-ca-x̀à-z

(16)   Relative clause with undergoer-coreference
    [a-xàc'a   yә̀-y-ba-(k°a)-z]_REL   à-ħ°sa
    ART-man   REL-3SG.M-see-(PL)-NFIN.PST.INDF   ART-woman.PL
    (ø-)z-dә̀r-wa-yt'
    3PL.F.PAT-1SG.A-know-DYN-FIN.PRS
    'I know the women whom the man saw.' (Hewitt 1987: 201)

(17)   Relative clause with actor-coreference
    [a-pħ°әs   dә-z-šә-z]_REL   a-xàc'a   d-aa-ø-yt'
    ART-woman 3SG.H-REL-kill-NFIN.PST.INDF ART-man 3SG.H-come-AOR-FIN
    'The man who killed the woman came.' (Hewitt 1987: 201)

(18)   Dependent clause
    a.   dә-z-ba-ø-yt'
        3SG.PAT-1SG.A-see-AOR-FIN
        'I saw him.'
    b.   [d-anә̀-z-ba-ø]   a-š°q°'ә̀
        3SG.PAT-when-1SG.A-see-NFIN   ART-book
        (ø-)lә̀-s-ta-yt'
        3SG.PAT-3SG.F.BEN-1SG.A-give-AOR.FIN
        'When I saw her, I gave her the book.' (Hewitt 1987: 138)

(19)   Dependent clause
    [(a-)àš°a   (ø-)yә-ħ°a-wà-**zar**]   zag'ә̀   r-xә
    ART-song 3SG.NH.PAT-3SG.M.A-say-DYN-COND all   their-head
    (ø-)rә̀-x'-wa-yt'
    3SG.NH.PAT-3PL.PAT-pain-DYN-FIN.PRS
    'If he sings, everyone's head aches.' (Hewitt 1987: 89)

Another language with a finiteness/nonfiniteness distinction based on illocutionary force is Kistane or Soddo (South Semitic, Gurage, North-Eastern Gurage). The morphological structure of the finite/independent verb in this language consists of inflectional formatives plus a declarative suffix as represented in (20) (Leslau 1992; Goldenberg 1969). Dependent verb forms are characterized by the omission of the declarative marker.

(20)   Stem + Inflectional Formatives + Declarative Suffix

The forms of the declarative suffixes are illustrated in Table 5.2 (for perfective and imperfective inflection). Table 5.3 presents the perfective forms of the verb *sfr* 'measure' and the imperfective forms of the verb *bdr* 'advance'.[1]

---

[1] The verbal forms presented here are subject to the following rules of elision: 1. ä + u → o. 2. ä + i → e.   3. e + i → e.

TABLE 5.2. The declarative suffixes in Kistane (Soddo) (Goldenberg 1969)

	Suffixed to PFV/IPFV	Suffixed to forms including objects
3SG.M	-u	-t
3SG.F	-i	-t
2SG.M	-u	-u
2SG.F	-in	-u, -in
1SG	-u (-ki/-hi in PFV)	-u
3PL.M	-n	-n
3PL.F	-n	-n
2PL.M	-n	-n
2PL.F	-n	-n
1PL	-u	-u

TABLE 5.3. The verb *sfr* 'measure' and *bdr* 'advance' in Kistane (Soddo) (Leslau 1992) (the morpheme analysis is added by me—W.B.)

	Perfective independent	Perfective dependent	Imperfective independent	Imperfective dependent
3SG.M	säffär-o	säffär-ä	yə-bädr-u	yə-bädər
3SG.F	säffär-ätt-i	säffär-ät	tə-bädr-i	tə-bädər
2SG.M	säffär-ko	säffär-kä	tə-bädr-u	tə-bädər
2SG.F	säffär-š-in	säffär-š	tə-b^{y}edr-in	tə-b^{y}edər
1SG	säffär-ki	säffär-k^w	ä-bädr-u	ä-bädər
3PL.M	säffär-mu-n	säffär-(ə)m	yə-bädr-əmu-n	yə-bädr-əm
3PL.F	säffär-ma-n	säffär-ma	yə-bädr-əma-n	yə-bädr-əma
2PL.M	säffär-kəmu-n	säffär-kəmu[2]	tə-bädr-əmu-n	tə-bädr-əm
2PL.F	säffär-kəma-n	säffär-kəma	tə-bädr-əma-n	tə-bädr-əm
1PL	säffär-no	säffär-nä	nə-bädr-u	nə-bädər

Example (21) presents a finite form with the declarative marker -*u* for the third person singular masculine. In examples (22–24), the predicates printed in bold have no declarative marker. They are in the position of a complement clause (22), of a sequential construction comparable to converb constructions in many other languages (23), of an adverbially subordinated clause (24):

(21) Independent clause
abi   yä-bayy-äw   **yə-wädd-u**
father.DEF   MOD-son-POSS.3SG.M   3SG.IPFV-love-DEC.3SG.M
'The father loves his son.'

---

[2] For the second person masculine perfective dependent Goldenberg (1969) expects the form -*kəm*; Leslau (1992 [1968]: 18) presents the form -*kəmu*.

(22) Dependent form in a complement clause
tä-kätäma-yy   yä-mäṭṭa-hom   ä-šl-u
to-city-towards MOD.PFV-come.3SG.M-COMP IPFV.1SG-know-DEC.1SG
'I know that he came to the city.' (Leslau 1992: 20)

(23) Dependent form in the sequential construction
bä-nat-aw   qəb   awänn-a-m   bämida tonnaw
on-head-POSS.3SG butter put.PFV-3SG.M-SEQ outside sit.PFV.DEC.3SG.M
'He put butter on the top of his head and sat outside.' (Leslau 1992: 19)

(24) Dependent form in a causal clause
maläs sälä-**hon**-ä   attuqann
small because-PFV.be-3SG.M hit.NEG.IMP.2SG.M.A.3SG.M.PAT
'Since he is small, don't hit him.' (Leslau 1992: 14)

The use of illocutionary-force markers in the context of finiteness is quite common in Gurage languages. Meyer (2005: 305–7, 335–6) describes the function of the declarative marker in Zay, an Eastern Gurage language (Ethiosemitic).

5.3.3.3 *Person and minus-asymmetry*   Minus-asymmetry with regard to person is attested in some Turkish converbs such as those in *-ip* and *-erek* (see Johanson 1995). Another example is Iatmul (a Papua language of New Guinea) with regard to dependent-coordinate forms:

(25)   Vɨ-laa   ya-wun.
       see-CVB   come-1SG
       'Having seen it I come.' (Staalsen 1972)

5.3.3.4 *Politeness and minus-asymmetry*   The Japanese polite forms in *-mas-* (*-mas-u* = POL.PRS, *masi-ta* = POL.PST) are the most clear instances of finite marking. They occur almost exclusively with finite as well as independent clauses. The forms which are marked for tense only without the politeness suffix added to them are good indicators of finiteness (see section 5.3.3.1). Nevertheless, we also find these forms in relative clauses. Example (26) shows the politeness suffix *-mas-* followed by the past marker *-ta* in a finite clause. Example (27a) shows the same verb form without the politeness marker. As can be seen from (27b) vs. (27c), only the plain past without the politeness marker can be used in relative constructions:

(26) ringo   o   tabe-masi-ta
      apple   ACC   eat-POL-PST
      '[He] ate an apple.'

(27) a. ringo   o   **tabe-ta**
         apple   ACC   eat-PST
         '[He] ate an apple.'

      b. **tabe-ta**   ringo
         eat-PST   apple
         'the apple [he] ate'

      c. *tabe-masi-ta   ringo
         eat-POL-PST   apple

In converb forms, neither tense markers nor politeness markers are allowed
(see also example 14):

(28) Koobe   e   it-te,   tomodati   ni   at-te,   issyo-ni
      Koobe   DIR   go-CVB   friends   DAT   meet-CVB   together-DAT
      gohan   o   tabe-**mas**-u.
      meal   ACC   eat-POL-PST
      '[I] go to Kobe, meet my friend, and [we] eat together.' (Hinds 1986: 85)

Korean differs from Japanese inasmuch as it cannot use tense for establishing asymmetry as is illustrated below by the converbs in *-unikka* (29), *-taka*
(30), and *-ko* (31). In each of these converb forms we find the past marker
-(e)ss- (also see Sohn 1995; Choi 1998):

(29) pi-ka   kuchi-**ess**-unikka   pata-ey   ka-ca
      rain-NOM   stop-PST-because   sea-to   go-PROPS
      'Let's go to the beach, since it's stopped raining.' (Sohn 1994: 324)

(30) Chelswu-nun kukcang-ey ka-**ss**-taka   chinkwu-lul manna-ss-ta
      Chelswu-TC cinema-DIR go-PST-CVB   friend-ACC meet-PST-DEC
      'Chelswu went to the cinema and there he met a friend.'

(31) ne-nun mwue-l   hay-**ss**-ko   Nami-nun eti-lul   ka-ss-ni
      you-TC what-ACC do-PST-CVB   Nami-TC where-ACC   go-PST-Q
      'What did you do and where did Nami go?' (Sohn 1994: 30)

Korean finite clauses are determined by a set of suffixes occurring in the
final slot of the verbal paradigm. These suffixes are characterized by the
interaction of illocutionary force and politeness. In the cases of intimate,
blunt, and polite (bold print), politeness seems to be the only criterion which
determines finiteness.

TABLE 5.4. Sentence-enders (from Sohn 1994: 8)

	Declarative	Interrogative	Imperative	Propositive
Plain	po-n-ta	po-ni	po-a-la	po-ca
	see-IND-DEC	see-Q	see-INF-IMP	see-PROPS
Intimate	po-a	po-a	po-a	po-a
	see-INF	see-INF	see-INF	see-INF
Familiar	po-ney	po-na	po-key	po-sey
	see-DEC	see-Q	see-IMP	see-PROPS
Blunt	po-o	po-o	po-o	—
	see-BL	see-BL	see-BL	
Polite	po-a-yo	po-a-yo	po-a-yo	po-a-yo
	see-INF-POL	see-INF-POL	see-INF-POL	see-INF-POL
Deferential	po-p-ni-ta	po-p-ni-kka	po-si-p-si-o	po-p-si-ta
	see-AH-IND-DEC	see-AH-IND-Q	see-SH-AH-RQ-IMP	see-AH-RQ-PROPS

5.4 Obligatoriness, grammaticalization, and the categories used for marking finiteness

The number of cognitive domains that are cross-linguistically amenable to grammatical categories is not very large; to some readers it may even appear surprisingly small at first glance. Slobin (2001) presents the following list, which is based on Talmy (1985):

(32)   List of 'grammaticizable domains typically marked on verbs'
        (Slobin 2001: 408):
        tense (temporal relation to speech event)
        aspect and phase (temporal distribution of an event)
        causativity
        valence/voice (e.g. active, passive)
        mood (e.g. indicative, subjunctive, interrogative, imperative)
        speech act type (e.g. declarative, interrogative, imperative)
        personation (action on self vs. other)
        person (1st, 2nd, etc.)
        number of event participants (e.g. singular, dual, plural)
        gender of participant
        social/interpersonal status of interlocutors
        speaker's evidence for marking claim (e.g. direct experience, hearsay)
        positive/negative status of an event's existence

As we have seen above, only a fraction of these domains is relevant to the finite/nonfinite distinction. Section 5.3.3 discussed the domains of tense, illocutionary force (speech act type), person (personation), and politeness (social/interpersonal status of interlocutors). Since none of these domains are semantically related, the question to be answered in this section is why all of them are used in the context of finiteness asymmetries.

Even from a perspective that is more general than finiteness, the small number of domains that make up grammatical categories calls for an explanation. Talmy (1985) raises the following two questions in this context. Why are some domains excluded from being grammatically relevant, and why is the number of distinctions within a grammaticalized domain restricted to a small number (e.g. a tense system consisting of the binary opposition of past vs. nonpast)? Slobin (2001; also see Slobin 1997) provides a solution to both questions. As can be seen from the following quotation, his explanation is based on obligatoriness, frequency of use, and rapid online processing. All three factors entail categorial domains with only a small number of unambiguous divisions:

If a domain is to be divided up such that each of the subcategories can be rapidly accessed online, by speaker and hearer, there cannot be too many divisions in the domain, nor can the deciding factors be infrequent or idiosyncratic. Typically, as forms become highly grammaticized, they divide up a domain exhaustively into a very small number of options: *singular* vs. *plural* (with possible additions of *dual*), *perfective* vs. *imperfective*, the six cases and three genders of Russian. Markers such as these are **obligatory**, which means they must be accessed in almost every utterance. The facts of language processing work against ambiguities of online access. The notions that evolve into such very small and obligatory sets must (1) unambiguously divide the domain, and (2) use criteria that are **generally relevant** to that domain. Thus it is no mystery that grammatical inflections do not indicate color or rate or ambient temperature: these are not aspects of experience that are universally applicable or memorable with regard to all of the event types that we talk about. That is, they are not aspects that are relevant to how we interpret and store events IN GENERAL. (Slobin 2001: 435; the bold print is mine—W.B.)

In my explanation, I shall concentrate on the first of Talmy's (1985) questions, which I shall narrow down to the phenomenon of finiteness. Thus the question to be analysed is why only a small number of categories is involved in the marking of finiteness. The crucial terms in my explanation are the ones printed in bold in the above quotation, i.e. obligatoriness and general relevance. Obligatoriness is defined as in section 5.3. The notion of 'general relevance' can be defined more precisely in terms of 'generality' as introduced by Bybee (1985):

(33)   Generality (Bybee 1985: 16; the bold print is mine—W.B.)
       By definition, an inflectional category must be applicable to all stems of
       the appropriate semantic and syntactic category and must obligatorily
       occur in the appropriate syntactic context. In order for a morphological
       process to be so general, it must have **only minimal semantic content**.

Generality is counterbalanced against relevance, which is defined as in (34)
below:

(34)   Relevance (Bybee 1985: 13)
       [A] meaning element is relevant to another meaning element, if the
       semantic content of the first directly affects or modifies the semantic
       content of the second.

   Generality entails that the semantics of a marker needs to be maximally
general if it is to be combined with a large class of lexical items. This criterion
is particularly pertinent for a category which is obligatory in every independent clause. Bybee's (1985) findings on the grammatical categories expressed
inflectionally and thus the ones which are the most general ones (inflection is
defined by obligatoriness) are summarized in Table 5.5, based on a sample of
fifty languages. It presents the percentage of languages that express the
grammatical functions listed in the leftmost column by inflection (second
column) or by derivation (third column).
   The categories which are exclusively or almost exclusively marked inflectionally are marked by italics in the above table. Although this table does not
fully cover the categories discussed in section 5.3.3, it nevertheless confirms
the high degree of generality of tense and person. The category of illocutionary force is not mentioned in the above list because it is rarely marked as a

TABLE 5.5. Inflectional/derivational marking (%) of some categories at the verb
(Bybee 1985: 30; italics are mine—W.B.)

	Inflectional	Derivational	Total
Valency	6	84	90
Voice	26	30	56
Aspect	52	22	74
Tense	48	2	*50*
Mood	68	0	*68*
Number agreement	54	12	66
Person agreement	56	0	*56*
Person agreement (Object)	28	0	*28*
Gender agreement	16	0	*16*

separate category in verbal morphology (Abkhaz and Kistane in section 5.3.3.2 are two comparatively rare examples). Given the wide scope of illocutionary force, it seems to be a straightforward candidate to occur obligatorily with every possible clause. A reflection of this is the fact that it takes the highest operator position in Role and Reference Grammar (Van Valin and LaPolla 1997) as well as in Functional Grammar (Dik 1997). Politeness does not semantically interact with the meaning of the clause and is thus of no relevance for it either. If the marking of politeness becomes compulsory for whatever social reasons, semantics certainly does not interfere with such a process. Other categories such as voice or valency seem to carry too much of their own semantic weight to be used obligatorily with every possible clause. In this sense, they are too relevant (see 34) to the semantics of the predicate they occur with.

Given the semantic character of generality, the question that remains to be answered is how the cognitive domains of tense, person, illocutionary force, and politeness can become significant to clausal syntax and finiteness. The answer to this question is related to frequency and parsing. Once a marker is frequent enough within a certain syntactic structure, it can be associated with that structure and thus become relevant to the human parser. At a next stage, obligatoriness becomes indispensable for a marker to be a reliable indicator of a syntactic structure to the parser. The process of association between the semantic function of a marker and a certain syntactic structure is not semantically motivated. The condition for a semantic category to become relevant to a syntactic structure seems to be that it is semantically general enough to be interpreted as coextensive with that structure. The categories of tense, person, illocutionary force, and politeness can all be associated with the syntactic unit of an independent clause, and they are semantically general enough to be applicable to any state or event expressed in that form. As soon as they are not present in a clause of a language in which they are compulsory sentence indicators, the parser can conclude that the clause is nonfinite. If this stage is reached, minus-asymmetry between finiteness and nonfiniteness is firmly grammaticalized.

The process of reanalysis by which linguistic units like tense markers become indicators of finiteness is not semantically motivated. This type of functionally non-motivated reanalysis is called 'regrammaticalization' by Greenberg (1991). It can be compared to what is called 'exaptation' by Lass (1990) and 'hypoanalysis' by Croft (2000). Given the semantic arbitrariness of regrammaticalization, the categories involved with finiteness need not necessarily be limited to tense, illocutionary force, person, and politeness. The only condition for a category to be relevant to finiteness is semantic generality. Other categories that can be found in markers that combine more than one function are number, aspect (see tense-aspect markers or aspecto-tempora) and modality (see Cristofaro, Chapter 4 above). Given my explanation in terms of regrammaticalization, it would not come as a surprise to me if still other categories relevant to finiteness were discovered.

5.5 Conclusion and outlook

I have tried to show that finiteness can be described as a discrete phenomenon in a functionalist approach. The function of finiteness is purely syntactic. It is used to indicate the dependency status of a clause, and thus supports the human parser in the analysis of the linguistic structure of utterances. Such an approach has its consequences for the status of finiteness in the universality discussion, for the role of semantics in finiteness, and for the overall pervasiveness of finiteness through the whole system of a language or across all the relevant constructions of a language. Each of these consequences will be addressed briefly in this conclusion.

If the selection of particular cognitive domains as indicators of finiteness can be accounted for in terms of obligatoriness, generality, and the parser's ability to associate them with a certain syntactic structure, the fact that T and Agr or the use of full or empty pronouns is associated with finiteness is to be expected. It is motivated by the same process of regrammaticalization (exaptation, hypoanalysis) as in functional linguistics. The difference between the formal and the functional approach is that the latter claims that there can be additional semantic domains involved with finiteness (politeness, illocutionary force—for the latter, see ForceP in Rizzi 1997). An even more important difference has to do with the universal status of finiteness. If finiteness is the product of regrammaticalization, this greatly reduces a priori specifications of grammatical categories in terms of innateness (Bisang 2001b). As was pointed out by Slobin (2001), it is not necessary to assume that any category is a priori excluded from becoming grammatically relevant:

The reason why languages have no grammatical markers for quantified categories of 'fixed distance, size, contour, and angle' (Talmy 1988: 171) is simply because human beings do not regularly code, store, and report their experience in these terms—not because these categories are *a priori* excluded from the grammar module. I would suggest, then, that anything that is important and salient enough for people to want to refer to it routinely and automatically most of the time, and across a wide range of situations, can come to be grammatically marked, within the constraints of online processing briefly alluded to earlier. (Slobin 2001: 437)

The phenomenon of reanalysis in the sense that something that is already there is used for a completely different function seems to be well known in evolutionary biology. Danchin (2000: 63) presents this phenomenon under the term of *bricolage* 'handicraft':

It is the aptitude for seizing an opportunity, for making a fire out of everything, that makes living organisms develop systematically by discovering new functions from what is at their disposal (for they cannot create anything from what is not at their disposal). What is particular about life is its capability to create new functions from everything. (Danchin 2000: 63; the translation from French is mine.[3])

From this point of view, it comes as no surprise to find a purely social criterion such as politeness in the syntactic context of finiteness. Once the encoding of the social relation between speaker and hearer has become compulsory in a culture, it can also serve as an indicator of finiteness. It would be interesting to see whether extra projections or extra features would be needed for at least some languages in which finiteness is based on politeness.

If finiteness is a syntactic phenomenon (i.e. related to the semantics of event integration to some extent) and if the categories used for marking it are selected by regrammaticalization, one would expect the semantics of the finiteness markers to vary cross-linguistically to the extent that their meaning is general enough to be associated with the syntactic status of a clause. Klein (1994; 1998; forthcoming) defines his well-known semantic/pragmatic definition of finiteness in terms of tense and assertion:

(35)   Finiteness in terms of Klein (1994; 1998; forthcoming)
       Assertion of the validity of a state of affairs p for some topic time
       (whereby topic time is the time span for which the speaker makes a
       claim). Assertion functions to link the state of affairs or entity denoted
       by the predicate of the utterance to its topic.

If tense is somehow associated with assertion in many Indo-European languages, this is not necessarily the case in all the languages of the world. My hypothesis is that assertion is conventionally inferred from the use of tense markers in a number of Indo-European languages, and that it is this combination of functions (tense plus inferred assertion) which children then

---

[3] The original version in French runs as follows: 'C'est une aptitude à l'opportunisme, à faire feu de tout bois, qui fait que les organismes vivants évoluent systématiquement en découvrant, à partir de ce dont ils disposent (puisqu'ils ne peuvent pas créer quelque chose dont ils ne disposent pas), des fonctions nouvelles. Ce qui est particulier dans la vie, c'est d'être capable, à partir de n'importe quoi, de créer des fonctions nouvelles' (Danchin 2000: 63).

integrate into morphosyntactic structures. In many languages, individual tenses can have a number of different functions. Wunderlich (1970) enumerates no fewer than thirteen functions for the present in German. This is not a problem for finiteness from the perspective adopted here as long as the grammatical category represented by the present tense is semantically general enough and its frequency is reliable enough for it to be associated with finiteness.

Finiteness does not seem to be fully pervasive within a language system as a whole (see Evans on insubordination, Chapter 11 below). Lasser (2002) presents a number of instances of root infinitives (jussives/hortatives, rhetorical questions, counterfactuals, anecdote registers). The use of these forms is more frequent in spoken language than one may expect (3 per cent of all the sentences with a verb uttered by adults; see Lasser 2002: 775). Lasser's paper shows that maturation theories (optionality of finiteness marking in the children's competence is replaced by a notion of obligatoriness) cannot account for the use of root infinitives. Lasser (2002: 791) thus argues that 'children have to acquire language-specific facts that will ultimately allow them to produce proper finite utterances as well as proper nonfinite utterances (both infinitival and verbless utterances)'.

If we take the perspective of grammaticalization in the sense that finiteness is not an innate property of language but a phenomenon that can emerge depending on the generality and the frequency of a marker (and thus its reliability as an indicator of finiteness to the parser), we do not need that marker to be fully (100 per cent) obligatory. In fact, a very high degree of obligatoriness causes its own problems. What if the speaker wants to make an utterance in which she just cannot/does not want to take any position with regard to an obligatory category? From this perspective, it does not come as a surprise if there are certain areas which remain unaffected by the process of grammaticalization. As Lasser (2002: 778) points out, 'in main-clause infinitivals no assertion is marked'. Thus, what is not expressed in the root infinitives of the languages analysed by her is exactly what is expressed by the much more frequent finite forms in the same languages, i.e. assertion (given the importance of assertion in the Indo-European languages she is dealing with). The areas which remain open for utterances which are neutral with regard to assertion are themselves strictly determined—they underwent their own processes of grammaticalization.

In this chapter, finiteness is understood as a discrete phenomenon operating in individual languages to create a morphosyntactic asymmetry between independent and dependent forms based on the obligatoriness of grammatical categories such as tense, illocutionary force, person, and politeness. From such a perspective, finiteness is not a specific category, nor is it a rule or a tendency. It is instead a device for overtly marking structural independence at the highest possible level of sentencehood. Cognitively, it is seen as a help to the human parser in recognizing sentences as maximal syntactic units. Finiteness is not universal, neither in the sense of individual grammatical categories that are used for its expression nor in the sense that it must be marked in some way in every language. Some languages make use of that option, others do not. If they do, grammatical markers which are semantically general enough to be coextensive with the independent clause can be selected for that purpose. For that reason, it does not come as a surprise that the features related to finiteness are T and Agr in the Minimalist Programme. One might even take the approach adopted here as a functional account of why features like T and Agr show up in the context of finiteness. Finally, understanding finiteness in terms of regrammaticalization or exaptation also explains why finiteness cannot be defined in terms of individual semantic (pragmatic) categories (see tense and assertion: Klein 1994; 1998; forthcoming), and why there may be exceptions like insubordination (Evans, Chapter 11 below) or root infinitives (Lasser 2002).

6

Constructional Economy and nonfinite independent clauses

IRINA NIKOLAEVA

6.1 Introduction

As nonfiniteness is commonly thought to correlate with the dependent status of the clause, most research on finiteness has concentrated on subordination. Some studies explicitly claim that a main/independent clause must be finite (Hornstein 1990: 146) and/or that the major function of nonfiniteness is signalling syntactic and semantic embedding (Givón 1990; Anderson 1997; 2001: 9; Cristofaro, Chapter 4 above). Yet it is also known that certain independent clauses exhibit reduction in tense/agreement morphology and the absence of a prototypical subject, both of which are crucially implicated in ensuring nonfiniteness.

The purpose of this chapter is to provide an explanation for why some independent clauses favour nonfinite patterns while others do not. Assuming that finiteness properties are interrelated, one way to account for this fact is to say that in nonfinite clauses a syntactic element responsible for finiteness is absent from the structure or negatively specified. In this view, a certain class of independent clauses is universally predicted to share a standard cluster of nonfinite properties. Here I shall explore another possibility. I will argue that finiteness properties in independent clauses do not have a common source and may occur in any combination. Their reduction is better understood as a cross-linguistic tendency motivated by the functional pressure for economic expression, which applies to some languages and constructions but not others.

I would like to thank Frans Plank, who was the first to turn my attention to finiteness in independent clauses. Thomas Mayer provided invaluable practical help during the writing of this chapter. Unless indicated otherwise, the French examples come from consultations with native speakers. I particularly thank Martine Lorenz-Bourjot for her judgements. For the German data I am very grateful to Thomas Mayer and Thomas Schöneborn. Latin examples mostly come from Contino (1977), while the primary source is not indicated.

In section 6.2, I present evidence that in many languages imperatives and hortatives/jussives demonstrate reduced finiteness as far as tense/agreement marking and cooccurrence with the subject is concerned. This leads to the understanding that reduction of finiteness in independent clauses is not random but has ultimately to do with the meaning/function of the clause. Section 6.3 examines some existing proposals on nonfinite independent clauses and shows that they are not universally applicable. In section 6.4, I introduce the theoretical framework adopted here, Construction Grammar, which defines grammatical construction as an integration of constraints on form, meaning, and use such that their combination is not shared by any other types in the grammar. I further suggest the principle of Constructional Economy, formulated as a functional tendency that prevents the doubling of constructional meaning by inflectional or phrasal means within the same construction. Section 6.5 shows how the notion of Constructional Economy accounts for the reduction of finiteness in non-assertive independent clauses. Section 6.6 concludes the chapter.

6.2 Reduction of finiteness properties

This section makes no claims to originality, but serves to summarize evidence for the contention that the imperatives, hortatives, and jussives demonstrate remarkable cross-linguistic parallels with prototypical nonfinite clauses. In the absence of opacity effects restricted to dependent clauses, two finiteness criteria will be taken into consideration: tense/agreement marking on the verb and subject licensing.

6.2.1 *Imperatives*

As has repeatedly been pointed out in the literature, imperatives have little inflectional morphology. Even in languages with rich agreement systems they tend to lack subject agreement, as has been noticed after Greenberg (1966: 47) by Sadock and Zwicky (1985: 159, 173–4), Palmer (1986: 29, 108), Bybee et al. (1994: 210), and others.[1] Bare imperatives occur in English, Aghul (Dobrušina 2003), Mongolian (Birjulin and Xrakovskij 2001: 23), and on transitive verbs in Jacaltec (Craig 1977: 70) and Ainu (Tamura 2000). Among these languages, Jacaltec and Ainu exhibit rich subject agreement in the indicative. Tense also

---

[1] A contrary observation comes from Birjulin and Xrakovskij (2001: 29–30) who suggest the following implication: if a language has a person/number distinction in the indicative it has this distinction in the imperative, but the reverse is not true. However, this claim is based on a non-standard definition of imperatives as denoting speech causations irrespective of person.

often remains unexpressed (Sadock and Zwicky 1985: 172). For example, indicative verbs in Swahili obligatorily host a tense prefix, but imperatives do not (Perrot 1957: 46–7). In Obdorsk Khanty indicative verbs are morphologically marked either as present or past, but imperatives bear no tense markers (Nikolaeva 1999).

Other languages do have subject agreement, but the set of agreement features differs from that expressed by non-imperative verbs. The agreement categories associated with imperatives are number and, less frequently, gender/class and honorification. In a number of languages the singular imperative is represented by a bare stem, but the plural and possibly dual are overtly marked. This situation is observed in many (otherwise highly inflecting) Uralic and Turkic languages (Korkina et al. 1982: 320; Lewis 1967: 137; Kurbatov et al. 1969: 237; Kononov 1960: 205; Nasilov et al. 2001) and is reconstructed for the respective proto-languages. Other languages belonging to this type are Latin, German,[2] French, Modern Greek (Joseph 1983: 14), Tukang Besi (Donohue 1999: 452), Yimas (Foley 1991: 269–73), and Salinan (Turner 1987: 161), as well as Nkore-Kiga (Taylor 1985: 163), Ewe (Agbojo and Litvinov 2001: 394), Bambara (Bergelson 2001: 490), and some other languages of Africa. Gender agreement is present in Biblical Hebrew, where the imperative has four forms, as in the following paradigm of the verb 'sit': singular masculine *shev*, singular feminine *shvi*, plural masculine *shvu*, and plural feminine *shevna* (Givón 2001: 313–14). Examples of languages that express honorification in the imperative are Korean and Maithili (Yadav 1997). However, person distinctions are never expressed, since most researchers agree that true imperatives are inherently 2nd person (Palmer 1986; Sadock and Zwicky 1985; Bybee, Perkins and Pagliuca 1994; Potsdam 1998).

Imperatives have limited co-occurrence with subjects. In a number of languages imperative subjects are completely excluded, independently of the presence of zero subjects elsewhere in the grammar, e.g. in Romance and Supyire (Carlson 1994). At least French is not a pro-drop language, as far as declaratives are concerned. The same holds for Babungo, which does not allow pro-drop unless the subject is identical to the one in the preceding clause, but in imperatives the subject must be absent (Schaub 1985: 22–4). Potsdam (1998: 238), referring to the sample of Zhang (1990), who surveys imperatives in forty-six languages from thirteen families, concludes that imperative subjects may be dropped in all but two of them. This parameter is independent of whether or not the imperative verb carries agreement. Sadock and Zwicky (1985: 174) observe that subject pronouns

---

[2] For this reason Donhouser (1986) refers to the German imperative as 'semi-finite'.

appear to be more frequently suppressed than agreement affixes: there are languages where the subject is dropped but the verb must carry agreement. Some languages allow under special conditions an overt NP expressing the first argument of the imperative verb, but whether or not it is a syntactic subject is in fact debatable (see section 6.3).

6.2.2 *Hortatives and jussives*

Unlike imperatives, hortatives are not primarily directive and there are no restrictions on the hortative subject: they can express exhortations to any person (Sadock and Zwicky 1985). The illocutionary functions differ when different persons are involved. When the subject is the 2nd person, hortatives express an indirect causation and are usually perceived as more polite or remote future imperatives. The function of the 1st person singular hortatives is to solicit the addressee's agreement (*Let me think*), while the 1st person plural involves a suggestion for a cooperative action (*Let's go*). Third person hortatives (jussives) express causation and wishes not directed at one of the interlocutors (*May he prosper!*). These types can be thought of as different speech acts, but they have a common component in their illocutionary meaning (see section 6.5.1) and are expressed by the same grammatical category in many languages, so I will reserve the general term 'hortative' for them.

In the languages where different semantic subtypes of hortative are expressed by the same category, hortatives show person agreement. For example, in Kolyma Yukaghir the imperative is encoded by the inflection *-k*, which may be preceded by the plural *-ŋi-*. The hortative takes the suffix *-gə*, followed by personal affixes: *-k* in the 2nd person and *-n* in the 3rd person. The 1st person singular form is missing and in the 1st person plural there is no personal inflection. The resulting hortative paradigm is as follows: 2SG *-gə-k*, 3SG *-gə-n*, 1PL *-gə*, 2PL *-ŋi-gə-k*, and 3PL *-ŋi-gə-n* (Nikolaeva 2005). In a similar way, a number of African languages have special forms usually referred to as the subjunctive, injunctive, hortative, or optative (see Carlson 1994 for Supyire; Dimmendaal 1983 for Turkana; Givón 2001: 315–16 for Bemba; and Bergelson 2001 for Bambara). Unlike imperatives, limited to the 2nd person and expressing direct prescriptions, hortatives occur in all three persons and two numbers, and convey the illocutionary meaning of inducement or wish, when used independently.

Yet in other languages hortatives show reduction of agreement compared to indicatives. The same form may be used to express several person/number distinctions. In a South Estonian dialect spoken in Karski the hortative is expressed by the affix *-ku/-kku* and is mainly used as an indirect command to the 3rd person (both singular and plural), but is also possible with the 1st person (Pajusalu 1996: 157–8). This language has a rich agreement in the indicative expressing the person/number of the subject, but the hortative exhibits no agreement morphology. A similar situation is observed in other Estonian dialects and a related Balto-Finnic language, Livonian. In Rapanui (Du Feu 1996) the 2nd person imperative expressed with the particle *ka* is opposed to the 1st and 3rd person hortative formed with the particle *ki*. In these languages one undifferentiated hortative form is used for several persons.

Hortatives may employ morphologically heterogeneous forms for different persons and numbers. The extent to which they form a single paradigm is questionable, but given that both a semantic and formal difference is involved, they are better thought of as different moods specialized in expressing a particular subtype of the hortative meaning and consequently lacking agreement distinctions. For example, Kannada has several forms expressing wishes (Sridhar 1990: 32–4). The optative form combines with the 3rd person subject. Unlike finite verbs in declarative clauses, the optative verb does not inflect for person/number (1a). The so-called suggestive is the 1st person plural hortative and is not marked for agreement either (1b).[3]

(1) a. huDugaru   modalu   u:Ta   ma:Dali
     children   first   meal   do.OPT
     'Let the children eat first!'

   b. horaDo:Na
     start.SUG
     'Let us start!'

The same holds for some North-Caucasian languages. Dobrušina (2003: 77) shows that in addition to an uninflected imperative, Aghul has an optative form to denote 3rd person exhortations (2a). This form is not used with other persons. The 1st person exhortation is expressed by a special periphrastic construction involving an infinitive (2b).

(2) a. (Ge)   ajč'-uraj!
     he   go.away-OPT
     'Let him (*me/us) go away!'

   b. šaw   (xin)   ajč'ʷ-a-s
     PART   we.INCL   go-IPFV-INF
     'Let's go away!'

---

[3] The suggestive is compatible with a dependent participle, in which case the subject may be 1st person singular.

Similar data are available for Tsakhur (Kibrik 1999) and Lezgian (Haspelmath 1993). Dobrušina (2003: 73) observes on the basis of a small typological sample that grammaticalization of 1st person plural hortatives is more common than grammaticalization of 3rd person hortatives (jussives).

The hortative subjects are less likely to be omitted than subjects in imperatives. For instance, in Ju/'Hoan (Snyman 1970: 25), Cambodian (Spatar 2001), Supyire (Carlson 1994), and Canela-Krahõ (Popjes and Popjes 1986: 159) the subject pronoun can be omitted in the imperative but is required in the 1st and 3rd person hortatives. However, subject drop does occur even if a language disallows it otherwise. This is especially common in the 1st person plural hortatives that express exhortations on the part of both the speaker and the addressee. For example, in Russian and French the 1st person plural hortative is mostly morphologically identical to the 1st person plural indicative present but, unlike the latter, prohibits the overt subject. Thus, *Nous lisons* can only be interpreted as 'We are reading/read', while *Lisons!* must mean 'Let us read!'. A few verbs in French employ special forms not identical to the indicative (e.g. *Sachons!* 'Let us know!') and the subject pronoun is omitted.

Finally, hortatives have little tense morphology. In some Indo-European languages hortatives are expressed by subjunctives, which convey a large array of irrealis meanings and are tensed. However, there are few languages where hortatives morphologically distinct from subjunctives are marked for tense. Carlson (1992) presents compelling evidence showing that hortatives in African languages do not co-occur with tense/aspect/modality auxiliaries. Even the opposition of immediate vs. remote future, which may be present in imperatives (see section 6.3.2), seems to be rare in hortatives. For example, in Nanai (Avrorin 1961) the 2nd person imperatives express tense distinctions, but hortatives limited to the 1st and 3rd person do not.[4]

6.3 The reductionist view

The previous section has summarized ample cross-linguistic evidence for the systematic reduction in tense/agreement morphology and co-occurrence with subject in imperatives and hortatives. Since these properties are a common indicator of nonfiniteness, this evidence argues for the finite/nonfinite distinction in independent clauses. The question is how it is to be represented. One way to look at it is to use what Kathol (2000: 136–141) referred to as 'the reductionist approach'. Under this view, finiteness properties are interrelated

---

[4] Avrorin analyses the 1st, 2nd, and 3rd person forms as members of the same paradigm, but the 2nd person form, on the one hand, and the 1st and 3rd person forms, on the other, are distinct both formally and functionally.

and are crucially associated with the syntactic presence of one relevant element, either a feature localized on a clausal head or a functional category. Hortatives have not been widely discussed in this context, but for imperatives two possibilities have been explored: that imperative INFL is syntactically present but has a different content from the finite INFL (e.g. Sawada 1980; Rupp 2003), or that imperatives altogether fail to project the relevant functional layers (e.g. Akmajian 1984). In this section I will discuss the proposal of Platzack and Rosengren (1998) (P&R), which falls under this latter category, but differs from other reductionist proposals in that it explicitly addresses finiteness.

6.3.1 *Platzak and Rosengren*

Assuming split CP *à la* Rizzi (1997), P&R argue that finiteness (FinP) in the CP-domain has a dual function. FinP indicates the existence of the event by anchoring it in time and space. Its presence is a necessary condition for the clause to refer. A finite utterance refers to an event existing in the speaker's world or in some other world, whereas in nonfinite utterances the existence of the event is not presupposed. At the same time finiteness gives rise to a predication relation between a prominent argument (the subject) and the rest of the clause. The subject is a participant of the event the clause refers to such that the utterance is construed to be about it. Since finiteness is associated with a semantic contribution of its own, this predicts that there are no major differences between languages when it comes to the finite/nonfinite distinction in independent clauses. The properties of each semantico-pragmatic type induced by FinP do not differ across languages.

The relationship between Finiteness, Tense, and Mood is captured by positing that Fin° attracts the features hosted in Tense° and Mood°. P&R reject Chomsky's (1995b) proposal that the feature ensuring the Extended Projection Principle is the strong D-feature. Instead they assume after Branigan (1996) that Tense, Mood, and Finiteness are related by the shared [finite] feature, and that the same feature may be carried by a DP. The [finite] feature of Tense, Mood, and Finiteness must be checked against a DP that satisfies the subject requirement. The Spec–head relation in FinP expresses the predication relation between the subject and the predicate. In regular finite clauses the subject DP is attracted to Spec-TP, Spec-MoodP, and Spec-FinP to check the [finite] features of Tense, Mood, and Fin respectively. The [finite] feature is strong on Finiteness and causes the overt movement of the subject to Spec-FinP position in most Germanic languages. When there is no Tense and Mood, the presence of Finiteness will cause the derivation to crash because the features hosted in Tense and Mood cannot be checked. The absence of Tense/Mood implies the absence of Finiteness and consequently the absence of a subject: there is no Spec-FinP position to host the subject. In other words, Tense/Mood and subject licensing are related through the notion of Finiteness.

In this theory the sentence type features are assumed to be merged in Force. Imperative clauses bear the strong [imp] feature. The same feature is carried by the imperative verb, which guarantees the movement of the verb to Force° in German and most other Germanic languages. The main difference between indicatives and imperatives is the lack of FinP in the latter. This has both interpretive and structural consequences. From a semantic viewpoint, this implies that imperatives do not refer to an event, do not express a proposition anchored in time and space, and do not involve a predication relation between the verb and its first argument. From the lack of FinP also follow the three syntactic properties of imperatives. First, the imperative verb has the morphologically meagre form. A clause lacking FinP cannot have TP or MoodP, so imperatives do not express any tense or mood distinctions. P&R support this point, referring to Zhang's (1990) forty-six-language sample. Although in some languages the imperative is compatible with a future suffix or particle, no language in this sample displays a tense distinction. Second, imperatives are characterized by the impossibility of embedding. P&R assume that embedded clauses are referring expressions that prototypically serve as arguments. Since in imperatives FinP is absent, they cannot refer to a specific time and therefore cannot be syntactically embedded.

The third property ensured by nonfiniteness is the lack of a prototypical subject. This follows from the semantics of imperatives: imperative utterances are not used to talk about the addressee, but rather to the addressee. There is no predication relation between the performer of the imperative action and the rest of the clause, and the first argument of the imperative verb is not anchored with respect to the actual world in the sense the finite subject is. This observation is corroborated by the structural account of imperatives given the absence of FinP and consequently Spec-FinP. Although the first argument NP may be overtly expressed, it is enumerated without the [finite] feature. P&R show that in Germanic it has a different distribution and interpretation from typical subjects, which leads them to assign it to a separate category, ImpNP. The ImpNP has a subset of properties of the subject in a corresponding finite clause but is not behaviourally similar to finite subjects, as it is not located in the typical subject position Spec-FinP. The absence of a strong Spec-FinP means that there is no position outside VP that attracts the ImpNP overtly. Instead P&R argue that it occupies a lower position, either Spec-AgrsP or Spec-VP. Since both positions are weak, the syntax does not force the ImpNP to realize overtly; its presence is a matter of pragmatic-informational considerations. The relevant structures for German are shown below. (3a) is the representation of the declarative *Peter kommt heute* 'Peter is coming today' typed as [−wh], where the subject is in the Spec of FinP position. (3b) is the structure of the imperative *Kauf das Buch* 'Buy the book!' adapted from P&R.

(3) a.

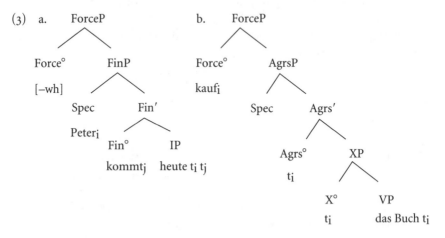

P&R base their claims mainly on Germanic data, and explicitly say that the possible universality of their proposal must be tested against other languages. In the rest of this section I will show that the cluster of properties they predict to play a role for the finite/nonfinite distinction in independent clauses is not universal.

6.3.2 *Finiteness features in imperatives*

The purpose of this subsection is to demonstrate that the proposed correlation between relevant nonfinite properties in imperatives does not always hold.

First, the crucial component of P&R's analysis is the incompatibility of imperatives with an ordinary subject, overt or covert. The absence of FinP and the subject position is motivated by the imperative semantics, and is therefore predicted to be a universal cross-linguistic property of imperative constructions. But the syntactic status of the ImpNP is controversial. Potsdam (1998), Han (2000), and Rupp (2003) argue that English imperatives contain behaviourally unexceptional subjects. Rupp (2003: 65) notices that, although the properties of the ImpNP can be explained in syntactic terms under P&R's analysis, it is unnecessary to assume a distinct new category on semantic grounds. In other words, the absence of the subject is not a universal property of imperative constructions, but depends on one's syntactic assumptions and the particularities of individual grammars. Rupp in fact argues for cross-linguistic variations in the realization of imperative subjects. The imperative subject needs not to be placed in SpecIP/SpecFinP for EPP/predication reasons, as in P&R's analysis, but may be forced by other factors. In Dutch, Danish, and West Flemish the subject moves to SpecIP to check agreement: the subject position is fixed in SpecIP by the specified [2nd] feature. In English the imperative subject need not occur in SpecIP to satisfy EPP, but may be present in lower syntactic positions. Its overt presence is not forced by anything in the computational system but lies in the properties of the PF and LF interfaces. That is, subject licensing is motivated by semantic or discourse/prosodic factors and serves a certain interpretive goal, whereas the subject position may vary accordingly.

Further, P&R themselves observe that, at least in Icelandic clipped imperatives, the subject is not omittable:

(4)   farð   *(þú)   út
      go   you   out
      'Go out!' (Platzack and Rosengren 1998: 196)

They provide no explanation for this fact. There are other languages where the imperative subject appears to be obligatory. According to Mortensen (1999), in Northern Embera the 2nd person pronoun must be overt as imperative subject even in the presence of an address, and the same holds for Tagalog. Schachter and Otanes (1972: 402) explicitly state that the imperative in Tagalog is formed by eliminating an aspect marker from the verbal form, but the 2nd person pronoun is retained:

(5)   a. wina-walisan   mo   ang   sahig
         IPFV-sweep   you   o   floor
         'You are sweeping the floor.'

      b. walisan   mo   ang   sahig
         sweep   you   o   floor
         'Sweep the floor!'

The pronoun may only be absent if the addressee of the imperative utterance is generic (Rachkov 2001: 442), and the same holds for Newari (Korolev 1989: 75). In both these languages the same verbal form is used to express the 2nd person imperative and the 3rd person jussive, so the subject pronoun is essential for disambiguation. Consider the following Newari examples (Korolev 1989: 740).

(6)   a. *(chaN)   na
          you   eat
          'Eat!'

       b. *(waN)   na
          he   eat
          'Let him eat!'

With non-imperative verbs, which exhibit more agreement in Newari, pronouns can be omitted. In Ndyuka (a creole language spoken in Surinam) the
imperative subject is impossible in the singular, but must be present in the
plural (Huttar and Huttar 1994: 46):

(7)   a. (*i)   Gwe
          you.SG   leave
          'Leave!'

       b. *(u)   Gwe
          1/2PL   leave
          'You (PL) leave!'

Pronominal subjects cannot be omitted in non-imperative finite clauses in
this language.

   Second, the claim that imperatives do not project tense is also problematic.
Although tense distinctions are indeed rare, some languages express the
opposition of near/immediate and distant/remote/indefinite future. This is
observed in a number of Tungus languages such as Evenki, Even, Nanai,
Neghidal, and Orok (Jarceva 1997; Xrakovskij 2001), as well as in Latin,
Maithili (Yadav 1997: 164–5), Tuscarora (Mithun 1976: 111–14), and Hua
(Haiman 1980: 162–3). To take one example, in Nanai (Avrorin 1961) the 2nd
person singular imperative expressing near or immediate future is marked
with the suffixes -ro/-ru-/-do-/du. In the plural this suffix (with some
phonological alternations) is followed by the regular marker of the 2nd person
plural -su. The 2nd person singular remote future imperative is indicated by
the suffix -xari/-xeri, while the 2nd person plural remote future uses the
combination of the same suffix in a truncated form and the plural -su. Thus,
the paradigm is symmetrical, as shown below using the verb ba- 'to find':

(8)   immediate future   remote future
       singular   ba-ru   ba-xari
       plural   ba-ro-su   ba-xar-su

The use of the immediate and remote future imperatives is demonstrated by
the following examples from Avrorin (1961: 128).

(9) a. esitul   min-či   di-du
        at.once   I-ALL   come-IMP.SG.IMM
        'Come to me at once!'

     b. čimana   xoton-či   ene-xeri
        tomorrow   city-ALL   go-IMP.SG.REM
        'Go to the city tomorrow!'

On the other hand, P&R (1998: 194–5) note that their account does not
make any predictions on behalf of the imperative verb with respect to the
features that are independent of the tense-mood-finiteness system. In particular, it does not predict restrictions on agreement. The reason is that FinP
does not attract agreement features as it attracts Tense features. Indeed, in
languages like German and Icelandic singular and plural imperatives have
different inflections. But P&R make a more general claim that agreement on
imperative verbs is cross-linguistically common. However, the evidence presented in section 6.2.1 rather demonstrates the opposite: imperatives do
exhibit restrictions on agreement. In a number of languages there is only
one unchangeable imperative form, which expresses no agreement. In other
languages imperative verbs may be marked for number, gender, or honorification, although person distinctions are never expressed. This asymmetry
between person on the one hand and number, gender, and honorification on
the other has not been accounted for by P&R's analysis.

Another asymmetry they have not addressed is between subject and object
agreement. While the former cannot employ the person feature, there are no
restrictions in the latter. For example, in Ainu (Tamura 2000) indicative verbs host
subject agreement (10a), but the intransitive imperative uses a bare verbal stem (10b).

(10) a. hinak   wa   e-ek
         where   from   2SG-come
         'Where did you come from?'

      b. te   un   ek
         here   towards   come
         'Come here!'

However, transitive verbs show agreement with the object in person and number.

(11) en-erampokiwen   wa   en-kore
      1SG.O-pity   PART   1SG.O-give
      'Pity me! (lit. Give me my pity)'

Such facts have not received an explanation in P&R's account.

To conclude, although there is a certain correlation between the lack of tense, agreement, and subject NP in imperatives, these properties can appear in any combination and seem to be empirically independent parameters.

6.3.3 *Finiteness features in hortatives*

P&R make a semantico-pragmatic distinction between the stating of a norm and setting of a norm. With respect to the 2nd person addressee, this difference is apparent in the following examples (Platzack and Rosengren 1998: 189):

(12)   a. You should visit your mother.
        b. Visit your mother!

Example (12a) states the necessity for the existence of the denoted event. The declarative modal verb licenses an existentially bound variable. In contrast, the imperative clause in (12b) does not state the necessity; instead the necessity is directly projected into the actual world. The existential operator is within the scope of the modal operator expressing necessity. This translates into the difference in finiteness: imperatives lack FinP, whose function is assumed to consist in anchoring the existentially presupposed event in time and space. Since the presence of FinP crucially depends on interpretation, this account predicts that it must be absent in other non-assertive clauses that fail to make a statement, in particular hortatives. Hortatives and imperatives have a common component in their meaning in that they both directly express a speaker's wish rather than a judgement about a state of affairs (see section 6.5.1), and therefore are not existentially bound. Hortatives, then, should display the same cluster of finiteness-related properties as imperatives.

Yet this prediction does not always hold. In some Tungus languages, for example Evenki (Nedjalkov 1995), hortatives express the opposition of immediate vs. remote future similar to that found in imperatives. As was mentioned in section 6.2.2, although the hortative subject is omitted more frequently than the indicative subject, in many languages it is in fact required. In Bambara (Bergelson 2001) the hortative/subjunctive is marked with the auxiliary *kà* or *ká* and must co-occur with the subject pronoun.

(13)   a. *(í)   ká   lívúrv̀   tà
            you   HORT   book   take
            'Why don't you take the book?'

        b. *(án)   ká   bámánánkáǹ   kàlàn
            we   HORT   Bambara   learn
            'Let's study Bambara!'

A number of languages such as Luo, Canela, or Kayardild distinguish between imperatives and hortatives by means of subject pronouns alone, which may be omitted in the former but must be present in the latter, as in the following Kayardild example cited in Dobrušina (2003: 74).

(14) a. *(ngakulda)   rabi-j
          we.INCL   get.up-IMP
          'Let's get up!'

      b. (nyingka)   rabi-j
          you   get.up-IMP
          'Get up!'

Another potential problem is that, unlike imperatives, hortatives are embeddable. Recall that in P&R's analysis nonfinite clauses lacking FinP cannot be embedded because they are not referentially anchored. If hortatives are taken to lack finiteness, they contradict this claim. According to Campbell (1985: 84–5, 116), Pipil has the undifferentiated imperative/optative/subjunctive. In the 2nd person it takes a distinctive prefix *xi-/x-* absent in other forms, so I believe such forms are better analysed as imperatives. In other persons there are no person markers (except the 1st person plural), but there is the plural marker *-kan*. These forms occur both as dependent subjunctives and as independent hortatives.

(15) a. ma: yawi
          HORT   go
          'Let him go!'

      b. xi-k-ilwi   ma: yawi
          IMP-him-tell   HORT   go
          'Tell him to go.'

This situation is reminiscent of Spanish, where subjunctives introduced by *que* are used independently as some kind of hortative, and may well have been influenced by the latter. But it also occurs in other parts of the globe, and it is not immediately obvious which function is historically primary.

As mentioned in section 6.2.2, a number of African languages have hortative/subjunctive forms used in independent clauses as indirect causations. At the same time, they may serve in dependent clauses as complements of modal or manipulative verbs, in clause-chaining, or in dependent purpose clauses (Carlson 1992). In fact, Bergelson (2001) states that the prototypical function of the hortative/subjunctive in Bambara is dependent, and refers to it as a dependent mood. Cf. (13) above and (16).

(16) a. Mádù   be´   sé   [kà   sò/ˋ   bòlì]
        Madu INCOMPL can SBJV horse   ride
        'Madu can ride a horse.'

     b. à   nà-ná   kà   à   mùsó` yé
        he come-COMPL.TR SBJV his wife   see
        'He came and saw his wife.'

In a similar vein, the hortatives in Kolyma Yukaghir are mostly used as exhortations, as in the following examples illustrating the 1st, 2nd, and 3rd persons.

(17) a. aj-na:-gə
        shoot-INCH-HORT-1PL
        'Let us start shooting!'

     b. eśe:-ŋin   qoŋ-ŋi-gə-k
        father-ALL   go-PL-HORT-2
        'Why don't you (PL) go to your father?'

     c. ta:tbən   o:-gə-n
        so   be-HORT-3SG
        'Let it be so.'

But the same forms are embeddable as different-subject purpose clauses
introduced by the complementizer *monut*.

(18) a. ńe:-ŋa: pundu-gə-n   monut   ...
        call-TR.3PL tell-HORT-3   COMP
        'They called him so that he could tell...'

     b. čoɣojə-pul tittə   čomo:l-ə ere   norqəɣə-nu-ŋi
        knife-PL   they.GEN will-INS PRT   jerk-IPFV-3PL
        əl-šejrej-gə-n   monut
        NEG-escape-HORT-3SG   COMP
        'The knives were moving by themselves to prevent him from
        escaping.'

This usage appears to be rather new, given that the complementizer *monut* has
grammaticalized from the converbial form of the verb *mon-* 'say', perhaps
under the influence of the neighbouring language Yakut, where the same
construction is used (Nikolaeva 2005).

In summary, although in P&R's sense hortatives are nonfinite in that they
do not express an existentially bound proposition, they do not necessarily
exhibit the cluster of grammatical properties predicted for nonfinite independent clauses by their analysis.

6.3.4 *Declarative infinitives*

P&R claim that a verb lacking Tense and Mood projections has no subject as a direct consequence of the lack of Finiteness. Infinitives in European languages have no Tense or Mood and are generally assumed to be nonfinite. Infinitives in root function typically have a non-declarative, non-assertive meaning and are subjectless (Reis 1995; Rizzi 1994a; Haegeman 1995), in conformance with P&R's predictions (see also Roberts 2004: 314–15, where Finiteness is said to be selected by Force). However, there is one root infinitival construction where the subject is in fact required. This construction traditionally referred to as the Narrative or Historical Infinitive is well attested in Romance, namely in French (Englebert 1998), Latin (Lombard 1936), Spanish (Sandoval 1986), Italian (Krenn 1996: 493), Portuguese (Maurer 1968: 123–4), and Catalan (Lombard 1936: 92–8), as well as in some Slavic languages (Miklosic 1926: 852). Below I present the data from Latin, French and Russian.

Narrative Infinitives are intended to report an event and have an assertive force (see Léard 1992 and Englebert 1998: 101 for French). The addressee may express disagreement with their truth value, and the construction is compatible with epistemics indicating the degree of the speaker's commitment to the truth, as is typical of declaratives. In French, Narrative Infinitives report an event that is the consequence of another situation immediately preceding it (Léard 1992: 203; Englebert 1998: 73ff.).

(19)   a. Marie   est   venue   et   Jean   est   parti.
          Marie   is   come   and   Jean   is   left
          'Marie came and Jean left.'

       b. Marie   est   venue   et   Jean   de   partir.
          Marie   is   come   and   Jean   to   leave.INF
          'Marie came and Jean left.'

In (19a), where the regular past is used, there is no implication that Jean left after Marie came, while the Narrative Infinitive in (19b) necessarily conveys this meaning. Cf. the following Russian example from Avrutin (1999).

(20)   Korol'   rasskazal   anekdot.   Carevna   xoxotat'.
          king   told   joke   princess   laugh.INF
          'The king told a joke. The princess started laughing.'

Example (20) must have a resultative reading and cannot be interpreted as two independent events: the princess started laughing because the king told a joke. Normally both events occur in the past, but Narrative Infinitives are marginally acceptable if the preceding verb expresses an habitual situation and the infinitive denotes events that follow each occurrence of the habitual situation in time.

(21)   Chaque fois que Jean embrasse Marie, Marie de rire.
        each   case that Jean kisses   Marie Marie to laugh.INF
        'Each time when Jean kisses Marie, Marie starts laughing.'

This semantics has several grammatical consequences for Russian and French, discussed in detail in Léard (1992), Englebert (1998), and Avrutin (1999: 138–52), but they are not directly relevant here.

The Latin Narrative Infinitive unambiguously refers to the past and behaves as a preterital tense with respect to the sequence of tenses, i.e. it requires secondary tenses in the embedded clause (Menge 2000: 189, 639; Rosén 1995: 540). For example, in (21) the embedded clause takes the imperfect to express simultaneity with the main clause event.

(22)   Graucus   primo   distinguere   et   dividere,
        Graucus.NOM   first   distinguish.INF and divide.INF
        quemadmodum   illa   dicerentur.
        as   they.NOM say.SBJV.IPFV.PASS.3PL
        'First Graucus distinguished and divided them in the way they were told.'

In contrast to Russian and French, the Latin Narrative Infinitive does not make reference to another event and is not perceived as the result of the latter. It is compatible with adverbial expressions denoting independent time in the past, and may open a new chapter or start a text (Rosén 1995: 543). It is not associated with any relative temporal value, but is simply used as a perfective or imperfective past.

In Latin and Russian the first argument of the Narrative Infinitive stands in the nominative and its syntactic status is fairly uncontroversial. All traditional Latin grammars analyse it as the subject (Blatt 1952: 199; Ernout and Thomas 1964: 270; Rosén 1995: 551–7; Menge 2000: 189), and this is supported by grammatical evidence. As shown below, the Nominative argument participates in passivization (23a), reflexive binding (23b), and the control of the *gerundium* (23c).

(23)   a. noctu   multa   domum   dimitti
           at.night many.NOM.PL   home.ACC.SG   send.INF.PASS
           'At night many were sent home.'
        b. et   inter   se   navigia   collidere
           and   among   REFL   ship.NOM.PL   collide.INF
           'And the ships collided among themselves.'

c. Affluere   ingens   multitudo   cum   luminibus,
flow.INF   huge.NOM.SG   multitude.NOM.SG   with   light.ABL.PL
atque   ubi   incolumem   esse   pernotuit,
and   as.soon.as   safe.ACC.SG   be.INF   become.known.3SG.PFV
ut   ad   gratandum   sese   expedire...
as.soon.as   to   wish.joy.GER.ACC   REFL.ACC   prepare.INF
'A vast multitude streamed to the spot with torches, and as soon as
all knew that she was safe, they at once prepared to wish her joy...'

Similar tests apply for Russian, where the nominative argument of Narrative Infinitives controls coreferential relations within the clause and clause-externally. I will not cite the relevant data for reasons of space, but the subject analysis for Russian is developed in Avrutin (1999).

The grammatical status of the first argument in French is more controversial, because personal pronouns appear in the strong form typical of non-arguments (objects of prepositions, predicates, or extraclausal topics):

(24)   Et   lui /*il   de   rire.
        and   him/he   to   laugh.INF
        'He started laughing.'

This led certain scholars to conclude that the first argument NP has a non-governable function. Barbaud (1987) suggested that it receives its case from the element *et* that functions as a kind of preposition, but Léard (1992) gave compelling arguments against this analysis. He pointed out that *et* can occur without a nominal, be separated from it by adverbs and appositions, or be altogether absent, and so is an unlikely case-assigner. Instead, assuming that subjects do not occur in non-tensed environments, Léard (1992: 202–12) suggests a topic analysis.[5] However, it can be excluded on prosodic grounds. Extraclausal topics are separated from the rest of the clause by a pause and an intonational break, but this is not the case in Narrative Infinitives (Englebert 1998: 112). Moreover, there are distributional differences. The external topic doubles an overt clause-internal argument, but Narrative Infinitives do not allow doubling of the pronoun by any clause-internal elements. Another difference is that the external topic may precede or follow the clause, but not simultaneously.

(25)   *Moi,   je   pars,   moi.
        me   I   leave   me
        'I am leaving.'

---

[5] See also Moignet (1975) and Rémi-Giraud and Basset (1988: 47–59). These authors claim that the infinitive is fully substantivized, so the construction represents a juxtaposition of two topics (in their terminology, themes). The function of *de* is to signal the absence of a syntactic bond between them.

In contrast, the first argument NP in Narrative Infinitives is compatible with the postposed topic:

(26) Et   moi de   me   débattre,   moi.
      and   me   to   REFL   struggle.INF me
      'I started struggling.'

This shows that it cannot bear the topical status itself.

Englebert (1998) argues that the NP in question has the predicative function and is the clausal head, whereas the infinitive is subordinated to it and serves as the secondary predicate, but this is also problematic. First, one of the head properties is obligatoriness. If the nominal in question were a syntactic head, it would be impossible to omit unless some kind of null element is assumed; but the only truly obligatory component of the construction is the infinitive preceded by *de*, as shown below.

(27) Et   de   rire.
      and   to   laugh.INF
      'He/she started laughing.' (Léard 1992: 205)

According to Englebert (1998: 198), in the absence of an argument NP the linking element such as *et* 'and' assumes the predicative role and becomes obligatory. She does not provide a satisfactory explanation of how conjunctions are predicativized, however. Moreover, she herself cites examples where both the nominal and the linker are absent (Englebert 1998: 68, 74, 199), e.g.

(28) Élise, un dimanche à midi, revient de la messe à jeune et il ne reste plus
      de lait.
      'One Sunday at noon, Elise returned from the mass hungry, but there
      was no milk left.
      De   fulminer   contre   la   cuisinière.
      to   threaten.INF against   DEF   cook
      She started threatening the cook.'

Second, Englebert's analysis does not account for the fact that the nominal in question displays the usual syntactic properties of subjects. It is typically interpreted as the agent, controls the gerund (29a) as well as agreement on the predicative adjective (29b), and can undergo passivization (29c).

(29) a. Et   Maigret de   grommeler, en   lui   prenant la
         and   Maigret to   growl.INF   by   him   taking   DEF
         cigarette des   lèvres.
         cigarette from.DEF   lips

'And Maigret started growling, having taken the cigarette from his lips.' (Englebert 1998: 185)

b. Et   elles   d'être   surprises.
   and   they.F   to.be.INF   surprised.F.PL
   'They started feeling surprised.'

c. Elle   d'être   mise   en   prison   par   la   police.
   she   to.be.INF   put.F   to   prison   by   DEF   police
   'She was put in prison by the police.'

In other words, it participates in all subject-related processes. What is more, it largely occurs in the places where one would expect the subject to occur. It is normally clause-initial or preceded by a conjunction or adverbial. Inversion may take place under the same conditions as the regular subject–predicate inversion, namely, in presentational constructions and when introducing direct speech (Englebert 1998: 69–70):

(30) a. Aussitôt   de   venir   un   prêtre.
        soon   to   arrive.INF   INDF   priest
        'Soon a priest arrived.'

     b. 'Et   aujourd'hui',   de   s'exclamer   le   Bon   Dieu   à
        and   today   to   exclaim.INF   DEF   good   God   to
        l'addresse   de   sa   confidente...
        DEF.address   of   his   confidante
        '"And today," God exclaimed to his confidante...'

Although Grevisse (2001: 1275) assesses this usage as archaic, these are attested examples from the modern language and they have been confirmed by native speakers. Yet Englebert does not clarify how inversion is compatible with her analysis. Examples like (30) provide an additional strong argument against analysing the nominal in question as a clause-external topic.

In sum, there are numerous processes in French grammar that treat the first argument NP of Narrative Infinitives like other subjects. Although none of them may be decisive on its own, taken together they provide a compelling body of evidence for the subject status of this NP. Therefore I conclude, after Touratier (1996: 187) and other grammarians, that this first argument NP is a subject, although its syntactic position is unclear.[6]

---

[6] In another paper Barbaud (1988) argues for the following structure: [C″ (et) NP [C′ *de* [I″ e AUX VP]]]. Under this analysis, the linker has no grammatical status, while *de* is a complementizer and a barrier for assigning the nominative case to the subject located in the Spec of CP. The subject takes a default non-governed form. As there is no requirement for the Spec of CP to be filled, the subject can be omitted. This analysis captures the subject-like properties of the nominal in question and accounts for the strong form of the pronouns, but faces other problems which I will not discuss here.

If finiteness has to do with overt subjects, Narrative Infinitives can be assumed to be finite in French, Russian, and Latin. In fact, there does not seem to be a syntactic sense in which they are nonfinite. From a structural viewpoint they seem to show properties of full-blown CPs. They are compatible with CP-related adverbs. Some authors have claimed that Narrative Infinitives in French cannot be questioned (Englebert 1998; LeGoffic 1994: 129; Barbaud 1988).[7] However, Léard (1992: 209–10) cites one example of a wh-question out of a Narrative Infinitive which he judges grammatical.

(31) Le   prof   a   demandé le   résultat. Et   qui   de
      DEF   teacher has asked   DEF   result   and   who   to
      répondre, tu   crois?
      answer.INF you think.2SG
      'The teacher asked the solution. And who do you think answered?'

According to Léard, questions are disallowed on semantic and stylistic grounds: the construction serves to report an event in narrative contexts, and therefore it is not really acceptable in dialogues and question–answer pairs. Yet questioning is marginally possible when the utterance is not intended as a search for information, but represents some kind of exclamation, as in (31). This is also true for Russian and Latin. Hofmann (1972: 368), Bennett (1966: 422), and Rosén (1995: 539) cite examples of questions made out of Narrative Infinitives in Latin, e.g.

(32) Qui   mori   timore   nisi   ego?
      who   die.INF terror.ABL.SG unless I.NOM
      'Who died from terror more than me?'

So although questioning is not easily compatible with the meaning of the Narrative Infinitive and may be bad for stylistic and register reasons, it is nevertheless syntactically available. Nothing precludes it in syntax. The same concerns the ability to be embedded. Narrative Infinitives are rarely embedded due to their narrative plot-advancing function, but embedding is not altogether impossible. In Latin, dependent Narrative Infinitives were introduced by Sallust (Schlicher 1914/15: 377). Although they were rather stylistically restricted, there is syntactic potential for embedding (cf. Rosén 1995: 547–8).

Thus, Narrative Infinitives demonstrate the following finite properties: they have overt referentially independent subjects, they express assertions, and

---

[7] In the framework Barbaud is assuming Narrative Infinitives cannot be questioned because the Spec of CP is a landing site for a wh-movement. If the subject is in the Spec of CP position, it blocks movement. However, the facts in Russian and Latin are basically the same, although these languages provide no evidence for the subject in the Spec of CP.

they have time reference. In French and Russian they express a relative tense, namely, posteriority with respect to an event completed by the time of speech. In Latin they express the deictic past and are primarily associated with stylistic and information-structural effects. The only obvious indicator of nonfinite-ness is morphology, namely, the infinitival verbal form that does not express tense and agreement distinctions.[8] Narrative Infinitive constructions present a counterexample to the claim that nonfinite independent clauses do not express existentially bound assertions and the predication relation between the subject and the rest of the clause.

To conclude this section, the major problem for P&R's account, as well as for other accounts which assume that the manifestations of finiteness are interrelated and come from a common source, is that such accounts lack generality: there is a significant range of data for which they fail to account. All possible combinations of relevant properties are attested. This suggests first, that they are empirically independent of each other and of any inter-pretive information, and second, that reduction of finiteness in certain types of independent clause is better understood as a cross-linguistic tendency than as a universal syntactic requirement. The question is then what motivates this tendency.

6.4 Constructions and economy

An analysis of nonfiniteness in independent clauses has to account for the fact that although finiteness properties are in principle independent, as was argued in section 6.3, they tend to come together, as was shown in section 6.2. In the rest of the chapter I will argue that the reduction of finiteness in some types of independent clause is motivated by the functional pressure for economic expression. This situation can be modelled within a constructional view of language. In the present section I introduce the notion of Construc-tional Economy that will be relevant for explaining the finiteness patterns in independent clauses in section 6.5.

6.4.1 *Constructional meaning*

In this chapter I assume the version of the Construction Grammar of Fillmore et al. (1988), Fillmore (1999), and Kay and Fillmore (1999). Its main features relevant to the subsequent discussion can be summarized as follows.

---

[8] Narrative infinitives provide additional support for the approaches that postulate a crucial distinction between morphological and syntactic aspects of finiteness and some kind of (indirect) mapping between the two (see Sell's and also Gretsch and Perdue's contributions to this volume (Chapters 3 and 12), as well as Nikolaeva 2003).

Grammatical knowledge takes the form of templates, as opposed to derivational rules. A fundamental unit of grammatical analysis is a grammatical construction. A grammar is basically viewed as a repertory of constructions, which form a taxonomic network. According to Fillmore (1999: 113), 'a construction is a set of formal conditions on morphosyntax, semantic interpretation, pragmatic function and phonology, that jointly characterize or license certain classes of linguistic objects'.

A definitional characteristic of constructions is that some aspects of their form and/or meaning and use are not shared by other grammatical patterns of the language. As stated by Goldberg (1995: 13), 'a construction is posited in the grammar if and only if something about its form, meaning, or use is not predictable from other aspects of the grammar, including previously established constructions'.

In other words, all constructions are idiomatic in the sense that each must have some idiosyncratic properties that do not follow from a knowledge of the rest of the grammar. Since constructions possess a collection of properties that are unique to each particular family of expressions, these properties must be specified in their representation.

Although the notion of construction may in principle refer to a conventional association of any kind of grammatical information, in most cases it is taken to represent a conventionalized pairing of form and meaning, meaning being understood broadly as comprising all conventionalized aspects of a construction's function, including the information about register and properties of the discourse and the situations of speech in which the construction occurs. Critically, then, a formal description of a construction may require the simultaneous representation of formal and interpretive information. Constructions are represented as tree structures with the attribute–value matrices at the nodes, where attributes and values correspond to features, while attributes may be syntactic, semantic, or pragmatic. The combination of constructions is regulated by the principles of unification, ensuring that attributes with contradictory values do not combine.

As distinct from lexical constructions, phrasal constructions or 'formal idioms' (Fillmore et al. 1988) are lexically open syntactic patterns dedicated to semantic and pragmatic purposes. In other words, they are complex structures which are larger than elementary lexical items and may be associated with idiosyncratic semantic content of their own. This content, referred to as 'constructional meaning', is not directly knowable from the form of the construction. This implies that, although linguistic forms provide cues for interpretation, meanings are rarely fully compositional and the meaning of the construction is not necessarily projected from the main verb. Verbs unify with linking constructions which denote event types. The number of valences specified by a given linking construction need not coincide with the number of valences specified by the verb. For example, the difference in argument configuration in ditransitive constructions has been traditionally associated with the argument structure of the verb; but Goldberg (1995) argues in detail that it can be attributed to the constructional meaning, since constructions themselves are capable of contributing arguments (cf. Jackendoff 1997), whereas the verb meaning is constant across different syntactic contexts.

So the information contributed by the construction and the information contributed by the verb are interrelated but independent. This leads to the partial understanding of compositionality: the meaning of a complex expression is motivated to varying degrees by patterns of composition applied to its sub-constituents, but is not fully predictable from them. The resulting meaning is comprehended partly from the meaning of specific words and partly from the constructional meaning. The two have been shown to interact in various complicated ways (Michaelis and Ruppenhofer 2001; Michaelis 2003).

The recognition of constructional meaning has a number of theoretical advantages. It eliminates implausible verb senses and therefore provides a non-circular and parsimonious description (Goldberg 1995). It offers a better account of polysemous syntactic patterns than the theories that rely on strict compositionality (Michaelis 1994). By postulating a construction which is itself associated with meaning, it accounts for the cases where the meaning of the whole is not built up from the meaning of the sub-parts in a straightforward way and explains the idiosyncratic semantic constraints associated with particular patterns (Michaelis and Ruppenhofer 2001). In the next subsection I will address another potential reason for preferring a constructional account, which has been somewhat less discussed in the existing literature. I will argue that an appeal to constructional meaning may prove useful in explaining the patterns of morphological marking and licensing of syntactic phrases.

6.4.2 *Constructional Economy*

An example of constructional meaning is the following French sentence:

(33) Il   ferme   les   yeux.
      he   closes   DEF.PL   eyes
      'He closes his eyes.'

In (33) the default interpretation is such that the entity encoded as the object is part of the body of the entity encoded as the subject, exactly as in its English translation. Crucially, although in both languages a body–part relationship is normally marked by possessives and so the regular expression for 'his eyes' in

French is *ses yeux*, the object in (33) is not compatible with a possessive. The possessive body–part relationship remains implicit.

Consider now the comitative constructions in Udihe (Nikolaeva and Tolskaya 2001). In this language the comitative relation is expressed by means of the instrumental case in *-zi* freely derived from all nouns. An instrumental noun expresses a number opposition (34a) and heads its own possessive phrase, in which case it bears a possessive affix and may be combined with an optional personal pronoun (34b).

(34) a. nuani   cawa:-ziga-zi   eme:-ni
          he   soldier-PL-INS   come.PST-3SG
          'He came with the soldiers.'

      b. nuani   (bi)   neŋun-zi-i   eme:-ni
          he   I   younger.brother-INS-1SG   come.PST-3SG
          'He came with my younger brother.'

Udihe additionally exhibits a more specialized comitative construction that employs the postposition *mule* 'with'. This construction is only used when there is a close (often symmetric) inalienable kinship or friendship relation between a person denoted by the subject and another person, such as *the mother with the child*, or *the older brother with the younger brother*. Thus *cawa: mule* in the intended reading 'with the soldier' would be impossible. This semantics is inherent to the construction and imposes certain restrictions on the properties of the base noun. The expression of possession is very regular on Udihe kinship terms, but the object of *mule* cannot head a possessive phrase and is not compatible with possessive affixes. Although there is no possessive affix in (35a), it cannot be understood as 'he with somebody else's younger brother', but only as 'he with his own younger brother'. Neither can the number be expressed, as the construction presupposes strictly two participants (35b).

(35) a. nuani neŋu /*neŋu-ni   mule eme:-ni
          he   younger.brother/*younger.brother-3SG   with come.PST-3SG
          'He came with his younger brother.'

      b. *nuani neŋu-ziga   mule eme:-ni
          he   younger.brother-PL   with come.PST-3SG
          'He came with his younger brothers.'

Udihe comitatives with *mule* are similar to the French example (33) in that the implied possessive relationship is not overtly expressed.

Langacker (1987a; 1991b; 1993) argues that the possessive relationship is based on an important aspect of cognitive processing: the ability to invoke the conception of one entity for purposes of establishing mental contact with another entity. This ability, referred to as a reference-point phenomenon, is so fundamental to the human mental experience that the possessive meaning makes up a part of the construction's conventional semantic value without being overtly expressed. In (33) possession need not be marked on the object because the possessive relationship is inherent to the construction. This relation is established between sub-parts of the component structures associated with the subject of the process and the person whose body part is affected. In Langacker's theory the inherent possessive relation in (33) is depicted as a line expressing the semantic correspondence in the schematic representation of the constructional pattern. Since it is included in the representation of the construction, there is no need for a separate possessive element to indicate the possessive relation. Presumably Udihe works in the same way. The very use of the postposition *mule* presupposes the inherent possessive (kinship) relationship between two participants; otherwise the construction with *mule* would not be used in the first place. Therefore the use of a possessive affix is redundant. So, as Langacker (1987a: 286–7) puts it, 'the presence vs. absence of a particular correspondence ... often has striking consequences for the construction's ... grammatical behaviour'.

I suggest that such considerations are not necessarily restricted to reference-point phenomena but play a role in motivating the surface form of other constructions as well. If constructional meaning is associated with the syntactic pattern as a whole and is inherently incorporated into its representation, expressing the same meaning with overt phrasal or morphological means within the same construction is superfluous and therefore non-economical. Thus we can formulate the following principle.

(36)   The Principle of Constructional Economy

   If two syntactic patterns are inherently associated with the same
   constructional meaning, the pattern that has less phrasal or
   morphological material expressing this meaning is to be chosen.

Constructional Economy is a tendency regulating the relation between form and function. Its purpose is to eliminate redundancy in form: it disfavours overt material expressing constructional meaning. As a tendency, it works on a language- and construction-specific basis and competes with other functional pressures, e.g. iconicity, which ensures the direct match between linguistic and conceptual structure (Haiman 1985; Givón 1991).

The understanding of economy relevant here is different both from the Minimalist economy dealing with minimizing the operations of the computational system (Chomsky 1995b) and from Goldberg's (1995) Principle of

Maximized Economy, which constrains the multitude of constructions in a language because of the general cognitive need for simplification. Rather it relates to Haiman's (1985) 'syntagmatic economy', i.e. the tendency to economize on the length and/or complexity of the utterance, and ultimately to Grice's maxim of quantity. The basic idea behind Haiman's economy and the Constructional Economy as understood here is the same: speakers tend to avoid constructions with redundant lexical or morphological material. However, there is one important difference. Haiman argues that less expression is given to the information that is familiar or predictable from the context, the situation of the speech, or a general knowledge of the world (Haiman 1985: 195; see also Givón 1990; Kibrik 1992). Predictability is here understood in terms of inference. A meaning can be inferred in the absence of overt marking because it is most likely in the given context. Predictable combinations are frequent and in this sense unmarked. As a result, economy motivations in typology largely based on Haiman's insights are mainly concerned with textual frequency which determines the patterns of functional markedness (Bybee 1985; Croft 2003; Aissen 2003). Bybee (1994) also associates morphological zeros with inference. She argues that zeros may have a positive semantic content equivalent in many ways to that of overt grams. Their meaning arises from the communicative context and can be inferred from it. As an overt marker becomes more frequent, the addressee can infer that its absence is intentional and meaningful.

The understanding of Constructional Economy suggested here is partly similar in spirit in that it maintains the importance of the semantico-pragmatic aspect for the ultimate shape of the construction. On the other hand, it departs from most other functional approaches in that it does not rely on inference, discourse context, or textual frequency. Under (36) predictable information does not come from anything outside that very construction but is contributed by the constructional meaning. Obviously, constructions are patterns of word combinations that are used for specific communicative purposes and therefore serve to convey typical communicative situations and human experiences. But the point is that they represent grammatical conventionalizations of the latter, so that constraints on meaning and use are directly tied to morphosyntax and included in the representation of the construction. The context in which the construction occurs and its frequency are not directly relevant for the shape of the construction, but the constructional meaning is. Since the description of the constructional pattern inherently contains the interpretation-relevant information associated with the pattern as a whole, economy considerations prevent it from being overtly expressed by means of morphology or overt phrasal material.

It is important to emphasize that the grammatical category absent from the construction in question may be systematically expressed in other constructions within the same language if its value is not pre-specified. The grammars of French and Udihe require the possessive relation to be signalled either by a free-standing possessive pronoun (French) or by a bound possessive suffix (Udihe). From this perspective, examples (33) and (35a) are anomalous and are difficult to explain without appealing to constructional meaning, which in this case involves an inherent positive specification for the possessive category. Constructional Economy, then, provides an answer to the question of why grammatical contrasts are present in some constructions but remain unexpressed in others in the same language.

6.5 Economy and finiteness

In the previous section I suggested that economy prevents the constructional meaning represented in the description of the constructional pattern from being overtly expressed by phrasal or morphological means or, more precisely, makes its overt expression typologically unlikely. This tendency was referred to as Constructional Economy. The purpose of this section is to argue that reduction of such features of finiteness as tense/agreement and subject licensing in some independent clauses is motivated by Constructional Economy.

6.5.1 *Illocutionary force constructions*

The reduction of finiteness in independent clauses is not random: as shown in section 6.2, it is largely restricted to non-assertive clauses. What we need, then, is a theory of how speech act distinctions are to be represented within the constructional view of language. Construction Grammar follows the traditional theory of sentence types (Sadock and Zwicky 1985) in that the illocutionary force is conveyed according to conventions of language rather than by a process of conversational reasoning, and must be accounted for by the grammar. It fully recognizes a correlation between form and illocutionary function, and accounts for the variety of illocutionary types by maintaining that the semantico-pragmatic properties of each type are directly included in its representation. But unlike the generative tradition, it does not rely on the idea that a clause is typed by the presence of an overt or covert force-carrying element.

In some versions of Construction Grammar and in HPSG, a related theory, illocutionary forces are properties of types paired with morphosyntax and represented as values for semantic attributes (Kathol 2000; Ginzburg and Sag 2001). This is the result of understanding constructions as basically bilateral form–meaning signs. For example, in Kathol (2000) the declarative clause is a construction whose CONTENT attribute is typed as *proposition*. It has some structural features, e.g. V2 and the absence of a wh-expression in German. Sells (Chapter 3 above) represents the declarative clause with the value *prop*(osition) for the attribute CONT and headed by the finite verb. The imperative type is headed by the imperative verb, and so on. This approach is confronted with the problem of indirect speech acts, which has not received a detailed treatment within HPSG. Kathol (2000: 142) mentions that in order for the addressee to recognize an indirect speech act, she must classify the utterance with respect to its primary illocutionary force; but even in this case some additional assumptions are needed to ensure indirect interpretation.

To avoid this complication, I will maintain that clauses are typed through a combination of grammatical properties, and that illocutionary forces are not semantic values but constructions in their own right. In this I follow Kay (n.d.), who postulates that a construction can remain exclusively interpretational. The existence of constructions that are not symbolic form–meaning pairs is consistent with Fillmore and Kay's version of Construction Grammar where, unlike in other versions, constructions are not necessarily bilateral signs in the sense of HPSG or Cognitive Grammar. Kay (2000; n.d.) further suggests that illocutionary forces are conventionally associated with a particular linguistic form and such associations become lower-level constructions. In a similar vein, Michaelis and Lambrecht (1996a; 1996b) argue that abstract illocutionary super-constructions are a part of the Construction Grammar model along with phrasal, lexical, and linking constructions. Such constructions are exclusively defined in pragmatic and semantic terms and lack any morphosyntactic content. However, they may motivate the morphosyntactic properties of their actual realizations.

Michaelis and Lambrecht postulate the abstract Exclamative Construction whose function is to express surprise at the high degree to which a given property has been manifested on some occasion, with the following semantico-pragmatic content: (a) presupposed open proposition, (b) scalar extent, (c) assertion of affective stance, (d) identifiability of described referents, and (e) deictic anchoring. The relationship between illocutionary function and form is one-to-many. For example, the following English sentences:

(37) a. It's amazing, the difference!
      b. God, my feet hurt!
      c. The things I do for this boy!
      d. It is so hot in here!
      e. What a day (I had)!

are all instances of the Exclamative Construction as far as their function is concerned, although their syntax differs. So constructions with different structures can be associated with the same complex of semantic and pragmatic properties. There are no common syntactic requirements for different representatives of an abstract illocutionary construction, except those that directly follow from its semantico-pragmatic characterization and must receive expression.

The constructions in (37) are licensed by the relationship of inheritance. The mechanism of prototype-based inheritance captures generalizations across different kinds of construction and provides a way of representing formal and semantic correspondences between them. The inventory of constructions is organized in such a way that more detailed constructions inherit formal, semantic, and pragmatic specifications from more general constructions. If a construction X inherits construction Y, then X inherits all the conditions on Y by virtue of being an instance of Y, but may impose individual restrictions on form or meaning. In this sense X may be a more or less prototypical representative of Y. Although abstract illocutionary super-constructions do not themselves license any actual sentences, their ultimate inheritors do. Abstract constructions are related to their inheritors by means of instance links (Goldberg 1995; Michaelis and Lambrecht 1996a): the latter are more fully specified instances of the former, differing in the level of schematicity. Constructions may have multiple parents and the relationship between them forms a multiple inheritance network. Multiple inheritance accounts for cases that appear to be simultaneously motivated by two distinct constructions, because each higher level construction only represents a partial specification of the grammatical structure of its daughter(s). For example, (37a) inherits both the abstract Exclamative Construction and Nominal Extraposition. In this network information is represented non-redundantly. It is specified only once in the construction taxonomy in the highest and most schematic node and then is passed down to its inheritors. Following Goldberg (1995), I will further assume default inheritance, which allows the mechanism of overrides: the default information can be blocked if it conflicts with information provided by a more specific construction.[9] With this the generalizations can be captured, but at the same time other constructions with exceptional properties are permitted.

So abstract illocutionary constructions are realized in a family of sub-constructions which inherit their basic meaning and are subject to different

---

[9] Default inheritance is not used in Fillmore and Kay's model; instead default values are left unspecified (Fillmore 1999: 115).

formal constraints. Conversely, the same formal structure may render various speech acts. Michaelis (2003) argues that sentence-type constructions can override the function of the sentence types with which they unify. In indirect speech acts, usage conventions block prototypical inheritance and a new, less prototypical association gets conventionalized. That is, the indirect association becomes a construction itself (cf. Kay, n.d.). Under this view indirect speech acts are idioms in their own right, a matter of convention rather than inference (see Levinson 2000 on a different view), so indirectness is only apparent.

Typological generalizations on clause types follow from the fact that languages share the abstract illocutionary constructions independently of the properties of individual grammars. Two illocutionary constructions will be relevant below, the Directive Construction and the Hortative Construction. The abstract Directive Construction licenses the family of imperative constructions. The actual imperative constructions are syntactic configurations whose structure contributes the semantic content associated with the Directive Construction and is to some extent motivated by it. The abstract Directive Construction is taken to be a grammatical corollary of the directive speech act, understood after Searle (1969) as an attempt of the speaker to get the addressee to do something. According to the standard view, the illocutionary intention of a directive utterance is that the speaker intends the hearer to take the utterance as a reason to perform action X, whereas the preparatory condition is that the speaker believes the addressee can do X (Allan 1986; 1994). It has been argued that the set of imperative denotations is the addressee's plan set or To-Do List, i.e. a set of propositions that specifies the addressee's future actions, and that by performing a directive act the speaker instructs the addressee to update it (Han 2000; Portner 2005). So the semantico-pragmatic frame associated with the Directive Construction involves the reference to the addressee and the action X which the speaker intends that the addressee should add to his/her plan set. This semantics is fairly general and does not account for various instantiations of the directive force such as requests, orders, wishes, or commands. I assume after Han (2000: 168–70) that they do not have to be encoded by the grammar but may be handled by processes of inference and reasoning.

The content of the abstract Hortative Construction can roughly be described as follows. The preparatory condition is that the speaker believes the situation X can take place and the illocutionary intention is that the speaker expresses his/her wish that X takes place and invites the addressee to consider the implications of X in a world in which X is the case. Imperatives and hortatives then have a common component in their meaning—the reference to a future event as intended by the speaker—but the illocutionary intentions differ. If imperatives are instructions and are meant to induce an (often immediate) action on the part of the addressee requiring the speaker's assumption that the addressee can carry out event X, hortatives do not necessarily presuppose a non-verbal response from the addressee, and for this reason have fewer agentivity restrictions. Instead they emphasize the affective emotional aspect used to display the speaker's wishes. In this sense they stand close to optatives, although (as noticed in Wilson and Sperber 1988) they differ from them as well. While both express wishes, only hortatives involve the belief that the desired state of affairs is achievable, so hortatives, unlike optatives, cannot refer to a past event, cf. *To have lived in Ancient Greece!* and **Let me have lived in Ancient Greece!* The content of the Hortative Construction then involves a reference to an achievable future event as desired by the speaker, but no reference to the addressee.

As was shown in section 6.2.2, a number of languages do not impose any restrictions on the identity of the hortative subject, but there are languages where several hortative constructions exist. For example, the suggestive construction in Kannada expresses exhortations with respect to the speaker and another person, while the optative construction expresses exhortations to a third person. I take such cases to be more specialized instances of the Hortative Construction, inheriting its basic content but imposing individual grammatical and pragmatic requirements, which in this case do not conflict with the information specified by the super-construction.

The next subsection shows how illocutionary force super-constructions and the principle of Constructional Economy account for nonfiniteness in independent clauses.

6.5.2 *Motivating nonfiniteness*

As far as tense/agreement and subject licensing is concerned, nonfiniteness is a matter of reduced expression, when some elements are omitted and some morphological contrasts are not available. It is commonly thought that the reduction of finiteness in dependent clauses signals the thematic dependence of the clause on the textual context (e.g. Givón 1990: 874–6). Since the value of the missing grams in dependent clauses may be provided by the main clause, an economic pattern requires uninflected or poorly inflected forms. The same applies to independent clauses with a sequential function which stand in the medial position in narratives. Carlson (1994) shows that in a number of African languages such clauses employ nonfinite forms, and explains this in terms of thematic continuity and the high degree of coherence with the previous discourse. By using nonfinite forms, reiteration of predictable information about participants and tense/aspect/modality is avoided, so the form of the clause is generally motivated by economy considerations.

I suggest that economy is also at work in imperatives and hortatives. They tend to show reduced finiteness because the expression of tense and subject is redundant. In this I draw in part on the insights of some functional works. Already Leech (1983: 25) noticed that the imperative subject may be absent for the reasons of economy, which simplifies the structure while maintaining recoverability of the message (see also Lyons 1977: 746–7). According to Givón (2001), the information about tense and subject identity in imperatives remains unexpressed, since it can be inferred from the situation of speech and the function of the clause. In other words, 'both aspects of reduced finiteness—subject marking and tense-aspect-modality—are predictable, given the norms of face-to-face verbal manipulation' (Givón 2001: 313). Similarly, Langacker (1991b: 495–504) argues that the participants and circumstances of the speech acts can play a role in characterizing an expression's meaning, and influence aspects of the respective form. For example, it follows from the very nature of a performative that the subject is the 1st person, the object is normally the 2nd person, and the verb is in the present tense. However, under the constructional approach adopted here the source of the missing values is neither the context of the utterance nor the situation of speech. Rather, the construction itself carries a value for a given feature. Since this information is inherently incorporated into the representation of the construction, Constructional Economy prevents it from being overtly expressed by morphological or phrasal means.

Following the reasoning of the previous subsection, we can assume that declarative clauses are instances of the abstract illocutionary Declarative Construction. This construction makes no reference either to a specific tense or to a subject participant. All that is specified in its semantico-pragmatic content is that it conveys assertion, i.e. it serves to add a proposition to the Common Ground (Stalnaker 1978). This requirement does not restrict the range of potential participants in the event or periods of time about which the assertion is made. As a result, constructions that inherit their force from the abstract Declarative Construction are semantically indeterminate as far as tense and the identity of subject is concerned. A prototypical inheritor of the Declarative Construction is the Declarative Sentence Construction suggested for English in Fillmore and Kay (1997):

(38) $\begin{bmatrix} \text{inherit} & \text{Spec-V} \\ \text{syn} & \text{vif fin} \\ \text{role} & \text{main} \end{bmatrix}$

The Declarative Sentence Construction is a Spec-V construct marked as the finite main clause. The information about subject identity and tense is associated with its ultimate inheritors, i.e. actual tokens of the constructional patterns, and has to be provided by phrasal means and/or feature specification on the verb.

The situation is different in imperatives and hortatives because the illocutionary force determines the interpretation of tense and the identity of the subject participant. Imperatives are instances of the abstract Directive Construction and some of their basic grammatical properties follow from this categorization. First, the constructional meaning specifies that the action denoted by the verb is intended to be added to the addressee's plan set. If a state of affairs X is planned, it will only obtain after the time of planning. In other words, imperatives are meant to bring about an event, which is therefore necessarily posterior to the time of the speech act itself. Therefore they are inherently future-oriented, as is confirmed by collocation with future time adverbials and future tag-questions. As the future tense is a necessary component of the constructional content, tense does not need to be specified on the verb, with the possible exception of the opposition between the remote and immediate future. This follows from the principle of Constructional Economy: an economical pattern avoids doubling by morphological means of the information contributed by the constructional meaning.

Second, the constructional meaning reflects the interaction between speech act participants. Since (i) the imperative proposes that the addressee brings about an event, (ii) the performer of an event is normally encoded as the subject, and (iii) the addressee is associated with the grammatical 2nd person, the prototypical imperative subject bears the 2nd person feature.[10] As noticed already by Schmerling (1982: 209), it is precisely the restriction to audience reference for subjects that distinguishes imperatives from other similar speech acts, in particular hortatives. Constructional Economy makes reference to the imperative subject's person cross-linguistically unlikely, hence many languages show no person agreement. However, there are no restrictions on agreement features compatible with the 2nd person such as number, gender, or honorification: as was mentioned in section 6.2.1, they are often expressed on imperative verbs. In a similar manner, imperatives rarely require an overt subject. The identity of the performer of the action is part of the inherent meaning of the construction. Since it follows unambiguously from the

---

[10] Potsdam (1998) argues that English imperatives contain the subject *pro*, whose 2nd person content is recovered from the core meaning of the imperative. This proposal is compatible with the proposal of my chapter, except that Construction Grammar does not use null elements. Instead, the constructional meaning assigns the 2nd person value directly to the first argument.

definition of the respective speech act and is represented as a feature of the imperative construction, the semantic argument may remain formally unexpressed without causing interpretational problems. Patterns without an overt subject NP are more economical and therefore preferred.

A simplified schematic representation of the Imperative Sentence Construction for English is as follows.

(39)

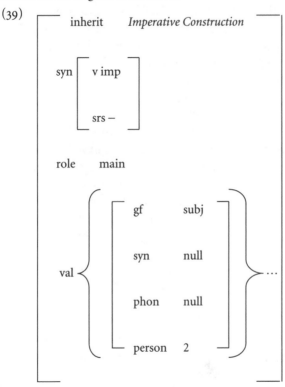

This representation indicates that imperatives have no overt subject but the first argument of the imperative verb bears the 2nd person feature. Null elements are not part of the Construction Grammar model and are replaced with the notion of definite null instantiation. In Fillmore's (1986) terminology, the semantic arguments that remain uninstantiated are 'definite omissible complements' or 'pragmatically controlled zero anaphora' that are licensed by particular constructions (see also Fried and Östman 2004: 68–9).[11] The representation of null subject in (39) follows Kay (2002: 469) and specifies

---

[11] In Fried and Östman's account the semantic and pragmatic attribute of the Imperative Sentence Construction contains an indication that the referent of the definite null instantiation corresponds to the hearer. In my account this property is inherited from the higher-level Imperative Construction.

that there is no overt syntactic element that satisfies the verbal valence slot, without positing any null categories in the way the generative grammar does. Additionally, the syntactic attribute of the construction contains the specification [srs −] that indicates that the specifier requirement is not satisfied.[12]

Although (39) prohibits an overt subject, in English and some other languages such as German, Russian, Bulgarian, Korean, Japanese, Bambara (Bergelson 2001: 490), and Ngiyambaa (Donaldson 1980: 159), an imperative subject may be present for emphatic purposes or when the first argument of the imperative verb corresponds to a quantified subset of the group of addressees and is grammatically the 3rd person. I take such cases to represent more specialized instances of the Imperative Sentence Construction which impose some individual constraints overriding the grammatical requirements inherited from the higher-level construction. The inherited information is blocked because it conflicts with the information provided by individual sub-constructions, as allowed by the mechanism of default inheritance. Note that the illocutionary function inherited from the illocutionary Imperative Construction is preserved even when the subject is grammatically the 3rd person. Potsdam (1998: 210–18) extensively argues for English that in this case the addressee must stand in a control relationship over the subject participant in a certain (social, political, economic, discourse, etc.) domain, cf. *Nobody leave the hall, sergeant!* and *#John, someone wash the dishes!* The latter example is infelicitous because the control relationship does not hold. If exercising a control over the state of affairs carried out by another individual is viewed as part of one's plan set, such cases fit the description of directive force provided above.

A similar reasoning applies to hortatives. As suggested in the previous subsection, the abstract Hortative Construction involves a reference to a future event as desired by the speaker. Since it is contributed by constructional meaning, the principle of Constructional Economy makes the expression of tense in lower-level hortative constructions typologically unlikely. Therefore hortatives do not normally express tense distinctions, with the exception of the remote and immediate future, just like imperatives. However, they differ in terms of subject agreement. As was shown in section 6.2.2, in languages like Kolyma Yukaghir hortatives are not specialized for person: the same hortative construction is used with different persons and numbers. In this case subject identity is not specified by the constructional meaning, and the verb inflects

---

[12] Although the subject is not internally specified, the grammatical construction provides a way of accounting for the subject-related phenomena. Binding relations in Construction Grammar are defined in terms of valence sets rather than constituent structure (Kay 1994). That is, they have a direct access to the argument structure. See a compatible HPSG proposal for binding by missing imperative subjects in Sag et al. (2003: 216–18).

for subject agreement and is likely to require an overt subject NP. In contrast, in languages like Kannada there are several specialized hortative constructions, each involving reference to different persons. Verbal inflections that mark moods and are the main morphological indicators of the constructional meaning cumulatively express reference to the subject. The optative inflection expresses both the optative and the 3rd person, while the suggestive inflection expresses both the suggestive and the 1st person plural.[13] In such cases the first argument of the verb has an inherent semantic value that follows from the function of the construction, and is unlikely to be cross-referenced by agreement or syntactically instantiated as the subject NP.

This account provides a unified functional explanation for nonfiniteness in dependent clauses and some non-assertive independent clauses. In both cases it is a matter of the omission of predictable information. In dependent clauses it involves contextual dependency. In non-assertive independent clauses the interpretation of tense and subject argument does not follow from the linguistic context, and neither do I attribute it directly to the situation of speech, as has been proposed in several functional works. Instead the explanation lies in recognizing the existence of constructional meaning and an economy tendency referred to as Constructional Economy. The relevant information is contributed by the semantico-pragmatic content of the construction and attributed to the constructional pattern as a whole. Hence in many languages economy considerations prevent it from being doubled either by a separate syntactic phrase or by inflectional morphology. Since Constructional Economy is only a tendency, one can expect to find languages and constructions where it is not applicable, as was shown in section 6.3.

6.5.3 *Nonfinite forms in independent clauses*

I have argued that the tendency for reduced tense and agreement and for null subjects in some non-assertive utterances is motivated by Constructional Economy: the function of relevant constructions is such that there is no need for the subject or tense to be expressed explicitly. This predicts that nonfinite verbal forms, which generally lack inflectional categories and are rarely compatible with subjects, are appropriate in independent non-assertive contexts. In this section I show that this prediction is correct: the use of such forms as imperatives and hortatives is a widespread cross-linguistic phenomenon.

---

[13] The connection between subject agreement morphology and the markers of non-assertive speech acts is supported by the fact that some languages demonstrate a diachronic relationship between them (see Paolillo 1994).

Imperative infinitives exist in many modern European languages, as well as in Latin (Hofmann 1972: 366–7; Menge 2000), Afrikaans (Donaldson 1993: 217), Ancient Greek (Riemann and Goelzer 1897: 640–41; Moore 2000: 88; Meillet and Vendryes 1924: 564; Blass and Debrunner 1976: 315–16; Smith 1968: 448), Eastern Armenian (Kozinceva 2001: 265–6), Middle Irish (Disterheft 1980: 182), Lithuanian (Ambrazas 1985: 324), Indic (Bhatia 1993: 35–6; Singh 1970: 60) and Slavic (Comrie and Corbett 1993: 431, 499, 658, 728, 917; Grappin 1963: 278) languages. They are directive, i.e. intended to give instructions to the addressee(s), but in most languages imperative infinitives do not pick up a specific member of the audience. Instead they are used for impersonalized instructions or recommendations, and there are a number of semantico-pragmatic differences between them and regular imperatives. Infinitives, gerunds, or other deverbal nouns serve as imperatives outside the Indo-European area as well, for example in Turkic (Tatar, Bashkir, Shor, and Yakut) (Nasilov et al. 2001: 204, 207, 213–14; Korkina et al. 1982: 321), Limbu (Van Driem 1987: 209–10), Maori (Polinsky 2001: 416–17), Modern Hebrew (Malygina 2001: 280–81), Kannada (Sridhar 1990: 239), and Kunama (Böhm 1984: 37).[14]

Independently used infinitives may have a hortative meaning, for example in Russian and German. Such hortatives are understood narrowly as involving adhortations to the 1st person, as in the following colloquial examples.

(40) a. Vot   i   stancija.   Pojti   napit'sja.
        here   and   station   go.INF   drink.INF
        'Here is the station. Let me go to drink something.'

     b. Den   Pullover   umdreh-en
        DEF.ACC sweater   turn-INF
        'Let me turn the sweater.' (Lasser 1997: 49)

According to Lasser (1997), (40b) is an attested example produced in a situation when the speaker was looking at a sweater put out on a radiator for drying. She analyses it as declarative, i.e. assertive, and translates example (40b) with the modal verb as 'I must turn the sweater'. However, these constructions do not pass the usual assertion tests: they cannot be embedded under assertive verbs (41) and do not allow epistemics and evidentials (42).

---

[14] Nonfinite forms are rather favoured in negative contexts as prohibitives (Sadock and Zwicky 1985: 175–7; Palmer 1986: 114; Han 2000, and the literature cited there). Han argues that negative imperatives may be unavailable for interpretational rather than syntactic reasons. An alternative explanation is suggested in Platzack and Rosengren (1998). I have no view on this issue.

(41) a. *Ja   govorju,   čto   pojti   napit'sja.
          I   say   that   go.INF   drink.INF
          'I am saying that I am going to drink something.'

      b. *Ich   sage,   dass   den   Pullover   umdreh-en.
          I   say   that   DEF.ACC   sweater   turn-INF
          'I am saying that I must turn the sweater.'

(42) a. *Očevidno   pojti   napit'sja.
          apparently   go.INF   drink.INF
          'Apparently I must go and drink something.'

      b. *Anscheinend   den   Pullover   umdreh-en
          apparently   DEF.ACC   sweater   turn-INF
          'Apparently I must turn the sweater.'

Hortative infinitives have no truth-value, as follows from the fact that they cannot be challenged by the answer *It's not true*. In other words, they do not assert a modal situation, but directly name an action which is desired by the speaker or makes sense for her and which the speaker is planning to attempt, normally, right after the time of the utterance. The first argument of the infinitive verb has a fixed interpretation: it is interpreted as the 1st person. The number feature plays no role, as it can be either 1st person singular or 1st person plural. In the latter case a group of individuals of which the speaker is a member is meant.[15]

Han (2000) proposes that imperatives and infinitives are interchangeable because they share some aspects of their semantics: they denote an irrealis situation located in the future. This also applies to subjunctives, which provide the same modal information as dependent infinitives and may be used for speech causation in independent clauses, so that there exists a close interpretational relation between imperatives, subjunctives, and infinitives. In a similar vein, Reis (1995) argues that indicatives bear the feature [+finite/+referential] ensuring the constative function. In her analysis, this feature is absent in German infinitives. When infinitives are used in independent clauses they acquire a non-epistemic modal meaning due to the 'communicative presumption' that a [−finite/−referential] construction with root status must have an irrealis interpretation. These accounts have in common the idea that the infinitive is associated with a meaning of its own, either

---

[15] In narrative contexts the first argument can be interpreted as the 3rd person. However, this appears to be caused by some kind of conscious or unconscious exploitation of the construction for stylistic purposes. By using the construction that requires the 1st person argument, the writer creates the effect of introspection. The 2nd person interpretation is totally excluded.

irrealis or [−finite/−referential], which translates into a non-assertive function when infinitives are used independently.

Yet this explanation seems insufficient. For one, nonfinite forms that express realis situations, such as realis converbs and past participles, can also function as imperatives. According to Vaxtin (2001), Asiatic Eskimo uses the converbs in *-lu*, which normally denote an accompanying situation, to express polite requests, cf.:

(43) a. aqumga-lu-ten   neqev-u-ten
         sit-CVB-2SG   get.up-INTR-2SG
         'After having sat down, you got up.'

    b. itegh-lu-ten
         come.in-CVB-2SG
         'Please come in!'

In the Turkic languages Shor and Tatar converbs also serve as polite requests (Nasilov et al. 2001). Tundra Yukaghir has a future imperative that expresses an attenuated request or one which does not have to be fulfilled immediately. It is etymologically based on the future action nominal in the locative case, optionally followed by the regular imperative marker. In its dependent function the locative action nominal serves as a temporal converb. The German perfect participles that express a categorical command with a number of verbs should also be mentioned here, e.g. *Still gestanden!* 'Stand still!' (Birjulin and Xrakovskij 2001: 14, 45–6).

Second, although infinitives are prototypically irrealis, I have shown in section 6.3.4 that in French, Russian, and Latin they can express realis situations in the past. Given this, it seems impossible to associate the infinitival form with one and the same meaning, but it is more reasonable to maintain that infinitives receive interpretation only within a construction. The constructional view advocated here separates the information provided by the verb and information provided by the construction. Under this approach, the illocutionary force is not necessarily projected from the specification of the main verb, but is a property incorporated into the description of the constructional pattern, whereas the verbal form is basically deprived of any illocutionary meaning of its own. This allows the same infinitival form to be used in a variety of independent functions, such as narrative, imperative, or hortative.

The relationship between abstract illocutionary constructions and constructions involving independently used nonfinite forms is a relation of inheritance. Constructions with independent nonfinite forms inherit illocutionary constructions, although they may have a more specialized meaning than their more prototypical inheritors. Commonalities in form and meaning between independently used nonfinite forms and other expressions of non-assertive speech acts result from common constructional sources. For example, in German and Russian both true imperatives and imperative infinitives inherit the Directive Construction, whereas hortatives and hortative infinitives inherit the Hortative Construction. The constructions involving independent infinitives do not only differ in illocutionary force, but also have a different syntax, as far as co-occurence with the overt subject and the interpretation of the understood subject is concerned. As was shown above, in narrative infinitives overt subjects are required, in imperative infinitives the subjects are interpreted as 2nd person although in some languages they can be expressed by a 3rd person quantifier, and in hortative infinitives they are interpreted as 1st person and are never overt.[16] This implies that root infinitives do not allow identical structural representations as assumed in some analyses (e.g. Rizzi 1994a; Haegeman 1995; Lasser 1997; Avrutin 1999), but form a natural class only inasmuch as they represent independently used nonfinite forms.

In sum, I suggest that the reason why nonfinites are often used in imperatives/hortatives is not related to the properties of the verbal form but rather lies in the properties of the relevant constructions. Historically, nonfinite forms in independent contexts could have arisen through the process of insubordination (see Evans, Chapter 11 below) after the main verb has ellipsed. But crucially, the very nature of these constructions is such that it does not require an overt expression of some contrasts, which makes the use of such forms appropriate.

6.6 Conclusion

This chapter has argued that relating the cluster of finiteness properties in independent clauses to the presence of one syntactic element is a purely theory-internal device not supported by empirical evidence if a broader cross-linguistic picture is taken into account. Some types of non-assertive independent clause show reduction of finiteness as far as tense/agreement inflection and subject licensing are concerned, but languages show different patterns of combinations of these properties, which suggests that

---

[16] Root infinitives may formally be disambiguated with respect to their illocutionary function by means of non-morphosyntactic clues. Lasser (1997: 205–6) emphasizes the role of particles, adverbials, or interjections that are typical of some constructions but not others. Intonational and prosodic factors are crucial in Sandoval's (1986) analysis of Spanish root infinitives.

they do not have a common source. Reduction of finiteness in independent clauses is better viewed as a cross-linguistic tendency than a universal syntactic generalization. The question then arises why in many cases nonfiniteness properties do come together.

I have argued that, although nonfiniteness tends to correlate with non-assertiveness, it has an independent motivation. Thus, the analysis suggested here does not directly relate finiteness to assertion, as suggested in some works (e.g. Klein 1994; 1998). Instead, the reason why some independent clauses tend to demonstrate reduced finiteness lies in the functional pressure for economy which regulates the relationship between form and function. In non-assertive independent clauses the information about subject identity and tense is provided by the meaning of the relevant syntactic pattern. For example, the semantics of the imperative imposes heavy restrictions on the available subjects because there is a strong connection between the subject and the addressee: either the addressee corresponds to the subject participant or she is expected to control the subject participant. This requirement directly follows from the function of the directive speech act. Since this information is predictable, economy considerations make it unlikely to be overtly expressed by phrasal or morphological means. Thus, the chapter provides evidence for the contention that grammar can become adapted to pragmatic constraints.

This situation was modelled within the theory of Construction Grammar, a non-derivational framework based on the notion of grammatical construction, i.e. a conventionalized association of various types of formal and structural information related to other constructions through an inheritance network. The essential point here is separating information provided by the verb and information provided by the construction. I have suggested that generalizations about illocutionary force follow from the network of inheritance between constructions. They are stated at a high node in the hierarchy of grammatical constructions and inherited by lower-level constructions. The illocutionary meaning may motivate the interpretation of the first argument and tense. Since this information is contributed by the construction as a whole and is specified in its representation, it is unlikely to be expressed by overt material due to economy considerations. I referred to this particular instance of economy as Constructional Economy. Constructional Economy prevents the doubling of constructionally predictable semantic information by penalizing its overt morphological or phrasal expression within the given construction. As far as I can see, this reasoning provides an additional argument for the approach to language that posits constructional patterns as basic building blocks of grammar.

As economy is a tendency and only determines the likelihood of certain patterns, we can expect to find some cross-linguistic variations in the relevant constructions. The ultimate shape of the construction is not strictly predictable but is determined by its individual grammaticalization path. This result is consistent with the grammatical archetypes model proposed in Ackerman and Webelhuth (1998), where the properties of individual constructions arise through the interaction of universal categorial archetypes and language- and construction-particular constraints involving different diachronic sources.

Part III
Finiteness in Individual Languages

7

Clause structure and verbal forms in Nakh-Daghestanian languages

ELENA KALININA AND NINA SUMBATOVA

7.1 Introduction

The notion of finiteness is one of those theoretical concepts that is widely used but vaguely defined. Traditionally, finiteness has often been understood in terms of morphological categories, i.e. as the ability of a verbal form to be marked for certain morphological categories such as subject agreement in person and number, or tense (e.g. Schwyzer 1939: 639; Heidolph et al. 1981: 498). Generative grammar also accepts that finiteness of a clause correlates, although indirectly, with verbal morphology (e.g Radford 1988: 287–92; Rizzi 1997: 284; Carnie 2002: 149–51, and Kornfilt, Chapter 9 below).

Another way of defining finiteness is through syntactic functions of a verbal form. Finite and nonfinite forms are defined via their unmarked syntactic position: finite forms prototypically function as the only predicate of an independent clause, participles as nominal attributes, infinitives as sentential arguments, and verbal nouns as arguments (Nedjalkov 1995: 97). Givón (1990: 852–60) suggested that finiteness is a gradual property of a clause and constructed the scale of finite features (p. 853). In his view, clauses can be more and less finite. The main clause is the 'most finite' in the sense that it realizes all finite features in full (see Cristofaro and Bisang, Chapters 4 and 5 above, for a discussion of the scalar approach to finiteness).

This chapter addresses finiteness in the languages of the Nakh-Daghestanian (East Caucasian) group. We argue that none of the approaches mentioned above yields satisfactory results when applied to the Daghestanian data. We claim that the important oppositions in the verbal system of

We would like to express our sincere gratitude to Irina Nikolaeva and the anonymous reviewers, whose valuable comments helped us to improve the paper. All mistakes and misrepresentations of the data are totally our fault.

the Nakh-Daghestanian languages are based on the illocutionary force and information structure of the sentences where the verbal forms occur, rather than on the dependent/independent distinction or the presence/absence of inflectional categories. Hence, the data of the Nakh-Daghestanian languages shed a new light on the definition of finiteness in terms of verb properties.

In section 7.2 we discuss the theoretical concepts we will need to analyse the data of the Nakh-Daghestanian languages. In section 7.3 we present general information on the Nakh-Daghestanian languages and a short overview of the verbal systems of Dargwa, Bagwalal and Tsakhur, three languages from different branches of the Nakh-Daghestanian group.[1] The data for each language are summarized at the end of the respective section. In section 7.4 we show how the theoretical notions discussed in section 7.2 can be applied to the languages in question. The last section provides conclusions on the sentence structure and verbal systems of the languages of the group, and discusses the relevance of the finite vs. nonfinite opposition for Nakh-Daghestanian.

7.2 Theoretical notions

Most concepts that we will need in order to discuss the Nakh-Daghestanian data relate to the theory of information structure. The term most widely used here is that of focus. We will also refer to different focus types. Since the focus expression in the Nakh-Daghestanian languages comes into interplay with the illocutionary force of the utterance, we now have to start with this well-known notion.

7.2.1 *Illocutionary force*

Illocutionary force is the basic purpose of a speaker when uttering a sentence. The lists of possible illocutionary forces suggested by different authors are not the same, but most contain at least declarations, commands/requests, and questions. Along with declaratives, questions, and commands, many authors include exclamations in the list of illocutionary forces.[2] In producing exclamations, the speaker's intention is to express her emotions. Here, we treat exclamatives as a distinct illocutionary type.

Declarations and questions are the utterances that involve operations with the state of knowledge of the communication participants. Declarations are

---

[1] Most of the Bagwalal and Tsakhur data have been collected by Elena Kalinina through fieldwork (1994–8) and published in the descriptive volumes on these languages (Kibrik 1999; 2001).

[2] For example, for Russian, Janko (2001: 22–3) distinguishes the following types of speech act: declaration, question, command, exclamation, and address.

produced in order to change the knowledge of the hearer. Questions are uttered to fill a gap in the knowledge of the speaker. Commands and wishes are different in this respect: commands are produced to influence the hearer's behaviour, while wishes are meant to influence the state of the real world.[3]

A special type of declaration consists of sentences that the speaker produces in order to remind the hearer of something and to make the corresponding proposition actualized in the discourse. The content of such utterances is familiar to both speech act participants, cf. the italicized sentence in the following example from *Stamboul Train* by Graham Greene:

(1)   ... It was my father who brought the business here.
      You found it a mistake?
      Oh, come now, Mr. Myatt, *you've seen the figures*. It wasn't as bad as that.
      But I want to sell out and retire while I can still enjoy life.

Utterances of this type we call 'actualizing utterances.'

Most languages have different sentence types according to the illocutionary force they are meant to carry. This is also the case in the languages of Daghestan. Most of them distinguish the following sentence types: commands, wishes, exclamations, declarations, and questions. As will be shown in section 7.3, actualizing sentences constitute a separate sentence type.

7.2.2 *Information structure*

7.2.2.1 *Presuppositions, assertions, and foci*   In this chapter we generally follow Lambrecht's (1994) view on information structure. Lambrecht's definition of focus is based on the concepts of presupposition and assertion.

There are two main approaches to the notion of presupposition. In logic and (formal) semantics, presupposition is mainly understood as the part of the meaning of the sentence that is not affected by polarity and modality (see Horn 1996 for a short survey of different views on the problem). However, the concept that is of relevance for us is that of pragmatic presupposition introduced by Stalnaker (1974) and Karttunen (1974). In our discussion of information structure, we exploit the notions of pragmatic presupposition ('common ground') and pragmatic assertion, as defined by Lambrecht (1994: 52):

---

[3] Other types of speech act such as commands and wishes may also change the state of the hearer's mind. For example, after hearing a command, the hearer obtains knowledge that the speaker wants something to be done. In our view, however, the state of the hearer's mind is irrelevant for the speaker when he or she utters a command or a wish.

Pragmatic presupposition: The set of propositions lexicogrammatically evoked in a sentence which the speaker assumes the hearer already knows or is ready to take for granted at the time the sentence is uttered.

Pragmatic assertion: The proposition expressed by a sentence which the hearer is expected to know or take for granted as a result of hearing the sentence uttered.

Consider the following example from Lambrecht (1994: 51–2, 55–6):

(2)   I finally met the woman who moved in downstairs.

When the speaker pronounces (2) he or she assumes, among other things, that the hearer takes for granted that someone moved in downstairs, and asserts that he or she finally met the new neighbour.

An utterance can be presented as a combination of its pragmatic pre-suppositions and an 'illocutionary component', which is a proposition under the scope of an illocutionary force operator. Generally, illocutionary force is a property of a given speech act, which is not conditioned by the previous discourse. That is why the illocutionary force cannot be presupposed.

The propositions encoded by the complement clauses of the factive verbs such as 'know', 'finish', or 'regret' are semantically presupposed. More than that, they can be shown to encode a pragmatic presupposition of the whole utterance. Even if these propositions have not been actualized in the previous discourse, the speaker behaves as if they have. This is a case of pragmatic accommodation of the presuppositional structure (Stalnaker 1973; Lewis 1979; Lambrecht 1994: 65–73).

Focus, in Lambrecht's framework, is 'the semantic component of a prag-matically structured proposition whereby the assertion differs from the presupposition' (Lambrecht 1994: 213). For Lambrecht, focus is essentially a semantic notion. The focused phrase 'stands in a pragmatically construed relation to the proposition such that its addition makes the utterance of the sentence a piece of new information' (p. 210). However, the term 'focus' is often used with respect to the syntactic constituent(s) expressing focus. As mentioned above, the focus can take scope over the whole sentence or over a smaller constituent. Lambrecht differentiates three types of focus articulation: predicate-focus, argument-focus, and sentence-focus:

The three focus-structure types correspond to three basic communicative functions: that of predicating a property of a given topic (predicate-focus: topic-comment function); that of identifying an argument for a given proposition (argument-focus: identificational function); and that of introducing a new discourse referent or of reporting an event (sentence-focus: presentational or event-reporting function). (Lambrecht 1994: 336)

The following examples from Lambrecht (1994: 223) illustrate these focus types:

(3)   Predicate-focus structure
      What happened to your car?
      My car/It broke *down*.

Predicate-focus structure is the most neutral and frequent focus type. The speaker makes an assertion about the topic of the sentence (in this case about the speaker's car).

(4)   Sentence-focus structure
      What happened?
      My *car* broke down.

In sentence-focus structures, 'no pragmatic presupposition is formally evoked except for some of the non-distinctive presuppositional features...(e.g. the proposition that the speaker has a car, that the speaker is a topic, etc.)' (Lambrecht 1994: 233).

(5)   Argument-focus structure
      I heard your motorcycle broke down?
      My *car* broke down.

In argument-focus (narrow-focus) sentences, both speech act participants share a knowledge of an open proposition: in example (5) this is 'speaker's x broke down.' The speaker asserts the relationship of identity between x (an entity determined by its participation in a known situation) and another entity, which is encoded as the focused phrase of an argument-focus sentence. In Lambrecht's example, this is the identity between the thing that broke down and the speaker's car.

Apart from the three focus types discussed by Lambrecht, many authors address the fourth type, the 'verificational' focus, 'which involves the polarity of a proposition rather than some semantic domain within it' (Lambrecht 1994: 236). Sentences with the verificational focus only assert the truth-value of the proposition, which is known to both speech act participants. Consider the following example from Klein (1998: 228):

(6)   The idea that he didn't love her is plainly wrong: John *did* love Mary.

Dik et al. (1980) call this focus type 'counterassertive' or 'counterpresuppositional'. For Russian, Janko (2001: 61–2) uses the term 'verificational meaning', and Kovtunova (1976) speaks about 'verificational rhemes.'

7.2.2.2 *Declarative assertions and declarative foci*   In Lambrecht's conception, assertions are expressed by all sentence types including non-declarative sentences.

> From the point of view of information structure, questions as well as orders and requests convey information, even though they are not statements. For example by asking a question, a speaker may inform his addressee of his desire to know something; by giving an order he may inform his addressee of the obligation to do something, etc. Within the present framework, non-declarative sentences, like their declarative counterparts, are viewed as having pragmatic presuppositions and as being used to make assertions. (Lambrecht 1994: 55)

However, the data of many languages suggest that focus marking differs in declarative and interrogative sentences, on the one hand, and all other sentence types, on the other. For example, in English, French, and other languages, cleft constructions are only possible in declarative and interrogative sentences. In Russian, the same holds for the focus construction with the demonstrative pronoun *éto*: cf. grammatical sentences (7a, b) and the ungrammatical imperative construction (7c):

(7) a. Éto   menja   bud-ut   po   televizoru   pokazyva-t'
        this   I.ACC   be.FUT-3PL   on   television.DAT   show-INF
        'It is *me* who will be shown on TV.'

     b. Éto   tebja   po   televizoru   pokazyva-l-i?
        this   you.SG.ACC   on   television.DAT   show-PST-PL
        'Is it *you* who was shown on TV?'

     c. *Éto   menja   pokaži!
        this   I.ACC   show.IMP
        'Show *me*!'

Languages like Russian draw a line between declarative and interrogative, on the one hand, and all other sentence types, on the other. Crucially important for the contrast is whether the primary intention of the speaker is to change his own or the hearer's state of knowledge or not.

Declaratives and interrogatives have to do with the state of knowledge of the speech act participants. Consequently, they involve operations with truth-values: declaratives assert a truth-value, while interrogatives provoke the hearer to assert a truth-value. On the other hand, non-declarative and non-interrogative sentences either express emotions (exclamatives) or are performative in the sense that they are social actions by themselves (commands, advice, wishes, and conventionalized expressions). As such, they do not have truth-values.

That is why, based on Lambrecht's definition of assertion, we introduce a similar, but somewhat different, notion of a declarative assertion:

Declarative assertion: the proposition expressed by a sentence which the hearer is expected to know or take for granted as a result of hearing the sentence, and this change of the hearer's state of knowledge is the main communicative purpose of the utterance.

Declarative focus will be found in the sentences containing declarative assertions only. These definitions restrict the domain of assertion, and hence the domain of focus, to declarative utterances. It rules out declarative foci in commands, exclamations, wishes, and other non-declarative utterance types.

We further maintain that only independent or complex sentences have assertions and foci; embedded clauses normally do not express independent assertions. However, some types of dependent clause seem to bear secondary assertions. In this case, the assertion of the sentence can be viewed as a conjunction of several assertions, possibly hierarchized according to their relevance for the speaker: cf. sentence (8) with a non-restrictive relative clause:

(8)   Fortunately, we had a map, without which we would have got lost.

This sentence asserts (i) that the speaker and his companions had a map and (ii) that they would have got lost if they did not have the map. In this case we say that the dependent clause expresses secondary assertion, which is part of the assertion of the whole sentence (the conjunction of (i) and (ii)).

Other types of dependent clause relevant for this discussion are complement clauses of the verbs of speech. In this case, the dependent clause has all the semantic features of a fully-fledged sentence, including its own illocutionary force and information structure.

Questions and their relation to focusing will be discussed in the following section.

7.2.2.3 *Question foci*   Roughly speaking, the focus of an interrogative utterance is the information sought. It is a variable that corresponds to the foci of all felicitous answers to the question. Below we discuss several basic question types.

Focus types matching declarative foci.   Generally, polar questions evoke most common and trivial types of presuppositions, such as those connected with the reference and definiteness of noun phrases within these questions. A polar question (9) from Lewis Carroll:

(9)   Do cats eat bats?

does not evoke any presuppositions except possibly relating to the existence of cats and bats. What is questioned here is the truth-value of the whole proposition. Questions about the truth-value of a proposition will be termed here 'truth-value focus' structures. This question type matches the counter-presuppositional or 'verificational' type of declaratives (section 7.2.2.1).

There are questions that correspond to declarative sentence-focus structures. The speaker is asking what situation is taking or took place as in the following well-known question from *Jesus Christ Superstar* (lyrics by Tim Rice):

(10)   What's the buzz? Tell me what's happening?

Interrogative sentences matching the predicate-focus structures are seman-tically similar to sentence-focus interrogatives: the only difference is the presence of a topic, cf.:

(11)   What are you doing? What's the matter with you?

Constituent questions are often supposed to have an open proposition as their presupposition where the variable corresponds to the question word, cf.:

(12)   a. Who killed Lord Gurney?

In (12a) the presupposition is that 'somebody (x) killed Lord Gurney', and the speaker asks for information about the identity of x. A presupposition of this type entails that a negative answer such as *Nobody* is highly improbable. If such an answer still appears, it means that the question was infelicitous and had a false presupposition:

(12)   b. Nobody. It was a suicide.

The information structure of the constituent questions of this type follows the pattern of the declarative sentences with a narrow focus. In many languages the morphosyntactic structure of constituent questions directly matches that of narrow focus constructions (e.g. French has cleft constructions in con-stituent questions). The question phrase, which corresponds to the variable in the presupposition, will be treated here as the question focus.

Double focus.   There are constituent questions that easily allow negative answers:

(13)   Who would like some coffee?
       Me. / Grandma. / Nobody.

In this example (suggested and commented on by Barbara H. Partee, p.c.), the answer *Nobody* is absolutely natural. The set of possible answers includes a negative answer and a number of positive answers pointing at different participants of the coffee drinking situation.

Semantically, such sentences are similar to polar questions with indefinite pronouns:

(14)   Did anybody call?

Question (14) presupposes one negative answer and a set of positive answers (*John, Your boss,* etc.). Neither (13) nor (14) suggests that the open proposition contained in the question is true. Uttering a question of this type, the speaker is simultaneously asking about two things: (i) is it true that somebody called / that somebody wants some coffee? and (ii) if yes, who was/is that person? In other words, such interrogative sentences amalgamate two questions: a question about the truth-value and—in the case of a positive answer—a constituent question about the denotatum of the interrogative/indefinite pronoun. Each of the two semantic components of the question has a focus of its own (the truth-value and the interrogative/indefinite pronoun). We will refer to questions of this type as double-focus questions.

Lambrecht (1994) mentions questions of this type as exceptions to the normal presuppositional structure of constituent questions. He shows that the difference between what we called 'narrow focus' and 'double focus' questions is explicitly marked in French via the form of the answer.

To answer a question like (5.43),[4] a speaker will normally use a cleft construction, as in (5.43'):

(5.43') Q: Qui (c'est qui) a mangé le biscuit? «Who ate the cookie?»
      A : C'est moi. "Me," "I did".

On the other hand, the question in (5.46), in which the final NP is indefinite, will typically be answered with a simple NP, as in (5.47):

(5.47) Q: Qui veut un biscuit? «Who wants a cookie?»
      A: Moi. "Me," "I do".

In sentences like (5.46) and (5.47), the question is perhaps best analyzed as a conventionalized shortcut for a more cumbersome sequence such as "Does anyone want a cookie, and if so, who?" (Lambrecht 1994: 285)

Combining a truth-value focus and a narrow focus is not the only possibility of double focus in questions. In the same way, a truth-value focus can be combined with a sentence-focus or a predicate-focus.

---

[4] Lambrecht's example (5.43) is *Who ate the cookie?*, example (5.46) is *Who wants a cookie?* (Lambrecht 1994: 282).

(15)   A: It's by way of being a parting present.
        B: Are you going away?

In example (15) from Somerset Maugham, the speaker (B) does not simply want to know whether the hearer (A) is going, but is rather trying to find out the motivations of the hearer's behaviour: he presented her with a precious gift without any obvious reasons. In this case a negative answer would be insufficient. A different case is presented by (16) from *Stamboul Train* by Graham Greene:

(16)   Was there any news on the train?
        Everything quiet in Belgrade,—said Lukitch.

What is being asked is not simply the truth-value of the proposition 'there was news on the train.' The speaker wants to know (i) if there was any news and if so (ii) what particular situation took place. In this case, just a positive answer would not suffice.

To sum up, the following types of focus domain are observed in questions: (i) in truth-value questions, the question focus only comprises the truth-value; (ii) in sentence-focus questions, the whole sentence belongs to the focus domain; (iii) in predicate-focus questions, the focus domain extends over the predicate; and (iv) in many constituent questions, the focus corresponds to the question word phrase. A number of questions has a double focus, which involves a truth-value focus and an additional focus domain (sentence-focus, predicate-focus, or argument-focus).[5]

In what follows—if not stated otherwise—we will use the term 'focus' for the declarative focus and the question focus only. This concept will not be applied to utterances other than declarative and interrogative.

7.3 The Daghestanian data

7.3.1 *Basics*

Most languages of Daghestan belong to the Nakh-Daghestanian (East Caucasian) language family. The genetic subgrouping of the Nakh-Daghestanian languages is as follows (Alekseev 2001: 156):[6]

---

[5] We did not mention the so-called alternative questions (e.g. *Would you like coffee or tea?*). Generally, their focus structure is similar to that of wh-questions. The difference is that the speaker explicitly offers a set of possible values of the question variable.

[6] In some alternative versions of genetic subgrouping: (i) there is the Daghestanian sub-branch which comprises all languages of the group except Nakh; (ii) Lak and Dargwa constitute a subgroup; and (iii) Khinalug belongs to the Lezgian subgroup.

Nakh (Bats, Chechen, Ingush)
Avaro-Andi-Dido: Avar (Avar), Andi (Akhvakh, Andi, Botlikh, Chamalal, Ghodoberi, Karata, Bagwalal, Tindi), Dido (Dido, Hinukh, Hunzib, Bezhta, Khvarshi)
Lak (Lak)
Dargwa (Dargwa)
Lezgian (Aghul, Archi, Budukh, Kryts, Lezgi, Rutul, Tabassaran, Tsakhur, Udi)
Khinalug (Khinalugh)

The Nakh-Daghestanian languages have a number of common features. All languages have extensive case systems. Most languages have class agreement, while some also show person agreement. The Nakh-Daghestanian languages are morphologically ergative, though many syntactic processes operate according to the accusative pattern. Subordinate clauses are typically headed by verbal derivatives (converbs, participles, infinitives, and verbal nouns or masdars). The languages show a flexible word order with the default SOV pattern.

Before we start describing the verbal systems of the languages in question, we need to touch upon two important grammatical points that characterize most or even all Nakh-Daghestanian languages and will be frequently referred to below.

First, the Nakh-Daghestanian languages have a special class of auxiliaries that we call 'predicative particles'. Most predicative particles are clitics hosted by the head of the focus phrase. Predicative particles express various grammatical meanings usually associated with finiteness such as tense (present/past), modality, certain illocutionary forces (primarily interrogative), polarity, and in some languages (e.g. Lak and Dargwa) also person. The words traditionally analysed as copulas are also members of this syntactic class. Morphologically, predicative particles are not homogeneous across languages and sometimes not even within one language. Some of them are marked for class or person, some are morphologically simple. The class of predicative particles is singled out on syntactic grounds. There are sentence types where predicative particles are disallowed and those where their use is obligatory. In the latter case they can be shown to be syntactic heads of the clause in which they occur (Kazenin 1997: 60–67). Predicative particles fall into several classes of mutually exclusive elements.

Second, the Nakh-Daghestanian languages show a tendency towards overt morphosyntactic marking of the focused constituent. In most cases it is marked by the position of the predicative particles, as shown in the following examples from Tsakhur:

(17) a. aIli   a=r=y   wo=r[7]
         Ali.ABS   come-M-PF   COP=M
         'Ali came.'

      b. aIli   wo=r   a=r=y
         Ali.ABS   COP=M   come=M=PF
         'It was Ali who came.' (Kibrik 1999: 583)

(17a) is a predicate-focus structure and the predicative particle glossed here as COP is located next to the verb. In contrast, (17b) is an argument-focus structure. The same predicative particle follows the focused constituent *Ali*.

Since predicative particles are allowed in certain clause types only (see below), morphosyntactic focus marking is also confined to the same class of clauses. Conditions of their use in Dargwa, Bagwalal and Tsakhur are discussed in more detail in sections 7.3.2–4.

7.3.2 Verbal forms in Icari Dargwa

All Dargwa data represent the dialect of Icari. The data has been collected by Nina Sumbatova and published in Sumbatova and Mutalov (2003).

7.3.2.1 *The verbal system: general*   The verbal system of Dargwa includes a number of forms traditionally treated as finite, as well as several participles, converbs, and deverbal nouns. Dargwa is one of the few languages of the group that show a well-developed category of person. As in most Nakh-Daghestanian languages, the verb in Dargwa agrees with the absolutive argument in class and number. The verb can be marked for aspect, tense, mood, evidentiality, and polarity. In some tense/aspect/mood forms the verb also expresses the oppositions of direct/inverse and transitive/ intransitive.

Most 'finite' indicative, and some non-indicative, forms in Icari consist of a verbal stem or a verbal derivative (a converb or a participle) and a predicative particle. In the indicative mood Icari Dargwa has only two simple tense paradigms, the past habitual and the general present (see section 7.3.2.4). 'Simple' means here that the forms from these paradigms cannot host predicative particles. Imperative, prohibitive, and subjunctive are simple forms (see section 7.3.2.4). Other non-indicative paradigms include one or two simple forms (e.g. *kattigulli* 'if we sit down' in 18) and a set of complex periphrastic forms, where the auxiliary is a simple verb form (e.g. *čarčisabihubli behedil* 'if it had turned' in 19).

---

[7] Following the tradition adopted in Caucasian linguistics, we separate the class marker by the equality sign.

(18) ži   ka.tt.ig-u-l-li,   ssika-l
     above   sit.1/2PL.PF-THM-1-COND   bear-ERG
     kkwalʕ   ač-ib-li,   jara   qqaraldi
     smell   take.PF-PRET-CVB   or   silhouette
     či.b.až-ib-li   čar.b.ih-ub-li,   arg-an-ni
     see.N.PF-PRET-CVB   become.N.PF-PRET-CVB   go.IPF-OBLG-FUT
     'If we sit down here, the bear will smell us or see our silhouettes,
     and it will go away.'

(19) ilttu=b   čar.či.sa.b.ih-ub-li   b=ehedil-ra,
     there-N   turn.N.PF-PRET-CVB   N-be.COND.PST-and
     nišša-la   b=uč'-an   b=elč'-un-ni-di
     we-GEN   N-read.IPF-OBLG   N-read.PF-PRET-CVB-PST
     'If it [the bear] had turned to us, the Koran would have been already
     read in our memory.' (lit. 'to-be-read would have been read')

Icari also has a number of nonfinite derivatives. These are simple and specialized converbs, short and full participles, and several deverbal nouns (see section 7.3.2.4).

When applying the term 'finite' to Dargwa, one faces certain difficulties: the morphological criteria of finiteness (person, tense, and mood marking) and the syntactic criteria (functioning in independent vs. dependent clauses) single out different classes, as shown in Table 7.1.[8] The last column of the table shows how the forms are classified in the traditional descriptions of Dargwa (Abdullaev 1954; Xajdakov 1985; Musaev 2001; 2002; Mutalov 2002). In these descriptions, all non-indicative simple forms, the generic/habitual forms of the present and past tense, as well as all grammatical combinations of any verb form with a predicative particle cliticized to it, are analysed as finite. Throughout section 7.3.2 we use the term 'finite' in this sense, traditional for Caucasian linguistics.

7.3.2.2 Predicative particles and focus marking As in other languages of Daghestan, predicative particles in Dargwa express sentence-level categories: person, tense (present vs. past), illocutionary force (interrogativity), and polarity. A sentence can contain no more than two predicative particles, which are never separated from each other.

The set of predicative particles is heterogeneous. The particles used in the present tense express person/number (-*di* for the 2nd person singular, -*da* for

---

[8] In Icari and some other dialects, subjunctives express person and are morphologically finite. The cognate forms of literary Dargwa and other dialects are uninflected (Abdullaev 1954; Van den Berg 2001). They are labelled infinitives and classified as nonfinite. In some earlier works (Mutalov 1992), the Icari-type subjunctives/infinitives are also treated as nonfinite verbal derivatives.

TABLE 7.1. Finite and nonfinite verb forms in Icari Dargwa

	Syntactic function	Person marking	Traditionally defined as
Simple form (generic/habitual, hypothetical, obligative/ irrealis, imperative, optative, noncurative)	Main clause	+	
Simple form (conditional, concessive)	Dependent clause	+	Finite
Verb stem/simple converb/full participle + non-past predicative particle	Main clause	+	
Verb stem/simple converb/full participle + past predicative particle	Main clause	−	
Simple form (subjunctive)	Dependent clause	+	
Simple converb, full participle, masdar in -*ni*	Dependent clause	−	Nonfinite
Deverbal noun in -*dexx*	Main clause	−	

the 1st person singular and plural and 2nd person plural). The 3rd person affirmative particle -*ca*=*b*, the existential auxiliaries (*le*=*b*/*te*=*b*/*že*=*b*/*če*=*b*/ *he*=*b*[9]), and the negative existential verb *b*=*ākku* 'not exist' show class agreement (see 20a with the 3rd person present particle -*ca*=*b* and 21 with the 1st person form of the negative auxiliary *akk$_w$i*[10]).

(20) a. murad-il   qu   b=ax-un-ca=b
         Murad-ERG   field.ABS   N-SOW-PRET-PRS.3-N
         'Murad has sown the field.'

(21) du ik'-ul-da: duččilla   w=išš-ib-lejkk$_w$i,
       I   M.say.IPF-CVB-1   at.night   M-sleep.PF-PRET-CVB.NEG.1
       arg-a-tta   du   qil
       go.IPF-PROG-CVB.1   I   home
       'I say: I had no sleep last night, so now I am going home.'

---

[9] We cite stems with the neutral class marker (*b* = in all three languages). If the neutral class marker is improbable for semantic reasons, we choose the masculine class marker (*w* = or zero in Dargwa, *w* = in Bagwalal, and *r* = or zero in Tsakhur). Most verbs in Dargwa have two basic stems (perfective and imperfective). For citing, we use the imperfective stem.

[10] When following the verb, predicative particles undergo sandhi at the stem boundary; see the forms *arg-a-tta* (<*arg-a-tti-da*) 'I am going' and *w*=*išš-ib-lejkk$_w$i* (<*w*=*išš-ib-li* + *akk$_w$i*) 'I did not sleep' in example (21).

In (20a), the predicative particle *-ca=b* expresses the present tense, 3rd person, and agrees in class with the absolutive noun *qu* 'field' of the neutral class, in (21) the 1st person negative particle *-akku* does not agree in class.

Other predicative particles, i.e. the past particle *-di*, the epistemic particle *-q'al*, and the interrogative particles *-ū* and *-n(i)*, do not show any type of agreement. This is illustrated in (22) for the past particle *-di*.

(22) ssa ištti Rabdan-qal sa.ka.b.iž-ib-li
yesterday these Rabdan-ASC.PL watch.HPL.IPF-PRET-CVB
b=už-ib-li-di, ižal q'alli ča.k'al w=ākk$_w$i
HPL-stay-PRET-CVB-PST today but.PRT nobody M-not.exist.PST
ehttu=w
there-M
'Yesterday that group of Rabdan and people with him were staying there and watching, but nobody was there today.'

The particle *-q'al* marks a sentence as actualizing (see section 7.2.1):

(23) ilttalli it b=ax-un b=ikk-ub ce-l-gu
they.ERG this N-SOW.PF-PRET N-burn.PF-PRET what-OBL-SUPESS
q'aʔ b=alx$_w$-a-tti b=už-ib-li,
radishes N-SOW.IPF-PROG-CVB N-stay-PRET-CVB
q'aʔ wanza-la gu.b.al b=ik-a-tti-q'al hēl q'aʔ
radish earth-GEN under.N N-grow.IPF-PROG-CVB-but that radishes
'They were sowing radishes under the burnt crops, (you know that) radishes grow downwards.'

Sentence (23) explains how the Icarians managed to deceive the Persian Shah Abbas. The Shah's army burnt all the crops, and the Shah hoped that the people would die of starvation. The Icarians, however, were sowing and eating radishes, which the Shah was not able to notice: this was because radishes grow under the earth. The fact that radishes grow 'downwards' is, of course, known to all communicants. The 'actualizing' function is also characteristic of the general present forms (see section 7.3.2.4).

The position of the predicative particles marks focus in the sense we developed in Sections 7.2.2.2–3: they appear in declarative and interrogative sentences only. The predicative particles are cliticized to the right edge of the head of the focus phrase. In most cases, this is the main predicate of the sentence. In argument-focus structures, predicative particles follow the focused phrase, which in this case does not include the main predicate. A predicate that does not belong to the focused part of the sentence obligatorily takes the participle marker *-ci* (SG) / *-ti* (PL). In example (20), sentence (a) is a predicate-focus structure, while (b) is an argument-focus structure (the actor argument is focused).

(20) b. murad-il-ca=b   qu   b=ax-un-ci
          Murad-ERG-PRS.3-N   field.ABS   N-SOW-PRET-ATR
          'It was Murad who sowed/has sown the field.'

In constituent questions, the predicative particles either follow the question phrase (24) or are cliticized to the main predicate of the sentence (25):

(24) čina=b-ni   di-la   qati?
      where=N-Q   I-GEN   cap
      'Where is my cap?'

(25) qil-i=b   b=irqʼ-an   ʕalčʼi hi-l   b=alrqʼ-ib-lēkku-ni?
      house-INESS-N   N-do.IPF-OBLG   work who-ERG   N-do.PF-PRET-CVB.NEG-Q
      'Who did not do their homework?'

Example (24) is a typical narrow-focus structure where the question focus is marked by the question word and the position of the predicative particle -*ni*. Example (25) is structured as a double-focus question, where the first focused constituent is expressed by the question word, and the predicate attaches the predicative particles -*akku* and -*ni*.

7.3.2.3 *Nominal predicate clauses*   The structure of the clauses with nominal predicates parallels that of verbal clauses containing predicative particles. In these two clause types predicative particles take the same linear and structural position, whereby the nominal predicate takes the position of the verb stem or verbal derivative in periphrastic forms: cf. (20) and (26).

(26) a. di-la   kkujab   ččakkwa-ci-ca=r
          I-GEN   fiancée   beautiful-ATR-PRS-F
          'My fiancée is pretty.'

      b. di-la   kkujab   ččakkwa   rirssi-ca=r
          I-GEN   fiancée   beautiful   girl-PRS-F
          'My fiancée is a pretty girl.'

      c. ila   kkujab   ččakkwa-cī?
          you.GEN   fiancée   beautiful-ATR.PQ
          'Is your fiancée pretty?'

Predicative particles are cliticized to the focused phrase, exactly the way they behave in verbal clauses. In this case, the focused phrase functions as the main predicate of the clause.

(27) du w=ik'-ul-da,   iž k'wi-īb-ci   qaIbc'a   ssika-di,
I M-say.IPF-CVB-1 this two-ORD-ATR having.white.neck bear-PST
it ssika ber-ci-di,   w=ik'-ul-da,
that bear brown-ATR-PST   M-say.IPF-CVB-1
niššij   ber-ci-di   HaIžat-ci
we.SUPLAT brown-ATR-PST need-ATR
'I say: the second bear had a white neck. [And] that [first] bear was
brown. We needed the brown one.'

In the first clause of (27) the predicative particle -*di* is cliticized to the noun
phrase *qaIbc'a ssika* 'bear with white neck', in the second and the last clause
the same marker is cliticized to the attribute *berci* 'brown'

7.3.2.4 Basic functions of the verbal forms   In this section we are going to
demonstrate that verbal forms in Dargwa do not yield a straightforward, neat
distribution over clause type (main ~ dependent, attributive ~ complement
~ adjunct).

Indicative.   Dargwa has two types of indicative form: simple forms and
periphrastic forms with predicative particles.[11] Both types are primarily
used as main predicates in independent clauses. However, they differ in
their ability to be used in argument-focus structures.

Generally, indicative is not used in dependent clauses. The only exceptions
are sentential complements of the verbs of speech, perception, and emotion
introduced by the complementizers *habībli* or *(w)=ik'ᵥil*. These are the only
types of dependent clause that have an illocutionary force of their own. In
(28), the dependent clause introduced by the complementizer *habībli* contains
the predicative particle -*da* (first person marker) cliticized to the obligative
verb stem *sērRan* 'will/should come.'

(28) du-l   ttatti-cci   [Rurš   sērR-an-da   habībli]
I-ERG father-IN.LAT tomorrow M.come.IPF-OBLG-1 that
b=urs-ib-da
N-say.PF-PRET
'I told the father that I would (FUT) come tomorrow.'

In the indicative mood, Dargwa has only two simple forms, i.e. the past
habitual and the general present, encoding past habitual and atemporal
situations respectively:

---

11 Dargwa also has complex periphrastic forms with an auxiliary verb. Their usage is determined by
the form of the auxiliary: if the auxiliary takes a simple form, the properties of the construction are
close to the properties of a clause headed by a simple form; if the auxiliary attaches a predicative
particle, the construction behaves like other constructions with predicative particles.

(29) harzamina   b=urs-iri   di-la   waba-l
      always   N-tell.IPF-HAB.PST.3   I-GEN   mother-ERG
      'My mother used to tell (this story).'

(30) ici   gu.d.ubkk-u,   q'ʷili   icc-u
      OX.PL   yoke.NPL.IPF-THM   COW.PL   milk.IPF-THM
      'Oxen are yoked, cows are milked.' ('Each thing has its own purpose.')

The 'atemporal' general present is normally used to encode propositions
generally known to the speech act participants, like proverbs (30) or common
norms of behaviour. However, the general present form has many functions;
semantically, most of them belong to the non-indicative domain. Except
for atemporal situations, the general present expresses threats, cautions, and
factive conditions (examples 31, 32, and 33 respectively).[12] It is also used in the
apodosis of generic conditionals (34).

(31) kūtti   dehc'et'   arž-aq-i-d-āli   hana!
      how   noise   go.IPF-CAUS-THM-1-IQ   now
      '(You come over here and) I'll give you one!' (a threat, lit. 'I will make noise')

(32) kērk-u-tt   raXXil!
      fall.down-THM-2   suddenly
      '(Be careful), do not fall down!'

(33) čirkalli   čaqēr-u-d   –   či.d=iž-aq-a-ca=d
      in.the.morning   M.stand.up.IPF-THM-1   see.NPL.PF-CAUS-PROG-PRS-NPL
      naIqq-bi
      hand-PL
      (Maxač, who was spending a night in the speaker's house, did not sleep
          well at night.) '(When) I stood up in the morning, he (immediately)
          showed (me) his hands.'

(34) na,   u-ra   nišša-la   mussa-n-ir   r=ih-u-tt-il,   ssika
      now you-and we-GEN   place-OBL-EL F-become.PF-THM-2-COND bear
      či.b.ig-an   zamana, qqil-leh   tti.r.ax-u-tt-ū?   –
      see.N.IPF-OBLG   time   tracks-OBL.POSTLAT follow.F-THM-2-PQ
      r=axax-u-tt
      F-go.NEG-THM-2
      'And you, if you were in our place and saw a bear, would you go along
          the tracks of another bear?' (lit. 'When you are in our place ... , do
          you follow ... ?')

---

[12] The term is introduced in Thompson and Longacre (1985).

The past habitual and the general present are not used in argument-focus constructions.[13]

Preterite is represented by a heterogeneous paradigm: the 3rd person is a simple form, the 1st and 2nd person forms host predicative particles indicating person:

(35) a. ʕalli-l   murad   uc-ib
          Ali-ERG   Murad.ABS M.catch.PF-PRET
          'Ali caught (3) Murad.'

      b. du-l   murad   uc-ib-da
          I-ERG   Murad.ABS M.catch.PF-PRET-1
          'I caught (1) Murad.'

The 3rd person preterite coincides with the forms used in relative clauses ('short' participles). In example (36) the preterite form *bursib* of the verb 'tell' heads an attributive clause; in (37) it functions as the main predicate of an independent clause.

(36) dul   cinicci   hel Xabar b=urs-ib   XXunul-li   hel Xabar
      I-ERG self.IN.LAT this story N-tell-PRET woman-ERG this story
      lebillellicci čibēRaIq-ib
      all.IN.LAT   retell.N-PRET
      'The woman who I told this story retold it to everybody.'

(37) rasul-li   hel   Xabar murad-icci   b=urs-ib
      Rasul-ERG   this story Murad-IN.LAT N-tell-PRET
      'Rasul told this story to Murad.'

Non-indicative moods.   The irrealis and obligative forms include predicative particles, and function as heads of independent clauses. In this respect they are similar to indicative forms. These two moods are possible in argument-focus structures, where the main verb takes the form of the obligative participle, and the predicative particle accompanies the focused constituent, as in (39), where the past particle *-di* follows the focused dependent clause headed by the specialized converb *wākk_warqqilla* 'because (you) were not.'

---

[13] Dargwa also has a system of periphrastic habitual forms where the auxiliary verb (*b=ug-* 'be, stay' or *b=ir-* 'be, become') takes the past habitual or general present form, and the lexical verb is a simple (progressive) converb. Functionally, and to a certain degree also formally, the past habitual and general present in Dargwa are close to non-indicative forms: on the one hand, they tend to express non-indicative modal meanings; on the other hand, like most non-indicative moods, they form a system of one simple and several periphrastic forms.

(38) Xalq'   b=ax-an-ēr   w=ax-an-di
      people   HPL-go.IPF-OBLG-as   M-go.IPF-OBLG-2SG
      'Walk the way your people do.' (lit. 'You should go the way the people do.')

(39) u   šša=w   w=ākk_war-qqilla-di
      you   village-M   M-not.exist.ATR-because.of-PST
      du   ila   pajla   jerga-llij   w=ax-an
      I   you.GEN   instead   turn-OBL.SUP.LAT   M-go.IPF-OBLG
      'I had to go and look after the herd for you (lit. 'in your turn'),
      because you were not in the village.'

The hypothetical mood is expressed by the forms that also include predicative
particles (the 1st and 2nd person markers or the past marker) and that
function as heads of independent sentences.

(40) ištaIH   b=ū-li   b=ehedil,
      wish   N-be-CVB   N-become.COND.PST
      beliki,   it-ra   ʕaIH-il   uč'-iž-di
      maybe   he-and   good-ADV   M.read.IPF-HYP-PST
      'If he had wanted to, he, too, would have probably done well in his
      studies.'

Hypothetical mood precludes argument focus constructions. The person and
tense markers are inseparable from the hypothetical mood forms (see footnote 20 below).

The imperative, optative, and non-curative[14] are incompatible with predicative particles. They are used to express commands and wishes, which have
no corresponding argument-focus structures.

(41) bicci-waIna-l   ka.tt.erxx_w-ab-a
      tasty-warm-ADV   get.old.1/2PL.PF-OPT-2
      'May you live till your older years in warmth and satiety!'
      (a traditional wish to a married couple)

(42) dehni   wajhat   b=uʕ-ikk.a
      child.PL   for.a.walk   HPL-go.PF-NCUR
      'Let the children go for a walk.' (the speaker does not object)

Dargwa also has several conditional forms; all of them are used exclusively in
dependent clauses: see examples (18), (19), and (40).

The subjunctive forms are functionally equivalent to the infinitives of other
languages of the group. They are mainly used as heads of either purpose

---

[14] Non-curative forms express the speaker's indifference to the possible realization of the situation.

clauses (43) or sentential complements of matrix predicates, such as 'want', 'necessary' (44), and the like.

(43)   u   XXibra-ccir   kejʕ-un-ci   insan   w=ih-u-tt-i,
       you   grave-EL   M.go.out.PF-PRET-ATR   person   M-become.PF-THM-2-COND
       w=aš-i   di-la   qil,   di-la   ttatti-j,   waba-j
       M-go.IPF-IMP   I-GEN   home   I-GEN   father-SUP.LAT   mother-SUP.LAT
       ci.k'al   b=alli   b=uqq-i-tt-aj
       something   N-with   N-take.PF-THM-2-SBJV
       'As you have come out of the grave, let us go to my house and pick up
       something for my parents.' (Magometov 1978: 276–7)

(44)   Rurš   qqaljc.'ik'ᵥ-ar-aj   kaI.ʕ-aIn-aj   Halžatil-ca=b
       tomorrow   search.IPF-ITR-SBJV   come.PF-ITR-SBJV   necessary-PRS-N
       '(It is useless to do it today,) we have to come and look for (it)
       tomorrow.' (lit. 'necessary to come to look for')

Neither conditional nor subjunctive forms take predicative particles. This is easily explained by the fact that they only head dependent clauses, which have no illocutionary force and no focus of their own.

All modal forms used in dependent clauses (subjunctive, conditional, and concessive[15]) differentiate person, whereas past indicative forms (pluperfect, evidential past, resultative past, etc.) do not. For instance, in (43) the verbs *wihutti* (the conditional of the auxiliary verb 'become') and *buqqittaj* (the subjunctive of the verb 'take') are both marked for 2nd person. Cf. (22), where the verb *bužiblidi* 'were staying' (pluperfect) does not indicate the 1st person of the subject. This violates the finiteness hierarchy suggested by Givón (1990: 853), which predicts that non-indicative forms used in dependent clauses should not be marked for more verbal categories than forms used exclusively in independent clauses.

Nonfinite derivatives.   Though most dependent clauses in Dargwa are headed by nonfinite derivatives, there is no clear correspondence between the syntactic type of the dependent clause and the verb form that usually heads it.

Dargwa has two types of converbs: simple converbs and specialized converbs.[16] Simple converbs are used both on their own and within periphrastic verbal forms. In the former case, they head adverbial clauses and sentential

---

[15] Concessive forms are derived from the conditionals by adding the particle -*ra* 'and'.

[16] According to the classification of V. Nedjalkov (1995), the former are contextual converbs and the latter are specialized converbs.

complements of aspectual verbs (45), as well as of the matrix verbs 'want/love', 'necessary', and the like. Within adverbial clauses, simple converbs in most cases encode sequences of actions (as *bužibli* 'staying', *čarsabihubli* 'having returned', *kk𝓌idēRibli* 'having penned', and *bukatti* 'eating' in 46). They can also express cause.

(45) murad-il   qal   b=erxx-ul-li   taman.b.aIrq'-ib
      Murad-ERG   house N-paint.PF-PRET-CVB   finish.N.PF-PRET
      'Murad finished painting the house.'

(46) xadiža   waba-ra   ca=w-ra   arilla   diči=b
      Hadiža   mother-and   self-M-and the.whole.day   herding-HPL
      b=už-ib-li,   nā   cinna   nisna   qil
      HPL-be-PRET-CVB   now   (self)   in.the.evening   home
      čar.sa.b.ih-ub-li,   kk𝓌.i.d.ēR-ib-li   HaIjwanti,
      return.HPL.PF-PRET-CVB   pen.NPL.PF-PRET-CVB   cattle.PL
      ka.b.iž-ib-ca.b   b.uk-a-tti
      sit.down.HPL.PF-PRET-PRS-HPL   HPL-eat.IPF-PROG-CVB
      'Mother Hadiža and he (Xan) *stayed* in the pasture the whole day, and in the evening they *returned* home, *penned* the cattle, and they sat and *ate*.'

Specialized converbs are used in dependent clauses expressing time, cause or manner. An example can be found in (39): *wākk𝓌ar-qqilla* 'because you were not (there)' is a specialized converb denoting cause.

Dargwa has two classes of participles, i.e. the so-called short participles[17] that coincide with the 3rd person preterite forms (see above) and 'full' participles, that are formed by adding the attributive marker -*ci* (SG)/-*ti* (PL) to short participles. There are also obligative participles: they are not marked by -*ci*/-*ti*, but belong to the syntactic class of full participles.

Full participles are used in different syntactic functions. In combination with predicative particles, they function as predicates of independent clauses. Without predicative particles, they function as nominal attributes (47) or arguments (headless attributes), as in (48).

(47) [ix𝓌lalla zaman-t-a-cci=b   b=aIrq'-ib-ci]   šši-ca=b
      old   time-PL-OBL-N.IN.ESS.   N-do.PF-PRET-ATR   village-PRS-N
      '(Icari) is a village that was built in old times.'

---

[17] 'Short' participles are relatively limited in their functions. When used as heads of relative clauses they are inseparable from the head noun. Further on we discuss only full participles.

(48) nišša-la   šša=b   b=už-ib-ti-ca=b   [d=eqel
      we-GEN   village-HPL   HPL-be-PRET-ATR.PL-PRS-HPL   NPL-many
      juz-i   d=elk'-un-ti],   [ʕaIrab-la
      book-PL   NPL-write.PL-PRET-ATR.PL   Arabic-GEN
      b=elč'-un-ti] ...
      NPL-read.PF-PRET-ATR.PL

'There have been in our village those who had written many books, those who could read Arabic...'

Full participles also head complements of the matrix verb 'know':

(49) ruslan-ni   [ttatti   nisna   sērR-an-ci]
      Ruslan-ERG   father   in.the.evening M.come.IPF-OBLG-ATR
      b=uXX-a-ca=b
      N-know-PROG-PRS-N

'Ruslan knows that father will come tonight.'

Full participles are the only possible forms of the predicate in argument-focus constructions (example 20b).

Dargwa has several deverbal nouns with very diverse functions. Optative nouns (= the bare verbal stem) are used as predicates of optative exclamative sentences. They are usual in traditional wishes, blessings, and curses.[18] In (50) *ag* is an optative noun.

(50) urk'i-la   wēr   murad   ag!
      heart-GEN   seven   wish   go.PF

'May seven wishes of your heart be fulfilled!'

The masdar in *-ni* is primarily used in argument positions (51). In particular, it heads sentential complements of the aspectual verbs *taman.b=irq'-* 'finish (*transitive*)', *taman.b=ir-* 'finish (*intransitive*)', and *w=igal* 'continue.'

(51) nā   uže   tupang-li-j   či.w.iX-ni   sa.b=aIR-ib   di-la
      now already   gun-OBL-SUP.LAT   trust.M.IPF-MSD   come.N.PF-PRET   I-GEN

'Now I already trust my gun.' (lit. 'trust has already come')

Action nominals with the suffix *-dexx* are semantically similar to the masdar, but show a different range of syntactic functions. They are used either as regular nouns taking all case markers or as main predicates of exclamative sentences:

---

[18] Optative nouns are also used in argument positions. In this case, they take regular case markers and refer to the person to whom the wish/curse is addressed (Sumbatova and Mutalov 2003: 122–4).

(52) iž-i-la   ha.r.ax-an-dexx!
      this-OBL-GEN   rock.F.IPF-OBLG-AN
      'Oh, that conceit of hers!'

Exclamative sentences headed by these nouns do not bear any predicative markers and do not allow argument-focus marking.

7.3.2.5 Dargwa: generalizations

Clause types and verbal forms.   Dargwa shows no direct correlation between clause types and verbal forms. Only a minority of forms are tied to a certain type of clause: imperative and prohibitive are used in the main clauses expressing commands; optative nouns and finite forms of the optative and non-curative mood are used in main clauses expressing wishes; conditional and concessive forms are used in conditional and concessive dependent clauses; specialized converbs are used in adjunct clauses; and action nominals in *-dexx* are used in main clauses of exclamative sentences. Other clause types (main declarative and interrogative clauses and dependent clauses except those headed by specialized converbs) allow different verbal forms.

Main clauses of declarative and interrogative sentences show the highest diversity of verbal forms. Declaratives can be headed by indicative forms and several non-indicative moods (obligative, irrealis, and hypothetical).[19] Interrogatives exploit the same forms additionally marked by an interrogative particle (*-ū* in polar questions, *-ni/-n* in constituent questions: cf. 24).[20] However, in both declarative and interrogative argument-focus constructions the diversity of verbal forms is confined to only one type, i.e. the predicative particle at the focused phrase and a full participle as the lexical part of the predicate.

Formally, Dargwa does not oppose nominal vs. verbal predicate clauses. Neither is there a clear opposition of main vs. dependent clause types. Instead, all clauses in Dargwa fall into those headed by a predicative particle and those headed by a verbal form (a simple form or a nonfinite derivative).

Dependent clauses.   The distribution of nonfinite derivatives over dependent clause types is not stipulated by the syntactic function of the clause

---

[19] In sentences headed by a hypothetical form the predicative particles are inseparable. We think the reasons are both semantic and formal. In the argument-focus structure with a hypothetical verb form, an epistemic modal operator would be a part of a presupposition, which seems impossible in Dargwa. On the other hand, Dargwa lacks a hypothetical participle, which should have been used in the argument-focus construction.

[20] Constituent questions have a predicative particle either on the question word or on the predicate. In the former case, the question is an argument-focus structure. Its predicate is a full participle. The same holds for polar questions with an argument-focus.

(attributive ~ complement ~ adjunct), but rather by the information structure of the sentence as a whole.

Relative clauses in Dargwa are normally restrictive and headed by short or full participles.[21] The latter, however, are more frequently used as headless attributes, where they function as heads of referential noun phrases: see (48).

Clausal complements of speech and perception verbs can be introduced by a complementizer (finite strategy): see (28). However, most clause complements lack a complementizer and are headed by a verbal derivative (simple converb, full participle, or masdar) or a subjunctive. Examples (53–55) illustrate these strategies.

(53) dam   uk-_wdaj/uk-un-ni   b=ikkul-da
      I.DAT   M.eat.IPF-SBJV.THM.1/M.eat.IPF-PRET-CVB   N=want-1
      'I am hungry' (lit. 'I want to eat').

(54) ruslanni   ttatti   nisna   sērR-an-ci/sērR-ni
      Ruslan.ERG   father   in.the.evening come-FUT-ATR/come-MSD
      b=uXXa-ca=b
      N-know-PRS-N
      'Ruslan knows that father comes tonight.'

(55) itil   du   xxarurR-ni   taman-b=alrq'-ib
      it-ERG   I   ask-MSD   finish-N-do-PRET
      'He finished asking me.'

Most matrix verbs allow several types of complement clause formation, as shown below:

'say'	finite form + complementizer	'think'	finite form + complementizer
'know'	masdar; participle	'want'	subjunctive; converb
'begin'	converb; subjunctive; masdar	'fear'	finite form + complementizer; subjunctive
'finish'	converb; masdar	'be able'	subjunctive
'see'	finite form + complementizer; converb		

Strictly speaking, the subordination strategy is a lexical property of the matrix verb. However, if a verb allows two or more strategies, the choice of the strategy is determined by certain semantic and pragmatic properties of the sentence as a whole. The main tendencies are as follows:

---

[21] In particular, relative clauses cannot modify personal names.

(i) Participles are only used with the verb *b=arh-* 'know' (note that the content of those clause complements is pragmatically and semantically presupposed).

(ii) Masdars tend to head clauses expressing situations known to both participants and viewed as facts. For example, a masdar clause is another possible strategy for the complements of the matrix verb *b=arh-* 'know'. Masdars are also governed by verbs like *šak.=irk-* 'guess', *qum.irt-* 'forget' (a fact), *w=ixx-* 'believe, trust'; predicates expressing estimates like *ʕalHil* 'good' or *waIl* 'bad'; and factive phasal verbs *taman.b=irq'-* 'finish (*transitive*)', *taman.b=ir-* 'finish (*intransitive*)' and *w=igal* 'continue'. Masdars are possible with the verb *b=aʔ.b=irxx-* 'begin', but only if the addressee is supposed to know that the event had to begin (pragmatically presupposed proposition).

(iii) Modal predicates (*w=ir-* 'can'; *HaIžatil* 'necessary'; *b=ikk$_{(w)}$-* 'want'; *Xajri.b=ik'-* 'allow, be possible', etc.) and the aspectual verb *b=aʔ.b=irxx-* 'begin' subcategorize for subjunctive clauses. These clausal complements often contain information new to the addressee, which is (part of) the sentence assertion.

(iv) Converbs are used with the predicates like *=urcc-* 'get tired', *b=ikk$_{(w)}$-* 'want/love', *HaIžatil* 'necessary', and with all aspectual verbs. The content of converbal subordinates is not presupposed and does not constitute a separate assertion.[22]

Clausal adjuncts form a very heterogeneous group, which includes (i) conditional and concessive clauses headed by special (morphologically finite) verb forms; (ii) clauses expressing cause and time and headed by specialized converbs; and (iii) purpose clauses headed by subjunctives. The rest are numerous clauses headed by simple converbs with a broad temporal or—less frequently—causal meaning (examples 46 and 18).

The syntactic argument-focus marking is ungrammatical in all types of dependent clause headed by verbal derivatives and subjunctives. However,

---

[22] Most matrix verbs can be used in sentences with different information structures. Some verbs allow only one subordination strategy for their sentential complements, and the tendencies formulated above can be violated: these verbs fix the most frequent strategy as the only one. However, many verbs allow more than one strategy. In this case, the choice of the complement-taking strategy is often determined by the information structure of the sentence:

(i)   it   du   xxar.urR-a-tti   w=aʔ.išš-ib
        he   I   M.ask.IPF-PROG-CVB M-begin.PF-PRET
        'He started asking me.'

(ii)   it-il   cin-na   xxar.b=urR-ni   b=aʔ.bišš-ib
        he-ERG   self-GEN   N.ask.IPF-MSD   N-begin.PF-PRET
        'He started his questioning.'

Sentence (ii) presupposes that both speech act participants know that the actor was going to interview or question the speaker, whereas sentence (i) does not have this presupposition.

some types of complex sentence allow focus marking on constituents within the dependent clause. In this case the focused constituent inside the dependent clause is marked by the predicative particle while the main clause predicate takes the form of a full participle:

(56) ila   ucci-di   sāR-ib-li   dam   ʕaIH.ka.b.icc-ur-ci
      you.GEN brother-PST M.come.PF-PRET-CVB   I.DAT like.N.PF-PRET-ATR
      'I was pleased that it was your brother who came.'

Dependent clauses selected by a complementizer can be argument-focus structures exactly like independent clauses:

(57) a. du-1   rabdan sāR-ib-lī   w=ik'ᵥil xxar.b.aIR-ib-da
         I-ERG Rabdan M.come.PF-PRET-CVB.PQ   M-that   ask.N.PF-PRET-1
         'I asked whether Rabdan had come.' (predicate-focus)
      b. du-1   rabdan-ū sāR-ib-ci   w=ik'ᵥil xxar.b.aIR-ib-da
         I-ERG Rabdan-PQ M.come.PF-PRET-ATR   M=that   ask.N.PF-PRET-1
         'I asked whether it was Rabdan who had come.' (subject-focus)

Predicate types.   Dargwa allows three types of predicate head: (i) simple (finite) forms; (ii) verbal derivatives; and (iii) predicative particles.

Predicative particles only head main clauses of declarative/interrogative sentences. This is the only predicate type that allows focus to be placed on any constituent other than the predicate. In argument-focus structures, predicative particles are separated from the lexical verb and placed next to the focused phrase. Though generally predicative particles can be combined with different verbal units (verb stems, simple converbs, full participles) as well as nouns, attributes and adverbials, the only possible form of the lexical verb in an argument-focus structure is a full participle.

Most simple forms head only main clauses. They are compatible with different clause types expressing different illocutionary forces: habitual/generic, hypothetical, obligative, and irrealis forms are used in declarations and questions; optative and non-curative forms are used in wishes and curses; while imperative and prohibitive forms are used in commands. Simple forms of the subjunctive, conditional, and concessive mood are used exclusively in dependent clauses. Simple forms cannot be used in argument-focus structures. In all sentence types headed by simple forms, the morphosyntactic marking of an argument-focus would be ungrammatical.

Most nonfinite forms head dependent clauses. However, deverbal action nominals in -*dexx* are used as heads of independent exclamative sentences. Full participles and simple converbs combine with predicative particles to

function in independent declarative and interrogative clauses. Only full
participles are allowed if the predicate does not belong to the focused part
of the sentence. Participles are also used as heads of (restrictive) relative
clauses and, more frequently, as headless attributes (arguments) and heads
of argument clauses governed by the verb *b=arh-* 'know'. Simple converbs,
when used in dependent clauses, head adjunct clauses of time and cause and,
very frequently, argument clauses with non-factive meaning (see Table 7.2).
The distribution of the three predicate types correlates with the opposition
of declarative/interrogative sentences vs. other illocutionary force type sentences (section 7.2.2.2). Generally, declarations and questions are headed by
predicative particles, which implies the possibility of morphosyntactic focus
marking, and other sentence types exclude it. The only exceptions are the
general present and the habitual forms, which can head declarative sentences
but are incompatible with predicative particles. We observed, however, that
the meaning of these forms is prototypically non-indicative and that they
tend to be used in non-declarative utterances at least as frequently as in
declarations and questions.

TABLE 7.2. Dargwa: the relationship between the predicate form and clause type

Verbal form	Bare form, no predicative particles	Form with an enclitic predicative particle	Predicative particle shifted away
Simple form	Main clause (habitual/ generic: predicate or sentence-focus; non-declarative)		
Verb stem			
Simple converb	Argument clause (non-factive) adjunct (time, cause)	Main clause (declarative/ interrogative: predicate-focus or sentence-focus)	
Participle	argument clause ('know') relative clause (restrictive)		Main clause (declarative/ interrogative: argument-focus)
Masdar (*-ni*)	argument clause (factive)		
Deverbal noun (*-dexx*)	main clause (exclamative)		

7.3.3 *Verbal forms in Bagwalal*

7.3.3.1 *The verbal system: general*   The Bagwalal verb is marked for tense, aspect, modality, evidentiality, and polarity. The verb agrees with the absolutive noun phrase in class[23] and number. The verbal system of Bagwalal consists of few simple forms and many periphrastic forms. In periphrastic formations the lexical verb takes the form of a nonfinite derivative (participle, converb, infinitive); the verbal auxiliary can be both a simple and a periphrastic form. Deverbal nouns never occur in periphrastic tense/aspect/mood forms: they head the complements of some matrix verbs. The auxiliary position in periphrastic formations can be occupied by any predicative particle. The set of predicative particles in Bagwalal includes the following elements: the present tense copula *ek'ᵥa*; the negative copula *woč'e*; question particles *ištō/ištā, ile, ilaX, jī/jō/jā, lassi*; and the epistemic particles[24] *Rā/Rō, Rassō/Rassā, Rabō/Rabā, Rabi,* and *Rala*[25].

Bagwalal also has a serial verb construction, where two simple forms equally marked for tense/aspect/mood are juxtaposed.

7.3.3.2 *Focus and the predicative particles in Bagwalal*   Focus is consistently marked in Bagwalal declarative and interrogative main clauses by the position of predicative particles. Focus marking in non-indicative utterances is disallowed. The principle focus marker is the copula *ek'ᵥa*. The unmarked position of the copula is clause-final. However, to mark argument-focus the copula is shifted next to the focused element:

(58) a. maHammad   w=ā=w=o   ek'ᵥa
          Mohammed   M-come-M-CVB   COP.PRS
          'Mohammed has come.'

      b. maHammad   ek'ᵥa   w=ā=w=o
          Mohammed   COP.PRS   M-come-M-CVB
          '*Mohammed* has come.' (Kazenin 2001: 683).

Another auxiliary in the verbal system of Bagwalal is the verb *b=isāss* 'find'. Its distribution is completely parallel to the distribution of the 'be' auxiliary: in both its forms (preterite and future) it combines with all types of nonfinite

---

[23] There are three noun classes: masculine, feminine, and neutral. In plural, the opposition of the masculine and feminine is neutralized, and human plural is opposed to non-human plural.

[24] Epistemic particles are particles expressing epistemic modal meanings. When talking about epistemic modality, we mean the degree and/or source of the speaker's commitment to the truth of the proposition (see Halliday 1970: 349; Palmer 1986: 54–5; Bybee and Fleischman 1995: 6; Drubig 2001: 44).

[25] Variations in the phonetic form of some particle depend on the addressee's sex: particles ending in -ō are used to address males, and those ending in -ā to address females.

forms that are involved in the formation of periphrastic constructions. The 'find' forms express the admirative meaning.

The negative copula *wečʼe* and simple forms of the verb *b=ukʼass* 'be' behave in the same way.

(59)   maHammad   wečʼe   w=ā=w=o
       Mohammed   COP.PRS.NEG   M-come-M-CVB
       'It's not *Mohammed* who has come.' (Kazenin 2001: 683)

(60)   maHammad   w=ukʼa   w=eł-ā-X
       Mohammed   M-be   M-walk-IPF-CVB
       '*Mohammed* was walking.' (Kazenin 2001: 683)

The same type of distribution is observed for a number of epistemic (61) and interrogative (62) particles. However, these particles can co-occur with the copula, as in examples (68) and (69) (Kazenin 2001: 686).

(61)   a. maHammad   w=ā=w=o=Rala
          Mohammed   M-come-M-CVB-PRT
          'Looks like Mohammed has come.'

       b. maHammad-Rala   w=ā=w=o
          Mohammed-PRT   M-come-M-CVB
          'Looks like *Mohammed* has come.' (Kazenin 2001: 683)

(62)   a. ʕisa=w   waša   w=ā-jišt?
          Isa=GEN.M   son   M=come-Q
          'Has Isa's son come?'

       b. ʕisa=w   waša-jišt   w=ā?
          Isa=GEN.M   son-Q   M=come
          'Is it Isa's son who has come?' (Kazenin 2001: 684)

In constituent questions, question words are sufficient to mark question focus:

(63)   den   heLʼi: "he=b-i-Re   du-ha   qʼoča=m=o ?"
       I.ERG   said   what-N-Q-QUOT   you.OBL-DAT   want-N-CVB
       'I said: "What do you want?"' (Kibrik 2001: 813)

Unlike in Dargwa, in Bagwalal argument-focus constructions, the verb does not obligatorily take the participial form, as can be seen from example (63). Argument-focus structures are compatible with the preterite forms (see 62b), where the question marker *-jišt* is shifted to mark argument-focus, while the verb retains its preterite form. Bagwalal also allows question words to co-occur with the simple preterite forms (example 64), but not with the future forms: in the latter case the verb is obligatorily represented by a participle (65):

(64) Ło-r-ō   o=b   misa   džē ?
      who.OBL-ERG-Q.M   this-N house   make
      'Who has built this house?' (Kazenin and Skobelkin 2001: 451)

(65) a. heštu=b=ī gur   pat'imat-i-r   b=al-ā-ł-o=b?
         [what-N-Q dress] patimat-OBL-ERG N-put.on-POT-FUT-PTCP-N
         'What dress is Patimat going to wear?' (Kazenin and Skobelkin
         2001: 451–2)

      b. *heštu=b gur-ī   pat'imat-i-r   b=al-a-ss?
         what-N   dress-Q Patimat-OBL-ERG N-put.on-POT-FUT

The verb can optionally take the participial form in constituent questions:

(66) a. Ło-r-ī   bišda   kumuk džē-rā-X   b=uk'a?
         who.OBL-ERG-Q   you.PL.DAT   help   make-IPF-CVB   N-be
         'Who is helping you?'

      b. Ło-r-ī   bišda   kumuk džē-rā-X   b=uk'a=b?
         who.OBL-ERG-Q   you.PL.DAT   help   make-IPF-CVB   N-be-PTCP.N
         'Who is helping you?' (Kazenin 2001: 694)

The copula and its negative counterpart, along with the auxiliary verb, are termed the 'polarity group' of focus markers in Kazenin (2001: 685). They are opposed to the 'illocutionary force group', which is made up of discourse particles. Kazenin shows that when the elements of the two groups co-occur, it is only the members of the 'illocutionary force group' that mark focus by shifting:

(67) a. maHammad-Rala   w=ā=w=o   ek'_wa
         Mohammed-PRT   M-come-M-CVB   COP.PRS
         'Looks like *Mohammed* has come.' (Kazenin 2001: 686)

      b. *maHammad ek'_wa   w=ā=w=o-Rala
         Mohammed   COP.PRS   M-come-M-CVB-PRT

Focus can also be marked jointly by the members of both groups:

(68) maHammad(-Rala ek'_wa   // ek'_wa-Rala)   w=ā=w=o
      Mohammed(-PRT   COP.PRS   // COP.PRS-PRT)   M=come=M=CVB
      'Looks like *Mohammed* has built a house.' (Kazenin 2001: 686)

Even if both the copula and the particle are shifted, this does not make the sentence ambiguous: it is always the member of the illocutionary force group that is interpreted as the focus marker:

(69) maHammad-R-ō   Xal-i-r   *ek'$_w$a*   č'ini=w=o
      Mohammed-PRT-M   Halil-OBL-ERG   COP.PRS   beat-M-CVB
      'Halil has beaten *Mohammed.*' (Kazenin 2001: 686)

(70) ło-r-ō   maHammad   *ek'$_w$a*   č'ini=w=o?
      who.OBL-ERG-Q   Mohammed   COP.PRS   beat-M-CVB
      'Who has beaten Mohammed?' (Kazenin 2001: 686)

Question words cannot co-occur with the particles of the illocutionary group either:

(71) *ło-r-ō   o=b   misa   džē-R-ō?
      who.OBL-ERG-Q.M   this=N   house   make-RO-M
      'Who has built this house?' (Kazenin and Skobelkin 2001: 452).

Kazenin observes one more type of focus construction that he terms 'quasi-focusing': the copula is shifted from the clause-final position, while semantically there is no argument-focusing. Rather, the construction signals that the whole sentence introduces new, unknown information. To us, this is an instantiation of the sentence-focus structure:

(72) bort-abi   r=uk'a=r=o   *ek'$_w$a*
      ramp-PL   NPL-be-NPL-CVB   COP.PRS
      šašan-ā-X,   sangut-abi-la   r=uk'a=r=o   *ek'$_w$a*
      reel-IPF-CVB   chest-PL-and   NPL-be-NPL-CVB   COP.PRS
      hāhani   r=eł-ā-X
      slide.apart   NPL-go-IPF-CVB
      '(The hook on the body of the car didn't close, so) the ramps were reeling and the chests in the body were sliding apart.' (Kibrik 2001: 766)

7.3.3.3 *Nominal predicate clauses*   Kalinina (1999; 2001a) shows that the copula in Bagwalal nominal predicate sentences is not an equation predicate, nor is it there to mark tense/aspect/mood. The Bagwalal copula functions on a par with other predicative particles—the negative copula (example 73b), question particles (example 73c), epistemic particles (example 73d), the particle -*Re* (example 73d)). As a rule, it is omitted in the presence of question words (example 74).

Normally, copula and other predicative particles follow the focused constituent (main predicate) of the nominal predicate sentence:

(73) a. c'inu=b   mašina   ek'ʷa   a=b
          new-N   car   COP   this-N
          'This is a new car.'

      b. c'inu=b   mašina   woč'e   a=b
          new-N   car   COP.NEG   this-N
          'This is not a new car.'

      c. c'inu=b   mašina-ile   a=b?
          new-N   car-Q   this-N
          'Is this a new car?'

      d. hešda-ji-Re   in-ššu=b   mašina   b=ič'-ir-ō=b,
          how-Q-RE   LOG-OBL.M-GEN.N   car   N=die-IPF-PTCP=N
          c'inu=b   mašina-Re   a=b
          new-N   car-RE   this-N
          'How can my car break down (=die), when it is a new car!'
          (Kibrik 2001: 793)

(74) q'adiHā: hindi-jō   čā?
      Qadimahammad   where-Q   tea
      'Qadimahammad, where is tea?' (Kibrik 2001: 811)

7.3.3.4 *Basic functions of the verbal forms*
Simple forms. The Bagwalal verb has two simple indicative forms: the preterite (75) and future (76). Simple tense forms (and their negative correlates) can only be used as main clause predicates.

(75) hē   sani   č'aruba   b=ełłi=r   iši
      then   together   plain   HPL-go-HPL   we
      'Then we all went (down), onto the plain.'   (Kibrik 2001: 762)

(76) mē   w=ič'a-ss
      you   M=die-POT-FUT
      (What happens if I eat these mushrooms?)
      'You will die.' (Tatevosov and Majsak 2001: 275)

Other simple forms are non-indicative moods: the imperative (77), prohibitive (78), optative and negative optative (79), and irrealis (80). Examples (77–80) illustrate the use of non-indicative forms in independent clauses.

(77) du-ba   b=ī-r-ō=b   boL'ara=b   istorija   b=as-ā
      you.OBL-AFF   N-know-IPF-PTCP-N   any-N   story   N-tell-POT.IMP
      'Tell any story you know.' (Kibrik 2001: 760)

(78) bišdi-r   he=b=ʕagila   b=asimi-sse-X-ō
      you-ERG   what-N-UQ   N-tell-PRH-PRT-M
      'Please, don't tell everything.' (Kibrik 2001: 820)

(79) q'oč-a-nā,   w=e-be-la,   q'očan-č'i-rā
      want-POT-COND   M-come-IMP-OPT   want-NEG-COND
      w=ēbi-sse-la,   o=b   o-ššu=b   iš   ek'_wa
      M-come-PRH-OPT   this-N   this-OBL.M-GEN.N   matter   COP.PRS
      'Let him come if he wants to, let him not come if he doesn't want
      to—it is up to him.' (Dobrušina 2001a: 327)

The meaning of the irrealis in main clauses is very close to that of the optative,
but irrealis expresses counterfactual wishes:

(80) eheli   di-č'   tup   b=isan-Ralir!
      today   I.OBL-CNT   gun   N-find-IRR
      'If only I had a gun today!' (uttered in the situation when the speaker
      did not have a gun at hand) (Dobrušina 2001a: 333)

The periphrastic forms in Bagwalal are formed with the auxiliary verb
b=uk'ass 'be' or with the copula *ek'_wa*. The auxiliary verb has two simple
forms, *b=uk'a* in the preterite and *b=uk'ass* in the future. The reference to the
moment of speech is performed by the copula *ek'_wa*; unlike the verb 'be', it has
no position for class/number marker.

The verb has several nonfinite derivatives: four converbs (preterite, imperfective, future, and prospective), two infinitives (potential and imperfective),
and three participles (preterite, imperfective, and future). Each nonfinite
form has a negative correlate. All but two infinitives participate in the formation of the periphrastic constructions, combining either with the forms of
the verb 'be' or with the copula. Table 7.3 shows all periphrastic forms of the
verb *hec'i* 'say, talk' involving the present tense copula; periphrastic formations with the preterite and future forms of the auxiliary are derived in a
similar way.

The auxiliary can take a periphrastic form too:

(81) eb-eb   han   eb-eb   tuXum-ła-ss   Xindi   sani-li=b=o
      self-self   village self-self   clan-LOC-EL   from   together-VRB-N-CVB
      b=uk'a=b=o   ek'_wa
      N-be-N-CVB   COP.PRS
      'Each village emerged when each clan had gathered (= each village
      emerged from having gathered each clan).' (Kibrik 2001: 727)

TABLE 7.3. Periphrastic verbal forms in Bagwalal

Nonfinite form		Corresponding finite form	
Past converb	*hec'i=b=o*	Perfect ('has said')	*hec'i=b=o ek'_wa*
Past participle	*hec'u=b*	Resultative ('is said')	*hec'u=b ek'_wa*
Imperfective converb	*hec'i-rō-X*	Present progressive ('is saying')	*hec'i-rā-X ek'_wa*
Future participle	*hec'-ā-ł-o=b*	Periphrastic Future ('will say')	*hec'-ā-ł-o=b ek'_wa*
Future converb	*hec'-ā-łi-X*	Intention ('is intended to say')	*hec'-ā-łi-X ek'_wa*
Prospective converb	*hec'-ā-di(=b=o)*	Prospective ('is going to say')	*hec'-ā-di(=b=o) ek'_wa*

In (81), the complex periphrastic form consists of the periphrastic perfect of the auxiliary verb *b=uk'ass* 'be' and the converb of the lexical verb.

As has been mentioned above, Bagwalal makes use of serial verb constructions where two simple finite forms are juxtaposed. In (82), the two juxtaposed forms are the preterites *eta* 'flew' and *bā* 'came.'

(82)   samalot   eta   b=ā
       plane   fly   N-come
       'The plane has arrived.' (Tatevosov 2001: 121)

Serial verbs show prominent dissimilarities to periphrastic verb constructions: first and foremost, semi-auxiliaries, unlike true auxiliaries and predicative particles, cannot be shifted to mark focus (see section 7.2.4.2).

Nonfinite derivatives. In Bagwalal there are two infinitives, which are termed the 'potential infinitive' and 'imperfective infinitive' in Kibrik (2001).

The imperfective infinitive is not used in main clauses. The potential infinitive can be used in independent clauses accompanied by predicative particles. These forms have the hortative meaning (a command addressed to the first person):

(83)   wela-X   hatu=b=łli-r   haš'aX   j=uk'-ā-Ra
       let.me-PRT   small-N-OBL-ERG   down   F-be-POT.INF-PRT
       'Let me sit for a while.' (lit. 'to be down') (Dobrušina 2001a: 332)

In dependent clauses, both infinitives head complements of modal and aspectual verbs. The majority of verbs take either the imperfective infinitive or the potential infinitive. For example, the verb 'begin, start' takes the imperfective infinitive only:

(84) ima   hur   Xabē-ra   aša
      father.ABS [wood cut-IPF.INF] start
      'Father started cutting wood.' (Kalinina 2001a: 515)

On the contrary, modal and desiderative verbs take the potential infinitive only:

(85) jaš-ła   behr-ō=b   jass   s'e-li-r-a-ł
      girl-OBL.DAT be.possible.IPF-PTCP-N [sister guest-VRB-MSD-OBL-GEN
      j=ah-ā
      F-take-POT.INF]
      'The girl can take her sister on a visit.' (lit. 'to be a guest') (Kalinina
      2001a: 515)

Participles (preterite and imperfective) can function as main clause predicates
on their own. In this case, imperfective participles express the habitual meaning:

(86) o-rā   heL'i-r-ō=b   wahabija-di
      this-OBL.HPL.SUP.LAT say-IPF-PTCP-N   Wahabit-PL
      'People call them Wahabits.' (lit. 'they say to them "wahabit"')
      (Kibrik 2001: 756)

Imperfective participles also head clauses containing generic statements:

(87) łē:hā=w-išš_wa   łē: iči-č'-u=b
      irrigate-PTCP.M-OBL.M.DAT   water.N give-NEG-PTCP-N
      'Those who had irrigated (their cornfields) cannot get (extra) water.'
      (lit. 'To those who had irrigated, water is not given.') (Kibrik 2001: 806)

Preterite participles refer to the well-known facts; for example, speakers resort
to independent preterite participles to retell some episodes of ethnic history:

(88) iłi=b   Soloq-abi   weč'-u=b-la   b=ija=b=o,
      [we.INCL-GEN.N young.man-PL   COP.NEG-PTCP-N]-and N-know-N-CVB
      č'ihi   k'anc'ur-u=ba
      upon   spring-PTCP-HPL
      'Knowing that our people are not there, they attacked (= sprang upon)
      us.' (Kibrik 2001: 738)

Independent preterite participles in combination with various particles also
occur in statements actualizing background knowledge known to both interlocutors and introducing it into the universe of discourse.

(89) ūšš-i-la-ss   Xindi b=ułu=ba-Rabi   iłi
      earth-OBL-SUP-EL   from   HPL-become-PTCP.HPL-PRT   we
      'We were made of earth (by Allah), you know.' (Kibrik 2001: 745)

For any Muslim, it is part of the common background that Allah made people of earth. Citing this fact in discourse, the speaker does not intend to inform the hearer of anything new. Instead, he or she says this to support statements with some common knowledge.

Finally, participles are main clause predicates in constituent questions:

(90) du-ba   lek'i   burik   han-č'i-le-di,
      you.OBL-AFF Avar.guy   Burik   see-NEG-Q-CIT
      di-ba   o=w   hešta-jī-Rala   w=is-an-ł-o=w ?
      I.OBL-AFF   this-M   how-Q-PRT   M-find-POT-FUT-PTCP-M
      'Have you seen this Avar guy Burik? How can I find him?'
      (Kibrik 2001: 748)

As expected, participles can head relative clauses. Relative clauses headed by participles tend to be restrictive. This can be best seen in examples where restrictive relative clauses refer to proper names. The proper name is a sufficient identifier on its own, so as a rule a further restriction is unnecessary. In example (91), where a proper name is modified by a restrictive relative clause, the resulting interpretation is that there were two girls called Patimat. In this case, the speaker is identifying the Patimat he is talking about by appealing to the fact that she found the ring on the road. This fact is supposed to be known to the hearer.

(91) miq'-a-la   hinc'ašul b=isã=j   pat'imat-i-r   o=b
      road-OBL-SUP ring   N-find-PTCP.F Patimat-OBL-ERG this-N
      b=aXa iči
      N-back give
      '(Of two girls named Patimat,) the Patimat who found a ring on the road gave it back.' (Ljutikova 2001: 508)

When the speaker needs to apply a property (expressed by a clause) such that this property is new information for the hearer, he or she uses an adverbial clause:

(92) miq'-a-la   hinc'ašul b=isa-m=o   pat'imat-i-r   o=b
      road-OBL-SUP ring   N-find-N-CVB   Patimat-OBL-ERG this-N
      b=aXa iči
      N-back give
      'Patimat, who found a ring on the road, gave it back.' (lit. 'Having found the ring on the road, Patimat gave it back')
      (Ljutikova 2001: 508)[26]

---

[26] In Bagwalal there is also a special restrictive particle =b=el that can be attached to all types of modifier in a noun phrase, except for verbal modifiers:

(iii) den   hac'a=b=el   b=išširi   gur
       I.ERG   white=N=RESTR   N=choose   shirt
       'I have chosen the white shirt'. (Daragan and Majsak 2001: 175)

Finally, participles head the complements of factive verbs (see example 88) with the matrix verb 'know.' In (93) the participle heads the complement of the verb 'finish' (the other option would be to use the verbal noun). An infinitive is unacceptable here.

(93) de w=ā-la   saʕit-i-r   t'ama gird-ō=b /
      I   M-come.POT-because said-OBL-ERG   roof   roll-CAUS.PTCP-N /
      *gird-ā-la   b=iR-ē
      *roll-POT-CAUS.INF   N-stop-CAUS
      'Because I came, Said stopped rolling the roof.' (Kalinina 2001a: 522)

Bagwalal deverbal nouns, or masdars, are used as predicates in exclamative sentences. They do not inflect for tense or any other finite category.

(94) di-ha   ongiri ek'ʷa=b   č'alʕa-n!
      I-OBL.DAT   here   be-PTCP.N   feed.up-MSD
      'How fed up I am with all that here!' (Kalinina 2001b: 427)

In dependent clauses, verbal nouns along with participles are complements of factive verbs.

(95) ʕali-r   bišał c'aXi-n /*c'aX-ā   e=b-da   b=eta
      Ali-ERG   ram   look.for-MSD/*look.for-POT.INF   self-N-EMPH   N-leave
      'Ali gave up (= left as is) looking for the (lost) ram.'

Besides factive complements, masdars head manner complements (about manner complements see Comrie and Thompson 1985; Koptjevskaja-Tamm 1993a).

(96) ʕali-la   q'oč-in-ō=b   ima-ššu=b   keč'   b=ihi-r
      Ali-DAT   like-IPF-PTCP-N   [father-OBL.M-GEN.N   song   N-take-MSD]
      'Ali likes (his) father's singing.' (Kalinina 2001a: 525)

Perhaps the 'manner' semantics of the verbal noun in Bagwalal underlies its use with non-factive verbs when the speaker's attention is centred on the way the action is performed:

(97) di=b   o=b bažēri-r   telewizar-łi   ahē-nā-X
      [I.OBL-GEN.N   this-N be.able-MSD]   television-INTER   show-IPF-CVB
      ek'ʷa
      COP.PRS
      'They are showing on TV how I could do that.' (Kalinina 2001a: 527)

So, Bagwalal consistently marks restrictive noun modifiers either by means of the relative clause construction or by specialized particles.

Like other languages of the group, Bagwalal has two types of converb: simple converbs and specialized converbs. The former have generalized meanings (perfective, imperfective, future, prospective, or intentional) and are used to build periphrastic forms. The latter have a specialized marker showing the exact nature of the semantic relationship between the two clauses in a complex sentence.[27] These are temporal converbs, conditional converbs, causal converbs, and so on. Specialized converbs are predicates of adjunct clauses. Example (98) shows an adjunct clause with the causal converb:

(98) aram-di   kutakila b=iXXi=r=o   b=uk'=ur... din
      person-PL very   HPL-be.pleased-HPL-CVB HPL-be-HPL religion
      b=ešta   b=et-a-la
      N-set.free N-leave-POT-CSL
      'People became pleased because they were allowed to practise their
      religion.' (Kibrik 2001: 754)

Simple converbs head non-factive complement clauses: complements of perception verbs (example 99) and propositional attitude verbs (100). In the latter case the copula slot is occupied by a complementizer:

(99) hā-m=o   ek'ʷa o-ru-ba   b=ełił-ā-X   ujsini poezd /
      see-N-CVB AUX   this-OBL.PL-AFF   N-come-IPF-CVB there train /
      *b=ełō=b   poezd
      N-come-PTCP.N   train
      'They saw a train come.' (Kibrik 2001: 792)

(100) o-ššu-r   heL'i di-lā   "tallah b=eta
      this-OBL.M-ERG   say   I.OBL-SUP.LAT   swear   N-think
      b=uk'a-Rala   mašina heraX b=ełi-łā-X-la"
      N-be-PRT   car   back   N-go-IPF-CVB-and
      'My word, I thought that the car was going backwards.'
      (Kibrik 2001: 764)

Finally, simple converbs are used when the speaker characterizes the entity with a certain property, and this characterization represents new information for the hearer. These adjunct constructions are the functional counterparts of non-restrictive relative clauses because true participial relative clauses in Bagwalal are normally presupposed and restrictive:

---

[27] This distinction is similar to that in Dargwa and to the opposition of contextual vs. specialized converbs in Nedjalkov (1995).

(101) hā=m=o   ek'ʷa   o-ru-ba
       see-N-CVB   COP.PRS   this-OBL.HPL-AFF
       b=eɬi-ɬā-X   uj-ssini   čiraq-abi-la   r=uka=m=o   poezd
       [N-come-IPF-CVB there-TRANS light-PL-and NPL-burn-N-CVB train]
       'They saw a coming train with burning lights.' (Kibrik 2001: 792)

7.3.3.5 *Bagwalal: generalizations*   As in Dargwa, in Bagwalal only a few forms show a direct correlation with functional clause types: imperatives and prohibitives are used in the main clause of command; optative and irrealis are used as in the main clause expressing a wish; specialized converbs are used as heads of adjunct clauses (each converb is reserved for a certain semantic type); and simple preterite and future forms are used in main clauses of declarative sentences.

Declarative and interrogative sentences can be headed by indicative forms (simple and periphrastic), non-indicative modalities (admirative), and verbal derivatives (participles). Interrogatives adhere to the same predicate types as declarative sentences, but they are additionally marked by an interrogative particle (examples 62, 63, 64, and 65). Only indicative forms (simple and periphrastic) are allowed in argument-focus constructions. In some cases, especially in interrogative sentences, participles appear when the main predicate is not within the focus domain. Main clauses of exclamative sentences are headed by masdars (verbal nouns). Main clauses of commands addressed to the first person have infinitival predicates accompanied by particles.

Relative clauses in Bagwalal are typically restrictive and headed by a participle. Normally they do not modify personal names and nouns that denote unique objects.

The strategies of complement clause formation in Bagwalal are similar to those in Dargwa. Speech verbs and propositional attitude verbs require their complement to have a complementizer head (the 'finite' strategy). The standard indirect speech complementizer is -*di*, though it can be accompanied by several other particles:

(102) čo-Rala   tak   mala-di,   heL'i
       what(*Russian*)-PRT so(*Russian*) little(*Russian*)-CIT say.PRET
       gaʔišnik-ššu-r
       traffic.warden-OBL.M-ERG
       ' "Why (are you giving me) so little (money)?"—said the traffic warden.'[28]
       (Kibrik 2001: 775)

---

[28] This example is taken from a narrative; in the story the traffic warden spoke Russian. The narrator renders the Russian quotation in accordance with the Bagwalal pattern of indirect speech marking.

In most cases, clausal complements do not require complementizers and are headed by a verbal derivative (simple converbs for perception verbs, full participles and masdars for factive verbs, and infinitives for implicative and modal verbs). These strategies have been illustrated by examples (99) for the converb, (95) and (96) for the masdar, (88) for the participle, and (84) and (85) for the infinitive.

So, matrix verbs allow several types of complement clause formation:

'say'	finite form + complementizer	'want'	potential infinitive
'know'	masdar; participle	'see'	converb
'begin'	imperfective infinitive	'be able'	potential infinitive
'finish'	participle; masdar	'think'	finite form; converb + complementizer
'fear'	finite form + complementizer; potential infinitive		

As in Dargwa, the subordination strategy is a lexical property of any complement-taking verb. Generally, we observe the following tendencies in Bagwalal:

(1) Participles are most often used with the verb *b=ija* 'know.'

(2) Masdars tend to head clauses expressing situations known to both participants of the conversation and viewed as facts. For example, masdars are another strategy used with the verb *b=ija* 'know'. They can be selected by other factive verbs denoting mental activities like *rak'ʷaɫi ek'ʷa* 'remember (a fact)', *b=oža* 'believe, trust'; predicates expressing estimates such as *hō=b ahan ek'ʷa* 'good' or *eč'u=b ahan ek'ʷa* 'bad', and the factive aspectual verb *biRē* 'finish'. Masdars also head manner clauses with the verbs *q'oča* 'like' and *ahE:* 'show'.

(3) Infinitive clauses are selected by modal predicates (*bažeri* 'be able'; *b=uku* 'be necessary'; *q'oča* 'want'; *behiri* 'allow, be possible'), implicative predicates (*maɫi* 'teach'), and by the aspectual verb *ašša* 'begin'. The content of these clausal complements is often new to the addressee.

(4) Converbs are used with the perception verbs *hã:* 'see' and *ahã:* 'hear'. Converbal dependent clauses in this syntactic context are very close to independent predications.

Clausal adjuncts include counterfactual conditional clauses headed by irrealis forms, causal, conditional, and temporal clauses headed by specialized converbs, and purpose clauses headed by the potential infinitive. Besides, adjunct clauses headed by simple converbs can have a temporal or a causal meaning.

Table 7.4 shows that there is no direct correlation between verbal forms and clause types. Starting with all possible types of syntactic predicate

TABLE 7.4. Bagwalal: predicate structure and clause type

Verbal form	Bare form, no predicative particles	Form with an enclitic predicative particle	Predicative particle shifted away
Serial verb	Main clause (declarative/ interrogative: predicate-focus)		
Simple form	Main clause (declarative/ interrogative: predicate or sentence-focus; non-declarative)		Main clause (non-future declarative/ interrogative: argument-focus; non-future declarative: sentence-focus)
Simple converb	Argument clause (non-factive perception verbs) adjunct (time, cause) adjunct corresponding to non-restrictive relative clauses	Main clause (declarative/ interrogative: predicate or sentence-focus)	
Participle	Argument clause ('know') Relative clause (restrictive) Main clause (habitual/ generic/facts)		Main clause (future declarative/ interrogative: argument-focus; non-future interrogative: argument-focus)
Masdar	Argument clause (factive, manner) Main clause (exclamative)		
Infinitive	Argument clause (implicative verbs, modal verbs, phase verbs)	Main clause (propositive, hortative)	

(clause head), we can distinguish three formal predicate types: (i) simple (finite) verbal forms; (ii) verbal derivatives; (iii) predicative particles. These types show a neat correlation with the illocutionary force (declarative/

interrogative vs. rest), on the one hand and the status of the clause in the information structure of the whole sentence (presupposition/assertion) on the other.

Predicative particles can only head main clauses of declarative and interrogative sentences. This is the only predicate type that allows focus to be placed on any constituent other than the predicate. In the argument-focus structures, predicative particles are separated from the lexical verb and placed next to the focused phrase. Predicative particles can be combined with different verbal forms (simple converbs, full participles, or infinitives) as well as with nouns, attributes, and adverbials. In argument-focus and sentence-focus structures, the lexical verb usually retains the same form it has in the periphrastic construction: the focus position is marked by simply shifting the particle next to the focused constituent in argument-focus constructions, or in the position between the subject and the predicate in sentence-focus constructions. Only simple future forms are unacceptable in argument-focus constructions and constituent questions—in these cases the verb is obligatorily turned into a participle. When multiple focus-marking particles co-occur in the same sentence, the markers of the 'illocutionary group' get priority in focus marking over the 'polarity group'.

Simple 'finite' forms also head only main clauses. They are compatible with different sentence types (different illocutionary forces) according to their modal semantics (indicative, imperative, or optative). Unlike Dargwa, simple indicative forms can be used in argument-focus structures and in constituent questions.

Most nonfinite forms head both dependent and independent clauses. Deverbal action nominals are used as heads of independent exclamative sentences. Full participles, simple converbs, and infinitives combine with predicative particles and function as predicates of independent declarative and interrogative clauses. Participles can function as the only predicate in habitual/generic statements and in sentences referring to well-known facts; in actualizing statements, participles are accompanied by various predicative particles of the epistemic group. Participles are also used as heads of (restrictive) relative clauses and heads of argument clauses selected by the verb 'know'. Simple converbs, when used in dependent clauses, head adjunct clauses of time and cause, adjunct clauses analogous to non-restrictive relative clauses, and, very frequently, non-factive complement clauses. Infinitives head complements of aspectual, modal, and implicative verbs; in main clauses, infinitives are used in 1st-person commands (hortative and propositive) accompanied by modal particles.

7.3.4 *Verbal forms in Tsakhur*

7.3.4.1 *The verbal system: general*   The Tsakhur verbal system has three simple indicative forms that can be used as independent clause predicates: aorist, present, and potentialis (103a, b, and c respectively; Tatevosov 1999: 86).

(103)   a.   maIhammad   qik'u
             Mohammed   M.die.AOR
             'Mohammed died.'

        b.   maIhammad   qek'a
             Mohammed   M.die.PRS
             'Mohammed is dying.'

        c.   maIhammad   qik'a-s
             Mohammed   M.die-POT
             'Mohammed will die.'

Each of the three indicative forms can combine with the focus marker *wo=b* and the auxiliary verb *yxes* 'be'. All possible combinations for the verb *āqas* 'open' are listed in Table 7.5 (after Kibrik 1999: 87). Each combination expresses a certain tense/aspect/mood meaning which is different from the meaning of the simple form. For instance, the simple aorist is used to describe the past situation as a whole, without emphasizing its internal structure. The combination of the simple form with the copula can be labelled 'perfect': it expresses an action whose result is relevant in the present.

Apart from indicative forms, there is a series of irrealis forms (irrealis proper, conditional, counterfactual imperative, and counterfactual optative) and a series of imperative forms (imperative, prohibitive, jussive, and optative).

7.3.4.2 *Focus marking and predicative particles*   In Tsakhur, there is a specialized focus marker, the copula *wo=b*. It marks predicate-focus and argument-focus in declarative and interrogative clauses. The focus marker occurs with both verbal and nominal predicates: in (104) the first part of the

TABLE 7.5.   Periphrastic forms in Tsakhur

	focus marker (*wo=b*)	'be': aorist (*yxa*)	'be': present (*ejxe*)	'be': potentialis (*yxes*)
Past	*āqy wo=b*	*āqy yxa*	*āqy ejxe*	*āqy yxes*
Present	*āqa wo=b*	*āqa yxa*	*āqa ejxe*	*āqa yxes*
Potentialis	*āqas-o=b*	*āqas yxa*	*āqas ejxe*	*āqas yxes*

sentence is a nominal predicate sentence, while the predicate of the other one is the verb. The copula marking focus is present in both.

(104) zy   lap   d̦oles-na   wo=r,   za-s   jāluR   wo=b
       I   very close-ATR   FOC-M   I.OBL-DAT headscarf FOC-N1
       qa.b.y
       N1.bring.PF
       (in the context of how presents are distributed at a wedding party)
       'I am a very close (relative), (but) I got only a headscarf.'
       (Kibrik 1999: 824)

In spontaneous spoken texts the focus marker most frequently occurs after the verb, in sentence-final position or right in front of the verb, after the direct object. In argument-focus sentences the marker is located next to the focused noun phrase, while the main verb retains its form:

(105) a. aIli   a.r.y   wo=r
          Ali.ABS   M.come.PF   COP=M
          'Ali came.'

       b. aIli   wo=r   a=r=y
          Ali.ABS   COP-M M-come-PF
          'It was Ali who came.' (Kazenin 1999b: 583)

All forms of the verb *ixes* 'be' can also be used to mark focus (example 106 illustrates the perfective form of *ixes* 'be'):

(106) a. dakk-i-s   maIhamad   Gadž-es   ykkan   yxa
          father-OBL-DAT   Mohammed   see-POT   M.want.IPF M.be.PF
          'Father wanted to see Mohammed.' (Kazenin 1999: 584)

       b. dakk-i-s   maIhamad   yxa   Gadž-es   ykkan
          father-OBL-DAT   Mohammed   M.be.PF   see-POT   M.want.IPF
          'Father wanted to see *Mohammed*.' (Kazenin 1999b: 584)

Focus is also marked by the negative copula *deš*, the epistemic particles *-jī* (example 107) and *-nī*, the question particles and the habitual marker *-xe* (example 108).

(107) a. aIl-ē   Xaw   alaʔ-a-jī
          Ali-ERG   house   N2.build-IPF-EM1
          'Ali is building a house.'

       b. aIl-ē   Xaw-jī   alaʔ-a
          Ali-ERG   house-EM1 N2.build-IPF
          'Ali is building a *house*.' (Kazenin 1999b: 586)

(108) a. aⅠl-ē   dakk-i-s   kumag haʔ-a-n-xe
          Ali-ERG   father-OBL-DAT   help   N2.make-IPF-ATTR-HAB
          'Ali used to help his father.'

       b. aⅠl-ē   dakk-i-s-xe   kumag haʔ-a-n
          Ali-ERG   father-OBL-DAT-HAB help   N2.make-IPF-ATTR
          'Ali used to help his *father.*' (Kazenin 1999b: 586)

In Tsakhur there is a special strategy for marking sentence-focus. As shown in Kalinina and Toldova (1999), the main predicate in thetic (sentence-focus) constructions is normally expressed by an attributive form (see 7.2.1). The attributive marker agrees in class and number with the absolutive argument of the clause. In example (109), the attributive form *qadīmmy* 'brought' has a nominal plural marker:

(109) i-ni   zaIʔf-ē,   haše-ni   magazin-ē nⱼaIXu=d=ē,
       this-AOBL   woman-ERG   that-AOBL   shop-IN   how-NPL-Q
       hamaIXu=d   t'ufli-by   qa.d.īm-my
       thus-NPL   shoe-PL   NPL.bring.PF.ATR-PL
       'The woman brought the shoes the way she did in that shop.'
       (Kibrik 1999: 790)

The attributive form as the marker of a sentence-focus structure is incompatible with the copula, which marks predicate-focus or argument-focus.[29]

(110) *i-ni   zaIʔf-ē   t'ufli-by qa.d.īm-my   wo=d
       this-AOBL   woman-ERG   shoe-PL   NPL.bring.PF.ATR-PL FOC-NPL
       'This woman brought the shoes.'

---

[29] For semantic reasons, the attributive form is incompatible with one of the so-called epistemic particles, namely -*jī*:

(iv)   *k'umk'um   qōx_war-in-ī
        cauldron   N2.boil-A.N2-EM1
        'The cauldron has boiled.' (Kalinina and Toldova 1999: 398)

Another particle, -*nī*, can crop up in sentences with attributive predicates:

(v)   gojne   dars-y-l-qa   aⅠhā-nGaI,   hamanke=r   jic'y-ni
       then   lesson.OBL-SUP-ALL   go.IPF-TEMP   then=COH.M   ten-AOBL
       minut-y-s   gedž-x-e-na-nī-xe
       minute-OBL-DAT   late-M.BE-IPF-ATR-EM2-HAB
       'Then, each time he went to a lesson, he was ten minutes late.' (Kibrik 1999: 779)

In Tatevosov and Majsak (1999a) the semantics of the particle -*jī* is described as the epistemic modal frame: 'I have just learnt P' (mirative). The particle -*nī* marks propositions that are part of the speaker's knowledge about the past. The latter meaning is compatible with the meaning of the attributive forms: they are often used to highlight facts.

Besides, the attributive form cannot be used to answer constituent questions: the answers to these questions again presume a different focus type (argument-focus or predicate-focus):

(111)   a. haššu-je   hek'$_w$-a?
          who-Q   M.sing-IPF
          'Who is singing?'

        b. alī   wo=r   hek'$_w$-a   / *alī   hek'$_w$-a-na
           Ali   FOC-M   M.sing-IPF   Ali   M.sing-IPF-ATR
           'Ali is singing.' (Kalinina and Toldova 1999: 407)

Question words and question particles cannot co-occur with the focus copula (neither positive nor negative) and with epistemic particles.

(112)   alī   a.r.y-ne?
        Ali.1   M.come.PF-Q2
        'Has Ali come?' (Kazenin 1999a: 452)

(113)   *gade-b-iš-e   čopp-ā-r   aʔ-u   wo=d-ne?
         boy-PL-OBLPL-ERG   lot-PL-NOMPL   NPL.cast-PF   FOC-NPL-Q2
         'Did the boys cast lots?' (Kazenin 1999a: 453)

(114)   all-ē   hidžō-ne   haʔ-as?
        Ali-ERG   what.N2-Q2   N2.do-POT
        'What will Ali do?' (Kazenin 1999a: 453)

(115)   *šawa-ne   čopp-ā-r   aʔ-u-nī?
         who.ERG-Q2   lot-PL-ABS.PL   NPL.cast-PF-EM2
         'Who cast lots?' (Kazenin 1999a: 453)

In (113), the focus copula combines with the question particle -*ne*, which makes the sentence ungrammatical; in (114) the same particle attaches to the question word *hidžō* 'what.N2' without producing a dispreferred combination.

   In questions the verb does not take the attributive form. However, attributive forms are possible in interrogative expressions with the question particle -*ne*. In questions with the particle -*jē*, attributive forms of the predicate are ungrammatical. This distribution of verbal forms and question particles follows the concurrence pattern of epistemic particles with the attributive predicate form (this pattern is determined semantically: see footnote 29 above).

(116)   a. gade-b-iš-ē   čopp-ā-r   aʔ-u-ne / aʔ-im-my-ne?
           boy-PL-OBLPL-ERG   lot-PL-NOMPL   NPL.cast-PF-Q2 / NPL.cast.PF-ATR-PL-Q2

        b. gade-b-iš-ē   čopp-ā-r   aʔ-u-jē /*aʔ-im-my-jē?
           boy-PL-OBLPL-ERG   lot-PL-NOMPL   NPL.cast-PF-Q1 / NPL.cast.PF-ATR-PL-Q1
           'Did the boys cast lots?' (Kazenin 1999a: 454)

7.3.4.3 *Nominal predicate clause*   Example (104), repeated here as (117), shows
that in nominal-predicate sentences focus is marked in the same way as in
verbal-predicate sentences:

(117) zy lap dⱼoles-na wo=r, za-s   jāluR   wo=b qa.b.y
       I very close-ATR FOC-M I.OBL-DAT headscarf FOC-N1 N1.bring.PF
       (in the context of how presents are distributed at a wedding party)
       'I am a very close (relative), (but) I got only a headscarf.'
       (Kibrik 1999: 824)

In nominal predicate clauses the copula, too, can be replaced by epistemic
particles (example 118); it is also dropped in constituent questions (119).

(118) t'āhir   jug-na   maIʔalim-nī/-jī
       Tahir   good-ATR   teacher-EM2/-EM1
       'Tahir was a good teacher.'
       (Kalinina 1999: 436)

(119) hammaz-ā-r=yb   nⱼaIX=b=um-my-ne ?
       friend-PL-NOMPL-COH.HPL   what-HPL-ATR-PL-Q2
       'What (were) (his) friends (like)?'
       (Kalinina 1999: 783)

So, in Tsakhur, nominal predicates do not require an obligatory copula for
tense/aspect/mood marking. Rather, the priority is the expression of illocutionary force. This is done by the standard array of elements marking
illocutionary force: the focus marker, the epistemic particles, the question
particles, and the question words.

Nominal-predicate sentences illustrate that, unlike lexical verbs, auxiliaries
and all other predicative particles are subject to word-order restrictions: they
cannot be freely scrambled with the nominal predicate. The predicate noun
phrase with predicative particles attached to it normally follows the subject:

(120) a. urudž   čoban-o=r
          Orudge.M   shepherd-FOC-M
          'Orudge is the shepherd.' //*'It is Orudge who is the shepherd.'

       b. urudž-o=r   čoban
          Orudge.M-FOC-M   shepherd
          *'Orudge is the shepherd.' // 'It is Orudge who is the shepherd.'

Example (121) shows that what is impossible for predicative particles is quite
normal for verbs: the auxiliary verb *yxana* 'was' stands in front of the
predicate noun phrase:

(121) ma-m-mi-š-di   arajl_j   yxa-na   sa... č'or-un
       this.H-A-PL-OBLPL-AOBL   among   M.be.PF-ATR   one   red-ATR
       č'aIr-na-na... insan
       hair-with-ATR   man.M
       'There was one red-haired man among them.' (Kibrik 1999: 798)

7.3.4.4 *Basic functions of the verbal forms*

Indicative forms. The aorist describes the event as a whole without any reference to its internal temporal structure. The present denotes situations simultaneous with the moment of speech, habitual situations, and planned future events. The present and aorist can function both as converbs and main clause predicates. Example (122) shows the aorist form in both functions: the dependent clause is embedded in the main clause, as is clearly demonstrated by the word order, but the form of the predicate does not show embedding: both main and dependent clause predicates are identical in form.

(122) fāt'imat, eminat-ē   hama-n   džuwab iwho,   č'aIraqīxa
       Fatimat Aminat-ERG this-ATR word   say.PF red.become.F.PF
       'Fatimat went red when Aminat said this word.' (Testelec 1999: 335–6)

Simple forms (present and aorist) also function as predicates in non-restrictive relative clauses:

(123) taXč-ej-l_j   gi.t'.k'yn   Gelilim-my wo=d   yxa
       shelf-OBL-SUP NPL.lay.out.PF shoes-PL   FOC-NPL NPL.become.PF
       magazin-ē
       shop-in
       'The shoes in the shop were laid out on a shelf.' (Kibrik 1999: 785)

In (123) the position of the prenominal modifier is occupied by a simple verbal form; in restrictive relative clauses, the attributive form is placed in the same slot (cf. example 140b).

Simple forms can function in complement clauses; nearly all matrix verbs allow the 'finite' strategy of this kind. Example (124) illustrates the matrix verb 'begin.'

(124) i-ni   pyl-y-l_j   alla   gi.b.Ryl   wo=b
       this-AOBL money-OBL-SUP because.of HPL.start.PF FOC-HPL
       i-ni   zaI?fa-j-s   indžikiwalla   hōl-e
       this-AOBL woman-OBL-DAT disturbance.N1   N1.give-IPF
       'They started to disturb this woman because of this money.'
       (Kibrik 1999: 786)

The potentialis form refers to the future, but sometimes it can have past tense reference denoting the epistemic estimate of the past situation:

(125) g$_j$oRī   g$_j$oR-as
rain.N2   N2.rain-POT
'It will rain.' // 'It must have rained.' (Tatevosov and Majsak 1999a: 251)

Besides, the potentialis can express the hortative meaning (the speaker tries to encourage the hearer to commit a joint action):

(126) aIlh-ās   Xā-qa!
go-POT   home-ALL
'Let's go home.' (Dobrušina 1999a: 285)

In dependent clauses the potentialis is used in the functions typical of the European infinitive, namely in purpose clauses (example 127), and in sentential complements of modal verbs (128), aspectual matrix verbs, and verbs expressing desire or intention (129):

(127) dak$_j$,   zy   qikk-e   qaI.t.q-as,   za-ss-e   aIX-as-yn
father I   M.take-IMP   N2.study-POT   I.OBL-AD-EL   N2.be.able-POT-ATR
'Father, take me (to town) to study, I can (study).' (Kibrik 1999: 778)

(128) Xiw-ni,   rajon-ni   toXtur-ā-ši-ss-e   hičču=d
village-AOBL   district-AOBL   doctor-PL-OBLPL-AD-EL   what.N2-COH.N2
ha?-as   d$_j$-aIX-a
N2.make-POT   NEG-N2.be.able-IPF
'Neither village doctors nor doctors in the regional hospital could do anything.' (Kibrik 1999: 776)

(129) sa.w.ales   w=ukkan   sa   džig-ē-qa
HPL.gather.POT   HPL-have.to.IPF   one   place-IN-ALL
'(We) have to gather in one place.' (Kibrik 1999: 797)

Non-indicative forms. Conditional forms are used in the protasis of conditional constructions:

(130) še-na   sa.r.k'yl-ē   zy   džu-s   baryš   ha?-i
that-ATR   M.come.back.PF-COND2   I   self-DAT   forgiveness   N2.make-IRR
'If he came back, I would forgive him.' (Dobrušina 1999b: 262)

Irrealis is used in the apodosis of irreal and counterfactual conditional constructions.

(131) šenke   zy   dawat-by   h.id$_j$.a?-im-my-xi   haIšde
then   I   wedding-PL   NEG.make-ATR-PL-CONJ   now

za-qa=b ušaR-ār d_j-ōx-i
I.OBL-POSS=HPL child-PL NEG-be-IRR
'If I had not got married then I would not have had children now.'
(Dobrušina 1999b: 263)

All forms of the imperative series (imperative, prohibitive, jussive, and optative) are used as main-clause predicates only:

(132) ac'a-xa-j-l-e qīRa hama-na balkan=yb
M.know-M.be.PF-MSD-SUP-EL after this-ATR horse.N1-COH.N1
džu-s w=ux-e-dže
self.OBL.M-DAT N1-be-IMP-JUSS
'After I see him, let this horse be his.' (Kibrik 1999: 798)

(133) saR=ra ix-e-na Ru, aj leonid maI?allim
healthy-ADV.M M.be-IMP-OPT you.M wow Leonid teacher
'Teacher Leonid, we wish you well.' (Kibrik 1999: 772)

Counterfactual imperative and counterfactual jussive are used in independent clauses expressing unrealized wishes:

(134) ali.w.š-i sa dawar
N1.buy-IRR one ram.N1
'You should have bought a ram.' (Dobrušina 1999b: 266)
(counterfactual imperative)

Attributive forms. Attributive forms in Tsakhur are quite common as main-clause predicates. In (135), the predicate of the embedded adjunct clause is the simple aorist form, while the position of the main-clause predicate is occupied by an attributive form:

(135) rasul eminat-ē ma-n džuwab iwho a.r.k'yn-na
Rasul Aminat-ERG this-ATR word say.PF M.leave.PF-ATR
'Rasul left because Aminat said this word.'
(Kibrik 1999: 335)

Attributive forms as main-clause predicates are quite frequent with 1st person subjects:

(136) zy mat-xa-na hama-n-Gu-ni
I be.amazed-M.become.PF-ATR this.M-ATR-OBL.M-AOBL
ek'wal-i-l-e
courage-OBL-SUP-EL
'I am amazed how brave he is (= I am amazed by his courage).'
(Kibrik 1999: 798)

The non-attributive form of the focus copula is unacceptable with 1st person subjects:

(137) zy   akka   āqy   wo=d=un //*wo=d
       I   door.N2   N2.open.PF   FOC-N2-ATR // FOC-N2
       'I have opened the door.' (Tatevosov and Majsak 1999a: 230)

This fact can be explained with reference to the function of attributive forms in focus-marking: when talking about themselves, speakers choose sentence-focus structures to avoid marking of the 1st person participant as the topic. As our language consultant explained, if you use non-attributive forms with the first person subject, 'you sound as if you are talking about yourself too much'.

In complement clauses, attributive forms are used with perception verbs, while the argument of the subordinate clause undergoes raising to the main clause:

(138) iči-k'le   Gadže-na   adamī bajram-y-k'le   Xaw
       girl-AFF   M.see-ATR   man.M Bayram-OBL-AFF   house.N2
       hag_w-a-na
       N2.show-IPF-ATR
       'The girl saw how the man was showing the house to Bairam.'
       (Ljutikova and Bonč-Osmolovskaja 1999: 492)

Attributive forms are normally used as heads of relative clauses, where they are placed in preposition to the head noun.

(139) teze=da   āli   maktab   Gatti.t.xyn-na   maIʔallim
       fresh-ADV.N2   high   school.N2   N2.finish.PF-ATR   teacher
       'a teacher who has just graduated from university' (Kibrik 1999: 775)

In example (124) above and in (140a), the modifying clauses are headed by non-attributive perfective and imperfective forms respectively.

(140) a. hamanke   akka-ss-e   džu-qa=d   Xod-a-l_j
          then   door-AD-EL   self.OBL.M-POSS-N2   move-OBL-SUP
          išlemiš-ex-e   mašin   yxa
          work-N2.become-IPF   car.N2   N2.be.PF
          'At that time, he had a car waiting behind the door with the
          engine started.' (lit. 'a car working on the move')
          (Kibrik 1999: 791)

However, the relative clauses in these sentences could also be constructed in a more typical way, i.e. with the attributive verb form:

(140) b. hamanke akka-ss-e džu-qa=d Xod-a-l_j
then door-AD-EL self.OBL.M-POSS-N2 move-OBL-SUP
išlemiš-ex-e-n mašin yxa
work-N2.become-IPF-ATR car.N2 N2.be.PF
'At that time, he had a car waiting behind the door with the engine started.'
(lit. 'a car working on the move') (Kalinina 2001d: 68)

The difference between (140a) and (140b) is that in sentence (a) the relative clause is non-restrictive. In (b), on the contrary, the relative clause is restrictive, which has been stated in our consultant's comment. The speaker in (140b) implies that the person had two cars, and that one of them was behind the door with the engine started.

Deverbal nouns. Deverbal nouns typically head the complements of factive matrix verbs:

(141) ma-n-Gu-qa=d kalle yxa-j-jī
this.M-ATR-OBL.1-POSS-N2 head.N2 N2.be.PF-MSD-and
d-exa-j xunaše-k'le jug=da ac'a-xe-s
NEG-N2.be-MSD wife-AFF good-ADV.N2 N2.know-N2.STAT-POT
'His wife must know well if he had a head or not.' (Kibrik 1999: 858)

The case forms of deverbal nouns head temporal and purposive adjunct clauses:

(142) jišš-in gyrgy=da išš-by Gatti.t.xyn-ī-l-e
our-ATR all-NPL business-PL NPL.finish.PF-MSD-SUP-EL
qīRa, aʔ-im-my šši čopp-ā-r
TEMP NPL.cast.PF-ATR-PL we.ERG lot-PL-ABS.PL
'After finishing with our business, we cast lots.' (Kibrik 1999: 852–3)

Converbs. Apart from participles and deverbal nouns there are several specialized converbs used exclusively in adjunct clauses of different kinds (temporal clauses, purpose clauses, concessive clauses, and some others).

(143) gojne dars-y-l-qa aIlhā-nGaI, hamanke=r jic'y-ni
then lesson.OBL-SUP-ALL go.IPF-TEMP then-COH.M ten-AOBL
minut-y-s gedž-x-e-na-nī-xe
minute-OBL-DAT late-M.BE-IPF-ATR-EM2-HAB
'Then, each time he went to a lesson, he was ten minutes late.'
(Kibrik 1999: 779)

This example illustrates the Tsakhur temporal converbs in *-nGaI* that denote events preceding those denoted by the main-clause verb.

7.3.4.5 Tsakhur: generalizations   Like Dargwa and Bagwalal, Tsakhur shows very few direct correlations between functional clause types and formal predicate types. These correlations are the following: the imperative, prohibitive, hortative, and jussive are used in the main clauses of commands; the optative, counterfactual imperative, and counterfactual jussive are used in main clauses expressing wish; and specialized converbs are used in adjunct clauses of various semantic types. Below we discuss the relationship between the verbal form and clause type for other clause types (main declarative and interrogative clauses, relative and complement clauses).

Main clauses.   Declarative and interrogative sentences can be headed by indicative forms and by attributives. Indicative simple forms can either function on their own or combine with predicative particles and auxiliary verbs. Attributive verbal forms disallow auxiliaries and certain types of predicative particle.

Dependent clauses.   Relative clauses are normally restrictive and headed by the attributive forms.

There are three basic complementation strategies: the finite strategy, the complementizer strategy, and the masdar strategy. The finite strategy uses simple forms and attributive forms, as both types can function as independent predicates. Simple forms are characteristic of modal and aspectual matrix predicates, though they are also possible with some factive predicates. Attributive forms head complements of factive matrix verbs (mental verbs and verbs of emotion). The complementizer strategy is characteristic of factive predicates and propositional attitude predicates. Masdars head sentential complements of factive verbs; they also function as predicates of manner clauses.

The following list shows complementation strategies for some typical matrix verbs:

'say'	simple from + complementizer	'be able'	potentialis
'know'	masdar, complementizer; finite strategy	'want'	potentialis
'begin'	imperfective	'finish'	imperfective
'see'	simple form (perfective or imperfective)	'think'	simple form + complementizer
'fear'	simple form + complementizer; potentialis		

Tsakhur contrasts factive verbs, perception verbs, propositional attitude verbs, and modal/aspectual verbs.

Clausal adjuncts form a non-homogeneous group, which includes (i) causal, conditional/concessive and temporal clauses headed by specialized converbs, (ii) adjunct clauses headed by simple forms (they can have temporal or causal meanings), and (iii) purpose clauses headed by potentialis forms (example 127).

Predicate types. In Tsakhur there are three types of predicate: (i) simple verbal forms, (ii) attributives, and (iii) predicative particles. The opposition of three clause types has certain semantic correlations, basing on the illocutionary force and/or information structure of the clause.

Predicative particles and auxiliaries can only head main declarative/ interrogative clauses. In argument-focus structures, predicative particles are separated from the lexical verb and placed next to the focused phrase. Predicative particles can be combined with simple verbal forms, attributives, nouns, and adverbials, though there are restrictions on co-occurrence of predicative particles with attributive forms. In argument-focus constructions the lexical verb usually retains the form it has in the periphrastic formation— i.e. argument-focusing is achieved by simply shifting the particle next to the focused constituent.

Simple forms head both main and dependent clauses. They are compatible with different sentence types (different illocutionary forces) according to their modal semantics (indicative, imperative, or optative). Simple indicative forms can be used in argument-focus structures and in constituent questions. Simple perfective and imperfective forms can function in paratactic structures with modal and aspectual matrix verbs and in non-restrictive relative clauses. Simple forms, when used in dependent clauses, head adjunct clauses of time, cause, and purpose.

Attributive forms head both dependent and independent clauses. Attributives are used in sentence-focus constructions, which in Tsakhur comprise constructions with 1st person subjects. They are also used as heads of (re-strictive) relative clauses and heads of argument clauses selected by the verb 'know'. This picture is summarized in Table 7.6.

7.4 Discussion

In this section we suggest that the data of the Nakh-Daghestanian languages examined in section 7.3 can be interpreted in terms of information structure and the speaker's intentions.

TABLE 7.6. The correspondence between the verbal form and clause type

Verbal form	Bare form, no predicative particles	Form with an enclitic predicative particle	Predicative particle shifted away
Simple form	Main clause (declarative/ interrogative: predicate-focus; non-declarative) Argument clause (non-factive modal, phasal, and perception verbs) Adjunct clause (time, cause) Adjunct corresponding to non-restrictive relative clauses	Main clause (declarative/ interrogative: predicate-focus)	Main clause (declarative/ interrogative: argument-focus or predicate-focus)
Attributive	Argument clause ('know') Relative clause (restrictive) Main clause (sentence-focus)	Main clause (declarative/ interrogative: sentence-focus)	
Masdar	Argument clause (factive)		

7.4.1 *Sentence types*

Dargwa, Bagwalal, and Tsakhur show no clear opposition of verbal and nominal predicate sentences. Nominal predicates do not require an auxiliary verb to be present. Most nominal-predicate sentences are fully marked for 'finite' categories in the way verbal sentences are (tense, modality, sometimes also person; see sections 7.3.2.3, 7.3.3.3, and 7.2.4.3, respectively). Focus is marked in the same way in both nominal and verbal predicate sentences. Other languages of the group are similar in this respect. For example, in Lak, as in Dargwa, nominal predicates attach 'verbal' person markers, which can also be moved to mark focus.

So, in all three languages in question we identified the following three basic sentence types: (a) sentences headed by predicative particles; (b) sentences headed by simple verb forms; (c) sentences headed by forms ambiguous in terms of finiteness. Class (a) contains only unambiguously declarative and interrogative sentences. Class (b) is heterogeneous: it mainly comprises non-declarative sentences (commands and wishes) and certain types of declarative: generic and past habitual sentences (Dargwa), as well as sentences headed by irrealis and aorist forms (Bagwalal). Class (c) comprises sentence-focus constructions in Tsakhur, exclamatives in Dargwa and Bagwalal, and backgrounded generic and actualizing sentences in Bagwalal. This opposition of sentence types is mainly based on illocutionary force, though some additional factors (like backgrounding) are in play. Only sentences of type (a) allow morphosyntactic focus marking: they consistently show the position of the declarative focus or question focus.

7.4.2 *The verbal system*

The three verbal systems described in sections 7.2.2–4 are essentially different. However, the distribution of verbal forms across clause types is similar in all three languages.

First, each language has simple forms which only head independent clauses and do not combine with predicative particles. Most of these forms explicitly express a non-indicative modal meaning (imperative, prohibitive, optative, and some others). Hence, they are limited to non-declarative sentences and semantically incompatible with focus in the sense in which we are using this term. As a result, these forms do not combine with predicative particles. They can be regarded as direct bearers of a non-declarative illocutionary force. Logically, the non-indicative simple forms lie within the scope of the main illocutionary force operator that determines the functional type of the utterance. Therefore they cannot be presupposed. Simple forms used exclusively in independent clauses also include the past habitual and the general present in Dargwa (see footnote 34 below) and the preterite forms of Bagwalal (see section 7.3.3.4).

Second, there are forms which only head dependent clauses and do not combine with predicative particles. This class comprises specialized converbs in all the three languages as well as the masdar in Dargwa and Tsakhur and the subjunctive forms in Dargwa. They are not used in independent clauses because of their highly specialized semantics.

Third, there are forms that head independent clauses and are used both with and without predicative particles: the third person preterite form (= the preterite stem) in Dargwa[30], participles and masdars in Bagwalal, and simple

---

[30] In Dargwa, the preterite forms (3rd person) coincide with 'short' participles. However, unlike its counterparts in Tsakhur and Bagwalal, the Dargwa preterite takes the 1st and 2nd person markers.

TABLE 7.7. Classes of verbal forms in Dargwa, Bagwalal, and Tsakhur

No predicative particles		With predicative particles (Independent clause only)
Independent clause	Dependent clause	

Class 1		
	Class 2	
Class 3		
	Class 4	

forms in Tsakhur.[31] These forms are also used as heads of dependent clauses without predicative particles. In other words, all forms in this class are ambiguous in terms of finiteness (see Evans, Chapter 11 below, for a typological survey of such constructions). Close to this class are the *dexx*-nominalizations in Dargwa, which head either noun phrases or exclamative sentences.

Fourth, there are forms that head dependent clauses when used on their own and independent clauses when combined with predicative particles:[32] full participles and simple converbs in Dargwa, and infinitives in Tsakhur and Bagwalal (see Table 7.7).

Two of four form classes (3 and 4) cover both dependent and independent clauses. What is even more important is that these two classes include the most frequently used and the least marked forms, such as the preterite and other indicative forms, the attributive forms, and the simple converbs. We can conclude, then, that in all three languages, verbal forms are not opposed on the basis of their syntactic functions but rather on the basis of their semantic and pragmatic features.

[31] Similar phenomena can be observed in Standard Avar, where the participles too can be used as finite predicates. In the following example, two future participles *č'ʷalarejin* 'will not kill' and *qʷelarejin* 'will not slaughter', function as main-clause predicates:

(vi) Hinq'u-ge-jin   mun,   Hinq'u-ge-jin,   č'ʷa-lar-e=j-in,
      be.afraid-PRH-PRT   you   be.afraid-PRH-PRT   kill-NEG.FUT-PTCP-F
      qʷe-lar-e=j-in   dica   mun
      slaughter-NEG.FUT-PTCP-F   I.ERG   you
      'Don't be afraid, don't, I won't kill you, I won't slaughter you.' (Bokarev 1949: 71)

In the Zakatal dialect of Avar the use of participles in independent clauses is triggered by the 1st person transitive subject (Isakov 1980; Saidova 1980; Helmbrecht 1996). Similarly, the use of the attributive form was stipulated by 1st person subjects in Tsakhur (see section 7.2.4.4).

[32] In Dargwa predicative particles can also be combined with verbal stems, which are not used on their own (see section 7.2.2.1).

Participles can be predicates not only in attributive clauses but also in main clauses and in certain types of complement clauses. In Bagwalal and Dargwa, they tend to encode presupposed propositions. This is especially clear in the argument-focus constructions where the participle is the principal way to encode a non-focused (hence, presupposed) predicate. Participles are quite common in constituent questions, which are often treated as a kind of argument-focus construction (see section 7.2.2.3). Participles also head the clausal complements of the verb 'know', which are normally factive and presupposed. In all languages, participles do not cover all types of relative clauses, being confined to restrictive clauses only. They are commonly used like referential nouns, in headless relative clauses. In Tsakhur, where attributive forms can be regularly derived from all lexical categories, they are used in restrictive relative clauses and in sentence-focus constructions.

A similar pragmatic function is characteristic of masdars, though the domain of their use is much more limited. In all three languages masdars head factive complement clauses. The idea that masdars tend to head clauses conveying presupposed propositions is not undermined by the fact that in Bagwalal masdars also head exclamative sentences. According to Michaelis (2001), exclamative speech acts refer to gradable situations: the fact that the situation is taking place is known to both participants (presupposed). Michaelis believes that exclamatives contain assertions: what is asserted in exclamatives is the high degree of some scalable property. Independently of whether one agrees with Michaelis on what constitutes assertion in exclamatives, what is important for us is that the very proposition expressed by the exclamative sentence is presupposed. In Dargwa, exclamative sentences are headed by a special deverbal noun (the *dexx*-noun: see section 7.3.2.4).

Simple converbs and infinitives (in Icari Dargwa, subjunctives) are functionally close: dependent clauses headed by these two form classes constitute part of the assertion, but they are not assertions on their own. In all three languages, infinitives (subjunctives) and simple converbs head non-factive complement clauses. They also head adjunct clauses that are functionally equivalent to non-restrictive relatives in Tsakhur and Bagwalal. In Tsakhur, we observe that when used with aspectual and modal verbs, infinitives (potentialis) are interchangeable with imperfective converbs (= simple forms). In Tsakhur and Bagwalal, infinitives are used in imperative clauses addressed to the 1st person singular and plural in combination with special particles. In this case, the particle is the carrier of the illocutionary force, while the infinitive just denotes the desired situation.

Simple converbs (when used independently) head 'secondary declaratives', i.e. dependent clauses that express secondary assertions (section 7.3.2.2). In

(46), repeated here as (144), the main clause encodes just one (probably the most pragmatically important) event in a chain, whereas all other events are encoded by converbal clauses.

(144) xadiža   waba-ra   ca=w-ra   arilla   diči=b
       Hadiža   mother-and   self-M-and   the.whole.day herding-HPL
       b=už-ib-li,   nā   cinna   nisna   qil
       HPL-be-PRET-CVB   now   (self)   in.the.evening home
       čar.sa.b.ih-ub-li,   kk_wi.d.ēR-ib-li   HaIjwanti,
       return.HPL.PF-PRET-CVB   pen.NPL.PF-PRET-CVB   cattle.PL
       ka.b.iž-ib-ca.b   b=uk-a-tti
       sit.down.HPL.PF-PRET-PRS-HPL   HPL-eat.IPF-PROG-CVB
       'Mother Hadiža and he [Xan] stayed in the pasture the whole day,
       and in the evening they returned home, penned the cattle, and they
       sat and ate.'

Other types of secondary declarative are converbal clauses that function as non-restrictive relative clauses: see example (101) from Bagwalal and example (140) from Tsakhur. This function is not characteristic of the infinitives (subjunctives).

7.4.3 *Predicative particles and focus marking*

As shown in sections 7.3.2.2, 7.3.3.2, and 7.3.4.2, in all the three languages predicative particles mark focus. In Dargwa, the argument-focus structure is additionally marked by the participial form of the main predicate. In Bagwalal, participles are optional in argument-focus constructions. In Tsakhur, attributive forms signal sentence-focus.[33]

---

[33] Similar phenomena have been observed in many languages of Daghestan (see e.g. Kazenin 1999; 2002). We have good reasons to believe that all or almost all Daghestanian languages overtly mark focus in indicative clauses. For example, Avar has the focus-marking particle -Xa, which is cliticized to the focused argument. Sentences with this particle never have a copula or a finite verb. The main verb takes the attributive form, as in Dargwa:

(vii) a. was-as   mašina   tunk-ana
          boy-ERG   car.ABS   break-PST
          'The boy broke the car.'
       b. was-as-Xa   mašina   tunk-ara=b
          boy-ERG-FOC car.ABS   break-PST.PTCP-N
          'It was the boy who broke the car.'

Constituent questions in Avar are encoded as inherent-focus constructions, where the focused constituent is the question word: they do not allow finite forms as main predicates.
In Mehweb (which is regarded either as a dialect of Dargwa or as a separate language: see Magometov 1982; Xajdakov 1985), focus is marked by the particle -$g_w a$, which is incompatible with finite verbs and the copula. Like Bagwalal, Mehweb allows both participles and converbs in sentences with an argument-focus.

Predicative particles are ungrammatical in non-declarative sentences, interrogatives being the only exception. In other words, they are designed to mark
focus in the narrow sense of the word (declarative focus and question focus).
They cannot be used to mark other focus types, such as focus in commands or
wishes. So the very presence of predicative particles is a sign of the declarative
or interrogative illocutionary force.

Emphasizing a constituent is possible in all sentence types, including non-
declarative and non-interrogative utterances: cf. the following example from
Dargwa:

(145) a. žal   ducca-n   ma-ʕ-u-tt
           today   woodcutting.place-IN.LAT   PROH-go-THM-2
           'Don't go for wood today!'

       b. žal   ducca-n   ma-ʕ-u-tt,   Rurš   uʕ-in
           today woodcutting.place-IN.LAT PROH-go-THM-2 tomorrow   go-IMP
           'Don't go for wood *today*, you better go *tomorrow!*'

However, this type of emphasis can only be marked with a special intonation
pattern, where the focused constituent is stressed. Marking focus with predicative particles is impossible because they are ungrammatical in these
sentences. Contrastive stress in Dargwa, as well as contrastive stress in Russian
or English, or emphasizing particles like the Russian *imenno*, do not impose
such restrictions, because they are in no way connected with the illocutionary
force of the utterance:

(146) Pokaži   imenno   menja!
       show.IMP   namely   I.ACC
       'Show *me!*'

They are equally possible in utterances of any illocutionary force.

We believe that these facts follow from the meaning of the overt focus
markers (predicative particles). In all three languages, the set of predicative
particles includes copulas and auxiliaries, along with their negative counterparts. Copulas and auxiliaries basically do not denote identification or class
membership, even in nominal predicate sentences. This component of meaning is conveyed by the predicate noun itself. First and foremost, the presence
of a predicative particle signals the assignment of a truth value. This claim is
supported by the following arguments.

First, nouns and verbs take the same syntactic positions when used
as predicates and attach the same set of predicative particles. At the same
time, the distribution of predicative particles is different from that of

morphological verbs: for instance, the possibilities of their scrambling are much more restricted (see example 120).

Second, in all three languages the affirmative and negative copulas belonging to the class of predicative particles have several morphological forms (present, past, attributive, converb, and person forms in Dargwa). However, in none of the languages do these copulas express non-indicative modalities (including imperative, prohibitive, or optative). They are morphologically deficient because they lack any modal forms that do not involve operations with truth values.

Third, predicative particles are used as functional counterparts of the European words 'yes' and 'no' (see esp. Kazenin 1997). In sentence (147) from Lak, the 3rd person particle functions as 'yes':

(147) zu   mulk   wa   bah-lu-n-ni-w   b.a.w.xx-u-ssa?
      you   property this price-OBL-DAT-3SG-Q   N.sell-PST-PTCP
      di
      3SG
      'Did you sell your property for this price?' 'Yes.' (translation of
      The Acts of the Apostles 5: 8; example from Kazenin 1997: 66)

The following example shows the interaction of the positive particle *ek'$_w$a* and the negative particle *weč'e* as 'yes' and 'no' words in Bagwalal:

(148) a. ek'$_w$a-R-ō,   di-ba   hā-nā-X   ek'$_w$a-R-ō
          COP.PRS-PRT-M   I.OBL-AFF   see-IPF-CVB   COP.PRS-PRT-M
          ss$_w$ard-ā-X
          go.round-IPF-CVB
          (The participants of the dialogue are trying to make out if the
          recorder is on.)
          'It [= the tape] is (going round), I can see it go round.'

      b. "weč'e-Radi", —   o-ššu-r-la   heL'-a-łab-ō...
          COP.NEG-PRT   this-OBL.M-ERG-and   say-POT-PRT-M
          (The participants of the dialogue are discussing whether the owner
          of the tape-recorder deliberately left it on to record their talk.)
          'He will certainly say "No, (the recorder is not on)".'

So although predicative particles express a cluster of grammatical meanings, different for different particles and in different languages, all of them share a common semantic component, the assignment of the truth value. Using a predicative particle, the speaker explicitly marks the proposition as true or false.

That is why predicative particles are only possible in declarations and questions: these are the only speech acts that operate with truth values.

There are also predicative particles that directly express interrogativity. These particles co-occur with other predicative particles and take the rightmost position in the sequence of particles; see the sequence *-ni-w* 3SG-Q in example (147) from Lak. In this case, the truth value assigned by the left particle lies within the scope of the interrogative operator.

A sentence can lack both predicative particles and other explicit illocutionary force markers (markers of non-indicative modalities such as imperative or optative). In this case, the sentence has the default interpretation and is understood as a declarative utterance with the predicate within the focus domain.[34]

The placement of predicate particles is stipulated by the information structure of the sentence. In most cases they are cliticized to the rightmost slot of the focused constituent, but in Tsakhur we also observed the phenomenon of focus projection (Selkirk 1995), when the focus marker attached to a constituent at the same time licenses focusing of a higher constituent. For example, in sentence (149) the copula *wo=b* stands after the direct object *byIt* 'tail', but marks the whole verb phrase as the focus domain:

(149) istaR   balkan-y-lⱼ   qēk-a-nGaI,
       bride.F   horse-OBL-SUP   F.take-IPF-TEMP
       hama-n-či-na   byIt   wo=b   i.w.īt'al
       this.N-A-OBL.N-ATR   tail.N1   FOC=N1   N1.tie.IPF
       'When (they) take the bride away on a horse, they tie (the horse's) tail (in a special way).' (Kibrik 1999: 822)

In all three languages we can observe consistent marking of different focus types: argument-focus, predicate-focus, and sentence-focus. In Dargwa, argument-focus constructions are opposed to predicate-focus and sentence-focus. In Tsakhur, sentence-focus is marked by attributive verbal forms, and in this way sentence-focus constructions are opposed to argument-focus and predicate-focus.[35] In Bagwalal, all three focus types are marked by the placement of the copula.

---

[34] This idea can account for the fact that in Dargwa the predicative particles are not used in generic and habitual sentences. These sentences are normally used to describe backgrounded or pragmatically less important events. The speaker is interested in asserting the truth of foregrounded sentences, tacitly assuming the background to be true but leaving its truth unmarked.

[35] A similar phenomenon is observed in Aghul: in sentence-focus constructions, the copula is normally absent and the main verb takes the participial form.

As for the focus marking in interrogative sentences, some Nakh-Daghestanian languages (Tsakhur and Bagwalal, as well as Avar) encode constituent questions as inherent argument-focus structures. In these languages, the predicative particles follow the question phrase, and the main predicate takes the form that is characteristic of the argument-focus structures (the participle in Avar). Other languages (Dargwa) have two options: an argument-focus structure (predicative particles at the question phrase) and a double-focus structure (predicative particle at the main predicate; see section 7.3.2.2). In the latter case, the predicative particles are cliticized to the main predicate.

7.5 Conclusions

In the words of Benveniste, 'avec la phrase on quitte le domaine de la langue comme système de signes, et l'on entre dans un autre univers, celui de la langue comme instrument de communication, dont l'expression est la discourse' (Benveniste 1974 [1966]: 129–30). That is, a sentence is a bilateral unit: on the one hand, it belongs to language as a system of signs; on the other, it is a means of communication. As distinct from other syntactic units such as noun phrases or verb phrases, a sentence expresses a proposition anchored to the immediate discourse situation. Anchoring may involve several components: expression of the speaker's intention, the relationship between the proposition and the real world, the relationship between the situation participants and the speech act participants, the relationship between the situation participants and the objects actualized in the discourse, the relationship between the utterance and other utterances of the discourse, and perhaps others. Anchoring propositions to the discourse situation is a strong condition of a normal discourse, though it is not necessary for all elements listed above to be overtly expressed in a sentence.

The components of anchoring tend to be expressed by special grammatical and/or lexical means, i.e. elements expressing (i) illocutionary force (question words and particles, imperatives and the like); (ii) tense; (iii) modality and evidentiality; (iv) person; (v) definiteness and other categories expressing referential properties of the noun phrases; and (vi) topic, focus, and emphasis. The set of obligatorily expressed categories varies across languages. For example, not all languages have the category of person. In languages that have person, personal agreement on the verb can be controlled by one or several participants, may differentiate or not differentiate inclusive and exclusive, and so on. Similar observations can be made regarding tense, modality, and other categories listed above. We have also observed that whereas most European languages obligatorily express tense, modality, and often person/number, in Nakh-Daghestanian languages the overwhelming majority of the sentences are overtly marked for illocutionary force and information structure.

In the Russian linguistic tradition, the formal means of proposition anchoring are referred to as *predikativnost'* or *skazuemost'* (Peškovskij 1956 [1914]), i.e. 'predicativity'. Predicativity is 'a property or a set of properties that differentiate sentences from other syntactic phrase types' (Testelec 2001: 231). This property results from the fact that sentences are the only phrase types that are designed to function as utterances in the discourse. The concept of predicativity is functional; that is why it is expected to be universally applicable.[36] At the same time, the morphosyntactic patterns of predicativity do not have to be the same cross-linguistically.

The Standard Average European (SAE) and Nahk-Daghestanian languages demonstrate two different types of predicativity, or anchoring patterns, which most likely do not cover all the range of typological diversity. Below, we give a brief summary of these patterns.

SAE languages. In the SAE languages, any independent (main) clause contains a finite verb, exactly as predicted by the 'syntactic' understanding of finiteness (see section 7.1). Nominal predicate sentences are made finite by adding a finite copular verb.[37] Finite verbs are obligatorily marked for a number of grammatical categories. Hence, in European-type languages predicativity is conceptualized as finiteness. To put it differently, finiteness is the European model of predicativity. This type of predicativity implies the following grammatical properties:

(1) A language has a set of obligatory grammatical meanings which have to be expressed in each sentence. These are usually tense, modality, person, sometimes polarity, evidentiality, and interrogativity.
(2) These categories are realized as inflectional categories of the verb.
(3) The verbal forms marked for these categories are called finite forms; these forms are used as heads of independent clauses.
(4) Finite forms are opposed to nonfinite ones; the latter are not able to head independent clauses; they usually express fewer verbal inflectional categories than the finite forms.

---

[36] Viewed from a cognitive perspective, predicativity appears to be very close to finiteness as defined by Givón. Finiteness is 'the systematic grammatical means used to express the degree of integration of a clause into its immediate clausal environment' (Givón 1990: 853). But, taken as a whole, Givón's approach is aimed at describing the European type of predicativity. Most importantly, his approach only applies to dependent clauses.

[37] Nominal predicate sentences without a copula are possible in SAE languages (*Alles klar, Omnia praeclara rara*), but they are marginal and largely idiomatic sentence types. Many authors classified these sentences as elliptical.

Nakh-Daghestanian languages.   The data of Nakh-Daghestanian languages show that the European style finiteness is just one anchoring possibility. In Nakh-Daghestanian languages we observe a different type of relationship between anchoring categories and morphosyntactic structures.

(1) As well as in European languages, Nakh-Daghestanian languages have a set of grammatical meanings that are obligatorily expressed in all sentences. Though this set may contain tense, modality, evidentiality, and person, it is different from the typical SAE, since it usually includes illocutionary force, polarity, and information structure marking.

(2) The obligatory grammatical meanings of this set do not have to be realized as inflectional categories of the verb. They can be expressed by various markers, such as verbal affixes, clitics, and particles which attach to different constituent types.

(3) There are no verbal forms designed for heading independent predications. Verbal forms that look like finite forms have a narrower range of functions than the finite forms of the European languages: the Nakh-Daghestanian 'finite' forms head main clauses only if the verb belongs to the assertive part of a categorical (as opposed to thetic) utterance.

(4) Participles, infinitives, converbs, verbal nouns and 'finite' forms are not opposed on the basis of their syntactic properties. The core property of their opposition is the ability to head clauses with certain information structure (e.g. presupposed vs. asserted vs. neutral).

Different anchoring patterns result in different statuses of the verb. In SAE the verb is highly significant. First, it always expresses obligatory grammatical categories, even when the main predicate of the clause is expressed by a non-verbal element. Second, the main verb bears the markers of obligatory categories also when it does not belong to the assertive part of the sentence. So predicativity markers in SAE necessarily cluster around the finite verb.

Unlike the SAE languages, in Nakh-Daghestanian languages predicativity markers do not stick to the finite verb or any other lexical class. The verb bears the markers of obligatory categories only under certain conditions, i.e. if it belongs to the asserted part of the sentence. The same could be said about any other lexical unit that is able to take the position of the main predicate. The verb is not opposed to other lexical classes in this respect. Predicativity in the Nakh-Daghestanian languages is therefore not rigidly tied to the verb as a lexical class. Instead, the expression of obligatory sentence-level categories in Nakh-Daghestanian sentences depends on the illocutionary type of the utterance. The Nakh-Daghestanian predicativity type is strongly oriented towards expressing the illocutionary force and information structure of the sentence, which allows the markers of the predicative categories to cluster around the focused constituent. In the declarative and interrogative sentences the markers of predicative categories appear on the focused component of the sentence, be it a verbal phrase or another constituent type.

Different approaches to finiteness mentioned in section 7.1 share a common bias: finiteness/nonfiniteness is related to the properties of the verb as a lexical class. This concept of finiteness is based on certain preconceptions about the language structure originating from the European linguistic tradition, and is hardly applicable to all languages different from SAE. If we follow this approach, we will have to admit that for the Nakh-Daghestanian languages the opposition of finiteness/nonfiniteness does not yield any meaningful generalizations.

An alternative approach would be to define the finite/nonfinite opposition as a particular pattern of anchoring propositions to the discourse context. This approach implies that finiteness is a property of an independent clause, whereby predicative categories appear as grammatical categories of the lexical verb. Under this approach, the Nakh-Daghestanian languages do not have the finite/nonfinite opposition, but employ a different anchoring pattern.

Another possible approach is to relate finiteness to predicativity. In this case finiteness can be understood as the ability of a sentence to function as an utterance in a discourse. All languages have finiteness, but finiteness patterns are different across languages. In particular, finiteness in Daghestanian languages is crucially different from the SAE type: the verb in the Nakh-Daghestanian languages does not enjoy a special status as the bearer of the finite categories.

8

In what ways can finite and nonfinite clauses differ? Evidence from Russian

DAVID M. PERLMUTTER

8.1 Goals

In what ways can finite and nonfinite clauses differ in a given language? To what extent do different languages manifest different contrasts between finite and nonfinite clauses? This chapter addresses these questions with respect to Russian, which displays striking contrasts between clauses headed by an infinitive and clauses headed by a finite verb. I apply the labels 'nonfinite' and 'infinitival' to the former and 'finite' to the latter.[1]

Our first—descriptive—goal is to document two such contrasts between finite and nonfinite clauses in Russian. We describe two constructions—the Unspecified Human Subject (UHS) construction and the unspecified *they* construction—and show that they have opposite distributions. The UHS construction occurs in nonfinite but not finite clauses, while the unspecified *they* construction occurs in finite but not nonfinite clauses. We then show that the latter construction has the same distribution as impersonal constructions, which cannot occur in nonfinite clauses (Perlmutter and Moore 2002).

I am greatly indebted to Maria Polinsky for putting her native command of Russian at my disposal and for commenting on sections of the manuscript, and to Irina Nikolaeva both for detailed comments on earlier versions of the manuscript and for checking the data against her native intuitions, as well as to John Moore for clarifying some theoretical points and to the participants of the Finiteness conference for discussion of both the data and the theoretical issues. None of these individuals is responsible for what is said here, for which I assume full responsibility.

[1] This working characterization of the two clause types in Russian does not present the kinds of difficulty that beset attempts to characterize the notions 'finite' and 'nonfinite' in a number of the languages discussed in the Introduction to this volume. However, controlled infinitival complements in Russian, which differ in certain crucial respects from the infinitival clauses investigated in this chapter, are not discussed here at all.

Our second goal is to explain these patterns in the data. Why do these gaps exist? Why can't the UHS construction occur in finite clauses? Why can't the unspecified *they* construction and impersonal constructions occur in nonfinite clauses? We argue that these constructions have phonologically null subjects whose properties play the key role in explaining the constructions' distribution.

Consequently, our third goal is to make explicit the kinds of evidence supporting the existence of phonologically null subjects. A grammar can account for the ways the three construction types contrast by giving their null subjects distinct semantic and morphosyntactic representations which are in turn evidence for their existence. The constructions' contrasting properties cannot be due to subjectlessness itself, since that would not account for the ways they contrast. Thus, the three contrasting null subjects provide an argument for null subjects that no one of them could provide alone.

Fourth, we seek to distinguish between genuine properties of the finite/nonfinite contrast and phenomena that may be correlated with it but follow from other properties of the finite/nonfinite contrast in a particular language. It is argued here that the gaps in various constructions' distribution are not to be included among the properties of finite or nonfinite clauses in Russian. Listing the construction types that finite or nonfinite clauses can host does not lead to an understanding of the patterns in the data. The gaps can be shown to follow from another, independent property of finite and nonfinite clauses: the case they require of their subjects. This is one of the ways that finite and nonfinite clauses can contrast cross-linguistically. Thus, Russian does not show that finite and nonfinite clauses can differ in the classes of constructions they allow. Rather, it illustrates the independently attested fact that finite and nonfinite clauses can differ in the case they require of their subjects.

8.2 The Unspecified Human Subject (UHS) construction

8.2.1 *A semantic property of root infinitival clauses*

Most *root* infinitival clauses in Russian have a meaning that can be captured in English with the 'be to' construction:

(1) a. Ètomu   ne   byvat'
        this   NEG   be.INF
        'That is not to be.'

     b. Čto   mne   prinesti?
        what   me   bring.INF
        'What am I to bring?'

   c. Byt'   svad'be
      be.INF   wedding
      'There is to be a wedding.'

Nikolaeva (2003) gives a typology of root infinitival clauses, with detailed observations about their semantics and their conditions of use (pragmatics). The 'be to' meaning is robust in root infinitival clauses and subsumes most of the cases she cites, including the following:

(2) a. Tebe   xodit'
       you   go.INF
       'You are to go.' (e.g. in a card game)

     b. "Začem ty   prišel?" "Mne pogovorit' s   učitelem."
       why   you   came   me   speak.INF with teacher
       'Why did you come?' 'I am to speak with the teacher.'

     c. Vsem   vstat'!
       all   stand.up.INF
       'Everybody (is to) stand up!'

Controlled infinitival complements and infinitival complements of raising clauses do not have this 'be to' meaning.

8.2.2 *Two key properties of the UHS construction*

The Russian Unspecified Human Subject (UHS) construction has two key properties:[2]

(3) a. The UHS construction is understood as having an unspecified human subject.
     b. The construction has no overt subject.

The UHS construction is illustrated by the questions in (4a–d):[3]

(4) a. Čto   delat'?
       what   do.INF
       'What is one to do?'

---

   [2] A more precise characterization of the construction is proposed in section 8.2.3 below. Russian also has other constructions with the properties in (3), e.g. the unspecified *they* construction discussed in section 8.3.

   [3] As will be seen in section 8.2.6, the UHS construction is not limited to questions. Although it is an inaccurate translation, *one* is used in some glosses here, *faute de mieux*. For (4a) the passive *What is to be done?* is a more accurate translation, but since passives cannot be used to translate the intransitives in (4b–d), the use of *one*, while inaccurate, keeps the translations uniform. One reason why *one* is an inadequate translation is given in n. 8 below. '*Unspec*' is often used here in glosses.

b. Kak   žit'?
   how   live.INF
   'How is one to live?'

c. Kuda   pojti?
   whither   go.INF
   'Where is one to go?'

d. Gde   načat'?
   where   begin.INF
   'Where is one to begin?'

As root-clause sentences, (4a–d) have the 'be to' meaning in addition to being questions. Because such sentences are understood as having human subjects, they are anomalous with predicates that are semantically anomalous with human subjects:

(5) *Kak   ne   rassypat'sja?
    how   NEG   get.spilled/scattered.INF
    'How is one not to get spilled?'

8.2.3 *The Lexical Subject Hypothesis (LSH)*

The UHS construction raises these related questions:

(6) a. Is the UHS construction syntactically anomalous in having no subject?

  b. How is a grammar to account for the fact that the UHS construction is understood as having a(n unspecified) human subject?

  c. How is the UHS construction to be characterized, i.e. what do all its exemplars have in common, and how does this construction differ from other constructions?

The key step in solving these problems is to realize that (6a, b) are related. The understood human subject and the UHS construction's apparent subjectless-ness are accounted for if it actually has a phonologically null human subject in syntactic representations:

(7) The Lexical Subject Hypothesis (LSH)

  a. The lexicon of Russian includes a lexical item (called '*Unspec*' here)[4] that serves as subject of the UHS construction in syntactic representations.

---

[4] This entity has at different times been identified with both PRO$_{arb}$ and *pro*$_{arb}$ in the literature on Government and Binding Theory and its descendants in attempts to use the Binding Theory's

    b. *Unspec* is a noun whose lexical entry includes the semantic specification: [Human].[5]

    c. *Unspec* has no phonological shape in Russian; it is phonologically null.

    d. In other respects, *Unspec* is like other lexical items. Thus, its lexical entry represents its semantic, syntactic, and morphosyntactic properties.

By including the specification [Human] in *Unspec*'s semantic representation, the LSH accounts for the fact that the UHS construction is understood as having a human subject. The LSH's answer to (6a) is that the UHS construction is *not* syntactically anomalous; it has a subject (*Unspec*). The LSH reduces what appears to be a syntactic anomaly of the construction in Russian to a phonological property of one lexical item: it is phonologically null.

    With (7a), the LSH provides a characterization of the notion 'UHS construction' in Russian, solving problem (6c):

(8)   The extension of the UHS construction consists of the set of clauses that have *Unspec* as subject. This is what they have in common and how they differ from other constructions.

The LSH brings out the parallel between the UHS construction in Russian and the corresponding constructions with the subjects *on* in French and *man* in German:

(9)   Ici   on   parle   français.
        here   *Unspec* speaks French
        'French is spoken here.' (lit. '*Unspec* speaks French here.')

(10)   Hier   spricht man   Deutsch.
        here   speaks *Unspec* German
        'German is spoken here.' (lit. '*Unspec* speaks German here.')

---

differential treatment of PRO and *pro* to account for its distribution in other languages. A key paper in this connection is Rizzi (1986), which posits pro_{arb} to account for its occurrence in governed positions in Italian. For examples like (39), Rizzi (1986: 520) identifies the Italian reflexive clitic *si* as the element corresponding to *Unspec* in Russian, positing that the subject is pro_{arb}, which gets the features associated with *arb* through linking with si_{arb}.

    [5] A more precise characterization might be 'mind-possessing entity'. In a fairy tale, for example, where animals and trees are endowed with human properties and speak to each other, they could use the UHS construction when speaking of unspecified animals or trees. Similarly, (5) would be normal in a fairy tale in which liquids, endowed with human properties, converse. We systematically ignore this refinement.

Under the LSH, the three languages' unspecified human subjects differ in phonological shape. As will be seen below, they differ in their morphosyntactic features as well.[6]

The key element of the LSH is phonologically null *Unspec*, an element not recognized in previous discussions of null subjects in Russian (e.g. Mel'čuk 1974; Franks 1995). Since null elements are still controversial, at key points in the exposition an LSH grammar will be contrasted with one mandated by the *WYSIWYG* ('what you see is what you get') Hypothesis:

(11)   WYSIWYG Hypothesis
        Phonologically null lexical items do not exist.

In a WYSIWYG grammar, the UHS construction lacks a subject.

As will be seen below, the LSH is a valuable tool for discovering the properties of the UHS construction. Further, it will provide an explanation. In positing *Unspec* as the subject of the UHS construction, the LSH explains its semantic, syntactic, and morphosyntactic properties as properties of this lexical item. It will also be shown that the LSH explains the UHS construction's distribution. What initially appear to be semantic, syntactic, morphosyntactic, and distributional problems are reduced to lexicon: the construction's properties follow from lexical properties of a single lexical item.

8.2.4 *Morphosyntactic evidence for* Unspec: *agreement in UHS clauses*

8.2.4.1 *What the WYSIWYG Hypothesis predicts*   In claiming that the UHS construction is subjectless, the WYSIWYG Hypothesis predicts *ohne Weiteres* that agreement phenomena dependent on the subject will be lacking in UHS clauses. We show here that, on the contrary, the full range of agreement phenomena dependent on the subject are found in UHS clauses. This has two important consequences. First, it is evidence that, contrary to the claims of the WYSIWYG Hypothesis, the UHS construction has a subject. Second, it provides evidence about *Unspec*'s morphosyntactic properties, which show up in agreement morphology.

8.2.4.2 *Predicate agreement in the UHS construction*   Adjectival predicates in Russian agree with their subjects in gender and number:

(12)   a. Kak   Borisu   stat'   bogatym?
          how   Boris.DAT   become.INF   rich.M.SG
          'How is Boris to become rich?'

---

[6] There are further differences in their conditions of use, their ability to have first-person reference, etc. that are not relevant here.

    b. Kak   Svetlane   stat'   bogatoj?
       how   Svetlana.DAT become.INF rich.F.SG
       'How is Svetlana to become rich?'

    c. Kak   im   stat'   bogatymi?
       how   them.DAT   become.INF rich.PL
       'How are they to become rich?'

The adjective *bogat-* 'rich' is masculine singular in (12a), feminine singular in (12b), and plural in (12c).[7] A grammar of Russian then must include a rule or constraint with this effect:

(13)   An adjectival predicate agrees with its subject in gender and number.

In the UHS construction there are three grammatical possibilities:

(14)   Kak   stat'   bogatym / bogatoj / bogatymi?
       how   become.INF rich.M.SG /F.SG /PL
       'How is *Unspec* to become rich?'

The human subject is understood to be male with *bogatym*, female with *bogatoj*, and plural with *bogatymi*.

    The LSH can account for (14) with no complication of the grammar. Since it claims that *Unspec* is a noun marked [Human] in the Russian lexicon, all that is needed is for *Unspec* to be capable of having either masculine or feminine gender features. Like other nouns, it can be either singular or plural. Consequently, (13), which is needed independently to account for sentences like (12a–c), will account for (14) as well.

    Why do we find this range of agreement behaviour in the UHS construction? The key fact is that the three sentences in (14) differ semantically. In contrast to the sentence with *bogatym*, with *bogatoj* the subject is understood to be female and with *bogatymi* it is understood to be plural; the morphosyntactic differences reflect a semantic difference. *Unspec* can be understood to designate an unspecified male or female human or more than one unspecified human, with corresponding agreement in each case.

    Independent evidence for *Unspec*'s ability to be understood as female comes from its ability to occur with predicates that are natural only with female subjects:

(15)   a. Kak   ne   stat'   beremennoj   (*beremennym)?
         how   NEG   become.INF pregnant.F.SG pregnant.M.SG
         'How is *Unspec_F* not to become pregnant?'

---

[7] In Russian there are no gender distinctions in the plural.

b. Kak   rožat'   bez   medicinskoj pomošči?
how give.birth.INF without medical   help
'How is *Unspec_F* to give birth without medical help?'

Similarly, the ability of *Unspec* to be plural can be seen in the fact that it can serve as subject of predicates that require a semantically plural subject:[8]

(16) a. Gde   sobrat'sja?
where   assemble.INF
'Where is *Unspec_{PL}* to assemble?'

b. Začem   zdes'   perestrelivat'sja?
why   here   shoot.at.one.another.INF
'Why should *Unspec_{PL}* shoot at one another here?'

Russian typically has distinct nouns for male and female humans—a pattern robust enough to extend to some loanwords, as in (17b).

(17) a. francuz 'Frenchman', francuženka 'Frenchwoman'

b. sportsmen 'male athlete', sportsmenka 'female athlete'

In such cases, morphosyntactic gender is not idiosyncratic: a noun that designates males is masculine, one that designates females is feminine. This also holds of the nouns in (18):

(18) kaleka   'cripple'   ubijca   'killer, murderer'
obžora   'glutton'   umnica   'smart person'
p'janica 'drunkard' zabijaka 'scrapper, bully'
sirota   'orphan'   zanuda   'bore'
tupica   'dunce'

As with *Unspec*, these nouns can refer to either males or females, which is reflected in their morphosyntactic gender and hence in gender agreement:

(19) Ètot   tupica prevraščaetsja   v   nesčastnogo.
this.M.SG dunce turn.into.PRS.3SG into unhappy.M.SG
'This (male) dunce is turning into an unhappy person.'

(20) Èta   tupica prevraščaetsja   v   nesčastnuju.
this.F.SG dunce turn.into.PRS.3SG into unhappy.F.SG
'This (female) dunce is turning into an unhappy person.'

The noun's gender shows up in the form of the demonstrative and of *nesčastn-* 'unhappy'. Different forms of either would be ungrammatical.

---

[8] Collective nouns are semantically plural, e.g. *A crowd assembled. Unspec*'s ability to be semantically plural is one of the reasons it is not equivalent to English *one*.

Alternatively, it might be thought that these nouns are simply unspecified for gender, and that (19, 20) are both grammatical because *tupica* has no gender features to clash with either masculine or feminine agreement morphology. There are clear arguments against this proposal. First, the gender features expressed on the demonstrative and the predicate must be the same; they can't be mixed:

(21) a. *Ètot   tupica   prevraščaetsja   v   nesčastnuju
          this.M.SG dunce   turn.into.PRS.3SG   into   unhappy.F.SG

      b. *Èta   tupica   prevraščaetsja   v   nesčastnogo
          this.F.SG dunce   turn.into.PRS.3SG   into   unhappy.M.SG

Second, *tupica* is not compatible with features of any gender; neuter forms are ungrammatical:

(22) *Èto   tupica prevraščaetsja   v   nesčastnoe/nesčastnogo/nesčastnuju.
      this.N.SG dunce turn.into.PRS.3SG into unhappy.N.SG/M.SG/F.SG

In addition, any such proposal must be able to capture the link between semantic gender and morphosyntactic gender: (19) is about a male dunce, (20) a female dunce. We conclude that the nouns in (18) can be masculine or feminine.[9]

The UHS construction exhibits the same agreement pattern as the nouns in (18); *Unspec* can be masculine or feminine (but not neuter):

(23) Kak   ne   prevraščat'sja   v   nesčastnogo/nesčastnuju /*nesčastnoe?
      how   NEG   turn.into.INF   into   unhappy.M.SG/F.SG/*N.SG
      'How is *Unspec* not to turn into an unhappy person?'

Unspec can also be plural, like the nouns in (18) and other count nouns:

(24) Kak   ne   prevraščat'sja   v   nesčastnyx?
      how   NEG   turn.into.INF   into   unhappy.PL
      'How [are] *Unspec* [individuals] not to turn into unhappy people?'

(25) Èti   tupici   prevraščajutsja   v   nesčastnyx
      these.PL   dunces   turn.into.PRS.3PL   into   unhappy.PL
      'These dunces are turning into unhappy people.'

The significance of these agreement patterns is that *Unspec* has morphosyntactic features that show up in agreement. This fact argues for its presence in

---

[9] The question of whether *Unspec* and the nouns in (18) have a single lexical entry or a pair of lexical entries is beyond the scope of this chapter.

syntactic representations. Under the LSH, nothing need be added to the grammar to account for this.

8.2.4.3 *Agreement of secondary predicates in the UHS construction*   *Unspec*'s morphosyntactic features argued for above show up in other types of agreement as well, e.g. the agreement of secondary predicates:

(26)   Boris   idet   domoj   p'janym
       Boris.NOM   go.PRS.3SG   home   drunk.M.SG
       'Boris is going home drunk.'

(27)   Svetlana   idet   domoj   p'janoj
       Svetlana.NOM   go.PRS.3SG   home   drunk.F.SG
       'Svetlana is going home drunk.'

The secondary predicates *p'janym* and *p'janoj* in (26, 27) are masculine and feminine singular, respectively, in agreement with their subjects. The NP with which a secondary predicate agrees need not be a surface subject:

(28)   My   našli   Svetlanu   p'janoj
       we.NOM   find.PST.PL   Svetlana.ACC   drunk.F.SG
       'We found Svetlana drunk.'

In UHS clauses parallel to (26, 27), we find the same agreement pattern as with predicates:

(29)   Kak   idti   domoj   p'janym/p'janoj/p'janymi?
       how   go.INF   home   drunk.M.SG/F.SG/PL
       'How is *Unspec* to go home drunk?'

This follows if the UHS construction has a subject, *Unspec*, with the morphosyntactic features we have posited for it.

8.2.4.4 *Agreement of semipredicatives in the UHS construction*   Another piece of evidence that *Unspec* has gender and number features comes from the semipredicatives *odin* 'alone' and *sam* 'oneself' discussed by Comrie (1974), Franks (1995), and others:

(30)   Kak   Borisu   rabotat'   odnomu?
       how   Boris.DAT   work.INF   alone.M.SG
       'How is Boris to work alone?'

(31)   Kak   Svetlane   rabotat'   odnoj?
       how   Svetlana.DAT   work.INF   alone.F.SG
       'How is Svetlana to work alone?'

In (30), the semipredicative *odnomu* is masculine singular in agreement with *Borisu*, while in (31), the semipredicative *odnoj* is feminine singular in agreement with *Svetlane*. In each case the semipredicative agrees with what we can call its 'antecedent'. This parallels the agreement of adjectives within the NP (NP-internal concord) and of external elements like floated quantifiers. The grammar needs a rule or constraint to account for this:

(32)   The semipredicatives *odin* 'alone' and *sam* 'oneself' agree with their antecedents in gender, number, and case.[10]

In the UHS construction, semipredicatives exhibit the same agreement pattern as predicates and secondary predicates:

(33)   Kak   žit'   odnomu/odnoj/odnim?
       how   live.INF   alone.M.SG/F.SG/PL
       'How is *Unspec* to live alone?'

Under a WYSIWYG grammar, in which the UHS construction has no subject, (32) must be complicated to account for this agreement pattern in UHS constructions like (33). Under the LSH, however, with *Unspec* as subject of the UHS construction, no complication is needed.

Thus, predicates, secondary predicates, and semipredicatives all provide evidence for the LSH and for the morphosyntactic features of *Unspec*, the subject of the UHS construction.

It might be thought that predicates and semipredicatives are not distinct entities, and therefore that what have just been claimed to be distinct sources of evidence are the same thing. However, such an analysis cannot be maintained. First, predicates can occur in simple sentences such as:

(34)   On   bogat
       he   rich.M.SG
       'He is rich.'

Evidence that the semipredicative *sam* 'oneself' is not a predicate comes from the fact that it cannot be the predicate of such a simple sentence:

(35)   *On   sam
        he.NOM   oneself.M.SG

(35) is a noun phrase that means 'he himself', but it is not a sentence.

---

[10]   *Odin* and *sam* are the semipredicatives' citation forms. So far we have been concerned only with their agreement in gender and number. Agreement in case is discussed in section 8.5.3.

It might be objected that semipredicatives are a type of predicate that is restricted to occurring as secondary predicates. This would account for their inability to be the sole predicate of a clause as well as their ability to appear in addition to a predicate. This analysis cannot be maintained, however, because semipredicatives and secondary predicates behave differently with respect to case. Secondary predicates appear in the instrumental case, while semipredicatives agree with their antecedents in case (as well as gender and number). The contrast in their behaviour can be seen in sentences like:

(36) **Boris**   idet   domoj *p'janym*   **odin**
     Boris.NOM go.PRS.3SG home   drunk.INS   alone.NOM
     'Boris is going home drunk alone.'

(37) Kak **Borisu**   idti   domoj *p'janym*   **odnomu?**
     how Boris.DAT go.INF   home   drunk.INS   alone.DAT
     'How is Boris to go home drunk alone?'

In both (36) and (37) the secondary predicate *p'janym* is in the instrumental case. Unlike secondary predicates, semipredicatives agree with their antecedents in case. In (36) the semipredicative is nominative (*odin*) in agreement with the subject *Boris*, but in (37) it is dative (*odnomu*) in agreement with the dative subject *Borisu*. Such examples clearly show semipredicatives to be distinct from secondary predicates.

Thus, semipredicative agreement provides an independent source of evidence for the morphosyntactic features of *Unspec*, the subject of the UHS construction under the LSH.

In defence of the WYSIWYG Hypothesis, it might be thought that, instead of having to complicate (13) and (32), the grammar could simply say:

(38) In subjectless clauses, all gender-number combinations are possible.

However, this will not work. If *Unspec* is understood to be female, as in (15a), agreeing constituents must be feminine singular. If *Unspec* is understood to be plural, as in (24), agreeing constituents must be plural. Sections 8.3.2, 8.4, and 8.7.3 give further arguments against (38).

Another kind of evidence for the lexical nature of the morphosyntactic features of the subject of the UHS construction comes from the fact that they vary to some extent cross-linguistically. For example, there is a contrast between Italian and Spanish, which, like Russian, have a UHS construction whose subject is phonologically null; the construction is marked by a reflexive clitic on the verb. In Italian, verbs that agree with *Unspec* are singular, while agreeing adjectives are plural:[11]

(39) Quando si   è   stanchi   (*stanco),...
      when   REFL is   tired.M.PL tired.M.SG
      'When *Unspec* is tired,...'

In (39) the verb *è* is (3rd person) singular, while the adjective *stanchi* is masculine plural. In Spanish, however, both the verb (*está*) and the adjective (*cansado*) must be singular:

(40) Cuando se   está cansado   (*cansados),...
      when   REFL is   tired.M.SG tired.M.PL
      'When *Unspec* is tired,...'

Thus, the morphosyntactic features of the subject of the UHS construction can be idiosyncratic in individual languages and vary to some extent cross-linguistically. This supports the LSH's claim that these features of *Unspec* are lexical in each language.

In brief, the morphosyntactic behaviour of the subject of the UHS construction supports the LSH's claims that there is a subject in this case whose morphosyntactic features are supplied by the lexicon of each language.

8.2.4.5 *Conclusions*   The UHS construction has a number of morphosyntactic properties that are accounted for without any additions to the grammar if the UHS construction has *Unspec* as subject, as the LSH claims. Under the LSH, the rules or constraints that account for agreement in clauses with specified subjects account for the morphosyntactic properties of the UHS construction as well.

8.2.5 *Syntactic evidence for* Unspec

The two key arguments that *Unspec* is present in syntactic representations come from raising and control—phenomena argued in Moore and Perlmutter (2000) to be true diagnostics of subjecthood in Russian.

The first argument comes from *Unspec*'s ability to raise, as in (41):

(41) Kak prodolžat'   [rabotat' odnomu]?
      how continue.INF work.INF alone.M.SG
      'How is one to continue to work alone?'

---

[11] Rizzi (1986) emphasizes the plurality of null *arb* objects in Italian that shows up in adjectival agreement, as in (39). The fact that the verb in this construction is singular must also be accounted for.

In (41) the complement subject *Unspec* is raised to subject of the raising predicate *prodolžat'*, a predicate with which raising is obligatory; sentences with verbs of this class with infinitival complements but no raising are ungrammatical (Moore and Perlmutter 2000). Under the LSH, the raising requirement is satisfied by the raising of *Unspec*. A WYSIWYG grammar, however, will have to be complicated in some way to accommodate these facts.

The second argument is based on control: *Unspec* can control into complement and adjunct clauses (including those that are obligatorily controlled), and it can be controlled. This can be seen in the obligatorily controlled complement of *starat'sja* 'try' in (42).

(42) Začem   starat'sja   [rabotat'   odnomu]?
      why   try.INF   work.INF   alone.M.SG
      'Why try to work alone?'

The occurrence of *Unspec* in the matrix clause controls the complement subject in (42), where both the matrix and gerund clauses are understood as having unspecified human subjects. Similarly, gerund clauses in Russian must be controlled . The gerund clause in (43) is controlled by *Unspec* in the matrix clause:

(43) Ne   pol'zujas'   lekarstvom,   kak   pobedit'   ètu   bolezn'?
      NEG   use.GER   medicine   how   defeat.INF   this   disease
      'Not using medicine, how is one to conquer this disease?'

(42, 43) show that the subject of the UHS construction can control and be controlled. Unlike the LSH, which need add nothing new to accommodate these facts, a WYSIWYG grammar will need some additional device(s) to do so.

Third, the evidence above that *Unspec* determines agreement on predicates, secondary predicates, and semipredicatives is evidence that it is present in syntactic representations as the subject of UHS clauses.

Finally, in frameworks in which the binding of reflexives is stated on syntactic structures, there is an additional argument based on the fact that *Unspec* can bind a reflexive:[12]

(44) Čto   kupit'   sebe?
      what   buy.INF   REFL.DAT
      'What is one to buy for oneself?'

---

[12] In frameworks in which the binding of reflexives is stated on argument structure rather than syntactic structure, this is obviously not evidence for the presence of *Unspec* in syntactic structure. Since Russian reflexives are not differentiated for gender or number, the reflexive *sebe* in (44) provides no information about *Unspec*'s morphosyntactic features.

The beneficiary and the agent of buying in (44) are understood to be the same, as in (45), where *sebe* is bound by the overt subject *im*.[13]

(45) Čto   im   kupit'   sebe?
      what   them.DAT buy.INF   REFL.DAT
      'What are they to buy for themselves?'

Thus, *sebe* in (44) is bound by the human argument understood as the agent of *kupit'* 'buy'. In frameworks that state binding conditions on syntactic representations, this means that the phonologically null subject of (44) binds the reflexive *sebe*. Under the LSH nothing in the binding conditions[14] needs to be changed to account for the binding of reflexives in the UHS construction. A WYSIWYG grammar, however, will need an additional *ad hoc* binding condition just to account for the UHS construction, which it analyses as subjectless. In such frameworks, this is evidence that the phonologically null subject *Unspec* is present in syntactic representations.

In sum, there is clear evidence that *Unspec* is present in syntactic representations as the subject of UHS clauses.

8.2.6 *A class of pseudo-imperatives and hortatives as instantiations of the UHS construction*

8.2.6.1 *An analysis of pseudo-imperatives and hortatives*   Like the sentences in (4), those in (46) and (47) are root-clause infinitivals with no overt subject.[15]

(46) a. Smotret'   v   knigu
          look.INF   into   book
          'Look at/into the book.'

      b. Vstat'!
          stand.up.INF
          'Stand up!'

(47) a. Dognat'   i   peregnat'   Ameriku!
          overtake.INF and   surpass.INF   America
          'Overtake and surpass America!'

---

[13] This makes reflexives like *sebe* in (44) different from reflexives unbound by an antecedent. Ackema and Schoorlemmer (1995) analyse such unbound reflexives, as in *Books about oneself never read poorly*, as logophoric.

[14] That NPs which are *not* surface subjects can antecede reflexives has been known at least since Peškovskij (1956). This point has been much discussed in the literature and is argued in detail in Moore and Perlmutter (2000). The same point has been made for controllers of subjects of gerund clauses at least since Ickovič (1974).

[15] These sentences have no exact equivalents in English. The glosses are approximate, in some cases including what comes from their pragmatics as well as their semantics.

b. Pjatiletku vypolnit' dosročno!
5.year.plan fulfill.INF ahead.of.schedule
'Fulfil the 5-year-plan ahead of schedule!'

The sentences in (46), which I call 'pseudo-imperatives', are interpreted as commands and have been treated as a kind of imperative by Vinogradov (1938), Xrakovskij (1999: 286–9), and others. Those in (47) are interpreted more as hortatives like English sentences with *let's*. They raise two problems:

(48) a. What is their syntactic structure?
  b. How are their interpretations to be accounted for?

We consider three accounts of such sentences. First, the WYSIWYG Hypothesis claims that they are subjectless. A second account claims that (46) and (47) have distinct structures that directly encode their status as imperatives and hortatives, respectively. We argue here for a third account—the LSH—under which (46) and (47) both instantiate the UHS construction, with *Unspec* as subject. Thus, (46b) realizes the structure:

(49) *Unspec* vstat'
  Unspecified.human stand.up.INF
  'Unspecified human is to stand up.'

The LSH straightforwardly accounts for the fact that (46) and (47) have the key properties of the UHS construction in (3):

(50) a. They have no overt subject.
  b. They are understood as having a human subject.

Given (50b), they are semantically anomalous with predicates that are anomalous with human subjects:

(51) *Rassypat'sja i ležat'
  get.spilled/scattered.INF and lie.INF
  'Get spilled and lie (there).'

Since *Unspec* is phonologically null and human, the LSH accounts for (50a, b). We now turn to (48b), proposing:

(52) The imperative or hortative interpretations of such sentences are due to the 'be to' meaning of root infinitival clauses (cf. 8.2.1) and to having *Unspec* as subject. An imperative or hortative interpretation may be strengthened in particular cases by pragmatic factors.

The role of the 'be to' meaning can be seen in root infinitivals with a 2nd person subject:

(53) Vam   vstat'!
      you   stand.up.INF
      'You are to stand up!'

Although syntactically not an imperative, (53) has imperative force, like (46a, b). Thus, the 'be to' meaning contributes imperative force. But does *Unspec* contribute to the imperative interpretation?

Xrakovskij's (1999: 286–9) discussion of pseudo-imperatives is revealing. He points out two ways they differ from true imperatives (in addition to having the infinitival rather than imperative form of the verb). First, true imperatives can be suffixed with -*ka*, which has a softening effect, making the imperative somewhat less of an order:

(54) a. Posmotri!
         look.IMP
         'Take a look!'

      b. Posmotri-ka!
         look.IMP-*ka*
         'Take a look!'

Pseudo-imperatives, however, cannot be suffixed with -*ka*:

(55) a. Posmotret'!
         look.INF
         'Take a look!'

      b. *Posmotret'-ka!

Second, Xrakovskij cites a sentence that parallels the pseudo-imperative (56).

(56) Prodvinut'sja   naskol'ko vozmožno
      advance.PFV.INF   as.much   possible
      '*Unspec* is to advance as much as possible; advance as much as possible.'

Xrakovskij says that unlike true imperatives, whose understood subjects are 2nd person, pseudo-imperatives can have 3rd person subjects, citing the following exchange (from A. Tolstoj):

(57) Ordinarec: Kto   rotnyj?
      orderly: who   company.commander
      Orderly: 'Who is the company commander?'
      Nečaev: Ja.

Nečaev:	'I am.'			
Ordinarec:	Rote	prodvinut'sja	naskol'ko	vozmožno.
orderly:	company	advance.INF	as.much	possible
Orderly:	'The company is to advance as much as possible.'			

(57) is simply a root-clause infinitival with an overt 3rd person subject. The imperative force of the 'be to' meaning of the root infinitival is strengthened by the pragmatics of the speech act: the addressee (the company commander) has control over the actions of the subject (the company).

This is the key to understanding *Unspec*'s contribution to the imperative interpretation of pseudo-imperatives. In pseudo-imperatives, the addressee of the speech act is told what the unspecified human subject is to do. As (57) makes clear, a felicitous interpretation with imperative force results where the addressee has control over the actions of the subject. This obviously holds if the addressee is interpreted pragmatically as the referent of the unspecified human subject, which strengthens the imperative force due to the 'be to' meaning of root infinitivals.

Hortatives such as (47) can be accounted for in like manner. Under the LSH, they are syntactically like pseudo-imperatives, with *Unspec* as subject. They have imperative force for the same reasons. The difference is that pragmatically the actions in (47) can be accomplished only by the entire society. Consequently, these sentences are interpreted as being addressed to the entire society, which alone can control the actions described. Combined with the 'be to' meaning of root infinitivals, this yields a hortative interpretation. Thus, there is no need to posit distinct syntactic structures for pseudo-imperatives like (46) and hortatives like (47). The 'be to' meaning of root infinitivals and the presence of *Unspec* as subject give them both imperative force. The apparent contrast between pseudo-imperatives and hortatives is due to pragmatic factors.

Two aspects of this analysis are new: the recognition of the phonologically null element *Unspec* as subject of this construction, and the analysis of its imperative and hortative interpretations as due not to specifically imperative or hortative structures but to the 'be to' meaning of root infinitivals and the presence of *Unspec*, strengthened by pragmatic factors.

8.2.6.2 *Morphosyntactic evidence for* Unspec *in pseudo-imperatives*   In 8.2.4 it was shown that *Unspec* has morphosyntactic features that show up in various kinds of agreement. It behaves like nouns such as *tupica* 'dunce' which can be either masculine or feminine. As a human noun it cannot be neuter, and as a count noun it can be either singular or plural. The LSH predicts that, as subject of pseudo-imperatives, *Unspec* will determine three types of agreement on agreeing constituents: masculine singular, feminine singular, and plural. This can be seen most clearly in (58):

(58) Ne   prevraščat'sja v   bol'nogo/bol'nuju/bol'nyx
      NEG   turn.into.INF   into sick.M.SG/F.SG/PL
      'Don't turn into a sick person / sick people.'[16]

The LSH's prediction is confirmed. As predicted, the neuter singular form is ungrammatical:

(59) *Ne   prevraščat'sja v   bol'noe
      neg   turn.into.INF   into sick.N.SG

Second, as predicted by the LSH, *Unspec* determines agreement on secondary predicates:

(60) Ne   rabotat' p'janym/p'janoj/p'janymi
      NEG   work.INF drunk.M.SG/F.SG/PL
      'Don't work drunk.'

An agreeing secondary predicate can be masculine or feminine singular, or plural.

Third, as the LSH predicts, *Unspec* as subject of pseudo-imperatives determines agreement on semipredicatives:

(61) Zakončit'   sočinenie odnomu/odnoj/odnim
      finish.INF   essay   alone.M.SG/F.SG/PL
      'Finish the essay alone.'

An agreeing semipredicative can be masculine or feminine singular, or plural.

Thus, agreement in pseudo-imperatives provides evidence that, although they appear to have no subject, there is a subject whose morphosyntactic features are those *Unspec* was shown to have in 8.2.4. This is exactly what the LSH predicts.

8.2.6.3 *Syntactic evidence for* Unspec *in pseudo-imperatives*   There is also syntactic evidence for the presence of *Unspec* as the subject of pseudo-imperatives,[17] as the LSH predicts.

First, there are grammatical pseudo-imperatives with predicates that require raising:

---

[16] Example (58) and subsequent examples are glossed as imperatives, although glosses such as '*Unspec* is not to turn into a sick person/sick people' would convey the Russian more literally.

[17] Analogous arguments can be given for hortatives like (47).

(62) Prodolžat'   čitat'
      continue.INF   read.INF
      'Continue to read.'

If pseudo-imperatives were subjectless, there would be no way to satisfy the requirement that there be raising in sentences with *prodolžat'*, since there must be some NP to raise. *Unspec* is that NP.

Second, *Unspec* can control into a complement, as in (63), and into a gerund clause, as in (64).

(63) Pytat'sja   ponjat'
      try.INF   understand.INF
      'Try to understand.'

(64) Rabotaja   s   kollegami,   zakončit'   rabotu   dosročno
      work.GER   with   colleagues   finish.INF   job   ahead.of.schedule
      'Working with colleagues, finish the job ahead of schedule.'

Unspec must be present as the subject of pseudo-imperatives in order to control.

Third, the fact that *Unspec* determines various kinds of agreement, as in (58–61), is evidence for its presence in syntactic structures.

Fourth, in frameworks in which the binding of reflexives is stated on syntactic structures, the fact that *Unspec* can bind a reflexive argues for its presence in syntactic structures:

(65) O   sebe   ne   bespokoit'sja
      about   REFL   NEG   worry.INF
      'One (*Unspec*) is not to worry about oneself.'

This is all evidence against the WYSIWYG Hypothesis and for the LSH, which correctly predicts that *Unspec* will behave like a subject in all these ways.

8.2.6.4 *Summary*   Under the LSH, sentences like (46) and (47) instantiate the UHS construction, with *Unspec* as subject. This correctly predicts agreement patterns and the syntactic behaviour of *Unspec* as subject. Imperative force is due to the 'be to' meaning of root infinitivals and the presence of *Unspec* as subject. The apparent contrast between imperative and hortative interpretations is due to pragmatic factors.

8.2.7 *The distribution of the UHS construction*

Infinitival clauses in Russian have a relatively wide distribution:

(66) (Partial) Distribution of Infinitival Clauses in Russian
      a. Root clauses
      b. Purpose clauses

c. Temporal clauses
d. Complements of raising predicates
e. Controlled complements

Having established the properties of *Unspec* and the UHS construction as instantiated in questions, pseudo-imperatives, and hortatives, we can now determine their distribution by seeing in what clause types these properties appear.

The UHS construction occurs productively in nonfinite clauses. We have seen it in root infinitival clauses, and it occurs in subordinate infinitival clauses as well: in a temporal clause in (67) and in a purpose clause in (68). In each case the masculine singular semipredicative *odnomu* agrees with the subject *Unspec* of the UHS construction.[18]

(67) Pered tem, kak   rabotat' odnomu,   nado   zaščitit'
      before   COMP work.INF alone.M.SG needs defend.INF
      dissertaciju
      dissertation.ACC
      'Before working alone one needs to defend a dissertation.'

(68) Čtoby   rabotat' odnomu,   nado   mnogo znat'
      in order work.INF alone.M.SG needs a.lot know.INF
      'In order to work alone one needs to know a lot.'

The UHS construction occurs in a gerund clause in (69) and in an obligatorily controlled complement in (70).

(69) Rabotaja   odnomu,   trudno   idti   vpered
      work.GER alone.M.SG difficult go.INF forward
      'Working alone, it is difficult to make progress.'

(70) Začem   starat'sja   [rabotat' odnomu]?
      why   try.INF   work.INF alone.M.SG.DAT
      'Why try to work alone?'

While the Russian UHS construction occurs in various types of nonfinite clause, we search in vain for the syntactic and morphosyntactic properties of *Unspec* in finite root clauses. There are no finite UHS clauses in Russian corresponding to the infinitivals in (4), (46), and (47). In this respect Russian

---

[18] As indicated above, plural and feminine singular agreement are possible as well. The fact that the semipredicative *odnomu* is in the dative case is explained in section 8.5.3.

contrasts with French, German, Italian, and Spanish, where the UHS construction occurs freely in finite clauses; (9, 10) and (39, 40) have no exact equivalents in Russian.

The UHS construction cannot occur in finite subordinate clauses either. Temporal and purpose clauses, for example, can generally be either finite or nonfinite. Examples (67, 68) illustrate the UHS construction in infinitival temporal and purpose clauses. Their finite counterparts, however, are impossible:

(71)   *Pered tem,   kak   rabotal   odnomu,   nado   zaščitit'
       before   COMP   work.SBJV   alone.M.SG   needs   defend.INF
       dissertaciju
       dissertation.ACC
       'In order to work alone one needs to defend a dissertation.'

(72)   *Čtoby   rabotal   odnomu,   nado   mnogo   znat'
       in order work.SBJV   alone.M.SG   needs   a.lot   know.INF
       'In order to work alone one needs to know a lot.'

The generalization in (73) yields the distribution in (74), raising the questions in (75).

(73)   The UHS construction cannot occur in finite clauses.

(74)   Clause type   UHS construction
       Finite clauses   *
       Infinitival clauses   OK

In section 8.5 I address the following questions.

(75)   a. Why does the UHS construction have the distribution in (74)
          rather than some other distribution?

       b. Why does its distribution depend on whether the clause is finite
          or nonfinite, rather than on something else? Is this one aspect
          of what characterizes finite vs. nonfinite clauses in Russian?

8.3 The unspecified *they* construction

8.3.1 *The construction*

In addition to the UHS construction, Russian has another construction with an unspecified human subject:

(76) **Govorjat,** čto   budet   vojna
      say.3PL   that   will.be war
      '[They] say there will be a war.'

(77) Vezde   **strojat**
      everywhere   build.3PL
      '[They]'re building everywhere.'

(78) Zdes' **umirajut** ot   goloda i   boleznej
      here   die.3PL   from   hunger and diseases
      'Here [people] are dying of hunger and diseases.'

This construction features a 3rd person plural verb but no overt subject. It is understood as having an unspecified human subject which we will call 'unspecified *they*'. Because the understood subject is human, this construction is anomalous with predicates that are anomalous with human subjects:[19]

(79) *****Rassypajutsja**   vo   vse   storony
      get.spilled/scattered.3PL in   all   directions
      '[People] get spilled/scattered in all directions.'

This construction is similar to the English construction with unspecified *they* as subject:[20]

(80) a. They're going to build a new highway through here.
      b. How much do they charge for parking on campus?
      c. They keep making better computers all the time.

The English sentences in (80) are ambiguous: *they* can be referential, referring to some particular human beings, or it can indicate unspecified human beings, with no specific referent.[21] On the latter reading, (80a–c) instantiate what we will call the 'unspecified *they* construction'.

   The unspecified *they* construction poses the same problems as the UHS construction in (4). We claim that, like the UHS construction, the unspecified *they* construction has a lexical subject, as proposed by Mel'čuk (1974), and that this solves these problems.

---

   [19] (79) is starred because it cannot be understood as having a human subject that needs no antecedent, parallel to (76–8). (79) could be interpreted as having a null inanimate 3rd person plural pronominal as subject if its referent is clear from the context.

   [20] This construction and the corresponding construction in Spanish are discussed by Jaeggli (1986). There are significant differences between the English and Russian constructions, as can be seen in the Russian examples below, many of which cannot be accurately rendered with *they* in English.

   [21] With extra stress on *they*, only the former reading is possible. This is analogous to use of the overt pronoun *oni* 'they' in Russian, described below.

(81) The Lexical Subject Hypothesis (LSH)

  a. The lexicon of Russian includes a lexical item (called 'unspecified *they*' here) that serves as subject of the unspecified *they* construction in syntactic representations.

  b. Unspecified *they* is phonologically null in Russian.

  c. In other respects, unspecified *they* is like other lexical items; its lexical entry represents its semantic, syntactic, and morphosyntactic properties.

The LSH answers the questions about the unspecified *they* construction that correspond to (6a–c) for the UHS construction. First, the properties of the unspecified *they* construction are attributed to the lexical properties of unspecified *they*. For example, the specification [Human] in the semantic representation of unspecified *they* accounts for the fact that the construction is understood as having a human subject. Second, the LSH claims that the unspecified *they* construction is *not* syntactically anomalous, for it has a subject (unspecified *they*) that will behave syntactically as subject. The LSH reduces what appears to be a syntactic anomaly of the construction to a phonological property of one lexical item: it is phonologically null. Third, the extension of the unspecified *they* construction consists of the set of clauses that have unspecified *they* as subject. This is what they have in common and how they differ from other constructions. Thus, the LSH provides a characterization of the notion 'unspecified *they* construction' in Russian.

It will be argued here that in positing a single lexical item as the subject of the unspecified *they* construction, the LSH accounts for its morphosyntactic and semantic properties, which it claims are properties of its subject (unspecified *they*). As with the UHS construction, the LSH reduces the properties of the unspecified *they* construction to those of a single lexical item: unspecified *they*.

8.3.2 *Contrasts between Unspecified* they *and* oni *'they'*

Unspecified *they* is always phonologically null. Since there is an alternation between phonologically constituted and null subject pronouns in Russian (so-called 'pro-drop'), it might be thought, following Franks (1995), that unspecified *they* is simply the null counterpart of the 3rd person plural pronominal *oni* 'they'. Contrasts between them, however, suggest that this is not the case.

First, unspecified *they* can be used for what is known to be a single individual:

(82)   a. **Stučat**   v   dver'
        knock.3PL   on   door
        'There is a knock on the door; someone is knocking at the door.'

      b. Počtu   **prinesli**
        mail.ACC   brought.PL
        'The mail has come.'

(83)   a. Menja   **priglasili**   na   večerinku
        me.ACC   invited.PL   to   party
        'I've been invited to a party.'

      b. **Pozvonili**   čtoby   skazat',   čto   èkzamen budet zavtra
        called.PL   in.order   say.INF   that   exam   will.be tomorrow.
        'Someone called to say that the exam will be tomorrow.'

(82a) is appropriate when the speaker can hear that only one person is knocking at the door, as is (82b) when the speaker knows that only one letter carrier brings the mail. (83a) is appropriate when only one person invited me, as is (83b) when only one person called. Unspecified *they* is also used with predicates that require a semantically plural subject:

(84)   Obyčno   **sobirajutsja**   k   semi   časam
       usually   assemble.3PL   toward   seven   o'clock
       '[People] usually assemble around seven o'clock.'

Semantically, then, unspecified *they* does not specify either singular or plural number, although the agreeing verb is always plural.

    The pronominal *oni*, on the other hand, can have only plural referents:

(85)   a. **Oni**   stučat   v   dver'
        they   knock.3PL   on   door
        'They are knocking at the door.'

      b. **Oni**   prinesli   počtu
        they   brought.PL   mail.ACC
        'They have brought the mail.'

(86)   a. **Oni**   priglasili   menja   na   večerinku
        they.NOM   invited.PL   I.ACC   to   party
        'They have invited me to a party.'

      b. **Oni** pozvonili čtoby   skazat',   čto   èkzamen budet   zavtra
        they called.PL in.order   say.INF   that   exam   will.be tomorrow
        'They called to say that the exam will be tomorrow.'

In none of these sentences can *oni* refer to a single individual.

Second, while *oni* has a definite, specific referent, unspecified *they* does not.

(87) a. Zdes' **rabotajut** ves'   den' i   vsju noč'
           here   work.3PL all   day and all   night
           'Work goes on here all day and all night.'

        b. **Oni** rabotajut (zdes') ves' den' i   vsju noč'
           they work.3PL (here) all   day and all   night
           'They work (here) all day and all night.'

(87b) predicates working all day and all night of the definite referent of *oni*: hence it means that the same individuals work all day and all night. (87a) does not predicate working all day and all night of anyone; it could describe a situation where there are three groups of workers each working an eight-hour shift. (87a) means only that all day and all night work is done (by human beings). Unlike *oni*, unspecified *they* is non-referential.

This non-referentiality is a fundamental difference between unspecified *they* and *oni*. In sentences with two instances of unspecified *they*, nothing in the sentence's linguistic representation either forces or excludes an interpretation of either sameness or distinctness of 'reference'. Speakers are consequently free to infer that the same or different sets of individuals are involved, on the basis of the pragmatics of the situation. In some sentences the most likely interpretation is that the same set of individuals is involved:

(88) Iz-za togo, čto **polučajut** men'še deneg ot   pravitel'stva,
        because   receive.3PL less   money from government
        teper' **berut** bol'še za   obučenie
        now   take.3PL more   for   instruction
        'Because they get less money from the government, they're now charging more for tuition.'

In some sentences the pragmatics of the situation point to different sets of individuals:

(89) Teper' v   stranu **vvozjat**   men'še narkotikov
        now   into country bring.in.3PL less   narcotics
        potomu, čto **uveličili** čislo   pograničnikov[22]
        because   increased.PL number border.guards
        'Now they're bringing less drugs into the country because they've increased the number of border guards.'

---

[22] Similar sentences in Spanish are cited by Jaeggli (1986).

(90) **Govorjat,** čto   zdes' **žili**   v   drevnosti
     say.3PL   that   here   lived.PL   in   antiquity
     'It is said that people lived here in antiquity.'

Some sentences may be interpreted either way:

(91) **Pozvonili** čtoby   skazat', čto   **izmenili**   raspisanie
     called.PL in.order say.INF   that changed.PL   schedule
     'Someone called to say that the schedule had been changed.'

The individual(s) who called may or may not be the individual(s) who changed the schedule. To whatever extent speakers assume sameness or distinctness of 'reference' in (88–91), this is due to inference rather than linguistic structure.[23]

Finally, unspecified *they* is semantically human, while *oni* and its null counterpart are not limited in this way:

(92) a. Položi   stranici vse   vmeste,   čtoby   **oni**   ne   rassypalis'
        put   pages   all   together in.order   they   NEG   scatter.PL
        'Put the pages all together so that they don't get scattered.'

     b. Položi   stranici vse   vmeste,   čtoby   ne   rassypalis'
        put   pages   all   together in.order   NEG   scatter.PL
        'Put the pages all together so that they don't get scattered.'

(92a, b) show *oni* and the corresponding null pronominal as subjects of *rassypat'sja* 'get spilled/scattered', which is anomalous with human subjects. Unspecified *they*, however, is understood as human and is anomalous as subject of such verbs (cf. 79). Example (92) thus shows that unspecified *they* contrasts not only with overt *oni* but also with its null counterpart. This supports the LSH's claim that unspecified *they* has its own lexical entry with its own properties.[24]

---

[23] One tends to think of unspecified *they* as occurring with imperfective verbs, just as in Government and Binding theory and its successors [+ Generic] is one of the usual specifications associated with *arb* interpretation (e.g. Rizzi 1986). Examples (82b), (83a, b), (89), and (91) make clear that there is no such restriction on unspecified *they*, which can serve as subject of perfective verbs.

[24] Franks's (1995: 323–8) analysis of unspecified *they* is parasitic on his analysis of null subject pronouns in Russian, which he claims result from optional deletion in the presence of a 'discourse antecedent'. He explicitly claims that (since the deletion is optional) in Russian the arbitrary reading (unspecified *they* in our terms) is possible regardless of whether the subject is overt (*oni*) or deleted, and that this supports his analysis of Russian null pronouns in general. What has been shown here is sufficient to show that this proposal is untenable. First, Franks's prediction is incorrect, as the contrasts between (82, 83) and (85, 86) and between (87a) and (87b) make clear. Overt *oni* does not have the unspecified reading his analysis claims it to have; it has a definite plural referent. Second, Franks's claim that unspecified *they* is a null pronominal is inconsistent with his claim that null pronominals in Russian require a discourse antecedent. All the examples of unspecified *they* cited here show that it does not require an antecedent.

8.3.3 *Morphosyntactic properties of unspecified* they

As with *Unspec*, evidence for the existence of unspecified *they* comes from the fact that it must be marked in the lexicon with certain morphosyntactic features.

The person, gender, and number features of pronominals have two functions. First, since the feature values of a pronominal must match those of the antecedent that binds it, they limit the class of possible antecedents in particular instances. Second, those feature values show up in agreement. Since unspecified *they* is not bound, its person, gender, and number features have only the latter function.

Although unspecified *they* is semantically neutral with respect to number, it is plural morphosyntactically; agreeing verbs must be plural, as in (76–8), (81–3), and (86–91). In this it contrasts with *Unspec*, which can be either singular or plural morphosyntactically.

The plural number of unspecified *they* can be seen in the agreement of adjectival predicates:

(93) Zdes' ne **starajutsja** stat'   **bogatymi** (*bogatym/ *bogatoj)
       here NEG try.3PL   become.INF rich.PL (*M.SG/*F.SG)
       'Here [people] don't try to become rich.'

In the UHS construction, by contrast, singular adjectival predicates are possible:

(94) S   takoj zarplatoj, kak stat'   **bogatym/bogatoj?**
       with such salary   how become.INF rich.M.SG/F.SG.
       'With that kind of salary, how is one to become rich?'

The same contrast can be seen in secondary predicates, which must be plural with unspecified *they*:

(95) Zdes' ne **xodjat** na rabotu **p'janymi** (*p' janym/*p'janoj)
       here NEG go.3PL   to work   drunk.PL (*M.SG/*F.SG)
       'Here [people] don't go to work drunk.'

In the UHS construction, on the other hand, singular adjectival predicates are possible:

(96) Začem idti   na rabotu **p'janym/p'janoj?**
       why   go.INF to work   drunk.M.SG/F.SG
       'Why go to work drunk?'

The difference in number between *Unspec* and unspecified *they* can also be seen in semipredicatives. Unspecified *they* requires a plural semipredicative:

(97) V   estestvennyx naukax   ne   **rabotajut odni** (*odin/*odna)
      in   natural   sciences NEG   work.3PL alone.PL(M.SG/F.SG)
      'In the natural sciences [people] don't work alone.'

In the UHS construction, as we have seen, singular semipredicatives are possible:

(98) Kak rabotat'   **odnomu/odnoj?**[25]
      how work.INF   alone.M.SG/F.SG
      'How is one to work alone?'

Thus, the lexical entry of unspecified *they* specifies that it has these properties:

(99) a. Phonological shape: Null
      b. Morphosyntactic properties: 3rd person, Plural[26]

Under the LSH, agreement with unspecified *they* is accounted for by the same rules or constraints that account for other instances of agreement; no complications of the grammar are needed. In a WYSIWYG grammar that does not recognize null lexical items, however, each agreement rule or constraint must be complicated to account for agreement in the subjectless unspecified *they* construction.

The fact that *Unspec* and unspecified *they* contrast with respect to number agreement means that a WYSIWYG grammar that claims both constructions are subjectless cannot simply designate one set of agreement features as the 'default' set that shows up in subjectless sentences. Whichever number feature was designated as the default, agreement in the other construction would not be accounted for.

8.3.4 *Syntactic evidence for unspecified* they

There is evidence that phonologically null unspecified *they* is present as subject of its clause in syntactic representations. As argued in detail in Moore and Perlmutter (2000), only true subjects can raise or be controlled, and both types of evidence show unspecified *they* to be a subject in syntactic representations.

First, unspecified *they* can raise, satisfying certain verbs' obligatory raising requirement:

---

[25] The nominative singular forms *odin* and *odna* are ungrammatical for reasons made explicit in section 8.5.

[26] Unspecified *they* is not marked for gender because Russian has no gender contrasts in the plural.

(100) Teper' **načinajut** prepodavat' anglijskij jazyk v mladšix klassax
now begin.3PL teach.INF English in younger classes
'Now [they]'re beginning to teach English in the lower grades.'

Unspecified *they* is the raisee in (100), where it is the surface subject of the 3rd person plural verb *načinajut*.

Second, unspecified *they* can control and be controlled:

(101) Teper' **starajutsja** prepodavat' anglijskij jazyk v mladšix klassax
now try.3PL teach.INF English in younger classes
'Now [they]'re trying to teach English in the lower grades.'

(102) Starajas' privleč' bol'še čitatelej, v gazetax **pišut**
trying.GER attract.INF more readers in newspapers write.3PL
vsjakuju erundu
any rubbish.ACC
'Trying to attract more readers, [they] write all kinds of rubbish in the papers.'

(101) shows control into an obligatorily controlled complement, (102) into an adjunct (gerund) clause, as well as into a complement within the gerund clause. In each of these examples unspecified *they* controls and is controlled.

Third, to account for the various kinds of agreement discussed in section 8.3.3, unspecified *they* must be present in syntactic representations.

Finally, unspecified *they* can bind a reflexive:

(103) O takix veščax daže **sebe** ne **govorjat**
about such things even REFL.DAT NEG speak.3PL
'About such things [people] don't speak even to themselves.'

In (103), phonologically null unspecified *they* binds the reflexive *sebe*. The individuals who speak and are spoken to are understood to be the same. In frameworks in which binding is stated on syntactic representations, the binder (unspecified *they*) and the reflexive (*sebe*) must be represented syntactically, which argues for the syntactic representation of unspecified *they* in those frameworks.

Thus, the same kind of evidence that showed *Unspec* to be present in syntactic representations supports the presence of unspecified *they* as well. It also shows unspecified *they* to be the subject of its clause.

Under the LSH, all of this data is accounted for with no need to complicate the grammar in any way. A WYSIWYG grammar, however, will need to complicate the rules or constraints responsible for each of the phenomena mentioned above to account for what it claims are subjectless sentences in the unspecified *they* construction.

8.3.5 *The distribution of the unspecified* they *construction*

The unspecified *they* construction occurs freely in finite clauses, as illustrated by all the examples in 8.3.1–4. However, it cannot occur in nonfinite clauses. To demonstrate this, we will show that a sentence can have distinct instances of unspecified *they* in distinct finite clauses. If one of these finite clauses is replaced by a nonfinite one, however, distinct instances of unspecified *they* are no longer possible. Either the nonfinite clause will be interpreted as a controlled clause, or the result will be ungrammatical.

First consider temporal clauses, which can be either finite or infinitival. The unspecified *they* construction is possible in finite temporal clauses, as in (104), but not in infinitival temporal clauses like (105):

(104) Do togo, kak **pol'zovalis'** kompjuterami, takix vyčislenij
       before   used.PL   computers   such   calculations
       ne **delali**
       NEG did.PL
       'Before [they] used computers, [they] didn't do such calculations.'

(105) *Do togo, kak pol'zovat'sja kompjuterami, takix vyčislenij
       before   use.INF   computers   such   calculations
       ne **delali**
       NEG did.PL
       'Before [to use] computers, [they] didn't do such calculations.'

(104) has two instances of the unspecified *they* construction, both in finite clauses. With the infinitival temporal clause in (105), however, the unspecified *they* construction is not possible.

To show the same thing for purpose clauses is somewhat more difficult, since a purpose clause is likely to be interpreted as having the same subject as the matrix clause in which it is embedded. Consider (89), repeated here for convenience:

(106) Teper' v   stranu   **vvozjat**   men'še narkotikov
       now   into   country bring.in.3PL   less   narcotics
       potomu, čto **uveličili**   čislo   pograničnikov
       because   increased.PL   number border.guards
       'Now they're bringing less drugs into the country because they've increased the number of border guards.'

Like temporal clauses, purpose clauses can be either finite or infinitival, and it is possible to construct a sentence similar to (106) but with a finite purpose clause:

(107) Čtoby   v   stranu   **vvozili**   men'še   narkotikov,
       in.order into   country bring.in.PL   less   narcotics
       uveličili   čislo   pograničnikov
       increased.PL   number   border.guards
       'In order that [they] bring less drugs into the country, [they]'ve
       increased the number of border guards.'

(107) has two instances of unspecified *they*; they occur as subjects of *uveličili* in the main clause and of *vvozili* in the purpose clause. (107) has an interpretation on which those who increased the number of border guards and those who bring drugs into the country are not the same individuals. If the purpose clause is infinitival, however, the resulting sentence does *not* have two instances of unspecified *they*:

(108) Čtoby   v   stranu   **vvozit'**   men'še   narkotikov,
       in.order into   country bring.in.INF less   narcotics
       uveličili   čislo   pograničnikov
       increased.PL   number   border.guards
       'In order to bring less drugs into the country, [they]'ve increased
       the number of border guards.'

The purpose clause in (108) is a controlled clause whose subject is controlled by the matrix subject. Consequently, (108) is pragmatically bizarre; it means that whoever increased the number of border guards did so in order to bring less drugs into the country. The key fact is that (108) contrasts with (107); (108) does not have an interpretation on which those who increased the number of border guards and those who bring drugs into the country are not the same individuals. Thus, lacking two uncontrolled instances of unspecified *they*, (108) illustrates the fact that unspecified *they* cannot occur as subject of an infinitival clause.

Thus, the unspecified *they* construction occurs in finite but not in nonfinite clauses.[27] The UHS and unspecified *they* constructions occur in complementary environments:

(109) | Clause type | Unspecified *they* | UHS construction |
       |---------------------|--------------------|------------------|
       | Finite clauses | OK | * |
       | Infinitival clauses | * | OK |

[27] There are additional restrictions on the distribution of this construction that are beyond the scope of this chapter.

This distribution raises the question of why the UHS and unspecified *they* constructions have this distribution rather than some other. In particular:

(110)   a. Why does the distribution of the UHS and unspecified *they* constructions depend on whether the clause is finite or nonfinite, rather than some other factor? Is this one aspect of what characterizes finite vs. nonfinite clauses in Russian?

      b. Why do the UHS and unspecified *they* constructions occur in complementary environments?

8.4 Another contrast between finite and nonfinite clauses: the distribution of impersonals

Impersonal constructions in Russian appear to lack a surface subject. In other constructions, predicates agree with their subjects in gender and number in the past tense and in person and number in the nonpast.[28] The predicates of impersonal constructions are neuter singular in the past (as in 111a) and 3rd person singular in the nonpast (as in 111b).

(111)   a. Morosilo
        drizzle.PST.3N
        'It was drizzling.'

      b. Morosit
        drizzle.PRS.3SG
        'It's drizzling.'

A striking asymmetry in the distribution of impersonal constructions is documented in Perlmutter and Moore (2002):[29]

(112)   Impersonal constructions cannot occur in nonfinite clauses.

This generalization, which brings out another asymmetry between finite and nonfinite clauses, can be illustrated for a variety of impersonal constructions.

Purpose clauses in Russian can be either finite (subjunctive), as in (113a), or nonfinite (infinitival), as in (113b):

(113)   a. Čtoby   studenty   rabotali   vmeste,...
        in.order   students.NOM   work.SBJV.PL   together
        'In order that the students work together,...'

---

[28] Adjectival predicates (including participles) agree with their subjects in gender and number.

[29] This work builds in part on a generalization noted by Conrad (1969); cf. also Comrie (1974). What initially appears to be a class of exceptions to this generalization is discussed in section 8.6 below.

      b. Čtoby   studentam   rabotat'   vmeste,...
        in.order   students.DAT work.INF together
        'In order for the students to work together,...'

With impersonal constructions, however, only a finite purpose clause is possible. This can be seen in the data below from Perlmutter and Moore (2002). The (a) sentences are grammatical finite (subjunctive) purpose clauses of impersonal constructions, while the (b) sentences are the corresponding ungrammatical infinitivals.

(114)   Impersonal unaccusative constructions
      a. Čtoby   v   prudu   ne   plavalo   kuvšinok,...
        in.order in   pond   NEG float.SBJV water.lilies.GEN
        'In order that there not be any water lilies floating in the pond,...'
      b. *Čtoby   v   prudu   ne   plavat'   kuvšinok,...
        in.order in   pond   NEG float.INF water.lilies.GEN
        'In order for there not to be any water lilies floating in the pond,...'

(115)   Impersonal passive constructions
      a. Čtoby   ne   bylo   opublikovano takix statej   za
        in.order NEG be.SBJV published   such   articles beyond
        rubežom,...
        border
        'In order that there not be any such articles published abroad,...'
      b. *Čtoby   ne   byt'   opublikovannym(i)[30] takix statej
        in.order NEG be.INF published   such   articles
        za   rubežom,...
        beyond border
        'In order for there not to be any such articles published abroad,...'

(116)   Impersonal I-clauses[31]
      a. Čtoby   nam   ne   bylo   nužno takix knig,...
        in.order we.DAT NEG be.SBJV need   such books.GEN
        'In order that we not need such books,...'
      b. *Čtoby   nam   ne   byt'   nužnym(i) takix knig,...
        in.order we.DAT NEG be.INF need.INS   such books.GEN
        'In order for us not to need such books,...'

---

[30] Adjectival predicates are in the instrumental case in nonfinite clauses. (115b) is ungrammatical, however, regardless of whether it is singular (*opublikovannym*) or plural (*opublikovannymi*). By the same token, (116b) is ungrammatical regardless of whether it is singular (*nužnym*) or plural (*nužnymi*).

[31] I-clauses have a nominal in the dative case that can bind reflexives and control into adjunct clauses but is not the surface subject (Perlmutter 1978; Moore and Perlmutter 2000).

(117)   Weather-verb constructions
  a. Čtoby   morozilo   na   Gavajax, . . .
     in.order   freeze.SBJV on   Hawaii
     'In order that it freeze in Hawaii, . . .'

  b. *Čtoby   morozit'   na   Gavajax, . . .
     in.order   freeze.INF   on   Hawaii
     'In order for it to freeze in Hawaii, . . .'

(118)   Accusative human experiencer constructions
  a. Čtoby   menja   tošnilo, . . .
     in.order   I.ACC   nauseate.SBJV
     'In order that I feel nauseous, . . .'

  b. *Čtoby   menja   tošnit', . . .
     in.order   I.ACC   nauseate.INF
     'In order for me to feel nauseous, . . .'

(119)   I-clauses with accusative objects
  a. Čtoby   Borisu   bylo   žal'   sobak, . . .
     in.order Boris.DAT   be.SBJV   sorry   dogs.ACC
     'In order that Boris feel sorry for dogs, . . .'

  b. *Čtoby   Borisu   byt'   žal'   sobak, . . .
     in.order Boris.DAT   be.INF   sorry   dogs.ACC
     'In order for Boris to feel sorry for dogs, . . .'

(120)   Productive impersonal I-clauses with verbs in -*sja*
  a. Čtoby   Borisu   rabotalos'   doma, . . .
     in.order Boris.DAT   work.SBJV.*sja* at.home
     'In order that Boris be able to work at home, . . .'

  b. *Čtoby   Borisu   rabotat'sja   doma, . . .
     in.order Boris.DAT   work.INF.*sja*   at.home
     'In order for Boris to be able to work at home, . . .'

(121)   Impersonal raising predicates
  a. Čtoby   okazalos',   čto   perevod   udačnyj, . . .
     in.order turn.out.SBJV   that   translation successful
     'In order that it turn out that the translation is successful, . . .'

  b. *Čtoby   okazat'sja,   čto   perevod   udačnyj, . . .
     in.order turn.out.INF   that   translation successful
     'In order for it to turn out that the translation is successful, . . .'

An additional impersonal construction—the accusative-instrumental construction, not mentioned in Perlmutter and Moore (2002)—features an object in the accusative case and an instrument in the instrumental. There appears to be no subject:

(122) Dorogu   zaneslo   snegom
       road.ACC   load.PST   snow.INS
       'The road was overblown with snow.'

Like other impersonals, the accusative-instrumental construction cannot be infinitival. (123a) with the finite verb *zaneslo* is grammatical, while (123b) with the infinitive *zanesti* is not:

(123) a. Čtoby   dorogu   zaneslo   snegom,...
           in.order   road.ACC   load.SBJV   snow.INS
           'In order that the road be overblown with snow,...'

       b. *Čtoby   dorogu   zanesti   snegom,...
           in.order   road.ACC   load.INF   snow.INS
           'In order for the road to be overblown with snow,...'

The fact that all these constructions behave alike with respect to the finite-nonfinite contrast is evidence for grouping them together as 'impersonal'.

What has been illustrated here with finite and infinitival purpose clauses could also be illustrated with finite and infinitival root clauses or with finite and infinitival temporal clauses; limitations of space prohibit citing all the relevant data here. The evidence for (112) in Russian is robust.

Impersonal clauses contrast with both the UHS construction and the unspecified *they* construction in ways that fall together under the hypothesis that they have an expletive as surface subject. Some of these contrasts follow from expletive subjects' lack of semantic content: they cannot control into complement or adjunct clauses or be controlled, they cannot bind reflexives, and they cannot antecede secondary predicates or semipredicatives. The fact that impersonal clauses display 3rd person singular neuter agreement can be attributed to the expletive subject having those features. Expletive subjects' lack of semantic content also explains why impersonal constructions are not understood as having human subjects.[32] Most strikingly, Perlmutter and Moore (2002) show that the expletive subjects of impersonal clauses behave like subjects in being able to raise. Impersonal clauses' expletive subjects also play a key role in their explanation of impersonal clauses' distribution:

---

[32] Impersonal passives such as (115) conform to this generalization, since they are not necessarily understood as having human surface subjects. This is a distinct issue from the interpretation of passives' unexpressed agents.

(124) Clause type   Impersonals Unspecified *they* UHS
       Finite clauses   OK   OK   *
       Infinitival clauses *   *   OK

8.5 The problem and a solution

8.5.1 *Why this distribution?*

The grammar could include constraints to state the distribution of the three construction types directly:

(125) a. The UHS construction cannot occur in finite clauses.
       b. The unspecified *they* construction cannot occur in nonfinite clauses.
       c. Impersonal constructions cannot occur in nonfinite clauses.

Such constraints, however, merely state the facts, raising further questions:

(126) a. Why do impersonals and the unspecified *they* construction occur in environments that are complementary to those in which the UHS construction occurs?
       b. Why does the distribution of these three construction types depend on whether the clause is finite or nonfinite, rather than on some other factor?

(127) a. Do nonfinite clauses have some property that excludes the unspecified *they* construction and impersonal constructions? If so, what is it?
       b. Do the unspecified *they* construction and impersonal constructions have some property that excludes them from nonfinite clauses? If so, what is it?

(128) a. Do finite clauses have some property that excludes the UHS construction? If so, what is it?
       b. Does the UHS construction have some property that excludes it from finite clauses? If so, what is it?

Answers to (126–8) will explain the distribution in (124).

8.5.2 *Subject case in finite and nonfinite clauses*

The solution proposed here has two key elements. The first is the case of subjects of finite and nonfinite clauses in Russian, which contrast in this respect, as (129, 130) show:

(129) **Boris**   ne   rabotaet   zdes'
       Boris.NOM   NEG   work.3SG   here
       'Boris doesn't work here.'

(130) **Borisu**   ne   rabotat'   zdes'
       Boris.DAT   NEG   work.INF   here
       'Boris is not to work here.'

Boris in (129), a finite clause, is nominative, while *Borisu* in (130), an infinitival clause, is dative.

The same contrast can be seen in temporal clauses in (131) and in purpose clauses in (132):

(131) a. Pered tem, kak   **deti**   ušli   guljat',
          before   COMP   children.NOM   go.out.PST.PL play.INF
          oni   nadeli   sapogi
          they.NOM   put.on.PST.PL   boots.ACC
          'Before the children went out to play, they put their boots on.'

       b. Pered tem, kak   **detjam**   ujti   guljat',
          before   COMP   children.DAT   go.out.INF   play.INF
          oni   dolžny   nadet'   sapogi
          they.NOM   ought.PL   put on.INF   boots.ACC
          'Before the children go out to play, they ought to put their boots on.'

(132) a. Oni   sdelajut   vse   vozmožnoe,   čtoby   **deti**
          they   do.3PL   all   possible   in.order   children.NOM
          učilis'   v   xorošej   škole
          study.SBJV   in   good   school
          'They will do everything possible so that the children study in a good school.'

       b. Oni sdelajut vse vozmožnoe, čtoby   **detjam**   učit'sja
          they do.3PL all possible   in.order children.DAT   study.INF
          v   xorošej   škole
          in   good   school
          'They will do everything possible for the children to study in a good school.'

The (a) sentences in (131, 132) are finite and their subjects (*deti*) are nominative, while the (b) sentences are infinitival and their subjects (*detjam*) are dative.

Sentences like (129–132) with overt subjects show clearly that in Russian the case of the subject is different in finite and nonfinite clauses:

(133)   a. The subject of a finite clause must be in the nominative case.
      b. The subject of a nonfinite clause must be in the dative case.

8.5.3 *An explanation of the distribution*

If we juxtapose (133) with (124), a clear pattern emerges:

(134)

Clause type	Subject case	Impersonals	Unspecified *they*	UHS
Finite clauses	NOM	OK	OK	*
Infinitival clauses	DAT	*	*	OK

(135)   Impersonal constructions and the unspecified *they* construction are grammatical only in environments where the subject is required to be nominative.

(136)   The UHS construction is grammatical only in environments where the subject is required to be dative.

An explanation of the distribution of impersonals has been proposed in Perlmutter and Moore (2002):

(137)   The Silent Expletive Hypothesis (SEH)
Impersonal clauses have a silent expletive subject whose case is nominative.

The lexical entry for the silent expletive subject of impersonal constructions includes these elements:

(138)

Phonological shape:	Null
Morphosyntactic properties:	3rd person singular neuter
	Nominative case[33]

The expletive must be 3rd person singular and neuter to account for agreement in impersonal clauses. The nominative specification in (138) means that impersonals will occur in finite clauses, where the subject must be nominative. In infinitival clauses, where the subject must be dative, the nominative case of the expletive subject will clash with this case requirement, resulting in ungrammaticality.

To account for the distribution of the unspecified *they* construction, all that is needed is for the lexical entry of unspecified *they*, like the silent

---

[33] Perlmutter and Moore (2002) claim that the expletive subject of impersonal clauses is one of the series of nominative null pronouns used in cases of 'pro-drop' in Russian. The claim that it is nominative is independent of the feature system used for Russian cases. Thus, the claim would be unaffected if nominative case is represented as a single feature [NOM], or as a combination of features such as [−Oblique, +Subjective] or as any other combination of features.

expletive in (138), to be marked for nominative case (alongside 3rd person and plural):[34]

(139)   Phonological shape: Null
        Morphosyntactic properties: 3rd person plural
                                      Nominative case

Unspecified *they*'s nominative case will clash with the requirement that subjects of infinitival clauses be dative, so the unspecified *they* construction will be ungrammatical in infinitival clauses.

To account for the distribution of the UHS construction, all that is needed is for the lexical entry for its subject *Unspec* to include the morphosyntactic feature(s) for dative case alongside its gender and number features:[35]

(140)   Phonological shape: Null
        Morphosyntactic properties:[36]   Dative case

Consequently, the UHS is grammatical in nonfinite clauses, where the subject must be dative. In finite clauses, where the subject must be nominative, *Unspec*'s dative case clashes with this case requirement, resulting in ungrammaticality. This captures the generalization in (136). Thus, the LSH explains the distribution of the three construction types. All that is needed is for the silent elements it posits as their subjects to be marked for case in the lexicon. Their distribution then follows from the independent case requirements on the subjects of finite and nonfinite clauses in Russian.

Our explanation of the distribution of the UHS construction correctly predicts the generalizations in (141):

(141)   a. A semipredicative modifying the subject of the unspecified *they*
           construction will be in the nominative case.
        b. A semipredicative modifying the subject of the UHS construction
           will be in the dative case.

---

[34] In positing that unspecified *they* is nominative, we follow Mel'čuk (1974), who posits a null noun marked for nominative case, plural number, and the semantic designation 'people' as the subject of this construction. Mel'čuk posits a series of such null elements, each of which is marked with a semantic label, case, and those morphosyntactic features that show up in agreement on finite verbs. For proper subsets of the constructions analysed here and in Perlmutter and Moore (2002) as impersonal, he posits distinct null elements marked neuter singular nominative with the labels 'the elements' (e.g. with weather verbs), 'personhood' (*ličnost'*) with experiencer predicates, and 'environment'. He also posits a null element labelled 'arbitrary' and marked for genitive, dative, and accusative case.

[35] As shown in section 8.2, these can be either masculine or feminine. Like other count nouns, they can be singular or plural. These properties are not included in (140).

[36] As with the nominative marking in (138, 139), the key claim is that *Unspec* is dative; it is not relevant what features are used to represent this. Thus, regardless of whether dative case is represented as a single feature [DAT], as [+Oblique, +Subjective], or as any other combination of features, the essential claim is unaffected.

(141) follows directly from the lexical case specifications of unspecified *they* and *Unspec* and from the fact that semipredicatives agree with their antecedents in case.[37] The correctness of this prediction can be seen in the nominative form *odni* in (97) and the dative forms *odnomu, odnoj,* and *odnim* in (33), (61), and (98).

It might be objected that null subjects' cases revealed by semipredicatives could result from syntactic case assignment to the subjects of finite and nonfinite clauses rather than to lexical case features. Without lexical case features, however, there would be nothing to prevent the occurrence of unspecified *they* as the subject of nonfinite clauses and *Unspec* as subject of finite clauses, which would leave these constructions' distribution unaccounted for.

The LSH takes advantage of the independently attested syntactic requirements on the case of subjects of finite and nonfinite clauses to explain the distribution of the three constructions. It answers the questions in (126), explaining why impersonals and the unspecified *they* construction occur in environments complementary to those in which the UHS construction occurs and why that distribution depends on whether the clause is finite or nonfinite. It explains why we find the distribution we find rather than some other distribution.

The LSH also answers (127, 128). What excludes the unspecified *they* and impersonal constructions from nonfinite clauses is the fact that the subjects of nonfinite clauses must be dative, while their subject is nominative. The property of finite clauses that excludes the UHS construction is the fact that they require their subjects to be nominative, while the subject of the UHS construction is dative.

The essence of the LSH's explanation lies in positing that the items that occur as subjects of the three constructions have lexical case specifications that clash with the case requirements imposed by the syntax in the environments in which they cannot occur. Both the former and the latter are particular to Russian. Explanation is thus achieved internal to Russian grammar, without relying on any putatively universal devices.

---

[37] A rule or constraint such as (32) that ensures agreement in gender and number will ensure agreement in case as well. Franks (1995: ch. 6, following earlier work with Greenberg and Hornstein) eschews this solution, based on considerations internal to the framework he adopts, proposing instead that a rule assigning dative case to 'sister of I' in Russian and Polish will assign dative case both to subjects of infinitives and to the class of semipredicatives that exhibit what Comrie (1974) called the 'second dative'. The issues this raises are beyond the scope of this chapter.

8.6 Predictions for the distribution of the UHS, unspecified *they*, and impersonal constructions in complements of raising predicates

8.6.1 *What the LSH predicts*

The explanation proposed here makes additional predictions:

(142) a. The unspecified *they* and impersonal constructions will be grammatical in any environment in which their subject occurs in a nominative position (and ungrammatical elsewhere).

   b. The UHS construction will be grammatical in any environment in which its subject occurs in a dative position (and ungrammatical elsewhere).

Thus, the LSH predicts that the real contrast that explains the distribution of the three construction types is not (143) but (144):

(143) The contrast between finite and nonfinite clauses

(144) The contrast between clauses whose subjects appear in nominative positions and those whose subjects appear in dative positions

We will now see that the LSH correctly predicts and therefore explains what would otherwise be puzzling data concerning what can occur in complements of the raising predicates *načinat'/načat'* 'begin', *prodolžat'/prodolžit'* 'continue', *perestavat'/perestat'* 'stop', and *prekraščat'/prekratit'* 'stop, cease', with which raising is obligatory.

8.6.2. *Predictions for infinitival complements of finite raising predicates*

8.6.2.1 *Impersonals in infinitival complements of finite raising predicates* An alternative to the LSH's account of the distribution of impersonals might claim that the gap is due to a purely morphological constraint:[38]

(145) Impersonal predicates have no infinitival form.

The LSH, however, actually predicts the grammaticality of certain infinitival impersonal clauses that (145) fails to account for.

---

[38] It is far from clear how such a constraint could be formulated, in view of the fact that many impersonal constructions (e.g. those with the genitive of negation, among others) have predicates that also occur in personal constructions that *can* occur in infinitival form. Since (145) is inadequate in other respects, as shown below, we will not dwell on this point.

Although barred from nonfinite clauses in general, impersonals are perfectly grammatical as infinitival complements of raising predicates:[39]

(146) Perestalo   morosit'
       stop.PST.N.SG   drizzle.INF
       'It stopped drizzling.'

(147) Borisa   načalo   tošnit'
       Boris.ACC   begin.PST.N.SG   nauseate.INF
       'Boris began to feel nauseous.'

(148) Borisu   prodolžalo   byt'   žal'   vsju   sem'ju
       Boris.DAT   continue.PST.N.SG   be.INF   sorry   all   family.ACC
       'Boris continued to feel sorry for the whole family.'

(149) Dorogu   načalo   zanosit'   snegom
       road.ACC   began   load.INF   snow.INS
       'The road began to become overblown with snow.'

(150) V stat'jax   prodolžalo   ne   pojavljat'sja   ssylok   na
       in articles   continued   NEG   appear.INF   references.GEN   to
       èmigrantov
       emigrants
       'In the articles there continued not to appear any references to
       emigrants.'

(145) is at a loss to account for such sentences, in which impersonals *are* infinitival. Indeed, the grammaticality of infinitival impersonals as complements of raising predicates is anomalous, given impersonals' inability to be infinitival elsewhere. The LSH, however, actually predicts the grammaticality of such sentences.

The LSH claims that impersonals have a nominative expletive subject. If an impersonal clause is embedded beneath a raising predicate, the expletive subject will raise and will be the surface subject of the raising predicate. As subject of the raising predicate, it will be required to be in the nominative case. Since it is marked nominative in the lexicon, there is no clash between its lexical case and that required in the environment in which it appears. In this way the LSH correctly predicts the sentences in (146–50) to be grammatical.

[39] This is shown for a larger range of impersonal constructions in Perlmutter and Moore (2002). In (147–50), *Borisa, Borisu, dorogu,* and *v stat'jax,* constituents of the complement, are fronted to shield the verb from initial position. An independent argument that this is due to fronting rather than raising is given in Perlmutter (2000).

Thus, the LSH predicts the grammaticality of infinitival impersonals as complements of raising predicates—a fact that would otherwise be anomalous.

8.6.2.2 *The unspecified* they *construction in infinitival complements of finite raising predicates* The LSH also predicts that the unspecified *they* construction can occur in the complement of a raising predicate: since unspecified *they* will be raised to subject of the raising predicate, where it will be in a nominative position and therefore will be grammatical. This prediction is confirmed:

(151) Načinajut   govorit', čto   budet   vojna
       begin.3PL.PRS   say.INF   that   will.be war
       '[People] are starting to say that there will be a war.'

This is possible because the nominative subject of the unspecified *they* construction surfaces in a nominative position as subject of a finite verb.

8.6.2.3 *Another gap: the UHS construction in infinitival complements of finite raising predicates* Although the UHS construction in general occurs in infinitival clauses, the LSH predicts another gap: it cannot occur in infinitival complements of finite raising predicates. Since the complement subject is obligatorily raised to subject of the raising predicate, it will surface as the subject of the finite raising predicate. Since *Unspec* is dative, and since the subject of a finite clause must be nominative, the resulting clash means that the UHS construction is predicted to be unable to occur in the complement of a finite raising predicate. And this is correct:

(152) *Načal(o)   žit'   odnomu
       begin.PST.M(N).SG   live.INF   alone/M.SG.DAT

Regardless of whether it is inflected for a masculine or neuter subject, (152) does not mean 'One began to live alone', as it would if the UHS were possible in the complement of a finite raising predicate.[40]

8.6.2.4 *The three constructions in infinitival complements of finite raising predicates* The infinitival complements of finite raising predicates illustrated above initially seem to show the opposite of the pattern found in other infinitival clauses. The LSH explains this by linking it to the case of subjects of these infinitival clauses:

---

[40] An anonymous reviewer claims it is necessary to show the ungrammaticality of sentences with an expletive subject of a raising predicate and the UHS construction in an infinitival complement. (152) with *načalo*, the neuter singular form of the verb, is one such ungrammatical sentence. However, its ungrammaticality can be attributed to the fact that with *načat'* 'begin' and the other raising predicates discussed here, raising is obligatory.

(153)   Clause type

Clause type	Subjects' case	Impersonals	Unspecified *they*	UHS
Finite clauses	NOM	OK	OK	*
Infinitival clauses	DAT	*	*	OK
Infinitival complements of finite raising predicates	NOM	OK	OK	*

Crucially, the environments in which impersonals and the unspecified *they* construction occur are complementary to those in which the UHS construction occurs. The crucial variable predicting the distribution is not the clause's finiteness, but whether its subject is nominative or dative. The LSH predicts and explains this fact.

8.6.3   *Predictions for infinitival complements of nonfinite raising predicates*

8.6.3.1 *The UHS construction in infinitival complements of nonfinite raising predicates*   Now suppose that the raising predicate is itself infinitival. What is possible in its complement? One might expect to find the same pattern as when the raising predicate is finite, but the LSH predicts that now the UHS construction will be possible in the complement. This is correct:

(154)   Kak   perestat'   bespokoit'sja   ob   ètom?
         how   stop.INF   worry.INF   about   this
         'How is one to stop worrying about that?'

(155)   Kak   načat'   rabotat'   odnomu/odnoj/odnim?
         how   begin.INF   work.INF   alone.M.SG.DAT/F.SG.DAT/PL.DAT
         'How is *Unspec* to begin to work alone?'

The LSH's claim that the key variable is the subject's case predicts this. Since the raising predicates *perestat'* and *načat'* are themselves infinitival, their subjects must be dative. *Unspec*, the raisee, is itself marked dative. Consequently, a dative NP occurs as subject of a clause that requires its subject to be dative. The result is grammatical. The LSH thus predicts and explains the grammaticality of the UHS construction as complement of a nonfinite raising predicate.

8.6.3.2 *Two further gaps: impersonals and the unspecified* they *construction in infinitival complements of nonfinite raising predicates*   Now consider impersonal complements of raising predicates, shown in (146–50) to be grammatical. In those examples, the raising predicate is itself finite. If the raising predicate is infinitival, however, the LSH predicts the corresponding sentences to be ungrammatical. The nominative expletive subject of impersonals will be raised to subject of a raising predicate which, being infinitival, will require its subject to be dative. The LSH predicts the resulting case clash to result in ungrammaticality.

This prediction is confirmed, as can be seen in purpose clauses, which can be either finite (subjunctive) or infinitival. If the raising predicate is finite, an embedded impersonal is grammatical, but if the raising predicate is infinitival, an embedded impersonal is ungrammatical, as shown in Perlmutter and Moore (2002).

(156)   a. Čtoby   prodolžalo   morosit',...
             in.order   continue.SBJV   drizzle.INF
             'In order that it continue to drizzle,...'

         b. *Čtoby   prodolžat'   morosit',...
             in.order   begin.INF   drizzle.INF
             'In order for it to continue to drizzle,...'

(157)   a. Čtoby   Borisa   načalo   tošnit',...
             in.order   Boris.ACC   begin.SBJV   nauseate.INF
             'In order that Boris begin to feel nauseous,...'

         b. *Čtoby   Borisa   načat'   tošnit',...
             in.order   Boris.ACC   begin.INF   nauseate.INF
             'In order for Boris to begin to feel nauseous,...'

(158)   a. Čtoby   Borisu   prodolžalo   byt'   žal'   vsju sem'ju,...
             in.order   Boris.DAT   continue.SBJV   be.INF sorry all   family.ACC
             'In order that Boris continue to feel sorry for the whole family,...'

         b. *Čtoby   Borisu   prodolžat'   byt'   žal'   vsju sem'ju,...
             in.order   Boris.DAT   continue.INF   be.INF sorry all   family.ACC
             'In order for Boris to continue to feel sorry for the whole family,...'

(159)   a. Čtoby   dorogu   prodolžalo   zanosit'   snegom,...
             in.order   road.ACC   continue.SBJV   load.INF   snow.INS
             'In order that the road continue to become overblown with snow,...'

         b. *Čtoby   dorogu   prodolžat'   zanosit'   snegom,...[41]
             in.order   road.ACC   continue.INF   load.INF   snow.INS
             'In order for the road to continue to become overblown with snow,...'

---

[41] Irrelevantly, (159b) is grammatical as a controlled clause, controlled by a human NP in the matrix clause, in which case it means 'In order for NP to continue to load the road with snow ...'. Crucially, (159b) is impossible as the infinitival counterpart of (159a), i.e. as an infinitival impersonal.

(160) a. Čtoby   v   stat'jax   prodolžalo   ne   pojavljat'sja
          in.order in   articles   continue.SBJV NEG   appear.INF
          ssylok   na   èmigrantov,...
          references.GEN to   emigrants
          'In order that there continue not to appear any references to
          emigrants in the articles,...'

       b. *Čtoby   v   stat'jax   prodolžat'   ne   pojavljat'sja   ssylok
          in.order in articles continue.INF NEG appear.INF   references.GEN
          na   èmigrantov,...
          to   emigrants
          'In order for there to continue not to appear any references to
          emigrants in the articles,...'

The LSH also predicts that the unspecified *they* construction cannot be
embedded beneath an infinitival raising predicate. Unspecified *they* would be
raised to subject of the raising predicate which, being nonfinite, requires its
subject to be dative. Since unspecified *they* is nominative, the resulting case
clash will cause ungrammaticality. This prediction is confirmed:

(161) a. Čtoby   prodolžali   govorit',   čto   budet   vojna,...
          in.order   continue.SBJV   speak.INF   that will.be war
          'In order that [people] continue to say that there will be a war,...'

       b. *Čtoby   prodolžat'   govorit',   čto   budet   vojna,...
          in.order   continue.INF speak.INF   that will.be war
          'In order to continue to say that there will be a war,...'

(161a) and (161b) contrast. (161a) is an example of the unspecified *they*
construction, but (161b) is not. It is grammatical as an example of a controlled
infinitival purpose clause, interpretable in terms of a controller in the matrix
clause, but not as an uncontrolled clause with unspecified *they* as subject.
Thus, it illustrates the impossibility of embedding the unspecified *they* construction beneath an infinitival raising predicate.

Exactly as the LSH predicts, neither impersonals nor the unspecified *they*
construction can be embedded beneath an infinitival raising predicate. In both
cases, their null subjects occur in positions where their nominative case fails to
satisfy the requirement that the subject of an infinitival clause be dative.

8.6.3.3 *The predictability of the data* The distribution of impersonals, the
unspecified *they* construction, and the UHS construction as complements of
raising predicates shows that what matters is not whether these constructions
are themselves finite or nonfinite. The variable that correctly predicts

grammaticality is the case requirement its surface structure position imposes on the subject:

(162)

Clause type	Subjects' case	Impersonals	Unspecified *they*	UHS
Finite clauses	NOM	OK	OK	*
Infinitival clauses	DAT	*	*	OK
Infinitival complements of finite raising predicates	NOM	OK	OK	*
Infinitival complements of infinitival raising predicates	DAT	*	*	OK

Where the subject must be nominative, impersonals and the unspecified *they* construction are grammatical and the UHS construction is not; where the subject must be dative, the UHS construction is grammatical and impersonals and the unspecified *they* construction are not. This is exactly what the LSH predicts.

8.7 Conclusions

8.7.1 *The distribution of the three construction types*

We have examined the distribution of three construction types in Russian that are sensitive to the contrast between finite and nonfinite clauses. We saw initially that the UHS construction occurs in nonfinite but not finite clauses, while the unspecified *they* construction and impersonal constructions have the opposite distribution, occurring in finite but not nonfinite clauses. Independently, subjects of finite clauses must be nominative, while subjects of nonfinite clauses must be dative. Hence the UHS construction occurs in those clauses whose subjects must be dative, while the unspecified *they* and impersonal constructions occur in those clauses whose subjects must be nominative.

Under the LSH, under which each construction type has a phonologically null subject drawn from the Russian lexicon, *Unspec*, which occurs as subject of the UHS construction, is marked dative in the lexicon, while unspecified *they* and the expletive subject of impersonal constructions are lexically nominative. This explains the distribution of the three construction types. The UHS construction cannot occur in finite clauses because its dative subject clashes with the syntactic requirement that subjects of finite clauses be nominative. The unspecified *they* and impersonal constructions cannot occur in nonfinite clauses because their nominative subjects clash with the syntactic requirement that subjects of nonfinite clauses be dative.

The distribution of the three construction types is explained by two devices:

(163)   a. The independent syntactic requirement that the subjects of finite and nonfinite clauses be nominative and dative, respectively.

   b. Phonologically null lexical items that are lexically marked for case.

All that is posited specifically to account for the distribution of the three construction types are the three items that serve as their subjects and their lexically marked case.[42] The LSH was then shown to make correct predictions about the distribution of the three construction types in complements of raising predicates.

Cross-linguistically common contrasting case requirements on subjects of finite and nonfinite clauses like those in Russian are discussed in Perlmutter and Moore (2002). In classical Greek, subjects of finite clauses are nominative, while subjects of infinitival clauses are accusative. There is also a nonfinite genitive absolute construction whose subjects are in the genitive case. In Latin as well, subjects of finite clauses are nominative, while subjects of infinitival clauses are accusative. There is also a nonfinite ablative absolute construction whose subjects are in the ablative case. In Turkish, subjects of finite clauses are nominative, while subjects of nonfinite participial clauses are genitive (Lewis 1967).[43] In Irish, subjects of finite clauses are nominative, while subjects of infinitival clauses are usually accusative but can also be dative under certain conditions (McCloskey 2001). Even in English, where only pronouns exhibit a contrast between subjective and objective case, in finite clauses subjects are in the subjective case, while in nonfinite clauses they are objective or possessive.

8.7.2 *Case as a lexical property*

Essential to the LSH is the claim that *Unspec* is lexically marked as dative and that unspecified *they* and the expletive subject of impersonals are lexically marked as nominative. This amounts to the claim that these are morphologically defective lexical items that lack other case forms. Such defective paradigms are widely attested in morphological systems. For Russian,

---

[42] The inventory of null elements in Russian certainly exceeds the three discussed here. First, the expletive subject of impersonal constructions is one of a series of phonologically null nominative pronouns that are needed independently to account for 'pro-drop' (e.g. Franks 1995; Perlmutter and Moore 2002). Second, Mel'čuk (1974) posits null objects (direct and indirect) like those posited for Italian by Rizzi (1986). Third, a null subject with 2nd person features appears in sentences like *Ves' den' rabotaeš' i za čto?* 'You work all day, and for what?'

[43] However, Kornfilt (Chapter 9 below) argues that at least some Turkish dependent clauses with genitive subjects are in fact finite, if finiteness is understood as syntactic opacity and subject licensing rather than being characterized in terms of verbal morphology.

Mel'čuk (1974: 353) cites *ščec* 'cabbage soup (diminutive)', *drovec* 'firewood', and *drožžec* 'yeast', all of which exist only in the genitive plural and must be so marked in their lexical entries. Mel'čuk (1974) and Perlmutter and Moore (2002) cite French *on* and German *man*, which appear only in nominative positions as subjects. Greenough et al. (1903: 42–3) list a number of Latin nouns that are defective in certain cases: nouns found in one case only (monoptotes), nouns found in only two cases (diptotes), nouns found in only three cases (triptotes), and nouns found in only four cases (tetraptotes), as well as nouns that are regular in the singular but defective in the plural and nouns that are regular in the plural but defective in the singular. Such nouns must be marked in the lexicon with case features that correctly characterize their defective paradigms. Under the LSH, *Unspec* and unspecified *they* are simply lexical items with defective paradigms. In giving them lexical case features, the LSH uses a device that is independently needed in grammars.[44]

The expletive subject of impersonals has a somewhat different status. It is argued in Perlmutter and Moore (2002) to be one of a series of phonologically null nominative pronouns independently needed to account for Russian sentences with null subjects. Thus, it belongs to a wider class of pronouns that share the same phonological shape (null) and the same case feature(s). Similarly, the French expletive *il* belongs to a series of nominative pronouns and occurs only in nominative positions:

(164) Il   pleut
       it.NOM   rain.PRS.3SG
       'It's raining.'

(165) Il   est   nécessaire que   vous partiez
       it.NOM   is   necessary   that you   leave.SBJV
       'It is necessary that you leave.'

In accusative positions we find a phonologically null expletive rather than the accusative form (*le* or *l'*) corresponding to the nominative *il*:

(166) a. J'entends   pleuvoir
           I.NOM.hear.PRS   rain.INF
           'I hear it raining.'

       b. *Je l'entends   pleuvoir.
           I   it.ACC.hear.PRS rain.INF

---

[44] Lexical marking for other morphosyntactic features is also widely attested. Lexical marking of gender features is so common, both in Russian and cross-linguistically, as not to require comment. Lexical marking of number features is independently attested in *pluralia tantum* nouns.

(167) a. Je trouve   nécessaire que   vous partiez
           I   find.PRS   necessary   that you   leave.SBJV
           'I find it necessary that you leave.'
       b. *Je le   trouve   nécessaire que vous partiez
           I   it.ACC   find.PRS necessary   that you   leave.SBJV

Thus, expletive pronouns with lexical case features are independently attested as well.

8.7.3 *Contrasting morphosyntactic properties as evidence for phonologically null lexical entries*

Crucial to our explanation of the distribution of the UHS, unspecified *they*, and impersonal constructions are the contrasting case, gender, and number features of their phonologically null subjects:

(168) | Lexical item | Case | Gender | Number |
       | --- | --- | --- | --- |
       | *Unspec* | DAT | M/F | SG/PL |
       | Unspecified *they* | NOM | – | PL |
       | Expletive pronoun | NOM | N | SG |

Like the nouns in (18), *Unspec* can be either masculine or feminine (but not neuter). Like other nouns that can be either singular or plural, *Unspec* need not be lexically marked for number. Plural unspecified *they* need not be marked for gender because Russian has no gender contrasts in the plural. The expletive pronoun is clearly neuter because it determines neuter agreeing forms on verbs and adjectives.

Together these null elements with contrasting morphosyntactic features provide an argument against the WYSIWYG Hypothesis that none of them could make alone.

If impersonal constructions were the only constructions with no overt subject, one could maintain the WYSIWYG Hypothesis by claiming that they are subjectless. To account for the fact that their predicates are 3rd person singular neuter, we could claim that *neuter singular* forms are 'unmarked' or default forms which occur when there is no subject to agree with. This, in essence, is the analysis proposed by Babby (1989).

Similarly, if the unspecified *they* construction were the only apparently subjectless construction, one could maintain the WYSIWYG Hypothesis by claiming that they are subjectless. To account for the fact that predicates and semipredicatives that ordinarily agree with the subject must be plural in the unspecified *they* construction, one could claim that *plural* forms are 'unmarked' forms that appear when there is no subject to agree with.

Since the UHS construction displays three types of agreement (masculine and feminine singular, as well as plural), the WYSIWYG Hypothesis cannot claim in this case that one type of agreement is the default. This difficulty is compounded when it attempts to account for the unspecified *they* and impersonal constructions as well. It cannot claim that one type of agreement is the default, for at most one set of morphosyntactic properties can be claimed to be the default. For the other two construction types it is necessary to posit a phonologically null subject with morphosyntactic features with which agreeing forms agree. Thus, the existence of three phonologically null lexical items with contrasting morphosyntactic features yields an argument against the WYSIWYG Hypothesis and in favour of phonologically null lexical items that no one of them could make alone.

The argument above is based on the null subjects' gender and number features. An analogous argument can be based on their contrasting case features which account for the constructions' distribution and show up on agreeing semipredicatives in the UHS and unspecified *they* constructions. If the WYSIWYG Hypothesis were to claim that nominative is the 'unmarked' or default case, the dative case of *Unspec* in the UHS construction would be unaccounted for. If dative were claimed to be the 'unmarked' or default case, the nominative case of the subjects of the unspecified *they* and impersonal constructions would be unaccounted for. Again, distinct null entities' contrasting morphosyntactic features make an argument against the WYSIWYG Hypothesis and in favour of phonologically null lexical items that no one of them could make alone.

Null subjects' morphosyntactic features contrast not only internally to Russian but cross-linguistically as well. Russian *Unspec*, French *on*, and German *man* contrast in their case features: *on* and *man* are nominative, occurring freely in nominative environments, while Russian *Unspec* is dative, which excludes it from nominative environments. The analogous element *Unspec* with null phonological shape serves as subject of the UHS in Italian, Spanish, and Serbo-Croatian, where it occurs in nominative environments as subject of finite clauses. Yet it has a different morphological effect in those languages: it engenders reflexive morphology on the verb. In addition, as pointed out in section 8.2.3, it determines plural agreement on adjectives in Italian but singular in Spanish.

8.7.4 *Further problems for the WYSIWYG Hypothesis*

8.7.4.1 *Accounting for agreement and raising*   All three phonologically null subjects posited by the LSH behave like subjects syntactically in two respects: they determine agreement and they raise.

We have discussed a class of predicates with which raising is obligatory; there are no grammatical variants of the relevant structures without raising. The LSH correctly predicts that when impersonal, unspecified *they*, and UHS constructions are embedded beneath these raising predicates, grammatical sentences with raising result. Since all three construction types have subjects under the LSH, nothing has to be added to the grammar to account for this. Since a WYSIWYG grammar claims that all three construction types are subjectless, it will be necessary to complicate the grammar in some way to explain why they can be embedded beneath predicates that require raising.

Thus, with respect to both raising and agreement, the LSH correctly predicts the data that a WYSIWYG grammar must devise complications to account for.

8.7.4.2 *Contrasts between impersonal constructions and the Unspecified Human constructions*   We have accounted for contrasts between impersonals and the unspecified human constructions by means of differences in their null subjects:

(169)	Impersonals	Unspecified *they*	UHS
Human subject understood	No	Yes	Yes
Can antecede secondary predicates	No	Yes	Yes
Can antecede semipredicatives	No	Yes	Yes
Can bind reflexives	No	Yes	Yes
Can control	No	Yes	Yes
Can be controlled	No	Yes	Yes

The LSH predicts these contrasts, which result from differences between the properties of lexical nouns and those of non-thematic expletives. The null human subjects behave just like phonologically constituted ones with respect to all relevant rules and constraints; nothing need be added to the grammar to account for them.

Since the WYSIWYG Hypothesis claims that all three construction types are subjectless, it must elaborate otherwise unnecessary devices in each case to account for the data. Further, in specifying such devices, it is unclear how to distinguish impersonal constructions from the UHS and unspecified *they* constructions, which behave differently.

8.7.4.3 *The constructions' distribution in finite and nonfinite clauses*   While in general the distribution of the three construction types depends on the finiteness of the clause in which they appear, in section 8.6 we saw that in infinitival complements of raising predicates their distribution depends on the finiteness of the matrix clause. These are the distributional generalizations:

(170)	Impersonals	Unspecified *they*	UHS
OK in finite root clauses	Yes	Yes	No
OK in infinitival root clauses	No	No	Yes
OK in infinitival complements of finite raising Vs	Yes	Yes	No
OK in infinitival complements of nonfinite raising Vs	No	No	Yes

The LSH's explanation of this distribution comes from the null subjects' case features, as made explicit above. A WYSIWYG grammar, which claims that all three construction types are subjectless, offers no explanation of their distribution and will need to be complicated in some way just to account for the data.

8.7.4.4 *Summary of problems for the WYSIWYG hypothesis* We have examined impersonal constructions and the unspecified *they* and UHS constructions with respect to the phenomena summarized in (171):

(171)	Impersonals	Unspecified *they*	UHS
Determine predicate agreement	Yes	Yes	Yes
Can raise	Yes	Yes	Yes
Human subject understood	No	Yes	Yes
Can antecede secondary predicates	No	Yes	Yes
Can antecede semipredicatives	No	Yes	Yes
Can bind reflexives	No	Yes	Yes
Can control	No	Yes	Yes
Can be controlled	No	Yes	Yes
OK in finite root clauses	Yes	Yes	No
OK in infinitival root clauses	No	No	Yes
OK in infinitival complements of finite raising Vs	Yes	Yes	No
OK in infinitival complements of nonfinite raising Vs	No	No	Yes

By positing that they all have phonologically null subjects, the LSH accounts both for the ways they behave alike and for their differences. In claiming that all three construction types are subjectless, a WYSIWYG grammar cannot make the properties of the three construction types follow from properties of their subjects. It therefore must be complicated in some way to account for the properties in (171). While we have not attempted to elaborate the devices a

WYSIWYG grammar would have to resort to, we have made explicit the domain of data it must account for without loss of generality.[45]

8.7.5 *In what ways can finite and nonfinite clauses differ?*

We now return to the questions that motivated this study:

(172)   a. In what ways can finite and nonfinite clauses contrast in a given language?
      b. To what extent do different languages manifest different contrasts between finite and nonfinite clauses?

The major contrast between finite and nonfinite clauses investigated here concerns the distribution of the UHS, unspecified *they*, and impersonal constructions in Russian, which initially appeared to depend on whether the clause is finite or nonfinite. If one were listing the properties of finite and nonfinite clauses in Russian, one might well include the distribution in (170) in the list.

An attempt to go beyond a mere listing of facts has led to the discovery that the distribution of these constructions is not due to the contrast between finite and nonfinite clauses, but is predicted by the case required of the subject. Consequently, the ability to host the unspecified *they* construction, impersonals, or the UHS construction is not a property that distinguishes finite and nonfinite clauses. The relevant contrast lies in the different cases finite and nonfinite clauses require of their subjects—a phenomenon widely attested cross-linguistically.

We conclude that the contrast between constructions that can occur in finite and nonfinite clauses in Russian does not lead us to expand the inventory of ways that finite and nonfinite clauses can differ. The clash between the syntactic case requirement on clauses' subjects and the lexical case of the subjects of the UHS, unspecified *they*, and impersonal constructions explains what would otherwise be a mysterious distribution.

---

[45] An anonymous reviewer criticizes this paper for positing phonologically null subjects, which s/he claims are 'undesirable entities'. This reviewer, however, provides no alternative account of the phenomena in (171). While readers are certainly entitled to their opinions about what is desirable or undesirable, it is incumbent on those who find null subjects undesirable to show that a grammar without them is superior to one that posits them. (171) can serve as a checklist of the phenomena that a grammar without null subjects must account for in a superior way in order to be preferable to a grammar incorporating the LSH.

9

Verbal and nominalized finite clauses in Turkish

JAKLIN KORNFILT

9.1 Introduction

Finiteness is a term used very often in traditional, typological, and formal literature in linguistics. Yet it is not completely clear whether this term expresses a discrete formal feature or even a unique phenomenon to which such a feature would correspond, or if finiteness is an epiphenomenon resulting from certain other properties of language, thus in need of formal analysis as a combination of features (see discussion in Adger, Chapter 2 above, as well as the contribution of Cristofaro, Chapter 4 above, where the view that finiteness is not one single, discrete phenomenon is also defended).

In generative approaches to language study, the term of finiteness has been used in syntactic, semantic, and morphological senses. Generally speaking, this term has been employed to characterize syntactic domains—usually clauses—which display, in one way or another, propositional independence. While such independence is, of course, a property of most root clauses, the issue of whether an embedded clause is finite or not can be a question of interesting inquiry, and thus the challenge arises in the quest for some overt syntactic and morphological correlates of finiteness.

As briefly mentioned above, the most recent thinking about this issue is that there is no single, discrete notion of finiteness that corresponds in a

This article corresponds only in part to the presentation I gave at the Konstanz conference on Finiteness, held in May 2001 at Konstanz University. I am grateful to the organizers of that conference, especially to Frans Plank and Irina Nikolaeva, for financial and logistic support which made my participation possible. I would further like to thank the audience at that presentation for their questions and comments, especially Josef Bayer. I am particularly grateful to two anonymous referees of a previous version of this text, as well as to Irina Nikolaeva, for insightful questions and suggestions. I am indebted to Mehmet Yanılmaz, Ayşe Yazgan, Demir Dinç, Akgül Baylav, and Cemal Beşkardeş for serving as additional native informants. Finally, I would like to express my gratitude to Irina for her patience and understanding of the delays that were unavoidable and for her help with the formatting of this chapter. All shortcomings are my own responsibility.

one-to-one fashion to any single morphological or syntactic expression. Propositionality was just mentioned as a relevant semantic notion corresponding to finiteness. While this relationship remains unchallenged, the notion of propositionality is itself less than clear-cut. The overt expression of finiteness therefore remains an interesting and challenging issue, especially because such expression also appears to be open to parametric variation.

In most Indo-European languages (especially many well-studied languages still in use in Europe), finiteness appears to correlate with subjects in the nominative case, and with a predicate which is marked for tense and agreement. The correlation of nominative subjects and of tensed predicates has led to proposals about a causal relationship. In most formal syntactic approaches to subject Case—independently of any particular theoretical model—tense (and agreement in those languages that express it) have been taken to be the licenser(s) of nominative (Chomsky 1981 and related work in the Government and Binding and the Principles and Parameters models). The same is true of structuralist approaches (e.g. Bloomfield 1933).

One repercussion of this view is to take nominative case as licensed clause-internally (rather than clause-externally) as a necessary (if perhaps not sufficient) condition for the finiteness of the clause, given that a finite clause would not be transparent to clause-external factors, due to its propositional, and therefore syntactic, independence from the clause it is embedded in. Further, a tense 'strong' enough in some sense to license the nominative case of the subject syntactically would also be sufficiently strong semantically to make the embedded clause independent from its syntactic context with respect to its temporal semantics, and thus contribute to the clause's propositionality.

On the basis of such considerations, the morphological realizations of nominative as well as of tense (and agreement) have been taken to be definitional for finiteness in traditional as well as formal literature, with the main difference that in traditional literature (see e.g. Hock 1991 and Jespersen 1924), with its morphology-based focus, finiteness has been a notion generally used for the morphology of tensed (and agreeing) predicates, while in more recent, formal literature, finiteness has been used as a term referring primarily to syntactic domains, usually clauses headed by morphologically finite predicates.[1]

---

[1] One of the anonymous referees comments that it is unlikely for such a view to have been expressed in traditional literature, especially because Latin had, in addition to nominative subjects, also non-nominative ones—the latter in the presence of tensed and agreeing predicates. While doubtlessly correct concerning Latin subjects and predicates, this remark does not take into account the fact that non-nominative subjects are rather rare in European languages, and where they do occur (such as in English and, to a lesser degree, in German), they occur with non-tensed (hence 'nonfinite') clauses. Thus, the identification of tensed predicates as finite ones co-occurring with nominative subjects and of non-tensed predicates as nonfinite ones co-occurring with non-nominative subjects

In this chapter, I would like to pursue two aims. First, I shall venture to show that in Turkish (as a representative of languages with similar properties), not just nominative but also genitive subject Case can be an expression of finiteness, however defined, as long as it can be shown that such genitive case is indeed licensed clause-internally (i.e. in similar ways to nominative), and that the genitive is dependent on the inflection of the predicate within that clause.

This further suggests that realization of finiteness with respect to subject Case licensing is not a particular case (such as the nominative, as widely assumed) but, more generally, clause-internally licensed subject Case (as a syntactic notion). The morphological realization of subject Case (as nominative or genitive in languages such as Turkish, or perhaps as yet another case in some other languages) is a matter that may depend on a number of other factors. In Turkish, I claim that the realization of this syntactic subject Case as either nominative or genitive depends on the categorial features of the predicate inflection (as either verbal or nominal, respectively) and does not affect the issue of finiteness.

Second, while earlier as well as more recent approaches to finiteness have taken tense as the most important semantic and syntactic property of a clause in determining its finiteness, it is possible that these duties are performed by overt agreement in certain languages such as Turkish, where agreement can show up independently from tense. A further conclusion would follow from this: since agreement (without tense) cannot represent a clause's temporal independence semantically, the notion of finiteness cannot be a monolithic one. In other words, semantic finiteness and syntactic finiteness, while coinciding in many instances, do not always go hand in hand. Thus, it is not surprising that the morphological realizations of finiteness (if finiteness has any syntactic relevance at all) are not expressions of a monolithic semantic notion.

This is a conclusion similar in spirit to Adger (Chapter 2 above), where finiteness is treated as a syntactic feature with a distinct position in the clausal architecture, but where finiteness as a general linguistic notion is viewed as an epiphenomenon. Note further that the conclusion that, in languages where agreement can occur independently from tense, it is agreement rather than

took hold in the traditional literature, despite the facts of Latin. It is further interesting to note that Latin infinitives can be analysed as lacking 'finite' agreement, although infinitival clauses do have morphological agreement. See Cecchetto and Oniga (2001), where it is claimed that infinitival agreement on these predicates differs from 'finite verbal' agreement, because it lacks person features, which finite verbal agreement does have. The authors argue that an inflection with the features [+T, −Agr] is too weak to license nominative subjects clause-internally; this is why the subject is accusative (in their account, due to an abstract Preposition). In their account, accusative subjects occur in 'nonfinite' clauses, and those clauses are nonfinite due to the absence of rich, fully-fledged agreement. Their account is thus compatible with the one proposed here for Turkish, where agreement is taken as the primary (if not always the only) feature that expresses finiteness, with finiteness understood as a composite phenomenon.

tense which gives rise to syntactic finiteness phenomena, is not limited to clauses with genitive subjects. I will argue this point in Turkish with respect to nominative subjects, too.

Furthermore, similar arguments in favour of the primacy of agreement over tense in these respects have been made for European Portuguese (Raposo 1987; 1989), Latin (Cecchetto and Oniga 2001), and, to a lesser degree, for Modern Greek (Cecchetto and Oniga 2001, basing their view on previous work by Iatridou 1993).[2]

In these languages, the subject Case licensed by agreement (rather than tense, or in addition to tense) is the nominative. This, then, offers an additional argument for viewing one syntactic (or morphosyntactic) expression of finiteness as clause-internally licensed subject Case in general, rather than just as the nominative, since similar generalizations hold for both nominative and genitive. Once again, a particular phenomenon correlated with finiteness, namely subject Case—whether nominative or genitive—is licensed clause-internally by agreement alone, or at least by agreement as the primary factor. Where tense plays a role, that role is secondary; furthermore, tense cannot determine finiteness by itself, i.e. without the presence of agreement.

In this study, I present my analyses in a loose Principles and Parameters framework with reliance on some aspects of the Minimalist Programme, whose details are presented in detail in Adger's contribution to this volume. This chapter is structured as follows. In section 9.2, I establish agreement as the main element setting up 'finite' clauses and licensing overt subjects in such clauses. I first discuss verbal embeddings with and without agreement (and with nominative vs. non-nominative subjects), showing that tense without agreement does not lead to syntactic finiteness. In section 9.3 I turn to nominalized embeddings, and show that agreement without any tense does lead to phrase structural domains that exhibit syntactic finiteness phenomena. I then show that, where both agreement and tense are exhibited by embedded clauses (especially in nominalized clauses), tense does contribute to finiteness

---

[2] In Modern Greek, the infinitival morphology has been lost; citation forms as well as constructions that would correspond to ECM/SOR use a tensed and agreeing form. Iatridou (1993) shows that the apparent finiteness of such forms is fake, and that syntactic opacity/finiteness is created when the morphological tense expresses genuine, syntactic tense. All tensed predicates, whether their tense is 'genuine' or 'fake', bear agreement morphology. Cecchetto and Oniga (2001) interpret these findings in a more general typological context, as follows. In European Portuguese, infinitives are untensed yet bear agreement, and they have nominative subjects (one of the hallmarks of finiteness, as discussed here). Hence, agreement is the primary subject licenser (and in my approach the primary finiteness inducer) in that language. In Modern Greek, too, nominative subjects are licensed by agreement. However, the requirements are stricter as compared with European Portuguese: the subject-licensing agreement must be accompanied by genuine tense.

phenomena syntactically, but only as a secondary source. Section 9.4 summarizes the results of this study.

I now turn to a discussion of the Turkish facts concerning embedded clauses and their syntactic finiteness. I start with tensed clauses and nominative subjects, before turning to a study of genitive subjects.

9.2 Embeddings in Turkish

9.2.1 *Fully finite verbal embeddings*

While the main focus of this paper is on nominalized embeddings, it is of interest to look at embeddings with verbal predicates as well, so as to capture any similarities between the two types with respect to finiteness.

It is well known that Turkish has borrowed an Indo-European pattern of embedding from Persian. In this pattern, the embedded clause is introduced by an overt complementizer (*ki*), and the clause itself has a verbal predicate which contains all relevant verbal morphology. In other words, such clauses look exactly like root clauses, with the exception of the complementizer, which of course does not show up on roots:

(1)   a. Ali   sınav-ı   geç-ecek[3]
         Ali   test-ACC   pass-FUT
         'Ali will pass the test.'

      b. Sen   sınav-ı   geç-ecek-sin
         you   test-ACC   pass-FUT-2SG
         'You will pass the test.'

(2)   a. San-ıyor-um   [ki [Ali   sınav-ı   geç-ecek]]
         believe-PRSPR-1SG   that   Ali   test-ACC   pass-FUT
         'I believe that Ali will pass the test.'

      b. San-ıyor-um   [ki [sen   sınav-ı   geç-ecek-sin]]
         believe-PRSPR-1SG   that   you   test-ACC   pass-FUT-2SG
         'I believe that you will pass the test.'

Assuming that the syntactic and morphological properties of root clauses clearly encode finiteness, it is clear that this borrowed pattern of embedding exhibits full finiteness.

---

[3] In the agreement paradigm for verbal predicates, the shape of the 3rd person singular agreement morpheme is null. In this paradigm, this is the only null morpheme; all other agreement morphemes in this paradigm are overt as well as distinct from each other, as expected in a Null Subject Language like Turkish. In the 'nominal agreement' paradigm found on embedded nominalized predicates, all the morphemes, including the one for third person singular, are overt, as well as distinct from each other.

I shall not be further concerned with this borrowed pattern for the purposes of this chapter. However, if we characterize this pattern as fully finite, then we should characterize the next pattern as fully finite, as well:

(3) a. [Ali   sınav-ı   geç-ecek]   san-ıyor-um
        Ali   test-ACC   pass-FUT   believe-PRSPR-1SG
        'I believe Ali will pass the test.'

     b. [Sen   sınav-ı   geç-ecek-sin]   san-ıyor-um
        you   test-ACC   pass-FUT-2SG   believe-PRSPR-1SG
        'I believe you will pass the test.'

Note that here, we do have an embedding which precedes rather than follows the matrix verb. This is the expected position of an embedded complement clause, as Turkish is a head-final language. As a matter of fact, the more typical nominalized clausal embeddings also precede the verb (in unmarked word orders).

Patterns as illustrated in (3) are therefore to be analysed as part of the native grammar. Their use appears to have widened lately. Nonetheless, they are limited in terms of the matrix verbs with which they can appear, which are essentially those of thought and belief.

These fully verbal embeddings have all the morphological properties of a root clause: the predicate can have the full array of tense, aspect, and mood markings; the agreement elements are those of the verbal (rather than nominal) paradigm; the subject is in the nominative (rather than the genitive or some other case). Thus, irrespective of our exact definition of finiteness, we cannot go wrong characterizing such embedded clauses as finite.

From the point of view of binding principles, such clauses also behave as fully finite:

(4) a. *Biz_i [kendi-miz$_i$/ birbir-imiz$_i$ sınav-ı   geç-eceğ-iz]
         we   self-1PL / each.other-1PL   test-ACC   pass-FUT-1PL
         san-ıyor-uz
         believe-PRSPR-1PL
         Intended reading: 'We believe ourselves/each other will pass the test.'

     b. Biz_i [biz$_i$[4]   / pro_i sınav-ı   geç-eceğ-iz]   san-ıyor-uz
        we   we   / pro   test-ACC   pass-FUT-1PL   believe-PRSPR-1PL
        'We believe we will pass the test.'

---

[4] The version with the overt 1st person plural pronoun sounds awkward. There are two reasons for this. First, the immediate repetition of the same pronoun, after the matrix token of the same pronoun, is stylistically awkward. Furthermore, the availability of *pro*, the phonologically unrealized pronoun, renders the overt pronoun in the same position awkward, as well. For the latter effect, see Chomsky (1981), Kornfilt (1984; 1996a), and related work, concerning the so-called 'Avoid Pronoun Principle', which stipulates that if a phonologically unrealized pronoun is licensed in a given syntactic position,

(5) *Öğrenci-ler_i [birbir-leri_i   sınav-ı   geç-ecek-ler] san-ıyor-lar[5]
student-PL   each.other-3PL test-ACC pass-FUT-3PL believe-PRSPR-3PL
Intended reading: 'The students believe each other will pass the test.'

According to Binding Theory, however formalized, anaphors (in the narrow
sense, i.e. reflexives and reciprocals) need to be bound in a local domain, and
pronouns have to be free in the same domain. If we define the relevant local
binding domain as a finite domain, the facts are just as predicted, given that
these embedded clauses are clearly finite, due to their resemblance to root
clauses.

In addition to these binding facts, these embedded clauses also conform to
the criterion that finite domains should be independent from the matrix with
respect to tense. Examples (4) and (5) show that the embedded clauses can be
future, while the matrix is in the present. The embedded clauses can bear
other tenses, too, with the same matrix clause, illustrated below, for past tense
on the embedded clauses:

(6) a. Biz_i [pro_i sınav-ı   geç-ti-k]   san-ıyor-uz
        we   pro   test-ACC pass-PST-1PL believe-PRSPR-1PL
        'We believe we passed the test.'

     b. [Sen   sınav-ı   geç-ti-n]   san-ıyor-um
        you   test-ACC pass-PST-2SG believe-PRSPR-1SG
        'I believe you passed the test.'

(7) Öğrenci-ler_i [pro_i sınav-ı   geç-ti-ler]   san-ıyor-lar
    student-PL   pro   test-ACC pass-PST-3PL believe-PRSPR-3PL
    'The students believe they passed the test.'

Now, the question that needs to be raised is: what is it about these embedded
clauses that makes them finite? Is it the verbal features of their predicates? Is it
the tense that they bear? Is it the agreement element?

With respect to Turkish, I would like to claim that the main factor is the
agreement element. Tense does play a role, but only secondarily, and only
together with agreement. I now turn to examples that will help establish the

an overt pronoun is ill-formed in that same position. This effect appears to be weaker for non-3rd
person pronouns. This sentence is acceptable, however, if the embedded subject pronoun is defocused
and backgrounded, i.e. if its intonation is low in pitch and unaccented.

[5] I did not include an example of a reflexive here, for the following reason: the reflexive in Turkish is
inflected for person and number, as also illustrated in (4a). However, for singular 3rd persons, two
forms are possible: inflected and bare. Only the bare form is a locally bound anaphor; the inflected
form is a logophoric pronoun (for discussion, see Kornfilt 2001). For 3rd plurals this distinction is
neutralized, as the reflexive has to be inflected in all instances. Therefore, the inflected reflexive in
embedded subject position in examples like (5) sounds quite acceptable, but under the reading of a
logophoric pronoun. Hence, such examples do not illustrate anaphoric binding effects.

claim of the primary relevance of agreement. I shall first compare the embedded, fully verbal and finite clauses we just saw with another type, closely related in having fully verbal and tensed predicates which, however, lack agreement. I shall then turn towards extending my claim to nominalized embedded clauses.

9.2.2 *Nonfinite verbal embeddings*

The same matrix verbs that allow for fully finite, verbal embedded clauses also allow for similar clauses that lack agreement and whose subjects are in the accusative, instead of the nominative we saw earlier (cf. Kornfilt 1977; 1996b; Moore 1998; Zidani-Eroğlu 1997).

(8) a. [Ali-yi   sınav-ı   geç-ti]   san-ıyor-um
         Ali-ACC   test-ACC   pass-PST   believe-PRSPR-1SG
         'I believe Ali to have passed the test.'

     b. [Sen-i   sınav-ı   geç-ti]   san-ıyor-um
         you-ACC   test-ACC   pass-PST   believe-PRSPR-1SG
         'I believe you to have passed the test.'

As mentioned earlier, the agreement morpheme for 3rd person singular subjects is, in the verbal paradigm, null. Therefore, (8a) does not show the point to be made. However, (8b) does, as comparison with (6b), repeated here as (9), clearly shows:

(9) [Sen   sınav-ı   geç-ti-n]   san-ıyor-um
     you   test-ACC   pass-PST-2SG   believe-PRSPR-1SG
     'I believe you passed the test.'

Note that here, the embedded predicate bears agreement morphology with the subject, and the subject is in the nominative.

It is further important to note that the possibility of accusative subjects as in (8) is not limited to past tense embeddings, as the following future tense embeddings show:

(8) c. [Ali-yi   sınav-ı   geç-ecek]   san-ıyor-um
         Ali-ACC   test-ACC   pass-FUT   believe-PRSPR-1SG
         Lit.: 'I believe Ali to pass the test (in the future).'

     d. [Sen-i   sınav-ı   geç-ecek]   san-ıyor-um
         you-ACC   test-ACC   pass-FUT   believe-PRSPR-1SG
         Lit.: 'I believe you to pass the test (in the future).'

The accusative-marked subject in examples like those in (8) behave as though they were part of the matrix domain rather than of the embedded domain:

(10) a. Ali_i kendin-i_i [t_i sınav-ı geç-ti] san-ıyor
      Ali self-ACC test-ACC pass-PST believe-PRSPR
      'Ali believes himself to have passed the test.'

    b. Sen kendi-n-i_i [t_i sınav-ı geç-ti] san-ıyor-sun
      You self-2SG-ACC test-ACC pass-PST believe-PRSPR-2SG
      'You believe yourself to have passed the test.'

(11) Öğrenci-ler_i birbir-lerin-i_i [t_i sınav-ı geç-ti] san-ıyor-lar
    student-PL each.other-3PL-ACC test-ACC pass-PST believe-PRSPR-3PL
    'The students believe each other to have passed the test'

These examples show that the embedded clause is 'transparent'; its subject participates in syntactic phenomena that belong to the matrix domain—accusative case as licensed by the matrix verb;[6] furthermore, the binding facts show that for the purposes of binding principles A and B, the relevant binding domain for the subject is the matrix clause rather than the embedded clause.

The bracketing I used above for the accusative-marked anaphoric elements in (10) and (11) reflects an analysis according to which the accusative subject has moved out of the embedded clause into the matrix. This was done to represent an approach based on accounts both preceding and following the Government and Binding model of syntax with its Exceptional Case Marking (ECM) analysis of such constructions, i.e. where the matrix verb exceptionally licenses the Accusative case on the embedded subject and does so directly (for Turkish, see Kornfilt 1984; 1996b; for the examples in (8) I have used a representation in line with such an ECM analysis). More recent approaches, such as in Moore (1998) and Zidani-Eroğlu (1997), as well as older ones (Kornfilt 1977), assume an analysis whereby the subject moves to a position in the matrix (usually referred to as a Subject-to-Object Raising (SOR) derivation), where that subject receives accusative case, and where its binding behaviour receives a straightforward explanation, given that it is now indeed in the matrix domain.

I shall not here address the issue of the nature of ECM in Turkish (i.e. whether the proper analysis of these accusative subjects is via ECM or via Raising). However, irrespective of whether we assume the accusative subject in such constructions to still be part of the embedded clause or whether we assume it to have moved out of that clause, the question about the finiteness of these tensed, verbal clauses without agreement morphology

---

[6] It should be noted that all the matrix verbs that allow for this construction are transitive verbs that can be shown independently to license accusative case.

remains an interesting and crucial one. Why and how should a tensed (i.e. not an infinitival) clause be accessible to syntactic phenomena that are part of the matrix domain? If the subject is still within the clause, this question is straightforward with respect to accusative case and the binding of the subject. If the subject has moved out of the clause, then the question is about how the subject could move out of a tensed clause to begin with.

It is well known that a number of languages, especially modern Balkan languages, allow for ECM constructions involving tensed embedded clauses. In those languages, however, there is no morphological infinitive (cf. also footnote 2 above). Thus, one particular tense is used instead of the infinitive in a variety of contexts: in Control constructions and in ECM constructions, as well as for citations. One could therefore say that in such languages, the ECM constructions involving tensed embedded clauses actually involve 'fake' tenses that represent infinitives.

In Turkish, however, the tense in ECM constructions is genuine. First of all, Turkish does have a morphologically special infinitival form (i.e. the suffix -*mAK*),[7] and it is this form that is used for citations as well as in Control constructions. Secondly, in ECM constructions a range of tenses can show up on the embedded predicate, as we just saw. Hence, we are not dealing with 'fake' tense here.

It is important to note that no speakers of Turkish allow for a nominative (instead of accusative) subject in constructions like (8) or (10) and (11), when the embedded predicate lacks overt agreement:

(12)   *[Sen   sınav-ı   geç-ti]   san-ıyor-um
        you.NOM   test-ACC   pass-PST   believe-PRSPR-1SG
        Intended reading: 'I believe you passed the test.'

This is despite the genuine tense on the embedded predicate. I therefore conclude that the relevant factor that creates a finite domain with respect to these embedded verbal, tensed clauses is the agreement morpheme rather than the tense morpheme.[8]

---

[7] I follow general Turkological conventions here by using capital letters to represent segments that vary according to well-established phonological processes, e.g. voicing alternations for consonants and vowel harmony for vowels.

[8] It should be mentioned that there are speakers who allow accusative subjects with such verbal embedded clauses, even when an agreement morpheme is present on the embedded predicate. Kornfilt (1977) and Moore (1998) discuss the existence of such speakers. Moore (1998) discusses them in depth and proposes that for such speakers, the accusative subject is in fact in the matrix clause, but that the embedded subject is a (resumptive) pronominal (phonologically empty) copy. If this analysis is on the right track, then this dialect is not problematic for my proposal that defines finiteness based on overt agreement, because the accusative constituent is not within the finite domain, and the construction is not a genuine movement construction, either, due to the (resumptive) pronoun. It is important to

Once we have established this point, we have to ask also whether a similar situation holds for nominalized clauses. I will now argue that this is indeed so.

9.3 Nominal embeddings and agreement

9.3.1 *Establishing agreement as the element inducing finiteness and licensing the subject*

As mentioned earlier, the most typical embedding pattern in Turkish involves so-called nominalized clauses. Turkish has a few different 'nominalization' types. I shall use the term 'nominalization' in this context as a characterization of clauses which have a verbal 'core', with verbal and lexical as well as functional projections, and with the addition of some nominal functional layers (cf. Borsley and Kornfilt 2000), rather than as a characterization of lexically derived verbal nouns, which I shall exclude from the discussion here.[9]

For the purposes of this chapter, I shall concentrate on two types of nominalization: one type where the clause exhibits the suffix -*DIK* in the morphological slot of tense, aspect, and mood morphemes of a fully finite verb, and the second type, where the suffix -*mA* shows up. It is not clear how best to label these two suffixes. I shall follow Lees (1968) in glossing -*DIK* as a factive nominal (FN), and, in contrast to this term, I shall gloss -*mA* as a non-factive nominal (NFN).[10] The reader should bear in mind, however, that these terms are somewhat misleading. While in many, probably most, instances, these nominalization morphemes indeed do head factive vs. non-factive domains and are thus selected by appropriate matrix verbs, there are numerous exceptions to these generalizations—a situation which leads to the difficulty of a satisfactory characterization. I shall continue using these terms for ease of

note that not all speakers accept such constructions anyway, while all speakers do accept accusative subjects in the absence of agreement morphology, and no speakers accept nominative subjects when that agreement morphology is absent. At this point in the exposition, therefore, the correlation between licensed subjects and overt agreement remains unchallenged.

[9] Analysing nominalized clauses as represented by nominal functional projections dominating lexical and functional verbal projections is different from representing some nominalizations as verbal nominals. I think that Turkish has nominals of both types. For a discussion of the differences between such verbal nouns and syntactic nominalizations in complete embedded clauses, cf. Kornfilt and Greenberg (2000) and Borsley and Kornfilt (2000).

[10] In some previous work, I have glossed these suffixes as 'nominal indicative' and 'nominal subjunctive', respectively. There is some obvious motivation for these terms as well; this comes in part from the semantics of the matrix verbs with which these complements typically appear, and in part from the fact that at least in some instances, these complements are in free variation with fully verbal complements that are in the indicative vs. subjunctive mood respectively, as we are about to see in the text. But there are some counterexamples to these generalizations, just as there are to the terms based on Lees's terminology.

reference, however; this should not be problematic, given that the issue of labelling these nominalized domains is tangential to our present concerns.

Each type is illustrated below, with the factive (= indicative) nominalized embedding first and the non-factive (= subjunctive) nominalized embedding second (see also footnote 10 above).

(13) [Sen-in   sınav-ı   geç-tiğ-in]-i   san-ıyor-um
      you-GEN   test-ACC   pass-FN-2SG-ACC   believe-PRSPR-1SG
      'I believe (that) you passed the test.'

(14) [Sen-in   sınav-ı   geç-me-n]-i   isti-yor-um
      you-GEN   test-ACC   pass-NFN-2SG-ACC   want-PRSPR-1SG
      'I want (that) you should pass the test.'

I also include corresponding fully verbal embeddings, so as to illustrate the similarities with respect to mood and factivity:

(15) [Sen   sınav-ı   geç-ti-n]   san-ıyor-um
      you.NOM   test-ACC   pass-PST-2SG   believe-PRSPR-1SG
      'I believe you passed the test.'

(16) [Sen   sınav-ı   geç-e-sin]   isti-yor-um
      you.NOM   test-ACC   pass-SBJV-2SG   want-PRSPR-1SG
      'I want (that) you should pass the test.'

Note that the factive (= indicative) nominalized clause corresponds to the fully verbal, root-like tensed and indicative clause, as in (13) vs. (15).

Likewise, the non-factive (= subjunctive) nominalized clause corresponds to the fully verbal, root-like subjunctive clause (cf. 14 vs. 16). Note further that the matrix verbs that select for the respective embedded clauses are the same: what is selected is the particular mood, and this works across the divide between nominalized and verbal embeddings.

At least in these examples (and many more like them), we see the motivation for the terminology concerning nominalized clauses with reference to either (non-)factivity or to indicativity versus subjunctivity.

Now, let us turn to the properties of the nominalized clauses and let us first note the similarities: In both types, the subject is in the genitive. In both, the tense or mood morpheme is replaced by an appropriate nominalization morpheme. In both, the agreement morphology is drawn from the nominal (rather than verbal) agreement paradigm. Both clauses are marked for the case marker that is licensed by the matrix verb.

All those properties are expected concerning nominal (rather than verbal) domains. However, note also that the nominalized verbs are still able to license structural case, i.e. the accusative on their direct objects. This means that the verbs still have verbal features, at least at lower levels of the clausal architecture. This property contrasts with lexically derived deverbal nouns, where an internal argument cannot show up in the accusative and where such an argument is externalized by the deverbal noun, without any passive morphology.[11]

Having noted the main similarities of these two nominalizations in embedded clauses, let us briefly discuss their differences.

9.3.2 *Differences in temporal independence*

The two types of nominalized embedding have different properties with respect to being temporally independent from their matrix clauses. I now turn to some examples that illustrate temporal dependence vs. independence of nominalized embedded domains.

Factive, indicative nominal embeddings are first shown to be independent from the matrix temporally:

(17) [Sen-in   sınav-ı   geç-eceğ-in]-i
      you-GEN   test-ACC   pass-FUTFN-2SG-ACC

      bil-iyor-um / bil-iyor-du-m
      know-PRSPR-1SG / know-PROG-PST-1SG
      'I know/knew that you will/would pass the exam.'

(18) [Sen-in   sınav-ı   geç-tiğ-in]-i
      you-GEN   test-ACC   pass-FN-2SG-ACC

      bil-iyor-um / bil-iyor-du-m
      know-PRSPR-1SG / know-PROG-PST-1SG
      'I know/knew that you passed the exam.'

In contrast, nonfinite, subjunctive embeddings are dependent on the matrix temporally, as they are formally neutral for tense:

(19) [Sen-in   sınav-ı   geç-me-n]-i
      you-GEN   test-ACC   pass-NFN-2SG-ACC
      isti-yor-um / iste-di-m / isti-yeceğ-im
      want-PRSPR-1SG / want-PST-1SG / want-FUT-1SG
      'I want/wanted/will want that you should pass the exam.'

---

[11] Indeed, in the clausal nominalizations under discussion here, an internal argument can be externalized only when the predicate bears passive morphology. From this point of view, too, these (transitive, nominalized) clauses are like regular (i.e. verbal) finite (transitive) clauses. For some examples and discussion of lexically derived deverbal nominals and their properties that contrast with those of clausal nominalizations, see Kornfilt and Greenberg (2000).

We see, then, that if temporal independence of an embedded clause is taken to be part of what defines finiteness, a different marker than that for agreement contributes to this aspect of finiteness.

I conclude, then, that while agreement and its overt expression is the primary factor in defining finiteness in Turkish embedded clauses—clauses that can be either verbal or nominal—temporal marking can also contribute to finiteness as a secondary marking.

Is this a problem for my agreement-based approach? The answer is 'no'. This only shows that temporal independence is expressed by the nominalization marker itself, just as in fully verbal clauses, where the tense marker is different from the agreement marker, but where the agreement marker contributes to the finiteness of the domain, as we saw clearly: without the agreement marker, even the fullest expression of tense cannot license the appropriate subject case, i.e. the nominative in those instances.

I now turn to evidence showing that in nominalized clauses, too, agreement delimits a finite domain.

9.3.3 *Infinitival embeddings and their subject*

A subset of matrix predicates that subcategorize for subjunctive argument clauses also co-occur with infinitival argument clauses. Such clauses share with the previously illustrated nominalized clauses the property of being case-marked.

Infinitival clause:

(20) a. Ben$_i$ [PRO$_i$ sınav-ı geç-mek]-ten kork-uyor-um
        I   PRO   test-ACC pass-INF-ABL fear-PRSPR-1SG
        'I am afraid to pass the test.'

Non-factive (subjunctive) nominal clause:

(20) b. Ben [Ali-nin sınav-ı geç-me-sin]-den kork-uyor-um
        I   Ali-GEN test-ACC pass-NFN-3SG-ABL fear-PRSPR-1SG
        'I am afraid that Ali might pass the test.'

Such infinitival clauses cannot bear overt agreement markers. Furthermore, overt subjects are not possible in infinitivals, irrespective of their case:

(21) *Ben [Ali / Ali-nin sınav-ı geç-mek]-ten kork-uyor-um
        I   Ali / Ali-GEN test-ACC pass-INF-ABL fear-PRSPR-1SG
        Intended reading: 'I am afraid for Ali to pass the test.'

Note that, no matter whether the embedded subject is in the nominative or in the genitive, an overt subject is not licensed when an overt agreement morpheme is absent. The last example can be saved when the infinitive is replaced by the non-factive nominalization morpheme, followed by a (nominal) agreement morpheme; cf. (20b), repeated as (22) for the reader's convenience:

(22) Ben [Ali-nin sınav-ı geç-me-sin]-den kork-uyor-um
     I   Ali-GEN test-ACC pass-NFN-3SG-ABL fear-PRSPR-1SG
     'I am afraid that Ali might pass the test.'

Thus, just as with verbal embedded clauses, we see that it is the agreement morpheme that is responsible for the licensing of an overt subject as well as of its case. The same generalization holds of yet another construction involving nominalized embeddings; I turn to such examples in the next subsection.

9.3.4 *Irrealis relative clauses*

Yet another construction that argues for the same point and does so in a similar fashion is the irrealis relative clause construction.

This is a construction which corresponds, in its semantics, rather closely to English infinitival relative clauses:

(23) Ben [[PRO iç-ecek] güzel bir bira] bul-du-m
     I   PRO drink-IRR nice a   beer find-PST-1SG
     'I found a nice beer to drink.'

The infinitive morphology does not permit a relative clause of this type, and can never head a modifier clause in a relative clause construction of any type.

(24) *Ben [[PRO iç-mek] güzel bir bira] bul-du-m
     I   PRO drink-INF nice a   beer find-PST-1SG
     Intended reading: 'I found a nice beer to drink.'

The subject of such irrealis relative clauses is always PRO, and the modifying clause can never bear an agreement element. As with infinitives, which, as we saw, exhibit these same two properties, it is not possible to have an overt subject, irrespective of whether it is in the nominative or in the genitive:

(25) *Ben [[sen / sen-in iç-ecek] güzel bir bira] bul-du-m
     I   you.NOM/ you-GEN drink-IRR nice a   beer find-PST-1SG
     Intended reading: 'I found a nice beer (for) you to drink.'

This construction can be rescued in two ways, both of them involving overt agreement morphology. The first way would be to add such agreement morphology to the embedded clause:

(26) Ben [[sen-in   iç-eceğ-in]   güzel bira]-yı   bul-du-m
      I   you-GEN   drink-FUTFN-2SG   nice   beer-ACC find-PST-1SG
      'I found the nice beer which you shall drink.'

The addition of the (nominal) agreement morpheme makes an overt subject possible, obviously along with the nominal subject Case, i.e. with the genitive. Note also that once we have the agreement morpheme, the relative clause becomes finite, at least in the sense of having temporal semantics, and in the possibility of exhibiting an overt subject. In part, this is due to the agreement morpheme itself. It is also due to the fact that the irrealis morpheme is homophonous with the nominalized factive marker in the future tense. In other words, the nominal factive marker -*DIK* we saw earlier has a general, impoverished tense feature, which is [−future]. Its [+future] counterpart is -*(y)AcAK*, which is, as just mentioned, homophonous with the irrealis marker, but which requires an agreement morpheme.

The second way of rescuing the ungrammatical irrealis relative clause is by changing the irrealis marker into the non-factive, subjunctive nominal marker (thus keeping, in essence, the same mood), and, once again, crucially adding overt agreement:

(27) Ben [[sen-in   iç-me-n]   için] güzel bir bira bul-du-m
      I   you-GEN   drink-NFN-2SG   for   nice   a   beer find-PST-1SG
      Lit.: 'I found a nice beer for your drinking' (i.e. 'I found a nice beer
      for you to drink/so that you (might) drink (it).'

This is obviously not a relative clause, but a construction where the non-factive (subjunctive) nominal clause is part of an adjunct (i.e. 'adverbial') postpositional phrase, headed by *için* 'for, with the purpose of'. The non-factive nominal type of embedding cannot host a relative clause construction in general; this is why the original relative clause structure could not be kept in this instance.

Note that in both versions of this 'rescue operation', the overt subject has been made possible by the agreement morphology. Also, given that the categorial features of that morphology are nominal, the licensed subject case is nominal as well, i.e. it is genitive.

We can now set up a general correlation that holds of both verbal and nominal embedded clauses:

When overt agreement morphology shows up, the overt subject is licensed via the corresponding subject Case.

I follow here a proposal I made in Kornfilt (2003), in suggesting that there is a general subject Case, licensed by overt agreement. The surface realization of this subject Case depends on the categorial features of this agreement morphology: if it has verbal features, then the licensed subject Case will be 'verbal' as well, i.e. nominative; if the agreement element has nominal features, then the licensed subject Case will be nominal, i.e. genitive.

9.3.5 *Binding and nominalized embeddings*

I now turn to binding facts and show that here, too, it is the overt agreement element which primarily participates in defining the relevant binding domain for an embedded subject, and which therefore, I suggest, also defines that domain as finite—at least for Turkish.

Starting with factive nominals, we see that their subjects cannot be anaphors in the narrow sense, i.e. neither reflexives nor reciprocals, when the embedded clause is headed by fully-fledged agreement, reflecting person and number features of the subject:

(28) a. *Biz$_i$ [birbir-imiz-in$_i$ sınav-ı   geç-tiğ-imiz]-i
          we   each.other-1PL-GEN   exam-ACC   pass-FN-1PL-ACC
          san-ıyor-du-k
          believe-PROG-PST-1PL
          Intended reading: 'We believed that each other passed the exam.'

      b. *Biz$_i$ [kendi-miz-in$_i$ sınav-ı   geç-tiğ-imiz]-i
          we   self-1PL-GEN   exam-ACC   pass-FN-1PL-ACC
          san-ıyor-du-k
          believe-PROG-PST-1PL
          Intended reading: 'We believed that ourselves passed the exam.'

The example with the reciprocal improves somewhat if the genuine agreement morpheme is replaced by a 'dummy' default (or weak) agreement morpheme which has the constant value for 3rd person singular, irrespective of the person and number features of the subject:

(29) a. (?)**Biz**$_i$ [**birbir-imiz-in**$_i$ sınav-ı   geç-tiğ-in]-i
             we   **each.other-1PL-GEN**   exam-ACC   pass-FN-3SG-ACC
          san-ıyor-du-k
          believe-PROG-PST-1PL
          'We believed that each other passed the exam.'

While native speakers' judgements vary somewhat, all speakers report that the reciprocal subject is better in these constructions than the reflexive subject. More importantly for our purposes here, native speakers report that the 'weak' agreement also improves constructions with reflexive subjects considerably:

(29) b. ?(?) **Biz**ᵢ **[kendi-miz-in**ⱼ sınav-ı   geç-tiğ-in]-i
       we   **self-1PL-GEN**   exam-ACC   pass-FN-3SG-ACC

       san-ıyor-du-k
       believe-PROG-PST-1PL
       'We believed that ourselves passed the exam.'

I suggest that the reason for the improvement is that the agreement we see here does not have features that genuinely agree, in a syntactic and semantic sense, with the relevant features of the subject, and that therefore the embedded clause is not finite either, leading to (relative) transparency of the embedded clause. Therefore, violations of locality with respect to binding are tolerated. Where the agreement morphology is genuine and does truly agree with the features of the subject, the embedded clause is finite, and locality violations are severe as a consequence.[12]

In accordance with what we have just seen with respect to reflexives and reciprocals (i.e. with respect to binding condition A phenomena),[13] we also find the expected facts (and thus reversed judgements) with respect to pronominal subjects, i.e. with respect to binding condition B. As expected, a pronominal subject is fine in a fully finite clause, but not in a non-(fully) finite clause, if we define a finite clause as one which is headed by genuine agreement.

Factive nominal embedded clauses with genuine agreement:

(30)   Bizᵢ [biz-imᵢ / proᵢ sınav-ı   geç-tiğ-imiz]-i   san-ıyor-du-k
       we   we-GEN   pro exam-ACC pass-FN-1PL-ACC believe-PROG-PST-1PL
       'We believed that we passed the exam.'

---

[12] Why should there be weak, or default, agreement at all? Why are the binding violations not 'saved' by simply leaving out overt agreement? I suggest that this is due to reasons of Case licensing; since the overt subject needs Case of some sort, the default agreement is needed to license subject Case. We see, then, that this default, weak agreement is too weak to create a syntactically finite domain, but that it is strong enough to license subject Case.

[13] For the Binding Conditions referred to here, see Chomsky (1981) and similar work in the Government and Binding model. In a nutshell, Principle A determines the distribution of anaphors in the narrow sense, i.e. mainly reflexives and reciprocals, and Principle B the distribution of pronouns. In that model, it is assumed that these two principles apply within the same syntactic domain (essentially a clause); Principle A states that anaphors must be bound in that domain (i.e. their antecedent must be in the same domain), while Principle B states that pronouns must be free in that domain (i.e. their antecedent must be outside that domain).

Factive nominal embedded clauses with default agreement:

(31)   *Biz_i [biz-im_i / pro_i sınav-ı   geç-tiğ-in]-i   san-ıyor-du-k.
       we   we-GEN / pro exam-ACC pass-FN-**3SG**-ACC believe-PROG-PST-1PL
       Intended reading: 'We believed that we passed the exam.'

Non-factive embedded clauses exhibit similar effects. I shall illustrate this with respect to binding condition A.

Non-factive embedded clauses with genuine agreement:

(32)   a. *Biz_i   [birbir-imiz-in_i   sınav-ı   geç-me-**miz**]-i
          we   each.other-1PL-GEN   exam-ACC   pass-NFN-1PL-ACC
          isti-yor-du-k
          want-PROG-PST-1PL
          Intended reading: 'We wanted that each other should pass the exam.'

       b. *Biz_i [kendi-miz-in_i sınav-ı   geç-me-**miz**]-i
          we   self-1PL-GEN   exam-ACC pass-NFN-1PL-ACC
          isti-yor-du-k
          want-PROG-PST-1PL
          Intended reading: 'We wanted that ourselves should pass the exam.'

Non-factive embedded clauses with default agreement:

(33)   a. (?)Biz_i [birbir-imiz-in_i   sınav-ı   geç-me-**sin**]-i
          we   each.other-1PL-GEN   exam-ACC   pass-NFN-**3SG**-ACC
          isti-yor-du-k
          want-PROG-PST-1PL
          'We wanted that each other should pass the exam.'

       b. ? Biz_i [kendi-miz-in_i sınav-ı   geç-me-**sin**]-i
          we   self-1PL-GEN   exam-ACC   pass-NFN-**3SG**-ACC
          isti-yor-du-k
          want-PROG-PST-1PL
          'We wanted that ourselves should pass the exam.'

We see that, with non-factive nominal embeddings too, the genuine agreement marker sets up a finite domain with respect to locality violations that concern condition A. The only difference with respect to factive, indicative nominal clauses is that the improvement noted with default agreement is greater for most speakers. This suggests that, in addition to agreement, tense and mood also play a role in setting up a finite domain, but that they are of secondary importance. It is a well-known fact that, in languages that make a distinction between indicative and subjunctive moods, subjunctive clauses are, in a number of ways, less finite than indicative clauses, with the understanding that finiteness is related to the opacity of clauses (i.e. with indicative clauses being more opaque with respect to processes that take place in higher domains). In addition to mood, the factive vs. non-factive nominal clauses in Turkish also differ with respect to tense. We saw earlier that the factive nominal has two distinct morphological shapes, with one morpheme expressing future and the other non-future. The non-factive nominal does not exhibit such differences. This difference makes factive nominal embeddings more independent temporally from the matrix than non-factive nominal embeddings. As discussed in the Introduction to this volume, such independence is another property that has often been linked to finiteness.

Since this aspect of finiteness is linked to the different nominalization morphemes rather than to agreement *per se*, I conclude here that, while agreement is, at least for Turkish, the primary element that sets up finite domains, there is also a relevant contribution made by morphemes expressing tense and mood. Later in the chapter I shall argue, however, that this additional contribution by tense and mood is possible only when agreement is present.

Distinctions between the two types of nominalized embedding similar to those seen with anaphoric and pronominal binding are also found with respect to the licensing of negative polarity items (NPIs).[14]

In Turkish, NPIs must be licensed, under c-command, by a local negation element:

(34) **Kimse**   geç   gel-**me**-di / *gel-di
      nobody   late   come-NEG-PST / come-PST
      'Nobody came late.'

(35) a. [**Kimse-nin**   geç   gel-**me**-diğ-in]-i   hatırla-dı-lar
         nobody-GEN   late   come-NEG-FN-3SG-ACC   remember-PST-3PL
         'They remembered that nobody came late.'

      b. *[**Kimse-nin**   geç   gel-**diğ**-in]-i   hatırla-dı-lar
         nobody-GEN   late   come-FN-3SG-ACC   remember-PST-3PL
         Intended reading: 'They remembered that nobody came late.'

The importance of locality is shown by the fact that a negation marker on the matrix verb does not save (35b) from ill-formedness:

(36) *[**Kimse-nin**   geç   gel-**diğ**-in]-i   hatırla-**ma**-dı-lar
      nobody-GEN   late   come-FN-3SG-ACC   remember-NEG-PST-3PL
      Intended readings: 'They didn't remember whether/that anyone/no body came late.'

---

[14] Some of the data on NPIs are taken from Kornfilt (1984), and some are recent, obtained as a result of polling native speakers in Oct. 2005. NPIs in Turkish have been studied in depth in Kelepir (2001).

It is obvious that the embedded clause is the relevant local domain for the purpose of the licensing of the NPI. However, once we compare examples involving factive embeddings with -*DIK* such as in (36), with non-factive embeddings headed by -*mA*, we realize that this generalization is too strong:

(37) [**Kimse-nin** geç gel-**me**-sin]-i iste-**me**-di-ler
nobody-GEN late come-NFN-3SG-ACC want-NEG-PST-3PL
'They didn't want (for) anybody to come late.'

This example is well-formed. This is not just a stray example: as long as the embedded clause is a non-factive -*mA*-clause, the same well-formedness is found with other (negative) matrix verbs (and other matrix tenses and aspects):

(38) [**Kimse-nin** sınıf-ta kal-**ma**-sın]-dan hoşlan-**ma**-m
nobody-GEN class-LOC stay-NFN-3SG-ABL like-NEG-1SG
'I don't like (for) anybody to repeat their grade.'

Furthermore, the ill-formed examples with a factive *DIK*-clause deteriorate even further when the NPI is a non-subject:

(39) **[Ali-nin **kimse-yi** sev-**diğ**-in]-i hatırla-**ma**-dı-lar
Ali-GEN nobody-ACC like-FN-3SG-ACC remember-NEG-PST-3PL
Intended reading: 'They didn't remember that/whether Ali likes anyone.'

(40) **[Ali-nin **hiçbir yer-e** git-**tiğ**-in]-i hatırla-**ma**-dı-lar
Ali-GEN no.one place-DAT go-FN-3SG-ACC remember-NEG-PST-3PL
Intended reading: 'They didn't remember that/whether
Ali had gone anywhere.'

No such deterioration is observed with the non-factive *mA*-clauses:

(41) [Ali-nin **kimse-yle** çık-**ma**-sın]-ı iste-**me**-di-ler
Ali-GEN nobody-with go.out-NFN-3SG-ACC want-NEG-PST-3PL
'They didn't want Ali to go out with anyone.'

(42) [Profesör-ler-in **kimse-yi** sınıf-ta bırak-**ma**-ların]-dan
professor-PL-GEN nobody-ACC class-LOC leave-NFN-3PL-ABL
hoşlan-**ma**-m
like-NEG-1SG
'I don't like (for) the professors to make anyone repeat their grade.'

While I don't have an explanation for this difference between the two complement types with respect to the subject–object asymmetry in non-local licensing of NPIs, it is interesting to note that when such licensing *is* possible, there is no subject–object asymmetry. This might be a property of verb-final languages; Korean and Japanese exhibit no such asymmetry in NPI-licensing either.[15]

We conclude, then, that at least as far as nominalized embeddings are concerned, tense does play a role in the permeability of the embedded clause with respect to non-local licensing of NPIs; the factive clauses with their (impoverished, but nonetheless present) tense are not permeable to such licensing, while the non-factive clauses with no tense at all are permeable. This seems to suggest that (nominal) agreement is irrelevant in this regard. This conclusion is implausible, however, in view of the relevance of nominal agreement with respect to anaphoric and pronominal binding.

Furthermore, non-local NPI-licensing in infinitival clauses suggests that nominal agreement *is* relevant, after all: non-local licensing of non-subject NPIs is particularly successful when the NPI is contained within infinitival clauses. Such clauses lack both tense and agreement, as we saw earlier; some relevant examples involving NPIs in infinitival clauses follow.

(43) pro$_i$ [PRO$_i$ **kimse-yi**   sınıf-ta   bırak-**mak**]-tan   hoşlan-**ma**-m
            nobody-ACC class-LOC leave-INF-ABL   like-**NEG**-1SG
      'I don't like to make anyone repeat their grade.'

(44) pro$_i$ [PRO$_i$ **kimse-yi**   üz-**mek**]   iste-**me**-di-ler
            nobody-ACC sadden-INF   want-**NEG**-PST-3PL
      'They didn't want to sadden anyone.'

While the instances of non-local licensing of the object NPIs in the tenseless (but agreeing) non-factive clauses in (41) and (42) are well-formed, the similar licensing of the object NPIs in the infinitival clauses (where there is no agreement) in (43) and (44) sound even better. This shows that nominal agreement is still relevant, while apparently not primarily so.

Let us now look at NPI licensing in fully verbal embeddings. Here, the fully-fledged verbal tense does not create any licensing or permeability effects; only agreement does. The facts, then, are similar to those we saw with respect to anaphoric and pronominal binding: an accusative-marked NPI, even where construed as the subject of a fully verbal and tensed embedded clause whose agreement element is typically missing, must be licensed in the matrix (given that it has undergone SOR/ECM); a nominative-marked NPI construed as the subject of a fully verbal and tensed embedded clause cannot be so licensed, and must be licensed within its own clause:

---

[15] I am indebted to Peter Sells and John Whitman for this information.

(45) **Kimse-yi**   geç gel-di   san-**mı**-yor-lar
     nobody-ACC   late come-PST   believe-NEG-PRSPR-3PL
     'They don't believe anyone to have come late.'

(46) *****Kimse-yi**   geç gel-**me**-di   san-ıyor-lar
     nobody-ACC   late come-NEG-PST   believe-PRSPR-3PL
     Intended reading: 'They believe nobody not to have come late.'

The facts concerning NPIs which are nominative subjects of a fully verbal embedded clause are opposite to what we just saw:

(47) *****Kimse**   geç gel-di   san-**mı**-yor-lar
     nobody   late come-PST   believe-NEG-PRSPR-3PL
     Intended reading: 'They don't believe anyone came late.'

(48) **Kimse**   geç gel-**me**-di   san-ıyor-lar
     nobody   late come-NEG-PST   believe-PRSPR-3PL
     'They believe nobody came late.'

I assume that in (45) and (46), the agreement element on the embedded verb is truly missing, and that this is what leads to the accusative marking on the embedded subject. I further assume that the agreement element is present in (47) and (48), thus leading to the nominative case of the embedded subject. Unfortunately, no morphological distinction between these two options can be found, given that the agreement marker on verbal predicates for 3rd person singular is null, as mentioned earlier. Furthermore, there are no NPIs that have person features other than 3rd person. However, we saw earlier that in general, verbal embedded clauses with 1st or 2nd person subjects mark their subject with nominative, when the agreement element is present, while the subject is in the accusative when the agreement element of such verbal embedded clauses is absent. Thus, my assumptions concerning the last four examples are independently motivated. In any event, we see that tense, even when it is the fully differentiated rich verbal tense, does not by itself create a local domain within which an NPI is licensed.

My preliminary conclusions are as follows. If one limits attention only to the two types of nominalized clause, then my proposal about the primacy of agreement over tense might be questioned, given that it is only tense that distinguishes between these two types of nominalized embedded clause. However, when we look at *all* the phenomena studied here, and when we attempt to offer an account that accommodates all those phenomena, it is clear that tense is irrelevant at least for some, while agreement is relevant for all.

It is especially interesting to note that, in ECM/SOR constructions, fully differentiated, rich verbal tense is insufficient to fulfil one of the main functions of a finiteness property, namely the licensing of nominative case of the subject. How can we then find a satisfying solution which takes care of both the ECM/SOR facts with respect to subject Case, where tense is irrelevant, and the facts of NPI licensing in subjunctive vs. indicative nominalized clauses, where tense does appear to play a role?

I propose the following account. Tense plays a role in finiteness phenomena only where agreement is also present, as it is in the two types of nominalized clause, where we saw clear distinctions between non-local NPI licensing with respect to presence vs. absence of tense. The same is true with respect to anaphoric and pronominal non-local binding, although the distinctions with respect to tense are, as we saw, less clear-cut—with agreement clearly the primary factor of opacity (and hence also of finiteness, insofar as we draw a connection between finiteness and the opacity of syntactic domains), and with tense creating weaker, secondary effects. Where agreement is absent, we saw that the syntactic domain in question is not finite, with tense unable to contribute to syntactic finiteness when it is present but agreement is not.

I conclude, then, that while agreement and its overt expression is the primary factor in defining finiteness in Turkish embedded clauses—clauses that can be either verbal or nominal—temporal marking can also contribute to finiteness as a secondary marking; however, it can do so only when agreement is present. When agreement is absent, tense is not a relevant factor in determining finiteness.

9.4 Summary and conclusions

I have proposed an account for finiteness for a language like Turkish where some of the properties of finite clauses referred to in the literature (fully verbal morphology, embedded clauses that look exactly like root clauses, and in particular nominative subjects) are found with certain types of embedding (i.e. the fully verbal embedded clauses) but not with others (i.e. not with the syntactically nominal clauses). Basing myself on properties that have been often cited in conjunction with finiteness (temporal independence from the matrix, opacity vs. transparency with respect to the binding of the subject position by a clause-external antecedent, and licensing of NPIs), I have concluded that Turkish, in addition to obviously finite verbal embeddings, also has nominal embeddings that can or should be called finite, despite the fact that they do not exhibit fully verbal morphology and have genitive rather than nominative subjects.[16]

Furthermore, I have proposed that the element that gives rise to 'finite' domains of both the verbal and the nominalized kind is the agreement element, if it is indeed a genuine, paradigmatic element fully agreeing with the subject of the domain, with the following proviso: when such an agreement element is present, then tense contributes to the computation of the finite domain. When a genuine agreement element is absent, then tense is irrelevant, and the domain is nonfinite, even if tense is present. Turkish is an interesting language in this regard, given that it is possible to have domains with tense but without agreement (i.e. in ECM/SOR constructions), and domains with agreement but without tense (i.e. the nominalized subjunctive, non-factive clauses).

The question now arises as to where to locate 'finiteness' in the phrase-structural architecture of the domains in question. At least as far as concerns the Turkish facts that we have studied here, it is not necessary to assume a position in addition to that of agreement (in contrast to the analysis of Scottish Gaelic, as proposed in Adger, Chapter 2 above). As a matter of fact, one could assume a [Fin]-head, projecting to a Fin-P(hrase). The morphological realization of such a [Fin]-head is, in languages such as Turkish, agreement. This would have the welcome consequence of not needing a separate syntactic head and projection for agreement; given that agreement has no semantic content, it is taken to be an 'uninterpretable' feature (Chomsky 1995b; 2001a) and thus it would be undesirable if it had a syntactic presence in the form of a projection. This would also accord well with an account such as Adger's in this volume, where Finiteness is a syntactic feature which is not co-extensive with agreement or tense; thus, in Celtic languages such as Scottish Gaelic, Finiteness would have a syntactic presence apart from

---

[16] It would be interesting to be able to identify domains that bear certain morphological properties of finite domains, such as exhibiting nominative rather than genitive subjects, but which can nonetheless be characterized as syntactically nonfinite; in other words, if it could be shown that the other side of the coin exists. As a matter of fact, Kornfilt (2003) claims that Turkish does have exactly such examples. Owing to space considerations I have not included those examples here. In a nutshell, the claim is as follows. In many adjunct (i.e. 'adverbial') clauses in Turkish, there is no agreement on the predicate. Nonetheless, the subject position can be occupied either by PRO or by an overt subject. In other words, PRO and overt subjects are not in complementary distribution in such clauses in the way they are in argument clauses, as we saw in this chapter. Such a breakdown is typically viewed as evidence that the overt subject in such instances bears default Case syntactically, rather than licensed Case. For independent motivation and discussion of default Case, the reader is referred to Schütze (2001), in addition to Kornfilt (2003). Given that, in the approach to finiteness advanced here, it is only *licensed* subject Case that contributes to syntactic finiteness, morphological nominative case which corresponds to syntactic default Case would not contribute to syntactic finiteness.

agreement and tense, while in Turkish, Finiteness, while having a syntactic presence as well, would be linked to the morphological presence of agreement. The difference between these two types of language would be in the morphological correlates of the common syntactic feature of Finiteness. Consequently, while both languages would have, in their clausal architecture, a [Fin]-head (and its projection), Scottish Gaelic would also have, in addition to such a head and its projection, an [Agr(eement)]-head, with its projection. Agreement morphology would be housed in [Fin] in Turkish, but in [Agr] in Scottish Gaelic.

Examples (49) and (50) offer two rough representations of the structure I am assuming and have described above, as realized for the nominalized clauses. I propose a Mood P(hrase) for both nominalization types; however,

(49)

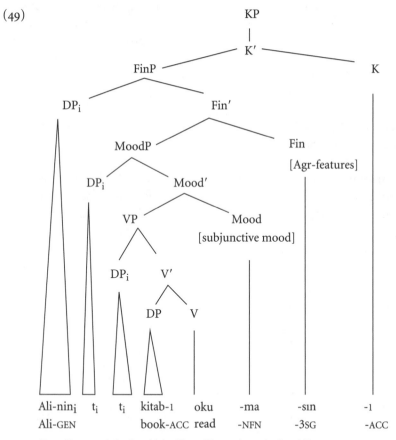

'for Ali to read the book' [= 'for Ali's reading the book']

(50)

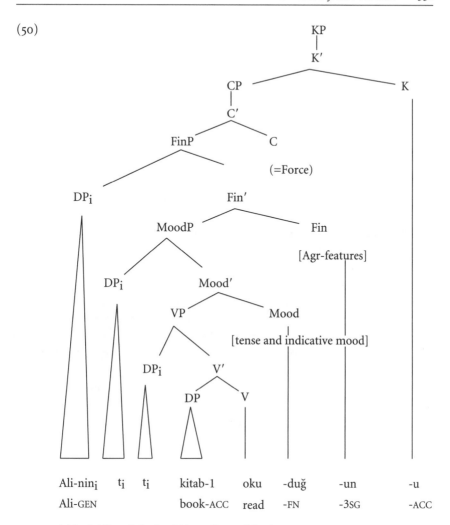

Ali-nin$_i$ t$_i$ t$_i$ kitab-1   oku   -duğ   -un   -u

Ali-GEN   book-ACC   read   -FN   -3SG   -ACC

' (that) Ali read the book'(as a direct object)

only the indicative/factive type has tense features in its MoodP. The rough representation for indicative nominalized clause is adapted from Borsley and Kornfilt (2000: 108).

These rough representations are very similar, with the exception of a CP- (or Force-Phrase) layer[17] between the Finiteness Phrase and the KP (the

---

[17] Here, I am following the proposed phrasal architecture in Rizzi (1997). The assumption that there is a Finiteness head, and that it can host agreement features, is also in the spirit of that approach.

highest layer of the nominal clause, i.e. a Case Phrase) in the representation for the nominal indicative clause in (50). The CP-layer is missing in the representation of the subjunctive clause.[18] The second difference is that in the indicative, finite nominalized clause, the Mood Phrase includes tense features, for the reasons we have seen earlier: this type of clause does have tense features, even if they are impoverished as compared to verbal clauses. In the subjunctive nominalized clause type, the Mood Phrase does not include tense features.

This treatment of the syntactic placement of Fin also accounts for the generalization I proposed for Turkish: Tense 'counts' as a defining factor for a 'finite' domain only when overt agreement is also present. If agreement is positioned in a Fin-head, as I have been assuming, and if Fin cannot be realized and cannot project in the absence of agreement, then it follows that tense features, even if they are fully realized, cannot determine a domain of finiteness: there simply would not be a Fin-head present into which the tense features could raise and thus contribute to syntactic finiteness. On the other hand, where agreement features are present, and are located in a Fin-head, then the contribution to Finiteness made by the tense features is explained under the reasonable assumption that those tense features raise to Fin, and thus, together with agreement, they play a role in determining the 'finiteness' of the domain in question, namely the FinP(hrase).

This account also has the additional advantage that it accommodates a view of syntactic finiteness where this notion can correspond to more than one morphological or syntactic phenomenon (here, tense as well as agreement), as mentioned also in Chapter 1 above. The account is flexible enough to accommodate different kinds of combined phenomena, as mentioned above for Scottish Gaelic.

---

[18] For motivation of this difference, see Kornfilt (2003). My assumption there is that tense, as a verbal category, is linked to C, also a verbal functional category. Therefore, the indicative/factive type of nominalized clause does have a C and a CP projection, given that it has tense features. The subjunctive/non-factive nominalized clause, lacking tense features, consequently also lacks a C and its projection, a CP.

Part IV

Finiteness in Diachrony and Language Acquisition

10

Diachrony and finiteness: subordination in the dialects of southern Italy

ADAM LEDGEWAY

10.1 Introduction

Although standardly recognized by linguists of many diverse theoretical persuasions, finiteness continues to figure among one of the most poorly understood concepts of linguistic theory (Ledgeway 2000: 187–9). Indeed, there appears to be no generally accepted view of how finiteness is manifested in natural languages, or to what precise entities or categories the terms 'finite' and 'nonfinite' readily apply (see Joseph 1983: 7–10; Vincent 1998: 146ff.; Nikolaeva, Chapter 1 above). While such issues are increasingly the subject of synchronic and comparative investigations, still very little attention has been given to exploring how finiteness and its correlates are affected by linguistic change. To this end, in what follows we shall undertake an in-depth examination of three distinct subordination types from the dialects of southern Italy that bear directly on a number of unresolved questions regarding the nature, trigger, and direction of changes involved in finiteness. The significance of such structures for our understanding of the nature of finiteness comes, among other things, from the fact that all three subordination types have been subject to changes which have ostensibly resulted in a change of the overall degree of finiteness borne by each clause type. More

The research reported here was conducted as part of a larger research project dedicated to the writing of a diachronic grammar of the Neapolitan dialect. I am grateful to the Arts and Humanities Research Council (AHRC) and the University of Cambridge for providing generous funding for this research project by way of research leave during the academic year 2005–6.
I use the following abbreviations for Italian sources: *Brancati* = Barbato (2001); *Ferraiolo* = Coluccia (1987); *de Spechio* = Compagna (1990); *LDT* = De Blasi (1986); *Lettera* = Sabatini (1993); *RDF* = McArthur (n.d.).

specifically, such structures will be demonstrated to provide us with a fertile test-bed in which to investigate the parameters involved in changes in finiteness, and at the same time will lead us to challenge and question some of the more orthodox views of finiteness widespread in the literature.

In particular, we shall deliberately adopt here, at least for initial working purposes, a traditional definition of finiteness (Ledgeway 1998: 2), according to which richness of overt verbal morphology (viz. morphological finiteness) and the availability of nominative Case (viz. syntactic finiteness) are assumed to rank among the key parameters in the proper assessment and evaluation of finiteness. Following a consideration of several cases ostensibly exhibiting superficial changes in the morphological and/or syntactic reflexes of finiteness, we shall, however, conclude and demonstrate (sections 10.5–6) that finiteness should be ultimately understood as a semantic notion, with only loose formal correlates at the morphological and syntactic levels which are subject, within the idiosyncratic limits of language-particular parameters, to considerable cross-linguistic variation.

The chapter is organized as follows. Section 10.2 begins with an examination of the significance of morphological correlates of finiteness in relation to infinitival subordination in the history of the Neapolitan dialect, investigating the causes and repercussions of a notable change in the latter's inflectional parameter which resulted in the loss of the inflected infinitive. This is followed in section 10.3 by a consideration of the syntactic correlates of finiteness, which are explored through an investigation of the development of southern Calabrian complement clauses, which, although remaining morphologically intact, have been subject to some noteworthy structural modifications. Section 10.4 charts the diachrony of Neapolitan asyndetic complementation, exemplifying the effects of changes simultaneously involving both morphological and syntactic parameters of finiteness. In addition to exploring what it is about finiteness that is subject to change, and the mechanisms involved therein, the investigation of Neapolitan asyndeton will also be profitably directed towards exploring directionality in change. Section 10.5 critically reviews some of the consequences of the results of the preceding sections, in particular the role of morphological and syntactic correlates of finiteness, evaluating their significance for an understanding of a number of more general questions about the nature of finiteness, before concluding that finiteness should be understood as a semantic notion. In support of this conclusion, section 10.6 returns to the old Neapolitan inflected infinitive and its development from an erstwhile conditional verb form, highlighting how changes operating at the levels of phonology, morphology, and syntax are all to be interpreted as superficial reflexes of an underlying downgrading in semantic finiteness. By way of conclusion, section 10.7 sketches a unified approach to semantic finiteness and its overt phonological, morphological, and syntactic correlates in terms of an analysis which privileges functional categories as the locus of finiteness.

10.2 Morphological finiteness: the Neapolitan inflected infinitive

Besides the canonical infinitive, old Neapolitan exhibits a species of infinitive morphologically inflected for person.[1] Although deriving from the Latin pluperfect indicative (Loporcaro 1986),[2] synchronically the inflected infinitive can be argued to consist of the canonical infinitival form (e.g. *ama-re* love-INF 'to love') augmented by a series of person inflections, as illustrated in Table 10.1. In contrast to other Romance varieties with inflected infinitives such as Portuguese (Maurer 1968; Raposo 1987) and Sardinian (Jones 1993: 278–82), the old Neapolitan inflected infinitive displays overt person marking only for the 1st, 2nd, and 3rd persons plural, the singular persons of the Latin

TABLE 10.1. Diachrony and synchrony of old Neapolitan inflected infinitive

	Latin pluperfect	Inflected infinitive
1SG	AMA(VE)RA(M)	*ama-re-Ø* love-INF-SG.AGR
2SG	AMA(VE)RA(S)	*ama-re-Ø* love-INF-SG.AGR
3SG	AMA(VE)RA(T)	*ama-re-Ø* love-INF-SG.AGR
1PL	AMA(VE)RAMU(S)	*ama-r(e)-**mo*** love-INF-1PL
2PL	AMA(VE)RA(TIS)=VO(S)	*ama-r(e)-**vo*** love-INF-2PL
3PL	AMA(VE)RAN(T)	*ama-r(e)-**no*** love-INF-3PL

[1] This system of person inflections extends equally to other verbal forms traditionally labelled as nonfinite such as present and past participles and gerunds. For a detailed discussion, see Vincent (1998: §2.2).

[2] Also relevant here is the question of how a finite verb form like the Latin pluperfect indicative was reinterpreted in Neapolitan as a less finite verb form, a question to which we return below in section 10.6. A similar change affected the Portuguese inflected infinitive, which (at least according to one hypothesis) developed from the Latin imperfect subjunctive (see e.g. Pires 2002, who analyses this change within a cue-based theory of acquisition).

pluperfect indicative converging in the undifferentiated form *amare* [a'marə],[3] which happens to coincide with the canonical (non-inflecting) infinitival form.

As for its distribution,[4] the inflected infinitive occurs in contexts of both obligatory control (OC) and, more frequently, non-obligatory control (NOC).[5] In the former case, the inflected infinitive occurs within a complement clause containing an implicit null subject (PRO) obligatorily controlled by an argument of the matrix clause. In sentences (1a, b), for example, below the matrix predicates *avertevamo* 'we had intended' and *se acordaro* 'they agreed' are subject control verbs that subcategorize for an inflected infinitival complement whose implicit 1/3PL subjects, evidenced in the agreement markers *-mo/-no* suffixed to the infinitive, are necessarily understood as coreferential with the matrix subject. In example (1c), by contrast, *placesse* 'it pleased' is an object control verb whose dative EXPERIENCER argument *ve* 'you' is obligatorily construed as coreferential with the understood subject of the inflected infinitival complement referenced in the 2PL inflection *-vo*.

(1) a. se nui avertevamo   de   le=anda-r-<u>imo</u>   appriesso,
        if we   consider.PST.1PL of.COMP them=go-INF-1PL   after
        non ne=scanpava   nissciu(n)o
        not us.DAT=escape.PST.3SG   not.one
        'If we had intended to go after them, not one of them would
        have got away.' (*Ferraiolo* 116r.3, *c.*1498, Coluccia 1987)

     b. se=acordaro   de   non   vole-re-<u>no</u>   re
        selves=agree.PST.3PL   of.COMP   not   want-INF-3PL   king
        'They agreed they would not want a king.' (*de Spechio* II.1.3, *c.*1468,
        Compagna 1990)

     c. se   ve=placesse   de   trasi-re-<u>vo</u>   mo'
        if   you.DAT=please.SBJV.PST.3SG of.COMP   enter-INF-2PL   now
        a   la   vattaglya
        to   the   battle
        'if you would now like to enter the battle' (*LDT* 214.16–17, *c.*1330,
        De Blasi 1986)

---

[3] Similar in this respect is the development of the inflected infinitive of standard Brazilian Portuguese, which only retains distinct person markings for the plural forms (Pires 2002: 143).

[4] See further Vincent (1996) and Ledgeway (1988: 41–6; 2000: 109–14).

[5] See Williams (1980) and Hornstein (1999).

In contexts of non-obligatory control, by contrast, the inflected infinitive is found in both complement and, more frequently, adjunct clauses. Here it occurs with an overt or covert (pro) nominative subject that is referentially free, insofar as control by an argument of the matrix clause is not obligatory, though indeed often possible, as demonstrated in (2):

(2) a. io   v'=aio   qua   fate   congriare   per   nuy
        io   you=have.PRS.1SG   here   make.PTCP   gather.INF   for   we

        ave-re-<u>mo</u>   ordene
        have-INF-1PL   orders
        'I have assembled you here for us to take our orders.' (*RDF* 24, first
        half 15th c., McArthur, n.d.)

     b. legya   cosa   serrà   a   perde-re-<u>vo</u>   le   persune
        light   thing   be.FUT.1SG   to.COMP   lose-INF-2PL   the   persons
        'You might easily die.' (*LDT* 55.24–5)

     c. speravano   in Dio, lo   dì   venenno,   d'   ave-re-<u>no</u>
        hope.PST.3PL   in God the   day coming   of.COMP   have-INF-3PL
        lo   castiello
        the   castle
        'They put their hope in God that, by daylight, they would capture
        the castle.' (*Ferraiolo* 128v.3)

In all three sentences the reference of the infinitival subject—which is explicit in (2a) although in most cases (cf. 2b, c) overt person agreement on the infinitive proves sufficient in referencing its identity—is not constrained by the semantics of the matrix predicate but, rather, is free to refer to any set of individuals. For example, in (2a) the reference of the infinitival subject includes both the speaker and his addressees, whereas in (2b) it refers exclusively to the addressees. In (2c), by contrast, the implied 3PL infinitival subject is controlled by the matrix subject, although, as illustrated in (3), *sperare* 'to hope' does not necessarily impose a subject control relation on the embedded subject of its inflected infinitival complement.

(3) presto   speramo   a   Dio   esse-re-<u>no</u>   rutte
     soon   hope.PRS.1PL   to.COMP   God   be-INF-3PL   routed
     'We hope to God that they will soon be routed.' (*Ferraiolo* 138v. 8–9)

By around the second half of the seventeenth century (De Blasi 2002: 113), however, the inflected infinitive had fallen entirely from usage. De Blasi identifies its loss with processes of phonological attrition that emerged during the same period. However, a more promising line of investigation, we believe, is to relate the loss of the inflected infinitive to the fact that in the singular persons of the paradigm (cf. Table 10.1 above) there are no overt markers for person or number, all three singular persons invariably coinciding with the canonical non-inflecting infinitive. Presented with examples such as (4a–d), which from a historical perspective arguably instantiate the undifferentiated singular form of the inflected infinitive deriving from the Latin pluperfect, it is conceivable that speakers would readily reinterpret the singular form of the inflected infinitive in such examples simply as the non-inflecting infinitive:

(4) a. ne=ave   voluto   assaltare   a   la   soa   citate,
         us=has.PRS.3SG want.PTCP   attack.INF   to   the   its   city

         senza   essere   a   lluy facto   oltrayo   per   nuy
         without   be.INF   to   it   do.PTCP   offence   through   us
         'They [=the enemy] wanted to attack us in their own city,
         although they had not been affronted by us.' (*LDT* 134.17–18)

     b. Non è   licito quillo   passar   certi   anni   de   la
         not be.PRS.3SG   licit   that.one   pass.INF   some   years of   the

         sua   vita
         its   life
         'It is not right that it [= the boa constrictor] should spend a
         number of years of its life like that.' (Brancati, 206v.17, *c*.1479,
         Barbato 2001)

     c. le=promise   mia   fede   de   tu   pillare
         him.DAT=promise.PST.1SG my   faith   of.COMP   you   take.INF
         sua   filla   per   molere
         his   daughter   for   wife
         'I gave him my word that you would take his daughter for
         your wife.' (*RDF* 225)

     d. oramay   ch'   ey   tienpo, de   te=maritare
         now   that   be.PRS.3SG   time   of.COMP   yourself=marry.INF
         'now that it is time for you to marry' (*RDF* 64)

     e. Per cierto   mello ey   questa battalla a   spinire
         for certain better be.PRS.3SG this   battle   to.COMP finish.INF
         luy   e   io   isema
         he   and I   together
         'It is certainly better for him and me to finish this battle together.'
         (*RDF* 26)

Once this reinterpretation takes places, speakers have the necessary cue to infer that non-inflecting infinitives license full lexical subjects (cf. 4a–c) and disjoint null (pro) subjects (cf. 4d). The next step, therefore, is for speakers to extend the use of the non-inflecting infinitive to non-coreferential plural subjects, an option extensively documented in early texts (see e.g. (4e) above and the discussion in Vincent 1996: §2),[6] ultimately leading to the loss of the inflected infinitive and the emergence of the so-called personal infinitive (Ledgeway 1998: 3–6; 2000: ch. 4). Consequently, in the modern period the inflected infinitive in both OC (cf. 5) and NOC (cf. 6) clauses is now replaced by the canonical (non-inflecting) infinitive:

(5) a. ite   fatto   male   a   ve=nzurà
         have.PRS.2PL do.PTCP   wrong   to.COMP   yourself=marry.INF
         n'-ata   vota
         an-other   time
         'You were wrong to get married again.'

     b. a   lloro c'=è   venuto   'o gulìo 'e
         to them   them.DAT=be.PRS.3SG   come.PTCP   the desire of.COMP
         se=da'   nu   poco 'e cunforto
         selves=give.INF   a   bit   of comfort
         'They feel like treating themselves a bit.'

     c. nun ve=mettete   scuorno 'e   m'='o=ddicere
         not yourself=put.PRS.2PL   shame   of.COMP   me.DAT=it=tell.INF
         n-faccia?
         in-face
         'Are you not ashamed to tell me to my face?'

(6) a. meh,   Carmè,   serve   pe   ce=vedé   n'-ata   vota
         come.on Carmela   serve.PRS.3SG for us=see.INF an-other   time
         'Come on, Carmela, it'll allow us to see one another again.'

     b. ma chist' è   'o   mumento 'e   v'=appiccecà?
         but this   be.PRS.3SG   the moment of.COMP   yourselves=argue.INF
         'Is this the right time for you to have an argument?'

---

6 *Pace* Miller (2002: 50), who claims that '[i]n languages with plain and inflected infinitives, a lexical subject is never licensed in the absence of Agr'. Similarly, modern Sardinian varieties with inflected infinitives are also reported to optionally allow lexical subjects in conjunction with the canonical (non-inflecting) infinitive (Jones 1992: 303–5; 1993: 281–2).

c. ce=vo   n'-ata   mez' ora   pe fernì   'e guagliune
it.DAT=want.PRS.3SG an-other half   hour   for finish.INF the boys
'The lads won't be finished for another half-hour yet.'

In (5a–c) the infinitival subject is obligatorily controlled by an argument of the matrix predicate, forcing it to surface as the anaphoric null pronominal PRO.[7] In (6), by contrast, the infinitival clause licenses a nominative subject, pro (cf. 6a, b) or a full lexical DP (cf. 6c), with independent reference that is not controlled by an argument of the matrix clause.

From a purely morphological perspective, it is indeed possible, then, to conclude that the development of infinitives in Neapolitan, and in particular the loss of inflectional marking for person, provides incontrovertible proof that finiteness—at least as traditionally employed in the description of Indo-European languages, where it is generally equated *tout court* with morphological richness (Joseph 1983: 17ff.; Koptjevskaja-Tamm 1993b: 256)—is susceptible to change. However, such a superficial interpretation of finiteness, though undoubtedly justified at the morphological level, may have less of an impact on other areas of the grammar, where its effects often prove more difficult to detect.[8] In particular, a comparison of the infinitival examples in (1) and (2) on the one hand and (5) and (6) on the other demonstrates beyond all doubt that finiteness cannot be exhaustively reduced to the availability of inflectional marking for such categories as person and number and its repercussions on nominative Case, as has been common practice in the generative tradition (Chomsky 1981: 52; Ledgeway 1998: 7–20; Mensching 2000). Rather, the change observed in the inflectional parameter of Neapolitan, ultimately resulting in the loss of person marking in conjunction with infinitives by the second half of the seventeenth century, has had no effect whatsoever on the syntax of the Neapolitan infinitive. The latter continues to license Caseless PRO in OC contexts (cf. 5) and nominative (covert/overt) subjects in NOC contexts (cf. 6), in striking contrast to the non-inflecting infinitive of related languages such as Italian and French, which, at least in the prescriptive standards,[9] does not license nominative subjects in NOC environments. In short, the surface manifestation of the original infinitival patterns, although modified, fails to

---

[7] According to a number of recent proposals, OC may be more conveniently analysed as a subcase of A-movement (O'Neil 1997; Hornstein 1999; Manzini and Roussou 1999; Ledgeway 2000: 94ff.). Accordingly, subjects in OC environments are obligatorily null on account of their being traces of NP-movement.

[8] See e.g. Vincent (1998: 136–51) and Ledgeway (2000: 187–9).

[9] See Ledgeway (2000: 120) and Mensching (2000: 22).

have any direct consequence on the underlying structure of infinitival subordination.

A reasonable assumption at this stage in our investigation, then, is that finiteness, although frequently viewed as a global property of the clause, might have distinct and unrelated manifestations in different areas of the grammar. Thus, what might legitimately be taken in this case as a reduction in finiteness at the level of morphology does not necessarily presuppose a concomitant downgrading in the syntactic (nominative-licensing) and semantic (obligatory vs. non-obligatory control) finiteness of the clause. Instead, it emerges that finiteness in those languages where it proves to be a relevant grammatical distinction may operate at different levels of the grammar, with, for example, morphological distinctions not necessarily impacting on syntax, and vice versa. In this respect, morphology is best viewed independently of other areas of the grammar, as highlighted by inflectional parameters such as that of person/number marking which are notoriously unreliable indicators of syntactic processes—witness the difficulties of generative attempts such as the 'Rich Agreement Hypothesis' (Bobaljik 2000) and the Mirror Principle (Baker 1985; 1988: 13) to relate overt morphological richness to the availability of syntactic operations such as verb movement and pro-drop phenomena.[10] Thus, while recognizing that morphological distinctions serve in the core cases to draw a linguistically relevant distinction between finite and nonfinite verb forms,[11] we conclude that there is not necessarily a one-to-one mapping between morphological correlates of finiteness, which we have seen are subject to linguistic change, and any corresponding syntactic categories or distinctions.[12] This point is also made by Anderson (2002: 273), who persuasively argues against the traditional 'assumption that syntactic and morphological (especially inflectional) structure ought to be isomorphic'.

[10] See e.g. Taraldsen (1980), Rizzi (1982: ch. 4), Chomsky (1991), Rohrbacher (1999), Jonas (2002), and Lightfoot (2002: 6–7). In recent work within the Minimalist Programme, syntactic operations are said to be morphologically driven (cf. Chomsky 1995a: 222, 253), insofar as operations such as movement take place to check uninterpretable morphological features such as Case and phi-features. Clearly, however, morphological features are to be interpreted here to mean abstract, formal (grammatical) features, completely divorced from the language-specific question of whether such features are given overt expression.

[11] Indeed, there is considerable cross-linguistic evidence to suggest that 'the finite class will always be the set which is marked morphologically and the nonfinite class the unmarked set' (Joseph 1983: 29); see also Vincent (1998: 147, 150–1) for further discussion of the implicational interaction between finiteness and marking for person/number and tense.

[12] Illustrative in this regard is Sells's discussion (Section 3.2 above) of raising structures in Japanese which, while exhibiting morphological finiteness, are devoid of any of the clausal semantic functions of finiteness.

In this respect, a comparison between the development of the Neapolitan inflected infinitive and that of contemporary colloquial Brazilian Portuguese (ColBP) proves instructive. Contrary to what has happened in Neapolitan (cf. 6a, b), in ColBP the loss of person inflection in conjunction with the inflected infinitive has blocked the licensing of null pronominal (pro) subjects in conjunction with the non-inflecting infinitive in NOC environments (cf. Pires 2002). Thus, although not excluded, the comparative evidence suggests that there is *a priori* no one-to-one correspondence between morphological and syntactic structures or, for that matter, between morphological and syntactic correlates of finiteness, to the extent that changes in the surface manifestation of given syntactic patterns do not inevitably result in a modification of their underlying syntactic structures.[13]

10.3 Syntactic finiteness: MODO-clauses

Further evidence that finiteness is indeed liable to change emerges from southern Calabrian complementation structures like that illustrated in (7a), taken from the Catanzarese dialect:

(7) a. èbbimu   'a possibilità [**ma**   stacimu   a lu liettu]
       have.PST.1PL the possibility [$_{CP}$ that [$_{IP}$ stay.PRS.1PL at the bed]]

   b. èbbimu   'a possibilità [**ma**=sta-cimu   a lu liettu]
       have.PST.1PL the possibility [$_{IP}$ INF.MRK= stay-1PL   at the bed]
       'We had the possibility of staying in bed.'

As convincingly argued by such scholars as Rohlfs (1969: §717; 1972a; 1972b; 1972c), structures like that in (7a) in the dialects of southern Calabria (south of the Nicastro-Catanzaro-Crotone isogloss),[14] historically part of the Greek-speaking area known as *Magna Graecia*, are originally calqued on an indigenous Greek finite structure headed by a complementizer derived from MODO 'now' > *ma* (cf. Greek *na*-clauses).[15] On a par with their Greek counterparts and other similar Balkan subordination structures (Joseph 1983), southern Calabrian MODO-clauses prove a serious competitor to the

---

[13] Cf. also Lightfoot (2002: 3): 'Sometimes morphological case systems or the inflectional properties of verbs change. They come to be manifested differently in childhood experience, and it may be that, when that happens, there are then structural changes in people's grammars. On the other hand, this might not be true.'

[14] Similar structures are also found in the dialects of north-eastern Sicily (province of Messina) and the Salentino peninsula (south of the Taranto–Ostuni isogloss).

[15] In other areas, reflexes of MODO have given *mu* (provinces of Catanzaro and Reggio Calabria) and *mi* (Reggio Calabria and province, north-eastern Sicily). In the dialects of the Salentino peninsula, by contrast, MODO is replaced by QUOD > *cu*.

traditional Romance infinitive in this and other areas of the extreme south of Italy,[16] to the extent that in the modern dialects the infinitive only survives, albeit subject to some degree of regional variation (for an overview, see Lombardi 1997: ch. 3; 1998), as an optional variant in conjunction with a restricted class of auxiliary verbs (modals, aspectuals, causatives).

However, an examination of the properties of such clauses in the modern dialects highlights that reflexes of MODO no longer behave synchronically as complementizers, but are instead more felicitously analysed as preverbal infinitival markers within Infl, as indicated by the structural representation in (7b).[17] The principal evidence for this conclusion comes from a consideration of a number of ordering and co-occurrence restrictions placed on reflexes of MODO with respect to other clausal elements. For example, assuming MODO to occupy the head of CP, we should expect it to precede canonical preverbal subjects in [Spec, IP] and the preverbal negator *non* incorporated into the verb under Infl. As the examples in (8a, c) demonstrate, however, MODO invariably follows both of these:

(8) a. vogghiu   **lu   diavulu** <u>mu</u>   ti=mangia
         want.PRS.1SG   the   devil   MODO   you=eat.PRS.3SG
         'I wish the devil would eat you up!'

     b. fa=lli   celati   e   **nudhu** <u>mu</u>   ti=vidi
         do.IMP=them   hidden   and nobody   MODO   you=see.PRS.3SG
         'Do them secretly and so that nobody sees you.'

     c. speriamu   **nom-<u>ma</u>**   nivica
         hope.IMP.1PL   not-MODO   snow.PRS.3SG
         'Let's hope it doesn't snow.'

That the subject in examples like (8a) is not left-dislocated is evidenced by examples like (8b), where the subject is a quantifier (*nudhu* 'nobody') and hence incompatible with left-dislocation (cf. Cinque 1990). Thus, even analysing such structures in terms of a more richly articulated CP space (Rizzi 1997), in which MODO would presumably occupy the head of FinP (Finiteness Phrase), would fail to predict the grammaticality of sentences like (8b).

---

[16] See Sorrento (1949), Trumper and Rizzi (1985), Pristerà (1987), Calabrese (1993), Leone (1995: §80), Cristofaro (1997), Loporcaro (1997: 346–7), and Trumper (1997: 364).

[17] Cf. Ledgeway (1998: 23ff.). An analogous analysis is also frequently proposed for many of the modern Balkan languages, where erstwhile complementizers like Greek *na*, Romanian *să*, and Bulgarian *da* are standardly treated as inflectional (subjunctive) particles (cf. Phillipaki-Warburton 1987; Rivero 1987; 1994; Terzi 1991; 1992; Dobrovie-Sorin 1994: 93ff.; 2001; Krapova 2001; Miller 2002: 93ff.).

Additional evidence for the Infl status of MODO comes from the observation that MODO co-occurs both with *wh*-phrases (cf. 9a) and the finite complementizers *chi* and *ca* (cf. 9c, d):

(9) a. non eppi   **cui**   '̱u[18]   si=pigghja   li   difesi
        not have.PST.1SG who MODO self=take.PRS.3SG the defences
        'I had nobody to take up my defence.'

   b. cu   sapa   **quantu**   (*ca) custanu?
      who know.PRS.3SG how.much that cost.PRS.3PL
      'Who knows how much they cost?'

   c. vi=promettu,   si non vi=pagu,   chi-<u>mmu</u>
      you=promise.PRS.1SG if not you=pay.PRS.1SG. that-MODO
      moru   schjettu!
      die.PRS.1SG   alone
      'I promise you that, if I don't pay you, would that I die a bachelor!'

   d. non facìa   autru **ca**   <u>mi</u>   ciangi
      not do.PST.3SG other that MODO cry.PRS.3SG
      'He did nothing but cry.'

Although a stipulation that proves difficult to implement theoretically, Chomsky and Lasnik's (1977) so-called Doubly-filled Comp Filter turns out to be a valid empirical generalization for the dialects of southern Calabria, as evidenced by the ungrammaticality of (9b), where the head of CP is filled by *ca* and its associated specifier position simultaneously hosts the *wh*-phrase *quantu* 'how much'. Nonetheless, the combination of a *wh*-phrase and MODO (cf. 9a) produces grammatical results, casting serious doubt once again on the complementizer status of MODO. Similarly, the well-formedness of the sequence *chi/ca* + MODO highlighted in (9c, d) is congruent with the view that MODO is not a complementizer.

On the basis of the evidence reviewed in examples (8) and (9),[19] we conclude that MODO in the modern dialects is best analysed as a preverbal infinitival marker (Ledgeway 1998: 47–56). As a concomitant of this categorial change from complementizer to infinitival marker (cf. 7a ⇒ 7b), erstwhile finite verb forms accompanied by a reflex of MODO, which came to be restricted to occurring in the present irrespective of the temporal specification of the matrix predicate, are now reinterpreted as infinitival forms augmented by overt marking for person/number, namely inflected infinitives (for a

---

[18] '*U* (just like '*i*) is a frequent phonologically reduced form of *mu* (and *mi*).
[19] For a more detailed discussion of all the evidence, see Ledgeway (1998).

detailed discussion, see Ledgeway 1998: 41–7).[20] Indeed, the formal and functional overlap between subjunctives and infinitives is further highlighted by Nikolaeva (2003), who persuasively argues that 'there is no apparent semantic distinction between the subjunctive and the infinitive, as both forms express exactly the same irrealis future situations when in complementation'. In syntactic terms alone, we conclude then that MODO-clauses, despite exhibiting no loss in the morphological realization of finiteness, have been de-categorialized and downgraded from finite to inflected infinitival clauses, demonstrating once again that the degree of finiteness borne by particular verb forms and constructions can be subject to attrition.

More significantly, however, MODO-clauses confirm our previous observation in relation to the Neapolitan infinitive that reflexes of finiteness are not necessarily uniformly mapped onto all areas of the grammar in an isomorphic fashion. In the case under investigation, we have witnessed how a reduction in syntactic finiteness, triggered by the categorial shift from tensed complementizer to infinitival marker undergone by reflexes of MODO, is not paralleled by a concomitant decrease in the surface morphological correlates of finiteness. This appears to be a prime example of *reanalysis*,[21] a mechanism of syntactic change involving a modification in the underlying structure of a given syntactic pattern, yet without any concomitant change in its surface appearance. Arguably, however, the syntactic changes affecting MODO-clauses are not without their consequences for semantic correlates of finiteness. In particular, the increased syntactic integration and dependency between matrix and complement clauses are paralleled by a commensurate degree of semantico-pragmatic integration between the two events/states (Givón 1990: 826). For instance, interlacing (cf. Lehmann 1988) between both clauses has resulted in the loss of the sequence of tense rule and the fossilization of the present indicative following MODO (Ledgeway 1998: 50–1), such that the temporal evaluation of MODO-clauses is now wholly determined by the

---

[20] The infinitival status of MODO-clauses is further supported by the observation that they license PRO subjects and obligatory control (cf. (i)a below), whereas subjunctive clauses (cf. the Italian example (i)b, as MODO-clauses have been traditionally defined, never license PRO and give rise to either variable control or obviation:

(i)   a.   Rina$_i$ si=mentiu   PRO$_i$/*pro$_j$/*'Ntoniu   m'   'i=lava
             Rina   self=put.PRS.3SG   PRO$_i$/pro$_j$ / Antonio   MODO   them=washes
             'Rina$_i$ began PRO$_i$/*pro$_j$/* Antonio to wash them.'

       b.   Lucia$_i$ si=aspetta   che pro$_{j/*i}$ /Antonio   pianga
             Lucia$_i$ self=wait.PRS.3SG   that pro$_{j/*i}$ / Antonio   cry.SUBJ.3SG.
             'Lucia$_i$ expects her$_{j/*i}$ / Antonio to be crying.'

[21] See Langacker (1977: 58), Timberlake (1977), Hopper and Traugott (1993: 40–56), and Harris and Campbell (1995: 50–1, 61 ff.).

temporal reference of the matrix clause. This sharing of tenses has contributed, in turn, to increased bonding between matrix and subordinate clauses, leaving the verbal inflection to be reinterpreted wholly as subject agreement on the infinitive.

10.4 Directionality of change: Neapolitan asyndeton

Our examination of Neapolitan infinitival clauses and southern Calabrian MODO-clauses has highlighted two distinct cases involving a reduction in finiteness, albeit operating at the levels of morphology and syntax respectively. This naturally raises the question of whether such changes are unidirectional, as suggested by the two preceding examples, which both involve a shift in the direction from finite to less finite, or whether changes can equally operate in the opposite direction. A consideration of the history of Neapolitan asyndetic structures consisting of the paratactic sequence of two juxtaposed imperatives demonstrates that linguistic change can indeed result in a shift from the less finite to the more finite. By way of example, consider the sentences in (10a, b):

(10) a. viene=te   [a   assettà]
          come.IMP.2SG=yourself to.COMP   seat.INF

      b. viene   [t'=assiétte]
          come.IMP.2SG yourself=seat.IMP\2SG
          'Come (and) sit down.'

Alongside familiar hypotactic infinitival structures like (10a), Neapolitan, on a par with most Italo-Romance varieties,[22] also makes considerable use of parataxis (cf. 10b) in conjunction with the two verbs of motion *jì* 'to go' and *venì* 'to come'. Superficially, such asyndetic structures display several puzzling properties (Ledgeway 1997: 257–9). First, they are restricted to the imperative mood, whereas in many other southern dialects they also occur in indicative contexts. Secondly, they are restricted to occurring in the 2nd person singular, again in contrast to other southern dialects, which license asyndeton in conjunction with all six grammatical persons. Thirdly, *jì* and *venì* obligatorily trigger restructuring in Neapolitan (Ledgeway 2000: 83), such that all clitic pronouns of embedded infinitival complements automatically climb to the matrix predicate (cf. the enclitic *-te* 'yourself' in 10a), yet no restructuring, and hence no clitic climbing, occurs in the asyndetic structure in (10b). Finally, although clitic pronouns in positive imperatives invariably

---

[22] See Ascoli (1896); Ledgeway (1997: 256).

attach enclitically to their verbal host, e.g. *assiétte=te* (seat.IMP=yourself) 'sit down', in asyndetic structures like (10b) all clitics exceptionally stand proclitic to the second imperatival verb.

Nonetheless, all these otherwise exceptional properties fall into place once the origin of Neapolitan asyndeton is established. Simplifying somewhat and leaving aside many of the details (though see Ledgeway 1997), alongside the canonical form of the infinitive (cf. 11a), Neapolitan also displays a specialized form of the infinitive (henceforth SFI) in which the expected oxytonic stress retracts to the verbal root (cf. 11b; cf. Bichelli 1974: 207–10):

(11) a. assett-à /   ver-é /   serv-ì
          seat-INF/   see-INF/   serve-INF

      b. assètte /   vére /   sèrve
          seat\INF /   see\INF /   serve\INF
          'to sit / to see / to serve'

These SFIs are typically employed in conjunction with clitic forms of a handful of auxiliary-like verbs, including the two aspectually marked verbs of motion *jì* and *venì* (see also Rohlfs 1966: §315). Thus, alongside canonical infinitival complements like (12a), it is also possible to find the SFI in the same context, although following verbs of motion it is increasingly judged to be marginal in the modern dialect (cf. 12b). The marginal status of such examples stems from the ambiguous status of the SFI, which in many cases, including (12b), coincides with the 2nd person singular imperatival form of the same verb. As a consequence of the ambivalent status of the embedded verb form, there arises a potential conflict between the syntax of the overall construction, since the second verb form, if interpreted as an imperative and hence a relatively finite verb form, will prove incompatible with the infinitival introducer *a* 'to' and will block restructuring and concomitant clitic climbing. Indeed, such a reanalysis of the SFI as an imperative appears to be well established among most speakers, leading to the subsequent loss of the infinitival marker *a* and resultant asyndetic structure (cf. 12c). Indeed, the imperatival status of the SFI is confirmed in modern Neapolitan by the fact that, where metaphonetic second person singular imperatival forms have emerged, these too can now appear alongside the original non-metaphonetic forms (cf. 12d):

(12) a. vatte   a   assett-à
          go.IMP.2SG=yourself   to.COMP   seat-INF

      b. ?vatte   a   assètte
          go.IMP.2SG=yourself   to.COMP   seat/SFI

    c. va   t'=assètte
        go.IMP.2SG yourself=seat/SFI.2SG (or seat/IMP.2SG)

    d. va   t'=assiétte
        go.IMP.2SG yourself=seat/IMP.2SG
        'Go (and) sit down.'

The developments outlined in examples (12a–d) instantiate therefore a gradual shift from an original, nonfinite hypotactic infinitival complementation structure towards an increasingly more finite, paratactic asyndetic structure consisting of two juxtaposed imperatives. The exceptional behaviour of clitic pronouns in asyndeton observed above thus represents the resolution of a conflict between an original nonfinite infinitival syntax and an incipient finite asyndetic syntax. Specifically, at some point the ambiguous second verb form (cf. 12c) is reanalysed as intermediate between a nonfinite (specialized) infinitival form and a 2nd person singular imperative,[23] before ultimately emerging unequivocally as an imperative (cf. 12d)—witness the appearance of the metaphonic rising diphthong. Nonetheless, such verb forms have not entirely jettisoned all their original infinitival properties, and may to some extent still be considered a hybrid of both verbal categories. From this perspective, the loss of clitic climbing can be viewed as a concomitant of the incipient imperatival reanalysis of the second verb form, since all finite verb forms block restructuring, whereas the unexpected proclisis to the embedded imperative may be interpreted as a residue of the latter's erstwhile infinitival status, since infinitives favour proclisis in Neapolitan. Consequently, proclisis becomes fixed, so that even when unequivocal metaphonetic forms of the 2nd person singular imperative subsequently emerge (cf. 12d), enclisis still fails to obtain.

By the same token, the superficial oddity of asyndetic complementation being restricted to the 2nd person singular of the imperative also finds a natural solution in light of the nonfinite hypotactic origin of such structures. In particular, the other persons of the imperatival paradigm, namely the 1st person plural *jammo/venimmo* 'let's go/come' and the 2nd person plural *jate/ venite* 'go/come', could not be readily assimilated into an asyndetic construction, since the SFI never coincides formally with the 1st/2nd person plural imperatival forms, the necessary catalytic condition that triggered the reanalysis of the SFI as a 2nd person singular imperative. We conclude therefore that a necessary condition for the genesis of the asyndetic construction is the

---

[23] This is a case of what Miller and Leffel (1994) term 'contextual reanalysis', an optional variety of reanalysis which occurs in a particular environment without, however, replacing the previously existing structure (cf. also Miller 2002: 3).

formal homophony of the SFI with another finite verbal expression. Only a 2nd person singular imperative form in the matrix clause (viz. *va/viene*) will thus ensure that the SFI invariably coincides with a non-infinitival verbal expression, ultimately giving rise to asyndetic structures.

Based on the strength of the Neapolitan data briefly reviewed above, we are forced to admit a much more fluid relationship between parataxis (finite clauses) and hypotaxis (nonfinite clauses) than is generally envisaged. It is traditionally assumed as a universal principle that hypotaxis, and hence nonfinite clauses, develop out of finite paratactic sequences, but that the reverse development, namely the change from hypotaxis (nonfinite) to parataxis (finite), does not occur.[24] Indeed, cross-linguistically this would generally appear to be the case, as witnessed by the fact that many subordinators develop out of erstwhile demonstrative pronouns (cf. Romance reflexes of QUID), which originally functioned as cataphoric markers of a loosely adjoined clause within a finite paratactic structure. However, the genesis of the Neapolitan asyndetic structure seriously impugns the so-called Parataxis Hypothesis, highlighting how the development from parataxis to hypotaxis, and consequently from finite to nonfinite, while undeniably extremely common cross-linguistically, is not necessarily a unidirectional development. Indeed, we have observed how a number of structural properties of Neapolitan asyndeton, otherwise inexplicable from a synchronic perspective, only become transparent once we recognize the hypotactic origin of asyndetic complementation. Without doubt, the outcome of the reanalysis in question results in a complement clause characterized by a greater degree of morphosyntactic finiteness, thereby providing persuasive evidence that changes in finiteness are indeed bidirectional.

As a final point, it is worth noting that, in contrast to the previous two examples, the developments witnessed in the development of Neapolitan asyndeton reveal how changes in the morphological and syntactic parameters of finiteness may operate in tandem. Specifically, the ambiguous status of the SFI, originally the result of a phonological rule of stress readjustment eliminating oxytonic stress in favour of preferred paroxytonic stress (Ledgeway 1997: 251–2), triggers a process of reanalysis whereby the category label 'infinitive' is eventually replaced by that of 'imperative'. In turn, this change in category in the underlying syntactic structure gives rise to a morphophonological readjustment manifested in the introduction of 2SG metaphonetic agreement in the second verb form.

---

[24] For an overview, see Hopper and Traugott (1993: 168ff.) and Harris and Campbell (1995: 25–7, 282–6).

10.5 Morphological and syntactic finiteness: an overview

The previous sections have served to present three case studies of changing subordination patterns in the dialects of southern Italy, the details of which have already been demonstrated to furnish some partial answers to a number of fundamental questions about the nature of changes affecting parameters related to finiteness. In what follows, we shall examine these and other questions in greater detail, considering what evidence the changes observed in the three subordination types outlined above provide for general issues in finiteness.

There can be no doubt that finiteness, or at any rate its surface manifestations, is liable to change. Already we have witnessed ample evidence to this effect from each of the three subordination types under examination which, considered together, additionally highlight the bidirectional nature of such changes. Given the subtle shifts involved, however, such as the development from inflected infinitive, a relatively finite form, to non-inflecting infinitive, a thoroughly nonfinite form, finiteness must necessarily be regarded as a gradient concept rather than as a simple finite/nonfinite dichotomy (Ledgeway 1998: 58; Vincent 1998: 152–3). This accords well with our previous observation that finiteness may surface in apparently conflicting ways across different areas of the grammar. For example, although morphologically nonfinite, failing to inflect for any of the traditional so-called finite categories such as person/number and tense, the modern Neapolitan personal infinitive (cf. 13a) nonetheless behaves to all intents and purposes like a finite tensed verb form (cf. 13b), licensing a nominative subject (*'o pullmanne* 'the bus') with independent reference that is not controlled by an argument of the matrix clause:

(13) a. primma 'e   se=fermà   'o pullmanne, 'o=chiammaje
       before   of.COMP self=stop.INF the bus   him=call.PST.1SG
       ncopp'   ô   cellulare
       on   the   mobile

   b. primma ca   se=fermava   'o pullmanne, 'o=chiammaje
       before   that   self=stop.PST.3SG the bus   him=call.PST.1SG
       ncopp'   ô   cellulare
       on   the   mobile
       'Before the bus stopped, I called him on my mobile.'

The existence of the personal infinitive construction therefore challenges the traditional dichotomy between finite and nonfinite verb forms and, in particular, the presumed correlation between nominative Case-licensing and the presence of overt inflectional morphology.

At the same time we are led to conclude that changes in finiteness may operate at different levels, for example at the level of morphology, as in the case of the loss of the old Neapolitan inflected infinitive, at the level of syntax, as in the case of southern Calabrian MODO-clauses, or indeed at the levels of both morphology and syntax, as witnessed by the genesis of Neapolitan asyndeton. It is doubtful, however, that developments applying at different levels of the grammar should be accorded equal status. As already observed, the change in the old Neapolitan inflectional parameter which gave rise to the loss of the inflected infinitive and the concomitant emergence of the personal infinitive, arguably a case of diminished morphological finiteness, failed to have any repercussions whatsoever on the syntax of Neapolitan infinitival structures. Conversely, the syntactic downgrading of MODO-clauses from finite subjunctive clauses to inflected infinitival clauses, though producing significant linearization effects, is not correspondingly mirrored at the level of morphology. In sum, while it is natural to expect a strong correlation between morphological and syntactic structures within the limits of language-specific morphological parameters, morphology cannot realistically be expected to exhaustively mirror all structural distinctions. In this respect, while overt morphological, and in particular inflectional, markings can generally be taken to faithfully reflect underlying syntactic structures, their absence, on the other hand, does not imply *a priori* the absence of corresponding syntactic distinctions or categories. By the same token, morphological correlates of finiteness, as we have seen, have a limited role to play in assessing the degree of finiteness borne by individual expressions and, at best, only indirectly reflect syntactic correlates of finiteness (cf. Nikolaeva, Chapter 1 above).[25]

Thus, what might be considered a reflex of finiteness at one level, for example morphology, may prove entirely irrelevant to other levels such as syntax, semantics, and phonology.[26] Such facts lead us to conclude that there may not be a direct mapping between the levels of morphology, phonology, syntax, and semantics, a fact which presumably has contributed to the often conflicting degrees of emphasis attributed to one or more of these areas by individual researchers analysing and interpreting finiteness in otherwise

---

[25] Cf. Joseph (1983: 13), who observes in relation to the Portuguese inflected infinitive that 'person/number markings...[cannot] be taken as a good determiner of finiteness/nonfiniteness in Portuguese, or, more important, universally'.

[26] In Ancient Greek, for example, reflexes of the finite/nonfinite distinction surface in the phonological component, as witnessed by the distribution of so-called recessive accent (cf. Joseph 1983: 17ff.).

similar constructions but across different languages.[27] For example, in languages like English and French a morphologically based approach suffices to capture the relevant generalizations between finite forms like the (simple) past on the one hand and nonfinite forms like the infinitive on the other. On the basis of such evidence, within the generative tradition finiteness is commonly held to follow from properties of the functional heads T and Agr, in turn correlatively responsible for the availability of nominative Case. In particular, infinitives are marked $[-T, -Agr]$, an impoverished Infl specification which underlies the impossibility of nominative Case assignment to the subject position and, at the same time, predicts that a null anaphoric pronominal subject (PRO) is licensed. Finite verb forms, in contrast, exhibit both tense and person/number marking, hence specified as $[+T, +Agr]$. Consequently, either T (Chomsky 1980: 250) or Agr (Chomsky 1981: §4.3) may be taken as responsible for the assignment of nominative to the subject position (Koopman and Sportiche 1991). Yet, in a language like Neapolitan the generative approach, which privileges morphological inflection as the relevant diagnostic, clearly proves inadequate in identifying supposedly nonfinite forms like the infinitive: not only can non-inflecting infinitives license nominative subjects (cf. 13a), but infinitives may equally occur in inflected form, though, conversely, not necessarily endowed with the ability to license nominative subjects (cf. 1a–c).

Equally problematic are contrasts between Neapolitan so-called finite clauses like that exemplified in (14a, b):

(14) a. Ciro$_i$ ricette   ca   Ø$_{i/j}$ / isso$_{i/j}$ veneva   cchiù doppo
           Ciro$_i$ say.PST.3SG that Ø$_{i/j}$ / he$_{i/j}$ come.PST.3SG more   after
           'Ciro$_i$ said that he$_{i/j}$ would come later.'

      b. Ciro$_i$ prummette   che   Ø$_{i/*j}$ / isso$_{j/*i}$ accatta 'e purtualle
           Ciro$_i$ promise.PRS.3SG that Ø$_{i/*j}$/he$_{j/*i}$ buys   the oranges
           'Ciro$_i$ promises PRO$_{i/*j}$ to buy the oranges / that he$_{j/*i}$ will buy
           the oranges.'

Verbs like *ricere* 'to say' in (14a), which select for the *ca* complementizer, yield NOC structures in which the understood embedded subject, presumably pro though represented here as Ø, may be controlled by an argument of the matrix clause (e.g. the matrix subject *Ciro*) or receive an independent interpretation. Consequently, if the embedded subject is overtly realized (e.g. *isso*

[27] Cf. Gretsch and Perdue (Chapter 12 below) and Nikolaeva (2003), who draw a distinction between M(orphological)-finiteness and S(emantic)-finiteness, and M(orphological)-finiteness and C(onstructional)-finiteness, respectively.

'he'), it too may be freely construed with the matrix subject or not. Given the non-complementary distribution of pro and *isso*, we conclude that nominative can be checked in the embedded subject position of *ca*-clauses. In contrast, verbs like *prummettere* 'to promise' in (14b), which select for the *che* complementizer, impose an OC relation on the understood null subject (here represented as Ø) of their embedded clause, such that it can only be interpreted as coreferent with the matrix subject, despite an intervening finite clause boundary (on the definition of binding domains, see Nikolaeva, Chapter 1 above, and Sells, Chapter 3 above, section 3.4.1).[28] To be interpreted as disjoint in reference, the embedded subject must be overtly realized (e.g. *isso* 'he'). The complementary distribution of covert and overt subjects in (14b) under the control reading suggests therefore that nominative cannot be licensed in the embedded subject position, thereby precluding the presence of pro. Rather, as a Caseless position, the embedded subject position in (14b) must host PRO, despite the fact it is ostensibly licensed by a finite verb (viz. 3SG present indicative).[29]

The Neapolitan data therefore highlight the dangers of interpreting finiteness in terms of morphological evidence alone, insofar as the availability of overt inflectional markings for person/number (Agr) and T(ense) are neither necessary nor sufficient conditions on licensing nominative, which clearly operates independently of such distinctions. At the same time, observed syntactic correlates of finiteness such as destructuring (cf. loss of clitic climbing in conjunction with Neapolitan asyndeton), categorial changes ($\text{MODO}_{\text{Comp}} > \text{MODO}_{\text{Infl}}$), and nominative-licensing appear devoid of any intrinsic value themselves, ultimately following from deeper semantic changes and distinctions. For instance, the destructuring process that accompanies the emergence of Neapolitan asyndeton, manifested in the dissolution of the clause union (restructuring) of the original infinitival hypotactic structure, signals a greater degree of semantic autonomy in the complement clause, whereas the categorial shift from complementizer to infinitival marker undergone by reflexes of MODO, in contrast, highlights an increased degree of semantico-pragmatic integration between matrix and embedded clauses and, by implication, the reduced autonomy of the latter. Similarly, the distribution of pro and PRO (and hence nominative Case) in Neapolitan infinitival (cf. examples 1, 2, 5, and 6) and *ca-/che-* (cf. examples 14a, b) clauses has

[28] The proper definition of binding domains in such cases as (14a, b) has also been characterized in the literature in relation to the different tense features of indicative and subjunctive clauses (cf. Anderson 1982; Giorgi 1983/4; Picallo 1984/5; Raposo 1985/6; Manzini and Wexler 1987), as well as a consequence of the differing finiteness features of the embedded clause (cf. Holmberg and Platzack 1995: 90ff.).

[29] See also the discussion of Sranan in Bisang (Section 5.4.1.1 above).

been demonstrated to follow as a consequence of the OC/NOC distinction, wholly independent of the presence of subject–verb agreement.

In short, the OC relation is a lexical property of the subcategorization frame of particular predicates, inasmuch as the subcategorization of a complement, be it infinitival or otherwise, imposes an obligatory relation of coreferentiality between the embedded subject (PRO) and an argument of the matrix clause. It follows from this that OC characterizes complement clauses, since these are s-selected by the matrix verb. On the other hand, NOC arises whenever the reference of an embedded subject (pro) is not independently recoverable from, or predetermined by, lexical properties of the matrix predicate, a situation which typically obtains in adjunct clauses which, not being s-selected, do not enter into a direct selectional relation with the matrix predicate. In this respect, the principled distinction between PRO and pro dissolves, the empty category in subject position now understood as a direct instantiation of the particular semantics (OC/NOC) of the matrix predicate (cf. also Culicover and Jackendoff 2001).

It would seem, then, that finiteness should be interpreted as a semantic notion, in essence a cover term for the varying degrees of semantic autonomy borne by individual clauses, correlating in turn with the [$\pm$ dependent] clause distinction (cf. Timberlake 1976). Under this interpretation, we can account very simply for the fact that those constructions traditionally classified as nonfinite are precisely those involving subordinate clauses, and, by the same token, that the greater semantic autonomy exhibited by main clauses calls for a so-called finite verb form.[30] There does not appear, however, to be any evidence to consider finiteness a linguistic primitive, reducible to any single category or structural position, as proposed, for example, within Rizzi's (1997) split-C system which identifies finiteness with a distinct functional projection *FinP*, indirectly replicating the core IP-related characteristics in accordance with parametric variation. Rather, finiteness can be envisaged more felicitously as a global semantic property of the clause whose formal representation can be variously marked, in accordance with parametric variation and the idiosyncrasies of individual grammars, on the verb (VP, e.g. person/number marking, clitic placement), at the level of the sentence (e.g. IP, MODO$_{Comp}$ > ma_{Infl}, pro vs PRO), and at the level of the clause (CP, e.g. *ca/che*, re-/destructuring).[31] On this view, finiteness can be interpreted as a scalar phenomenon, spelling out the cumulative effect of a number of variable features manifested in language-particular grammatical generalizations of a

---

[30] Cf. Vincent's (1998: 151–2) conclusion that mood and finiteness represent sub-parts of the same overall grammatical category (see also Miller 2002: 1, 68–9).

[31] Cf. Vincent (1993: §7.6.1).

phonological, morphological, and/or syntactic nature that correlate with some deeper semantic clausal property.

The inescapable conclusion is that finiteness, in those languages where it is visible, should be viewed as the phonological and/or morphosyntactic encoding of the degree of semantic autonomy exhibited by individual clauses.[32] Significantly, though, under this interpretation overt correlates of finiteness are treated purely as the phonological and/or morphosyntactic reflex of the degree of semantic autonomy displayed by particular clauses, devoid of any intrinsic value themselves. Consequently, while finiteness (= semantic autonomy) emerges as a universal, its realization finds itself subject to considerable cross-linguistic variation, as is well documented.

10.6 Semantic finiteness: the genesis of the old Neapolitan inflected infinitive

By way of reinforcing our conclusion that finiteness should ultimately be viewed as a purely semantic notion, we now briefly return to the old Neapolitan inflected infinitive examined above and, in particular, to its genesis. Previously it was noted, following Loporcaro (1986), that the old Neapolitan inflected infinitive derives from the Latin pluperfect indicative. More specifically, following the weakening of all final atonic vowels, centralized to [-ə], the syncopated singular forms of the Latin pluperfect, which continue into old Neapolitan with conditional value (Rohlfs 1968: §603), namely, AMA-(V-E) RA-(M/S/T) (love-PRF-PST-1/2/3SG) 'I/you/(s)he had loved' > *ama-r-a* [a'marə] (love-COND-SG.AGR) 'I/you/(s)he would love', came to formally coincide with the active form of the infinitive, namely AMA-RE > *ama-re* [a'marə] (love-INF) 'to love'. This formal merger of the two paradigms subsequently opened the way for the original singular conditional forms to be reinterpreted as infinitives, a reinterpretation which presumably would have been particularly favoured in contexts such as (15a, b), where the forms and functions of the conditional and the infinitive appear to overlap:

(15) a. non saccio   dove   lo=trovara
          not know.PRS.1SG where it=find.COND.1SG
          'I don't know where I would find it.'

      b. non saccio   dove   lo=trovare
          not know.PRS.1SG where it=find.INF
          'I don't know where to find it.'

---

[32] Similarly, Givón (1990: 853) sees the overt reflexes of finiteness as a means of marking 'the degree of integration of a clause into its immediate clausal environment'.

Once such a reinterpretation had taken place, the plural forms of the conditional paradigm (< Latin pluperfect) could then also be similarly integrated as infinitival forms transparently augmented by the person markers -*mo* (1PL), -*vo* (2PL), and -*no* (3PL), together with a concomitant stress retraction in the first two persons (cf. AMA(VE)RÀMU(S)/-(TIS)=VO(S) > *ama-ré-mo/-vo* love-COND-1/2PL), namely *amà-re-mo/-vo/-no* love-INF-1/2/3PL. By way of further illustration of the formal overlap between the conditional and the inflected infinitive, Loporcaro (1986: 215) cites the example in (16) where only the first underlined verb form is to be interpreted as an inflected infinitive, despite being morphologically indistinguishable from the subsequent underlined forms with conditional value:

(16) se ve=placesse   de   <u>trasi-re-vo</u>   mo' a la vattaglya,
      if you=please.SBJV.PST of.COMP enter-INF-2PL now to the battle,
      certamente vuy le=<u>ruppe-re-vo</u>   tutti et <u>acquista-re-vo</u>
      certainly you them=rout-COND-2PL all   and acquire-COND-2PL
      perpetuamente una grande glorya [...] Perzò   che vuy
      perpetually   a   great   glory   therefore that you
      co la gente vostra ve=<u>trova-re-vo</u>   frisco [...]
      with the people your   yourselves=find-COND-2PL fresh
      'If you would now like to enter the battle, you would certainly rout
      them all and would be remembered for it for all eternity [...] You
      and your men would therefore be at a disadvantage [unless ...]'
      (*LDT* 214.16–9)

To sum up, then, the genesis of the old Neapolitan inflected infinitive ostensibly exemplifies a case of downgrading in semantic finiteness, whereby an erstwhile semantically autonomous verb form specified [± dependent] is radically reanalysed as a [+dependent] verb form ('conditional' ⇒ 'infinitive'). At the root of this development, we can then identify a single semantic change in the intrinsic temporal properties of this verbal form, whose distinctly deictic temporal specification *qua* conditional (cf. 17a) is ultimately replaced by a non-deictic specification *qua* inflected infinitive, correlating in turn with the [± dependent] ⇒ [+dependent] shift. More specifically, in the absence of an internally organized tense the verbal form in its new inflected infinitival guise comes to invariably assume an anaphoric temporal interpretation strictly anchored to the tense of the matrix clause, such that the temporal frame of the infinitive can only be located in relation to the reference time of the matrix verb with which it coincides (cf. 17b), or fixed as unrealized with respect to the matrix tense (cf. 17c):

(17) a. io fecera   per suo amore onne cossa
          I   do.COND.1SG   for her love   every thing
          'I would do anything for her love.' (*RDF* 176, 1400–50)

      b. ave   plazuto   a   li   nuostri Diey de
         have.PRS.3SG   please.PTCP to   the   our   gods   of.COMP
         nuy esseremo   in   questa parte
         we   be.INF.1PL in   this   part
         'It has pleased our Gods for us to be in these parts.' (*LDT* 69.35)

      c. non foy   la   vostra principale intentione de
         not be.PST.3SG the your   principal   intention   of.COMP
         mettereno   a   ffine questa briga
         put.INF.3PL to   end   this   dispute
         'It was not your main intention that they should put an end to this
         dispute.' (*LDT* 120.8)

The primacy of this single semantic reanalysis is such that it acts as the
catalyst, and indeed is solely responsible, for a number of significant structural repercussions in other areas of the language, as schematized in Table
10.2. More specifically, once reanalysed as an inflected infinitival form, there
follows a series of concomitant processes of readjustment and levelling that
operate at the levels of phonology, morphology, and syntax to accommodate
and realign this verbal form in accordance with its new semantic categorization. Thus, the paroxytonic stress characteristic of the 1PL and 2PL conditional
forms, inherited directly from the corresponding Latin pluperfect indicative
forms (AMA(VE)RÀMUS > *amarèmo* and *AMA(VE)RÀ(TIS)=VO(S) > amar-
èvo*), retracts to the thematic vowel (i.e. *amàremo/-vo*) in line with the regular

TABLE 10.2. From Conditional to Inflected infinitive

Conditional (AMAVERAMUS ⇒ *amarèmo*)	Inflected infinitive (*amàremo*)	
T_Deictic	T_Anaphoric	Semantics
(1/2PL) Paroxytonic stress	(1/2PL) Proparoxytonic stress	Phonology
T formative -R- > -r-	Infinitival formative -r-	Morphology
Singular number Agr formative -a-	Infinitival formative -ə	Morphology
Stem allomorphy	Regular infinitival stem	Morphology
−N	+N	Syntax
+Nom	±Nom	Syntax
High V-movement	Low V-movement	Syntax

stress placement of the majority of infinitives (e.g. *amàre* 'to love'). Similarly, the erstwhile tense -R- > -*r*- and singular Agr(eement) -*a*- formatives of the original conditional verb form, namely, *ama-r-a* (love-COND-SG.AGR) 'I/you/(s)he would love', are correspondingly reanalysed as a single portmanteau infinitival formative -*rə*, viz. *ama-rə* (+-*mo/-vo/-no*) love-INF(+1/2/3PL.AGR). A more conspicuous morphological reflex of the reanalysis in question is manifested in the loss of stem allomorphy associated with the original Latin pluperfect forms. As noted by Loporcaro (1986: 215–16), the reanalysis from conditional to inflected infinitive would have first taken root in those verbs characterized by a regular perfective stem (notably those derived from the Latin I conjugation) where there was perfect formal correspondence with the infinitive, before eventually extending to verbs originally characterized by an irregular perfective stem (notably those derived from the Latin II conjugation) formally distinct from that of the infinitive, e.g. RUPE-RA(TIS)=VO(S) (break\PRF-PST=2PL) 'you had broken/routed' > *ruppere-vo* (break\COND-2PL) 'you would break/rout' (cf. 16a above) ⇒ *rompe-re-vo* (break-INF-2PL) 'you to break/rout' (cf. RUMPERE > *rompere* 'to break, rout').

The effects of the semantic reanalysis surface also in several significant syntactic areas. Underlyingly, the shift from conditional to inflected infinitive correlates with a radical change in the latter's categorial feature specification [-N] ⇒ [+N] in line with the greater nominal nature of the resulting verb form. As a consequence, the reanalysed verb form now occurs, for example, as the complement of preposition(al complementizer)s, witness the use of *de* 'of' in (17b, c) above. Furthermore, as an infinitival verb form, the nominative Case properties of the verb are also subject to significant changes directly derivable from the deictic-to-anaphoric change in its temporal specification. Whereas nominative Case was invariably licensed by the relevant verb form under its former conditional reading, nominative is now only licensed by the inflected infinitive in a subset of environments in accordance with its differing obligatory and non-obligatory control uses, as already identified above in section 10.5.

Finally, a more subtle but nonetheless important superficial syntactic reflex of this downgrading in semantic finiteness is observable in the differing degrees of verb movement that characterize both semantic instantiations of the relevant verb form. On the assumption that finite verb forms such as the conditional target specific heads within the rich IP-related functional structure above *v*-VP in accordance with their need to license particular agreement, temporal, and modal features (for a recent implementation of this idea, see Cinque 1999), we might a priori expect to find a difference in the movement properties of ostensibly less finite verb forms such as infinitives. Indeed, Cinque (1999: 110–11, 143ff.) demonstrates that Italian lexical infinitives, surprisingly, target higher positions within the IP-space than canonical finite lexical verbal forms such as the present indicative and the future, which raise to lower positions above the *v*-VP. On the other hand, Cinque (1999: 143–4) and Ledgeway and Lombardi (2005: §3) demonstrate, for French and the southern Italian dialect of Cosenza respectively, that infinitival verb forms in these varieties target lower positions than canonical finite verb forms. Although further research in this area is urgently required, there is some evidence to suggest that the observed downgrading in semantic finiteness is correlatively spelt out in the differing positions targeted by both verb forms. For instance, examples such as (18a) demonstrate that under the conditional reading the relevant verb form (*putere*) raises at least to a position to the left of so-called lower VP-adverbs like *already, still, always, nothing* (cf. Cinque 1999: §1.1). In contrast, in their inflected infinitival function these same verb forms would appear to target a lower clausal space, as demonstrated by (18b) where the inflected infinitive *vedereno* now occurs to the right of lower VP-adverbs such as *may* 'never', on a par with canonical non-inflecting infinitives (cf. 18c):

(18) a. et   no   si=putere   niente   ricollire
        and not self=be.able.COND.3SG nothing gather.INF
        'and nothing could be taken back' (*Lettera* 124.41–2, 1356;
        Sabatini 1993)

    b. yà   non credevano   de   may lo=vedereno   plu
       already not believe.PST.3PL of.COMP ever him=see.INF.3PL anymore
       'Already they believed that they would never see him again.'
       (*LDT* 66.33)

    c. né   se=potte   may   devisare   la   forma in che
       nor   self=be.able.PST.3SG ever imagine.INF the shape in what
       muodo fo   facto
       way   be.PST.3SG   do.PTCP
       'Nor could the way in which it was done ever be imagined.'
       (*LDT* 250.5–6)

We conclude, then, that the surface phonological, morphological, and syntactic changes witnessed in the genesis of the old Neapolitan inflected infinitive are all semantically induced. More specifically, these are adaptive changes that have a deeper structural significance, inasmuch as they signal and spell out in each of the various components of the language the diminished semantic autonomy borne by the erstwhile conditional verb form which, as a consequence of its loss in temporal autonomy, is downgraded to a dependent verb form. By contrast, in the case of some other subordination developments, such as the change from inflected to non-inflecting infinitive discussed in section 10.2, we are not dealing with semantically induced changes but with developments whose effects are variously confined to (a combination of) the areas of phonology, morphology, and syntax, but which fail to have any impact whatsoever on the semantic autonomy, and hence finiteness, of the construction in question. For instance, in the resulting non-inflecting infinival subordination type the overall semantics of the construction is not minimally affected, and hence it seems inappropriate to associate any deeper significance or relevance to such (albeit essentially arbitrary) superficial changes which operate independently of considerations of finiteness. We are thus left to conclude that whereas changes in finiteness, strictly understood here as a gradable semantic property of the clause, are mapped isomorphically onto phonological, morphological, and syntactic structures in accordance with language-particular parameters, isolated changes in one or more of these same areas do not a priori presuppose an inverse correlation with an up- or downgrading in clausal semantic autonomy, albeit finiteness.[33]

10.7 Changing finiteness: concluding remarks

Our synopsis of the semantically induced changes presented in Table 10.2 allows us at the same time to identify and assess the susceptibility of different areas of the grammar to be affected by changes in finiteness. In short, we have seen that phonology, morphology, and syntax are all readily amenable to change as a result of semantic downgrading (and upgrading: see section 10.4) in finiteness, and can arguably be viewed, on the strength of the evidence reviewed here, as necessary readjustments to take account of developments in the semantic component. More specifically, an increased degree of semantic integration between a given dependent event and its associated higher clause tends to be iconically mirrored by changes operating at the phonological and morphosyntactic levels (Givón 1990: 853), giving rise to a process of desententialization typically manifested in the loss of core verbal properties of the dependent verb. Thus, while there do not appear to be any particular identifiable constraints on which phonological, morphological, and syntactic aspects of language can adapt to reflect changes in semantic finiteness within the idiosyncratic limits of language-particular parameters, prototypically

---

[33] In a similar fashion, Gretsch and Perdue (section 12.1.3.1) and Nikolaeva (2003) observe, following Lasser (1997: 84), that the absence of Morphological finiteness does not a priori imply the absence of Semantic finiteness.

such changes, although far from being entirely predictable in view of the considerable cross-linguistic variation witnessed in the individual combinations of finiteness features, tend to surface in the reduction of verbal morphology (i.e. tense, aspect, mood, and agreement markings) and the rise of obligatory subject coreferentiality (typically translated in the loss of nominative Case). These properties are ultimately correlated, in turn, with the increased nominal nature of the dependent clause, as highlighted, for example, by its compatibility with such categories as Case, prepositions, and determiners.

In structural terms, the formal correlates of changes in semantic finiteness can be conveniently viewed within the verbal domain as the loss or deactivation of particular functional projections (e.g. AgrP, MoodP, NegP, FinP) or entire domains (CP and IP) which, once rendered inaccessible, become unavailable to the syntactic component to license particular operations (and hence have no reflex at PF). There thus emerges an iconic relationship between full semantic clausal autonomy and a matching full array of accessible functional projections, such that any attrition in the former is commensurately mirrored by a reduction in the latter. Typically, such attrition is translated in a restriction of the operation Move, such that individual items may undergo shorter movements to reach lower functional projections, as we saw to be the case with our comparison of verb movement in relation to the old Neapolitan conditional and inflected infinitive. In extreme cases, this might result in the outright loss of the operation Move, with particular items now directly merged in lower positions, increasingly restricted to the lexical structure of the clause. One such case might be the controlled null subject (viz. PRO) of the inflected infinitive in OC environments which, at least under one interpretation (cf. Baltin 1995: 244), fails to raise to the specifier position of the appropriate functional projection (e.g. T or Agr) responsible for nominative Case-checking, instead remaining in situ within the (specifier of) *v*-VP.

In an apparently conflicting manner, diminished semantic finiteness resulting in the deactivization of clausal functional projections might at the same time actually trigger movement operations, as is presumably the case in raising structures such as the Italian example (19), where the infinitival subject *Gianni*, unable to check Case and phi-features against the functional projections of the infinitival complement clause, is forced to raise to the vacant matrix subject position:

(19) Gianni sembra   [t_{Gianni} capire]
      Gianni seem.PRS.3SG   understand.INF
      'Gianni seems to understand.'

The inert nature of the embedded functional structure in examples like (19) is such that subject raising proves necessary and clause boundaries are consequently blurred,[34] iconically reflecting the underlying pragmatico-semantic integration of the dependent event into the higher clause.

Interpreted in this way, changes in language-particular manifestations of finiteness can simply be viewed as a consequence of changes in properties of particular functional projections (or domains), the morphological and lexical realization of which are independently known to be subject to considerable cross-linguistic variation (Cinque 1999). Thus, if as a consequence of semantic downgrading a particular functional projection or domain becomes inaccessible in a given construction, it follows that the overt reflexes of this inaccessibility can potentially surface in all areas of the grammar. Syntactically, if a position becomes inaccessible, this can result in the loss of items which previously filled, or were licensed in, that position under the operations Merge or Move, be they independent lexical heads (e.g. auxiliaries, complementizers), bound morphemes (e.g. suffixal agreement and tense markings), or free morphemes (e.g. TAM particles). Alternatively, the same items might be retained but merged in, or moved to, lower (possibly functional) positions, as we saw to be the case with reflexes of the Calabrian erstwhile complementizer MODO subsequently reanalysed as an infinitival marker merged within Infl. In such cases, the surface output might appear the same as in the original construction; on the other hand, it might be characterized by distinct surface linearization effects. Assuming furthermore that formal features of individual functional heads correlate in the core cases with specific phonological features at PF, it is legitimate to expect items now merged or moved into higher or lower functional projections to display some degree of morphophonological modification in accordance with language-specific parameters. Illustrative in this respect is Neapolitan asyndeton, where the original embedded infinitival verb form, once reanalysed as an imperative, presumably comes to target a higher functional space (see discussion of verb movement in section 10.6 above), possibly including Agr heads, as witnessed by the emergence of metaphonetic agreement on the relevant verb form.

---

[34] The inaccessibility of the embedded functional structure in (19) is further highlighted by the impossibility of merging a lexical complementizer (viz. *di* 'of') in the embedded complementizer position ($C°$ or, in a more richly articulated structure, $Fin°$), in contrast to infinitival complements to *sembrare* 'to seem' *qua* object control predicate (cf. (i) below), which display a lesser degree of pragmatico-semantic integration between main and embedded clauses:

(i)   mi$_i$=sembra   [$_{CP}$[Comp di   [PRO$_i$ capire]]]
      me$_i$.DAT=seem.PRS.3SG   of.COMP   PRO$_i$ understand.INF
      'I think I understand.'

To sum up, by recognizing the essential semantic import of functional projections and their domains, transparently matched to different semantic classes of adverb hosted in their associated specifier positions (Cinque 1999), finiteness can be interpreted as the cumulative semantic effect of such projections and domains which may variously be semantically, and hence also morphosyntactically, active or dormant. Thus, although it appears a priori to be a reasonable expectation that semantic finiteness be commensurately spelt out by the associated phonological and morphosyntactic features of the functional projections or domains involved,[35] the morphophonological and lexical realization of functional structure is notoriously characterized by considerable cross-linguistic variation in accordance with language-specific parameters. This allows us in turn to capture the empirical observation that overt manifestations of finiteness fail to display perfect homogeneity across languages, although the underlying functional structure they variously spell out is held to be universal.

---

[35] For example, if a functional projection XP is rendered inactive, it follows that any phonological or morphosyntactic features normally associated with the same will also be unavailable.

11

Insubordination and its uses

NICHOLAS EVANS

11.1 Introduction

Prototypical finite clauses are main clauses—indeed, the ability to occur in a main clause is often taken as definitional for finiteness, e.g. by Crystal (1997: 427)[1]—and prototypical nonfinite clauses are subordinate clauses. Problems thus arise when clauses that would by standard criteria be analysed as non-finite are used as main clauses; examples are the use in main clauses of the English bare infinitive *go* (1a) or Spanish *ir* in (1b) (both from Etxepare and Grohmann 2005: 129), or the Italian and German infinitives used to express commands in (2).

(1) a. John go to the movies?! No way, man.
    b. ¿Yo ir   a   esa   fiesta?!   ¡Jamás!
       1.SG go.INF to   this party   never
       'Me go to that party? Never!'

(2) a. Alza-r-si,   porc-i, av-ete   cap-ito?   Rifa-re
       get.up-INF-REFL   pig-PL   have-2PL   understand-PSTPTCP   make-INF
       i   lett-i,   ma presto! Puli-r-si   le   scarp-e
       the.M.PL   bed-PL   but quickly clean-INF-REFL   the.F.PL   shoe-PL

This chapter has had a long gestation, and earlier versions were presented at the Monash University Seminar Series (1989), the inaugural conference of the Association for Linguistic Typology in Vitoria Gasteiz (1995), and at the Cognitive Anthropology Research Group of the Max Planck Institut für Psycholinguistik (1995). I thank Frans Plank for inviting me to revise it for the present volume, thereby rescuing it from further neglect, and Irina Nikolaeva for her subsequent editorial comments. For data, analyses, and references on specific languages I thank Mengistu Amberber (Amharic), Winfred Bauer (Mon), Melissa Bowerman (Dutch), Sue Duncan (Chinese), David Gil (Modern Hebrew), Sotaro Kita and Shigeko Nariyama (Japanese), Alan King (Basque), Bill McGregor (Gooniyandi), Miren Oñederra (Basque), and Anna Wierzbicka (Polish). Bruce Rigsby, Sandy Thompson, Scott Schwenter, and Tony Woodbury drew other crucial papers to my attention, and I am indebted to Eve Danziger, Mark Durie, Masha Koptjevskaja-Tamm, Steve Levinson, Marianne Mithun, Irina Nikolaeva, Eric Pederson, Lesley Stirling, Claudia Wegener, David Wilkins, and two anonymous referees for a range of other critical comments on various versions of this paper.

[1] See Kalinina and Sumbatova (Ch. 7 above) for the quoted definition and fuller discussion.

'(To) get up, pigs, understand? (To) make your beds, and hurry!
(To) clean your shoes!' (Source: P. Levi, *La tregua*: 14, cited in
Moretti and Orvieto 1979: 19)[2]

b. Bei-m   Eintritt   tief   verneig-en!
   on-DEF.DAT entry   low   bow-INF
   '(To) bow low on entering!' (Weuster 1983: 79)

Such clauses are clearly problematic for typologies of finiteness. The two
commonest solutions to the conundrum they pose are either to ignore
them altogether or to treat them as underlying subordinate clauses from
which some sort of main clause has been ellipsed. A third solution would
involve admitting them to the category of finite clauses, concurrently broad-
ening the definition of finiteness in various ways, such as allowing, as finite,
verb forms that fail to show tense, mood, or subject person. A fourth solution
is to dissociate the assumed necessary link between main clause status and
finiteness, allowing certain types of main clause to be nonfinite; see the
chapters in this volume by Nikolaeva and by Kalinina and Sumbatova (Chapters 6 and 7 above) for strong arguments in favour of this position.

My contention here will be that such constructions are much more widespread than is commonly believed. In fact I will be casting my net more
widely, looking generally at the main clause use of (prima facie) subordinate
constructions, whether nonfinite or not. This is because the relevant cross-
linguistic patterns are more discernible if you examine the main clause use of
subordinate constructions more generally, rather than restricting your pur-
view just to that subset of subordinate clauses which happen to be nonfinite
constructions in some languages—especially since the category 'subordinate
clause', though not without its problems, is nonetheless cross-linguistically
more robust than the category 'nonfinite clause'.

I will apply the term 'insubordination' to *the conventionalized main clause
use of what, on prima facie grounds, appear to be formally subordinate clauses*.
In surveying the uses of insubordination cross-linguistically, I have three main
goals:

- To establish the range of formal manifestations of insubordination
  (section 11.2), e.g. main clause use of infinitives, but also main clause
  subjunctives, subordinate word order or characteristic subordinating
  complementizers or conjunctions in apparent main clauses, logophoric

[2] Translations are mine for the Italian, Spanish, German, and Kayardild material, and for the
citations from Buscha, Weuster, and Schwenter. Bracketed material in the translations, such as the
'(to)' in (2a) and (2b), is simply a guide to the source grammatical structure, not to the best English
translation.

pronouns, or switch-reference in main clauses. As this list indicates, these include both types of nonfinite construction, such as infinitives, and those that are not normally considered to manifest nonfiniteness, such as subordinating conjunction, as well as categories that are intermediate or disputed.

- To establish the range of functions that are served by insubordinated clauses (section 11.3). These include:

  (a) Various expressions of interpersonal coercion, including commands, as in (2), but also permissives, abilitatives, threats and warnings. These are discussed in Section 11.3.1.

  (b) Modal framing of various types, including the unattributed evocation of quotation or belief (as in 1), and other kinds of deontic and evidential use. Here a main clause predicate expressing quotation, perception, thought, emotion, or inference is omitted. In some cases the semantics of this kind of insubordination goes beyond modality proper to tense. These are discussed in section 11.3.2.

  (c) Marking of various discourse contexts, such as negation, contrastive statements, and reiteration, all high in presuppositionality, through the adaptation of devices for expressing interclausal relations to the expression of discourse relations more generally. These are discussed in section 11.3.3.

- To examine the diachrony of how these functions arise through a three-step process of (a) ellipsis, (b) conventionalized restriction of interpretation, (c) development of conventionalized main clause use.

This will lead back to the issue of how realistic it is to maintain a strict distinction between syntactic (inter-clausal) and discourse (inter-sentential) relations in natural language.

11.1.1 *Insubordination: delimiting the phenomenon*

A number of grammarians of individual languages have discussed the problems posed for analysis by what I am calling insubordinated clauses.[3] Yet there has not, to my knowledge, been any detailed typological study of the

---

[3] The most thorough and succinct discussion of the phenomenon is in the literature on German; see esp. Buscha's (1976) treatment of *isolierte Nebensätze*, 'isolated subordinate clauses', and the lengthier discussion of 'non-embedded clauses with verb-final order' in Weuster (1983). Within the Spanish literature, discussion of independent if-clauses (see section 11.2.2 below) goes back to Bello (1847), who offered an ellipsis-based account (1984 [1847]: §1272), against which a number of investigators in the past two decades have argued that the relevant construction must be considered a main clause (Almela Perez 1985; Montolío Durán 1999; Schwenter 1996; 1999).

phenomenon, so it will be helpful to begin with some overall problems thrown up by this definition.

Many of the examples I will discuss lie at the uncomfortable boundary between parole and langue, where it is not always clear when grammar has emerged from discourse, and this leads to marginalized treatments in descriptions of particular languages. As a result, it is premature to attempt a fully systematic typological survey of the phenomenon, since in many cases the relevant constructions are considered too marginal or elliptical to be described in the standard reference grammars that need to be consulted over a structured sample in mature typological research. The 'if' request in English described below, for example, receives its first mention in an English reference grammar in Huddleston and Pullum (2002),[4] though it is earlier mentioned in two analyses based on conversational corpora, Ford and Thompson (1986) for American English and Stirling (1999) for Australian English, who discusses it in detail. Likewise, crucial data on certain uses of independent *daß*-clauses in German come from specialized discourse studies rather than reference grammars.

My purpose, therefore, is rather to sketch out some emerging patterns in an initial set of languages for which I have been able to obtain relevant information. Although twelve language families are represented, the initial impetus for this survey came from my attempts to make sense of the relevant constructions while writing a reference grammar of the Australian language Kayardild (Evans 1995a). To help with this I consulted the literature on other Australian languages and on Indo-European languages for which detailed work on the pragmatics–syntax interface was available, later adding in material from other languages around the world as I became aware of comparable constructions in them. This leads to a strong bias towards data from Australian and Indo-European languages, which between them account for twenty-four of the thirty-seven languages considered here. (For

Other relevant treatments dealing with particular languages or subgroups are Kettunen's (1924) early discussion of the subordinate clause origin of Estonian indirect (modus obliquus) constructions, Lakoff's (1968) generative semantic treatment of the Latin 'independent subjunctive', Kroskrity's (1984) discussion of formally subordinate negative clauses in several Tanoan languages, Merlan's (1981) discussion of formal links between mood, tense, and subordination in several Australian languages, and McGregor's (1988) discussion of 'non-subordinated' subjunctives in Gooniyandi (Kuniyanti). Some cross-linguistic discussion of indirection in imperatives is in Sadock and Zwicky (1985) and Brown and Levinson (1987). I will discuss this work in more detail below.

[4] Quirk et al. (1985) discuss a few of what I would term insubordinated clauses under the rubric 'subordinate clauses as irregular sentences' (11.41); they discuss *if only* sentences of the type *If only I'd listened to my parents*, but otherwise do not discuss independent *if*-clauses. Earlier grammars such as Leech and Svartvik (1975) do not mention the phenomenon.

substantial further data on comparable phenomena in Daghestanian languages see Kalinina and Sumbatova, Chapter 7 above.) I hope this bias will eventually be corrected by further research built on a more representative sample, at the stage when more attention to the phenomenon in descriptive work makes a wider range of data available.

11.1.2 *Insubordination and depragmaticization*

In my definition above I used the hedge 'on prima facie evidence' to my criterion 'appears to be a formally subordinate clause'. The need for this hedge generally arises because of the following paradox. Insubordinated clauses usually look like subordinate clauses, because of the presence in them of prototypically subordinate characteristics, such as infinitive, participial or subjunctive inflections on their verbs, subordinate word order, complementizers, and so on. But to the extent that, over time, they get reanalysed as standard constructions, those features will no longer be restricted to subordinate clauses, so that the term 'subordinate' means, at best, 'having diachronic origins as a subordinate clause'.

The historical trajectory that leads to the formation of insubordinated clauses follows four steps:

Subordination	Ellipsis	Conventionalized ellipsis	Reanalysis as main clause structure
(1)	(2)	(3)	(4)
Subordinate construction	Ellipsis[5] of main clause	Restriction of interpretation of ellipsed material	Conventionalized main[6] clause use of formally subordinate clause (Constructionalization)

---

[5] Theories of ellipsis differ widely on the degree to which ellipsed material is recovered. As a matter of definition, for example, Quirk et al. (1972: 536) restrict the use of the term as follows: 'words are ellipted only if they are uniquely recoverable, i.e. there is no doubt about what words are to be supplied ... What is uniquely recoverable depends on the context.' This is not a position I accept, for reasons to be discussed later in the chapter. I would rather define ellipsis as involving 'some recoverable elements that are grammatically acceptable', and then allow a range of situations from uniquely recoverable to non-uniquely recoverable (with perhaps an infinite range of possibilities).

[6] In one respect, this panchronic definition involves some circularity once stage (d) is reached. If such clauses are now normal main clauses, why include them in the survey? One reason is that analysts are traditionally reluctant to treat them as full main clauses: typically, grammars will include them in the section on subordinate clauses, and then make an aside that they can also be used independently on occasion. As typologists dependent on secondary sources, we cannot always simply reanalyse the data. A second reason is that by including such cases in our survey we may be able to show that such awkward cases display many regularities cross-linguistically, and in this way lead to a better and more consistent treatment of them across languages.

The most detailed discussions of the phenomenon (though under different names) are in the literature on German, perhaps because the existence of special subordinate word order makes such constructions particularly obvious there (see e.g. Buscha 1974; Weuster 1983; Schwabe 1994; Reis 1995; 2002; 2003; Schlobinski n.d., and references therein). Drawing on examples and analyses from Buscha and Weuster we may illustrate the four phases above.

Full construction with overt main clause. This phase is simply the normal situation where a subordinate clause is used as such; note that the subordinating conjunction *ob* 'whether' in (3) requires that its clause have subordinate word order, with the verb in clause-final position.

(3) Ich   erinner-e   mich   nicht,
     I   remember-1SG   REFL   not
     ob   sie   eine   Karte   gekauft   hatte
     whether she   INDF.F.NOM   ticket   bought   had
     'I don't remember whether she bought a ticket.' (Durrell 1997: 387)

Ellipsis of main clause. Any grammatically compatible main clause can be 'reconstructed' by the hearer. I have developed elsewhere (Evans 1993) the concept of 'grammatical placedness' which amounts to a grammatical projection limiting possible main clauses (e.g. to predicates governing the subjunctive, or logophoric contexts). Exactly which main clause is restored is determined by processes of conversational inference.

For German, this is the situation where any grammatically compatible main clause could potentially be restored. I am not aware of any published arguments demonstrating this specifically, but the literature contains some suggestive examples. The discussion of insubordinated *ob* clauses in Buscha and Weuster contains such a wide range of reconstructed elements—with great variation in both the subject and the verb of the ellipsed clause—that there appear to be no grounds for claiming semantic restrictions on the restored materials:

(4) [Was   mein-st   du   dazu,]   Ob   ich   mal   wegen   meiner
     what   think-2SG   you   to.it   if   I   just   because   my
     Galle   frag-e?[7]
     gall.bladder   ask-1SG
     '(What would you think), if I just ask about my gall bladder?'
     (Buscha 1976)

---

[7] For these examples, the English translations are my own; occasionally they are slightly non-literal in the interests of idiomaticity.

(5) [Ich   zweifl-e,]   Ob   wir   richtig   sind?
     I   doubt-1SG   if   we   right   are
     '(I doubt), whether we are right?' (Buscha 1976)

(6) Ob diese Wortstellung zulässig   ist? [, erschein-t mir   fraglich]
     if   this   word.order   permissible is   appear-3SG I.DAT doubtful
     'Whether this word order is permissible (, seems doubtful to me).'
     (Weuster 1983: 33)

(7) [Dieser   Aufsatz   macht   deutlich,]   ob   diese   Wortstellung
     this   article   makes   clear   whether   this   word.order
     zulässig   ist[?]
     permissible is
     '[This article makes it clear, as to] whether this word order is acceptable.'
     (Weuster 1983: 38)

Although Buscha (1976) claims that such clauses express 'an uncertainty regard-ing the opinion of the interlocutor or regarding objective possibilities',[8] she does not demonstrate that this exceeds the general semantic conditions on the use of subordinated *ob* clauses, and examples like (7) from Weuster (1983: 38) demonstrate that all that is needed is a main clause that frames a polar ques-tion—which is the general semantic condition on the use of *ob* clauses anyway.

Determining whether regular ellipsis is the best analysis, in a given lan-guage, requires rather sensitive language-specific tests. For example, there may be various types of syntactic evidence for the underlying presence of a main clause, such as the presence of negative polarity items like 'ever' or 'any' in an English clause like *that I'll ever give you any money?*, whose presence can only be accounted for by an ellipsed negative matrix clause like *You don't believe*. The application of the negative polarity to test insubordinated Span-ish if-clauses is discussed in Schwenter (1999), see below. More difficult to test, because of the very large number of candidate ellipsed clauses, is the question of whether there are any limits on which ellipsed clauses can acceptably be reconstituted. When there are significant restrictions on this, as a result of the conventionalized use of the construction, we move to the next stage.

Conventionalization of ellipsis. Certain syntactically permitted reconstructions become excluded by convention.

There is considerable range in the degree to which restoration of material is conventionalized to a subset of the grammatically tolerated possibilities. This may be extremely general, such as restrictions to a positive rather than a negative consequence in 'if requests' (17, 18), 'if wishes' (8), and 'if offers' (9).

---

[8] 'Eine Unsicherheit hinsichtlich der Meinung des Partners oder hinsichtlich der objektiven Möglichkeiten.'

(8) a. [Es wäre schön,] / Wenn ich deine Statur hätte
it be.3SG.SBJV lovely if I your build had
'[It would be lovely] / if I had your build.'

b. [Ich wäre froh,] /
I be.1SG.SBJV glad
'[I would be glad]'

c. *[Es wäre schlimm,] /
it be.3SG.SBJV bad
'[It would be bad]'

(9) Wenn Sie sich vielleicht die Hände wasch-en möchten?
if you self perhaps the hands wash-INF might

a. [, können Sie das hier tun]
could you that here do

b. [, wäre das sehr nett von Ihnen]
were that very nice of you

c. *[, können Sie das nicht tun]
could you that not do

d. *[, wäre das nicht sehr nett von Ihnen]
were that not very nice of you

'If you would maybe like to wash your hands.
[, that would be very nice of you]
[, you can do it here]
*[, you cannot do it]
*[, that would not be very nice of you]'

Or it may be very specific, such as the restriction of the main clause to 'what happens' in (10). Here Buscha comments that 'the matrix clause can be eliminated, without any change of meaning. The isolated subordinated clauses of this group [of sentences] need no linguistic or situational context for a monosemous interpretation'.[9]

(10) Und wenn ich nicht von ihr loskomm-e?
and if I not from her get.away-1SG
'And if I don't get away from her?'

[< Was geschieh-t, wenn ich nicht von ihr loskomm-e?]
what happen-3SG if I not from her get.away-1SG

---

[9] 'Der Matrixsatz kann eliminiert werden, ohne daß sich eine Bedeutungsveränderung ergibt. Die isolierte Nebensätze dieser Gruppe brauchen zur Monosemierung keinen sprachlichen oder situativen Kontext.'

Conventionalization of the whole construction (Constructionalization). The construction now has a specific meaning of its own, and it may not be possible to restore any ellipsed material. A clear case where the construction has been conventionalized to the point where restoration of ellipsed material is not possible—at least in a way that allows all the overt material to be preserved— is the concessive use of *wo* (where) clauses with subordinate verb order. Buscha (1976), in discussing examples like (11a), is unable to supply a paraphrase from which this can be derived by simple deletion, and replaces *wo* by the subordinating concessive conjunction *obwohl* in her expansion (11b):[10]

(11) a. Wo   Zehntausende   verreck-en   müss-en
         where   ten.thousands   die-INF   must-3PL
         Lit.: 'Where tens of thousands must die'

      b. Obwohl   Zehntausende   verreck-en   müss-en,
         although ten.thousands die-INF   must-3PL
         mach-en   sie   sich keine   Gedanken   darüber
         make-3PL   they   self no   thoughts   about.that
         'Even though tens of thousands must die, they don't think twice
         about it.'

Another nice example of conventionalized meaning going hand in hand with increasingly main-clause-like behaviour is the insubordinated use of *si* clauses in Spanish, historically conditionals, but which can now function as main clauses putting forth a proposition at odds with that articulated or presupposed by the preceding speaker (see 20 below). Arguments for their main clause status are presented by Almela Pérez (1985), Montolío Durán (1999), and Schwenter (1999). In contrast to the subordinate use, which typically suspends factivity, the insubordinated use signals certainty on the part of the speaker (Schwenter 1999: 89), fails to activate negative polarity items such as postnominal placement of *alguna* 'any', is limited to one occurrence per utterance (whereas true conditional *si* can be repeated, one per condition), is impossible to embed under a speech act verb, and cannot appear inside the scope of sentence adverbs like *obviamente* 'obviously'.

Note that the four-stage pathway proposed above zigzags between an opening up, then a closing, of the role of pragmatics. First a previously syntacticized subordinate clause, made independent, becomes available for

---

[10] Note Weuster's comment (1983: 56) on this construction: '*Wo* verweist [in this example] nicht auf einen Ort; es handelt sich vielmehr um das Konzessive *wo*': *wo* [where] refers not to a place; rather it is a matter of concessive *wo* [i.e. English whereas].

pragmatic interpretation; in this phase grammatical formatives get opened up to the pragmatics and become 'less grammatical'. Only in the second phase does 'depragmaticization' occur, as the newly independent clause acquires a more specific constructional meaning. For example, a switch-reference marker originally interpreted in simply grammatical terms (e.g. tracking identity between subjects in main and subordinate clauses) may take on more general functions of tracking contrasts in discourse, the exact nature of which is to be determined pragmatically. An examination of insubordination is thus instructive for 'interactionist' functional typologies that do not seek to replace structural with functional accounts, but rather examine the ways in which various functions (including pragmatic interpretation) intricately interdepend with language-particular structures.

In addition to its typological importance for the relation between finiteness and subordination, insubordination is also of great interest for theories of historical morphosyntax. The extensive literature on morphosyntactic change—whether as grammaticization or reanalysis—largely concentrates on diachronic developments in the opposite direction, i.e. the development of subordinate constructions from material in main clauses. It has been widely asserted, particularly in the functionalist and grammaticization literatures, that there is a unidirectional pathway from pragmatics to syntax to morphology, one consequence of which is that loose paratactic 'pragmatic' constructions become syntacticized as subordinate clauses.

[G]rammaticalization is unidirectional [...]. [I]t leads from a 'less grammatical' to a 'more grammatical' unit, but not vice versa. A few counterexamples have been cited (e.g. ... Campbell, in press.)[11] They concern either degrammaticalization or regrammaticalization ... The former is present when the direction of grammaticalization is reversed, that is, when a more grammatical unit develops into a less grammatical one, while the latter applies when forms without any function acquire a grammatical function. Although both degrammaticalization and regrammaticalization have been observed to occur, they are statistically insignificant and will be ignored in the remainder of this work. Note that many cases of alleged degrammaticalization found in the literature on this subject can be shown to be the result of an inadequate analysis (see Lehmann 1982: 16–20). (Heine et al. 1991a: 4–5)

From the diachronic point of view, [grammaticalization—*N.E.*] is a process which turns lexemes into grammatical formatives *and renders grammatical formatives still more grammatical.* (Lehmann 1982: v, italics mine)

[Grammaticalization is a process] whereby linguistic units lose in semantic complexity, pragmatic significance, syntactic freedom, and phonetic substance, respectively. (Heine and Reh 1984: 15)

---

[11] = Campbell (1991), discussed below.

Discussions of reanalysis have been a bit more willing to admit developments from subordinate to main clause status:

> The discussion so far has focused on unidirectionality, and what kinds of unidirectionality are characteristic of grammaticalization. Virtually nothing is exceptionless, and there are of course instances of change in languages that are counterexamples of tendencies that can be characterized as 'less > more grammatical', 'main clause > subordinate clause', etc. In these volumes the papers by Campbell and Greenberg explicitly raise counterexamples to unidirectionality... It is likely that all these examples are strictly speaking actually not cases of grammaticalization (although once they have occurred they may be subject to the generalization, reduction, loss, and other changes typical of grammaticalization). Rather, the examples Campbell and Greenberg cite can be regarded as instances of reanalysis. (Traugott and Heine 1991c: 6–7)

It is not my concern here to situate insubordination within the grammaticalization/reanalysis dichotomy. Some scholars suggest that grammaticalization is not a logically independent type of morphosyntactic change, but merely a cluster of other processes such as sound change, semantic change, and reanalysis (Campbell 2000). On the reanalysis side, it is not clear that the normal definitions of reanalysis apply clearly to the phenomenon of insubordination,[12] and, as outlined above, the complex trajectory followed in insubordination, with its successive opening and restriction of pragmatic interpretation, may leave room for suitably redefined versions of each process to be identified.[13] However, wherever we situate it within a taxonomy of morphosyntactic change, it is clear that insubordination goes against the usual direction of change by recruiting main clause structures from subordinate clauses.

---

[12] Langacker's oft-cited definition of reanalysis treats it as 'change in the structure of an expression or class of expressions that does not involve any immediate or intrinsic modification of its surface manifestations' (Langacker 1977: 59). Heine et al. basically follow this definition. Traugott (1980: 49) focuses on the reinterpretation of boundaries: 'another well-known source of grammaticalization is reanalysis ... in which old boundaries are reinterpreted.' It takes a bit of massaging to apply these to any stage of the insubordination trajectory I have outlined above. Conceivably stage (b) could be seen as an example of a sentence boundary being realigned with a clause boundary, but it all seems rather forced and unilluminating.

[13] It would certainly be consistent, for example, with Hopper's salvationist allegory: 'Grammaticalization ... is the tragedy of lexical items young and pure in heart but carrying within them the fatal flaw of original sin; their inexorable weakening as they encounter the corrupt world of Discourse; their fall into the Slough of Grammar; and their eventual redemption in the cleansing waters of Pragmatics' (Hopper 1998: 147–8).

11.2 Formal realizations

Recall that we define insubordination as the conventionalized independent use of a formally subordinate clause. The criterion 'formally subordinate' can refer to any formal feature primarily associated with subordinate clauses in the relevant language: non-finite verb forms; subordinating conjunctions and other complementizers (e.g. case markers with clausal scope); logophoric pronouns and long-distance reflexives; switch-reference markers; or special word order normally confined to subordinate clauses.

The rider 'primarily associated' in the preceding paragraph is important here, since the more an insubordinated clause allows independent use, the less its formal features can be taken as uniquely distinctive of subordinate clauses. This means that arguments of the form 'clause type X is subordinate because it has formal features Y which are characteristic of subordinate clauses' will be circular. Weuster (1983), for example, shows the fallacy of taking V-final clauses in German to be subordinate simply on the basis of their word order, since for some types at least embedding under a putatively ellipsed main clause is either impossible or arbitrary.[14] At the same time, as the independent use of erstwhile subordinate clauses becomes increasingly conventionalized, the relevant constructions may exhibit a mix of subordinate and main clause features. For example, some types of 'suspended' clause discussed for Japanese by Ohori (1995), which fall into my category of insubordinated constructions, behave like subordinate clauses in taking the participial ending *-te*, but like complete sentences in taking the pragmatic particle *-ne* (see further discussion below). Finally, it may be the case that historical developments leading to formal similarity between main and subordinate forms have run in the opposite direction, such as the development of the West Greenlandic intransitive participle from the pan-Eskimo intransitive indicative, as discussed by Woodbury (1985).

The fact remains that virtually all cases discussed here are treated as basically subordinate in their morphosyntax by the sources, and discussed in the section on subordination as a special case. In defence of this position (though this is not always made explicit) there are three types of argument.

---

[14] 'Dabei ist es das Ziel der Arbeit, zu zeigen, daß eine Klassifizierung finiter Sätze mit Verb-Endstellung als "isolierte" bzw. "nicht-elliptische" oder "hauptsatzwertige Nebensätze" syntaktisch nicht überzeugend gerechtfertigt werden kann. Es soll deutlich gemacht werden, daß es sich um selbständige Sätze handelt ... Es erscheint vielmehr sinnvoll anzunehmen, daß auch hier unabhängige Sätze mit Verb-Endstellung vorliegen' (Weuster 1983: 21).

First, it may be demonstrable by comparative or historical evidence that the construction originated as a subordinate clause; this is the case for the Arizona Tewa examples discussed below, for example, where at the same time the analyst makes it clear that the construction in question is no longer so regarded synchronically.

Secondly, subordinate or main clause status is typically demonstrated on the basis of a cluster of tests, not all of which may yield a positive result in the case of insubordinated clauses; their anomalous position may be demonstrable through their non-prototypical performance here. Related to this are cases where the insubordinated use is semantically restricted compared to standard subordinate uses: an example would be the clear semantic restrictions on insubordinated *if*-clauses, such as the restriction to positive outcomes, compared to their corresponding subordinate clauses.

Finally, in cases where the first two arguments fail, we may argue that such clauses are basically subordinate by resorting to typological analogy, from the two facts that (a) nominalized clauses bearing case affixes on their nominalized verbs are typically a subordinate structure cross-linguistically, and (b) the complementizing use of case markers is, logically, an extension of their two-place predicate use to one in which both arguments are clauses.

The danger of circularity when arguing on such typological grounds is greatest in the case of certain categories that have entered the metalinguistic vocabulary with analyses of languages where they happen to occur in subordinate clauses, but where the cross-linguistic grounds for associating them with subordinate constructions are weak. Logophoric pronouns, for example, were first discussed in connection with African languages, where they are primarily found in subordinate clauses (see below), but subsequent work on Central Pomo (Mithun 1990) suggests that occurrence in subordinate clauses is not a necessary defining feature of logophoric pronouns. Similarly, the 'subjunctive' category has always been defined in a way that vacillates between structural grounds (in terms of particular types of subordinate clause, reflecting the term's origin as a translation of the Greek *hypotaktikē* 'subordinate'—see Palmer 1986: 22) and semantic grounds, such as Lavandera's (1983: 211) characterization of the Spanish subjunctive as referring to states of affairs 'whose occurrence could easily be denied or affirmed, but is instead left unasserted'.

My inclusion of a particular construction as insubordinate typically follows decisions in the primary sources to group them as special independent uses of subordinate clauses, or as descendants of subordinate clauses in previous language states; the component 'independent use' in my definition allows for the fact that there will be language-specific arguments for treating the construction as a main clause, and indeed the process of insubordination may have been so far-reaching that, synchronically, they have full main clause status.

We now pass to a survey of the various formal characteristics, normally associated with subordinate clauses in the relevant language, for which insubordinated uses have been reported.

11.2.1 *Special subordinate verb forms*

These are forms such as the subjunctive in Italian (12a, b) or Icelandic (25 below), participles in Lithuanian (13a, b) or Japanese (14a, b),[15] and the so-called 'lest' or apprehensive forms in many Australian languages, e.g. Diyari (15a-b) and Kayardild (49 below).

Typically such verb forms are either nonfinite or can be analysed as containing an old complementizer such as a case marker. For each language I give an example of a 'typical', subordinate use, followed by an 'insubordinated', independent use.

(12) a. Non vogl-io   che   venga   domani
         not want-1SG that   come.3SG.SBJV tomorrow
         'I don't want him to come tomorrow.'

      b. Che   venga   domani
         that come.3SG.SBJV tomorrow
         '(It's possible/likely/I hope/believe etc.) that he'll come tomorrow.'

(13) a. Mókytojas   sāko,   kàd   tù   tìngi̇s   mókytis
         teacher.NOM say.3   that   you   be.lazy.PRS.PTCP study.INF
         'The teacher says that you are lazy in studying.' (Comrie 1981)

      b. Traukinỹs išeĩn̨as   lýgiai   septiñt̨a   vāland̨a
         train.NOM leave.PRS.PTCP prompt.ADV seventh.ACC hour.ACC
         '(It is said that) the train will leave promptly at seven o'clock.'
         (Comrie 1981)

---

[15] (14b) is taken from Ohori (1995) and follows his glosses. (14a) is a 'full' version that corresponds maximally to his insubordinated example, though according to Shigeko Nariyama (email of 22 May 2002) 'this sounds a little awkward, though people do say this', and a more natural full version would be *tukaretyatta-kara, zyugyoo yasumu yo*, i.e. where the particle -*te* 'and so' is replaced by -*kara* 'because'. This is typical of the structural slippage that frequently accompanies insubordination, as the now main clauses become detached from their original complex structures and take on main clause features in their own right.

(14) a. Tukare-tyat-te,   zyugyoo   yasumu   yo
         exhausted-PRV-PTCP class   skip   PRT
         'Being exhausted, (I)'ll skip class.'

      b. A: Zyugyoo yasumu   no?   B: Tukare-tyat-te   ne
            class   skip   PRT   exhausted-PRV-PTCP   PRT
         'Are (you) going to skip the class?' '(I'm) exhausted.'
         (Ohori 1995: 202) (lit. 'Being exhausted.')

(15) a. Makita paḍaka-Ø-mayi,   wanku   yundu   wala   ṇayi-yaṭi
         gun   take-IMP-EMPH   snake.ACC 2SG.ERG soon   see-APPR
         'Carry a gun, in case you see a snake.' (Austin 1981a: 225)

      b. Ṉulu-ka   kiṇtala-li yinaṉa   maṭa-yaṭi
         3SG.F.ERG-TOKEN dog-ERG   you.ACC bite-APPR
         'This dog might bite you.' (Austin 1981a: 229)

11.2.2 *Subordinating conjunctions and complementizers*

Examples are the use of the word 'if' for polite requests in French (16),
English[16] (17, 18), or Dutch (19).

(16) Si   on   allait   se   promen-er?
      if   one   went   REFL   walk-INF
      'What if we went for a walk?'

(17) a. (I wonder) If you could give me a couple of 39c stamps please
      b. If you could give me a couple of 39c stamps please,
         (I'd be most grateful)

(18) (A milkman's sheet about Xmas deliveries, including:[17])
      If you would kindly indicate in the boxes below your requirements
      and then hand the completed form back to your Roundsman by no
      later than the 16th December 1995

(19) Hans, of   je   even   naar   Edith   zou   lopen
      Hans   whether you   just   to   Edith   will   go
      'Hans, would you just go to Edith?'[18]

Though the commonest function of insubordinated conditionals is to express
polite requests, they may have other conventionalized functions, such as

---

[16] Alan King (p.c.) raises the question of whether the source is the conditional use ('if X, (then) I'd
be grateful') or the embedded-question use; the lack of a paraphrase with 'whether', which would suit
the embedded-question use but not the conditional use, suggests the former, but English speakers who
I have consulted are divided on their intuitions here. In Basque (see below) the two are formally
distinct, and both are available for elliptical requests.

[17] I thank Grev Corbett for this example.

[18] I am indebted to Melissa Bowerman for this example.

expressing disagreement, as in Spanish (20). As an explanation for this development Schwenter (1999: 8), who furnishes this example, suggests that the link from conditionality to disagreement is via an ellipted main clause along the lines of (in this example) 'If it's horrible, how can you say it's great?'.

(20)   (Sisters Q and R are looking at clothes in a shop window.)
    Q: Ah,   ¡mira   qué   chaqueta   más   chula!
          ah   look.IMP   what   jacket   INT   great
    R: Si   es   horrible.
        if   is   horrible
    Q: 'Hey, look what a great jacket!'
    R: 'But it's horrible!'

Conversely, the same function (polite requests) that is expressed by the insubordination of conditionals in some languages may be expressed by insubordination of complementized purpose clauses in others, e.g. by insubordinated *żeby* 'in order that' in Polish (21) or *supaya* (also 'in order that') in Indonesian (36 below).

(21)   Żeby   ciocia   teraz   może   zadzwoni-ła
     COMP   auntie   now   perhaps   telephone-PST.F
     'If you (auntie) could perhaps make a phone call for me?'

Insubordinated clauses may also involve 'complementizing case' markers on verbs and/or other clausal constituents, which normally signal interclausal temporal or modal relations (Dench and Evans 1988). Compare the use of the complementizing dative in Yukulta, where it marks purpose clauses and is restricted to subordinate clauses (e.g. 22), with the etymologically corresponding clauses in Kayardild, where it may either function as a subordinate clause of purpose (23) or be used in an independent clause as a hortative (24).

(22)   kira   warra-ja-rna,   [dathin-inja makurrarra-ntha burldi-j-inja-yi]$_{DAT}$
     close   go-IMP-3SG.O   that-DAT   wallaby-DAT   hit-THM-DAT-2SG
     'Go close to him, so you can hit that wallaby!' (Keen 1983: 247)[19]

---

[19] Some of the Australian languages I cite use phonetic symbols (Diyari, Dyirbal). Some use a practical orthography employing digraphs to show retroflex, lamino-dental, and lamino-palatal articulations: Kayardild, Gooniyandi, and Mparntwe Arrernte use leading *r* for retroflex, following *h* to show lamino-dental, and following *y* or *j* to show lamino-palatal, and Mparntwe Arrernte uses following *w* to show consonantal labialization. Western Desert dialects use underlining to show retroflexion. Ngiyambaa employs a mixture of these strategies. In general, voicing is non-phonemic and individual orthographies arbitrarily choose the voicing values. I normally follow the orthography employed in the source, to which readers are referred for phonological details, except that I have retranscribed Yukulta in the same practical orthography as the closely related Kayardild to facilitate comparison of morphemes.

(23) wuu-ja   ngijin-ji,   wadu-ntha   baa-jinj
     give-IMP   me-LOC   smoke-OBL   bite-PURP
     'Give me (the tobacco), so that I can have a smoke.'

(24) Wirdi-jinja-da   dathin-a   dukurduku   binthu
     stay-HORT-yet   that-NOM   moist.NOM   prepuce.NOM
     'Let those freshly circumcised foreskins wait a while yet (before burying them).'

Note that the complementizing case spreads to any object NPs present in the complementized clause: the dative to 'that wallaby' in (22), and the oblique to 'smoke' in (23); the Yukulta dative is cognate with the Kayardild Oblique. In addition, the relevant verb inflection, *th.inja* or *j.inja* in both languages according to conjugation, can be broken down into a conjugation marker *th/j* plus the dative/oblique suffix *inja/ntha*. In section 11.3.2.4 we examine a series of changes of this type that have occurred in the Tangkic languages, giving rise to new main clause tense/mood categories.

11.2.3 *Logophoric pronouns and long-distance reflexives*

These are normally restricted to subordinate clauses, but may in some languages be used independently to indicate reported speech or thoughts in a *style indirect libre*. An example from Icelandic is (25), in which all clauses after the first, though not overtly embedded, exhibit such subordinate clause features as the use of the subjunctive and of long-distance reflexives (LDRs). They are used in the 'logophoric domain' in which 'the speech, thought, perception, etc., of an individual, distinct from the speaker or the narrator, is reported on' (Sigurðsson 1986:13)—in this case, the chairman—and would be translated by something like *he expressed* in English. Further examples of insubordination with logophoric pronouns will be given in section 11.3.2.1.[20]

(25) Formaðurinn   varð   óskaplega   reiður.   tillagan   væri
     the.chairman   became   furiously   angry   the.proposal   was.SBJV
     svivirðileg   og   væri   henni   beint   gegn sér
     outrageous   and   was.SBJV   it   aimed   at   self(LDR)
     persónulega.   ser   væri   reyndar   sama
     personally   self(LDR)   was.SBJV   in.fact   indifferent
     'The chairman became furiously angry. (He felt) the proposal was outrageous and was directly aimed at himself personally. In fact, he (self) did not care...' (Sigurðsson 1986: 12)

---

[20] Note here that while subordinate clauses always presumably originate as such, logophoric pronouns may have a main clause origin—a point I shall return to later.

11.2.4 *Switch-reference markers*

Such markers are normally restricted to subordinate clauses but used, in special cases, with main clauses, as in the Australian language Arrernte. Examples of this will be given in (113–16) below.

11.2.5 *Special subordinate word order*

Special subordinate word order may also occur in insubordinated clauses. An example is the German use of the verb-final subordinate word order when repeating a question, but with the main clause *ich sagte* or *ich fragte* omitted, as in (26), as well as the various other examples given in section 11.1.2 above.

(26) Aber   wo   komm-st   du   denn   jetzt   her?
      but   where   come-2SG you   then   now   hither
      'But where are you coming from now?'
      Wie   bitte?
      how   please
      'What's that?'
      Wo   du   jetzt   herkomm-st?
      where   you   now   come-2SG
      '(I asked) Where you're coming from(?)'

11.2.6 *Combinations of subordinate features; minimal types*

We have already seen examples where more than one feature characteristic of subordinate clauses is found—such as a complementizer and the subjunctive in Italian (12b), or the subjunctive and a logophoric pronoun in Icelandic (25). Example (27) illustrates the combination of a subordinating conjunction plus subordinate clause (verb-final) word order in German.

(27) Ob   er   krank   ist?
      whether   he   sick   is
      '(You're asking/wondering // I wonder) whether he is sick?'

Or it may happen that a word that is ambiguous between main and subordinate clause functions is shown to be used with its subordinate clause function by its occurrence with some other subordinate clause feature, such as subordinate clause word order, as in (28). The German word *warum* can function as a main clause interrogative meaning 'why', with main clause (V-second) word order, or as an interrogative subordinator meaning '(as to) why', with subordinate (V-final) word order; in (28) the V-final word order shows clearly that it is being used in the second function.

(28) Warum er   noch nicht da   ist?
      why   he   still not   there is
      '(You're wondering/asking // I can't understand) why he still isn't
      there (?)'

Japanese illustrates perhaps the most extremely reduced example of an insubordinated clause: (29) consists of just a subordinating conjunction, the word for 'also', plus an illocutionary particle, thanks to ellipsis of subordinate clause predicates and arguments in addition to ellipsis of the whole main clause:

(29) Ka   mo   ne
      whether   also PRT
      'Possibly', lit. '[I wonder] whether [it's true].' (Sotaro Kita, p.c.)

11.2.7 *Scope and limits of the present survey*

I shall exclude from this survey, for reasons of scope, formally coordinated clauses used independently, exemplified by the following sentence from Ewe (30). But it may well turn out that they have rather similar functional properties to insubordinated clauses. The overt cohesive contrasting of propositions expressed by different speakers is reminiscent of the 'insubordinated switch reference' to be discussed in section 11.3.3.3, while in terms of interpersonal pragmatics the function of independent or-clauses is reminiscent of many insubordinated requests (section 11.3.1.1).

(30) ma-vá   fiẽ   sia   lóó
      1SG.IRR-come   evening DEM   or
      'Should I come this evening or?' (Ameka 1991: 54)

My definition also requires that the resultant construction draw its material from only the old subordinate clause. This is to distinguish it from cases of clause union which end up including elements of an erstwhile subordinate clause (e.g. participial forms, or a causativized verb root) in addition to elements of the erstwhile main clause (e.g. an auxiliary, or a causativizing element). This requirement excludes from consideration such English sentence types as *What if it rains?* (of underlying biclausal nature, from *What happens if it rains*, according to Quirk et al. 1985) and *What if they ARE illiterate?* (from *What does it matter if they ARE illiterate?*), or Russian and other Slavic past forms based on the past participle, with historic loss of the auxiliary verb. It also excludes the plethora of forms in many Cariban languages, discussed at length in Gildea (1998), where the verbs of main clauses are historically nominalizations of various types, once part of copular clauses from which the copula has disappeared.[21] Cf. the Panare examples (31a), with the nominalization functioning as a habitual present, and no copula, with (31b), exemplifying what Gildea argues is the original construction, where the habitual nominalization is linked to the subject by an overt copula (Gildea 1998: 236).

(31) a. t-ipán-sen   iye
          IRR-dry-HAB   tree
          '(This kind of) pole/tree dries.'

      b. a-t-ama-sen   kəh   məh
          2-ADP-kill-HAB   3.be   this
          'This could kill you.' (Nominal interpretation: 'This could be your killer.')

Also excluded are cases where former main verbs are reduced to particles or suffixes to an erstwhile subordinate verb which has become the new main verb; an example would be the change from Latin *cantare (h)a(b)eo* to Italian *cantaró*, or the derivation of evidential affixes in many languages from reduced verbs, such as the Maricopa 'non-visual sensory evidence' marker, *-ʔa*, which is a reduced form of the verb *ʔav-* 'hear', and the 'visual evidential' *-ʔyuu*, which derives from the verb *yuu-* 'see' plus the 1st person prefix *ʔ-* (Willett 1988: 79). Similarly, it excludes cases like Teso (Nilotic), discussed by Heine and Reh (1984: 104–5), where the reconstructed main clause negative verb **e-mam* 'it is not' gets reduced to a negative particle *mam* 'not'. As a result the originally subordinate verb remains the only full verb (32b); in the process this introduces a change from original VSO word order to SVO, as VS[VO] reduces to PartSVO.

(32) a. e-mam   petero   e-koto   ekiᵃok
          3SG-not Peter   3SG-want   dog
          'Peter doesn't want a dog.' (Heine and Reh's reconstruction for pre-Teso)

      b. mam   petero   e-koto   ekiᵃok
          not   Peter   3SG-want   dog
          'Peter doesn't want a dog.'

Finally, I exclude instances where complement-taking predicates embedded in main clauses reduce to formulaic particles, parenthetical phrases etc. This is illustrated in Thompson and Mulac's (1991) discussion of reduction of *I think* from complement-taking predicate (*I **think** that we're definitely moving*

---

[21] For a comparable case in the Cupan languages (Uto-Aztecan), where nominalized structures plus copula have been reanalysed as finite verb forms, see Jacobs (1975).

toward being more technological) to a sort of epistemic adverb, as in *It's just your point of view you know what you like to do in your spare time I think.*

Although there is some functional overlap between all the above cases and insubordination, there is a crucial formal difference. Clause union condenses a main and a subordinate clause while retaining semantic elements of both, and examples of reduction of main clause verbs to either affixes (Maricopa) or formulaic phrases (English *I think*) likewise retain material from both clauses. In cases of insubordination, on the other hand, only material from the subordinate clause is overtly expressed.[22] The missing material is merely alluded to—signalled by the presence of subordinate morphosyntax—and must be restored inferentially.

To conclude this section, it is worth repeating that, under 'formally subordinate', I include cases where the evidence for formal subordination is synchronically obvious, as well as those where it is only diachronic. My main reason for doing this is that the rapid turnover of some types of construction in particular directives can bleach the indirection from an 'indirect' insubordinated request and leave it unacceptably direct. In addition, there are many cases where it is not analytically clear how far insubordination has become conventionalized. As we have seen there exists a continuum from subordinate clauses only used as such, to free-standing subordinate clauses for which an ellipsed main clause can be readily supplied, to insubordinated clauses which can be supplied with main clauses though it sounds somewhat unnatural or pedantic, to insubordinated clauses which have become so conventionalized that they are felt to be quite complete in themselves. Once this last point has been reached, there may be disagreement among analysts as to whether 'insubordinated' clauses should be treated as deriving from subordinate clauses at all, since an alternative analysis in which they are just another main clause type becomes more plausible.

11.3 Functions of insubordination: towards a typology

In this section I survey the functions of insubordination, as defined above, in a variety of languages. For each functional type I first discuss the attested range of formal realizations, and then look at some functional reasons why insubordination should occur. It should be noted that although, for expository purposes, functions have been treated as distinct, there are many languages in which a single 'generalized insubordinate' type covers a number of

---

[22] We shall see one partial exception to this: cases where focused-object constructions derive from a fronted object and an old subordinate clause, reanalysed as a single clause. The crucial difference is that there is no retention of predicate material from the main clause.

functions. Some examples of this multifunctionality will be discussed in section 11.4, where I look at the question of whether a unified semantics, or a unified set of functions, can be given for insubordinated clauses.

11.3.1 *Indirection and interpersonal control*

By far the commonest type of insubordination is found in various types of clause concerned with interpersonal control—primarily imperatives and their milder forms such as hints and requests, but also permissives, warnings, and threats. All such clauses are, to a greater or lesser extent, 'face-threatening acts' (Brown and Levinson 1987), and insubordinating ellipsis has the effect of putting the face-threatening act 'off the record'. In fact Brown and Levinson (1987: 227) explicitly include the strategy 'be incomplete, use ellipsis' in their section on 'off the record' ways of politely handling Face Threatening Acts:

[Off-record] Strategy 15: Be incomplete, use ellipsis.
This is as much a violation of the Quantity Maxim as of the Manner Maxim. Elliptical utterances are legitimated by various conversational contexts—in answers to question, for example. But they are also warranted in F(ace) T(hreatening) A(ct)s. By leaving an FTA half undone, S can leave the implication 'hanging in the air', just as with rhetorical questions.

Sadock and Zwicky (1985: 193), in their discussion of how requests are characterized by indirection, include the use of formally subordinate clauses in their typology:

Indirection usually serves a purpose in that it avoids—or at least gives the appearance of avoiding—a frank performance of some act that the speaker wishes to perform. For this reason certain sorts of effects are more likely to be targets for indirect accomplishment than others. Most cultures find requests somewhat objectionable socially and these are therefore frequently conveyed by indirect means... Numerous languages use some typically subordinate clause form, a free-standing infinitive or subjunctive, for example, as a circumlocution for the imperative.

Insubordinated clauses of this type most commonly take the form of complements of request, desire, or possibility predicators, purpose clauses with an implicit 'I say this (in order that X)', and conditional clauses with an implicit 'It would be nice / You would make me happy / I would like it' etc.

11.3.1.1 *Ellipsed predicates of desire*   To begin with an example of ellipsed request or desire predicates, consider the well-discussed example of the independent subjunctive in Latin (cf. Lakoff 1968), for which it is claimed that (33b) is a paraphrase of (33a):

(33) a. Imper-o / vol-o   ut   ven-ias
         order-1SG want-1SG that come-SBJV.2SG
         'I order/I want you to come.'

      b. Ven-ias
         come-SBJV.2SG
         'Come!/May you come!'

The clear syntactic relationship between (33b) and (33a) is illustrated by the selection of negators: main clauses of command or desire select *ne*, while main clauses of possibility select *non*; these selections carry over into the corresponding insubordinated clauses (34). Note that epistemic interpretations are also available with the Latin independent subjunctive, as with (35b).

(34) a. Imper-o/ vol-o   ut   ne   ven-ias
         order-1SG want-1SG that NEG   come-SBJV.2SG
         'I order/want you not to come.'

      b. Ne   ven-ias
         NEG   come-SBJV.2SG
         'Don't come! / May you not come!'

(35) a. Potest fieri   ut   non   ven-ias
         can.3SG become   that NEG   come-SBJV.2SG
         'It may be that you won't come.'

      b. Non   venias
         NEG   come-SBJV.2SG
         'Maybe you won't come.'

11.3.1.2 *Ellipsed enabling predicate* Enabling predicates are also commonly ellipsed, leaving behind an insubordinated purpose clause. An Indonesian example is (36), while the Kayardild example (37) is similar: a literal translation would be 'in order to bring that bird back'.

(36) supaya   di-baca   halaman lima   puluh
      in.order.that PASS-read   page   five   ten
      'If you could read page fifty.'

(37) dathin-a   yarbud-a   thaari-juru-y
      that-NOM   bird-NOM   bring.back-POT-COMP.LOC
      '(Eat it in such a way that) you can bring that bird back (i.e. don't eat it all).'

One specialized type of request realized by an insubordinated purposive clause in the Yankunytjatjara dialect of the Western Desert Language (Australian;

Pama-Nyungan) is the request for permission, as in (38b) below; (38a) illustrates a canonical subordinate clause use of the purposive nominalized verb.

(38) a. ngayulu Yami-nya   nyaku-nytja-ku   paṭa-ṇi
          1SG.NOM Yami-ACC   see-NMLZ-PURP   wait-PRS
          'I'm waiting to see Yami.' (Goddard 1985: 165)

      b. ngayulu ngalku-nytja-ku / kuli-nytja-ku?
          1SG.ERG eat-NMLZ-PURP   listen-NMLZ-PURP
          'May I eat / listen?' (Goddard 1985: 166)

Goddard (1985: 166), who notes of this construction that '[a] purposive clause
with rising intonation may constitute a complete sentence in itself', goes on to
suggest that 'these utterances are probably best interpreted as "indirect speech
acts", for they implicitly request the addressee to do something, so that the
situation they depict may become possible'.

An equally widespread type of insubordination found in polite requests is
the independent if-clause, already exemplified above for French (16), English
(17, 18), and Dutch (19); see Stirling (1999) for a detailed discussion of this
phenomenon in Australian English.[23] Among the many other languages using
independent if-clauses for polite requests are Spoken Mon (39) and Japanese
(41). In all of these languages non-elliptical versions are also possible; the
ellipsed portion is typically something like '[It would make me happy] if X', as
in the non-elliptical (39a) or '[I think it would be a good idea] if X' (40).

(39) a. (yɔ raʔ) ʔa wòiŋ kwan   mòn məkɛh, (ʔoa) cat   mìp
          if PRT go visit village Mon if   I   mind happy
          '(I) would be happy if (you) would visit a Mon village.'
          (W. Bauer, p.c.)

      b. ʔa wòiŋ kwan   mòn   məkɛh
          go visit village Mon   if
          '(You) should visit a Mon village.' (W. Bauer, p.c.)

(40) oishasan ni   it-tara   ii   to   omo-u
      doctor   LOC   go-if   good   COMP   think-PRS
      'I think that it would be good to go to a doctor.'

---

[23] Ford and Thompson (1986: 365) find that, in their conversational data, 7% of their initial
if-clauses express polite directives. Although they state that '[s]ince this use of the conditional form
is one of the least compatible with logical interpretation, it is not surprising that in many cases a
consequent clause is very difficult to isolate', the examples they cite do in fact have an overt consequent
and would hence not count as insubordinated clauses by my definition; an example is 'If you could get
your table up with your new sketches just as soon as this is over I would like to see you'.

(41) oishasan ni   it-tara?
      doctor   LOC   go-if
      'Why don't you go to a doctor?'

The more such subordinated if-clauses become conventionalized, the less speakers are sure of exactly what has been ellipsed. When asked to supply a source main clause for a construction like *If you could give me a 39c stamp*, for example, English speakers I have asked split between two alternatives, corresponding to the conditional and question-embedding uses of English *if*: *I wonder if. . .* and *If. . . it would be good*. One argument against the first interpretation is that English speakers do not permit parallel examples with *whether*, as in (42):

(42) *Whether you could give me a 39c stamp.

However, one could dismiss this by claiming that selection applies to the process of insubordination, such that not all possible subordinate clauses can be used with ellipsed main clause, and that English only allows insubordination to occur with *if*, not *whether*. It becomes relevant to ask whether there are other languages that allow insubordinated requests with both types; and in fact we find that in Basque, which has distinct constructions for the two types, employing distinct auxiliary forms, both are permitted as insubordinated requests:

(43) a. 39 pezta-ko   bi   seilu   ematen   ba-dizkidazu
         39 peseta-ADJ two   stamp   give.IMP SUBOR-AUX
         Lit. 'If you give me two 39 peseta stamps.' (condition)

      b. Ea   39 pezta-ko   bi   seilu   emango   dizkidazu-n.
         DUB 39 peseta-ADJ two   stamp   give.FUT AUX-SUBOR
         Lit. 'If you give me two 39 peseta stamps.' (embedded question)
         (Alan King, p.c.)

11.3.1.3 *Ellipsed result clauses*   Another common source of requests is the omission of main clauses stating a consequence of result, leaving explicit only a reason clause, or more generally a clause giving background. In Kayardild, insubordinated reason clauses—formally, a complementized version of immediate, past, future, or resultative clauses, without any main clause—can be used as hints. The reason is stated, but not the suggested course of action, which is pragmatically obvious.

(44) mala-ntha   bala-thurrka   kamarr-urrk
      sea-COBL   hit-IMM.COBL   rock-IMM.OBJ.COBL
      '(Let's leave here,) because the sea is hitting the rocks now.'

(45) dathin-inja   kunawun-inja   rabi-jarra-nth   rik-urrk,
     that-COBL   child-COBL   get.up-PST-COBL   crying-LOC.COBL
     rila-thirrin-inj
     wake-RES-COBL
     '(Someone/you should comfort that child), because it's got up, because
     it's crying, because it's been woken up.'
     (Context: addressing the child's mother in middle of night.)

Kita Sotaro (p.c.) reports that in Japanese insubordinated 'because' clauses
can be used in a similar way. An example with at least two quite different
interpretations is (46), which includes both request and other interpretations;
similar interpretations are available with the structurally parallel but more
polite version (47).[24]

(46) Boku   wa   ik-u   kara
     I   TOP   go-PRS   because
     'Since I am going, [please don't bother / don't worry /etc.].'
     'Since I am going, [nobody else has to do it / the problem there will
     be solved etc.].'

(47) Boku   wa   iki   masu   node
     I   TOP   go   ADR.HON   because
     'Since I am going, so ... [= (46)]'

11.3.1.4 *Free-standing infinitives*   The use of free-standing infinitives for
requests is extremely widespread. Examples have already been given in
Italian (2a) and German (2b); see also the data from Russian discussed by
Perlmutter (Chapter 8 above) and from various Daghestanian languages
discussed by Kalinina and Sumbatova (Chapter 7 above). In many languages
it is confined to written notices and other specialized contexts. But a good
example of a language allowing free-standing infinitives in the spoken form is
modern Hebrew. David Gil (p.c.) gives the following example of a lifeguard
who would continually admonish the bathers (over the megaphone) to move,
using an independent infinitive (48a); occasionally, when he felt he wasn't
being paid attention, he would elaborate by 'restoring' a matrix sentence (48b);
if he still was not obeyed, he would lose his temper and resort to a real
imperative, in this particular case employing the colloquial Hebrew option
of using the future as an imperative:

---

[24] Ohori (1995: 210) gives an example of an insubordinated *-kara* clause being used to furnish an
excuse for declining an invitation: A: 'Are (you) free today?' B: 'Yes, but because (I')m tired (+ > I can't
make it).

(48) a. laʕavor   mul   hamigdal!
         INF.move opposite   DEF.tower
         'To move in front of the tower!' (i.e. 'Move opposite the watch-
         tower!')

      b. ani mevakeʃ   laʕavor   mul   hamigdal
         I   request.PRS.M.SG INF.move opposite DEF.tower
         'I request (bathers) to move in front of the tower.'

      c. taʕavru   mul   hamigdal!
         FUT.2.PL.move opposite   DEF.tower
         'Move in front of the tower!'

In addition to infinitives, other nonfinite verb forms such as verbal nouns and masdars frequently occur in main clauses in a number of Daghestanian languages (see Kalinina and Sumbatova, Chapter 7 above).

11.3.1.5 *Warnings and admonitions*   Another type of interpersonal coercion widely expressed by the use of insubordinated clauses is the warning, admonition, or threat. In many unrelated languages this is expressed by an independent subordinate clause of purpose or negative purpose, spelling out the consequences to be avoided. Many Australian languages, for example, have a special type of subordinate clause, typically labelled 'lest', 'apprehensive', or 'evitative' in grammars, which is used to express undesirable consequences to be avoided by carrying out the main clause action. An example from Diyari has already been given in (15). For Kayardild, (49a) illustrates the subordinate use, while (49b) exemplifies an insubordinated use for giving a warning. See also example (50) from Basque, and (51) from Polish, where negative subjunctive clauses complementized by *żeby* can be used as warnings. Although Polish clauses of this type normally occur insubordinated, it is possible to insert *uważaj* 'look out, pay attention' before them.

(49) a. walmathi karn-da   rajurri-n,   ba-yii-nyarra
         on.top   grass-NOM walk-NEG.IMP bite-PASS-APPR
         yarbuth-iiwa-nharr!
         snake-V.I.ALL-APPR
         'Don't walk across the grass, in case you get bitten by a snake.'

      b. nyingka   ba-yii-nyarra   kulkiji-yiwa-nharr
         you.NOM   bite-PASS-APPR   shark-V.I.ALL-APPR
         '(Watch out/Do something,) you might get bitten by a shark.'

(50) erori   gabe,   e!
      fall.NON.FIN without   INTERJ
      Lit. 'Without falling, huh!', i.e. 'Mind your step!' (Alan King, p.c.)
      (As spoken, say, by a mother to a small child as they walk along a
      narrow path or down the garden steps.)

(51) Żeby-ś   się tylko nie wywroci-ł-a
     in.order.that-you REFL only   not fall-PST-F
     'Make sure you don't fall! You might fall!'

In most of these languages there is good comparative evidence that the subordinate use is historically prior; in Kayardild, for example, the apprehensive verb form -*NHarra* derives from a verb complementized by the 'having' case, -*marra*. The extension to independent use then probably occurs through omission of the imperative, whose content is usually obvious if one knows the undesirable consequence, and which is in any case a face-threatening act.

Insubordinated if-clauses may also be used as threats and warnings, as in English (52); the use of 'threatening intonation' and frequent presence of such lexical items as 'dare' distinguishes it from the 'if' requests.

(52) If you (dare) touch my car!

11.3.1.6 *Insubordinated requests and politeness*   It is appropriate to end this section with some reservations about oversimplifications implicit in the account with which we began it, namely that insubordinated requests are favoured in requests for reasons of politeness by virtue of playing down the explicit interpersonal control made evident in imperatives and other direct commands.

The first problem is that some insubordinated requests actually sound more imperious than commands; an example is the French independent subjunctive.

A second problem is that insubordination may actually remove some markers of politeness; an example of this in Japanese is the ellipsis of *kudasai* 'please', etymologically meaning 'give'. Thus (53a), with a full main clause, is considerably politer than the casual (53b):

(53) a. Are-o mi-te   kudasa-i.
         that-ACC look-PTCP give-PRS
         'Look at that (for me), please.'

      b. Are-o   mi-te.
         that-ACC look-PTCP
         'Look at that (for me).'

What seems more likely, then, is that the face-threatening nature of requests and commands places strong pressures on the language system to come up with new variants whose pragmatic force is freed from the history of existing formulas, and that insubordination provides one fertile source for this, but that the actual pragmatic value of insubordinated clauses need not be more 'polite' than a more direct form.

11.3.2 *Modal insubordination*

Another widespread use of insubordination is to express various kinds of modal meaning, both epistemic—having to do with belief, truth, knowledge about the proposition—and deontic, i.e. 'concerned with action, by others and by the speaker himself' (Palmer 1986: 96) to bring about a state of affairs denoted by the proposition. Although both types of meaning get expressed by insubordinated clauses, there are interesting differences in the source constructions: whereas epistemic insubordination involves 'pure' markers of subordinate status, implicating ellipsed main clauses of reporting, thinking, perceiving, or asserting, deontic insubordination frequently involves complementizers with additional semantic content, such as showing tense/mood relations between clauses.

In this section I also consider the frequent use of insubordinated clauses to express speaker reaction to the proposition, such as astonishment or disapproval, since they frequently display similar formal patterning. As Palmer (1986: 119) puts it: 'if Evaluatives are defined as attitudes towards known facts, they are not strictly modal at all. But they must be briefly considered, because they are sometimes included within, or as semantically closely related to, modal systems.'

Finally, because there are frequently further semantic developments from mood to tense, such as from purposive to future,[25] the use of insubordination to yield new tense markers will also be discussed in this section.

11.3.2.1 *Epistemic and evidential meanings*   Probably the commonest type of evidentializing insubordination involves the representation of indirect speech—whether of an identified participant in *style indirect libre*, or simply of unidentified hearsay—by an independent subordinate form. Well-studied European examples are the use in indirect discourse of the accusative subject plus infinitive construction in Latin without overt framing quotative verb (54), or the subjunctive in German or Icelandic (25). As Hall (1964: 220–1) puts it, 'indications of subordination in parataxis can be used, in some languages, throughout long stretches of discourse to indicate their status as quotations or otherwise dependent elements'. He cites, as an example, the following Latin passage with its 'indirect discourse marked by sequences of infinitives in clauses printed as independent sentences'. I give it here as transcribed in the

---

[25] Or else direct developments to tense marking from the same set of constructions as yield the deontic insubordinated clauses.

Loeb Classical Library edition, and followed by two alternative translations: one from the Loeb edition (by H. J. Edwards), which uses an initial quotative 'he said' followed simply by the use of quotation marks throughout, and one from the Penguin Classics translation (by S. A. Handford) that uses an initial quotative, then no other marks of quotativity at all.

(54)   Locutus   est   pro   his   Diviciacus   Aeduus: Galliae   totius
       said   is   by   these   Diviciacus   Aeduan   in.Gaul   all
       factiones   esse   duas: harum   alterius   principatum   tenere
       factions   be.INF   two   of.these   one   leadership.ACC   hold.INF
       Aeduos,   alterius   Arvernos.   Hi   cum   tantopere
       Aedui.ACC   one   Arverni.ACC   these   when   so.much
       de   potentatu   inter   se   multos   annos   contenderent,
       for political.power   among   self   many   years   vied
       factum   esse,   uti   ab   Arvernis   Sequanis-que
       made.ACC   be.INF   how   by   Arverni   Sequani-and
       Germani   mercede   arcesserentur
       Germans   for.pay   were.summoned
       (Caesar, *de Bello Gallico*, Book I:31, Loeb Classical Library edition)

Edwards translation (p. 47 of Loeb Classical Library edition):
Diviciacus the Aeduan spoke on their behalf. 'In all Gaul,' he said, 'there are two parties; in one of them the Aedui have the primacy, in the other the Arverni. For many years there was a vehement struggle between the two for the dominon; then it came about that the Arverni and the Sequani summoned the Germans to their aid for a price...' (Quote continues into following paragraphs, not given here.)

Handford translation (p. 56 of Penguin Classics edition)
Their spokesman was the Aeduan Diviciacus. The Gauls, he said, were divided into two parties, one dominated by the Aedui, the other by the Arverni. After a fierce struggle for supremacy, lasting many years, the Arverni and Sequani hired some German mercenaries to help them.

Similar phenomena, though with different formal markers of subordination, are found in a wide range of languages. In Lithuanian, for example, indirect speech is normally reported with participles (see 13a). However, as an independent sentence, one could say (55), 'without accepting responsibility for the punctual departure of the train, by the use of the participle *išeĩnąs*' (Comrie 1981: 153).

(55)   traukinỹs   išeĩnąs   lýgiai   septiñtą   vãlandą
       train.NOM   leave.PRS.PTCP   prompt.ADV   seventh.ACC   hour.ACC
       '(It is said that) the train will leave promptly at seven o'clock.'

In Latvian as well (Comrie 1981: 153–4) the active past participle can be used to describe situations whose authenticity is not vouchsafed by the speaker; consequently it is common in fairy tales. See Comrie (1981: 153) for examples. While the participle form is noncommittal with respect to authenticity of the statement, there is a separate form, involving the suffix -*ot*, which is used to express uncertainty about the veracity of a statement, as in (56) as opposed to (57).

(56)   Viņš   esot   bagāts
       he.NOM   be.PRS.INFER   rich.NOM
       'he is supposed to be rich'

(57)   Viņš   ir   bagāts
       he.NOM   be.PRS.3   rich.NOM
       'he is rich'

Etymologically, this is a participial ending; like the past participle it can also be used in indirect speech; compared to the quotative use of the past participle it has moved further towards syntactic independence (with its classification as a participle now being etymological rather than synchronic, according to Comrie 1981: 54), and semantically it now expresses uncertainty directly, rather than by implicature from the fact of quotation.

Next door, in Estonian,[26] free-standing clauses with quotative force, in the *modus obliquus* or 'indirect', as in (58), originated as subordinate clauses embedded under speech act verbs, as in (59), by a process of insubordination similar to those already discussed. See Campbell (1991) for a clear discussion of how this construction evolved, including evidence that the original 'modus obliquus' construction was an Estonian innovation that took place at a stage when the construction was still exclusively subordinate and had not yet been extended to main clauses, and which involved a reinterpretation of participles as finite verbs with a concomitant change in subject case marking from genitive to nominative. Wälchli (2002) contains further discussion in broader Baltic perspective.

(58)   Ta   tege-vat   töö-d
       he.NOM   do-PRS.INDIR   work-PARTV
       'They say he is working.' (Campbell 1991: 287)

(59)   Sai   kuul-da,   (et)   seal   üks   mees   ela-vat
       got   hear-INF   that   there   one.NOM   man.NOM   live-MOD.OBL
       'He came to hear/he heard that (they say) a man lives there.'
       (Campbell 1991: 287)

---

[26] Areal influence is obviously a possibility here, though determining the direction of diffusion is problematic—see Campbell (1991), Wälchli (2000), and Dahl and Koptjevskaja-Tamm (2001).

To illustrate a similar development from a totally different part of the world, in Sierra Miwok (Freeland 1951: 87–8), there are two 'narrative tenses', characteristically used in formal narrative when relating whole myths or anecdotes of old days. Although they occur in free-standing clauses, they have a number of formal features in common with subordinate constructions, lacking the pronominal subject suffix characteristic of normal main clauses. Freeland (1951: 87) comments: 'The narrative mode is obviously simply an extension in use of the subordinate mode... and illustrates the Miwok tendency to use as independent verbs, forms originally subordinate in character.' Presumably this originated as embedding under a main clause speech act verb, something like 'the old people said', although Freeland does not go into details on the exact mechanism.

Another manifestation of 'evidentializing' insubordination may involve the extension of logophoric pronouns to independent clause use. The canonical use of logophoric pronouns is in subordinate clauses embedded under matrix verbs of communication, thought, psychological state, or perception,[27] to indicate coreference between a subordinate clause argument and the 'epistemic source' of the main clause (the sayer, knower, etc.). (60a) and (60b) contrast the use of logophoric and non-logophoric pronouns in Ewe subordinate clauses.

(60) a. Kofi   be   yè-dzo
        Kofi   say   LOG-leave
        'Kofi$_i$ said that he$_i$ left.'

   b. Kofi   be   e-dzo
        Kofi   say   3-leave
        'Kofi$_i$ said that (s)he$_j$ left.'

Now in some languages with logophoric pronouns it is possible to use them in main clauses to show 'represented speech' or 'style indirect libre' (Coulmas 1986: 7). In Tuburi, for example (Hagège 1974), logophoric pronouns may continue to be used at a great distance from the original locutionary verb that introduced them. Hagège (p. 298) cites an example in which an account of the origins of a clan, which began with the locutionary clause 'my elders taught me that...', continues to use logophoric pronouns thirty minutes into the text, as exemplified below. Here the logophoric acts as a sort of spoken inverted commas:

---

[27] This list represents an implicational hierarchy, with types to the left more likely to trigger logophoric contexts (Stirling 1993: 259).

(61) sā:rā dús   sō
      LOG   disperse then
      'Then they dispersed.'

In fact, logophoric pronouns in Tuburi need not be introduced by a main clause locutionary verb at all. They may be used to indicate point of view, or to dissociate the speaker from the proposition (p. 300), in other words, they may have quotative evidential force.

In the case of such independent clause use of logophorics the historical arguments for regarding this as insubordination are weaker than with, say, participles, since we cannot be sure there was ever a stage where they were uniquely associated with subordinate clauses. It is equally possible that the constraint on their use has always been semantic (they can occur in utterances framed as thought or quotation), and that their statistical association with subordinate constructions is an epiphenomenon of the fact that these are the commonest grammatical contexts for such framing. We will not be able to answer this question until we have a better understanding of the historical syntax of logophorics.

Long-distance reflexives present a similar picture to logophorics. Typically found in subordinate clauses, they may also occur in insubordinated clauses, again typically accompanied by an independent subjunctive, and again, the semantic effect is to express represented speech or viewpoint. An Icelandic example using the long-distance reflexive *sig*, construed as coreferential with an ellipsed 'thought' verb, was exemplified in (10) above. Sigurðsson (1986) cites such examples as evidence against a specifically syntactic account of Long Distance Reflexives in Icelandic, since they need have no syntactic antecedent. Such LDRs are, he argues, interpreted semantically as referring to the 'story-experiencing self' in *style indirect libre*, the *erlebte Rede* or 'represented speech and thought'. With their direct and conventionalized semantic interpretation of formally subordinate clauses, these represent a further possible case of insubordination. As far as the Long Distance Reflexives are concerned, there are the same caveats on whether they do in fact originate as subordinate constructions; but in this case they additionally involve independent uses of subjunctives, for which a subordinate clause origin is usually assumed.[28]

A semantically comparable case, but where the evidence for subordinate origins is much stronger due to the proliferation of overtly subordinating morphology in the form of 'complementizing case' suffixes distributed over

---

[28] For further examples and discussion see Maling (1984: n. 27) on Icelandic and Kameyama (1984: 235) on Japanese.

all words in the clause is Kayardild (Evans 1995a). Here, insubordinated complementized clauses (enclosed in square brackets in the examples below) may, for certain combinations of tense and person, carry various kinds of evidential force:

- direct perception in the case of clauses that are 'immediate' (62), involve non-verbal predicates (63) or present-tense negatives that are formally nominalizations bearing the privative (64);
- inference from observed facts in the case of past clauses (65);
- prediction based on knowledge in the case of future clauses (66).

(62) [dan-kurrka   ri-in-kurrka   dali-jurrka   budubudu-nth]
     here-LOC.COBL east-from-LOC.COBL come-IMMED.COBL boat-COBL
     '(I can hear/see) the boat coming from the east.'
     (Context: a group of people waiting on a beach, watching and listening for a boat.)

(63) [dan-kurrka   marrkathu-nth]
     here-LOC.COBL aunt-COBL
     'Here's aunty. (I can see/hear her coming).'

(64) [kajakaja-ntha   dali-n-marri-nja-d]
     daddy-COBL   come-NMLZ-PRIV-COBL-yet
     '(I see that/it seems that) daddy hasn't arrived yet.'
     (Context: speaker is returning disappointed from the airstrip, where he had hoped to meet the hearer's father.)

(65) [thabuju-ntha   warra-jarra-nth]
     big.brother-COBL go-PST-COBL
     '(There's no one here,) because big brother has gone.'
     (Context implies: there's no one here, so big brother must have gone.)

(66) [banga-ntha bijarrba-ntha balung-kuu-ntha   thula-thuu-nth]
     turtle-COBL dugong-COBL westward-MPROP-COBL descend-POT-COBL
     '(I know that) the turtle and dugong will go down to the west.'
     (Context: speaker has seen the 'spouts' where they have broken the surface en route.)

The source of knowledge could in each case be made explicit by restoring the ellipsed main predicate, e.g. *ngada kurrij / ngada marrij* 'I see / I hear' in the case of (62) and (63). The restored predicates would in each case govern a clause of the appropriate form. Note the parallel with the skewing in interpretation of English *see/hear* between *I (can) see/hear the boat coming*, with a true perception-verb interpretation, vs. *I hear/see that the boat has come* and *I heard / saw / could hear / could see that the boat had come*, in which the basis of knowledge may be more indirect, for example resulting from hearsay or inference.

We now turn to the question of why insubordinated clauses should be used for this range of functions, rather than simple clauses on the one hand or explicitly biclausal constructions ('I think that X', 'It seems to be the case that X', etc.) on the other. I shall begin by considering the very insightful account by Schlobinsky (n.d.) of independent *daß* clauses in German client-centred therapeutic discourse. Then I shall extend the discussion to a more general level, and show why there are good pragmatic reasons, not limited to the specialized domain of client-centred therapy, why insubordinated clauses should be used in this way.

In German client-centred therapeutic discourse, therapists regularly follow turns by the client with insubordinated *daß* clauses which restate, suggest interpretations of, or clarify material in the client's turn. Such insubordinated *daß* clauses are associated with a weakly rising intonation, which has the effect of passing back the turn to the client for further restatement. For example:

(67)   Client: Ich glaub, also, ich geb erstmal klein bei, um (.) wenn ich
                  jetzt nochmal was dagegen sage, kann ich mir einfach nicht
                  erlauben, dann wird er wieder laut. Also muß ich schon
                  mal klein beigeben.
                  I think I pull in my horns at first, inorder (.) if I say
                  something against that again, I just can't allow myself to
                  do that, then he'll start yelling. That's why I have to pull in
                  my horns a bit.

       Therapist: Daß Sie doch jetzt das Gefühl haben, sich ducken zu
                  müssen.
                  That you already have the feeling now you have to
                  knuckle under. (Schlobinsky n.d.)

In Rogerian therapeutic discourse, insubordinated *daß* clauses are always connected to a client's utterance, forming the second pair-part of an adjacency pair. The most significant thing about these clauses, from both a semantic and sociolinguistic point of view, is that they are unspecified with regard to facticity: 'the attitude of the speaker remains unspecified because of the absence of the modal operator' (p. 12). The epistemic status of the proposition can only be interpreted through context, which may allow the speaker's attitudes to be recovered inferentially.

Schlobinsky proposes the following functional reason why, in the context of client-centred therapy, insubordinated *daß* clauses are preferable to more explicit constructions with an overt main clause with an epistemic verb:

> One could also imagine an utterance like 'I think you are trying to play that down a bit.' Here however the therapist would raise himself qua SubjectAgent to the discourse agent, and lessen the focus on the client. His utterance would therefore be more directive. By deleting the attitude operator in the superordinate clause the therapist takes his role back and takes the role of the client or reflects her conversational work without attributing a specific attitude to the client such as 'you believe, are convinced, that p...' It is exactly here that the two-party monologue is continued. As opposed to an utterance like 'you have the feeling...' the *daß* clause is unspecified with regard to facticity and thus allows the client to personally evaluate the proposition. The client is forced to take a position on the part of discourse in focus. (Schlobinsky n.d.: 17)

Schlobinsky thus stresses the specific social features of client-centred therapy as a reason for favouring the independent *daß* clause construction, in particular the non-directiveness of the therapist and the method of arriving at an analysis by joint focusing. But in fact similar characterizations could be made of normal conversation in many small-scale societies, such as Australian Aboriginal societies, in which conversation is normatively non-directive and epistemic statements are arrived at by negotiation of essentially equal conversational participants rather than clear assertion by a more knowledgeable person.

11.3.2.2 *Deontic meanings* A number of languages use insubordinated clauses to express various deontic meanings. In Latin, Italian, French, etc., the independent subjunctive can have a hortative meaning, while in several Baltic languages necessity is expressed by 'debitive' verbal nouns or infinitives (see Wälchli 2000 for a survey of the Baltic data).

An Italian example of the use of an independent subjunctive with hortative meaning is:

(68) Si   aggiunga   poi   che   l'uomo   è   pedante
     3REFL add.SBJV.3SG then   that   DEF.man   is   pedant
     'And then may it be added that the man is a pedant.'
     (M. Bontempelli, cited in Moretti and Orvieto 1979)

An explanation of how independent subjunctives acquire hortative meanings is offered in a discussion of Icelandic by Sigurðsson. Here the preterite subjunctive is sometimes insubordinated, particularly with auxiliaries like 'want', 'may', 'have to', 'can', and 'need'. An example is:

(69) Jón   θyrfti   að fara heim
     John   had.sbjv.3sg   to   go   home
     'John should (/would need to) go home.' (Sigurðsson 1986: 21)

According to Sigurðsson,

main clause subjunctives reflect the speaker's feelings, opinions, etc.: the speaker feels
that John should go home and uses the preterite subjunctive to express this (epistemic
modality)…The speaker claims [the indicative equivalent] to be true in our (past)
world, whereas he claims [69] to be true in the 'world' of his own feelings, opinions,
desires, etc. (Sigurðsson 1986: 22).

In Dyirbal 'implicated clauses' are basically subordinate and derive historically (in the *y*-conjugation at least)[29] from the addition of a complementizing
purposive case marker -*gu* to the verb (this is cognate with the Yankunytjatjara purposive -*ku* exemplified in 38). Normally they indicate that the subordinate clause is a consequence of the main clause, as in:

(70) balan   ḍugumbil   baŋgul   yaṛa-ŋgu balga-n, baḍi-gu
     DEM.II.ACC woman.ACC DEM.I.ERG man-ERG hit-NP   fall-IMPL
     'Man hits woman, causing her to fall down.' (Dixon 1972: 68)

However, implicated clauses may also be used independently with the meaning 'must' or 'has to', as in the following examples:

(71) balan   ḍugumbil   miyanda-ygu
     DEM.II.NOM woman.NOM   laugh-IMP
     'The woman wants to laugh (i.e. something has happened to make her
     want to laugh, and she will have to restrain herself to avoid doing so).'
     (Dixon 1972: 69)

(72) bayi   yaṛa   yanuli
     DEM.I.NOM   man.NOM   go.IMP
     'The man has to go out (for some reason).'

Dixon offers a plausible explanation for the development of subordinate
implicated clauses to insubordinated deontic clauses: the obligation arises
from a causal (or 'implicating') connection between an earlier, unreported
event and the obligatory event. In other words, insubordination allows the
causal relationship expressible by interclausal morphosyntax to be harnessed
for the expression of the causal element present in all deontics of obligation.

---

[29] Dyirbal has two conjugations, *y* and *l*. The origin of the *l*-conjugation form -*li* is obscure, though
with apparent cognates in Ngiyambaa (see below).

Another Australian language, Ngiyambaa (Donaldson 1980), uses the same form in subordinate clauses of purpose (73) and as a deontic, usually translated 'must' (74) or 'has got to' (75), in main clauses. Although Donaldson does not analyse the main clauses as derived by ellipsis from the purposive construction, the fact that this is the only main clause inflection also serving in nonfinite subordinate clauses suggests that the main clause construction originates from an insubordinated clause, with a similar semantic development to Dyirbal. Interestingly, verbs in the -*l*- conjugation have the same form, -*li*, as implicated verbs in the Dyirbal -*l*- conjugation, suggesting a form of some antiquity given that the two languages are not closely related.

(73) ŋadhu-na   ŋiyiyi   / girma-l-i   ŋinu:
      1SG.NOM-3ABS say.PST   wake-CM-PURP   you.OBL
      'I told her to wake you.' (Donaldson 1980: 280)

(74) ŋadhu   bawuŋ-ga   yuwa-giri
      1SG.NOM   middle-LOC   lie-PURP
      'I must lie in the middle.' (Donaldson 1980:162)

(75) bura:-dhu   dhiŋga: dha-l-i
      child-ERG   meat.ABS   eat-CM-PURP
      'The child has got to eat meat.' (Donaldson 1980: 162)

11.3.2.3 *Exclamation and evaluation*   Insubordinated *that* clauses in English, *daß* clauses in German, and subjunctives in Italian can be used to express evaluation, with reconstructable main clause predicates such as 'I am amazed', 'I am shocked', or 'I would not have expected'. Quirk et al. (1985: 841) comment in this regard on 'the omission of the matrix clause...being mimetic of speechless amazement'. For further discussion and data in this volume, see also the discussion of nonfinite exclamative clauses in Bagwalal and Dargwa in the chapter by Kalinina and Sumbatova (Chapter 7 above).

Examples for English (76) are from Quirk et al. (1985)—who do not, however, supply reconstructions of the ellipsed material—and for German (77), from Buscha (1976).

(76) a. [I'm amazed and shocked] That he should have left without asking me!
     b. That I should live to see such ingratitude!

(77) a. [Ich wundere   mich,] Daß du   immer noch Witze
        I   am.amazed REFL   that you   still   still   jokes
        mach-en   kann-st!
        make-INF   can-2SG
        '[I am amazed] that you can still make jokes (about it).'

b. Daß ich dich hier treff-en   würde!   [, habe ich nicht
   that I   you here meet-INF would.SBJV have   I   not
   erwartet]
   expected
   '[I didn't expect] that I would meet you here!'

Similar constructions using a range of wh-questions with subordinate word order also exist in both languages (78, 79); both examples in (78) were heard from speakers of Australian English in Melbourne, January 1996. Buscha (1976) and Weuster (1983) discuss comparable examples in German in some detail (they are not discussed in Quirk et al.). The reconstructable ellipses are basically comparable in both languages, and express astonishment or surprise, with either 1st person or indefinite 3rd person subjects: 'I'm amazed at [how...]', 'I don't understand [how...]', 'No one understands [why...]'. Frequently exclamative intonation is also used.

(78) a. [I don't understand] How they can bet on a bloody dog like that!
      b. [Can anyone tell me] Why they don't schedule the under 11s first!

(79) a. [Ich wundere   mich,] Wie du   das   nur   mach-st?
         I   am.amazed REFL   how you   that only   do-2SG
         '[I'm amazed at] how on earth you can do that?' (Buscha 1976)

      b. [Niemand begreif-t,]   Warum du   wohl   nie   zu Potte
         no.one   understand-3SG why   you   well   never to potty
         komm-st
         come-2SG
         '[No one understands] why you can never get going.'
         (Weuster 1983: 56)

A third type of insubordinated clause, employing a main clause infinitive, can be used to express surprise in English (80):

(80) a. To think that she should be so ruthless! (Quirk et al. 1985)
      b. To think that I was once a millionaire! (Quirk et al. 1985)

Quirk et al. (p. 841) argue that '[t]he implied subject in such sentences is the first person pronoun', although they later broaden this to include indefinite subjects in their analysis of the reconstructed material as 'It surprises me to think...' or 'It surprises one to think...'. The tendency of ellipsed subjects to be construed as 1st person will be returned to in section 11.4.2.

A further nonfinite structure used in English, Spanish, and other languages to express hypothetical events (often then repudiated in a further sentence)

was illustrated in example (1), and originally discussed for English by
Akmajian (1984). See Etxepare and Grohmann (2005) for discussion of their
meaning and syntactic properties.

11.3.2.4 *New tense categories through deictic recentring*   Given the cross-
linguistic tendency for obligation to develop into future tense, it is not
surprising that there should be constructions which develop from
(subordinate) purpose clause to (insubordinated) deontics with meanings
of obligation or intention and on to (insubordinated) markers of futurity.
Blake (1976: 422–3) discusses the development of purposive case markers in
Australian languages to complementizers on purpose clauses to markers of
desiderative and on to future in some languages; the dative/purpose case
suffix -*ku* in Australian languages of the Pama-Nyungan family is a well-
known example, and has been exemplified with purpose-complement and
permissive uses above for Dyirbal and Yankunytjatjara, but in some other
languages it occurs as a future marker, as with the Pitjantjatjara dialect of the
Western Dialect language (Blake 1976: 422).

(81)   minyma   yula-ku
       woman   cry-FUT(*-DAT)
       'The woman will/may cry.'

A comparable but independent series of developments has occurred with the
suffix -*kur(l)u* in another Australian family, Tangkic. Basically a proprietive
case suffix marking 'having', it is used in all Tangkic languages to mark
intentional goals, e.g. 'look for kangaroo-PROP', i.e. 'look for, having a
kangaroo (in mind)'. In all modern Tangkic languages and therefore almost
certainly in proto-Tangkic it can also be used for purpose clauses, being
added both to the verb stem[30] and its non-subject arguments. The following
example is from Yukulta, which appears to preserve the proto-Tangkic structure in all essential respects:

(82)   wanji-ja-kadi   [marliyan-kurlu   bala-th-urlu]$_{PROP}$
       go·up-IND-PRS.1SG   possum-PROP   hit-THM-PROP
       'I'm climbing up to hit that possum.'

In addition to this original complementizing use of the proprietive, Kayardild
and Lardil have evolved an independent, insubordinated use. The carrying of
complementizing case marking on NPs into main clause constructions has
given rise to the strange phenomenon of 'modal case', by which non-subject

---

[30] i.e. the root plus the conjugational 'thematic'; it is possible this stem functioned as a participle-
type base.

NPs take case-type suffixes encoding mood and tense choices (see Dench and Evans 1988; Evans 1995a; 1995b).

In Kayardild, whose verbal semantics are known in most detail, and where the gloss 'potential' is used for this inflection, the insubordinated use has a wide semantic range that includes future, prescription, desire, and ability, as attested by (83). *-thu* and *-wu* are the Kayardild equivalents of Yukulta *-thurlu* and (in another declension) *-kurlu* (see Evans 1995a).

(83) dathin-a   dangka-a   bala-thu   bijarrba-wu
      that-NOM   man-NOM   hit-POT   dugong-MPROP
      'That man will/must/wants to/can hit the dugong.'

The development to future is likely to have been the endpoint of a shift that began, at the time insubordination occurred, with a shift from relative to absolute 'intentional' meanings, i.e. from 'at the time of the main clause, X intended to do Y' to 'now X intends to do Y'; this was followed with a semantic extension from intention to futurity.

The developments just described clearly involve modality evolving from the semantics of the case marking complementizer, and are comparable to the evolution of various deontic modal categories from insubordinated purposives, already described in section 11.3.2.2. But in parallel to this development, Kayardild and Lardil applied similar processes of insubordination to other subordinate clauses using complementizing case markers to show relative tense; in the process new categories of absolute tense evolved, as 'immediate present' evolved from 'simultaneous' subordinate clauses marked with a complementizing locative, and 'past' evolved from 'prior' subordinate clauses marked with a complementizing ablative.

For example, 'prior' subordinate clauses are found in Yukulta. They are marked by an ablative case on non-subject NPs in the subordinate clause, and a special 'prior' form of the verb, *-jarrba/-tharrba*, which is etymologically analysable into conjugational thematic *th/j* plus the consequential case suffix *-(ng)arrba*, closely linked semantically to the ablative. Comparative evidence suggests the subordinate clause construction in proto-Tangkic allowed NPs to take either the ablative or the consequential case, but that Yukulta has eliminated the second possibility. Such 'prior' subordinate clauses express events that began before the main clause; they may overlap, as in the case of (84), or precede it entirely (see Keen 1972; 1983 for examples).

(84) kurri-ja-nganta   [kabaj-inaba   jawi-jarrba]
      see-IND-1SG.A.PST   sand-ABL   run-PRIOR
      'I saw you running on the sand.'

Kayardild and Lardil still allow the subordinate clause use, but have additionally extended such clauses to main clause use through insubordination. In both languages, the resultant clause type serves as a marked way of describing past events (the unmarked way is to use the 'actual' verb inflection which does not distinguish past from present); an example is (85). Non-subject NPs bear the 'modal ablative' case (in Kayardild), and the past verb inflection is a reduced form of *-jarrba/-tharrba*: [31]

(85) ngada   yakuri-na   jungarrba-na   raa-jarr
      1SG.NOM   fish-MABL   big-MABL   spear-PST
      'I speared a big fish.'

Insubordination, in this case, has led to a recentring of the relationship of temporal priority. Instead of holding between the main clause and the subordinate clause, it now holds between the speech act and the insubordinated clause. Comparable deictic recentring has applied to the old simultaneous clause construction, whose insubordinated reflex in Kayardild has an 'immediate present' reading. These changes form part of a suite of insubordinations that have given rise to the majority of tense/mood inflections in Kayardild and Lardil, with their unusual patterning of marking tense/mood both on the verbal inflection and on non-subject NPs through the device of 'modal case'.

The changes described above have run to completion in the sense that the resultant clauses have no synchronic formal reason to be described as subordinate in Kayardild or Tangkic—in fact, as a result of the prevalence of this method for recruiting new tense/mood categories, they are now the canonical main clause type (see Evans 1995a: ch. 10 for details).

In addition to this 'first round', however, there is a second round of insubordination still taking place in Kayardild, and producing a new 'relevant present' construction. This construction is used for a present situation, usually newly arisen, that motivates the speaker's comment (86) or curiosity (87); informants always translate these clauses with 'now'.

(86) [dathin-inja   dangka-ntha   natha-wurrk]
      that-COBL   man-COBL   camp-LOC.COBL
      'That man is married now (i.e. sleeps in his own camp, with his new wife).'

---

[31] As with the proprietive, processes of final truncation make the correspondence with the Yukulta forms less than perfect, but the forms found in phonologically protected environments, i.e. before further case suffixes, show the cognation more clearly. For example the Kayardild proprietive, normally *ku* or *wu*, becomes *kuru* or *wuru* before an outer locative case (and the descent of proto-Tangkic *rl* as *r* in Kayardild is regular); similarly the ablative, normally *-(k)ina* in Kayardild, becomes *-(k)inaba* before a following locative case suffix. See Evans (1995a) for details.

(87) A: [jina-wurrka   ngakin-maan-inj?]
          where-LOC.COBL   our-begetter-COBL
      B: [riya-thi-wurrka   ngakin-maan-inj]
          east-REM-LOC.COBL   our-begetter-COBL
      A: 'Where's our dad now?'   B: 'Our dad's way over in the east now.'

Such clauses clearly pattern formally as subordinate clauses. In terms of their morphosyntax they are identical to the 'complementized clauses' whose various other functions have been described above in section 11.3.2.1: they bear a complementizing case (oblique or locative according to the person of the clause's subject) outside all other inflections, and their subjects, if pronominal, have special forms for the complementizing oblique. In terms of their semantics, it is most likely that they have developed from the 'perceptual complement' clauses discussed in section 11.3.2.1—from '(I see/hear) X happening now' to 'X [is] happening now' as the matrix perception predicate underwent ellipsis—but the link to present experience and relevance remained.

Unlike most of the functional types of insubordination described above, which have independent attestation in a range of language families, the use of insubordination to recruit new tense categories is largely limited to the Tangkic group; it may have arisen as a response to the paucity of tense/mood categories in the proto-language (McConvell 1981). However, there are occasional parallels from other languages.[32]

In Dyirbal (Dixon 1972: 104), dependent relative clauses in -*ŋu*- (which is probably related to an ablative formative -*ŋu*- widespread in Pama-Nyungan) have a perfective reading. As subordinate relatives, ongoing or completive interpretations are allowed:

(88) baŋgu   yugu-ŋgu   [gunba-ŋu-ru   baŋgul
      DEM.ERG.IV   tree-ERG   cut-REL-ERG   DEM.ERG.IV
      yaṛa-ŋgu]   ŋayguna   biriḏu   balga-n
      man-ERG   1SG.ACC   nearly   hit-PRS/PST
      'The tree which the man cut nearly fell on me.'

(89) ŋaḏa   [balan   ḏugumbil   ɲina-ŋu]   buṛa-n
      1SG.NOM   DEM.ABS.II   woman.ABS   sit-REL   see-PRS/PST
      'I am watching the woman who is sitting down.'

---

[32] For another Australian example, see Dench (forthcoming), who discusses the development, in Nyamal, of an original dative-marked nominalized construction into a narrative present, via independent purposive, to a use to describe culmination points in sequential narratives ('narrative prospective'), to narrative present more generally, to standard present.

But they may be also used as main clauses, in which case only the completive interpretation is allowed:

(90) ŋaɟa   babil-ŋa-ŋu   ba-gu-m   miraɲ-gu
      1SG.NOM   scrape-ANTIPASS-REL   DEM-DAT-III   black.bean-DAT
      'I've scraped the beans.'

There are many languages around the world where perfect or perfective-type constructions, which originated as copula plus completive or resultative participle, lose the copula through time so that the synchronic past perfective is etymologically a participle of some type. The perfective in most Slavic languages has arisen in this way; in section 11.2.7 we excluded these from being considered 'insubordination' because they have a biclausal (or at least biverbal) origin. Functionally, however, the Dyirbal and Kayardild examples discussed above may be very similar, except that the lack of a copula in their previous language states meant that participles and nominalizations of various types could serve directly as a nonfinite predicate, without needing an auxiliary verb.

A non-Australian example of nominalized / gerundive forms developing an incipient independent use in a way that is reminiscent of Dyirbal and Kayardild is in the South Semitic language Tigrinya. Here what Leslau (1941: 85) calls the 'gerundive' (*gérondif*),[33] which can be used in subordinate clauses to express simultaneity or anteriority with respect to the main clause, may also be used independently to express a resultant state. Although Leslau's description actually cites the independent use first, other authors emphasize that the dependent use is primary. Kogan (1997: 439) states:

Used independently, the gerund denotes the result of an action in the past (mostly from verbs with stative meaning)...In most cases, however, the gerund is found followed by another verb in the perfect or imperfect and denotes an action simultaneous or anterior to this one [the action expressed by the main verb].

It is also possible to use the gerund independently in the closely related Amharic:

---

[33] In discussing the historical origins of the gerund, in turn, Leslau proposes (1995: 356), for the closely related Amharic, that a form like *säbr-o* 'having broken.3M', derives 'through a process such as 'his breaking' > 'he breaking' > 'he having broken' '. This elaborates the earlier position taken by Cohen, who asserted for Amharic: 'Le gérondif, ancien nom verbal conjugué au moyen des pronoms régimes de nom, ne sert normalement, lorsqu'il est seul, qu'à constituer des sortes de propositions subordonnées incidentes' (Cohen 1936: 181).

At times the gerund stands alone at the end of the sentence without a principal verb. It then behaves like a finite verb. This usage of the gerund occurs when it refers to, or is a continuation of, a thought expressed in the preceding statement, or in answer to a question. The gerund is then uttered with a rising-falling tone on the last syllable. (Leslau 1995: 363)

For example, in replying to the question *käbbädä yät allä* [Kebbede where exist.3M.PFV] 'where is Kebbede?', a possible reply is the 3rd masculine gerundive form *hed-o*, lit. 'his having gone', but translatable in this context as 'Why, he has already left.' Given the availability of ample textual material in the liturgical language Ge'ez, ancestral to both Amharic and Tigrinya, a diachronic study of how this construction developed would be fascinating, but as far as I know has yet to be carried out: Leslau (1999: 81) writes: 'The details on the gerund in the various Ethiopian languages still await a thorough investigation.'

11.3.3 *Signalling presupposed material*

A third function of insubordinated clauses is to signal high levels of presupposed material in the insubordinated proposition, i.e. signalling relatively specific presuppositions about the discourse context in which the sentence can occur (see also Chapter 7 above by Kalinina and Sumbatova for a discussion of the impact of high presuppositionality in the use of nonfinite forms in Daghestanian main clauses). Specific examples of this use of insubordination are (a) negation, (b) focus constructions, (c) discourse contrast, (d) stipulated conditions before assenting to preceding assertions in interaction, (e) reiterations, (f) disagreement with assertions by the previous speaker. I shall discuss each in turn below.

11.3.3.1 *Negation*   Givón (1979: 107) has observed that 'negative assertions are used in language in contexts where the corresponding affirmative has been mentioned, deemed likely, or where the speaker assumes that the hearer—erroneously—holds to a belief in the truth of that affirmative.' Leech (1983: 298–9) makes a similar point in terms of implicature from negatives to positives: 'If X is a negative proposition, and if F is the most communicatively significant feature within the "scope of negation" in X and if Y is a proposition identical to X except that it is positive and does not contain F, then X implicates Y.' We shall see below that many languages display formal similarities between negatives and subordinate forms, and will account for this by proposing that such negatives were originally subordinated to main clauses bearing the main assertion.

Kroskrity (1984) proposes this line of analysis for Arizona Tewa (Tanoan, Kiowa-Tanoan).[34] In this language negative verbs combine a prefix *we-* with a suffix *-dí* which is formally a subordinator. Compare (92), which exemplifies a subordinate adverbial clause, with (93), a simple negative clause:

(91)   he'i   se   na-mɛn-dí   'o-yohk'ó
       that   man   3.STAT-go-SUBOR   1.STAT-be.asleep
       'When that man went, I was asleep.' (Kroskrity 1984)

(92)   sen   kwiyó   we-mán-mun-dí
       man   woman   NEG1-3>3.ACTIVE-see-NEG.2
       'The man did not see the woman.'

It is important to note that in Arizona Tewa there is no grammatical means for indicating the scope of the negation within the clause itself, unlike in the Isletan Tiwa dialect, where different negation scopes are shown by different placements of the negative affix (Leap 1975; Kroskrity 1984).[35] Instead it simply conjoins, as a main clause, an assertion which implicates the scope of the negative. Examples (93–5) below exemplify the use of this construction to negate subject/agent, object and predicate respectively. Note that the reanalysis of *-dí* as a negative suffix means that, in modern Tiwa, it must be followed by a homophonous doublet acting as a subordinator.

(93)   Kada   we-mán-mun-dí-dí   dó-mun
       Kada   NEG-3/3ACTIVE-see-NEG-SUBOR   1/3.ACTIVE-see
       'Kada did not see her/him/it, I did.'

(94)   sæ'éwe   we-dó-ku:p'e-wan-dí-dí   t'ummele
       pottery   NEG-1/3ACTIVE-sell-COMPL-NEG-SUBOR   plaque
       dó-ku:p'e-wan
       1/3ACTIVE-sell-COMPL
       'I didn't sell pottery, I sold a (wicker) plaque.'

(95)   he'i   kwiyó   sen   we-mán-he:-'an-dí-dí
       that   woman   man   NEG-3/3ACTIVE-sick-COMPL-NEG-SUBOR
       mán-hey
       3/3ACTIVE-kill
       'That woman didn't make the man sick, she killed him.'

Kroskrity proposes that, at an earlier phase of the language, negatives were typically biclausal structures with the following structural analysis:

[34] Kroskrity imputes this to Uto-Aztecan, following Whorf and Trager (1937), but recent classifications do not support this lumping and consider it part of Kiowa-Tanoan (Campbell 1997: 138–9). I thank Marianne Mithun for this information.

[35] Kroskrity argues that the availability of positional options is an Isletan innovation.

(96)

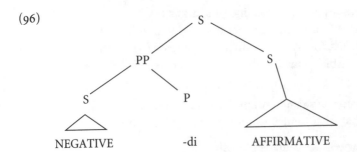

The *-di* subordinator, through association with negation, was probably reanalysed as a negative suffix. A further reanalysis saw 'elliptical negatives' (the negative S plus subordinator but without any following affirmative S) reanalysed as simple negatives through insubordination, and the *-di* reanalysed as a negative rather than a subordinate marker. Once this reanalysis had taken place, overtly subordinated clauses then needed to be marked by a second *-di*, as exemplified in (93–5).

Kroskrity cites a number of other languages in which negatives are morphologically associated with subordinate clauses. In the Numic language Kawaiisu (Munro 1976: 308), part of the Numic branch of Uto-Aztecan (Campbell 1997: 134), negatives differ from affirmatives in three ways: by an overt negative marker, by assigning object case to their subject, and by employing 'series II' verb endings, characteristic of embedded or nominalized clauses. An example is:

(97)   ta'nipazi-a   yuwaati   pikee-keene-neena   momo'o-na
      man-O   NEG   see-PST.SERIES.II-3ANIM>3ANIM   woman-O
      'The man didn't see the woman.'

In Western Mono (Bethel et al., n.d.), another Numic language within Uto-Aztecan (Campbell 1997: 134), negative imperatives take a subordinating suffix on the verb.

A number of Australian languages display similar correlations. In the Warburton Ranges dialect of Western Desert (Douglas 1964: 53), negatives usually juxtapose a positive verb bearing tense/mood/aspect with a negated nominalized verb. (98) and (99) illustrate negative imperatives; (100) a negative indicative.

(98)   wangka-ntja-maal-pa   kanmara-ri-ø!
      talk-NMLZ-NEG-NOM   quiet-INCH-IMP
      'Don't talk, be quiet! ' (Lit. 'Not talking, be quiet.')

(99) tjarpatju-nkutja-maal-tu   yila-la!
      insert-NMLZ-NEG-ERG   pull-IMP
      'Don't insert it, pull it!'

(100) ngayulu wangka-ntja-maal-pa   kanmara-ri-ngu
      I   talk-NMLZ-NEG-NOM   quiet-INCH-PST.COMPL
      'I didn't talk, but became quiet.'

In some related dialects all negative verb forms are historically nominalizations suffixed with the privative ('without') case; it is no longer necessary
to conjoin an affirmative. In the Yankunytjatjara dialect, negation simply
involves privativized nominalization:

(101) katja-lu   wangka   ngayi-nya   kuli-ntja   wiya
      son-ERG   talk.ACC me-ACC   listen-NMLZ   not
      '(My) son doesn't heed my words.'

Similar historical processes may be assumed to have applied in other
languages, such as Kaytetye (not closely related to Western Desert), where
negative forms of the verb employ a privative nominalized form:

(102) ape-nge-wanenye
      go-NMLZ-PRIV
      'not go' (Lit. 'without going')

It seems likely that in all these languages the use of insubordinated verb forms in
negative clauses arose in the way outlined by Kroskrity. At first subordinate
negative verbs were conjoined with main clause affirmatives; then the affirmatives were ellipsed; then the originally elliptical negative was reanalysed as a free-
standing main clause, and the subordinating morphology was reanalysed as
negative morphology. The synchronic result is that one type of main clause, high
in presuppositionality, shows morphological affinities with subordinate clauses.

11.3.3.2 *Contrastive focus constructions* Negative clauses presuppose the
existence of some affirmative clause which is being disconfirmed by the
negative. Contrastive focus[36] clauses are high in presuppositionality for
another reason: they presuppose a clause which is similar, but predicated of
another referent. For example, the relative clause *It's John who I saw*
presupposes the relevance of a clause asserting that I saw someone other
than John.[37] Many languages develop focus clauses from subordinate clauses

---

[36] The term 'focus' is plagued with many interpretations in linguistics; here it is being used solely in
the sense of 'contrastive focus'.
[37] See Schachter (1973) on formal relations between focus and relativization.

by a route something like the English cleft, without the initial presentative: 'John SUB I saw.'

An example of a language using subordinate forms for marked focus constructions is the Australian language Ngandi (Heath 1985). Like many Australian languages, Ngandi has a single generalized subordinate clause type, marked formally by the prefix *ga-* inside the verbal word. Typically 'a simple subordinated *-ga-* clause functions to provide background for the juxtaposed (usually directly following) matrix clause' (p. 98). This meshes with a leisurely discourse style in which each previous clause is reiterated as background to the next, as in:

(103) gu-wolo-yuŋ   bulkuy   ɲar-uḍu-ni   ɲar-ga-ruḍu-ni
       GU.class-that-ABS indeed   1PL.EXC-go-PRS   1PL.EXC-SUB-go-PRS
       ɲar-waɳʔḍu-ni
       1PL.EXC-look-PRS
       '...then indeed we go along; going along, we take a look...'

Alongside this genuine subordinate use, we find formally subordinate verbs in *-ga-* also used for what Heath calls 'focus constructions', in which 'a constituent other than the verb is highlighted as clause focus'. These may be translated into English by inversion constructions (104), passives (105), or cleft constructions (106). From a discourse perspective, what is important is that the non-focused sections are presupposed, but the connection of the focus with the non-focused part is newly asserted.

(104) gu-ḍawal-gic   ŋa-ga-ruḍu-ŋi
       GU.class-country-ALL   1SG-SUB-go-PST.CONT
       'I went to the country', 'To the country I went.'

(105) gu-mulmu   ɲigu-ga-ra-ŋi   ni-ḍeremu-ṯu
       GU.class-grass 3M.SG.GU-SUBOR-see-PST.CONT   M.SG-MAN-ERG
       'The man saw the grass', 'The grass was seen by the man.'

(106) Q: ba-ɲja   ba-ga-ruḍu-ŋi
           PL-who   3PL-SUB-go-PST.CONT
       A: ni-ḍeremu   ni-ga-ruḍu-ŋi
           M.SG-man   3M.SG-SUB-go-PST.CONT
       Q: 'Who went? A: 'The man went / It was the man who went.'

It seems likely that constructions like these have evolved via a cleft-type construction in which a NP was presented simply by mentioning it (i.e. with no overt presentative), and followed by a relative clause: '(it's) the man (who) went (SUBOR)'. Subsequently a merger of intonation contours yielded a single clause with a marked informational status. What is important for our analysis here, and parallel to the case with insubordinate negative clauses, is that the insubordinated part (here, the *ga*-verb) is presupposed, not asserted.

Similar focusing uses of a generalized subordinate clause type are found in several other Gunwingguan languages of Arnhem Land, including Rembarrnga (McKay 1975), Ngalakan (Merlan 1983), Mangarayi (Merlan 1981; 1982) and Jawoyn (Merlan 1981).

In Rembarrnga subordination is signalled by a special series of pronominal pronouns to the verb. Subordinate clauses have a wide range of functions, both adnominal and adverbial, with the exact interpretation determined by context and by the TAM categories. Of interest here is the fact that subordinate clauses can be used independently for contrasted objects, as in:

(107) yaṛap:aʔ-waɲʔ-miɲ   muṭulŋu-kaɲa-kaɲaŋʔ ken
       1unit.AUG-look-PST.PUN saratoga.fish-DIM-small woops
       muṭulŋu-kaɲa-kaɲaŋʔ?   dirmar-kaɲa-kaɲaŋ?   biri-ḍoḷʔ-miɲ
       saratoga-DIM-small   barramundi-DIM-small 3AUG.SUBOR-float-
                                                      PST.PUN
       'We saw a lot of little saratogas... Woops! Little saratogas?... It
       was little barramundis which were floating.' (McKay 1975: 346)

In Ngalakan such generalized subordination is achieved by suffixing -*gVn* to the verb. Historically this probably derives from a complementizing use of a dative/purposive case marker, which has the form -*gan*, -*gen*, or -*gin* in other Gunwinyguan languages of the area. (108) illustrates a true subordinate use—here interpreted as a relative clause—while (109) illustrates an object-contrasting use in an insubordinated clause.

(108) ŋunbu-yiniʔ-ganiɲ   ju-goʔje-ʔgen ju-bolo-ʔgon
       3/1-tell-AUX.PST.CONT F-that-DAT   F-old.person-DAT
       meɲeri   Ø-maniɲ-miɲ-gin   mu-juḷuʔ
       Hodgson.Downs   3/3-make-PST.PUN-SUBOR   VEG-lancewood
       'They told me about the old woman who made the lancewood at
       Hodgson Downs.'

(109) ṇu-gunʔbiri baṛamunu   ŋur-ne-ŋa-gan
       M-that   sand.goanna   1INCL.PL-cook-FUT-SUBOR
       'It's the sand goanna we will cook.' / 'We'll cook *the sand goanna*.'

Merlan (1981), whose article describing these constructions explicitly addresses the relationship between mood, focus, and subordination, argues that:

subordination simply acts as an instruction to relate the subordinate clause to some other part of the message, the precise relation being subject to interpretation by a variety of textual and other cues. Subordination in languages like Mangarayi is thus directly and primarily a part of the language system for expressing the relation of parts of the message to other parts. In view of its function in information structuring it is perhaps not surprising to find that in a number of northern languages with general-ized subordinate clauses, that which marks subordination also functions at the intra-clause level in structuring focussed configurations. (p. 200)

In Kayardild (Evans 1995a: 534), object-focused clauses (used, for example, when the object is given but not the subject) are insubordinated; the focused NP is either omitted or escapes case marking:

(110)   ngijuwa   mima-tharra-nth
         1SG.COBL   beget-PST-COBL
         'He's my son.' (Lit. 'I begot (him)'; '(He's the one whom) I begot')

11.3.3.3 *Trans-sentential contrast and switch-reference*   Switch-reference is primarily a device for indicating whether relations of coreference or non-coreference, and perhaps also of temporal or modal equivalence, hold between a matrix and subordinate clause. A clause marked with SR morphology thus presupposes a matrix whose subject differs from its own, or whose tense or modality bears a significant relationship of sameness or difference to its own. In many Australian languages, including the Mparntwe Arrernte case discussed below, there is evidence of a subordinate origin for switch-reference markers, which originate as case markers with clausal scope (Austin 1981b; Dench and Evans 1988).

An example of such canonical SR use from the Central Australian language Mparntwe Arrernte (Wilkins 1988), is the contrast between 'same-subject' (SS) marking on the subordinate clause in (111) and 'different-subject' (DS) marking in (112):

(111)   artwe-le   alye-lhe-me-le   kere   ite-ke
         man-ERG   sing-DTR-NPST.PROG-SS   meat   cook-PST.COMPL
         'The man cooked the meat while singing.'

(112)   artwe   alye-lhe-me-rlenge   ayenge   petye-me
         man   sing-DTR-NPST.PROG-DS   1SG.NOM   come-NPST.PROG
         'I'm coming while the man is singing.'

But switch-reference marking is also sometimes found on independent clauses, where it functions as a cohesive device for indicating tense relations between subsequent independent clauses, or common or disjoint reference across turns by different speakers. Wilkins (1988: 155) cites the following example:

(113) tayele   renhe   kemparre   twe-mele   arlkwe-tyeme
      tail   3SG.ACC   first   hit-ss   eat-PST.PROG
      [long pause]
      ikwere-tayeme   kwele,   arrentye   re   arrate-tyelhe-rlenge
      3SG.DAT-time   HEARSAY   demon   3SG.NOM   appear-go.and.do-DS
      'He chopped up the tail and was eating it. [Long pause]. It was then,
      they say, when the cannibal arrived on the scene.' (Wilkins 1988: 155)

He comments: 'the split into two sentences in this way presumes the
"simultaneity" of the two events, most commonly expressed through
switch-reference clauses, and also serves to highlight the entrance of
a character who is to play an important role as the text unfolds.'

Such uses of SR markers in independent clauses may also be a powerful
device for integrating successive conversational turns: 'a participant in a
conversation may interject, add to, or question the statement of another
participant, by using a sentence that is a clause morphologically subordinated
(marked for same- or different-subject) to a sentence uttered by another
participant.' An example is:

(114) A: yeah,   ikwere-kerte,   re   pente-ke   kwete,
         INTERJ   3SG.DAT-PROP   3ERG   follow-PST.CONT   still
         bullock   re
         bullock   3SG.DEF
         'Yeah, (they walked along) with it. That bullock, he kept on
         following (them).'
      B: nhenge   kaltyirre-mele, eh?
         remember   learn-ss   INTERJ
         'Was (that one we're talking about) learning (as he followed along)?'

Different-subject markers may also indicate contrasting activities or direc-
tions, and as such may become conventionalized at event boundaries such as
leave-takings. John Henderson (p.c.) reports that two common leave-taking
expressions in Mparntwe Arrernte involve different subject markers attached
to independent verbs:

(115) kele   yenge   lhe-me-nge
      OK   I   go-PRS-DS
      'As for me, well I'm off.' (I don't know what you're up to, but...)

(116) urreke   are- tyenhe-nge
      later   see-FUT-DS
      'See you later.'

The function of SR morphology may thus be extended from the grammaticalized linking found in complex sentences to the pragmatically presupposed linking found in conversational turns, and adjacency pairs like leave-taking sequences. In some cases, such as (115), it may be possible to plausibly supply ellipsed material, in which cases we may simply wish to analyse these as cases of ellipsis. In others like (116), however, a stage of conventionalization appears to have been reached where it is no longer normal or even possible to supply the missing material, so we may wish to consider this a case of insubordination.

11.3.3.4 *Conditions on preceding assertions in interaction*   Very similar to the insubordinated SR clause is the adaptation, for cohesive purposes, of other constructions normally associated with subordinated clauses, such as the use of 'if' clauses to limit agreement with a previous speaker by laying down a particular condition (117). As Ford and Thompson (1986: 368) put it in their discussion of this example, 'the speaker who states the condition does not repeat the main clause, but merely gives the condition which relates to a preceding proposition (albeit not the speaker's own claim).' In this case, however, it seems likely that we are only dealing with ellipsis, harnessed to interactional cohesion, since there is obviously recoverable ellipsed material, along the lines of 'I admit that it's possible, if...' in this example.

(117) S: Is it practically impossible to have that [a certain demand curve]?
       I: If you have this base.

11.3.3.5 *Reiteration*   A further example of insubordination in cases high in presuppositionality involves their use in reiteration: clauses of a subordinate form appropriate to embedding under a main clause such as 'I said [ ]' or 'I asked [ ]' may be used independently, with ellipsis of the main clause reporting the speech act. Here the context of mutually manifest repetition makes the restoration of the ellipsed speech act verb quite clear.

We have already seen an example of this from German in section 11.2.6, with verb-final word order being used independently when repeating a question, and the speech act main clauses *ich fragte* 'I asked' or *ich sagte* 'I said' ellipsed. A more intricate example comes from Basque, which uses different subordinate forms for statements, questions, and commands.[38] The basic form of a verb such as *dator* 'is coming' (118) will be changed, when embedded under an epistemic or reportative predicate, to the subjunctive

---

[38] I am indebted to Alan King (1993 and p.c.), from whose work the Basque examples and analysis are adapted.

form *datorrela* (119); when a question (120) is so embedded, the form will be *datorren* (121).

(118) Jon   d-a-tor
       John   3SG.ABS-PRS-come
       'John's coming.'

(119) Uste   d-u-t   Jon   d-a-torr-ela.
       think   3ABS-AUX-1SG.ERG   John   3ABS-PRS-come-DEC.SBJV
       'I think John's coming.'

(120) Jon   d-a-tor?
       John   3SG.ABS-PRS-come
       'Is John coming?'

(121) Ez   d-a-ki-t   (ea)   Jon   d-a-torr-en
       not   3ABS-PR-know-1ERG   DUB   John   3SG.ABS-PRS-come-INT.SBJV
       'I don't know whether John is coming.'

In cases of reiteration, the appropriate subordinate form may be used independently: the declarative subjunctive for a reiterated statement (122) and the interrogative subjunctive for a reiterated question (123). Note that this means that the reiterated, insubordinated clauses make explicit formal distinctions with regard to speech-act type that are not made in the case of the primary main clause.

(122) A: Jon   d-a-tor
          John   3SG.ABS-PRS-come
       B: Zer?
          what
       A: Jon   d-a-tor-**ela**
          John   3SG.ABS-PRS-come-SBJV
       A: 'John's coming.' B: 'What?' A: '(I said) That John's coming.'

(123) A: Jon   d-a-tor?
          John   3SG.ABS-PRS-come
       B: Zer?
          what
       A: Ea   Jon   d-a-torr-en
          DUB   John   3SG.ABS-PRS-come-INT.SBJV
       A: 'Is John coming?' B: 'What?' C: 'Whether John is coming.'

With commands, the main clause imperative construction exemplified in the first line of (124) is replaced by an 'imperative subjunctive' form, as in the third line;[39] the already-insubordinated use of the infinitive for a command, exemplified by the first line of (125), gets replaced under reiteration with the gerundive form in -*tzeko*, in the third line.

(124) A: Etor   zaitez   hona
            come   AUX   here

       B: Zer?
           what

       A: Etor   zaitez-**ela**   hona
            come   2SG.FORMAL.IMP.AUX-IMP.SBJV   here

       A: 'Come here!' B: 'What?' A: '(I said) to come here!'

(125) A: Etorr-i   hona
            come-PTCP   here

       B: Zer?
           what

       A: Eto-**tzeko**   hona
            come-GER   here

       A: 'Come here!' B: 'What?' A: '(I said) to come here!'

In the case of reiterated statements and questions, the subject of the ellipsed main clause is taken to be the 1st person. With reiterated commands, however, the subject may be either the 1st person or a 3rd person, since this pattern of reiteration is not restricted to cases where the speaker who reiterates is the originator of the original speech act. If a mother tells her daughter Mila, for example, to go and tell Mila's sister Pili to come to the house to eat lunch, the command could be reiterated by Mila using the gerundive as follows:

(126) MOTHER: Mila, esan   Pili-ri   etortzeko   bazkaltzera
                 Mila   tell.PTCP   Pili-DAT   come.GER   have.lunch.GER

       MILA: Pili, etortzeko   bazkaltzera!
                Pili   come.GER   have.lunch.GER

       MOTHER: 'Mila, tell Pili to come to eat lunch.'

       MILA: 'Pili, to come to eat lunch.'

Mila thereby conveys quite explicitly that she herself is not the originator of the command, as she would be if she had said:

---

[39] Though Alan King, who supplied these examples, points out that (124) is rather less likely than (125) to occur colloquially because 'colloquially … the forms *etor zaitez* and *etor zaitezela* just aren't used that much (in speech)', creating a stylistic clash between the informality of the structure and the literary sound of this form of the verb (Alan King, email of 4 Apr. 2002).

(127)   MILA: Pili,   etorri   bazkaltzera!
                 Pili   come.PTCP   have.lunch.GER
                 'Pili, come to eat lunch!'

The reiterations discussed here superficially resemble the insubordinated clauses found with free indirect speech discussed in section 11.3.2.1 above, a use that develops into quotative or hearsay evidentials in many languages. However, there are significant differences: reiterations are much more context-specific, presupposing both a preceding question like 'what?' and, before that, the statement, question, or command being reiterated. In addition, reiterations are semantically more specific, in the sense that the subject of the ellipsed clause in reiterations is 1st person (except in the special Basque case of reiterated commands, where it may be either 1st person or a 3rd person close at hand), whereas the subject of the ellipsed clause in evidentializing insubordination is usually a nonspecific 3rd person; 'they', or 'people' or 'the elders'.

The very specific alignments between the various forms of subordinate marker on the Basque verb and corresponding complex-clause structures point to clear sources in elliptical structures in each case. However, the limitations on the person of the subject of the ellipsed clause, and of the ellipsed verb itself, illustrate the transition between stages 2 and 3 of our scenario, in the sense that conventionalized restrictions on interpretation have begun to accrue.

11.3.3.6 *Disagreement with assertions by the previous speaker*   The use in Spanish of insubordinated conditional clauses with *si* (originally 'if') has already been discussed and exemplified (20). Recall that syntactic tests for the main clause status of this construction, such as its behaviour with negative polarity items, were summarized in section 11.1.2, and that the likely development has been from 'if X, (then how can you say Y)' to 'but in fact it's the case that X'. It is worth reiterating here, though, the characterizations that have been given by authors examining this construction. According to Schwenter (1996: 328), uses of insubordinated *si* 'all deal with correcting or modifying underlying pragmatic presuppositions that have been evoked (or inferred) in conversation'. Almela Perez (1985: 8) puts it slightly differently: 'the *si* we are concerned with is adversative: in every case it signifies a frustration of the previous turn; it therefore always allows, before it, the form *pero* [but].'[40] Although there is, in one way, a similarity to the

---

[40] 'El *si* del que nos ocupamos es adversativo: en todos los casos significa una frustración del miembro anterior; por eso siempre admite, precediéndole, la forma *pero*.'

'contrast' use of switch-reference markers discussed in section 11.3.3.3, in those cases there is no perceived incompatibility between the propositions put forth by successive speakers: it is simply a matter of them pointing out some contrast that holds between them, e.g. between what two different participants under discussion are doing. With insubordinated *si* in Spanish, by contrast, the proposition being put forward by the speaker using *si* is logically incompatible with the one it is aimed against. In the first case, then, the first speaker's proposition is presupposed and serves as a point of departure for a contrasting proposition about something else, while in the second case the fact that the first speaker's proposition has been asserted is presupposed, but its truth is then disputed, bringing this usage closer to the use of insubordination with negatives.

11.3.3.7 *Presuppositionalizing insubordination: summary*   In the first three cases discussed above—negatives (11.3.3.1), focus constructions (11.3.3.2), and trans-sentential contrast (11.3.3.3)—the tight grammatical conditions attached to particular subordinate clause constructions become loosened so that they can be satisfied by the broader discourse context rather than by a governing main clause. Negative clauses in Tewa and Western Desert move from needing an overt main clause explicitly expressing the contrasted positive to implicating some general positive state of affairs calculable from context. Focusing subordinate clauses in a number of Australian languages move from requiring a contrasted clause, or the overt equational element of a cleft construction, to implicating such a component: roughly, from 'It was X which were floating' to 'X which were floating'. Generalizations from switch-reference proper to trans-sentential contrast more generally in languages like Mparntwe Arrernte involve the ellipsis of the contrasted element: '[X is/may be Ving], while C-SR.'

Free-standing conditions (11.3.3.4) and reiterations (11.3.3.5) remain closer to the original construction: their context-specificity means that the candidate ellipsed clause is heavily restricted. The 'disagreeing *si*' construction in Spanish (11.3.3.6), like free-standing conditions and reiterations, remains tightly bound in terms of being restricted to second turns, though its semantics has moved further away from what can be readily stated by restoring a conversationally restricted main clause.

In each of these six subtypes, grammatical machinery that originally developed around overt relations between a main and subordinate clause, often using the inherently two-place predicate expressed by complementizing case, is subsequently generalized to encode similar relations between the insubordinated clause and some other part of the discourse. This latter may be unexpressed, or no longer involved in a subordinating grammatical relation to the insubordinated clause.

11.4 Multi-purpose insubordination, constructional indeterminacy, and pragmatic interpretation

In a number of languages, insubordinated clauses have what at first sight seem to be a bewilderingly wide range of functions. In this section I examine two Australian languages—Gooniyandi and Kayardild—with such 'multi-purpose' insubordination. I show that the functional range of insubordinated clauses is essentially the union of the three higher-level functions above: indirectionalizing, modalizing, and presuppositionalizing. I also examine the extent to which the precise interpretation can in large measure be recovered pragmatically because of predictable interactions with verbal tense/aspect/mood categories.

11.4.1 *Gooniyandi* [41]

In this non-Pama-Nyungan language (McGregor 1988; 1990) so-called 'subjunctive' clauses, marked by an enclitic *-ja*, can occur either as subordinate clauses or independently. I shall assume that the subordinate function is primary and that the independent use results from insubordination. [42] McGregor identifies the following 'common core of meaning' for subjunctive clauses in Gooniyandi, whether main or subordinate:

[T]he speaker is not asserting or proposing the propositional content of the clause; he is neither asserting/proposing that the situation will occur (realized by future tense), nor that it might have occurred (realized by potential mode). Rather, what he is asserting/proposing is that the propositional content of the clause is hypothesized, supposed, reckoned, guessed, hoped and so on ... The enclitic *-ja* functions like the logical operator |-. In other words, the speaker is not asserting/proposing a proposition about the world, but rather, a proposition about a proposition about the world, in effect that he will entertain its validity. (p. 41)

[41] In spelling the language name I am employing the practical spelling now preferred for this language, and used in McGregor's (1990) reference grammar, but which differs from the spelling Kuniyanti used in McGregor (1988). Examples retain the orthography of the source.

[42] Because there is no other formal marker of subordination, McGregor avoids taking the subordinate use of subjunctives as primary, and implies that they share the same multifunctional characteristics whether they are subordinate or independent. The analysis I propose here suggests they would have originated as subordinate clauses, a question that can only be answered by historical work on related languages.

The specific nature of this 'second order proposition', however, results from interaction of the subjunctive clitic with the tense markers—past, present, and irrealis—and with the person of the subject.

Combined with the past tense, the subjunctive suggests a statement about the past made on the basis of inference, as in (128).

(128)   (A police posse discovers the recently vacated dinner camp of a
        group of Aborigines they are following. The head tracker asserts
        (to the policemen):)
        ngapjawirra   ngamunyali
        eat.SBJV.3PL   before.REPET
        'They were eating here not long ago.' (McGregor 1988: 42)

Combined with the future, the subjunctive can produce a request for permission with a 1st person subject (129; cf. the Yankunytjatjara example (38b)), and a prediction with a non-1st person subject (130).

(129)   nganyi   wartngiri   mikarliminhi   majayu
        I   go.PRS.1SG   I.told.him   boss
        wartjawulunayi   ngarraki   yawarta
        go.SBJV.FUT.1SG>3DU   my   horse
        kay   wartpinayi   mikamingarra
        OK   go.FUT.3DU   he.told.me
        '"I'm going", I told the boss.
        "I might (would like to) take the two horses."
        "OK, take them", he told me.' (McGregor 1988: 40)

(130)   paplikajnhingi   ngilangku   palma   yuwarni   thutjawingkani
        pub.ABL   east   creek   one   descend.SBJV.FUT.2SG
        'From the pub you'll go east, and cross one creek.' (McGregor 1988: 39)

Combined with the present, the subjunctive is used 'to avoid stating the obvious by intruding his own attitude'; this may have the effect of strengthening the epistemic status of the proposition rather than weakening it, along the lines of English *I reckon I walk*.

(131)   wartjangiri
        go.SBJV.PRS.1SG
        'I walk hard.'

Combined with the irrealis, the subjunctive suggests that the speaker 'may suppose or entertain the notion that the situation occurred even though he knows it didn't':

(132) yuwulungka   marniwa   kartjayuni
       man   his.sister hit.SBJV.IRR
       'The man might have hit his sister (though I know he didn't).'

The subjunctive in Gooniyandi, then, signals that the speaker is not asserting/ proposing a proposition about the world, but rather, a proposition about a proposition about the world. The exact nature of the second order proposition, however, is not directly asserted but left to inference: it may involve circumstantial evidence (128), an indirect seeking of permission (129), or even strengthened assertion (131).

11.4.2 *Kayardild*

The functional range of the Gooniyandi independent subjunctive covers certain indirectionalizing uses (requests for permission) and a number of evidentializing or modalizing ones (hearsay, inference, assertion of conviction, prediction), but not the presuppositionalizing or deictic-recentring sets. In Kayardild the problem is more complicated still, since all main functional types of insubordination are present: interpersonal coercion, modal (both deontic and epistemic), and presuppositionalizing.[43]

Presuppositionalizing insubordination in Kayardild, in the form of object-topicalized clauses, is always formally distinctive: the object is either omitted, as in (113) above, or appears in the nominative (133) instead of the usual object-marking (which would here take the form of the modal proprietive plus complementizing oblique case, giving the form *ngaarrkuuntha* were it not for the rule assigning object topics the nominative—see Evans 1995a).

(133) kambuda   barji-j,   ngaarrka   barji-ja
       pandanus.fruit.NOM fall-ACT   pandanus.nut.NOM   fall-ACT
       rar-umban-da   warmarr.   [mutha-wuu-ntha
       south-ORIG-NOM   wind.NOM   much-MPROP-COBL
       darr-u-ntha   diya-juu-ntha   ngaarrk]COBL
       time-MPROP-COBL   eat-MPROP-COBL   pandanus.nut.NOM
       'The pandanus fruit falls, the pandanus nut falls at the time of the south wind. (One) can go on eating pandanus nut for a long time.'

Even though the odd-topic formal pattern—absent or nominative object— always overtly signals the presence of a presuppositionalizing function in the

---

[43] The historical operation of insubordination, in the form of 'modal case', which results from deictic recentring of tense/mood categories, was discussed in section 11.3.2.4; since the latter clauses have no particular synchronic evidence for primarily subordinate status, being insubordinated purely in a diachronic sense, they will not be discussed further here.

sense of object-focusing, it does not follow that this is the only function of such clauses. In (37), for example, there is simultaneous signalling of the utterance's function as an indirect request (through the choice of potential verb plus complementizing case), and as an object-focused construction (through the appearance of the object in the nominative).

So although an algorithm for interpreting insubordinated clauses in Kayardild can begin by searching for the manifestations of 'odd-topic marking' and assigning any insubordinated clauses with this feature to the object-topicalized category discussed in section 11.3.3.2 above, it cannot then conclude that this is the only aspect of insubordinated interpretation to be given to such a clause, since there may be other aspects (e.g. indirect request) motivating the choice in addition to the fact of object topic.

Nor does this exhaust the possibilities of using insubordinated clauses for a presupposed discourse context. For example, insubordinated clauses in the potential may be used to give consequences of a prior assertion, comparable to the independent use of a *so* or *so that* clause in English. An example from a Kayardild argument between two women—D, who is voicing her grievance at having lost her husband to M—is the following, which involves insubordinated clauses in the second and third turns (see Evans 1995a: 626–30 for the full text). In the second turn, by M, the insubordinated clause, in conjunction with the stress on the subject pronoun, expresses contrastive focus on the subject: '*I've* taken him.' But in the third turn the insubordinated clause, which here has no arguments in the nominative or ellipsed, is expressing the consequence of the action described in the preceding two turns: 'so that I'll be left with nothing':

(134) D: ngijin-jina   dun-kina   nyingka   buru-tharr !
           my-MABL   husband-MABL   2SG.NOM   take-PST
           'You've taken my husband!'

       M: [ngijuwa   buru-tharra-nth,   natha-maru-tharra-ntha
           1SG.SBJV.COBL   take-PST-COBL   camp-V.DAT-PST-COBL
           ngijin-maru-tharra-nth!]_{COBL}
           my-V.DAT-PST-COBL
           'I've taken (him), to my camp!'

       D: [ngijuwa   wirdi-juu-ntha   warirra-ntha   wirdi-juu-nth!]_{COBL}
           1SG.SBJV.COBL   remain-POT-COBL   nothing-COBL   remain-POT-COBL
           'So I'll be left with nothing!'

This leaves the problem of determining the meaning of insubordinated clauses lacking object topic marking. Table 11.1 summarizes the interpretive

options available for three selected TAM categories in Kayardild insubordinated clauses. Note that for the past tense two interpretations are possible,
and for the potential and immediate, three each. How far can these various
functions of insubordinated clauses be derived from functions of regular
subordinate clauses? Can we derive the insubordinated meanings from the
subordinate ones, via main clause ellipsis? Or is there a sufficient difference
that we should attempt to associate constructional meanings directly with
the various types of insubordinate clause?

In support of an ellipsis analysis one can cite the many constructions,
exemplified in the preceding sections, where appropriate main clauses can
readily be supplied. To the insubordinated *yaluluntha karnajurrka niwanjurrk*
[flame burns him]$_{COBL}$, for example, we can supply a main clause *ngada
kurrija* 'I see'. This would account for the presence of complementizing case,
the immediate verb inflection, and the meaning supplied on the occasion of
the utterance: 'I see him being burned by the flames.'

Further support for the ellipsis analysis comes from the many interpretations available for a given insubordinated clause, as represented partially
in Table 11.1. Although I have given very specific translations to the

TABLE 11.1. Interpretive options for insubordinated Kayardild clauses in the
immediate, potential, or past

Interpretation of reconstructed clause	Tense/mood of insubordinated clause		
	Immediate	Potential	Past
Epistemic	Perception (62, 63) I see/hear etc. that X	Knowledge (65) I know/assume that X	Inference (64) What I behold must result from X
Directive	Hint: (do something) because X is happening now (44)	Hint: (do something) so that X will happen (37)	Hint: (do something) because X has happened (45)
Discourse context		Consequence of previously stated fact: (V has happened) so X will happen (134)	
Tense	X is the case now (86, 87)		

insubordinated clauses in my examples, it must be borne in mind that these are utterance rather than sentence translations, and involve interpretations of the particular contexts in which they were recorded. Many would, in other contexts, be given quite a different interpretation. This makes it impossible to pair insubordinated clauses directly with constructional meanings (e.g. those summarizable as 'perception evidential' or 'polite command').

Such a wide range of interpretations is available for two main reasons. First, there is a range of possible matrix predicators, e.g. 'see', 'hear', 'smell' in the case of perception predicates. Secondly, some tense/moods in the insubordinated clause are potentially compatible with several types of matrix predicator. For example, potential clauses are compatible with main clause imperatives (giving rise to the 'hint' use exemplified in 37), and with actual main clauses of different types (giving rise to the 'inference' and 'consequence' meanings exemplified in 65 and 134 respectively). Only hortative and desiderative insubordinated clauses (not shown in Table 11.1) have a single reconstructed clause type, although even there the actual predicate ('say' vs. 'ask' vs. 'warn') is not specified.

Against the pure form of the ellipsis analysis one can make two arguments. First, it is rather difficult to relate some insubordinated meanings (such as the 'relevant present') directly to those found in complex clauses, and even in some other cases (such as the 'inferential' use of the past and potential) some semantic bridging is necessary. In such cases it seems more reasonable to see ellipsis as a first step in the development of the construction, as outlined in section 11.1.2, but to attribute the detailed semantic characteristics to 'depragmaticization', the conversion of pragmatic enrichment (such as perceptual comments being most commonly made of present events) to constructional meaning.

Secondly, there appear to be restrictions on what may be the subject of the 'restored' main clause predicate if this is a perception verb: the subject of the higher clause is always interpreted as 1st person in a declarative and second person in a question. There are good pragmatic reasons for this—a perceptually based assertion about an ongoing situation naturally implicates that the perceiver is the speaker, and a perceptually based question naturally implicates that the perceiver is the addressee[44]—and these extra constraints appear to have accrued to the relevant constructions by depragmaticization.

---

[44] See Hargreaves (1991) for a discussion of how evidentials in Kathmandu Newari take the speaker as epistemic source in statements, and the hearer in questions.

The balance of evidence, then, supports a hybrid position. On the one hand, in many cases the presence of complementizing case seems to signal simply that the hearer should interpret an insubordinated clause by inferentially restoring an ellipsed, contextually appropriate main clause that is grammatically compatible with the insubordinated clause (in the sense that it would assign complementizing case, and use an appropriate sequence of tenses). On the other hand, there are further, conventionalized constraints on the interpretation of some insubordinated clauses that suggest they have been grammaticized: the meaning of these constructions is more specific than one would expect if it were simply a matter of restoring ellipsed material.

11.5 Conclusion

This chapter has been a heuristic one, concerned with exploring constructions which tend to get marginalized in linguistic analysis and description. As a result, it is hard to get a systematic picture across the world's languages. If the phenomena have eluded description in English, it is certainly likely that less well-described languages will have examples of the phenomenon that have yet to be made available for typological comparison, although working in their favour is that corpus- and fieldwork-based descriptions are less likely to dismiss relevant data in the way that Matthews (1981: 40–42) dismisses incomplete utterances as 'of no concern to syntax, except as a source of confusion in our data'. I hope that the preliminary systematization of data presented here will encourage linguists to take these constructions more seriously, and have no doubt that we will see further formal and functional types being identified.

Insubordination is an important phenomenon because of the unusual way the direction of diachronic change runs: from subordinate clause to main clause, from morphosyntax to discourse, and (in its initial stage) from grammar to pragmatics. In each of these, it is a sort of backwash against the prevailing direction in which historical developments are supposed to occur. For functionalists who have shown us in how many ways grammar can emerge from discourse, it is a reminder that elaborate grammatical structures can also be partly disassembled and co-opted as discourse devices. For theories of pragmatic implicature, it illustrates how projected grammatical structures can act as a scaffold for the inferencing process.

The material we have surveyed here is relevant to debates about finiteness in several ways. First is the issue of how far main clause status entails finiteness. Just as insubordination can make it harder to maintain a crisp categorical distinction between subordinate and main clauses, so it can blur the boundary between finite and nonfinite clauses. In particular cases, however, we want to know what motivates the discrepancy: should we appeal to characteristics of nonfiniteness in particular (such as lack of assertativity)? Or should we see it as following from broader characteristics of insubordination, as sketched here, which happen to bear nonfinite constructions up into main clause structures along with others which it would be artificial to term nonfinite, such as clauses introduced with complementizers or general markers of subordination?

Secondly, we want to know whether the changes from subordinate to main clause status necessarily entail changes in finiteness as part of the reanalysis process. Again, considering a broader range of insubordination types, only some involving nonfinite constructions, makes it seem less of an automatic consequence that change to main clause status would automatically increase the finiteness of a construction. The redeployment of linkages from intraclausal to general discourse links, for example, has nothing to do with finiteness as it is normally defined. Accepting insubordination as a common process makes it clearer what is special about finiteness, by dissociating it from the main vs. subordinate clause parameter.

Thirdly, finiteness, like any other semantic value, is subject to diachronic change. Speakers draw on nonfinite constructions to detach themselves from speech-act or epistemic commitments, whether by presenting infinitives as impersonal alternatives that avoid making the command stance overt or by using participles in cases of hearsay to avoid taking responsibility for direct assessment of epistemic value. This process of sign-building means that the contexts and communicative intentions behind these initially disembodied nonfinite statements gradually attach to the constructions themselves, turning infinitives into normal imperatives, and erstwhile participles into hearsay evidentials. Once this process occurs, we do indeed see a semantic shift towards finiteness as insubordination occurs.

Returning to the general problem posed by insubordination for grammatical description, as reanalysis of erstwhile subordinate clauses (nonfinite or otherwise) into main clauses proceeds, at least some of their morphosyntactic characteristics are no longer sufficient conditions for identifying a clause as subordinate. In the first stage of the process, the distinction can be saved by treating insubordinated clauses as underlying subordinate clauses whose main clauses have been ellipsed but can plausibly be restored for analytic purposes. At the second stage, while the structure itself may still be adequately described by treating it as an underlying subordinate clause, this can only be achieved by turning a blind eye to the greater semantic specificity associated with the insubordinated clause, and ignoring the fact that certain logically possible 'restored' meanings or functions are never found with the insubordinated construction. By the final stage these clauses have been so nativized as main clauses that the generalizations gained by drawing parallels with subordinate structures are outweighed by the artificiality of not including them in the muster of main clause types.

12

Finiteness in first and second language acquisition

PETRA GRETSCH AND CLIVE PERDUE

12.1 Survey on finiteness in language acquisition

12.1.1 *The role of finiteness in the adult language*

Finiteness is traditionally associated with the categories of person and tense. The notion of finiteness has however much wider ramifications, as the other contributions to this volume make clear. The aim of this chapter is to unfold the complexity of the label 'finiteness' by splitting it up into a structural component, morphological finiteness, and an interpretational component, semantic finiteness. Both components may be conflated in individual target languages, but we can show that they pose separated steps for children as well as adults in language acquisition. This unexpected similarity of first and second language acquisition confirms theoretical considerations which keep the formal and the functional side of finiteness apart, assuming that the main function of finiteness is being the carrier of assertion (cf. Klein 1998).

In this chapter, we concentrate on the acquisition of finiteness in Germanic languages (German for L1 and Dutch/English/German as target for L2), and merely base our general discussion of finiteness in this section on the following problems that will be relevant for the analyses we discuss further on.

- Finiteness has been traditionally discussed on the level of morphology, for languages which display a verbal morphology. A problem that arises here is whether it is generally possible to formulate an inflectionally based definition of finiteness.
- Recent syntactic work has pointed to an interplay between verbal morphology and the licensing of subjects, verb placement (including

the Germanic V2-rule), and constraints on gapping. The inflection category is seen to be obligatory.

- On the semantic level, finiteness has been shown to affect the interpretation of indefinite noun phrases, and much recent work has analysed the interplay of finiteness and temporality, often inspired by the Reichenbachian distinction between speech time, reference time, and event time.
- The relation between finiteness and the assertive force of a sentence is a well-studied phenomenon in enunciative approaches to language, and has led more recently to the analysis of the interaction of finiteness with other scope-inducing elements: finiteness and focus particles such as English *also* and the like, especially in the languages to be discussed in this contribution.

We therefore understand finiteness as a notion to be analysed from structural, semantic, and pragmatic points of view, and adopt Lasser's (1997: 77) terminology, distinguishing between 'the overt form that finiteness takes and the invisible function that finiteness serves', respectively M(orphological)-finiteness versus S(emantic)-finiteness.

For our concerns, there are two sides to M-finiteness: the (finite) inflectional morphology of the Germanic languages, and the syntax that goes hand in hand with the finite/infinite morphological split. As we shall see, these two levels must be kept apart—not only for developmental studies but also for diachronic studies (see Ledgeway, Chapter 10 above). Thus we will use the term M-finiteness restrictively to denote (finite) verbal inflection, and speak of the syntactic/structural correlates of M-finiteness.

Whereas grammatical form is treated at the level of sentence structure, with the sentence basis as its kernel, semantic interpretation is bound to the utterance. In a very preliminary way S-finiteness can be defined as the condition for an independent interpretation of a sentence: an independently interpretable sentence is semantically finite. Thus semantic finiteness is related to the utterance and concerns all questions of reference, i.e. the mapping of the sentence onto the context of the utterance. This will be called in the following the 'anchoring' of a sentence. Anchoring sets the deictic binding (reference) of the actants of the scenario, and the temporal (spatial) anchorage of the event or the state designated by the sentence basis: in the simple declarative case, this descriptive content is asserted to be true at the moment of temporal anchorage. We develop this idea immediately below. Thus in a certain tradition of semantic reasoning semantic finiteness corresponds to the pragmatic (contextual, enunciative) specification of a sentence.

S-finiteness centrally involves the speaker's making a claim about a time span. Klein (1994; 1998) terms this operation 'assertion' (ASN),[1] and illustrates it with the following example:

(1)   The book WAS on the table.

In this example, *WAS* is marked by contrastive stress, and the contrast can involve either the time-span ('the book WAS on the table, but isn't any longer'), or the claim ('you said it wasn't, but in fact the book WAS on the table'). Thus the M-finite element *WAS* 'carries (at least) two distinct meaning components: (1) the tense component: it marks past, in contrast to present or future; (2) it marks the 'claim'—the fact that the situation described by the utterance indeed obtains, in contrast to the opposite claim' (Klein 1998: 227).

Following Klein (1994), we will call the time span for which the speaker makes a claim the topic time (TT), in contrast to the time of situation (TSit), i.e. the interval occupied on the time axis by the situation talked about. The notional category of tense then expresses the relation of TT to the deictically given time of utterance (TU), and the notional category of grammatical aspect expresses the relation between TT and TSit. Starren (2001) uses the metaphor of the video camera to explain TT—it is the time the camera is 'shooting'. Imagine you are a witness in court, and the judge asks you, 'What did you see when you entered the room?' The crucial time span corresponds to your entering the room, and just this time span is filmed by the camera. You answer, 'A man was trying to open the safe. He looked Japanese.' The time span occupied by 'man try to open safe', and indeed the time span occupied by 'man look Japanese'—the two situation times—are considerably longer than it took you to enter the room. It would indeed be surprising if the man did not still look Japanese as you speak. But this was not what you were asked. The TT is your entering the room, and your and the judge's use of past tense puts this TT, but not necessarily the TSit, before the time of utterance. The time of the action of trying to open the safe, TSit, encompasses the TT: TT ϵ TSit. This aspectual relation is imperfective, and explains the use of the past progressive aspect in your answer. Imperfective aspect contrasts with perfective aspect, where TSit is within, or coincides with, TT.

---

[1] '[B]eing the carrier of [assertion] is the main function of finiteness' (Klein 1998: 225). This idea is standard in enunciative approaches. For example, Culioli (1995[1983]: 106) states: 'In an assertion, we can see that this [predicative relation] ... will be located with respect to Sit ([the enunciative situation]), with respect to ... a system of spatio-temporal co-ordinates, as well as the subject of the utterance. This will enable me to say that such and such a relation is validated for a specific moment.' We will however stick with Klein's formulation, although Culioli's usual terms, 'validation of' or 'taking charge of' an utterance, are perhaps better suited to an operation which is neutral in relation to mood (declarative, interrogative, imperative) and modality.

As its name suggests, TT belongs to the topic of an utterance, which may, but need not, also contain a topic entity (in canonical versus thetic sentences, respectively), and a topic place. The operation ASN functions therefore to link the state of affairs or entity denoted by the predicate of the utterance to its topic.

As developed so far, the morphological vs. semantic distinction cannot be mapped directly onto syntactic structure. Although anchoring does not refer to a syntactic constituent, this does not preclude its being expressed by syntactic constituents in the following way. On the syntactic level the sentence basis can be distinguished from its periphery. The sentence basis consists of the predicate and its arguments. Its kernel is the predication, which is a semantic notion, independent of questions of word classes. Bloomfield (1933: 173) distinguishes qualitative predication from narrative predication. The traditional terminology for this distinction presupposes universal word classes, referred to as nominal and verbal sentences respectively. Qualitative predication (nominal sentences) is the basis for the traditional definition of the sentence as a relation between subject and predicate. Narrative predication (verbal sentences) articulates an event, for which the predicate mounts a scenario, which must be anchored. The periphery allows for this anchoring, as left-adjacent topical elements act as frame-makers for the utterance interpretation (cf. the examples to follow in the L1 and the L2 section respectively).

With these distinctions we enter language-specific structures. Different languages use different linguistic and discourse-based means to express S-finiteness.[2] Whereas possibly all languages use adverbials and discourse-organizational principles, more specific morphosyntactic means such as particle use and verb morphology are confined to specific subsets of languages. All Germanic (and Romance) languages have a more or less rich verbal morphology to express finiteness. Work in the generative framework (e.g. Pollock 1989) has established a relation between the richness (or 'strength') of the inflectional paradigm and the placement of the lexical verb with respect to certain adverbs and negation. This relation has an important role in discussions of the acquisition of finiteness. This holds for first as well as second language acquisition, as we shall see below.

However, as Lasser points out for German root infinitives (which are S-finite), the fact that a language has specific means to mark S-finiteness

---

[2] These different means render it problematic to define a clear-cut borderline between finite structures on the one hand and nonfinite and infinite structures on the other. If a morphological marking for M-finiteness is not obligatory or ambiguous, then this particular marking is less significant for a learner.

does not entail that all S-finite clauses are so marked. She draws the following generalizations as to the relationship between S- and M-finiteness (Lasser 1997: 84):

a. M-finiteness implies [S-finiteness].
b. The absence of M-finiteness does not imply the absence of [S-finiteness].

The question then arises (which is crucial for acquisition studies) of what means other than verb morphology can be used by learners to mark semantic finiteness.

Concerning the role of S-finiteness in acquisition, an array of precursors has been found for L1 and L2 which allow for the lexicalized expression of assertion without exhibiting target-like grammatical means (in our case, M-finiteness). Among others, the elements *auch/aussi* ('also'), *noch/encore* ('still' or 'more'), and *wieder/re+V* ('again') have been shown to mark early S-finiteness (see Penner et al. 1999; Perdue et al. 2002; Nederstigt 2002; Dimroth 2002; Dimroth et al. 2003). These elements and their function in learner language make it particularly clear that S-finiteness and M-finiteness need not go hand in hand—especially when talking about language systems under construction. So this form–function bifurcation within the notion of finiteness is not only a powerful tool in theory (see also Klein 1998) but highlighted by developmental research.

Moreover, the detachment of S-finiteness from M-finiteness has the advantage of not restricting the analysis of finiteness to that particular set of languages which exhibit overt morphological finiteness. This allows for Asian languages such as Chinese which have no M-finiteness to contribute to the finiteness discussion in theory and in acquisition. In Klein et al. (2000), Chinese aspectual markers such as *le* are analysed as bearing the function of early S-finiteness in child language. By treating markers like *le* as assertion markers within the time-relational analysis of Klein (1994), the range of interpretations of utterances exhibiting these elements can be captured in a parsimonious and coherent treatment. This is due to the notion of S-finiteness at the intersection of information about how TT relates to TSit and what the scope of the assertion part is. In addition, this split may also invite a fresh view on the acquisition of finiteness in the case of English with its impoverished M-finiteness.

With respect to early topological analyses of utterance structure, a further major advantage of the M-finiteness/S-finiteness distinction is that it accounts for the information-structural split of topical material (the periphery) and assertive material (the predication/sentence basis) via the abstract linking element of grammaticalized S-finiteness. This introduces a theory-independent perspective on the verb-second property of Germanic languages and its status in the process of acquisition.

Thus, in order to express the semantic function of finiteness, any learner of a language has to come to master:

(i) the devices which allow the utterance to be appropriately embedded in the context, i.e. the **anchoring** devices, and

(ii) the devices expressing the relation between the context-embedding and the state of affairs expressed in the utterance, i.e. the **linking** devices.

The verb 'master' then involves both understanding the concepts involved in these operations, and knowing how to use the relevant devices. The learning task is both conceptual and structural, and it is precisely its dual nature that makes the child learner/adult learner comparison interesting.

What also makes finiteness a particularly interesting case for acquisitional studies is the fact that the expression of S-finiteness via M-finiteness is obligatory, or forms at least a grammatical default in the target languages to be discussed in this chapter. Nevertheless, learners hardly ever start with this grammatical default but produce superficially nonfinite utterance structures to express S-finiteness in first as well as in second language acquisition. Hence, the issue of finiteness poses an acute problem for UG-based accounts which assume continuity in language acquisition.

12.1.2 *Previous work in L1*

The role of finiteness in language acquisition has been acknowledged especially in the work on root infinitives which gave rise to intense debate in the 1990s. As has been made clear in the section above, finiteness is a multi-level phenomenon which associates heterogeneous properties across different levels of analysis. Nevertheless, this view does not represent the mainstream perspective on finiteness, which focuses on its structural manifestation—our M-finiteness, with its syntactic correlates.

For the presentation here, we first focus on selected accounts of the acquisition of M-finiteness which mostly subsume research done in the generative framework, before giving selected accounts of the acquisition of S-finiteness, from a pragmatic, discourse-oriented point of view.

12.1.2.1 *Formal approaches to finiteness-related phenomena* In general, two different perspectives can be traced within the generative tradition towards the issue of unfolding M-finiteness and its syntactic ramifications in acquisition data.

On the one hand, there exists the Structure-building view which assumes the expansion of the syntactic tree as a 'telescoping process' in development. Thus, the functional categories associated with INFL—person and tense—and those associated with a sentence's left periphery—complementizers and wh-phenomena—have to be acquired. Moreover, the order of acquisition is implicational: from VP, functional categories are built up according to a syntactic hierarchy VP > IP > CP, with the implicational constraints that IP must be acquired before acquisition of CP can commence.[3] Proponents of this idea include Radford (1990) under the heading of 'minimal trees', Clahsen and Rothweiler (1993), Meisel (1997b), Fritzenschaft et al. (1990), and Tracy (1991).

On the other hand, it has been argued that learnability considerations suggest an UG-given syntactic tree from the very beginning of grammatical acquisition, including the whole set of hierarchically ordered, functional nodes. For acquisitional data to be compatible with a basically target-like tree configuration, the underspecification of individual nodes (Wexler 1994, and onwards) or the truncation of the syntactic tree (Rizzi 1994b; Hamann 1996) has been proposed.

Starting with the study of Clahsen (1988), the developmental association of productive subject–verb agreement and INFL-related grammatical properties has been shown to hold in German child language (see also Clahsen and Penke 1992). These INFL-related properties include target-like verb-second placement which also requires the acquisition of topicalization. INFL, short for 'inflection', labels a functional node (and in later work, a cluster of functional nodes) which associates with verbal inflection, in particular subject–verb agreement, tense, and aspect information (see also the articles in Clahsen 1996). This correlation between verb morphology and syntactic INFL-effects is corroborated by findings reported in Meisel (1997b) for French. Here, productive subject–verb agreement and the correct placement of the negation marker *pas* emerged in parallel. For this correct placement to be achieved, finite marked verbs have to be distinguished from infinitival ones not only inflectionally but also topologically. This common factor of verb placement in French and German makes the French data on negation comparable to the case of verb-second acquisition in German.

This view of a correlation of productive agreement and INFL-related properties is partly contradicted by the data presented in Fritzenschaft et al. (1990) and Gawlitzek-Maiwald et al. (1992), where a dissociation of agreement and the verb-second rule is found in the corpus of the child Benny. This

---

[3] Much in the spirit of the ZISA study (Meisel et al. 1981).

finding is also corroborated by the study of Schaner-Wolles (2001) on the child Nico, where a dissociation of the two factors in the data is also reported.

Nevertheless, broad stages are discernible concerning a distinct developmental progression for INFL-related phenomena and CP-related phenomena. The latter comprise the acquisition of wh-questions and complementizer-introduced embedded clauses, which usually follow the acquisition of agreement. As a consequence, a subsequent parameter-setting of INFL- and CP-features has been evoked to explain the successive emergence of clusters of properties associated with the INFL- and the CP-node. In the same vein, specific syntactic structures can be predicted to be excluded, i.e. those which exhibit CP properties without IP properties. Among these excluded structures are questions with root infinitives (Weissenborn 1992), subject clitics in French root infinitives (Rizzi 1994b), negation preceding finite marked verbs in English (Radford 1990), and finite verbs in verb-end position in German (Clahsen 1988). In contrast to the agreement discussion, these empirical facts seem to be robust and undisputed.

Focusing on the root infinitive discussion more closely, the factor 'utterance interpretation' has become more and more crucial. Whereas Poeppel and Wexler (1993) and Wexler (1994) argue for a random use of finite or nonfinite verb forms at the root infinitive stage due to early optionality in grammar, the majority of subsequent articles acknowledge that interpretation matters. So, Ingram and Thompson (1996: 115) argue that 'the omission of functional projections cannot be truly optional in the sense intended by Rizzi (1994b) and Wexler (1994), because the selection of the finite verb results in a semantically distinct sentence from the nonfinite alternative'.

In consequence, the modality of nonfinite utterances has been captured in various hypotheses:

- the 'Modal Drop Hypothesis' which assumes that the omission of a modal element in the AUX position explains the existence of root infinitives (Boser et al. 1992);
- the 'Modal Hypothesis' which states a correlation between using a root infinitive and expressing a modal interpretation (Ingram and Thompson 1996); and
- the association of root infinitives with a temporal non-here-and-now reference (Hoekstra and Jordens 1994).

12.1.2.2 *Functional approaches to finiteness-related phenomena*   Although finite structures are equated with tensed structures in the Germanic languages, the above approaches scarcely touch on the temporal side of the 'finiteness' coin. Thus, it is in the realm of functional approaches that the issue of

S-finiteness—the semantic/pragmatic side of finiteness—is related to the acquisition of M-finiteness. Here, the semantic debate mirrors the syntactic 'underspecification' approaches of section 12.1.2.1. The debate concerns hypotheses like the 'Defective Tense Hypothesis' which implicates the broader 'Aspect before Tense Hypothesis' (see Bronckart and Sinclair 1973; Antinucci and Miller 1976; Bloom et al. 1980).[4] But since the notion of aspect is not relational in these works, i.e. not related in a principled way to the notion of tense, it is unclear why the acquisition of the first should have a structural implication for the latter at all.

For us, the notion of S-finiteness sets our focus of attention on:

(i) the means with which children 'link' their topical elements to a predicate; and

(ii) the point in development when they achieve a grammatical setting of TT (and with it, grammatically induced assertive force).

This touches directly the question whether grammatical tense and/or aspect are acquired, a question which is closely tied up with the standard inflectional expression (M-finiteness) of S-finiteness in Germanic (and Romance) languages. To some extent, this takes us back to the question of the modality status of root infinitives, since the axis of modality crosses the temporal axis at the irrealis/future boundary. So, situational and co-textual information has to be taken into account to get a grip on the intentions behind child utterances and their interpretations.

For German, an influential study by Behrens (1993) compared morphological steps of development with aspects of temporal/modal reference, and established a first grid for the interpretation of finite vs. infinitival utterance structures in child language. Early preferences of temporal interpretation are associated with individual inflectional forms of verbs, from which it is tempting to conclude that the M-finiteness distinction [+/−finite] may convey more than person and number specification in German child language.

Coming back to point (i) above, the question of linking devices, research has examined the function of early focus particles like *auch* 'also' and *noch* 'still, yet, more'. Nederstigt (2002) elaborates on the idea of Penner et al. (1999) that these focus particles serve as lexical predecessors of the

---

[4] An elegant solution to reconcile the 'Aspect before Tense Hypothesis' with the temporal stage model given in Weist (1986) is presented in Schlyter (1990: 99), where it is argued that 'the Event Time System (i.e. the second of the Temporal Systems, ...), defined as non-separation of R and S, but allowing for the separation of E, is not necessarily different from an aspectual system. Both can be considered as two aspects of the same phenomenon.'

abstract element finiteness. They are assumed to involve S-finiteness without M-finiteness because:

> Caroline's particle use clearly reflects a conflict between AUCH and the finite verb. This conflict between the location of the particle and the finite verb provides evidence for the analysis of AUCH as an overt assertion marker because without this function the emergence of the finite verb in AUCH-utterances would be without consequences. (Nederstigt 2002: 275)

Surprisingly, these relational, scope-inducing elements with complex semantic properties are acquired very early (around the age of 1;05 in German) and occur very frequently. This means that they play a prominent role at the verbless stage even before root infinitives are attested. Nevertheless, these particles provoke a multitude of semantic/pragmatic consequences with a minimal amount of syntax. It is also noteworthy that pitch accent and particle placement is closely modelled (and interpreted) on the target from early on. This suggests strongly that S-finiteness is mastered before M-finiteness.

This view is also attested by findings of early TT specification in German (see Gretsch 2003), where a specification of TT distant from the default here-and-now setting is achieved without inflectional means. Some children mirror adult language acquisition in signalling a topical constituent via topological (and probably also intonational) means. This topical constituent specifies TT by virtue of exhibiting temporal adverbs, overt markers of time spans as dates, or time-related NPs as 'vacation'. Compare the following example of this sort of L1-untypical but attested TT specification under (2) with an example of an L1-typical TT specification as encoded in verbal inflection under (3):

(2)   Benny (2;02.15)[5]
       (Context: Benny had soup the day before when he visited his
       grandma; at utterance time, the family sits at the dining table,
       Benny's mother is serving soup.)
       Benny: oma   hause,   suppe   au
                 grandma   home,   soup   too
                 'When I was at grandma's house yesterday, we had soup, too.'

Consider now the following example, a stretch of conversation between a German-speaking child, Valle (age 1 year, 11 months, 25 days), his mother, and another adult interlocutor. The topic of this part of their conversation is their visit to a nearby city, Reutlingen, which took place earlier that same day:

---

[5] The (CHILD) data stem from the DFG project *Erwerb der komplexen Syntax* under the leadership of Rosemarie Tracy at the University of Tübingen, Germany.

(3) Valle (1;11.25)

    Mo: Weißt noch was ma gemacht ham? (...)
           'Do you remember what we have done?'

    Va: Eis   kauf-**en**
           ice.cream   buy-INF   (anterior reference)

    Mo: Ein Eis gekauft, ja!
           'An ice-cream (we) bought, yes!'

    Interl: (...) Was warn des fürn Eis?
           'What kind of ice-cream was it?'

    Va: nomal eis   ess-**en**
           again ice.cream eat-INF   (future reference/wish)

    Mo: Nomal Eis essen? Du, wenn wir wieder in die Stadt kommen.
           '[You want to] eat ice-cream again? Well, if we get back to
           the city.'
           (V throws over the basket with the farm toys uttering:)

    Va: valle   mach-**t**
           Valle   makes-FIN   (here-and-now reference)

    Va: sütt-**et**   alles   alles   um
           pours-FIN everything everything out (here-and-now reference)

Hence, a three-stage model of finiteness acquisition that would naturally fall out of the discussion so far could look as follows. The first step involves the lexically driven acquisition of S-finiteness via early focus particles (Stage 1), then the morphologically driven acquisition of the [+/−finite] distinction starts to play a syntactic and an interpretational role, and subsequently the subject–verb agreement paradigm builds up, i.e. M-finiteness emerges (Stage 2); lastly, S-finiteness and M-finiteness have to be brought into grammatical interaction leading to a grammatical default form of expressing S-finiteness via M-finiteness (Stage 3). In the two case studies following this general introduction, we refer to a specific model which is closely related to the three-stage model just proposed.

12.1.3 *Previous work in L2*

As in the L1 studies, the majority of functional analyses have concentrated on aspects of S-finiteness and all formal (generative) analyses have concentrated on M-finiteness. This section therefore also contains two parts, dealing first with functional, then with formal approaches. Some more recent studies have, however, tried to bridge the formal–functional gap. These studies will be dealt with in a separate section, 12.1.4, as they encompass analyses comparing first and second language acquisition.

12.1.3.1 *Functional approaches to finiteness-related phenomena*   The expression 'finiteness-related phenomena' in the title of this section is intended to capture a possible misfit between forms and structures (for our present interests, verb morphology in particular) used in the target language (TL) to express finiteness, and the use a learner may make of these forms on the way to the TL.

There is a way of classifying functional approaches to L2 acquisition which is a simplification, but for our present purposes a convenient simplification, and which we will adopt: the distinction is between 'form to function' (Fm>Fn) approaches, and 'function to form' (Fn>Fm) approaches. Fm>Fn approaches analyse the surface distribution of verbal morphology as an indication of the underlying semantic system of the learner's variety, and from this, retrace the semantic and communicative factors determining the acquisition of this aspect of the L2. Fn>Fm approaches select certain semantic concepts—finiteness, for our concerns—and see what the surface linguistic manifestations of the concept are over the acquisition process. Obviously, these approaches are complementary.

We start with the latter, the 'function to form' approaches. Right from the beginning of the acquisition process, it is necessary for an adult to validate the state of affairs talked about in relation to a TT. As we said in section 12.1.1 this involves the operations of anchoring and linking. Relevant previous work (e.g. Stutterheim 1991; Dietrich et al. 1995) in the functional tradition involves the expression of tense, i.e. how the learner establishes the relation between TT and the time of utterance.

In contrast to the standard case of inflectional-based TT specification in child language,[6] the temporal relation of an utterance to the moment of speech or to another reference time can be specified by an utterance-initial adverb.[7]

(4) a. SF: Gloria   aujourd'hui   ici   + quatre familles
                        today   here + four   families
         TD: Ergün   vandaag   + hoofdpijn
                        today   + headache

     b. AF: Abdel   après + avec   le   police
                        after + with (=there was)   the   policeman
         TD: Mahmut   en   dan   + politie   komen
                           and   then   + policeman   come

---

[6] But note the example from the child Benny in section 12.1.2.2. As set out in Gretsch (2004), adults and children share in principle the lexical and grammatical means of TT specification but they exhibit different weightings as to what is considered as standard for each of the acquisition processes.

[7] Examples come from Starren (2001). The initials are read as follows: S = Spanish, T = Turkish, A = Arabic for the source language, and F = French, D = Dutch, for the target languages. The sign '+' represents a short, silent pause.

In (4a, b) we have a case of referent introduction. In (4a) the entities *quatre familles* and *hoofdpijn* are related to a deictic temporal adverb; in (4b) *police* is related to an anaphoric temporal adverb, and it is remarkable that adult learners very quickly acquire a stock of temporal adverbials of position which allow them to express the TT–TU relation.

These initial utterances rarely contain recognizable verbs. However, in early varieties that do contain verbs, these verbs are uninflected; utterances completely lack the usual grammatical means to express tense and aspect. Learners nevertheless manage to produce sophisticated temporal structures in their discourse with the means available, which allow the specification of some time span and certain relations between time spans. What learners do at the beginning of their discourse is establish an initial TT either implicitly, by taking over the time proposed by the interlocutor or using TU as a default case, or explicitly, by means of an utterance-initial adverb as in (4a). This initial TT serves as a point of departure, and is maintained or shifted, depending on the type of discourse. If it is shifted (as in a narrative, for example), then this shifted time is marked by an initial anaphoric adverb, as in (4b), or follows on from discourse-organizational principles such as the principle of natural order (PNO, Clark 1971), whereby events are recounted in the order in which they occur. Adults have already mastered such principles from their L1. With this organization, the time of situation is always more or less simultaneous with TT, as there are no linguistic means allowing the learner to dissociate them. We return to this communicative restriction below, in the discussion of Starren's (2001) study.

Now, we turn to the complementary form-to-function approaches. As we said, Fm>Fn approaches trace the distribution of a form in the learner's variety, and then define its function from the distribution. This work mirrors the 'aspect before tense' hypothesis of L1 studies (section 12.1.2.2). Two hypotheses are proposed to explain the emergent verbal morphology:

- The (lexical) 'aspect-driven' hypothesis: morphological marking is governed by the verb's *Aktionsart*. Hence, those verbal morphemes which mark pastness, perfect(iveness) or anteriority in the target language are first associated with punctual or telic predicates, before spreading to durative and atelic predicates, whereas those morphemes which mark imperfectivity first appear with the latter predicates.
- The 'discourse-driven' hypothesis, whereby morphological marking is determined by narrative structure. Verbal morphemes marking perfectivity are first associated with foregrounded predicates,

whereas those marking imperfectivity are first associated with back-grounded predicates.

Starren (2001: 98) sums up the debate with reference to Bardovi-Harlig's (1998a) work, and concludes:

that lexical aspect and narrative structure both shape the distribution of tense-aspect morphology in second language acquisition. And nothing can be more true (and less surprising) than her [Bardovi-Harlig's] general conclusion that: 'A point of departure for further research is the understanding that interlanguage temporal systems are shaped by both the semantics of lexical aspect and the pragmatics of discourse' (K. B.-H. 1998: 501).

This brief survey of the Fm>Fn work warrants two remarks. First, the hypotheses and results have been criticized by Stutterheim (1991) and Starren (2001), amongst many others, for being restricted to lexical as opposed to grammatical aspect, and to narrative structure, to the exclusion of other text types. Secondly, the implication from the point of view of finiteness is that the development of verbal morphology described here has little to do with M-finiteness. The emergent verbal morphology neither specifies a TT nor links up a predicate to a TT. The TT is established by other means than verbal morphology, which serves other functions only indirectly related with finiteness. To paraphrase Lasser, M-finiteness does not imply S-finiteness.[8] Only later does verbal inflection come to mark tense and grammatical aspect. It is worth developing these criticisms, as they are relevant for the case studies of the following sections, by looking in more detail at Starren's study.

Starren (2001) describes and compares the acquisition of temporality by Turkish and Moroccan learners of Dutch, and by Moroccan learners of French, over a thirty-month longitudinal study.

As we have seen in examples (4a, b) above, learners use the utterance-initial adverb to specify the TT for which the (rather minimally expressed) state of affairs of the utterance is valid. Starren (2001) analyses the very early productions of Turkish and Moroccan learners of L2 Dutch or French from the European Science Foundation (ESF) corpus (cf. Perdue 1993), and finds a regular use of a *second* adverb of time, specifying the time span filled by the state of affairs, i.e. TSit:

---

[8] One could argue that the use of morphological perfective marking on telic predicates allows the speaker to assert that the situation is over, or that use of the same marking in foregrounded utterances asserts that the corresponding event is completed at TT. L2 researchers have indeed stressed the importance of boundary marking for making temporal inferences (Andersen 1991; Stutterheim 1991; Bardovi-Harlig 1998a), but were not directly concerned with the notion of assertion. We return to this in the conclusion of the L2 case studies.

(5) a. TD: Mahmut **altijd**   ik wakker   **om 8 uur**
                    always I   wake.up at   8 o'clock

  b. MF: Zahra **toujours** moi [fe] la   cuisine   ce   **soir**
                    always   me make the cooking   this (=in the) evening

(6) AD: Fatima **vandaag** ik **altijd**   weg   met   auto
                    today   I   always   here.and.there with   car

(7) MF: Abdel **hier**   le   capitaine bateau   **toujours** [regarde]
                    yesterday the captain   the ship always   look

Starren's analysis of many such early utterances allows a distinction to be drawn between the (lexical) aspectual values of habituality, continuity and iterativity, by the interplay of adverbs denoting TT and TSit. For habituality, as in (5a), one time of situation *om 8 uur* is linked to a series of topic times within the TT *altijd*; or (5b) for all the sub-intervals of *toujours, moi [fe] la cuisine ce soir.* Example (7), which contains an activity verb, expresses continuity ('the time span *yesterday* is filled by the activity of supervising'). This example can be contrasted with (6), where the particle *weg* conveys a bounded event, which provokes the iterative reading: a complex TSit expressed by *altijd* is linked to one TT span: *vandaag.*

Even without verbal morphology, it is therefore possible to make some aspectual distinctions, by means of an adverb distribution which owes less to source language (SL) or TL organization than to the information structure of the utterance: TT adverb in topic, TSit adverb in focus. But Starren (2001) also shows that the major communicative limitation of this interplay of adverbs is that it does not suffice on its own to dissociate TT and TSit. Learners thus cannot focus on the pre-state of an event (prospective: TT < TSit) or the post-state of an event (perfect: TT > TSit). In order to be able to do this, learners must go beyond this basic variety and develop a verbal morphology which allows for the independent specification of TT. Thus Starren sees the development of M-finiteness as indeed motivated by learners' need to express grammatical aspect and tense.

More precisely, the morphology-less system allowed a temporal adverb in the topic component of an utterance which had scope over the whole utterance, while the adverb in the focus component affected just the focus information—the predicate. The first finitely marked verbal forms to develop are auxiliary verbs and the copula, whose distribution can be traced back to the previous distribution of the adverbials. Starren's hypothesis is that the basic information structure with its clear topic-focus partitioning serves as a scaffold for subsequent morphological development, the first stage of which is the appearance of free finitely marked, verbal morphemes. Utterances such as the following are attested in the production of learners who have not (yet) attained TL competence:

(8) a. TD: Ergün | en | dan | **is** hij | **heeft** | werk | aanvragen
| | and | then | is he | has | work | ask.for

   b. TD: Ergün | dan | **is** | deur | **is** | zo | kapot
| | then | is | door | is | like.this | broken

   c. MD: Mohamed | toen | **was** | meisje | **heeft** | brood | stelen
| | then | was | girl | has | bread | steal

In these utterances we see (in bold) two finite auxiliaries, the first of which, on the topic/focus boundary, links the predicate to the TT (assertion), while the second form gives the temporal relation between TT and the TSit (grammatical aspect).

The overall picture which emerges from Starren's study is of a developing system which first allows temporal relations to be marked by discourse means and simple adverbs. At this stage finer temporal distinctions can be expressed through the interplay of adverbs marking both TT and TSit, in conjunction with the internal temporal characteristics of the event denoted in the utterance. The development of verbal morphology later allows TT and TSit to become dissociated, and grammatical aspect to be expressed. At this stage, we also see a finite verb form acting as an explicit link between the predicate and the TT specification.

12.1.3.2 *Formal approaches to finiteness-related phenomena*   This section also concerns 'finiteness-related phenomena', but for a different reason: the preference of individual authors goes either to the traditional tense category (does the verb carry past tense in obligatory past-time contexts?) or to the person category (subject–verb agreement, nominative case assignment).

The acquisition of M-finiteness is seen as an important test in a more general debate: whether the adult's language acquisition capacity is still intact or not. In generative terminology this amounts to whether the adult still 'has access' to 'universal grammar' (UG) or not.

As we saw in section 12.1.2, there is general agreement in first language research that children acquire morphological and syntactic properties of their language as clusters (the 'parameters' are set). Meisel (1997b: 239) formulates this generalization in terms of phenomena that are of direct interest to us. He states that 'the acquisition of sentence negation happens fast and virtually without errors' in L1 acquisition: 'As soon as one finds evidence for the productive use of finite forms, NEG is placed clause-internally. This indicates that the subject and the finite verb have been raised to their appropriate positions in a functional projection.'

Many L2 studies also attempt to establish whether or not there is a chronological correlation between the acquisition of different finiteness-related phenomena: verbal morphology, case assignment, word order (including NEG placement).[9] Establishing such a correlation has implications for a characterization of the adult learner's 'initial state', formulated in terms of what is transferable from the L1 grammar versus what must be (re-)acquired. For some studies (Meisel 1997b is a good example), it also has implications for whether the adult learner still has access to UG.

There is general agreement that during the initial stages of L2 acquisition (of Romance and Germanic languages), morphology is almost entirely absent from the learner's production. Vainikka and Young-Scholten (1996: 16) evoke the absence from early learner varieties of 'verb raising, auxiliaries, and agreement paradigm'. What is controversial, however, is what organizing principles explain this lack of morphology. The authors just cited hypothesize that only lexical categories and the syntactic organization of VP is transferable from the L1. This position corresponds to Radford's (1990) 'minimal trees' hypothesis for L1 acquisition (see 12.2.1), where an implicational progression for acquisition has been evoked following the syntactic hierarchy VP > IP > CP. Hence, morphological and syntactic acquisition goes hand in hand in L2 acquisition: M-finiteness has to be reacquired. These authors' position is challenged by researchers such as Schwartz and Sprouse (1996) and Lardière (1998a), for whom an adult learner has access to the full range of UG possibilities: the functional categories are 'there', and determine the syntax of the learner's utterances, but processing limitations explain the absence of an overt morphology. Lardière's (1998a) study is directly relevant for our review.

Lardière (1998a) studies the interlanguage of Patty, a Chinese immigrant long resident in the United States, whose interlanguage has fossilized. She looks at Patty's suppliance of tense morphology, as compared with her use of nominative vs. oblique pronouns, with the hypothesis (p. 10) that 'perfect distribution of nominative versus accusative pronouns . . . would provide much clearer evidence for the representation of a Tense projection

---

[9] For Bisang (Ch. 5 above) these finiteness-related phenomena consist cross-linguistically of the cognitive domains of tense, person, illocutionary force, and politeness.

in the grammar'.[10] The results indeed show a perfect (100 per cent target-like) distribution of nominative and accusative pronouns, whereas past tense marking was supplied in only (averagely) 34 per cent of obligatory contexts in the three available recordings, which spanned eight years, allowing the author to conclude that this interlanguage is indeed fossilized. Furthermore, Lardière found robust evidence of CP projection in a large number of explicit embeddings (if CP is acquired, then, implicationally, the tense projection is acquired). Patty has the target language functional categories, but not their TL morphological marking. This dissociation of morphological and syntactic development is not contradictory, for Lardière, with the hypothesis of access to UG, as the morphological deficiencies do not imply the absence of functional categories. Indeed, she reproaches Vainikka and Young-Scholten (1996) and Eubank (1993/4) for their assumption 'that the *absence* (or incorrectness) of morphological realization in the production data reflects the *absence* of the corresponding structure' (Lardière 1998: 4, her emphasis).

For Meisel (1997a), however, the dissociation of finiteness (subject–verb agreement) marking and verb placement follows from the assumption that (even if available[11]) UG plays no role in adult language acquisition. Looking at longitudinal data of the acquisition of French and German as L1 and L2, he examines the 'emergence of the +/− finite distinction and verb placement and consequently also target-like placement of the finite verb with respect to the negative element' (1997a: 257). While these phenomena cluster in the L1 analyses (see section 12.2.1), they do not in the L2 analyses, where the negator is found to be placed both pre- and post-verbally, this placement not being dependent on the presence or absence of subject–verb agreement: 'learners, rather than using structure-dependent operations constrained by UG, resort to linear sequencing strategies which apply to surface strings.'

Parodi (2000), on the basis of partially overlapping data from the ZISA project (Meisel et al. 1981), attempts to show that, on the contrary, verb placement in L2 German *is* related to finiteness, interpreted (as with Meisel) as subject–verb agreement (S-V Agr). Unlike Meisel, Parodi sees the distinction between auxiliary and lexical verbs (respectively 'non-thematic' and

---

[10] She chooses tense rather than agreement morphology because tense is closer to VP in the standard clausal phrase structure, and therefore should be acquired earlier than agreement, according to Vainikka and Young-Scholten's (1996) implicational hypothesis.

[11] Given the state of the theory in 1997, Meisel sees the 'accessibility' of UG as perhaps impossible to demonstrate, while adding (1997a: 259) that 'the burden of proof is on those who wish to defend this position'.

'thematic' verbs, in her terminology) as crucial to understanding the relationship between finite verb morphology and verb placement.

She divides the longitudinal data into three periods (beginning, intermediate, and final), and calculates first the percentage of correct subject–verb agreement (S-V Agr) for each period for the thematic and non-thematic verbs (modals, auxiliaries, the copula, and possessive *have*), finding virtually 100 per cent correct agreement for the latter over the three periods, whereas there was a low percentage of S-V Agr for thematic verbs at the beginning, this percentage increasing over time. She then demonstrated that, although the morphology of German modals is like that of German strong lexical verbs, there is S-V Agr on the former, but not on the latter, which pattern with weak lexical verbs: the syntactic category, rather than morphological conjugation, seems the important distinction. She then analyses the utterances showing sentence negation in order to see whether there is a relation between S-V Agr and negation patterns. Non-thematic verbs, which have already been established to show S-V Agr, show in negative utterances the V + NEG order in seventy out of seventy-two cases. The distribution for thematic verbs in negative utterances is (with a few exceptions) that NEG + V order is attested in the absence of S-V Agr, whereas the V + NEG order patterns with S-V Agr. Parodi concludes (2000: 376): 'there is a relationship between the placement of the negator with respect to the finite verb, on the one hand, and subject-verb agreement, on the other', and interprets this result, together with the overall S-V Agr shown by non-thematic verbs, in the following way:

> L2 speakers are dealing with lexical and syntactical information separately: at initial stages thematic verbs are responsible for lexical information, while non-thematic verbs are the main carriers of syntactical information.

She further points out that this is an option attested in natural languages, but not in TL German nor in SLs Italian and Spanish: adult learners do still have access to universal grammar.

12.1.4 *Conclusion: parallel studies of L1 and L2*

In this intermediate conclusion we concentrate on the methodological problems involved in the cited studies, whether they concern L1 or L2. The problem of contextual interpretation of learner utterances runs through the whole of the discussion due to their nature as production data. Such corpus data pose, of course, not only the traditional problem of interpretation (how can one be sure of the communicative intentions of a toddler?) but also the problem of completeness (does the corpus entirely reflect the learner's capabilities?), and, related to this, of productivity (what are the criteria, given a limited corpus, allowing the researcher to say that a particular item or rule is acquired?). These problems are compounded by the tendency of some researchers to interpret learner utterances as closely as possible to a 'corresponding' TL utterance, with the risk of (over-)interpreting learner performance in the direction of TL categories. This problem becomes even more crucial the more one wishes to attribute 'UG-given' knowledge to the beginning learner.

Nevertheless, we want to point out that such problems are mitigated by the longitudinal perspective taken by most researchers, which allows them to analyse comparable performances through time. This comparability can be enhanced in the case of adult learners by direct comparison over time of the same complex verbal tasks, such as apartment and picture descriptions, retellings, and the like. Such methodology allows further comparative checks, in the form of the analysis of cross-linguistic performances on identical tasks, as has been demonstrated in the analysis of the ESF data. But for child language the interpretation poses a general challenge, especially during the earliest stages of L1 acquisition.

The completeness problem is also recurrent, as generalizations are sometimes made on the basis of relatively scant data. But methodologically, can one answer the question of how many corpora make a generalization? And, given generalization, what kind of data are needed to falsify it?

The above questions are methodological. But they have more theoretical mirrors in the problem of deciding what the initial state of a (child or adult) learner is, and whether it is more parsimonious to assume a strong (innate) interpretation of UG-given or not. These are questions which results of L1 developmental studies should be able to address by comparing their results with the strong continuity hypothesis, for example.

We will not pursue these questions here, but rather turn to the possibility of comparing L1 and L2 studies. In the previous section it was assumed that the (adult) L2 learner masters S-finiteness from his or her L1, and results show that adults quickly acquire temporal adverbs which allow them, together with directly transferable discourse organization principles, to manage TT. Results from recent L1 studies (Nederstigt 2002; Jordens 2002; Gretsch 2004) also suggest that mastery of S-finiteness does *not* presuppose the mastery of M-finiteness. Hence, the three-stage model of finiteness proposed in 12.2.2 for L1 acquisition can be extended here in a preliminary way to include the L2 process as well:

- The first step involves the lexically driven acquisition of S-finiteness via early focus particles (Stage 1), together with temporal adverbs and the (already mastered) discourse organization principles of the adult learner.
- Then the acquisition of the [+/−finite] distinction on verbs (subject–verb agreement, tense) starts to play a syntactic and an interpretational role and M-finiteness emerges (Stage 2).
- Lastly, S-finiteness and M-finiteness have to be brought into grammatical interaction, leading to a grammatical default form of expressing S-finiteness via M-finiteness (Stage 3). This grammatical default may be highly language-specific, as with the (finite) V2 restriction in German and Dutch.

Within the case studies to follow this section, we refer to a specific model which is partly based on the three-stage model just proposed. This specific model has been laid out in Dimroth et al. (2003), Perdue et al. (2002), and Jordens (2002), where it is argued that the acquisition of the structural and functional properties of finiteness proceeds in three consecutive stages: the Holistic Stage, the Conceptual Ordering Stage, and the Finite Linking Stage. This model will be taken up in the following sections.

12.2 A case study on the acquisition of L1 German

12.2.1 *Bootstrapping into the system of grammatical finiteness*

Following the three-stage model as sketched above, this part focuses on the onset of S-finiteness, the onset of M-finiteness, and the onset of grammaticalized finiteness, i.e. the successful interlocking of S-finiteness and M-finiteness plus its syntactic correlates in German child language. To adhere to chronological order of acquisition, first a developmental path towards S-finiteness and then a developmental path towards M-finiteness will be discussed. We will follow the German monolingual child Benny on his way towards grammaticalized finiteness, the stage when finiteness marking becomes obligatory. This stage allows the learner to conflate anchoring properties (appropriate context embedding via the specification of minimally a TopicTime) and linking properties (creating a relation between the context embedding and the state of affairs expressed via assertive force in the basic case), whereas in the earlier stages, anchoring and linking occur independently of each other.

Table 12.1 sums up the developmental steps that can be shown to exist in German and to some extent also in Dutch child language (see Jordens 2000; Gretsch 2003; Nederstigt 2002). We shall describe the development of the

TABLE 12.1. Steps of acquisition related to M-/S-finiteness

Steps of acquisition related to M-finiteness	Steps of acquisition related to S-finiteness
Verbal particles like *auf* 'open'	Deictic elements like *da/des/dann* 'there, this, then'
Infinitival marked verbs, bare verb stems as *aufmach* 'open-make'	Adverbs like *hier* 'here'
	Auch with pitch accent as in *ich AUCH hose* 'I ALSO trousers' *Auch* and finite marked verbs occur in complementary distribution
Finite marked verbs occur (auxiliaries, copula, and selected main verbs)	*Auch*-use plus verbs as in *AUCH heilemachen* 'ALSO whole-make'
Topological distinction between finite and infinitival marked verbs traceable	Interpretational distinction between [+/−finite] marked utterances traceable
Productive use of finite marked verbs	Lexical assertion enhancer like *doch, wohl* 'indeed'
V2-properties and 'Assertion' focus, i.e. stressing a finite marked verb to highlight the validity of the assertion as in *He DID it!*	

child Benny more closely within this stage-model of the acquisition of finiteness as developed in section 12.1.4. In contrast to the articles cited in section 12.1.2, we will focus here on the relation between the acquisition of M-/S-finiteness as indicated in Table 12.1 and the acquisition of syntactic milestones to convey a coherent and integrative picture of the acquisition of finiteness against an uncontroversial developmental background grid (see also Gretsch 2004). To this end, the elementary steps within the acquisition of S-finiteness are analysed first, then the acquisition of M-finiteness is presented.

12.2.2 *The acquisition of S-finiteness*

As discussed in Penner et al. (1999), Perdue et al. (2002), Nederstigt (2002), and Dimroth et al. (2003), the emergence of scope-inducing elements like *auch* 'also' and *noch* 'more/still' signals more than the mere inclusion of another lexeme in the lexicon in L1. The characteristics of these particular lexemes indicate, on the one hand, that children in the earliest stages of acquisition are in command of a fairly abstract semantics ('Add x to the list in y'), and on the other hand, that intricate rules of topological ordering, focusing, and intonational highlighting combine already (mostly successfully) together to achieve a mutual understanding about what is added to what. Consider the following array of examples:

(9)   Benny (2;02.15)
        context: Benny and his family visited a funfair the day before
        Interloc: Bisch Karussell gefahren? ('Have you been on a
                    merry-go-round?')
        Mo: Autobus. ('Bus.')
        Benny: autoSUS\ ('Bus.')
        Interloc: Autobus? Au auf' m Karussell. ('Bus? Also on
                    the merry-go-round?')
                    Und Motorrad? ('And motorbike?')
        Benny: momomomoTOa:d/   **AUCH**\
                    motorbike   too

(10)   Benny (2;02.15)
        context: Benny wants his mother to play soccer with
                   him and the interlocutor
        Benny: mama   **AUCH**   tortor\
                   mummy   too   goal-goal
        Interloc: Soll d'Mama mitspielen? ('Shall mummy play with us?')

(11)   Benny (2;02.15)
        context: Benny's mother brings coffee to the table
        Benny: ich   **AU**   will   FE:\
                   me   too   want   coffee
        Benny: ich   **AUCH**   FE: will\
                   me   too   coffee   want
        Benny: ich   **AU**   will   FE:\
                   me   too   want   coffee
        Mo: Ja!! ('Yes!!')
        Benny: ja\
        Benny: APFLsaft   **AU**   **AU**\
                   apple juice   too   too
        Benny: **AU**   **AU**   apəlsapt   ap/
                   too   too   apple juice   have(?)
        Mo: Ne, ne kein Apfelsaft. ('No, no, no apple juice.')

Whereas the intonation contour under (9) still signals a non-integrated,
holistic structure, (10) exemplifies an integrated one with postposed, pitch-
accented *AUCH*. The latter example shows a conceptual ordering structure
(COS) par excellence: *mama*, the topical element, occurs left-adjacent to the
linking element *AUCH*; the rudimentary 'VP' or sentence base *tortor* occurs to
the right.

The example under (11) illustrates Benny's topological crisis which persists through the COS. On the one hand, the finite verb should be placed before the direct object mimicking V2; on the other hand, this position is already occupied by the phrasal head *AUCH* with its assertive force which is adopted together with the informational structuring from the previous utterance. Thus, the finite verb—the auxiliary *will* here—oscillates between a base position as familiar from root infinitival clauses, i.e. verb-end placement, and a blended V2/V3 position. Due to this conflict of verbal placement, verbs hardly occur in *AUCH* constructions at all which leads to the phenomenon of a complementary distribution of *AUCH* and finite verbs—see again (9) and (10). This positioning conflict carries over to *AUCH* structures without verbs as the two turns about apple juice in (11) indicate.

The next examples from later time points still demonstrate that this conflict is unsolved:

(12)   Benny (2;6.25)
     context: It's snowing.
     Interloc: Wie des schneit, ganz große Flocken, gell?
                'How it is snowing, very large flakes, isn't it?'
     Benny: Opel **AUCH**\
                Opel too   (Opel = German brand name of a car)
     Interloc: Auf'm Opel liegt auch Schnee. ('On top of the Opel is also snow.')

(13)   Benny (2;09.19)
     context: Benny and the interlocutor are playing with plasticine. The interlocutor is forming a big ball and puts it on the table.
     Benny: ich   **AUCH**   ein   bauch   möchte
                me   too   a   belly   want ('I want a belly, too.')

(14)   Benny (2;09.19)
     context: Benny and the interlocutor are playing with a puzzle
     Benny: nein   **AUCH**   nich   paßt\
                no   too   not   fits   ('[This one] does not fit, too.')

(15)   Benny (2;09.19)
     context: Benny talks about a house built by Benny's father
     Interloc: Wer wohnt denn da in dem Haus?
                'who lives there in that house?'
     Benny: AU   weiß   net
                too   know   not   ('I don't know, too')

Example (12) exemplifies again the familiar reduced XP-*AUCH* structure at this later stage of acquisition. In (13), *AUCH* occurs also integrated into a bigger structure together with the finite verb *möchte* and its direct object *ein bauch*. As found before, *AUCH* occupies here the superficial 'V2' position, whereas the finite verb is placed at the end (in generative terms in its assumed base position). The same pattern can be observed in (14). The competition between finite verb and *AUCH* for the V2 position might also lead to juxtaposition structures as illustrated in (15) and (11) before. The topical *I* has been target-adequately omitted in the utterance in (15), but the resulting word order *AU* before the finite verb *weiß* is again target-inadequate. The examples (12–15) illustrate again the COS typical structuring: topic first (maybe empty), then the linking element (here *AUCH*), and then the sentence base, the predicate. Other linking elements can be found in (16) and (17):

(16) Benny (2;09.19)
      context: Benny and the interlocutor are modelling a snowman
      Interloc: Braucht er noch was?   ('Does he need anything else?')
      Benny: ja ('yes')
      Interloc: Was? ('What?')
      Benny: **nomal** du   sag
                  again   you   say   ('Say it again.')

(17) Benny (2;09.19)
      context: The interlocutor holds Benny up towards the ceiling
      Interloc: Und jetzt? ('And now?')
      Benny: WEIterhoch
                  further high/up ('[Put me] higher up.')

Other early illocutionary markers still occur left-adjacent to their domain of application, here in (18) a rudimentary propositional phrase—this structuring points back to the holistic stage.[12] Note also the precursor of a subordinate structuring under the matrix verb *know* in the last turn of Benny in (18). This illustrates nicely the coexistence of simple, holistic structuring 'far below the IP' and complex structuring pointing already 'above the IP' level at one and the same data point.

(18) Benny (2;09.19)
      context: The interlocutor and Benny are modelling with plasticine
      Benny: jetzt was BAUN?   ('Now something build?')
      Interloc: Was machn wir jetzt?   ('What will we do now?')

---

[12] A list of these illocutionary markers for Dutch and German can be found in Dimroth et al. (2003).

Benny: **BITTE**   bau-n
          please   build-INF   ('Please build something')
Interloc: Ich bau jetzt eine Schlange. ('I am going to build a
          snake now.')
          [xxx]   (short part not understandable)
Benny: weiß   es   net   was   ich   mache
          know   it   not   what   I   make   ('I don't know what I
          [can/shall] do.')

Around his third birthday, the positioning conflict between *AUCH* and the
finite marked verb is solved. Moreover, combinations of scope-inducing
elements occur (*auch* + *noch*):

(19) Benny (3;00.01)
      context: Benny shows the interlocutor a broken door in his
                cardboard box home
      Benny: die   TÜR   is   **AUCH**   noch   kaputt\
                the   door   is   too   still broken   ('The door is
                broken, too.')

(20) Benny (3;00.01)
      context: Benny and the interlocutor look at self-made paper flowers
      Benny: darf ich   **AU**   mal/   papier/
                may I   too   once   paper   ('May I [build some], too?
                [Out of]   paper?')

The finite linking stage (FLS) is reached. *AUCH* is downgraded from a linking
element to a regular, additive scope-inducing particle whereas finite marked
verbs target-adequately conflate anchoring and linking properties in FIN2 or
FIN3 position. So, Benny has still to figure out the target-like set of classical
V2-properties—topologically and inflectionally speaking. Compare the following utterance structures with those in (19) and (20):

(21) Benny (3;00.01)
      context: Benny talks about the broken door in his cardboard box home
      Benny: die   tür   net   mehr   **geh-t**   zu\
               the   door   not   anymore   closes-FIN   PRT
               ('The door does not close any more.')

(22) Benny (3;00.01)
      context: Benny wants to go into his cardboard box home
      Benny: dann   dann   mich   **laß-t**   daHIN\
               then   then   me   let-FIN   PRT   ('Then let me in there.')

(23) Benny (3;00.01)
      context: The interlocutor wants to go into the cardboard box
              home of Benny
      Benny: aber net – du   kann   da   nich HIN\
              but   no   you can-*INF there   not   PRT
              ('No, you cannot go in there.')

Concerning the issue of S-finiteness, this sketch of Benny's development reveals the ability to juggle with assertive/illocutionary force-indicating elements without exhibiting the IP-typical structural correlates, i.e. flawless inflection and narrowed-down placement possibilities of the finite verb (V2). During a stage where his grammar still shows traces of the placement conflict, scope-reversing elements (*AUCH* bearing pitch accent) are differentiated from non-reversing elements (*nomal, weiter*) with target-like positioning and highlighting properties. Since early *AUCH*, *nomal*, and *weiter* serve as linking elements between topical elements and the sentence base, inducing assertive force into the utterance, they are prototypical markers of S-finiteness. Surprisingly, markers of early S-finiteness like *AUCH* emerge already at a stage where hardly any intonationally integrated phrases are documented (in Benny's case around 2;02)—see above. Now let us turn to the complementing issue of M-finiteness.

12.2.3 *The acquisition of M-finiteness*

Before the development of verbal morphology gets productive according to criteria as laid out, for example, in Jordens (2002), a relational clustering of forms to meanings can be observed. So, the 'modal bias' of root infinitives (see the overview in section 12.2.2 above) has been discussed extensively—a cover term to capture the tendency of the infinitival morphology to convey a modality-related interpretation. In the case of early child language, this amounts to request interpretation and wish interpretation. An example for this form–meaning correlation is presented under (24). A counterexample to this modality orientation complements this with a non-modal interpretation of the infinitival morphology, see (25).

(24) Benny (2;02.15)
      context: Benny wants to sit on a cardboard box.
      Interloc: Geh bitte von dem Karton runter.   ('Please go away
              from the box.')
      Benny: nain DA   sitsa\
              no   here sit.INF
              ('I want to sit here.')

(25) Benny (2;02.15)
      context: talking about mowing the lane.
      Interloc: Wer macht denn das bei Euch? ('Who does this in your
                  family?')
      Benny: de papa   mach-n   sens-en\
                  the daddy   make-INF   scythe-INF
                  ('Daddy mows with a scythe/he 'scythes'.')

Now the question arises of the extent to which this modal bias occurs (how many occurrences make a bias?) and whether it would be in principle a suitable candidate for an early form–meaning correlation in child language. For the analysis of the form-meaning development of the [+/−finite] distinction to be presented here, three data points within Benny's corpus have been chosen which fall into the 'root infinitive stage' of Benny. These data points represent roughly the onset, the peak, and the offset of root infinitival structures which are typical for the COS: see Figure 12.1. As the proportions shift from mainly verbless via (partly) infinitival to mostly finite utterance structures, a baseline assumption along the lines of the 'Optionality of Tense' account from Wexler would be that the range of interpretations expressed by the respective structures stays the same. On the other hand, accounts like Hoekstra and Hyams (1999) based on the 'Modal Reference Effect' (to give modal bias a more elegant label) predict an (allegedly statistically significant) preference for the infinitival morphology to convey modal interpretations in comparison to other non-modal interpretations.

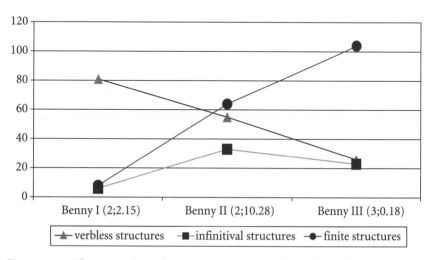

FIGURE 12.1. The proportion of utterance structures in Benny's development

Here a short note is useful on the methodological issues on (a) how to determine a root infinitive and (b) how to determine its interpretation. For the form–interpretation analysis, a verbal element was counted as finite if the pronunciation of the verb ending showed either a target-adequate or potentially also a target-inadequate agreement form. Thus, agreement errors and changes between standard and dialectal variants of finiteness marking were allowed for. Concerning the positioning factor, a finite marked verb could be placed in any position but the verb end position. Therefore, the acquisition of the strict verb-second rule of FIN-placement in German assertive root clauses was not a precondition for verbal elements to count as potentially finite. The placement of verbal particles played no role if the agreement marking was adequate and the non-verb end positioning of the verb unambiguous.

Infinitival verbal elements require a target-like pronunciation of the verb ending, allowing also for the dialectal variant, i.e. a *schwa* ending, spoken in the area where Benny lives. Moreover, the positioning of the verb should not contradict the placement patterns of the German target which restricts [−finite] marked verbs to verb end placement with some additional cases of rightward extraposition if other factors (information-structural status, intonation contour) corroborate this analysis. For verbal particles, they had to occur affixed to the verbal element in infinitival structures. It was also possible for infinitival structures to occur as one-word utterances. In consequence, the form determination of finite and infinitival structures was maximally independent from meaning factors.

Coming to the interpretational side, the following categories have been distinguished to classify the utterances: (i) requests/wishes, (ii) narratives, (iii) existentials/descriptions, and (iv) comments on ongoing events.[13] The modal interpretation is exclusively associated with category (i), requests and wishes; all other categories are non-modal. Together with questions and exclamatives, these categories include the bulk of utterances. The two latter were excluded from the analysis, since their form and interpretation aspects do not enlighten the issue of root infinitives. Additionally, the data have been cleared of onomatopoeic utterances, discourse fillers like *hm*, *äh*, immediate repetitions of the input, yes/no answers, and utterances with unclear structure and/or interpretation. Moreover, it is crucial for the case of *root* infinitives to exclude the category of context-coherent elliptical answers following turn-adjacent questions, although this constitutes a frequent category in child language. Otherwise, these cases of grammatical ellipsis would weaken the analysis in counting potentially finite utterance structures as infinitival.

---

[13] For a more detailed justification of this classification see Gretsch (2004).

All these exclusions lead to a major drop in numbers available for analysis. As can be deduced from Figure 12.1, 400 utterances eventually entered the form–interpretation grid. The age window covered for the M-finiteness analysis ranges from 2;2 to 3;0, since Benny has a comparatively late and extended root infinitive stage.

Let us now turn to the individual form–interpretation correlations in Benny. First, the interpretational distribution of the utterance total is presented. This serves as a background against which the interpretational biases of individual forms can be judged. Then the distribution of interpretations in the form type of verbless structures, infinitival structures, and finite structures follows. The idea is here to present the distribution of interpretational categories across the three data points for each form type to represent developmental progression, i.e. developmentally directed shifts of form–interpretation correlations.

Generally speaking, the picture of form–interpretation correlations does not exhibit one-to-one mapping, but instead different arrays of interpretations, which are covered by a particular form type at a data point, can be depicted. At the beginning of the relevant age window, the category of verbless utterances (Figure 12.3) closely represents the distribution of the interpretation of the utterance total (Figure 12.2). This is due to the obviously unbiased form type: verbless structures are completely nonspecified with respect to interpretational properties.

Turning to the form type of infinitival structures—the root infinitives—a comparison between Figure 12.4 and the background Figure 12.2 reveals that requests and narratives are preferred, whereas the descriptive category is more or less excluded. On the other hand, finite structures (see Figure 12.5) attract precisely this category of descriptives, as one would expect after the emergence of copula constructions. The last data point within the finite structures

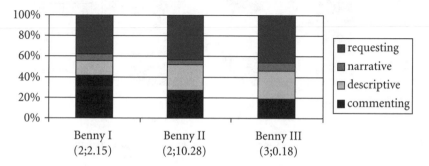

FIGURE 12.2. The interpretational distribution across all structures (Benny)

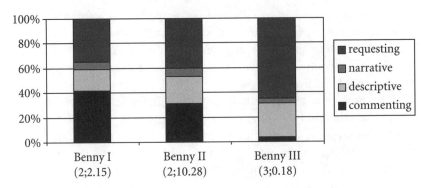

FIGURE 12.3. The interpretational distribution across the verbless structures (Benny)

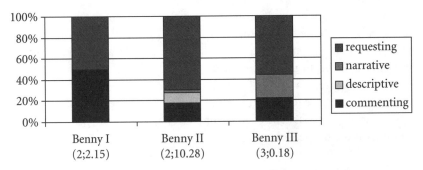

FIGURE 12.4. The interpretational distribution across the infinitival structures (Benny)

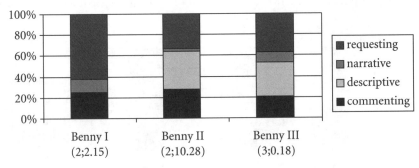

FIGURE 12.5. The interpretational distribution across the finite structures (Benny)

(Figure 12.5) shows the same interpretational distribution as the background Figure 12.2. Hence, the finite utterance organization eventually covers the whole range of interpretations in an unbiased way. This signals the acquisition of a grammaticalized M+S finiteness: finiteness marking becomes obligatory, and therefore independent from earlier transitory links to semantic/pragmatic meaning.

To sum up the presentation of the data, the overall picture of emerging form–interpretation correlations might not be as clear-cut as (for example) a feature-based grammar would require. If we assume that it is the notion of modality that invokes the major fission of forms, we are faced with the following problems: (i) How can we account for request interpretation in the non-infinitival domains, especially in the case of verbless structures? (ii) What induces the modal interpretation in verbless structures? (iii) How is this feature-mapping '[−finite] implies [+modal]' instantiated? (iv) How to retract from such a feature-setting later? And, last but not least: (v) Is this modal bias of the infinitival form significant after all?

Starting with the last question, the data of Benny's root infinitive stage show no significance in this direction. The probability of a request or wish being conveyed via an infinitival marked utterance is $\chi^2 = 2.06$ for $p < .05$, $df = 1$, critical value $= 3.84$.[14] Interestingly, the complementing probability of finite structures occurring with non-modal interpretation is likewise not significant, again $\chi^2 = 2.06$ for $p < .05$. The statistics of the pooled database of Benny's data plus the data of another child at comparable points in development lead to the same result with respect to the alleged 'Modal Reference Effect': the correlation between infinitival utterances and modal interpretation is not significant in the pooled data set ($\chi^2 = 0.78$ for $p < .05$, $df = 1$, critical value $= 3.84$). Concerning the complementing correlation of finite utterances and non-modal interpretation, the χ^2-analysis of the pooled data revealed, surprisingly, a highly significant value: ($\chi^2 = 67.16$ for $p < .05$). This points towards an 'Anti-Modal Reference Effect' of finite utterances instead of a 'Modal Reference Effect' for root infinitives if it comes to statistics.

An alternative account, as laid out in Gretsch (2004), captures the biases of forms to interpretations in the figures above within a system of broader semantic/pragmatic notions: this account sets up a frame for coarse clusters of temporal/aspectual/modal reference such as here-and-now reference vs. non-here-and-now reference. The latter comprises wish worlds (modal

---

[14] This analysis is based on the [+/− finite] marked structures, excluding the case of verbless structures. This is because the latter category is assumed to be marked for [Ø finite].

interpretation) as well as anterior reference as in personal narrations. The general case made is that [−finite] forms attract non-here-and-now reference whereas [+finite] forms attract here-and-now reference. This cluster-bound model of acquisition on the one hand reflects the coarse semantic/pragmatic categories we encounter in early child language, such as the future/modality conglomerate or the undifferentiated 'pastness' interpretation. On the other hand, it mirrors the distributional properties of forms to interpretations and their shifts during development as the clusters involved get more and more differentiated. This view is corroborated by the statistical data, which are significant in both ways for the individual and the pooled data sets. We will present the pooled data here: the here-and-now-based split reaches significance for the [−finite] domain correlating with non-here-and-now ($\chi^2 = 5.9$ for $p < .05$, df = 1, critical value = 3.84) and even a stronger significance for the finite form type correlating with here-and-now reference ($\chi^2 = 23.2$ for $p < .05$).

What does all this contribute to the issue of M-finiteness? A pairing of forms to interpretation can be traced in the domain of [+/−finite] marked structures from early on, whereas verbless structures stay truly unbiased. It is not the 'Modal Reference Effect' which is responsible for this split but a broader distinction of clusters of temporal/aspectual/modal reference. As soon as the pairings of individual forms to individual reference clusters become relevant (or significant), the distinction between [+/−finite] matters.[15] And it matters regarding the interpretation of the overall utterance concerning the topical/contextual specification of such pairings as depicted in the crude clusters of reference above. In that sense, early M-finiteness allows for a minimal specification of TT, pointing to 'pastness', 'present', or 'potential/desired future'. Whereas the section on S-finiteness above showed an early *linking* of topical elements and the state of affairs expressed via assertive force, the section on M-finiteness here presented data and a statistical analysis which substantiate early *anchoring* properties. This anchoring was defined above as an appropriate context embedding via the specification of minimally a TT, which is precisely achieved by the [+/−finite] split as discussed here.

12.2.4 *Interlocking S-finiteness, M-finiteness, and syntactic correlates*

It is important to note that the phenomena of S-finiteness and M-finiteness occur independently of each other in the examples above (with the exception of examples 19 and 20, which already depict a target-like organization). The

---

[15] Depending on the criteria for productive finiteness marking, this might even occur before the onset of true productivity. But this aspect might easily lead into a fruitless chicken vs. egg discussion.

fact that *AUCH* and finite marked verbs occur in complementary distribution in early stages of development makes it clear that the acquisition of S-finiteness and M-finiteness present the learner with two distinct problems of acquisition. But the conflict between *AUCH* and finite marked verbs bears also a major developmental potential in forcing the learner to invent his or her grammar anew, at least with respect to the opening of meta-levels within the tree hierarchy.[16] So, the complete acquisition of 'the IP-level' covers the interlocking of S-finiteness and M-finiteness in the finite marked verb in V2 position as the obligatory (base) case for root clauses in German.

The acquisitional path of Benny demonstrates compellingly the independence of S-finiteness and M-finiteness in development. Speaking about one corpus here, it is unjustified to generalize this specific acquisitional sequence to 'the German path'. But from what we know from comparable data presented in Penner et al. (1999), Nederstigt (2002), and Dimroth et al. (2003), the precedence of S-finiteness over M-finiteness in German L1 seems to be a stable fact. This implies that M-finiteness and S-finiteness only happen to fall together in the German target language, but a grammatical description of the phenomenon of finiteness has to allow for their separation on principled grounds. The syntactic correlates of finiteness as most prominently V2 placement—or, better, FIN2 placement—plus syntactic topicalization and correct person/number agreement do not necessarily fall in place as soon as M-finiteness and S-finiteness are acquired. It is a major developmental achievement to interlock all three linguistic levels (morphology, syntax, and semantics/pragmatics) in a target-adequate manner.

In Table 12.2 the developmental paths of S-finiteness and M-finiteness are depicted against the overall acquisition of major syntactic milestones which allows for an overview of Benny's linguistic development.

In Benny's development, the following stepping-stones for S- and M-finiteness can be isolated. Concerning S-finiteness, the element *AUCH* plays a crucial role in detecting the invisible function served (eventually) by finiteness. The addition of either focal material (contrasting 'VP') or topical material (contrasting topical entity/person) includes the adoption of the assertive force of the previous utterance without further qualification. The non-representational nature of *AUCH* points to an early abstractness in child language already at the stage of 'telegraphic speech' in adding material according to its information structural status plus an implicit expression of (the adoption of the previous) validity, i.e. the assertive (or modal) force of the utterance. In effect, *AUCH* is prone to serve as a linking element during

---

[16] See also Tracy (1991; 2002) for the important role of conflicts and crisis in development.

TABLE 12.2. Benny's development in a nutshell

Age	Stage	Developmental steps	FIN and V2 (%)
2;02	Holistic stage/ COS S-finiteness emerges	Proto-finite formulae, verbal particles occur in isolation	$3.4(V^{fin})$ $2.7\ (V^{inf})$
		AUCH with pitch accent in XP-*AUCH* structures	
		Deictic elements, TT marking (early *anchoring*) *Oma hause suppe au*	
2;07	COS M-finiteness emerges	[+/−finite] differentiation traceable (+finite marked are AUX, copula, and selected main verbs)	$3.8(V_2^{fin})$ $10.1\ (VE^{inf})$
	Covert conflict of M- with S-finiteness	*AUCH* and finite marked verbs occur in complementary distribution (early *linking*)	
		No stable V2 Still erroneous inflection	
2;9	Overt conflict of M-finiteness with S-finiteness	*AUCH* plus finite verb in verb-end position or in adjacency position ('enlarged V2')	$23.7(V_2^{fin})$ $0.2\ (VE^{inf})$ $3.2(V_3^{fin})$
		V3 occurs due to double filled topic position or to double filled V2 position *etz ich hebe des\\ Ø AU weiß net*	
2;11	,,	FIN conflicts and erroneous inflection persist *auch ich weiß AU net* *was du machen/ was macht du/ was machst du/ was ich kann machen*	$27.2(V_2^{fin})$ $7.3\ (VE^{inf})$ $27.2(V_2^{fin})$
3;0	FLS but no strict V2	Still problems with inflection and V2 but *AUCH* now occurs with V2 in a target-adequate manner	$32.8\ (V^{fin})$ $8.4\ (VE^{inf})$ $2.0\ (V_3^{fin})$
	M/S-conflict solved	V2 problems because of first complementizer-introduced subordinate clauses	
	M+S-finiteness acquired	True focus occurs (conflation of anchoring and linking visible) *hier SIND keine katze(n)*	

3;1		Variety of complementizers, subordinate structures but still FIN conflicts at the 'CP level' *weil hab ich mich auch naßgespritzt* *wenn han i au mal burtstag habt*	23.9 (V2^{fin}) 12.6 (VE^{inf}) 1.2 (V3^{fin})
3;4	FLS + V2	Target-adequate FIN placement in independent and subordinate clauses	

the COS until finite marked verbs become obligatory at the FLS. This analysis of the prominent role of *AUCH* for the acquisition/expression of S-finiteness is strongly corroborated by L2 findings (see the case study on L2 below). If we interpret S-finiteness as 'the condition for an independent interpretation of a sentence' (Maas 2004), the case of *AUCH* in L1 and L2 shows that independence (and with it S-finiteness) is gradual at the COS. The temporal anchorage still hinges on the previous utterance. So, an utterance like *mama AUCH tortor* ('mummy too goalgoal', see example 10) can be interpreted as a personal narration ('mummy **was** playing soccer'), as a comment on ongoing action ('mummy **is** playing soccer'), or as a wish/command/obligation ('I **want** mummy to play soccer/mummy **has to** play soccer'), depending on the context.

With respect to M-finiteness, the early differentiation of [+/−finite] leads to a sensitivity regarding verbal morphology. Even before verb placement patterns get stable, a topological and a semantic/pragmatic bifurcation can be traced at the COS. As one of the authors has argued elsewhere (Gretsch 2004), the earliest functional split occurs between [+finite] marked structures referring to the here-and-now and [−finite] marked structures referring to the non-here-and-now. The latter comprises a conglomerate of future/modal reference (wish-worlds) and temporal 'pastness' reference, until the integration of past participles disambiguates the forms for temporal directionality. Benny's development argues sharply for an independence of the emergence of M-finiteness and its syntactic correlates. It takes him nearly a year from the onset of M-finiteness to the target-adequate array of V2-related grammatical properties.[17]

---

[17] Nevertheless, it should be noted that children differ in how conservative or permissive they are at moments of grammatical conflict (see e.g. Fritzenschaft et al. 1990; Gretsch 2000). Whereas Benny allows for a range of verb-placement possibilities over a longer period, other learners prefer to stick to a single placement pattern (see e.g. Jordens 2002 for Dutch L1).

Although the functions of anchoring and linking are eventually fused in the finite verb form, both predecessors can do without verbs, i.e. AUCH in the case of linking, and early topical nominals (*hause oma*) in the case of anchoring. Nevertheless, it should be noted that the anchoring exclusively via topical XPs is typical for L2 but rather untypical for L1. The standard case for early anchoring in L1 exploits the [+/−finite] distinction to convey information about temporal/modal reference along the lines discussed above under the heading of M-finiteness.

In the next section we turn to the L2 counterpart of acquisition and examine two case studies of adult immigrants, concentrating on finiteness and its correlates.

12.3 Two case studies on the acquisition of L2 English

12.3.1 *Introduction to the adult data*

We will examine from a longitudinal perspective the development of finiteness-related phenomena in the varieties of Santo and Andrea, two Italian learners of L2 English who cooperated in the European Science Foundation's project on second language acquisition by adult immigrants (Perdue 1993). We concentrate on Andrea, and use Santo's data for comparative purposes. Both learners followed a similar developmental path up to the 'basic variety' (see below). Santo stabilized at this level, while Andrea's variety showed considerable grammatical development beyond (Perdue and Klein 1992).

Santo arrived in England in 1983 for work, and also to join his Italian girlfriend, expecting to stay indefinitely. He was first interviewed seven months later. He was working in an Italian restaurant and during the course of data collection was promoted to first cook. He attended no classes in England. Andrea arrived in 1982 and worked mainly as an electrician. He was first interviewed one year later, at which time he had already abandoned, through pressure of work, the English classes he had sporadically attended. Both learners lived in an overwhelmingly Italian-speaking environment, and were virtually beginners at the time of their first interview. But their command of English did develop over the months, through their mainly bureaucratic and instrumental contacts with English speakers: job applications, estate and travel agents, the health service, and the administration that goes with owning a motor vehicle. Both participated willingly in the project, which obviously also provided a regular opportunity to practise their English. It involved monthly interviews over the space of eighteen months in Santo's case and thirty months for Andrea, during which some more guided activities such as film retellings and picture descriptions were carried out. The recorded interviews were organized into 'cycles'—a series of regular encounters during which the different activities were carried out in a fixed order. Two such cycles were carried out for Santo, and three for Andrea. The recordings were subsequently transcribed and stored on a computer.

In the light of the considerations of section 12.1, the learning task for the adult learner can be metaphorically formulated as some general questions he (Santo and Andrea in this case) asks of the target language. What are the means that the TL gives me for expressing S-finiteness? Are any of these means grammaticalized, i.e. does M-finiteness play a role? If so, does this M-finiteness affect other aspects of utterance structure?

We assume (somewhat simplistically, perhaps) that such questions are asked on the basis of the learner's previous linguistic experience, which includes immediately transferable knowledge of language-neutral discourse-organizational principles, such as the principle of natural order (Clark 1971), which allows the implicit establishment of temporal relations. Their SL being Italian, both learners are also familiar with a rich verbal morphology (and the 'null subject' phenomenon), with auxiliary verbs expressing different grammatical aspects and with mainly lexical verbs expressing modality. We start by looking at the acquisition of the English 'equivalents' of these more specific means.

12.3.2 *Verbal morphology (does M-finiteness play a role?)*

Table 12.3 documents the emergence of M-finiteness, in the form of recognizably conjugated verbs. The columns are to be read from top to bottom (1:1 = cycle 1, recording 1, to 3:1 = cycle 3, recording 1). The columns mark the recording in which a particular conjugated verb form first appears spontaneously in declarative affirmative utterances. 'V' in the table indicates a main lexical verb, and 'Mod', the English defective modals. Learners' use of inflected *be*, of modals + V, of the present and past perfect, and of the past tense are given.

From this table, it is clear that M-finiteness emerges gradually, first on auxiliaries and only for Andrea on main verbs: the simple past emerges in the second cycle at 2:4. Andrea is a faster learner, who masters English tense oppositions in affirmative utterances by the beginning of the third cycle of data collection, with the exception of the 3rd person present -*s*. Santo left the project before the third cycle, but his development in this area stopped before the end of the second cycle, his only conjugated verbs being *be* and *have*. Note that, unlike Andrea, he does not correctly produce the present perfect, using *have* with the bare verb stem (*I have go*).

TABLE 12.3. First appearance of some conjugated forms in affirmative utterances (adapted from Perdue et al. 2002)

Recording	Santo	Andrea
1:1	*is*	*am, is*
1:2	*am*	
1:3		
1:4		
1:5	*are, have*	
1:6		*have, are*
1:7		
1:8		
1:9		
2:1	*have* + V	
2:2		
2:3		Mod + V
2:4		Present perfect, past
2:5		
2:6		
3:1		Past perfect

12.3.3 *Negation (does M-finiteness affect other aspects of utterance structure?)*

We have seen in sections 12.1.3 and 12.1.4 that in the TL, M-finiteness has syntactic correlates involving verb placement. One of the major indicators of topological development is the placement of negating elements. In contrast to the steady progression of the two learners in the realm of conjugated verb forms their development of negation is more heterogeneous (Figures 12.6 and 12.7). We see in both learners' data (more clearly in Andrea's) the negator *no* gradually being supplanted by unanalysed *don't*, which is complemented by the emergence of negated copula and *have* structures.[18] Interestingly, the use of the negative construction lags slightly behind the corresponding affirmative form. Only Andrea uses the complex 'AUX/Mod + *not* + V' construction (see example iii below, p. 474), towards the end of the period of observation.

The overview in Table 12.4 (p. 472) retraces the progression shown in Table 12.3, while showing the (non-)correspondences between the learners' production of conjugated verb forms and their expression of negation. The header and first row ('verb morphology') recapitulate the recording numbers, and the first appearances of inflected verb forms. The following lines give the occurrences of the negator

---

[18] Silberstein's (2001) counts of *no* + V vs. *don't* + V in Santo's data show the following development over the two cycles: Cycle 1, *no* + V = 72%; *don't* + V = 28%. Cycle 2, *no* + V = 56%; *don't* + V = 44%.

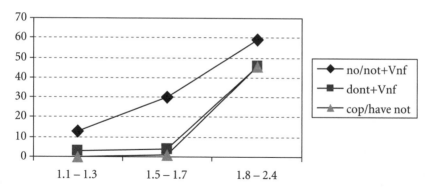

FIGURE 12.6. Development of negation in Santo

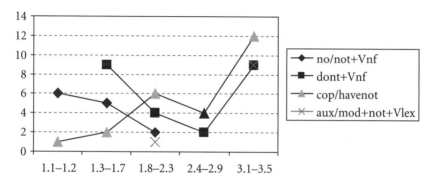

FIGURE 12.7. Development of negation in Andrea

preceding the nonfinite verb: *no/not* + V, *don't* + V. Underneath these are given the occurrences of negation to the right of the conjugated copula. The final row gives occurrences of complex verbal groups consisting of conjugated auxiliaries or modals, NEG, and the main verb. Whereas the temporal progression points from left to right as indicated by the subsequent recording sets, the structural progression points downward, i.e. eventually the negating element can be placed right-adjacent to a finite marked verb. So, Table 12.4 shows that the array of affirmative forms influences the structure of negation in L2 learners.

Summarizing so far, we may say that both learners initially build up two basic utterance patterns, given below. Santo does not go beyond this 'basic variety', whereas in Andrea's production, their major constituents subsequently complexify:

TABLE 12.4. Negative utterances containing verbs: English L2 learners all stages (adapted from Perdue et al. 2002)

Santo	Recording session		
	1.1–1.3	1.5–1.7	1.8–2.4
Verb morphology	*is, am*	*are, have*	*have* +V
no/not + V_{nonfin}	13	30	59
don't + V_{nonfin}	3	4	46
Cop/*have not*	–	1	46
Aux/mod + *not* + V_{lex}	–	–	–

Andrea	Recording session				
	1.1–1.2	1.3–1.7	1.8–2.3	2.4–2.9	3.1–3.5
Verb morphology	Cop		Mod	PresPerf/past	PastP
no/not + V_{nonfin}	6	5	2	–	–
don't + V_{nonfin}	–	9	4	2	9
Cop/*have not*	1	2	6	4	12
Aux/mod + *not* + V_{lex}	–	–	1	–	9

(A)   NP1 – V – (NP2) – (NP3)

(B)   NP1 – copula – AdjP/ NP2

In pattern A, the NPs in parentheses represent arguments of lexical verbs that take two or three arguments, and NP3 is an abbreviation for the third argument of *verba dicendi* and dative verbs. A third declarative pattern;

(C)   (ADV) – V – NP2

is also attested. It later dies out in Andrea's production, but Santo uses it very frequently (about 10 per cent of all his declarative utterances are so structured) throughout the observation period, often with the *have* first attested in 1.5: *have the one family* ('there is/was a family').

This initial stage corresponds to Klein and Perdue's 'basic variety'. The learner's repertoire consists mainly of lexemes: nouns, verbs, adjectives, (mainly spatial and temporal) adverbs, and a very small number of functional elements: a couple of prepositions, definite and indefinite articles, personal pronouns (where *I* and *you* clearly precede 3rd person pronouns), a negator, some (other) scope particles such as *also, only,* and the copula. This variety lacks inflectional morphology, and hence there is no tense, no agreement (with the exception of the copula), and no case marking (with the rare exception of *me*). This led Klein and Perdue to characterize learners' utterances as showing a 'nonfinite utterance organization' (NFUO), which only gradually gives way to a 'finite utterance organization' (FUO).

At this initial stage, the verbs of patterns A and C therefore show no morphological oppositions. The negator is most often *no*, and less often *don't* at this stage. It precedes V. Only the copula is inflected, for person and number agreement, and the negator *not* is to the right of these inflected forms. In general, the scopal items are placed immediately to the left of their domain of application; some authors (Meisel 1997a; Bardel 1999; Bernini 2000) see this phenomenon as resulting from a strategy of language use. As Meisel (1997a: 248) puts it for the negator: 'the strategy consists in placing the negator immediately before the element to be negated, in constituent as well as phrasal negation... NEG + X strategy.'

In going beyond this basic variety Andrea starts using AUX + V patterns in A. These auxiliaries and the copula of B start showing tense oppositions, and concomitantly, present/past tense oppositions are attested on the main V. The negator is found to the right of the auxiliaries, but in this data set, unanalysed *don't* continues to negate the lexical verb.[19]

As we have said, Santo stabilizes at NFUO, whereas Andrea develops significantly beyond this level. For Santo, post-verbal negation is limited to the copula and (twice) *have*,[20] the only inflected verbs he produces. The *no* + lexical verb sequence does not disappear. One can see a further difference between these two learners in pronoun development, to which we briefly turn.

12.3.4 *3rd person pronouns (does M-finiteness affect other aspects of utterance structure?)*

Both learners set up a basic system of nominal reference: *the/this* + Noun for definites, *(the) one* + Noun for countable indefinites, and bare nouns for uncountable indefinites. Both use the pronouns *I* and *you* from the very beginning of the observation period, but 3rd person pronouns develop much more slowly.[21] The following developmental pattern is based on

---

[19] This is an artefact of the data set. Giuliano (2003) retraces the subsequent analysis of *don't* into *doesn't, didn't*, and so on in more successful learners of English.

[20] These occurrences are conflated in Table 12.4.

[21] It is worth pointing out that this development, and developmental differences, have a functional rather than syntactic motivation. For the 1st and 2nd person pronouns, nominative case is attested from the beginning, whereas there are no 3rd person pronouns. Andrea ends up virtually mastering the pronoun system of English, whereas Santo does not. Santo gets less far along a similar developmental path, and the difference in progress between the two learners only concerns 3rd person pronoun use. In Lardière's (1998a) description of pronoun use in the fossilized variety of her subject Patty, correct 1st and 3rd person pronoun use is attested, but it is of course impossible to know how Patty got there.

Andrea's attempts at reference maintenance in film retellings, in comparison to Santo (the film retelling data was chosen for this analysis, as the task imposes reference maintenance to third person entities).

For Andrea, reference to humans is maintained in the following ways:

(i)   By an NP of identical form (e.g. *this woman...this woman*): the blonde friend tell *other woman*...and *other woman* call the emergency

(ii) By zero anaphora (o) in the restricted conditions:
      a. NP – V – X – *for/to* – O – V – X
      that woman knock very strong the door *for o* open or break the door
      b. NP – V – X – (*and*) – O – V – X
      the blonde girl help that woman *and o* explain to the police
      c. V – NP – (*and*) – O – V – X
      arrive the brigade fire and *o* open the door

(iii) By pronouns:
      other woman call the emergency but *she* can't to explain.

Table 12.5 gives the expressions Andrea uses to maintain reference to a human (singular or plural) referent or to an inanimate referent over the cycles of data collection. The place occupied by the referring expression (NP1 or NP2 in the corresponding utterance patterns A, B, C above) in successive utterances is linked by an arrow. 'det' is used in the table to indicate *the/this*. 'Pro' indicates a pronominal form: NP1 or 2 => NP1 gives nominative case, NP2 or 2 => NP2 gives oblique case. Zero anaphor is not included in the table: the configurations for o anaphor given in (ii) above remain constant over the period of observation.

Table 12.5 sets out the times, types and contexts of the different overt means that Andrea uses to maintain reference. Use of these means varies considerably. As can be seen from the table, (i) is the rule and (iii) the exception at the beginning of the observation period, whereas the opposite is true for the period 2.4–2.9, when the use of zero anaphor (ii) is also restricted, as pronouns encroach on configuration (ii) b (above). (i) actually makes a slight reappearance in cycle 3, where use of a pronoun would be confusing to the listener. Pronominal reference to inanimates is virtually nonexistent. To sum up the development of pronoun use for reference maintenance:

(i)   singular appears before plural;
(ii) nominative appears before oblique;
(iii) pronouns referring to humans appear before pronouns referring to inanimates.

TABLE 12.5. Andrea's means of overt reference maintenance from utterance to utterance (adapted from Perdue and Klein 1992)

	1.1–1.7	1.8–2.3	2.4–2.9	3.1–3.5
Human sg.				
NP1 → NP1	det + N	Pro	Pro	Pro
NP2 → NP1		det + N	Pro	Pro
NP1 → NP2		det + N	Pro	Pro
NP2 → NP2		det + N	Pro	Pro
Human pl.				
NP1 → NP1			Pro	Pro
NP2 → NP1		det + N		Pro
NP1 → NP2		det + N		Pro
NP2 → NP2				
Inanimate				
NP1 → NP1			Pro (1x)	
NP2 → NP1			det + N	det + N
NP1 → NP2		det + N	det + N	det + N
NP2 → NP2	det + N	det + N	det + N	det + N

Santo's development stops at Andrea's level of approximately the end of the first cycle (1.8). Only a handful of examples of *he* are attested in the retellings, and that is all. On the other hand, zero anaphora (o in example 26) continues to be very frequently used by Santo during the period of observation which, together with a contrastive use of patterns A–C, allows referent introduction and reference maintenance, for example:

(26) IE: Santo   have the one young girl +
                  and o take in the window in the shop the bread
                  and go away

Santo introduces a referent with *(the) one* + noun in a pattern (C) utterance, then maintains reference by o in the two following pattern (A) utterances. This difference possibly explains why pattern (C) continues to be used by Santo, whereas it disappears from Andrea's production.

These learners are adult speakers of Italian, who master S-finiteness and M-finiteness (the means to express S-finiteness) in their L1. Neither learner comes completely to master M-finiteness in the L2, although the paths the learners follow are structurally very similar in the initial stage. To sum up this descriptive paragraph, we have seen a common development for these two learners up to a 'basic' level of utterance organization, which Klein and Perdue (1992) termed 'nonfinite utterance organization', characterized by a lack of inflectional morphology (except on the copula), by NEG placement before the lexical verb (and after the copula), and a lack of third-person pronouns. In Andrea, we see a subsequent development of the three phenomena: verb morphology, in particular of auxiliaries, develops concomitantly with changes in verb placement, and the development of a 3rd person pronoun paradigm, to form a 'finite utterance organization' (Klein and Perdue 1992), showing case, and tense and agreement on the verb. We concentrate on these two latter phenomena in what follows.

12.3.5 *Discussion of the adult data*

This section will discuss the two main questions arising from the preceding descriptions: Why does the acquisition sequence look like it does? And how is S-finiteness conveyed in L2 English in the absence of the TL-morphological means?

12.3.5.1 *Why does the acquisition sequence look like it does?*   We have retraced an acquisitional sequence where finiteness marking first occurs on *be* and auxiliary *have*, before any morphological marking is attested on lexical verbs.[22] The auxiliaries show subject–verb agreement. The negator *not* follows the inflected auxiliaries, whereas the uninflected lexical verbs are preceded by *no*, *no* gradually giving way to unanalysed *don't*. There is, then, an interaction between use of inflected forms and placement of the negator— it appears to the right of the inflected auxiliaries, and to the left of the uninflected lexical verbs.

This tendency is now well attested in empirical L2 work. Giuliano (2003) gives the most detailed account (including analyses of Andrea and Santo) of the development of verb inflection and NEG placement for English L2, and we return to her study below. Her results are supported by Silberstein (2001), who does her own analysis of Santo's data, which she compares with other Italian learners of English and German: in her study, we see clearly that NFUO is directly comparable in English and German L2. Becker's (2005) results go in the same direction for the same L2s.

Bernini (2000) found the same (pragmatic) organization of negative utterances (the NEG + X strategy mentioned above) in the initial stages of acquisition of Italian L2 by learners of different L1s. As the sentence negator is systematically found before the finite verb in Italian, progress beyond the

---

[22] Space precludes our dealing with the English modal auxiliaries. Giuliano (2003) points out that Italian learners of English typically use paraphrases up to basic variety level (Santo: *for six months this possible drive* 'I can drive with this [temporary certificate] for six months'), and the reader is referred there for further details.

basic variety has however essentially to do with acquiring the TL distinction between holophrastic *no* and pre-verbal *non*:

(i) Verbal elements favour the use of *non* more than non-verbal ones.
(ii) Among verbal elements, use of *non* is found early with the predicate of existence... and the copula. (Bernini 2000: 421)

He concludes:[23]

Acquisition of negation in Italian is characterized in the early stages by the same strategies found in L2 acquisition of French... and German... However, the [Italian] target structures are reached... in a short span of time with no real transitorial constructions abandoned in the process of acquisition... Preposition of the negator to the verb as a non-marked structure in typological terms and scope domain on the right in both clause and constituent negation may be the major factors effecting ease of acquisition. (Bernini 2000: 431)

In all of these studies, non-thematic verbs, to use Parodi's (2000) terminology, play a specific role. They are the first verbs to appear in Bernini's study, and overall the first to be inflected. There is a contrastive order 'NEG + thematic verb' versus '(finite) non-thematic verb + NEG' attested for all Romance and Germanic languages studied, except for Bernini's study of L2 Italian,[24] where the distinction nevertheless has morphological consequences: *non* is first used before the copula. For all studies but Bernini's, therefore, Parodi's conclusion cited in section 12.1.3.2 and repeated here seems to be plausible: 'L2 speakers are dealing with lexical and syntactical information separately: at initial stages thematic verbs are responsible for lexical information, while nonthematic verbs are the main carriers of syntactical information' (Parodi 2000: 373).

Giuliano (2003) fleshes out Parodi's hypothesis in the following way, remarking that the non-thematic verbs ('relational predicates' in Giuliano's terminology) are not only the first to carry subject–verb agreement but also the first to carry tense distinctions:

---

[23] More surprising are the results of Bardel's (1999) study of the acquisition of Italian by a Swedish learner, Karl. Bardel sums up her results thus (p. 186): 'Karl seems to have a negation system which does not correspond totally either to the Swedish or to the Italian one, since he distinguishes between lexical verbs on the one hand, and copula and *avere* on the other ... Karl seems to have great difficulties in splitting up the NegX unit and placing a verb form inside it. He never places negation before the copula or possessive *avere*, which would be the target-like placement. In fact the copula is often missing in non-target-like ellipses, or, if the copula is present, negation is placed in post-verbal position.'

[24] And Meisel's (1997b) study, of course.

Relational predicates appear in a specific informational configuration: they are situated at the topic-focus barrier and mark the Topic Time, namely the time span for which the utterance makes an assertion... Now, with respect to negation, we have observed that:

1. the negator always follows *avoir*/have and *être*/*be*, which are inflected;
2. ... the use of inflected forms of *avoir*/have and *être*/be is relatively precocious...

The observation that *avoir*/have and *être*/be are systematically situated on the topic-focus barrier and mark the Topic Time has an extremely important implication for negation: the negator cannot have scope over the Topic Time because the non-validity of a propositional content must be asserted for a given time span. As a consequence, the negator follows *avoir*/have and *être*/be, i.e., the elements which carry topic time information, from early stages onwards, but in that same phase, it precedes the lexical verbs on which temporal markings are lacking. In other words, the lexical verb without clear Topic Time reference follows the negator and is IN its scope.

Giuliano's conclusion can be compared with Starren's study, discussed above in section 12.1.3.1. One of the proto-verbal elements she analyses in TL Dutch also occurs at the T/F boundary, linking the predicate to the TT adverbial. We give here a further example where the learner describes an ongoing action:

(27)   TD: Ergün   die man   hier   *is*   gewoon   werk   aanvragen
            (this man   here   is   just   work   ask)

In this example, *is* functions to link complex (topical) information comprising entity and place, the TT here being TU.

Benazzo (2003) sees a further reason for the development of verbal inflection. She observes that, while adult learners quickly build up a stock of temporal adverbs, these typically do not include temporal adverbs of contrast (TACs) which are virtually absent at NFUO level. She explains the acquisition of such adverbs, and their integration into FUO in the following way. The semantics of these adverbs are aspectual: they relate two time spans, one of which is the TT for which an assertion is made. *Still*, for example, indicates that the event of the utterance it occurs in carries on from a previous, adjacent time span, while *already* marks the transition from a negative to a positive phase of the same event. A functional verbal morphology is therefore necessary to specify one of the time intervals, the TT, over which these adverbs quantify.

We have seen, then, that M-finiteness comes progressively to express the two operations underlying S-finiteness, linking (through tense and person agreement) the predicate to the topic, or independently anchoring the utterance, through tense specifying TT.

12.3.5.2 *The expression of S-finiteness in 'nonfinite' L2 English*   We finally come to the way learners express the operations of anchoring and linking before M-finiteness emerges, i.e. at NFUO. As was already pointed out in section 12.1, learners can rely from the outset on discourse organizational principles, and quickly acquire a stock of temporal adverbs in order to be able to specify TT. The following example shows how Andrea initially relies on such means. It is part of a conversation taken from his first cycle, after about eleven months in England (Bhardwaj et al. 1988: 65):

(28)   a. NS: How did you find this house? Through Adorno?
      b. AN: before + I live together Adorno + the first time
      c. AN: after...Brixton two month
      d. AN: after + Tufnell Park
      e. AN: now here
      f. AN: at Christmas in Enfield
      g. NS: When did you live in Tufnell Park?
      h. AN: only two three weeks in Tufnell Park
      i. AN: because I change one job in Highgate village

The verbs used (*live, change*) are not conjugated; both are used in a past time context. Note also the presence of the 1st person pronoun with these verbs. Andrea sets up (b) a TT with *before,* paraphrased by *the first time,* i.e., 'first of all in the past'. In (c), anaphoric *after* shifts the TT, and the predicate *I live* is understood. *two months* gives the TSit: 'I live in Brixton for two months' is asserted as valid for the shifted TT. In (d), *after* functions in the same way, and (e) brings the story to the here and now (!); thus with the chronological time shift, *at Christmas* in (f) is understood as referring to future time 'At (TT) Christmas, I will live in Enfield.' The native speaker's question in (g) then takes the conversation back to a previously established TT, and *only two three weeks* gives the TSit of (h). Then in (i), the end of the period *two three weeks in Tufnell Park* functions as TT for *I change one job,* the (probable, in Bhardwaj's contextual analysis) reason for his leaving.

Thus, the interplay of temporal adverbs of position and duration, together with the chronology scaffolding this sequence, allows Andrea very economically to link up a series of situations to successive TTs, or to a TT (re)introduced by the interlocutor.

Temporal adverbs of contrast are typically absent from NFUO, as we saw above. Benazzo (2003) observes that some learners developing out of NFUO use such adverbs idiosyncratically—not with a contrastive value, but rather as compensatory means to express either tense or grammatical aspect. Such use is one means of overcoming certain communicative limitations of NFUO. Take this example from Alfonso, a Hispanic learner of French, who is clearing up a misunderstanding in the interviewer's question:

(29) a. NS: tu y es allé? + ou tu iras?   ('you did go there, or you will?')

    b. AL: je **déjà** je [ale] là-bas oui
           'I already I go there yes'

    c. AL: et après je [ale] otra fois
         'and after I go again'

Benazzo (2003) points out that *déjà* in such examples situates a predicate with
a past or perfect, not contrastive, reading. Andrea's data also contains idiosyncratic uses of *again* and *still* in the last part of the second cycle, as his
variety develops beyond NFUO: *again* (from Italian *ancora*) is used with the
value of English *still*, while *still* is used as an idiosyncratic auxiliary with
imperfective value. Benazzo gives the following examples. In (30) Andrea is
talking about the town he comes from, and in (31) he is describing a picture
where someone is buying apples:

(30) a. AN: when I had ten years
    b. AN: twenty years ago + a lot of woods
    c. NS: and now all the woods have gone?
    d. AN: no there are + **again** but no like before

(31) AN: this man **still** to take some apples into his bag

Up to NFUO, we have seen adverbs functioning to anchor an utterance. They
establish a TT, and the predicate is linked to this TT by juxtaposition, i.e.
implicitly. Other studies (Dimroth 2002; Perdue et al. 2002; Dimroth et al.
2003) have tried to establish whether, at NFUO level, learners use means other
than simple juxtaposition to lexically link the predicate to its TT. Dimroth
(2002) studies L2 learners' use of the German particles *auch* 'also', *noch*
'another time', *wieder* 'again', and *immer noch* 'still' in a picture retelling
task, and observes that the stressed variants of these particles have scope
over the topic information of the utterances they appear in:

In the underlying information structure, the validity of some given state of affairs for
the present topic must be under discussion. Topic-related additive words then express
that the state of affairs indeed applies to this topic, their function therefore coming
close to the function of assertion marking. (Dimroth 2002: 891)

This observation is reinforced, in the data analysed by Dimroth, by an
observation that has arisen in three other studies we have discussed—Penner
et al. (1999), Nederstigt (2002), and Bardel (1999)—where it is argued that the
negator is placed systematically after the copula (or possessive *avere* in
Bardel's case) or the copula is omitted altogether, both of which contradict

the target structure. Additive words, and also negation, appear at some stage to be in complementary distribution with the first finitely marked verbs. Thus, to quote Dimroth on *auch*, learners' attempts to go beyond NFUO result in a 'tendency to use stressed, topic-related *auch* and finiteness marking (finite auxiliaries) in complementary distribution' (Dimroth 2002: 900). Here is one of her examples, from a Turkish learner of German retelling the story of the film *Modern Times:*

(32) und die mädchen und der Chaplin *sind* aufgestanden
      and the girl   and the Chaplin have stood.up
      und die polizei   *auch* aufgestanden
      and the policeman also   stood.up

She speculates (Dimroth 2002: 901) that the ability of these additive particles 'to incorporate the abstract assertion operator might be one of the reasons why adult second-language learners acquire them quite early'. Just as child L1 learners do.

This part of the discussion has allowed us to see how, in the absence of a functional verbal morphology, adult learners of a second language use the means that they have—discourse-organizational principles, temporal adverbs of various types, additive words, negation—to mark the two operations which are central to S-finiteness, namely, anchoring and linking. We attempt in the final section to place these results, and the results from the L1 studies, into a common developmental model.

12.4 Conclusion for the analysis of finiteness and its acquisition

12.4.1 *Learning about finiteness*

Finiteness is a functional property of Germanic (and Romance) languages. It is carried by auxiliaries and lexical verbs. In order to explain processes of the acquisition of finiteness, we have found it necessary to distinguish between the semantic concept of finiteness and its formal representation (Klein 1998). The semantic concept of finiteness entails two properties of information structuring: anchoring and linking. Anchoring is the pragmatic operation which establishes the identification of what is talked about and the embedding of the actual utterance in a discourse world. Linking is the operation which validates the relation between a particular state of affairs described in the predicate part of an utterance and a topic element. While both functions are fused in one finite verb form in the target languages investigated, they are clearly separated in learner varieties of both children and adult learners.

We have therefore distinguished here between S-finiteness and M-finiteness, and we have shown that the acquisition of these two levels does not go hand in hand. For the adult, this is unsurprising, as such learners already understand S-finiteness from knowledge of their L1; their learning task is to acquire a new means of marking S-finiteness. But for children, too, it appears from the data analysed that these two levels represent independent learning tasks. These findings complement the theoretical considerations in Nikolaeva (2003), where she argues not only for a necessary separation of linguistic levels in the description of finiteness but also for an intricate correlation between assertive force and finiteness vs. non-assertive force and nonfinite structures. Moreover, our L1 and L2 data reveal that 'syntactic properties normally associated with finiteness do not necessarily have well-defined morphological corollaries' (Nikolaeva, Chapter 1 above) in our learner varieties.

We have concentrated on two stages of utterance organization, the first of which is termed 'Nonfinite Utterance Organization' (NFUO) in Klein and Perdue (1992) and the 'Conceptual Ordering Stage' (COS) in Dimroth et al. (2003). The former term emphasizes the absence of inflectional morphology, the central means for M-finiteness in the languages we have examined. The latter term emphasizes the fact that there is a very close fit between information structure and its linguistic form. Dimroth et al. characterize the COS in the following way. Utterances consist of three informational units: Topic—Link—Predicate, and the link is realized either implicitly, in the default assertion, or by lexical means (lexical linking).

The second stage is called 'Finite Utterance Organization' (FUO) by Klein and Perdue (1992) and 'Finite Linking Stage' (FLS) by Dimroth et al. (2003). It is at this stage that the two operations of anchoring and linking become conflated into one linguistic form, i.e. finite inflectional verb morphology. We have seen that this marking has different syntactic correlates in the different target languages: verb placement, nominative case assignment, and so on—from the generative perspective, the operations associated with INFL.[25]

We now summarize what is common in the utterance organization of children and adults at these two stages, adopting the terminology of Dimroth et al. (2003).

12.4.2 *A stage model for early L1 and L2 development*

Stage 1. At the conceptual ordering stage (COS) child and adult utterances consist of three structural positions for constituents, each with a particular

---

[25] For a detailed account of the acquisition of INFL from our 'stage model' perspective, see Jordens (2002).

informational function. The topic occurs in initial position. It establishes external reference to the outside world or to the previous utterance; it has, as we have seen, an anchoring function. The constituent in final position is termed the predicate. A predicate can be a VP or a VP-like expression, referring to a particular state of affairs. The relation between the predicate and the topic element is established by a closed class of linking elements. Linking devices used to validate relations between the predicate and the topic comprise (a) elements expressing positive or negative assertion, (b) scope particles such as *auch* 'also', *noch* 'still', *noch* 'more' in German, and finally, (c) modal phrases expressing volition, ability, possibility, and obligation. In German L1, we have examined *bitte* and *will*, which belong to this category.

Following this reasoning, our stage model could even be extended to cover cases of recalcitrant structures in regular target languages. Take the case of the Swedish *kanske* ('maybe') form in V2 position where the form clearly shows no marking of tense but bears finite values (see Sells, Chapter 3 above). Structures like these can be interpreted as remnants of a structural organization along the lines of the COS where certain adverbs exceptionally can take over the function of otherwise morphologically finite elements.

Stage 2. Validation of the relation between the state of affairs and the topic element is grammaticalized at the finite linking stage (FLS). Elements of the target functional category of auxiliaries are used to express both tense and assertion (and its modalized variants). Because the finite verb has come to be used as a grammatical linking device, scope particles and zero marking cannot be used any more as a means of validation. The same holds for the negator and other target adverbial elements. We have seen that this restriction constitutes a distinct acquisition problem for both children and adults, by virtue of the complementary distribution of the lexical and grammaticalized linking devices, as the learner progresses towards FLS. We repeat Nederstigt's explanation:

Caroline's particle use clearly reflects a conflict between AUCH and the finite verb. This conflict between the location of the particle and the finite verb provides evidence for the analysis of AUCH as an overt assertion marker because without this function the emergence of the finite verb in AUCH-utterances would be without consequences. (Nederstigt 2002: 275)

The FLS is characterized by the functional interaction of M- and S-finiteness through TL syntax. TL syntax can override the information structure regularities of the previous stage; for example, part of the lexical content of the predicate occurs before the finite element in the case of tensed main verbs, the finite element occurs to the right of NEG in TL Italian, informationally topical items may have to occur behind the finiteness marker in the case of the V2 Germanic languages.

To conclude, the COS, which is attested in both child and adult data, shows learners' attempts to express two distinct functions—anchoring and linking—which together allow a speaker to assert: to validate a state of affairs with respect to a TT. These attempts show learners striving for a one-to-one correspondence between form and function (and this is not the first time that such correspondences have been reported in work on language acquisition). In this respect, acquisitional data constitute supporting evidence for theories which see the double operation behind assertion as the central aspect of finiteness: 'Being the carrier of [assertion] is the main function of finiteness' (Klein 1998: 225). These two operations are conflated in the TL expression of finiteness, and this presents an acquisitional problem for both types of learner. Thus, although the standard assumption of the differences in the expression of finiteness between child and adult acquirers is that the former quickly and effortlessly develop the necessary verbal morphology and the latter do not, we have tried to give a more nuanced picture, showing that there are more similarities in the process than is usually assumed.

References

Abdullaev, S. N. (1954). *Grammatika Darginskogo Jazyka: Fonetika i Morfologija* [A Grammar of Dargwa: Phonetics and Morphology]. Maxačkala: DagNIIJaLI.

Abraham, W. (1989). 'Futur-Typologie in den germanischen Sprachen', in W. Abraham and T. Janssen (eds.), *Tempus-Aspekt-Modus: Die lexikalischen und grammatischen Formen in den germanischen Sprachen*. Tübingen: Niemeyer, 345–89.

Ackema, P., and Schoorlemmer, M. (1995). 'Middles and nonmovement', *Linguistic Inquiry* 26: 173–97.

Ackerman, F., and Webelhuth, G. (1998). *A Theory of Predicates*. Stanford, CA: CSLI.

Adger, D. (1994). 'Functional heads and interpretation'. Ph.D. thesis, University of Edinburgh, Centre for Cognitive Science.

—— (1996). 'Agreement, aspect and measure phrases in Scottish Gaelic', in R. Borsley and I. Roberts (eds.), *The Syntax of the Celtic Languages*. Cambridge: Cambridge University Press, 200–22.

—— (2000). 'VSO clause structure and morphological feature checking', in R. Borsley (ed.), *Syntactic Categories*. New York: Academic Press, 79–100.

—— (2003). *Core Syntax*. Oxford: Oxford University Press.

—— and Ramchand, G. (2003). 'Predication and equation', *Linguistic Inquiry* 34: 325–59.

Agbojo, K., and Litvinov, V. (2001). 'Imperative sentences in Ewe', in Xrakovskij (2001: 390–403).

Aissen J. (2003). 'Differential object marking: iconicity vs. economy', *Natural Language and Linguistic Theory* 21: 435–83.

Akmajian, A. (1984). 'Sentence types and the form–function fit', *Natural Language and Linguistic Theory* 2: 1–23.

Alekseev, M. E. (2001). 'Naxsko-Dagestanskie jazyki' [The Nakh-Daghestanian languages], in M. E. Alekseev (ed.), *Jazyki mira: Kavkazskie jazyki*. Moscow: Akademija, 156–66.

Allan, K. (1986). *Linguistic Meaning*, vol. 2. London: Routledge & Kegan Paul.

—— (1994). 'Speech act classification and definition', in R. E. Asher (ed.), *The Encyclopaedia of Language and Linguistics*, vol. 8. Oxford: Pergamon Press, 4124–7.

Allwood, J., Andersson, L.-G., and Dahl, O. (1977). *Logic in Linguistics*. Cambridge: Cambridge University Press.

Almela Pérez, R. (1985). 'El *si* introductor de oraciones independientes en español', *Lingüística española actual* 7: 5–13.

Ambrazas, V. (ed.) (1985). *Grammatika Litovskogo Jazyka* [A Grammar of Lithuanian]. Vilnius: Mokslas.

Ameka, F. (1991). 'Ewe: its grammatical constructions and illocutionary devices'. Ph.D. thesis, Australian National University.

Andersen, R. (1991). 'Developmental sequences: the emergence of aspect marking in second language acquisition', in C. Ferguson and T. Huebner (eds.), *Second Language Acquisition and Linguistic Theories.* Amsterdam: Benjamins, 305–24.

—— and Shirai, Y. (1994). 'Discourse motivations for some cognitive acquisition principles', *Studies in Second Language Acquisition* 16: 133–56.

Anderson, J. M. (1997). 'Finiteness and auxiliarihood', in M. Rydén et al. (eds.), *From Runes to Romance: A Festschrift for Gunnar Persson on his Sixtieth Birthday, November 9, 1997.* Umeå: University of Umeå, 1–20.

—— (2001). 'Finiteness, in Greek, and elsewhere', *Poznań Studies in Contemporary Linguistics* 37: 5–33.

Anderson, S. (1982). 'Types of dependency in anaphors: Icelandic (and other) reflexives', *Journal of Linguistic Research* 2: 1–22.

—— (2002). 'Syntax and morphology are different: commentary on Jonas', in D. Lightfoot (ed.), *Syntactic Effects of Morphological Change.* Oxford: Oxford University Press, 271–5.

Andersson, L.-G. (1985). *Form and Function of Subordinate Clauses.* Gothenburg: Gothenburg University, Department of Linguistics.

Andrews, A., and Manning, C. (1999). *Complex Predicates and Information Spreading in LFG.* Stanford, CA: CSLI.

Antinucci, F., and Miller, R. (1976). 'How children talk about what happened', *Journal of Child Language* 3: 167–89.

Ascoli, G. (1896). 'Un problema di sintassi comparata dialettale', *Archivio glottologico italiano* 14: 453–68.

Asher, R. (1985). *Tamil.* London: Croom Helm.

Austin, P. (1981a). *A grammar of Diyari, South Australia.* Cambridge: Cambridge University Press.

—— (1981b). 'Switch reference in Australia', *Language* 57: 309–34.

—— (ed.) (1988). *Complex Sentence Constructions in Australian Languages.* Amsterdam: Benjamins.

Avrorin, V. (1961). *Grammatika Nanajskogo Jazyka* [A Grammar of Nanai], vol. 2. Moscow: Nauka.

Avrutin, S. (1997). 'EVENTS as units of discourse representation in root infinitives', in J. Schaeffer (ed.), *The Interpretation of Root Infinitives and Bare Nouns in Child Language.* Cambridge, MA: MIT, 65–91.

—— (1999). *Development of the Syntax–Discourse Interface.* Dordrecht: Kluwer.

Babby, L. (1989). 'Subjectlessness, external subcategorization, and the Projection Principle', *Zbornik Matice Srpske za Filologiju i Lingvistiku* 32: 7–40.

Baker, M. (1985). 'The mirror principle and morphosyntactic explanation', *Linguistic Inquiry* 16: 373–416.

—— (1988). *Incorporation: A Theory of Grammatical Function Changing.* Chicago: University of Chicago Press.

Baltin, M. (1995). 'Floating quantifiers, PRO and predication', *Linguistic Inquiry* 26: 199–248.

Barbato, M. (ed.) (2001). *Il Libro viii del Plinio Napoletano di Giovanni Brancati*. Naples: Liguori.

Barbaud, P. (1987). 'Chaînes pronominales et positions non-argumentales', *Revue canadienne de linguistique* 32: 1–46.

—— (1988). 'De la modernité de la grammaire dans le style indirect: le cas de l'infinitif de narration', *Revue québécoise de linguistique théorique et appliquée*, 33: 113–28.

Bardel, C. (1999). 'Negation and information structure in the Italian L2 of a Swedish learner', *Acquisition et interaction en langue étrangère*, numéro spécial: *Proceedings of 8th EUROSLA Conference*, 2: 173–88.

Bardovi-Harlig, K. (1995). 'A narrative perspective on the development of the tense/ aspect system in second language acquisition', *Studies in Second Language Acquisition* 17: 263–91.

—— (1998a). 'From morpheme studies to temporal semantics: tense-aspect research in SLA', *Studies in Second Language Acquisition* 21: 341–82.

—— (1998b). 'Narrative structure and lexical aspect: conspiring factors in second language acquisition of tense-aspect morphology', *Studies in Second Language Acquisition* 20: 471–508.

Bar-Shalom, E., and Snyder, W. (1999). 'On the relationship between root infinitives and imperatives in early child Russian', in A. Greenhill, H. Littlefield, and C. Tano (eds.), *Proceedings of the 23rd Annual Boston University Conference on Language Development*. Somerville, MA: Cascadilla, 56–67.

Bäuerle, R., and von Stechow, A. (1980). 'Finite and non-finite temporal constructions in German', in C. Rohrer (ed.), *Time, Tense, and Quantifiers: Proceedings of the Stuttgart Conference on the Logic of Tense and Quantification*. Tübingen: Niemeyer, 375–421.

Bayer, J. (1983/4). 'COMP in Bavarian syntax', *Linguistic Review* 3: 209–74.

Becker, A. (2005). 'The acquisition of negation and the acquisition of finiteness', in H. Hendriks (ed.), *The Structure of Learner Varieties*, vol. 28. Berlin: Mouton de Gruyter, 263–314.

Becker, M., and Hyams, N. (2000). 'Modal reference in children's root infinitives', in E. C. Clark (ed.), *Proceedings of the 30th Annual Child Language Research Forum*. Stanford, CA: CSLI, 113–22.

Behrens, H. (1993). *Temporal Reference in German Child Language: Form and Function of Early Verb Use*. Zutphen: Koninglijke Wöhrmann.

Belletti, A. (1990). *Generalized Verb Movement: Aspects of Verb Syntax*. Turin: Rosenberg & Sellier.

Bello, A. (1984) [1847]. *Gramática de la lengua castellana*. Madrid: EDAF.

Benazzo, S. (2000). 'L'acquisition des particules de portée en français, anglais et allemand L2: étude longitudinale comparée'. Ph.D. thesis, Université Paris VIII.

—— (2002). 'Communicative potential vs. structural constraints: explanatory factors for the acquisition of scope particles', *Eurosla Yearbook* 2: 187–204.

Benazzo, S. (2003). 'The interaction between the development of verb morphology and the acquisition of temporal adverbs of contrast', in Dimroth and Starren (2003: 187–210).

—— and Giuliano, P. (1998). 'Marqueurs de négation et particules de portée en français L2: où les placer?', *Acquisition et interaction en langue étrangère* 11: 35–61.

Bennett, C. E. (1966). *Syntax of Early Latin*, vol 1: *The Verb*. Hildesheim: Olms.

Benveniste, E. (1974) [1966]. *Problèmes de linguistique générale*. Paris: Gallimard.

Bergelson, M. B. (2001). 'Imperative constructions in Bamana', in Xrakovskij (2001: 485–98).

Bergström A. (1997). 'L'influence des distinctions aspectuelles sur l'acquisition des temps en français langue étrangère', *Acquisition et interaction en langue étrangère* 9: 52–82.

Bernini, G. (2000). 'Negative items and negation strategies in non-native Italian', *Studies in Second Language Acquisition* 22: 399–440.

Bethel, R. et al. (n.d.). 'A practical dictionary for Western Mono'. MS, University of California, Los Angeles, American Indian Studies Centre.

Bhardwaj, M., Dietrich, R., and Noyau, C. (eds.) (1988). 'Second language acquisition by adult immigrants: temporality'. Final Report 5 submitted to the European Science Foundation, Strasbourg.

Bhatia, T. K. (1993). *Punjabi: A Cognitive-Descriptive Grammar*. London: Routledge.

Bianchi, V. (2000). 'On finiteness and nominative case licensing', *Quaderni del Laboratorio di Linguistica* (nuova serie) 1: 145–67.

—— (2003). 'On finiteness as logophoric anchoring', in J. Guéron and L. Tasmovski (eds.), *Temps et point de vue/Tense and Point of View*. Nanterre: Université Paris X, 213–46.

Bichelli, P. (1974). *Grammatica del dialetto napoletano*. Bari: Pégaso.

Birjulin, L., and Xrakovskij, V. (2001). 'Imperative sentences: theoretical problems', in Xrakovskij (2001: 3–50).

Bisang, W. (1995). 'Verb serialization and converbs: differences and similarities', in König and Haspelmath (1995: 137–88).

—— (1998). 'The view from the Far East: comments on seven thematic areas', in J. Van der Auwera with D. P. Ó Baoill (eds.), *Adverbial Constructions in the Languages of Europe*. Berlin: Mouton de Gruyter, 641–812.

—— (2001a). 'Finite vs. non finite languages', in M. Haspelmath, E. König, W. Oesterreicher, and W. Raible (eds.), *Language Typology and Language Universals*, vol. 2. Berlin: Mouton de Gruyter, 1400–1413.

—— (2001b). 'Areality, grammaticalization and language typology: on the explanatory power of functional criteria and the status of Universal Grammar', in W. Bisang (ed.), *Language Typology and Universals*. Berlin: Akademie, 175–223.

—— (2002). 'Classification and the evolution of grammatical structures: a universal perspective', *Sprachtypologie und Universalienforschung* 55: 289–308.

—— (2004). 'Grammaticalization without coevolution of form and meaning: the case of tense-aspect-modality in east and mainland Southeast Asia', in W. Bisang,

N. P. Himmelmann, and B. Wiemer (eds.), *What Makes Grammaticalization? A Look from its Fringes and its Components*. Berlin: Mouton de Gruyter, 109–38.

Blake, B. (1976). 'Rapporteur's introduction and summary (The bivalent suffix -*ku*)', in R. M. W. Dixon (ed.), *Grammatical Categories in Australian Languages*. Canberra: Australian Institute of Aboriginal Studies, 421–4.

Blass, F., and Debrunner, A. (1976). *Grammatik des Neutestamentlichen Griechisch*. Göttingen: Vandenhoeck & Ruprecht.

Blatt, F. (1952). *Précis de syntaxe latine*. Lyon: IAC.

Blom, E. (2002). 'On the use and interpretation of root infinitives in early child Dutch', in S. Barbiers, F. Beukema, and W. van der Wurff (eds.), *Modality and its Interaction with the Verbal System*. Amsterdam: Benjamins, 103–32.

Bloom, L., Lifter, K., and Hafitz, J. (1980). 'Semantics of verbs and the development of verb inflection in child language', *Language* 56: 386–412.

Bloomfield, L. (1933). *Language*. New York: Holt.

Bobaljik, J. (2000). 'The rich agreement hypothesis in review'. MS, McGill University.

—— and Carnie, A. (1996). 'A Minimalist approach to some problems of Irish word order', in R. Borsley and I. Roberts (eds.), *The Syntax of the Celtic Languages*. Cambridge: Cambridge University Press, 223–40.

Böhm, G. (1984). *Grammatik der Kunama-Sprache*. Vienna: Institut für Afrikanistik.

Bokarev, A. A. (1949). *Sintaksis avarskogo jazyka* [The Syntax of Avar]. Moscow: Akademija Nauk.

Borer, H. (1989). 'Anaphoric AGR', in O. Jaeggli and K. Safir (eds.), *The Null Subject Parameter*. Dordrecht: Kluwer, 69–109.

Borsley, R., and Kornfilt, J. (2000). 'Mixed extended projections', in R. Borsley (ed.), *The Nature and Function of Syntactic Categories*. New York: Academic Press, 101–31.

Boser, K., Lust, B., Santelmann, L., and Whitman, J. (1992). 'The syntax of CP and V2 in early child German: the Strong Continuity Hypothesis', *Proceedings of NELS* 22: 51–66.

Bowerman, M. (1985). 'What shapes children's grammars?', in D. I. Slobin (ed.), *The Crosslinguistic Study of Language Acquisition*, vol. 2. Hillsdale, NJ: Erlbaum, 1257–1319.

Bowers, J. (1993). 'The syntax of predication', *Linguistic Inquiry* 24: 591–656.

Brandner, E. (2004). 'Head-movement in Minimalism and V2 as FORCE-marking', in H. Lohnstein and S. Trissler (eds.), *Syntax and Semantics of the Left Periphery*. Berlin: Mouton de Gruyter, 97–138.

Branigan, P. (1996). 'Verb-second and the A-bar syntax of subjects', *Studia Linguistica* 50: 50–79.

Bresnan, J. (ed.) (1982). *The Mental Representation of Grammatical Relations*. Cambridge, MA: MIT Press.

—— (2001). *Lexical-Functional Syntax*. Oxford: Blackwell.

Bronckart, J. P., and Sinclair, H. (1973). ' Time, Tense and Aspect', *Cognition* 2: 107–30.

Brown, P., and Levinson, S. L. (1987). *Politeness: Some Universals in Language Usage*. Cambridge: Cambridge University Press.

Brun, D., Avrutin, S., and Babyonyshev, M. (1999). 'Aspect and its temporal interpretation during the optional infinitive stage in Russian', in A. Greenhill, H. Littlefield, and C. Tano (eds.), *Proceedings of the Boston University Conference on Language Development*. Somerville, MA: Cascadilla, 120–31.

Burt, M. K., and Dulay, H. (1980). 'On acquisition orders', in S. W. Felix (ed.), *Second Language Development: Trends and Issues*. Tübingen: Narr, 265–327.

Buscha, A. (1976). 'Isolierte Nebensätze im dialogischen Text', *Deutsch als Fremdsprache* 13: 274–79.

Bybee, J. L. (1985). *Morphology: A Study of the Relation between Meaning and Form*. Amsterdam: Benjamins.

—— (1994). 'The grammaticalization of zero', in W. Pagliuca (ed.), *Perspectives on Grammaticalization*. Amsterdam: Benjamins, 235–53.

—— (1997). 'Semantic aspects of morphological typology', in J. Bybee, J. Haiman, and S. A. Thompson (eds.), *Essays on Language Function and Language Type*. Amsterdam: Benjamins, 25–37.

—— and Fleischman, S. (1995). 'Issues in mood and modality: introductory essay for the volume', in J. Bybee and S. Fleischman (eds.), *Modality in Grammar and Discourse*. Amsterdam: Benjamins, 1–14.

—— Perkins, R. D., and Pagliuca, W. (1994). *The Evolution of Grammar: Tense, Aspect and Modality in the Languages of the World*. Chicago: University of Chicago Press.

Caesar, Julius (1917). *The Gallic War*, with an English translation by H. J. Edwards. London: Heinemann.

—— (1951). *The Conquest of Gaul*, trans. S. A. Handford. Harmondsworth: Pengin.

Calabrese, A. (1993). 'The sentential complementation of Salentino: a study of a language without infinitival clauses', in A. Belletti (ed.), *Syntactic Theory and the Dialects of Italy*. Turin: Rosenberg & Sellier, 29–98.

Calder, G. (1990) [1923]. *A Gaelic Grammar*. Glasgow: Gairm.

Campbell, L. (1985). *The Pipil Language of El Salvador*. Berlin: Mouton.

—— (1991). 'Some grammaticalisation changes in Estonian and their implications', in Traugott and Heine (1991a: 285–99).

—— (1997). *American Indian Languages: The Historical Linguistics of Native America*. New York: Oxford University Press.

—— (2000). 'What's wrong with grammaticalisation?', *Language Sciences* 4: 1–49.

Carlson, R. (1992). 'Narrative, subjunctive, and finiteness', *Journal of African Languages and Linguistics* 13: 59–85.

—— (1994). *A Grammar of Supyire*. Berlin: Mouton de Gruyter.

Carnie, A. (2002). *Syntax: A Generative Introduction*. Oxford: Blackwell.

Cecchetto, C., and Oniga, R. (2001). 'Consequences of the analysis of Latin infinitival clauses for the theory of case and control'. MS, University of Milano-Bicocca and University of Udine.

Choi, Y.-S. (1998). 'Das Konverb im Koreanischen'. MA thesis, University of Mainz.

Chomsky, N. (1973). 'Conditions on transformations', in S. R. Anderson and P. Kiparsky (eds.), *A Festschrift for Morris Halle*. New York: Holt, Rinehart & Winston, 232–86.

—— (1980). 'On binding', *Linguistic Inquiry* 11: 1–46.

—— (1981). *Lectures on Government and Binding: The Pisa Lectures*. Dordrecht: Foris.

—— (1986a). *Barriers*. Cambridge, MA: MIT Press.

—— (1986b). *Knowledge of Language*. New York: Praeger.

—— (1991). 'Some notes on the economy of derivation and representation', in R. Freidin (ed.), *Principles and Parameters in Comparative Grammar*. Cambridge, MA: MIT Press, 167–217.

—— (1993). 'A Minimalist Program for linguistic theory', in K. Hale and S. Keyser (eds.), *The View from Building 20*. Cambridge, MA: MIT Press, 1–52.

—— (1995a). 'Categories and transformations', in Chomsky (1995b: 219–394).

—— (1995b). *The Minimalist Program*. Cambridge, MA: MIT Press.

—— (2000). 'Minimalist inquiries: the framework', in R. Martin, D. Michaels, and J. Uriagereka (eds.), *Step by Step: Essays on Minimalist Syntax in Honour of Howard Lasnik*. Cambridge, MA: MIT Press, 89–115.

—— (2001a). *Beyond Explanatory Adequacy*. Cambridge, MA: MIT, Department of Linguistics and Philosophy.

—— (2001b). 'Derivation by phase', in M. Kenstowicz (ed.), *Ken Hale: A Life in Language*. Cambridge, MA: MIT Press, 1–52.

—— and Lasnik, H. (1977). 'Filters and control', *Linguistic Inquiry* 11: 1–46.

—— —— (1993). 'The theory of principles and parameters', in J. Jacobs et al. (eds.), *Syntax: An International Handbook of Contemporary Research*. Berlin: de Gruyter, 506–69.

Chung, S., and Timberlake, A. (1985). 'Tense, aspect, and mood', in Shopen (1985: 3. 202–58).

Cinque, G. (1990). *Types of A-Bar Dependencies*. Cambridge, MA: MIT Press.

—— (1999). *Adverbs and Functional Heads: A Cross-Linguistic Perspective*. Oxford: Oxford University Press.

Clahsen, H. (1988). *Normale und gestörte Kindersprache. Linguistische Untersuchungen zu Syntax und Morphologie*. Amsterdam: Benjamins.

—— (1996). *Generative Perspective on Language Acquisition*. Amsterdam: Benjamins.

—— Eisenbeiss, S., and Penke, M. (1996). 'Lexical learning in early syntactic development', in Clahsen (1996: 129–59).

—— and Muysken, P. (1986). 'The availability of Universal Grammar to adult and child learners: a study of the acquisition of German word order', *Second Language Research* 2: 93–119.

—— and Penke, M. (1992). 'The acquisition of agreement morphology and its syntactic consequences: new evidence on German child language from the Simone-Corpus', in J. Meisel (ed.), *The Acquisition of Verb Placement: Functional Categories and V2 Phenomena in Language Acquisition*. Dordrecht: Kluwer, 181–223.

Clahsen, H. and Rothweiler, M. (1993). 'Inflectional rules in children's grammar: evidence from German participles', in G. Booij and J. van Marle (eds.), *Yearbook of Morphology 1992.* Dordrecht: Kluwer, 1–34.

Clark, E. (1971). 'On the acquisition of the meaning of "before" and "after"', *Journal of Verbal Learning and Verbal Behavior* 10: 266–75.

Cohen, M. (1936). *Traité de langue amharique.* Paris: Institut d'Ethnologie.

Coluccia, R. (ed.) (1987). Ferraiolo, *Cronaca.* Florence: Accademia della Crusca.

Compagna, A. M. (ed.) (1990). Lupo de Spechio, *Summa dei re di Napoli e Sicilia e dei re d'Aragona.* Naples: Liguori.

Comrie, B. (1974). 'The second dative: a transformational approach', in R. Brecht and C. Chvany (eds.), *Slavic Transformational Syntax.* Ann Arbor: University of Michigan, 123–50.

—— (1976). 'The syntax of action nominals: a cross-language study', *Lingua* 40: 177–201.

—— (1981). *The Languages of the Soviet Union.* Cambridge: Cambridge University Press.

—— and Corbett, G. (eds.) (1993). *The Slavonic Languages.* London: Routledge.

—— and Thompson, S. A. (1985). 'Lexical nominalization', in Shopen (1985: 3. 349–98).

Conrad, R. (1969). *Transformationsanalyse russischer Infinitivkonstruktionen.* Halle (Saale): Niemeyer.

Contino, S. (1977). *L'infinito storico latino.* Bologna: Pàtron.

Cottell, S. (1995). 'The representation of tense in Modern Irish', *GenGenP* 3: 105–24.

Coulmas, F. (ed.) (1986). *Direct and Indirect Speech.* Berlin: Mouton de Gruyter.

Craig, C. G. (1977). *The Structure of Jacaltec.* Austin: University of Texas Press.

Cristofaro, S. (1997). 'Aspetti diacronici e sincronici della subordinazione infinitiva in alcuni dialetti calabresi e pugliesi e nelle lingue balcaniche: una prospettiva tipologico-funzionalista', in P. Ramat and E. Roma (eds.), *Sintassi storica: atti del XXX Congresso della Società di Linguistica Italiana, Pavia, 26–28 settembre 1996.* Rome: Bulzoni, 495–518.

—— (1998). 'Deranking and balancing in different subordination relations: a typological study', *Sprachtypologie und Universalienforschung* 51: 3–42.

—— (2003). *Subordination.* Oxford: Oxford University Press.

Croft, W. (1991). *Syntactic Categories and Grammatical Relations.* Chicago: University of Chicago Press.

—— (2000). *Explaining Language Change: An Evolutionary Approach.* Harlow, Essex: Longman.

—— (2001). *Radical Construction Grammar.* Oxford: Oxford University Press.

—— (2003) [1990]. *Typology and Universals.* Cambridge: Cambridge University Press.

—— and Cruse, A. (2004). *Cognitive Linguistics.* Cambridge: Cambridge University Press.

Crystal, D. (1997). *The Cambridge Encyclopedia of the English Language.* Cambridge: Cambridge University Press.

Culicover, P., and Jackendoff, R. (2001). 'Control is not movement', *Linguistic Inquiry* 32: 493–512.

Culioli, A. (1995) [1983]. *Cognition and Representation in Linguistic Theory*, texts selected and introduced by Michel Liddle. Amsterdam: Benjamins.

Dahl, Ö., and Koptjevskaja-Tamm, M. (eds.) (2001). *The Circum-Baltic Languages: Their Typology and Contacts*. Amsterdam: Benjamins.

Dalrymple, M. (1993). *The Syntax of Anaphoric Binding*. Stanford, CA: CSLI.

—— (2001). *Lexical Functional Grammar*. New York: Academic Press.

Danchin, A. (2000). 'L'identité génétique', in Y. Michaud (ed.), *Qu'est-ce que la vie?*, vol. 1. Paris: Jacob, 59–68.

Daragan, J. V., and Majsak, T. A. (2001). 'Častitsy, Sojuzy i Transkategorial'nye Pokazateli' [Particles, conjunctions and transcategorial markers], in Kibrik (2001: 173–84).

De Blasi, N. (ed.) (1986). *Libro de la destructione de Troya: volgarizzamento napoletano trecentesco da Guido delle Colonne*. Rome: Bonacci.

—— (2002). 'Notizie sulla variazione diastratica a Napoli tra il'500 e il 2000', *Bollettino linguistico campano* 1: 89–129.

Déchaine, R.-M. (1995). 'Zero tense in Standard and African American English', *Proceedings of NELS* 25: 63–77.

den Besten, H. (1983). 'On the interaction of root transformations and lexical deletive rules', in W. Abraham (ed.), *On the Formal Syntax of the Westgermania*. Amsterdam: Benjamins, 47–131.

Dench, A. (2003). 'From purposive/future to present: shifting temporal categories in the Pilbara languages of north west Western Australia', in B. Blake and K. Burridge (eds.), *Historical Linguistics 2001*. Amsterdam: Benjamins, 105–32.

—— (2006). 'Case marking strategies in subordinate clauses in Pilbara languages: some diachronic speculations', *Australian Journal of Linguistics* 26: 81–105.

—— and Evans, N. (1988). 'Multiple case-marking in Australian languages', *Australian Journal of Linguistics* 8: 1–48.

Derbyshire, D. (1979). *Hixkaryana*. Amsterdam: North-Holland.

de Villiers, J., and de Villiers, P. (1973). 'A cross-sectional study of the acquisition of grammatical morphemes', *Journal of Psycholinguistic Research* 2: 267–78.

Dietrich, R., Klein, W., and Noyau, C. (1995). *The Acquisition of Temporality in a Second Language*. Amsterdam: Benjamins.

Dik, S. (1981). 'On the typology of focus phenomena', in T. Hoekstra (ed.), *Perspectives on Functional Grammar*. Dordrecht: Foris, 41–74.

—— (1997a). *The Theory of Functional Grammar*, part 1: *The Structure of the Clause*. Berlin: Mouton de Gruyter.

—— (1997b). *The Theory of Functional Grammar*, part 2: *Complex and Derived Constructions*. Berlin: Mouton de Gruyter.

—— et al. (1980). 'On the typology of focus phenomena', *Leids Taalkundig Bulletin GLOT* 3: 41–74.

Dimmendaal, G. J. (1983). *The Turkana Language*. Dordrecht: Foris.

Dimroth, C. (1998). 'Fokuspartikeln und Informationsgliederung im Diskurs', Ph.D. thesis, Freie Universität Berlin.

—— (2002). 'Topics, assertions, and additive words: how L2 learners get from information structure to target-language syntax', *Linguistics* 40: 891–923.

—— Gretsch P., Perdue, C., Jordens, P., and Starren, M. (2003). 'Finiteness in Germanic languages: a stage model for first and second language development', in Dimroth and Starren (2003: 65–93).

—— and Lasser, I. (2002). 'Finite options: how L1 and L2 learners cope with the acquisition of finiteness', *Linguistics* 40: 647–51.

—— and Starren, M. (eds.) (2003). *Information Structure, Linguistic Structure, and the Dynamics of Language Acquisition.* Amsterdam: Benjamins.

Disterheft, D. (1980). *The Syntactic Development of the Infinitive in Indo-European.* Columbus, OH: Slavica.

Dixon, R. M. W. (1972). *The Dyirbal Language of North Queensland.* Cambridge: Cambridge University Press.

—— (1994). *Ergativity.* Cambridge: Cambridge University Press.

Dobrovie-Sorin, C. (1994). *The Syntax of Romanian.* Berlin: Mouton de Gruyter.

—— (2001). 'Head-to-head merge in Balkan subjunctives and locality', in M. L. Rivero and A. Ralli (eds.), *Comparative Syntax of Balkan Languages.* Oxford: Oxford University Press, 44–73.

Dobrušina, N. (1999a). 'Formy Imperativnoj Serii' [Imperative forms], in Kibrik (1999: 278–85).

—— (1999b). 'Formy Irreal'nogo Naklonenija' [Irrealis forms], in Kibrik (1999: 261–9).

—— (2001a). 'Formy Imperativnoj Serii' [Imperative forms'], in Kibrik (2001: 319–31).

—— (2001b). 'Irrealis', in Kibrik (2001: 332–3).

—— (2003). 'Imperative deictic reduction', in P. Suihkonen and B. Comrie (eds.), *International Symposium on Deictic Systems and Quantification in Languages spoken in Europe and North and Central Asia. Udmurt State University, Iževsk, Udmurt Republic, Russian, May 22–25, 2001. Collection of papers.* Iževsk: Udmurt State University and Max Planck Institute for Evolutionary Anthropology, 68–83.

Donaldson, B. (1993). *A Grammar of Afrikaans.* Berlin: Mouton de Gruyter.

Donaldson, T. (1980). *Ngiyambaa: The Language of the Wangaaybuwan.* Cambridge: Cambridge University Press.

Donhauser, K. (1986). *Der Imperativ im Deutschen: Studien zur Syntax und Semantik der deutschen Modussystems.* Hamburg: Buske.

Donohue, M. (1999). *A Grammar of Tukang Besi.* Berlin: Mouton de Gruyter.

Douglas, W. H. (1964). *An Introduction to the Western Desert Language.* Sydney: Oceania Linguistic Monographs.

Drubig, H. B. (2001). 'Towards a typology of focus and focus constructions', in E. Göbbel and C. Meier (eds.), *Focus Constructions: Grammatical and Typological Aspects of Information Structure.* Sonderheft der Zeitschrift *Linguistics*, 1–50.

Dryer, M. (1996). 'Grammatical relations in Ktunaxa (Kutenai)', the Belcourt Lecture delivered before the University of Manitoba, 24 Feb. 1995, Winnipeg, Canada. http://linguistics.buffalo.edu/people/faculty/dryer/dryer/dryer.htm

—— (1997). 'Are grammatical relations universal?', in J. Bybee, J. Haiman, and S. A. Thompson (eds.), *Essays in Language Function and Language Type*. Amsterdam: Benjamins, 115–43.

Du Feu, V. (1996). *Rapanui*. London: Routledge.

Durrell, M. (1997). *Hammer's German Grammar and Usage*. London: Arnold.

Egerland, V. (1998). 'On verb-second violations in Swedish and the hierarchical ordering of adverbs', *Working Papers in Scandinavian Syntax* 61: 1–22.

Emonds, J. (1978). 'The verbal complex V'-V in French', *Linguistic Inquiry* 9: 151–75.

—— (2004). 'Unspecified categories as the key to root constructions', in D. Adger, C. de Cat, and G. Tsoulas (eds.), *Peripheries: Syntactic Edges and their Effects*. Dordrecht: Kluwer, 75–120.

Englebert, A. (1998). *L'Infinitif dit de narration*. Paris: Duculot.

Erjavec, T. (1994). 'Formalizing realizational morphology in typed feature structures', in G. Bouma and G. van Noord (eds.), *Proceedings of 4th Computational Linguistics in the Netherlands Meeting*. Groningen: University of Groningen, 47–58. (http://odur.let.rug.nl/~vannoord/Clin/Clin4/toc.html)

Ernout, A., and Thomas, F. (1964). *Syntaxe latine*. Paris: Klincksieck.

Etxepare, R., and Grohmann, K. K. (2005). 'Towards a grammar of adult root infinitives', *West Coast Conference on Formal Linguistics* 24: 129–37.

Eubank, L. (1993/4). 'On the transfer of parametric values in L2 development', *Language Acquisition* 3: 183–208.

—— (1996). 'Negation in early German–English interlanguage: more valueless features in the L2 initial state', *Second Language Research* 12: 73–106.

—— and Beck, M.-L. (1998). 'OI-like effects in adult L2 acquisition', in A. Greenhill et al. (eds.), *Proceedings of the 22nd Annual Boston University Conference on Language Development*. Somerville, MA: Cascadilla Press, 189–200.

—— and Grace, S. (1996). 'Where's the mature language? Where's the native language?', in Stringfellow (1996: 189–200).

—— and Schwarz, B. (1996). 'What is the L2 initial state?', *Second Language Research* 12: 1–5.

Evans, N. (1993). 'Code, inference, placedness and ellipsis', in W. A. Foley (ed.), *The Role of Theory in Linguistic Description*. Berlin: Mouton de Gruyter, 243–80.

—— (1995a). *A Grammar of Kayardild*. Berlin: Mouton de Gruyter.

—— (1995b). 'Multiple case in Kayardild: anti-iconicity and the diachronic filter', in F. Plank (ed.), *Double Case: Agreement by Suffixaufnahme*. Oxford: Oxford University Press, 396–428.

Fantuzzi, C. (1996). 'The acquisition of tense and temporal reference', in A. String-fellow, D. Dahana-Amitay, E. Hughes, and A. Zukowski (eds.), *Proceedings of the 20th Annual Boston University Conference on Language Development.* Somerville, MA: Cascadilla, 201–12.

Felix, S. (1989). 'Finite infinitives in Modern Greek', in C. Bhatt, E. Löbel, and C. Schmidt (eds.), *Syntactic Phrase Structure Phenomena in Noun Phrases and Sentences.* Amsterdam: Benjamins, 113–32.

Fillmore, C. J. (1986). 'Pragmatically controlled zero anaphora', *Berkeley Linguistic Society* 12: 95–107.

—— (1999). 'Inversion and constructional inheritance', in G. Webelhuth, J.-P. Koenig, and A. Kathol (eds.), *Lexical and Constructional Aspects of Linguistic Explanation.* Stanford, CA: CSLI, 113–28.

—— and Kay, P. (1997). 'Berkeley Construction Grammar'. http://www.icsi.berkeley.edu/ ~kay/bcg/ConGram.html

—— —— and O'Connor, C. (1988). 'Regularity and idiomaticity in grammatical constructions: the case of *let alone*', *Language* 64: 501–38.

Fisher, K. (1988). 'Agreement and the distribution of anaphora', in M. Hammond, E. Moravcsik, and J. Wirth (eds.), *Studies in Syntactic Typology.* Amsterdam: Benjamins, 25–36.

Foley, W. A. (1991). *The Yimas Language of New Guinea.* Stanford, CA: Stanford University Press.

Ford, C. E. (1988). 'Grammar in ordinary interaction: the pragmatics of adverbial clauses in conversational English'. Ph.D. thesis, University of California, Los Angeles.

—— and Thompson, S. A. (1986). 'Conditionals in discourse: a text-based study from English', in E. C. Traugott, A. ter Meulen, J. S. Reilly, and C. A. Ferguson (eds.), *On Conditionals.* Cambridge: Cambridge University Press, 353–72.

Fortescue, M. D. (1984). *West Greenlandic.* London: Croom Helm.

Franks, S. (1995). *Parameters of Slavic Morphosyntax.* New York: Oxford University Press.

Freeland, L. S. (1951). *Language of the Sierra Miwok.* Baltimore: Waverley Press.

Fried, M., and Östman, J.-O. (2004). 'Construction grammar: a thumbnail sketch', in M. Fried and J.-O. Östman (eds.), *Construction Grammar in a Cross-Linguistic Perspective.* Amsterdam: Benjamins, 11–86.

Fritzenschaft, A., Gawlitzek-Maiwald, I., Tracy, R., and Winkler, S. (1990). 'Wege zur komplexen Syntax', *Zeitschrift für Sprachwissenschaft* 9: 52–134.

Gawlitzek-Maiwald, I. (1998). *Der monolinguale und bilinguale Erwerb von Infinitiv-konstruktionen: ein Vergleich von Deutsch und Englisch.* Tübingen: Niemeyer.

—— Tracy, R., and Fritzenschaft, A. (1992). 'Language acquisition and competing Linguistic representations: the child as arbiter', in J. Meisel (ed.), *The Acquisition of Verb Placement: Functional Categories and V2 Phenomena in Language Acquisition.* Dordrecht: Kluwer, 139–80.

Gazdar, G., Klein, E., Pullum, G., and Sag, I. (1985). *Generalized Phrase Structure Grammar.* Oxford: Blackwell.

George, L. M., and Kornfilt, J. (1981). 'Finiteness and boundedness in Turkish', in F. Heny (ed.), *Binding and Filtering*. London: Croom Helm, 105–27.

Gildea, S. (1998). *On Reconstructing Grammar: Comparative Cariban Morphosyntax*. Oxford: Oxford University Press.

Ginzburg, J., and Sag, I. A. (2000). *Interrogative Investigations: The Form, Meaning, and Use of English Interrogatives*. Stanford, CA: CSLI.

Giorgi, A. (1983/4). 'Toward a theory of long distance anaphors: a GB approach', *Linguistic Review* 3: 307–61.

—— and Pianesi, F. (1997). *Tense and Aspect: From Semantics to Morphosyntax*. New York: Oxford University Press.

Giuliano, P. (2000). 'L'acquisition et l'expression des fonctions négatives en français et en anglais comme langues secondes'. Ph.D. thesis, Université Paris VIII.

—— (2003). 'Negation and relational predicates in French and English as second languages', in Dimroth and Starren (2003: 119–57).

Givón, T. (1979). *On Understanding Grammar*. New York: Academic Press.

—— (1980). 'The binding hierarchy and the typology of complements', *Studies in Language* 4: 333–77.

—— (1984). *Syntax: A Functional-Typological Introduction*, vol. 1. Amsterdam: Benjamins.

—— (1990). *Syntax: A Functional-Typological Introduction*, vol. 2. Amsterdam: Benjamins.

—— (1991). 'Isomorphism in the grammatical code: cognitive and biological considerations', *Studies in Language* 15: 85–114.

—— (2001). *Syntax: An Introduction*, vol. 2. Amsterdam: Benjamins.

Goddard, C. (1985). *A Grammar of Yankunytjatjara*. Alice springs: Institute for Aboriginal Development.

Goldberg, A. E. (1995). *Constructions: A Construction Grammar Approach to Argument Structure*. Chicago: University of Chicago Press.

Goldenberg, G. (1969). 'Kəstanəňňa: studies in a Northern Gurage language of Christians', *Orientalia Suecana* 17: 61–102.

Grappin, H. (1963). *Grammaire de la Langue Polonaise*. Paris: Institut d'Etudes Slaves.

Greenberg, J. H. (1966). *Language Universals: With Special Reference to Feature Hierarchies*. The Hague: Mouton.

—— (1978). 'How does a language acquire gender markers?', in J. H. Greenberg (ed.), *Universals of Human Language*, vol. 3. Stanford, CA: Stanford University Press, 47–82.

—— (1991). 'The last stages of grammatical elements: contrastive and expansive desemanticization', in Traugott and Heine (1991a: 301–14).

Greenough, J., Kittredge, G. L., Howard, A. A., and D'Ooge, B. L. (1903). *Allen and Greenough's New Latin Grammar*. Boston: Ginn.

Gretsch, P. (2000). *Fokale Ellipsen in Erwachsenen- und Kindersprache*. Tübingen: Niemeyer.

—— (2003). 'On the similarities of L1 and L2 acquisition: how German children anchor utterances in time', in Dimroth and Starren (2003: 95–117).

—— (2004). 'What does finiteness mean to children? A crosslinguistic perspective on root infinitives', *Linguistics* 42: 419–68.

Grevisse, M. (2001). *Le bon usage: grammaire française*. Paris: Duculot.

Guillaume, G. (1929). *Temps et verbe: théorie des aspects, des modes et des temps*. Paris: Libraire Ancienne Honoré Champion.

Haegeman, L. (1986). 'INFL, COMP and nominative case assignment in Flemish infinitivals', in P. Muysken and H. van Riemsdijk (eds.), *Features and Projections*. Dordrecht: Foris, 123–37.

—— (1992). *Theory and Description in Generative Syntax: A Case Study in West Flemish*. Cambridge: Cambridge University Press.

—— (1995). 'Root infinitives, tense, and truncated structures in Dutch', *Language Acquisition* 4: 205–25.

—— (1997). 'Elements of grammar', in L. Haegeman (ed.), *Elements of Grammar: Handbook of Generative Syntax*. Dordrecht: Kluwer, 1–71.

—— (2004). 'The syntax of adverbial clauses and its consequences for topicalisation'. MS, Université Charles de Gaulle, Lille.

Hagège, C. (1974). 'Les pronoms logophoriques', *Bulletin de la Société de Linguistique de Paris* 69: 287–310.

Haiman, J. (1980). *Hua: A Papuan Language of the Eastern Highlands of New Guinea*. Amsterdam: Benjamins.

—— (1985). *Natural Syntax*. Cambridge: Cambridge University Press.

Håkansson, G. (2001). 'Against full transfer: evidence from Swedish learners of German', *Lund University Linguistics Working Papers* 48: 67–86.

Hale, K., and McCloskey, J. (1984). 'On the syntax of person–number inflection in Modern Irish', *Natural Language and Linguistic Theory* 1: 487–533.

Hall, R. A. Jr. (1964). *Introductory Linguistics*. Philadelphia: Chilton Books.

Halliday, M. A. K. (1970). 'Language structure and language function', in J. Lyons (ed.), *New Horizons in Linguistics*. Harmondsworth, Middlesex: Penguin, 140–64.

—— (1994). *Functional Grammar*. London: Arnold.

Hamann, C. (1996). 'Null arguments in German child language', *Language Acquisition* 5: 155–208.

Han, C. (2000). *The Structure and Interpretation of Imperatives: Mood and Force in Universal Grammar*. New York: Garland.

Hargreaves, D. (1991). 'The conceptual structure of intentional action: data from Kathmandu Newari', *Berkeley Linguistics Society* 17: 379–89.

Harris, A., and Campbell, L. (1995). *Historical Syntax in Cross-Linguistic Perspective*. Cambridge: Cambridge University Press.

Haspelmath, M. (1993). *A Grammar of Lezgian*. Berlin: Mouton de Gruyter.

—— (1995). 'The converb as a cross-linguistically valid category', in Haspelmath and Konig (1995: 1–56).

—— and König, E. (eds.) (1995). *Converbs in Cross-Linguistic Perspective*. Berlin: Mouton de Gruyter.

Heath, J. (1985). 'Discourse in the field: clause structure in Ngandi', in J. Nichols and A. Woodbury (eds.), *Grammar Inside and Outside the Clause: Some Approaches to Theory from the Field*. Cambridge: Cambridge University Press, 89–110.

Heidolph, K. E., Flämig, W., and Motsch, W. (eds.) (1981). *Grundzüge einer deutschen Grammatik*. 1980. Berlin: Akademie.

Heine, B., Claudi, U., and Hünnemeyer, F. (1991a). *Grammaticalisation: A Conceptual Framework*. Chicago: University of Chicago Press.

—— —— —— (1991b). 'From cognition to grammar: evidence from African languages', in Traugott and Heine (1991a: 149–88).

—— and Reh, M. (1984). *Grammaticalisation and Reanalysis in African Languages*. Hamburg: Buske.

Helmbrecht, J. (1996). 'The syntax of personal agreement in East Caucasian languages', *Sprachtypologie und Universalienforschung* 49: 127–48.

Hendriks, H. (1999): 'The acquisition of temporal reference in first and second language acquisition: what children already know and adults still have to learn and vice versa', *Psychology of Language and Communication* 3: 41–59.

Hengeveld, K. (1998). 'Adverbial clauses in the languages of Europe', in J. Van der Auwera with D. P. Ó Baoill (eds.), *Adverbial Constructions in the Languages of Europe*. Berlin: Mouton de Gruyter, 335–419.

Hessen, B. (1984). *Der historische Infinitiv im Wandel der Darstellungstechnik Sallusts*. Frankfurt am Main: Lang.

Hewitt, B. G. (1979). *Abkhaz*. Amsterdam: North-Holland.

—— (1987). *The Typology of Subordination in Georgian and Abkhaz*. Berlin: Mouton de Gruyter.

Hinds, J. (1986). *Japanese*. London: Routledge.

Hock, H. H. (1991). *Principles of Historical Linguistics*. Berlin: Mouton de Gruyter.

Hoekstra, T., and Hyams, N. (1998a). 'Aspects of root infinitives', *Lingua* 106: 81–112.

—— —— (1998b). 'Agreement and the finiteness of V2: evidence from child language', in A. Greenhill, M. Hughes, H. Littlefield, and H. Walsh (eds.), *Proceedings of the 22nd Annual Boston University Conference on Language Development*. Somerville, MA: Cascadilla, 360–73.

—— —— (1999). 'The eventivity constraint and modal reference effects in root infinitives', in A. Greenhill, H. Littlefield, and C. Tano (eds.), *Proceedings of the 23rd Annual Boston University Conference on Language Development*. Somerville, MA: Cascadilla, 240–52.

—— —— and Becker, M. (1999). 'The role of specifier and finiteness in early grammar', in D. Adger et al. (eds.), *Specifiers: Minimalist Approaches*. Oxford: Oxford University Press, 251–70.

Hoekstra, T., and Jordens, P. (1994). 'From adjunct to head', in T. Hoekstra and B. Schwartz (eds.), *Language Acquisition Studies in Generative Grammar: Papers in Honor of Kenneth Wexler from the GLOW Workshops*. Amsterdam: Benjamins, 119–50.

Hofmann, J. B. (1972). *Lateinische Syntax und Stilistik: mit dem allgemeinen Teil der Lateinischen Grammatik*. Munich: Beck.

Hogg, R. M. (ed.) (1992). *The Cambridge History of the English Language*, vol. 1: *The Beginnings to 1066*. Cambridge: Cambridge University Press.

Holmberg, A. (1986). *Word Order and Syntactic Features in the Scandinavian Languages and English*. Stockholm: University of Stockholm, Department of Linguistics.

—— Nikanne, U., Oraviita, I., Reime, H., and Trosterud, T. (1993). 'The structure of INFL and the finite clause in Finnish', in A. Holmberg and U. Nikanne (eds.), *Case and Other Functional Categories in Finnish Syntax*. Berlin: Mouton de Gruyter, 177–206.

—— and Platzack, C. (1995). *The Role of Inflection in Scandinavian Syntax*. Oxford: Oxford University Press.

Hooper, J., and Thompson, S. (1973). 'On the applicability of root transformations', *Linguistic Inquiry* 4: 465–97.

Hopper, P. (1998). 'The paradigm at the end of the universe', in A. G. Ramat and P. Hopper (eds.), *The Limits of Grammaticalisation*. Amsterdam: Benjamins, 147–58.

—— and Thompson, S. A. (1984). 'The discourse basis for lexical categories in Universal Grammar', *Language* 60: 703–52.

—— —— (1985). 'The iconicity of the universal categories noun and verb', in J. Haiman (ed.), *Iconicity in Syntax*. Amsterdam: Benjamins, 151–83.

—— and Traugott, E. (1993). *Grammaticalization*. Cambridge: Cambridge University Press.

Horn, L. R. (1996). 'Presupposition and implicature', in S. Lappin (ed.), *The Handbook of Contemporary Semantic Theory*. Oxford: Blackwell, 299–319.

Hornstein, N. (1990). *As Time Goes By: Tense and Universal Grammar*. Cambridge, MA: MIT Press.

—— (1999). 'Movement and control', *Linguistic Inquiry* 30: 69–96.

Huang, C.-T. (1984). 'On the distribution and reference of empty pronouns', *Linguistic Inquiry* 15: 531–74.

Huddleston, R. D. (1988). *English Grammar: An Outline*. Cambridge: Cambridge University Press.

—— and Pullum, G. K. (2002). *The Cambridge Grammar of English*. Cambridge: Cambridge University Press.

Huebner, T. (1983). *A Longitudinal Analysis of the Acquisition of English*. Ann Arbor, MI: Karoma.

Huttar, G. L., and Huttar, M. L. (1994). *Ndyuka*. London: Routledge.

Hyams, N. (1996). 'The underspecification of functional categories in early grammar', in H. Clahsen (ed.), *Generative Perspectives on Language Acquisition*. Amsterdam: Benjamins, 91–128.

Iatridou, S. (1993). 'On nominative case assignment and a few related things', *MIT Working Papers in Linguistics (Papers on Case and Agreement II)* 19: 175–96.

Ickovič, V. A. (1974). 'Očerki Sintaksičeskoj Normy' [Studies in syntactic norms], in G. A. Zolotova (ed.), *Sintaksis i Norma*. Moscow: Nauka.

Ingram, D. and Thompson, W. (1996). 'Early syntactic acquisition in German: evidence for the modal hypothesis', *Language* 72: 97–120.

Isakov, I. A. (1980). 'Èlement Klassno-Ličnogo Sprjaženija v Kusurskom Dialekte Avarskogo Jazyka' [An element of class and person agreement in the Kusur dialect of Avar], in *Glagol v Jazykax Dagestana*. Maxačkala: DagNIIJaLI, 1–19.

Jackendoff, R. (1977). *X'-Syntax: A Study in Phrase Structure*. Cambridge, MA: MIT Press.

—— (1997). 'Twistin' the night away', *Language* 73: 534–59.

Jacobs, R. A. (1975). *Syntactic Change*. San Diego: University of California Press.

Jaeggli, O. (1986). 'Arbitrary plural pronominals', *Natural Language and Linguistic Theory* 4: 43–76.

Janko, T.E. (2001). *Kommunikativnje Strategii Russkoj Reči* [Communicative Strategies of Russian Discourse]. Moscow: Jazyki Russkoj Kul'tury.

Jarceva, V. (ed.) (1997). *Jazyki Mira. Mongol'skie Jazyki, Tunguso-Man'čžurskie Jazyki, Japonskij Jazyk, Korejskij Jazyk.* [Languages of the World. Mongolian Languages, Tungus-Manchu Languages, Japanese, and Korean]. Moscow: Indrik.

Jespersen, O. (1924). *The Philosophy of Grammar*. New York: Norton.

Johanson, L. (1995). 'On Turkic converb clauses', in Haspelmath and König (1995: 313–47).

Johns, A., and Smallwood, C. (1999). 'On (non-)finiteness in Inuktitut', *Toronto Working Papers in Linguistics* 17: 159–70.

Jonas, D. (1995). 'On the acquisition of verb syntax in child Faroese', *MIT Working Papers in Linguistics* 26: 265–80.

—— (2002). 'Residual V-to-I', in D. Lightfoot (ed.), *Syntactic Effects of Morphological Change*. Oxford: Oxford University Press, 251–70.

Jones, M. (1992). 'Infinitives with specified subjects in Sardinian', in C. Laeufer and T. A. Morgan (eds.), *Theoretical Analyses in Romance Linguistics*. Amsterdam: Benjamins, 295–309.

—— (1993). *Sardinian Syntax*. London: Routledge.

Jordens, P. (1990). 'The acquisition of verb placement in Dutch and German', *Linguistics* 28: 1407–48.

—— (ed.) (1997). 'Introducing the basic variety', *Second Language Research* 13.

—— (2000). 'Particles in child Dutch'. MS, Vrije Universiteit Amsterdam.

—— (2002). 'Finiteness in early child Dutch', *Linguistics* 40: 687–765.

Josefsson, G. (1999). 'Non-finite root clauses in Swedish child language', *Working Papers in Scandinavian Syntax* 63: 105–50.

Joseph, B. D. (1983). *The Synchrony and Diachrony of the Balkan Infinitive: A Study in Areal, General, and Historical Linguistics*. Cambridge: Cambridge University Press.

Julien, Marit (2000). 'Optional *ha* in Swedish and Norwegian', *Working Papers in Scandinavian Syntax* 66: 33–74.

Jung, I. (1984). 'Grammatik des Paez. Ein Abriß'. Ph.D. thesis, University of Osnabrück.

Kalinina, E. J. (1999). 'Predloženija s Imennym Skazuemym' [Nominal predicate sentences], in Kibrik (1999: 420–48).

—— (2001a). 'Predloženija s Imennym Skazuemym' [Nominal predicate sentences], in Kibrik (2001: 430–43).

—— (2001b). 'Predloženija s Glagol'nym Skazuemym' [Verbal predicate sentences], in Kibrik (2001: 425–9).

—— (2001c). 'Aktantnye predloženija' [Complement clauses], in Kibrik (2001: 512–54).

—— (2001d). *Nefinitnye Skazuemye v Nezavisimom Predloženii* [Nonfinite Predicates in Independent Clauses]. Moscow: IMLI RAN.

—— and Toldova, S. J. (1999). 'Atributivizacija' [Attributivization], in Kibrik (1999: 377–419).

Kameyama, M. (1984). 'Subjective/logophoric bound anaphor Zibun', *Chicago Linguistic Society* 20: 228–38.

Karttunen, L. (1974). 'Presuppositions and linguistic context', *Theoretical Linguistics* 1: 181–93.

Kathol, A. (2000). *Linear Syntax*. Oxford: Oxford University Press.

Kay, P. (1994). 'Anaphoric binding in construction grammar', *Berkeley Linguistic Society* 20: 283–99.

—— (2000). 'Construction grammar', in J. Verscheuren, J.-O. Östman, and J. Blommaert (eds.), *Handbook of Pragmatics: Manual*. Amsterdam: Benjamins, 171–7.

—— (2002). 'English subjectless tagged sentences', *Language* 78: 453–81.

—— (n.d.) 'Pragmatic aspects of grammatical constructions'. MS. http://www.icsi.berkeley.edu/~kay/cg.prag.pdf

—— and Fillmore, C. J. (1999). 'Grammatical constructions and linguistic generalizations: the *What's C doing Y?* construction', *Language* 75: 1–33.

Kayne, R. S. (1994). *The Antisymmetry of Syntax*. Cambridge, MA: MIT Press.

Kazenin, K. I. (1997). 'Sintaksičeskie Ograničenija i Puti ix Ob"jasnenija' [Syntactic restrictions and their explanations]. Ph.D. thesis, Moscow State University.

—— (1999a). 'Ličnoje Soglasovanije v Lakskom Jazyke: Markirovannost' i Nejtralizacija' [Person agreement in Lak: markedness and neutralization], in E. V. Raxilina and Y. G. Testelec (eds.), *Tipologija i Teorija Jazyka: ot Opisanija k Ob"jasneniju* [Typology and Linguistic Theory: From Description to Explanation]. Moscow: Jazyki Russkoj Kul'tury, 383–99.

—— (1999b). 'Fokusnaja Konstrukcija' [The focus construction], in Kibrik (1999: 582–607).

—— (1999c). 'Voprositel'nye Predloženija' [Interrogative sentences], in Kibrik (1999: 452–7).

—— (2001). 'Fokusnaja konstrukcija' [The focus construction], in Kibrik (2001: 682–701).

—— (2002). 'Focus in Daghestanian and word order typology', *Linguistic Typology* 6: 289–316.

—— and Skobelkin, A. N. (2001). 'Voprositel'nye Predloženija' [Interrogative sentences], in Kibrik (2001: 444–56).

Keen, S. (1972). 'A description of the Yukulta language'. MA thesis, Monash University.

—— (1983). 'Yukulta', in R. M. W. Dixon and B. J. Blake (eds.), *Handbook of Australian Languages*, vol. 3. Canberra: Australian National University Press, 190–304.

Kelepir, M. (2001). 'Topics in Turkish syntax: clausal structure and scope'. Ph.D. thesis, MIT.

Kettunen, L. (1924). *Lauseliikmed Eesti Keeles* [Constituent Structure in Estonian]. Tartu: University of Tartu.

Kibrik, A. E. (1992). *Očerki po Obščim i Priladnym Voprosam Jazykoznanija* [Studies in General and Applied Linguistics]. Moscow: MGU.

—— (ed.) (1999). *Elementy Caxurskogo Jazyka v Tipologičeskom Osveščenii* [Studies in Tsakhur: A Typological Perspective]. Moscow: Nasledie.

—— (ed.) (2001). *Bagvalinskij jazyk. Grammatika. Teksty. Slovari* [Bagwalal: Grammar. Texts, Dictionaries]. Moscow: Nasledie.

Kim, J.-B. (2000). *The Grammar of Negation: A Lexicalist, Constraint-Based Perspective*. Stanford, CA: CSLI.

—— and Sag, I. (2002). 'Negation without head movement', *Natural Language and Linguistic Theory* 20: 339–412.

King, A. (1993). 'Communicative grammar of the Basque verb (selected aspects)'. Ph.D. thesis, University of London, Queen Mary Westfield College.

Klein, W. (1994). *Time in Language*. London: Routledge.

—— (1998). 'Assertion and finiteness', in N. Dittmar and Z. Penner (eds.), *Issues in the Theory of Language Acquisition: Essays in Honor of Jürgen Weissenborn*. Bern: Lang, 225–45.

—— (forthcoming) 'On finiteness', in V. Van Geenhoven (ed.), *Semantics Meets Acquisition*. Dordrecht: Kluwer.

—— and Dittmar, N. (1979). *Developing Grammars*. Berlin: Springer.

—— Hendriks, H., and Ping, L. (2000). 'Aspect and assertion in Mandarin Chinese', *Natural Language and Linguistic Theory* 18: 723–70.

—— Li, P., and Hendriks, H. (2000). 'Aspect and assertion in Mandarin Chinese', *Natural Language and Linguistic Theory* 18: 723–70.

—— and Perdue, C. (1992*). Utterance Structure: Developing Grammars Again*. Amsterdam: Benjamins.

—— —— (1997). 'The basic variety', *Second Language Research* 13: 301–41.

Kogan, L. (1997). 'Tigrinya', in R. Hetzron (ed.), *The Semitic Languages*. London: Routledge, 424–45.

Köhler, K., and Bruyère, S. (1996). 'Finiteness and verb placement in the L1-acquisition of German', *Wiener Linguistische Gazette* 53/54: 63–86.

Kononov, A. N. (1960). *Grammatika Sovremennogo Uzbekskogo Literaturnogo Jazyka* [A Grammar of Modern Literary Uzbek]. Moscow: Akademija Nauk.

Koopman, H., and Sportiche, D. (1991). 'The position of subjects', *Lingua* 85: 211–58.

Koptjevskaja-Tamm, M. (1993a). 'Finiteness', in R. E. Asher and J. M. Simpson (eds.), *Encyclopedia of Language and Linguistics*. Oxford and Aberdeen: Pergamon Press and Aberdeen University Press, 1245–8.

—— (1993b). *Nominalizations*. London: Routledge.

Korkina, E. I. et al. (eds.) (1982). *Grammatika Sovremennogo Jakutskogo Literaturnogo Jazyka. Fonetica i Morfologija* [A Grammar of Modern Literary Yakut: Phonetics and Morphology]. Moscow: Nauka.

Kornfilt, J. (1977). 'A note on subject raising in Turkish', *Linguistic Inquiry* 8: 736–42.

—— (1984). 'Case marking, agreement, and empty categories in Turkish'. Ph.D. thesis, Harvard University.

—— (1996a). 'Turkish and configurationality', in B. Rona (ed.), *Current Issues in Turkish Linguistics* 1. Ankara: Hitit, 111–25.

—— (1996b). 'NP-movement and restructuring', in R. Freidin (ed.), *Current Issues in Comparative Grammar*. Dordrecht: Kluwer, 121–47.

—— (2001). 'Long-distance and local reflexives in Turkish', in P. Cole, J. Huang, and G. Hermon (eds.), *Long-Distance Reflexives*. New York: Academic Press, 197–226.

—— (2003). 'Subject case in Turkish nominalized clauses', in U. Junghanns and L. Szucsich (eds.), *Syntactic Structures and Morphological Information*. Berlin: Mouton de Gruyter, 129–215.

—— and Greenberg, G. (2000). 'Changing argument structure without voice morphology: a concrete view', in A. Göksel and C. Kerslake (eds.), *Studies on Turkish and Turkic Languages: Proceedings of the Ninth International Conference on Turkish Linguistics*. Wiesbaden: Harrassowitz, 51–5.

Korolev, N. I. (1989). *Nevarskij Jazyk* [Newari]. Moscow: Nauka.

Kovtunova, I. I. (1976). *Sovremennyj Russkij Jazyk. Porjadok Slov i Aktual'noe Členenije Predloženija* [Modern Russian: Word Order and Information Structure]. Moscow: Vysšaja škola.

Kozinceva, N. (2001). 'Imperative sentences in Armenian', in Xrakovskij (2001: 245–67).

Krämer, I. (1993). 'The licensing of subjects in early child language', *MIT Working Papers in Linguistics (Papers on Case and Agreement II)* 19: 197–212.

Krapova, I. (2001). 'Subjunctives in Bulgarian and Modern Greek', in M. L. Rivero and A. Ralli (eds.), *Comparative Syntax of Balkan Languages*. Oxford: Oxford University Press, 105–26.

Kratzer, A. (1996). 'Severing the external argument from its verb', in J. Rooryck and L. Zaring (eds.), *Phrase Structure and the Lexicon*. Dordrecht: Kluwer, 109–38.

Krenn, H. (1996). *Italienische Grammatik*. Ismaning: Hueber.

Kroskrity, P. K. (1984). 'Negation and subordination in Arizona Tewa: discourse pragmatics influencing syntax', *International Journal of American Linguistics* 50: 94–104.

Kurbatov, K. R. et al. (1969). *Sovremennyj Tatarskij Literaturnyj Jazyk. Leksikologija, Fonetika, Morfologija* [Modern Literary Tatar: Lexicology, Phonetics, and Morphology]. Moscow: Nauka.

Lakoff, R. (1968). *Abstract Syntax and Latin Complementation*. Cambridge, MA: MIT Press.

Lambrecht, K. (1994). *Information Structure and Sentence Form: Topic, Focus and the Mental Representation of Discourse Referents*. Cambridge: Cambridge University Press.

Landau, I. (2004). 'The scale of finiteness and the calculus of control', *Natural Language and Linguistic Theory* 22: 811–77.

Langacker, R. W. (1977). 'Syntactic reanalysis', in C. Li (ed.), *Mechanisms of Syntactic Change*. Austin: University of Texas Press, 57–139.

—— (1987a). *Foundations of Cognitive Grammar*, vol. 1: *Theoretical Prerequisites*. Stanford, CA: Stanford University Press.

—— (1987b). 'Nouns and verbs', *Language* 63: 53–94.

—— (1991a). *Concept, Image, and Symbol: The Cognitive Basis of Grammar*. Berlin: Mouton de Gruyter.

—— (1991b). *Foundations of Cognitive Grammar*, vol. 2: *Descriptive Application*. Stanford, CA: Stanford University Press.

—— (1993). 'Reference-point constructions', *Cognitive Linguistics* 4: 1–38.

—— (1997). 'Syntactic reanalysis', in C. Li (ed.), *Mechanisms of Syntactic Change*. Austin: University of Texas University Press, 59–139.

Lapointe, S. G. (1985). *A Theory of Grammatical Agreement*. New York: Garland.

Lardière, D. (1998a). 'Case and tense in the "fossilized" steady state', *Second Language Research* 14: 1–26.

—— (1998b). 'Dissociating syntax from morphology in L2A', *Second Language Research* 14: 359–75.

Lasnik, H., and Saito, M. (1992). *Move Alpha*. Cambridge, MA: MIT Press.

Lass, R. (1990). 'How to do things with junk: exaptation in language change', *Journal of Linguistics* 26: 79–102.

Lasser, I. (1997). *Finiteness in Adult and Child German*. Wageningen: Ponsen & Looijen.

—— (2002). 'The roots of root infinitives: remarks on infinitival main clauses in adult and child language', *Linguistics* 40: 767–96.

Lavandera, B. (1983). 'Shifting moods in Spanish discourse', in F. Klein-Andrew (ed.), *Discourse Perspectives on Syntax*. New York: Academic Press, 209–36.

Leap, W. (1975). 'On negation (and what you can do with it) in Isletan Tiwa', paper presented at the Annual Meeting of the Friends of Uto-Aztecan, Flagstaff, Arizona.

Léard, J.-M. (1992). *Les gallicismes: étude syntactique et sémantique*. Paris: Duculot.

Ledgeway, A. (1997). 'Asyndetic complementation in Neapolitan dialect', *Italianist* 17: 231–73.

—— (1998). 'Variation in the Romance infinitive: the case of the southern Calabrian inflected infinitive', *Transactions of the Philological Society* 96: 1–61.

—— (2000). *A Comparative Syntax of the Dialects of Southern Italy: A Minimalist Approach.* Oxford: Blackwell.

—— and Lombardi, A. (2005). 'Verb movement, adverbs and clitic positions in Romance', *Probus* 17: 79–113.

Leech, G. N. (1983). *Principles of Pragmatics.* London: Longman.

—— and Svartvik, J. (1975). *A Communicative Grammar of English.* London: Longman.

Lees, R. B. (1968) [1963]. *The Grammar of English Nominalizations.* Bloomington and The Hague: Indiana University and Mouton.

LeGoffic, P. (1994). *Grammaire de la phrase française.* Paris: Hachette.

Lehmann, C. (1982). *Thoughts on Grammaticalisation: A Programmatic Sketch*, vol. 1. Cologne: Universität zu Köln, Institut für Sprachwissenschaft.

—— (1988). 'Towards a typology of clause linkage', in J. Haiman and S. Thompson (eds.), *Clause Combining in Grammar and Discourse.* Amsterdam: Benjamins, 181–225.

—— (1995). *Thoughts on Grammaticalization.* Munich: Lincom Europa.

Leone, A. (1995). *Profilo di sintassi siciliana.* Palermo: Centro di Studi Filologici e Linguistici Siciliani.

Leslau, W. (1941). *Documents Tigrinya.* Paris: Klincksieck.

—— (1992) [1968]. 'Outline of Soddo', in W. Leslau (ed.), *Gurage Studies: Collected Articles.* Wiesbaden: Harrassowitz, 153–80.

—— (1995). *Reference Grammar of Amharic.* Wiesbaden: Harrassowitz.

—— (1999). *Zway Ethiopic Documents: Grammar and Dictionary.* Wiesbaden: Harrassowitz.

Levinson, S. C. (2000) [1983]. *Pragmatics.* Cambridge: Cambridge University Press.

Lewis, D. (1979). 'Scorekeeping in a language game', in R. Bäuerle, U. Egli, and A. von Stechow (eds.), *Semantics from Different Points of View.* Berlin: Springer, 172–97.

Lewis, G. L. (1967). *Turkish Grammar.* Oxford: Clarendon Press.

Li, Y.-H. A. (1990). *Order and Constituency in Mandarin Chinese.* Dordrecht: Kluwer.

Liceras, J., Valenzuela, E., and Diaz, L. (1999). 'L1/L2 Spanish grammars and the Pragmatic Deficit Hypothesis', *Second Language Research* 15: 161–90.

Lightfoot, D. (2002). 'Introduction', in D. Lightfoot (ed.), *Syntactic Effects of Morphological Change.* Oxford: Oxford University Press, 1–19.

Ljutikova, E. A. (2001). 'Otnositel'nye Predloženija' [Relative clauses], in Kibrik (2001: 491–511).

—— and Bonč-Osmolovskaja, A. A. (1999). 'Aktantnye Predloženija' [Complement clauses], in Kibrik (1999: 481–537).

Lombard, A. (1936). *L' infinitif de narration dans les langues romanes: étude de syntaxe historique.* Uppsala: Almqvist & Wiksells.

Lombardi, A. (1997). 'The grammar of complementation in the dialects of Calabria'. Ph.D. thesis, University of Manchester.

—— (1998). 'Calabria greca e Calabria latina da Rohlfs ai giorni nostri: la sintassi dei verbi modali-aspettuali', in P. Ramat and E. Roma (eds.), *Sintassi storica: atti del XXX Congresso della Società di Linguistica Italiana, Pavia, 26–28 settembre 1996*. Rome: Bulzoni, 613–26.

Longacre, R. E., and Thompson, S. A. (1985). 'Adverbial clauses', in Shopen (1985: 2. 171–234).

Loporcaro, M. (1986). 'L'infinito coniugato nell'Italia centro-meridionale: ipotesi genetica e ricostruzione storica', *Italia dialettale* 49: 609–65.

—— (1997). 'Puglia and Salento', in M. Maiden and M. Parry (eds.), *The Dialects of Italy*. London: Routledge, 338–48.

Luhtala, A. (2000). *On the Origin of Syntactical Description in Stoic Logic*. Münster: Nordus.

Lyons, J. (1977). *Semantics*, vol. 2. Cambridge: Cambridge University Press.

Maas, U. (1997). *Infinitive: Sprachtypologische Studien*. Osnabrück: Secolo.

—— (2004). ' "Finite" and "nonfinite" from a typological perspective', *Linguistics* 42: 359–85.

Magometov, A. A. (1978). 'Ličnye Formy Infinitiva v Darginskom Jazyke' [Person forms of the infinitive in Dargwa], *Iberijsko-Kavkazskoe Jazykoznanie* 20: 264–79.

—— (1982). *Megebskij dialekt darginskogo jazyka* [The Megeb dialect of Dargi]. Tbilisi: Metsniereba.

Maling, J. (1984). 'Non-clause-bounded reflexives in Modern Icelandic', *Linguistics and Philosophy* 7: 211–41.

Malygina, L. (2001). 'Imperative sentences in Modern Hebrew', in Xrakovskij (2001: 268–86).

Manzini, R., and Roussou, A. (1999). 'A Minimalist theory of A-movement and control', *University College London Department of Phonetics and Linguistics Working Papers in Linguistics* 11: 403–40.

—— and Wexler, K. (1987). 'Parameters, binding theory and learnability', *Linguistic Inquiry* 18: 413–44.

Martin, R. (2001). 'Null case and the distribution of PRO', *Linguistic Inquiry* 32: 141–66.

Martineau, F., and Motapanyane, V. (1996). 'Hypothetical infinitives and crosslinguistic variation in continental and Québec French', in J. R. Black (ed.), *Microparametric Syntax and Dialect Variation*. Amsterdam: Benjamins, 145–68.

Matthews, P. H. (1981). *Syntax*. Cambridge: Cambridge University Press.

—— (1997). *The Concise Oxford Dictionary of Linguistics*. Oxford: Oxford University Press.

Maurer, T. H. (1968). *O infinito flexionado português: estudo histórico-descritivo*. São Paulo: Comp. Ed. Nacional.

McArthur, D. (ed.) (n.d.). '*Il Romanzo di Francia*. Une version du *Libro di Fioravante*, édité d'après le manuscrit unique conservé à la Bibliothèque Nationale'. Ph.D. thesis, Université de Paris.

McCawley, J., and Momoi, K. (1986). 'The constituent structure of -*te* complements', in S.-Y. Kuroda (ed.), *Working Papers from the First SDF Workshop in Japanese Syntax*. San Diego: University of California, San Diego, Department of Linguistics, 97–116.

McCloskey, J. (1984). 'Raising, subcategorization and selection in Modern Irish', *Natural Language and Linguistic Theory* 1: 441–85.

—— (1996). 'On the scope of verb movement in Irish', *Natural Language and Linguistic Theory* 14: 47–104.

McConvell, P. (1981). 'How Lardil became accusative', *Lingua* 55: 141–79.

McGregor, W. B. (1988). 'Mood and subordination in Kuniyanti', in Austin (1988: 37–67).

—— (1990). *A Functional Grammar of Gooniyandi*. Amsterdam: Benjamins.

McKay, G. R. (1975). 'Rembarnga: a language of central Arnhem Land'. Ph.D. thesis, Australian National University.

Meillet, A., and Vendryes, J. (1924). *Traité de grammaire comparée des langues classiques*. Paris: Librairie Ancienne Edouard Champion.

Meisel, J. (1997a). 'The acquisition of the syntax of negation in French and German: contrasting first and second language development', *Second Language Research* 13: 227–63.

—— (1997b). 'The L2 basic variety as an I-language', *Second Language Research* 13: 374–85.

—— Clahsen, H., and Pienemann, M. (1979). 'On determining developmental stages in natural second language acquisition', *Wuppertaler Arbeitspapiere zur Sprachwissenschaft* 2: 1–53.

—— —— (1981). 'On determining developmental stages in natural second language acquisition', *Studies in Second Language Acquisition* 3: 109–35.

Mel'čuk, I. A. (1974). 'O Sintaksičeskom Nule' [On the syntactic null], in A. A. Xolodovič (ed.), *Tipologija Passivnyx Konstrukcij*. Leningrad: Nauka, 343–61.

Menge, H. (2000). *Lehrbuch der lateinischen Syntax und Semantik. Völlig neu bearbeitet von Thorsten Burkard*. Darmstadt: Wissenschaftliche Buchgesellschaft.

Mensching, G. (2000). *Infinitive Constructions with Specified Subjects: A Syntactic Analysis of the Romance Languages*. Oxford: Oxford University Press.

Merlan, F. (1981). 'Some functional relations among subordination, mood, aspect and focus in Australian languages', *Australian Journal of Linguistics* 1: 175–210.

—— (1982). *Mangarayi*. Amsterdam: North-Holland.

—— (1983). *Ngalakan Grammar, Texts and Vocabulary*. Canberra: Pacific Linguistics.

Meyer, R. (2005). *Das Zay. Deskriptive Grammatik einer Ostguragesprache (Äthiosemitisch)*. Cologne: Köppe.

Michaelis, L. A. (1994). 'A case of constructional polysemy in Latin', *Studies in Language* 18: 45–70.

—— (2001). 'Exclamative constructions', in M. Haspelmath, E. König, W. Oesterreicher, and W. Raible (eds.), *Language Typology and Language Universals: An International Handbook*, vol. 2. Berlin: Mouton de Gruyter, 1038–50.

—— (2003). 'Word meaning, sentence meaning and constructional meaning', in H. Cuyckens, R. Dirven, and J. Taylor (eds.), *Cognitive Perspectives on Lexical Semantics*. Amsterdam: Mouton de Gruyter, 163–210.

—— and Lambrecht, K. (1996a). 'Toward a construction-based theory of language function: the case of nominal extraposition', *Language* 72: 215–47.

—— —— (1996b). 'The exclamative sentence type in English', in A. Goldberg (ed.), *Conceptual Structure, Discourse and Language*. Stanford, CA: CSLI, 375–89.

—— and Ruppenhofer, J. (2001). *Beyond Alternations: A Constructional Model of the German Applicative Patterns*. Stanford, CA: CSLI.

Miklosic, F. (1926). *Vergleichende Grammatik der slavischen Sprachen*, vol. 4: *Syntax*. Osnabrück: Biblio.

Miller, G. (2002). *Nonfinite Structures in Theory and Change*. Oxford: Oxford University Press.

—— and Leffel, K. (1994). 'The Middle English reanalysis of *do*', *Diachronica* 11: 171–98.

Mithun, M. (1976). *A Grammar of Tuscarora*. New York: Garland.

—— (1990). 'Third-person reference and the function of pronouns in Central Pomo natural speech', *International Journal of American Linguistics* 56: 361–76.

Miyagawa, S. (1987). 'Lexical categories in Japanese', *Lingua* 73: 29–51.

Moignet, G. (1975). 'Existe-t-il en français une proposition infinitive?', in A. Joly, W. H. Hirtle, and S. Clarke (eds.), *Grammaire générative transformationnelle et psychomécanique du langage*. Villeneuve-d'Ascq: Publications de l'Université de Lille.

Monachesi, P. (2001). 'Head-driven phrase structure grammar and the interfaces', ESSLLI course materials, University of Helsinki. http://www.helsinki.fi/esslli/courses/HDPSGaI.html

Montolío Durán, E. (1999). '¡Si nunca he dicho que estuviera enamorada de él! Sobre construcciones independientes introducidas por si con valor replicativo', *Oralia* 2: 37–69.

Moore, J. (1998). 'Turkish copy-raising and A-chain locality', *Natural Language and Linguistic Theory* 16: 149–89.

—— and Perlmutter, D. M. (2000). 'What does it take to be a dative subject?', *Natural Language and Linguistic Theory* 18: 373–416.

Moore, R. W. (2000). *Comparative Greek and Latin Syntax*. Bristol: Bristol Classical Press.

Moretti, G. B., and Orvieto, G. R. (1979). *Grammatica italiana*, vol. 2: *Il verbo*. Perugia: Benucci.

Mortensen, C. A. (1999). *A Reference Grammar of Northern Embera Languages*. Arlington, TX: SIL International and University of Texas at Arlington.

Munro, P. (1976). 'On the form of negative sentences in Kawaiisu', *Berkeley Linguistic Society* 2: 308–18.

Muraki, M. (1978). 'The *sika nai* construction and predicate restructuring', in J. Hinds and I. Howard (eds.), *Problems in Japanese Syntax and Semantics*. Tokyo: Kaitakusya, 155–77.

Musaev, M.-S. M. (2001). 'Darginskij jazyk', in Alexseev (2001: 257–369).

—— (2002). *Darginskij jazyk* [The Dargwa Language]. Moscow: Academia.

Mutalov, R. O. (1992). Icarinskij dialekt darginskogo jazyka. Ph.D. thesis, Daghestanian State University, Maxachkala.

—— (2002). *Glagol Darginskogo Jazyka* [The Verb in Dargwa]. Maxačkala: Dagestanskij Gosudarstvennyj Universitet.

Nakau, M. (1973). *Sentential Complementation in Japanese*. Tokyo: Kaitakusya.

Nasilov, D., Isxakova, X., Safarov, Š., and Nevskaja, I. (2001). 'Imperative sentences in Turkic languages', in Xrakovskij (2001: 181–220).

Nederstigt, U. (2002). '*Auch* and *noch* in child language and adult spoken German'. Ph.D. thesis, Humboldt Universität, Berlin.

Nedjalkov, I. (1995). *Evenki*. London: Croom Helm.

Nedjalkov, V. P. (1995). 'Some typological parameters of converbs', in Haspelmath and König (1995: 97–136).

Newmeyer, F. J. (1992). 'Iconicity and generative grammar', *Language* 68: 756–96.

Nikolaeva, I. (1999). *Ostyak*. Munich: Lincom Europa.

—— (2003). 'Finiteness in independent clauses: a constructional view'. MS, University of Konstanz.

—— (2005). Review of Elena Maslova, *A Grammar of Kolyma Yukaghir* (Mouton Grammar Library 27, Berlin: Mouton de Gruyter), *Linguistic Typology* 9: 299–325.

—— and Tolskaya, M. (2001). *A Grammar of Udihe*. Berlin: Mouton de Gruyter.

Noonan, M. (1985). 'Complementation', in Shopen (1985: 2. 42–140).

—— (1992). *A Grammar of Lango*. Berlin: Mouton de Gruyter.

Noyau, C. (1989). 'The development of means for temporality in the unguided acquisition of L2: cross-linguistic perspectives', in H. Dechert (ed.), *Current Trends in European Second Language Research*. Clevedon, Avon: Multilingual Matters, 143–70.

Ohori, T. (1995). 'Remarks on suspended clauses: a contribution to Japanese phraseology', in M. Shibatani and S. Thompson (eds.), *Essays in Semantics and Pragmatics: In Honor of Charles J. Fillmore*. Amsterdam: Benjamins, 201–18.

O'Neil, J. (1997). 'Means of control: deriving the properties of PRO in the Minimalist Program'. Ph.D. thesis, Harvard University.

Pajusalu, K. (1996). *Multiple Linguistic Contacts in South Estonian: Variation of Verb Inflection in Karski*. Turku: University of Turku.

Palmer, F. R. (1986). *Mood and Modality*. Cambridge: Cambridge University Press.

Paolillo, J. C. (1994). 'The co-development of finiteness and focus in Sinhala', in W. Pagliuca (ed.), *Perspectives on Grammaticalization*. Amsterdam: Benjamins, 151–70.

Paradis, J., Le Corre, M., and Genesee, F. (1998). 'The emergence of tense and agreement in child L2 French', *Second Language Research* 14: 227–56.

Parodi, T. (2000). 'Finiteness and verb placement in second language acquisition', *Second Language Research* 16: 355–81.

Penner, Z., Tracy, R., and Wymann, K. (1999). 'Die Rolle der Fokuspartikel *auch* im frühen kindlichen Lexikon', in J. Meibauer and M. Rothweiler (eds.), *Das Lexikon im Spracherwerb*. Tübingen: Francke, 229–51.

Perdue, C. (ed.) (1993). *Adult Language Acquisition: Cross-Linguistic Perspectives*, vol. 1: *Field Methods*; vol. 2: *The Results*. Cambridge: Cambridge University Press.

—— (1996). 'Pre-basic varieties: the first stages of second language acquisition', *Toegepaste Taalwetenschap in Artikelen* 55: 135–50.

—— Benazzo, S., and Giuliano, P. (2002). 'When finiteness gets marked: the relation between morpho-syntactic development and use of scopal items in adult language acquisition', *Linguistics* 40: 849–90.

—— and Klein, W. (1992). 'Why does the production of some learners not grammaticalize?', *Studies in Second Language Acquisition* 14: 259–72.

Perlmutter, D. M. (1978). 'Evidence for inversion in Russian, Japanese, and Kannada', MS, MIT.

—— (2000). 'A new way to distinguish raising from fronting in Russian'. MS, University of California, San Diego. http://ling.ucsc.edu/Jorge/perlmutter.html

—— and Moore, J. (2002). 'Language-internal explanation: the distribution of Russian impersonals', *Language* 78: 619–50.

Perrot, D. (1957). *Teach Yourself Swahili*. New York: McKay.

Pesetsky, D., and Torrego, E. (2001). 'T to C movement: causes and consequences', in M. Kenstowicz (ed.), *Ken Hale: A Life in Language*. Cambridge, MA: MIT Press, 355–426.

Peškovskij, A. (1956 [1914]). *Russkij Sintaksis v Naučnom Osveščenii* [Russian Syntax in the Scientific Perspective]. Moscow: Gosudarstvennoe Učebno-Pedagogičeskoe Izdatel'stvo Ministerstva Prosveščenija RSFSR.

Phillipaki-Warburton, I. (1987). 'The theory of empty categories and the pro-drop parameter in Modern Greek', *Journal of Linguistics* 23: 289–318.

Phillips, C. (1996). 'Root infinitives are finite', in Stringfellow et al. (1996: 588–99).

Picallo, C. (1984/5). 'Opaque domains', *Linguistic Review* 4: 279–88.

Pierce, A. (1992). *Language Acquisition and Syntactic Theory: A Comparative Analysis of French and English Child Grammars*. Dordrecht: Kluwer.

Pires, A. (2002). 'Cue-based change: inflection and subjects in the history of Portuguese infinitives', in D. Lightfoot (ed.), *Syntactic Effects of Morphological Change*. Oxford: Oxford University Press, 143–50.

Platzack, C. (1986). 'COMP, INFL, and Germanic word order', in L. Hellan and K. Koch Christensen (eds.), *Topics in Scandinavian Syntax*. Dordrecht: Reidel, 185–234.

Platzack, C. and Holmberg, A. (1989). 'The role of AGR and finiteness in Germanic VO languages', *Working Papers in Scandinavian Syntax* 43: 51–76.

—— and Rosengren, I. (1998). 'On the subject of imperatives: a Minimalist account of the imperative clause', *Journal of Comparative Germanic Linguistics* 1: 177–224.

Poeppel, D., and Wexler, K. (1993). 'The Full Competence Hypothesis of clause structure in Early German', *Language* 69: 1–33.

Polinsky, M. S. (2001). 'Imperative and other means of expressing exhortation in Maori', in Xrakovskij (2001: 404–19).

Pollard, C., and Sag, I. (1994). *Head-Driven Phrase Structure Grammar.* Chicago and Stanford, CA: University of Chicago Press and CSLI.

Pollock, J.-I. (1989). 'Verb movement, Universal Grammar and the structure of IP', *Linguistic Inquiry* 20: 365–424.

Popjes, J., and Popjes, J. (1986). 'Canela-Krahõ', in D. C. Derbyshire and G. K. Pullum (eds.), *Handbook of Amazonian Languages*, vol. 1. Berlin: Mouton de Gruyter.

Portner, P. (1997). 'The semantics of mood, complementation, and conversational force', *Natural Language Semantics* 5: 167–212.

—— (2005). 'The semantics of imperatives within a theory of clause types', in K. Watanabe and R. B. Young (eds.), *Proceedings of Semantics and Linguistic Theory* 14. *Ithaca, NY: CLC.*

Potsdam, E. (1998). *Syntactic Issues in the English Imperative.* New York: Garland.

Prévost, P., and White, L. (1999). 'Missing surface inflexion or impairment in second language acquisition? Evidence from tense and agreement', *Second Language Research* 16: 103–34.

Pristerà, P. (1987). 'Per la definizione dell'isoglossa *ca/mu* nei dialetti calabresi mediani', *Quaderni del Dipartimento di Linguistica, Università della Calabria* 2: 137–47.

Quirk, R., Greenbaum, S., Leech, G., and Svartvik, J. (1972). *A Grammar of Contemporary English.* Harlow: Longman.

—— —— —— —— (1985). *A Comprehensive Grammar of the English Language.* London: Longman.

Rachkov, G. E. (2001). 'Imperative and prohibitive constructions in Tagalog', in Xrakovskij (2001: 438–84).

Radford, A. (1988). *Transformational Grammar: A First Course.* Cambridge: Cambridge University Press.

—— (1990). *Syntactic Theory and the Acquisition of English Syntax: The Nature of Early Child Grammar of English.* Oxford: Blackwell.

—— (1997). *Syntax: A Minimalist Introduction.* Cambridge: Cambridge University Press.

Ramchand, G. (1997). *Aspect and Predication: The Semantics of Argument Structure.* Oxford: Oxford University Press.

Raposo, E. (1985/6). 'Some asymmetries in the Binding Theory in Romance', *Linguistic Review* 5: 75–110.

—— (1987). 'Case Theory and Infl-to-Comp: the inflected infinitive in European Portuguese', *Linguistic Inquiry* 18: 85–109.

—— (1989). 'Prepositional infinitival constructions in European Portuguese', in O. Jaeggli and K. Safir (eds.), *The Null Subject Parameter*. Dordrecht: Kluwer, 277–305.

Rappaport, G. (1986). 'Arbitrary plural pronominals', *Natural Language and Linguistic Theory* 4: 97–120.

Reis, M. (1995). 'Über infinite Nominativkonstruktionen im Deutschen', in O. Önner-fors (ed.), *Sprache und Pragmatik. Arbeitsberichte. Festvorträge anlässlich des 60. Geburtstags von Inger Rosengren.* Lund: Almqvist & Wiksell, 114–56.

—— (2002). 'What are we doing...?', *Georgetown University Working Papers in Theoretical Linguistics* 2: 287–341.

Rémi-Giraud, S., and Basset, L. (1988). *L'infinitif: une approche comparative.* Lyon: Presses Universitaires de Lyon.

Rice, K. (1989). *A Grammar of Slave.* Berlin: Mouton de Gruyter.

Riemann, O., and Goelzer, H. (1897). *Grammaire comparée du grec et du latin: syntaxe.* Paris: Colin.

Rivero, M. L. (1987). 'Barriers and the null subject parameter in Modern Greek', *Proceedings of North East Linguistic Society* 18: 412–25.

—— (1994). 'Clause structure and V-movement in the languages of the Balkans', *Natural Language and Linguistic Theory* 12: 63–120.

Rizzi, L. (1982). *Issues in Italian Syntax.* Dordrecht: Foris.

—— (1986). 'Null objects in Italian and the theory of *pro*', *Linguistic Inquiry* 17: 501–57.

—— (1994a). 'Early null subjects and root null infinitives', in T. Hoekstra and B. Schwartz (eds.), *Language Acquisition Studies in Generative Grammar.* Amsterdam: Benjamins, 151–77.

—— (1994b). 'Some notes on linguistic theory and language development: the case of root infinitives', *Language Acquisition* 3: 371–93.

—— (1997). 'The fine structure of the left periphery', in L. Haegeman (ed.), *Elements of Grammar.* Dordrecht: Kluwer, 281–337.

Roberts, I. (2004). 'The C-system in Brythonic Celtic languages, V2 and the EPP', in L. Rizzi (ed.), *The Structure of CP and IP: The Cartography of Syntactic Structures,* vol. 2. New York: Oxford University Press, 297–328.

—— (2005). *Principles and Parameters in a VSO Language.* Oxford: Oxford University Press.

—— and Roussou, A. (2002). 'The Extended Projection Principle as a condition on tense dependency', in P. Svenonius (ed.), *Subjects, Expletives, and the EPP.* Oxford: Oxford University Press, 125–55.

Rohlfs, G. (1968). *Grammatica storica dell'italiano e dei suoi dialetti, vol. 2: Morfologia.* Turin: Einaudi.

—— (1969). *Grammatica Storica dell'italiano e dei suoi dialetti, vol. 3: Sintassi e formazione delle parole.* Turin: Einaudi.

—— (1972a). 'La perdita dell'infinito nelle lingue balcaniche e nell'Italia meridionale', in *Studi e ricerche su lingua e dialetti d'Italia.* Florence: Sansoni, 318–32.

Rohlfs, G. (1972b). 'La congiunzione *mi* (in sostituzione dell'infinito) in Sicilia', in *Studi e ricerche su lingua e dialetti d'Italia*. Florence: Sansoni, 333–38.

—— (1972c). 'Problèmes de linguistique balkanique et ses rapports avec l'Italie méridionale', in *Studi e ricerche su lingua e dialetti d'Italia*. Florence: Sansoni, 339–48.

Rohrbacher, B. (1994). *Morphology-Driven Syntax: A Theory of V to I Raising and Pro-Drop*. Amsterdam: Benjamins.

Rosén, H. (1995). 'The Latin infinitivus historicus revisited', *Mnemosyne* 48: 536–64.

Roussou, A. (2001). 'Control and raising in and out of subjunctive complements', in M. L. Rivero and A. Ralli (eds.), *Comparative Syntax of Balkan Languages*. Oxford: Oxford University Press, 74–104.

Rouveret, A. (1994). *Syntaxe du gallois: principes généraux et typologie*. Paris: CNRS.

Rupp, L. (2003). *The Syntax of Imperatives in English and Germanic: Word Order Variation in the Minimalist Framework*. Basingstoke, Hampshire: Palgrave Macmillan.

Sabatini, F. (1993). 'Lettera del re Luigi d'Angiò-Taranto e di Giovanni I a Roberto d'Angiò, imperatore titolare di Costantinopoli e principe di Acaia, trascritta in una lettera degli stessi sovrani a Nicola Acciaiuoli, in "Volgare "civile" e volgare cancellersco nella Napoli Angioina"', in P. Trovato (ed.), *Lingue e culture dell'Italia meridionale (1200–1600)*. Rome: Bonacci, 109–32.

Sadler, L., and Nordlinger, R. (2004). 'Relating morphology to syntax', in L. Sadler and A. Spencer (eds.), *Projecting Morphology*. Stanford, CA: CSLI, 159–85.

—— and Spencer, A. (2001). 'Syntax as an exponent of morphological features', in G. Booij and J. van Marle (eds.), *Yearbook of Morphology 2000*. Dordrecht: Kluwer, 71–96.

Sadock, J. M., and Zwicky, A. M. (1985). 'Speech act distinctions in syntax', in Shopen (1985: 1.155–97).

Sag, I. A., Wasow, T., and Bender, E. M. (2003). *Syntactic Theory: A Formal Introduction*. Stanford, CA: CSLI.

Sagawa, M. (1978). '*Sika-nai* construction and *ne-que* construction', *Descriptive and Applied Linguistics* 12: 119–35.

Saidova, P. A. (1980). 'K Sprjaženiju Glagola v Zakatal'skom Dialekte Avarskogo Jazyka' [On verbal conjugation in the Zakatal dialect of Avar], in *Glagol v Jazykax Dagestana*. Maxačkala: DagNIIJaLI, 4–11.

Sandoval, M. (1986). 'Infinitive sentences in Spanish'. Ph.D. thesis, University of Arizona.

Sano, T., and Hyams, N. (1995) 'Agreement, finiteness, and the development of null arguments', *Proceedings of NELS* 24: 543–58.

Sauter, A. et al. (eds.) (1968). *Oxford Latin Dictionary*, vol. 1. Oxford: Clarendon Press.

Sawada, H. (1980). 'The category status of imperative *do*, *don't* and *let's* in the English modality system', *Descriptive and Applied Linguistics* 13: 137–51.

Schachter, P. (1973). 'Focus and relativisation', *Language* 49: 19–46.

—— and Otanes, F. T. (1972). *Tagalog Reference Grammar.* Berkeley, CA: University of California Press.

Schaner-Wolles, C. (2001). 'Am Anfang ist das Verb, finit markiert ist es erst später. Zum erstsprachlichen Erwerb von Finitheit im Deutschen', Bericht der AG 'Der Begriff der Finitheit', Universität Marburg.

Schaub, W. (1985). *Babungo.* London: Croom Helm.

Schlicher, J. J. (1914/15). 'The historical infinitive', *Classical Philology* 9: 279–94, 374–94; 10: 54–74.

Schlobinsky, P. (n.d.). 'The function of non-embedded *daß*-clauses in therapeutic discourse'. MS.

Schlyter, S. (1990). 'The acquisition of tense and aspect', in J. M. Meisel (ed.), *Two First Languages: Early Grammatical Development in Bilingual Children.* Dordrecht: Foris, 87–121.

Schmerling, S. F. (1982). 'How imperatives are special, and how they aren't', in R. Schneider et al. (eds.), *Papers from the Parasession on Nondeclaratives, Chicago Linguistic Society.* Chicago: University of Chicago Press, 202–18.

Schumann, J. (1978). *The Pidginization Process.* Rowley, MA: Newbury House.

Schütze, C. (2001). 'On the nature of default case', *Syntax* 4: 205–38.

—— and Wexler, K. (1996). 'Subject case licensing and English root infinitives', in Stringfellow et al. (1996: 670–81).

Schwabe, K. (1994). *Syntax und Semantik situativer Ellipsen.* Tübingen: Narr.

Schwartz, B. D., and Sprouse, R. A. (1996). 'L2 cognitive states and the full transfer/full access model', *Second Language Research* 12: 40–72.

Schwenter, S. (1996). 'The pragmatics of independent *si*-clauses in Spanish', *Hispanic Linguistics* 8: 316–51.

—— (1999). 'Sobre la sintaxis de una construcción coloquial: oraciones independientes con *si*', *Annuari de Filologia* 21: 87–100.

Schwyzer, E. (1939). *Griechische Grammatik,* vol. 1: *Allgemeine Teil, Lautlehre, Wortbildung, Flexion.* Munich: Beck.

Searle, J. R. (1969). *Speech Acts.* Cambridge: Cambridge University Press.

Seiler, H. (1983). 'Possessivity, subject and object', *Studies in Language* 7: 89–117.

Selkirk, E. (1995). 'Sentence prosody: intonation, stress, and phrasing', in J. Goldsmith (ed.), *The Handbook of Phonological Theory.* New York: Blackwell, 550–69.

Sells, P. (1995). 'Korean and Japanese morphology from a lexical perspective', *Linguistic Inquiry* 26: 277–325.

—— (1996). 'The projection of phrase structure and argument structure in Japanese', in T. Gunji (ed.), *Studies on the Universality of Constraint-Based Phrase Structure Grammars.* Osaka: Osaka University, Graduate School of Language and Culture, 39–60.

—— (2001). *Structure, Alignment and Optimality in Swedish.* Stanford, CA: CSLI.

—— (2004). 'Syntactic information and its morphological expression', in L. Sadler and A. Spencer (eds.), *Projecting Morphology.* Stanford, CA: CSLI, 187–225.

Sells, P. (2005). 'Morphological and constructional expression and recoverability of verbal features', in C. O. Orgun and P. Sells (eds.), *Morphology and the Web of Grammar: Essays in Memory of Steven G. Lapointe*. Stanford, CA: CSLI, 197–224.

—— and McCloskey, J. (1988). 'Control and A-chains in Modern Irish', *Natural Language and Linguistic Theory* 6: 143–89.

Shopen, T. (ed.) (1985). *Language Typology and Syntactic Description*, vol. 1: *Clause Structure*; vol. 2: *Complex Constructions*; vol. 3: *Grammatical Categories and the Lexicon*. Cambridge: Cambridge University Press.

Sigurðsson, H. A. (1986). 'Moods and (long distance) reflexives in Icelandic'. MS, Nordisches Institut der Christian Albrechts Universität, Kiel.

—— (1996). 'Icelandic finite verb agreement', *Working Papers in Scandinavian Syntax* 57: 1–46.

Silberstein, D. (2001). 'Facteurs interlingues et spécifiques dans l'acquisition non-guidée de la négation en anglais L2', *Acquisition et interaction en langue étrangère* 14: 25–58.

Singh, J. D. (1970). *A Descriptive Grammar of Bangru*. Kurukshetra: Kurukshetra University.

Slobin, D. I. (1997). 'The origins of grammaticizable notions: beyond the individual mind', in D. I. Slobin (ed.), *The Cross-Linguistic Study of Language Acquisition*, vol. 5: *Expanding the Contexts*. Mahwah, NJ: Erlbaum, 265–323.

—— (2001). 'Form–Function relations: how do children find out what they are?', in M. Bowerman and S. C. Levinson (eds.), *Language Acquisition and Conceptual Development*. Cambridge: Cambridge University Press, 406–49.

Smith, C. S. (1980) 'The acquisition of time talk: relations between child and adult grammars', *Journal of Child Language* 7: 263–78.

Smith, H. W. (1968). *Greek Grammar*. Cambridge, MA: Harvard University Press.

Snyman, J. W. (1970). *An Introduction to the !Xu (!Kung) Language*. Capetown: Balkema.

Sohn, H.-M. (1994). *Korean*. London: Routledge.

Sohn, S.-O. (1995). *Tense and Aspect in Korean*. Hawai'i: University of Hawai'i Press.

Sorrento, L. (1949). *Sintassi romanza: ricerche e prospettive*. Varese-Milan: Cisalpino.

Spatar, N. M. (2001). 'Imperative constructions in Cambodian', in Xrakovskij (2001: 475–84).

Sprouse, R. (1998). 'Some notes on the relationship between inflectional morphology and parameter setting in first and second language acquisition', in M.-L. Beck (ed.), *Morphology and its Interfaces in Second Language Knowledge*. Amsterdam: Benjamins, 41–68.

Sridhar, S. N. (1990). *Kannada*. London: Routledge.

Staalsen, P. (1972). 'Clause relationships in Iatmul', *Pacific Linguistics* A.31: 45–69.

Stalnaker, R. (1973). 'Presuppositions', *Journal of Philosophical Logic* 2: 447–57.

—— (1974). 'Pragmatic presuppositions', in M. K. Munitz and P. Unger (eds.), *Semantics and Philosophy*. New York: New York University Press, 197–213.

—— (1978). 'Assertion', *Syntax and Semantics* 9: 315–32.

Starren, M. (2001). *The Second Time: The Acquisition of Temporality in Dutch and French as a Second Language.* Utrecht: LOT.

—— (2003). 'Morphosyntactic doorways in the acquisition of tense and aspect in French L2: information structure, linguistic structure, and the dynamics of language acquisition', in Dimroth and Starren (2003: 95–118).

—— and van Hout, R. (1996). 'Temporality in learner discourse: what temporal adverbs can and what they cannot express', *Zeitschrift für Litteraturwissenschaft und Linguistik* 104: 35–50.

Stassen, L. (1985). *Comparison and Universal Grammar.* Oxford: Blackwell.

Stephany, U. (1981). *Aspekt, Tempus und Modalität: Eine Studie zur Entwicklung der Verbalgrammatik in der neugriechischen Kindersprache.* Tübingen: Narr.

—— (1995). 'Function and form of modality in first and second language acquisition', in A. G. Ramat and G. C. Galèas (eds.), *From Pragmatics to Syntax: Modality in Second Language Acquisition.* Tübingen: Narr, 105–20.

Stern, C., and Stern, W. (1907). *Die Kindersprache: Eine psychologische und sprachtheoretische Untersuchung.* Leipzig: Barth.

Stirling, L. (1993). *Switch-Reference and Discourse Representation.* Cambridge: Cambridge University Press.

—— (1999). 'Isolated *if*-clauses in Australian English', in P. Collins and D. Lee (eds.), *The Clause in English: In Honour of Rodney Huddleston.* Amsterdam: Benjamins, 273–94.

Stowell, T. (1982). 'The tense of infinitives', *Linguistic Inquiry* 13: 561–70.

Stringfellow, A., Dahana-Amitay, D., Hughes, E., and Zukowski, A. (eds.) (1996), *Proceedings of the 20th Annual Boston University Conference on Language Development.* Somerville, MA: Cascadilla.

Stump, G. (2001). *Inflectional Morphology: A Paradigm Structure Approach.* Cambridge: Cambridge University Press.

Stutterheim, C. von (1986). *Temporalität in der Zweitsprache: Eine Untersuchung zum Erwerb des Deutschen durch Türkische Gastarbeiter.* Berlin: Mouton de Gruyter.

—— (1991). 'Narrative and description: temporal reference in second language acquisition', in T. Huebner and C. A. Ferguson (eds.), *Crosscurrents in Second Language Acquisition and Linguistic Theories.* Amsterdam: Benjamins, 385–403.

Sumbatova, N. R., and Mutalov, R. O. (2003). *A Grammar of Icari Dargwa.* Munich: Lincom Europa.

Svenonius, P. (1994). 'Dependent nexus: subordinate predication structures in English and the Scandinavian languages'. Ph.D. thesis, University of California, Santa Cruz.

Swift, M. (2000). 'The development of temporal reference in Inuktitut child language'. Ph.D thesis, University of Texas, Austin.

Tallerman, M. (1996). 'Fronting constructions in Welsh', in R. Borsley and I. Roberts (eds.), *The Syntax of the Celtic Languages.* Cambridge: Cambridge University Press, 97–124.

—— (1998). 'The uniform case-licensing of subjects in Welsh', *Linguistic Review* 15: 69–133.

Talmy, L. (1985). 'Lexicalization patterns: semantic structure in lexical form', in Shopen (1985: 3. 36–149).

—— (1988). 'The relation of grammar to cognition', in B. Rudzka-Ostyn (ed.), *Topics in Cognitive Linguistics*. Amsterdam: Benjamins, 166–205.

Tamura, S. (2000). *The Ainu Language*. Tokyo: Sanseido.

Tang, T.-C. (2000). 'Finite and nonfinite clauses in Chinese', *Language and Linguistics* 1: 191–214.

Taraldsen, K. (1980). *On the Nominative Island Condition, Vacuous Application, and the That-Trace Filter*. Bloomington, IN: Indiana University Linguistics Club.

Tatevosov, S. G. (1999). 'Sostav i Organizacija Glagol'noj Paradigmy' [The verbal paradigm and its organization], in Kibrik (1999: 86–91).

—— (2001). 'Nekanoničeskie Glagol'nye Predicaty' [Non-canonical verbal predicates], in Kibrik (1999: 118–26).

—— and Majsak, T. A. (1999a). 'Sistema Grammatičeskix Kategorij Glagola' [The system of verbal categories], in Kibrik (1999: 202–60).

—— —— (1999b). 'Markery Èpistemičeskogo Statusa' [Epistemic status markers], in Kibrik (1999: 690–715).

—— —— (2001). 'Vremja' [Tense], in Kibrik (2001: 273–92).

Taylor, C. (1985). *Nkore-Kiga*. London: Croom Helm.

Terzi, A. (1991). 'Pro and obviation in Modern Greek', *Proceedings of WCCOL* 10: 471–82.

—— (1992). 'PRO in finite clauses: a study of the inflectional heads of the Balkan languages'. Ph.D. thesis, CUNY.

Testelec, J. G. (1999). 'Sočinitel'nye Konstrukcii' [Coordinate constructions], in Kibrik (1999: 458–60).

—— (2001). *Vvedenie v Obščij Sintaksis* [Introduction into General Syntax]. Moscow: RGGU.

Thompson, S. and Longacre, R. (1985). 'Adverbial Clauses', in Shopen (1985: 2, 171–234).

—— and Mulac, A. (1991). 'A quantitative perspective on the grammaticisation of epistemic parentheticals in English', in Traugott and Heine (1991b: 313–29).

Timberlake, A. (1976). 'Nonfiniteness in Finnish', in R. Harms and F. Karttunen (eds.), *Papers from the Transatlantic Finnish Conference, Texas Linguistics Forum* 5: 129–50.

—— (1977). 'Reanalysis and actualization in syntactic change', in C. Li (ed.), *Mechanisms of Syntactic Change*. Austin: University of Texas University Press, 141–77.

Touratier, C. (1996). *Le système verbal français (description morphologique et morphématique)*. Paris: Colin.

Tracy, R. (1991). *Sprachliche Strukturentwicklung: Linguistische und kognitionspsychologische Aspekte einer Theorie des Erstspracherwerbs*. Tübingen: Narr.

—— (2002). 'Growing (clausal) roots: all children start out (and may remain) multilingual', *Linguistics* 40: 653–86.

Trask, R. L. (1993). *A Dictionary of Grammatical Terms in Linguistics*. London: Routledge.

Whorf, B. L., and Trager, G. L. (1937). 'The relationship of Uto-Aztecan and Tanoan', *American Anthropologist* 37: 609–24.

Wijnen, F. (1997). 'Temporal reference and eventivity in root infinitivals', in J. C. Schaeffer (ed.), *The Interpretation of Root Infinitives and Bare Nouns in Child Language*. Cambridge, MA: MIT, 1–25.

—— and Bol, G. (1993). 'The escape from the optional infinitive stage', in A. de Boer, J. de Jong, and R. Landeweerd (eds.), *Language and Cognition 3: Yearbook of the Research Group for Theoretical and Experimental Linguistics of the University of Groningen*. Groningen: Groningen University Press, 239–48.

Wilkins, D. (1988). 'Switch-reference in Mparntwe Arrernte (Aranda): form, function and problems of identity', in Austin (1988: 141–76).

Willett, T. (1988). 'A cross-linguistic survey of the grammaticization of evidentiality', *Studies in Language* 12: 51–97.

Williams, E. (1980). 'Predication', *Linguistic Inquiry* 11: 203–38.

Wilson, D., and Sperber, D. (1988). 'Mood and the analysis of non-declarative sentences', in J. Dancy, E. Moravcsik, and C. Taylor (eds.), *Human Agency: Language, Duty, and Value: Philosophical Essays in Honour of J. O. Urmson*. Stanford, CA: Stanford University Press, 77–101.

Woodbury, A. C. (1985). 'Noun phrase, nominal sentence and clause in Central Alaskan Yupik Eskimo', in J. Nichols and A. Woodbury (eds.), *Grammar Inside and Outside the Clause: Some Approaches to Theory from the Field*. Cambridge: Cambridge University Press, 61–88.

Wunderlich, D. (1970). *Tempus und Zeitreferenz im Deutschen*. Munich: Hueber.

Wurmbrand, S. (2003). *Infinitives: Restructuring and Clause Structure*. Berlin: Mouton de Gruyter.

Xajdakov, S. M. (1985). *Darginskij i Megebskij Jazyki. Principy Slovoizmenenija* [The Languages of Dargwa and Mehweb: Derivation]. Moscow: Nauka.

Xrakovskij, V. (1999). 'Povelitel'nost'' [Imperativity], in *Teorija Jazykoznanija: Rusistika: Arabistika*. St Petersburg: Nauka.

—— (ed.) (2001). *Typology of Imperative Constructions*. Munich: Lincom Europa.

Yadav, R. (1997). *A Reference Grammar of Maithili*. New Delhi: Munshiram Manoharlal.

Zhang, S. (1990). 'The status of imperatives in theories of grammar'. Ph.D. thesis, University of Arizona.

Zidani-Eroğlu, L. (1997). 'Exceptionally case-marked NPs as matrix objects', *Linguistic Inquiry* 28: 219–30.

Zwart, C. J.-W. (1997). *Morphosyntax of Verb Movement: A Minimalist Approach to the Syntax of Dutch*. Dordrecht: Kluwer.

Author Index

Subject and language index